Hidden Lives of Jews and Africans

Underground Societies in the Iberian Atlantic World

Hidden Lives of Jews and Africans

Underground Societies in the Iberian Atlantic World

BY JONATHAN SCHORSCH

Markus Wiener Publishers
Princeton

Copyright © 2019 by Jonathan Schorsch for the updated text
Copyright © 2009 by Brill Publishers, Leiden for two volume edition

All rights reserved. No part of this book may be reproduced or transmitted in any form or by any means, whether electronic or mechanical—including photocopying or recording—or through any information storage or retrieval system, without permission of the copyright owners.

For information write to:
Markus Wiener Publishers
231 Nassau Street, Princeton, NJ 08542
www.markuswiener.com

Library of Congress Cataloging-in-Publication Data

Names: Schorsch, Jonathan, 1963- author.
Title: The Hidden Lives of Jews and African: Underground Societies in the Iberian Atlantic World.
Other titles: Swimming in the Christian Atlantic
Description: Princeton : Markus Wiener Publishers, [2019] | "Title of the original two-volume edition: Swimming in the Christian Atlantic : Judeoconversos, Afroiberians and Amerindians in the Seventeenth Century, 2009 by Brill Publishers, Leiden Netherlands" | Includes bibliographical references and index.
Identifiers: LCCN 2019000213 | ISBN 9781558766303 (paper back : alk. paper)
Subjects: LCSH: Church history—17th century. | Conversion—Christianity—History. | Christian converts. | Slaves—Religious life. | Montezinos, Antonio de, -approximately 1650. Classification: LCC BR440 .S46 2019 | DDC 909/.0971246—dc23
LC record available at https://lccn.loc.gov/2019000213

Cover design by Cheryl Mirkin.
Cover image excerpts from Casta system of hierarchical race classification created by Españoles in Hispanic America (oil on canvas), Mexican School, (18th century) / Museo Nacional del Virreinato, Tepotzotlan, Mexico / Bridgeman Images.

Markus Wiener Publishers books are printed in the United States of America on acid-free paper, and meet the guidelines for permanence and durability of the Committee on Production Guidelines for Book Longevity of the Council on Library Resources.

Contents

Acknowledgements vii
Foreword ix

INTRODUCTION 1

CHAPTER 1
The Whirlpool of Otherness: Judeoconversos, Judaism,
Afroiberians and Christianity 13

CHAPTER 2
The Free and Not so Free, the Christian and Not so Christian 47

CHAPTER 3
Some Incidents in Cartagena de las Indias 67

CHAPTER 4
Masters and Slaves Under the Stare of the Cross 95

CHAPTER 5
Slaves and the Downtrodden Religion of Their Masters 119

CHAPTER 6
Judaizers and Blacks: Alliances, Real and Imagined 143

CHAPTER 7
Esperanza Rodríguez, A Mulata Marrana in Mexico City,
and Other Afroiberian 'Jews' 169

Postscript I 201
Postscript II 211
Afterword 219
Notes 223
Bibliography 285
Index 297
About the Author 301

Acknowledgements

I would like to thank the many teachers who helped educate me in the course of this project: Ramón Aizpurua, Ida Altman, Gil Anidjar, Miriam Bodian, Harm den Boer, Thomas M. Cohen, Natalie Zemon Davis, Seymour Drescher, Mercedes García-Arenal, Matt Goldish, Tobias Green, Jonathan Israel, Yosef Kaplan, Wim Klooster, Lisa Moses Leff, Julia R. Lieberman, Murdo MacLeod, Gérard Nahon, Louise Newman, Ronnie Perelis, Peter Sahlins, Benjamin Schmidt, Adam Shear, Kenneth Stow, Daviken Studnicki-Gizbert, José Alberto Tavim, Odette Vlessing, and Michael Zeuske. Their generous input vastly improved this book and saved me from many mistakes.

For their translation help with Italian, I thank Francesca Bregoli and Francesca Trivellato; with Latin, Patrick Glauthier; with Baroque Spanish difficulties, Carmen Cordero, Hazel Gold, and Viviana Grieco.

Special thanks for various kinds of help go to several individuals. Before his untimely passing, Elias Lipiner very generously shared some of his time and expertise with me and allowed me to borrow a number of rare items from his collection. Daviken Studnicki-Gizbert very kindly shared with me copies of various documents, not least of them a large cache of business letters between various New Christian merchants that he had collected from the files of the Lima Inquisition. Dennis C. Landis, Susan Danforth and Lynne A. Harrell of the John Carter Brown Library, have been a perennial source of help and guidance, for which I am most grateful. As usual, the staffs of the Jewish Theological Library's Rare Book Room and the Klau Library at Hebrew Union College-Jewish Institute of Religion helped me find and copy many items.

Rebecca Rubin-Shlansky gathered materials for me at the Archivo Histórico Nacional in Madrid. Carlos López waded through the Archivo General de Indias in Seville on my behalf. For several months as I was completing this project Eugenia Albina served admirably and patiently as my intrepid girl Friday research assistant.

Most importantly, I want to make use of this free and relatively lasting discursive space to acknowledge my youngest child, Jacob Eliyahu Zelman, born too late for mention in my previous book. His names allude to and honor the memory of one of his grandfathers and of two great-grandfathers. May he be guided by the knowledge that his ancestors made their best efforts to live gracefully and to give the world more than they took from it. So may all of us. Jacob and my other four children — Emanuel, Michal, Gedalia and Nava — growing in every way, continue to shape me into the kind of person I should be.

One needs a sturdy and black sense of humor (pun very much intended) to cope with the kinds of matters raised in the seemingly distant historical sources with which my investigations deal. My wife Gail, who soothes away the occasional nightmares I experience, which I am convinced result at least in part from my studies, remains the foundation-stone of my world. Learning may well increase heartache (Ecclesiastes 1:18), but only by opening up to the world can we realize how good it is that we are not alone (Gen. 2:18) and thus that love is indeed stronger than death (Song of Songs 8:6).

Foreword

This book is a new edition of most of my *Swimming the Christian Atlantic: Judeoconversos, Afroiberians and Amerindians in the Seventeenth Century*, 2 vols. (Leiden: Brill, 2008). I am delighted that Markus Wiener approached me and suggested acquiring the rights from Brill in order to produce a reprint. A large thanks go to Craig Leisher, the editor of this edition, who viewed the text, discovering numerous typos and suggesting many improvements.

To fit the text into one volume, we decided to include only chapters that deal with Judeoconversos and Afroiberians.

Given the new format, we have come up with a new and more suitable title. The original title was an error in any case. "Swimming" had been my attempt to add activity, reflecting the ways individuals coped with and refashioned the world into which they were thrown, à la Michel de Certeau's *The Practice of Everyday Life*. My wife detested my active title, but by the time I found this out, my editors at Brill would not allow me to drop the verb.

I have modified the original text slightly here and there, updated it where appropriate, made corrections, and expanded some material based on information that came my way since the original publication. This work was made possible by a grant from the Gomez Mill House Foundation, for which I am most grateful. On the other hand, I have not systematically updated the references to include material published since the original edition, which would have necessitated an enormous amount of effort. The original Introduction and Postscript have been retained. Due to space constraints, only a selective Bibliography and Index have been provided. Readers wanting to see the full Bibliography and Index should consult the original edition, large parts of which are available online via Google Books.

New York City, 2019

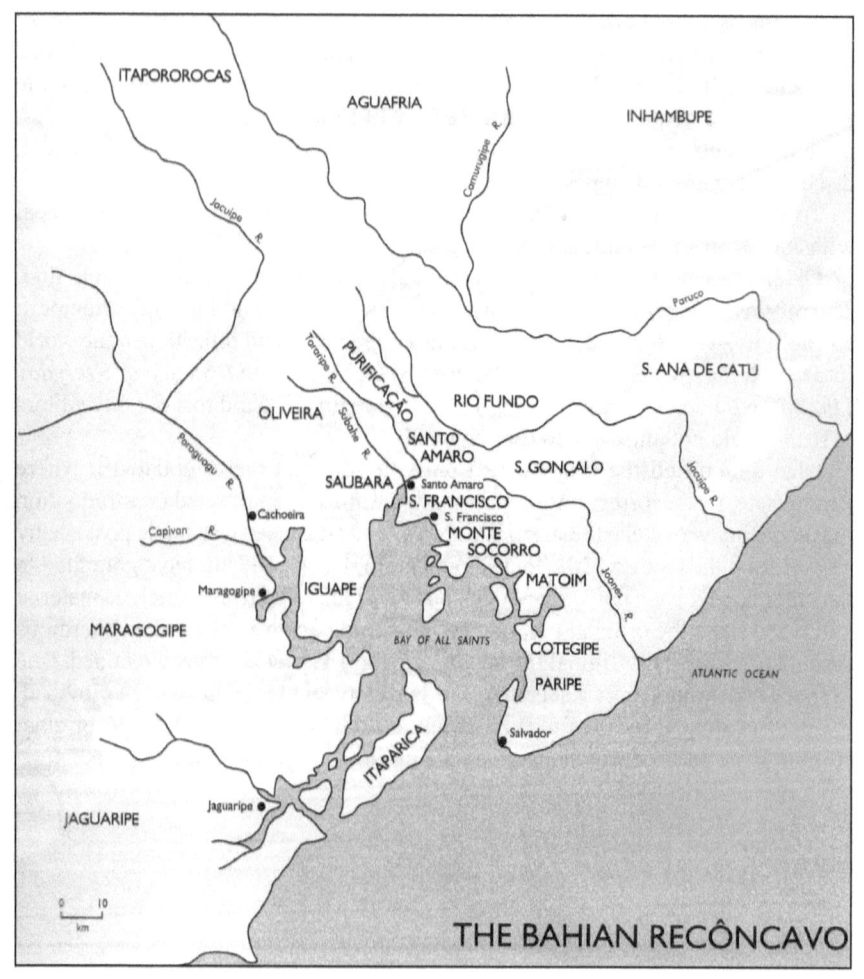

Map of Brazil

Introduction

From the beginning, the natives offered resistance to the Spanish, worried that they "would corrupt and alter their ancient customs; they called [the Spanish] 'seafoam,' fatherless people, men without repose, who cannot stay in any one place to cultivate the land to provide themselves with food."
—Jean de Léry, History of a Voyage to the Land of Brazil, 103

There are those who say [Panama] derives from [...] the Cuna Indian phrase *panna mai* (far away), in the hope that Spanish soldiers asking where gold was located would be told *panna mai* (far away) in the hope they would go "far away."
—Caesar E. Farah, An Arab's Journey to Colonial Spanish America, 24, n. 74

The French missionary Jean-Baptiste Labat [whose travel narratives have informed countless scholars] designed sugar mills and waterworks in the slave plantations of Martinique; in the islanders' memories, he lived on as a spook to frighten children.
—Marina Warner, Fantastic Metamorphoses, Other Worlds, 139

The entire history of ethnic struggle, victory, reconciliation, fusion, everything that precedes the definitive ordering of rank of the different national elements in every great racial synthesis, is reflected in the confused genealogies of their gods, in the sagas of the gods' struggles, victories, and reconciliations.
—Friedrich Nietzsche, *On the Genealogy of Morals*, II, 20

Despite the expansive title of this book, I seek to explore a few specific matters. First and foremost, I try to understand the way in which two dominated groups within the Spanish and Portuguese empires — Judeoconversos and Afroiberians — perceived one another and interacted with each other. A growing body of studies analyzes the vertical relations between each of these subject populations or a combination of them and the dominant socio-political elites of Spain and Portugal. Though I investigate the political, religious, and social contexts in which individuals from these subaltern groups circulated in the Atlantic world of the seventeenth century, I am more concerned with the less-studied horizontal relations *between* Judeoconversos and Afroiberians. This book presents not a sweeping overview but a series of chapters on textual moments and physical sites of interaction between members of these groups. The material presents an immanent view, exploring mostly statements and sentiments of members of these groups.

Among my goals in this project, I wanted to further delineate how the racial attitudes that we associate with the dominant elite circulated also among members of dominated populations in the *sistema de castas*, the caste system of the Spanish and Portuguese empires. These empires were in many respects the first European examples of what Nicholas Dirks calls "the ethnographic state."[1] It remains important to nuance the physical and ideological domination of these two groups as not merely due to monolithic, top-down, hegemonic systems but as more diffuse circulatory patterns. While it is clear that the racial imagination flowed across sociological borders of the caste system, it is critical not to ignore the realities of societal power differentials, and how they function and what they mean. Alida Metcalf's work on colonial go-betweens importantly shifts focus from the stereotypically dyadic relations of White Europeans with native Others to the triadic relations that depended on the mediation of third parties who were often mixtures of the other two forces and therefore to some degree foreign *and* bound to both.[2] Though serving empire in different ways, and constituted in different ways as admixtures of the European Christian and the non-European Other (and containing pluralities within each group), both Judeoconversos and Afroiberians functioned as cultural and political intermediaries, taking advantage of their status for their own benefit but also suffering accordingly.

I have been interested in 'Black-Jewish relations' over the *longue durée* and wanted to know whether the topic as a twentieth-century topos has any parallel or roots in a century that in many respects saw the rise of the globalized, multicultural world we know today. The answer appears to be both yes and no, as I discuss briefly in the Postscript. An analysis of racial discourse in the lives and writings of Judeoconversos permits a useful triangulation with racial discourse among Catholic Iberians and open Jews, just as Afroiberian statements regarding 'Jews' or 'judaizers' allows comparison with those stemming from White Iberians. This gives a sense of the fluidity of "Othering" while delineating the differences in usage within specific communities. In this study, I aim to take what often passed for exoticism in nineteenth- and early twentieth-century scholarship, to reclaim the encounter with the Other as a moment of hope, laying out exempla ripe with promise, however often disappointed.

Fuzziness, omissions and limits notwithstanding, I take it for granted that talk of an Atlantic world makes conceptual and methodological sense, particularly with regard to the Spanish and Portuguese empires. Paradoxically, though many studies of the Atlantic world-in-formation treat its origins through religious discourse, it is easy to forget this in the face of its eminently political identities. Yet the basic analytical ground of the Atlantic world — the populated coasts of western Europe and West Africa, the populated eastern shores and even hinterlands of South and North America and the Caribbean islands — is the fact that Catholicism and, not long after, Protestantism were made into, in the synopsis of anthropologist Webb

Keane, "what Marcel Mauss would have called a 'social fact.' [...] Christianity, its ideas, institutions, social formations, political identities, hopes, desires, fears, norms, and practices, both everyday and extraordinary, *exist* for an [sic] remarkably large and varied number of people."[3] As is well known, though worth repeating, the Atlantic world was to a great extent discovered, constructed, and defended as a *Christian* space, something I seek to re-emphasize even while attending to certain groups that resisted or remade that definition. Beginning with the Spanish *Reconquista*, whose mentality and methods were spurred by expansionist Catholicism and spurred it in turn, the great challenge posed to Christendom by the lands and peoples beyond Europe comprised nothing less than the rethinking of Christianity in the face of non-Christians, defined, in motion, as non-Europeans, people who were not White. This new stage in what Peter Van der Veer calls "the globalization of Christianity," this combination of geographic, ethnographic, theological, psychological and intellectual streams itself marked the beginning of modern Europe, erected in opposition to the Other(s).[4] The early colonial empires, including those of the Atlantic sphere, entailed spaces conceived and policed from the perspective of political theology.

From the perspective of Judeoconversos (if not Jews as well) and those of African descent, the seventeenth century Atlantic remained all too monolithically Christian. Working from Atlanticist premises, recent scholarship has sought to undo the assumptions of nationalist historiographies — English, Dutch, Spanish, Jewish/Israeli, etc. — that tend to proffer exceptionalist theses for the nation of each historiographical tradition. Yet, as Jorge Cañizares-Esguerra has argued, Catholic and Protestant colonizers shared the view that the New World and its inhabitants posed a satanic challenge requiring a crusade of forcible chivalric cleansing, if not extirpation.[5] Barbara Fuchs also posits a shared culture of conquest among the various European colonizing powers.[6] A number of other scholars have contributed to our understanding of the web of transnational and transcontinental symbologies that helped configure the polities, societies, and cultures of the Atlantic.

As recent scholarship has shown, despite top-down efforts at homogenization and social engineering, the polyglot world created in the wake of the overseas expansion of Europe is not just a retrojection of today's consciousness. Indeed, the top-down efforts in certain respects resulted from this very cosmopolitanism. The medieval world that was ever so gradually dissipating was one that prized homogeneity, feared and even hated outsiders, foreigners, others. The seventeenth century, on which this book focuses, witnessed the continued playing out of the seismic confrontations and couplings erupting throughout the sixteenth century, an era treated by now in numerous seminal works of scholarship. It behooves us to remember, however, just how far-reaching the repercussions were in Euroamerican discourse and daily life. Assumptions of caste and race (and class) were ubiquitous. They led to the fact that from 1580 to 1820 the vast majority of immigrants to the Americas arrived involuntarily. Regarding the period between 1580 and 1640, according to David Eltis, 67 percent of the immigrants were slaves, 6 percent servants (indentured servants or contract migrants) and 1 percent convicts, while between 1640 and 1700 65 percent were slaves, 18 percent servants and 2 percent convicts.[7] The original inhabitants of nearly every American colony first served for the most part as a source for slaves or forced labor for the extraction of the natural resources of what had been their homelands.

The caste system that created race and races was one invented in the late Middle Ages by an expansionist Christendom that in order to construct the community's boundaries increasingly measured the conflated circulation of blood and money, sanctity, purity and worth; blood became "the site and marker of theological [...] investments."[8] It was, to paraphrase Bruno Latour, a network, constructed by communities of jurists, scientists, political authorities, theologians, clerics, writers, law enforcement experts who claim to have 'discovered' it in nature, though they had in fact constructed it, a confused fusing "of 'nation' with religion, of religion with ancestry, and of ancestry with political loyalty." Yet, despite its intensely social and political manifestations, they paradoxically "dissimulated its impact upon the fabric of society."[9] Race was/is both real and constructed, "much more than an illusion and much less than an essence."[10] Nonetheless, my study will not delve into the ancient or medieval story of European attitudes and behavior toward Africa, Africans and Amerindians, all explored in a steadily growing body of literature. Neither is there space to survey the history of the Atlantic slave trade or the resulting diaspora of enslaved and liberated Africans in Europe, the Americas and elsewhere and its demographic, political, cultural faces; nor the parallel destruction of Amerindian societies and cultures and the transformations of the world of the survivors — topics investigated by increasingly numerous authors. I also do not devote much space to the ways in which those who (were) converted to Catholicism and their descendants, including, most centrally, the Judeo-conversos, were constructed as a tainted, poorly Christian or even anti-Christian race.

While the fixing of racial categories may have reflected merely bureaucratic imposition through the caste system, as R. Douglas Cope has argued,[11] consciousness of racial difference permeated daily life and discourse high and low, print and oral, as I hope to show. Racism and racialism were not solely impositions from some monolithic governmental apparatus. For an example of the kind of racialism purveyed by Catholic preachers, seeking to bolster the orderly society desired by both Church and Crown, see Irene Silverblatt's treatment of the Quechua sermons delivered over the course of the early seventeenth-century by Francisco de Avila and Fernando de Avendaño in and around Lima. The sermonizers explicitly and repeatedly lay out for their Amerindian audiences the significance of the different 'races' in the new global hierarchy: Spanish, Black and Amerindian, as well as Jews, Muslims (*moros*), and Turks.[12] Quito's bishop, Pena Montenegro, held that as far as intelligence and rationality went, "Peruvians (along with Mexicans and Chileans) were somewhere in the middle — distinct, on the one hand, from the more polished natives of China and Japan and, on the other, from the savages who 'run around naked in the jungle.'"[13]

This kind of top-down racialism has received extensive coverage by scholars. What I will argue, however, is that whether they agreed or not, many 'ordinary' people seem to have been quite aware of racialist thinking, if not participants in it themselves. Those subject to the caste system — Mulatos, Mestizos, Judeoconversos — also wielded it for their own ends in constructing their own identities and for constructing the identities of others in defending, competing with, or confronting them.

The topics at hand conjure a mood as much as an analytic modality, a dark mood, informed by cruelties, brutalities, the stuff of nightmares so horrific as to make the averting of the eyes in Maimonidean negative theology seem by comparison a game of coquetry. Attack dogs such as mastiffs used against women and children, sometimes just for sport. Men, slaves, of course, hung by their testicles as a form of control and cruelty. People, including youths, burned while still alive as punishment for upholding the wrong form of religion. I think of the life story of Cataline de Erauso, even if it is part self-mythologizing, remarkable not just for its rip-roaring woman's escape from oppressive Catholic femininity, its casual violence and globe-trotting, its confusion of gender (and sexual?) identity, but for the seeming unremarkability of it all.[14] This is Hernán Cortés with the sex left in and the official, 'state' police action left out. Survivors and sociologists have taught us about the upside-down world of the Nazi concentration or death camps. Was the early modern Atlantic a long-term equivalent for many of its inhabitants?

All this derives in part from the frontier terrain in question; frontiers ethnic, cultural and territorial, the unimagined, unintended spawn of physical movement, for Europeans (and Africans in different ways), new possibilities allowed by the distance from the centers of the old and 'real' world. It resulted from ports, meeting points, nodes of transit, movement, circulation, gathering. Joseph Penso de la Vega, a late-seventeenth-century writer whose family had managed to leave Spain for the Netherlands, where he lived and worked amid Amsterdam's relatively new Sephardic community, penned a typically Baroque sequence of novellas with a typically Baroque title reflective of current realities: *Rumbos peligrosos, por donde navega con titulo de Novelas, la çosebrantes nave de la temeridad temiendo los peligrosos escollos de la censura surca este tempestuoso mar*. This might be translated as something like: Dangerous Routes by which the Capsizing Ship of Recklessness, with the Title of Novellas, Navigates, Sails the Tempestuous Sea, Fearing the Dangerous Reefs of Censor.

I am reluctant, however, to over-prioritize colonial frontiers or places frequented by ships. Ports have no monopoly on clashing, hybridity, violence. Certainly, speed itself is a marker of modernity. I think of the rapidity of spreading trends. Black slaves imported as aesthetic appurtenances as far as the courts of the Hapsburgs and Sweden, by the sixteenth century; 'judaizers' hiding and hounded as far as São Tomé or Goa or the Philippines.[15] Perhaps this too was nothing remarkable. I consider the extremity and near-constant difficulty of life for most people in and around the Europe at the time as "the center:" the daily lives of the peasantry; the Chmielnicki massacre of thousands of Jews; Protestants and Catholics battling furiously and eating each other's organs in urban France (granted, an acute moment); and the drawing and quartering of thousands of smugglers.

It might well be that precisely the escape from the known forms of violence and misery in the Old World led to the creation of new forms, acted out upon new Others. While a proud and patriotic scholarship until recently produced grand narratives of discovery and conquest, only a quarter-century later authors rediscovered the pessimism of the Spanish Baroque, yielding the equally modern noir perspective of Josiah Blackmore's study of shipwreck narratives.[16] The social interactions and mutual imaginings explored within the following pages stem from the transportation of people under the coercion of governments as well as freely in search of better opportunities. That is, what Maurice Merleau-Ponty calls "geometrical space," a "homogeneous and isotropic spatiality" of distance and ocean, producing what he calls "anthropological space."[17] Physical movement and cultural translocation helped produce a discourse of "disruptive impulses," in the words of Robert Harbison, characterized "by an interest in movement above all, movement which is a frank exhibition of energy and escape from classical restraint." Shuttling between the old and the new, Harbison speculates that the Baroque may have suited the colonial scene so well because it "thrives on contradictions and flowers in those perverse enterprises which try to insert contrary motives into a prescribed format, prefiguring European genres as the medium for rambunctious native imagination. In fact, the authoritarian intentions of the Baroque seldom entirely conceal its origins in anxiety and spiritual conflict."[18]

My analysis contains sections that offer local histories and others that convey more global surveys and therefore almost inevitably it leaps between continents over the span of several centuries. Of necessity, I have flattened out many geographical and temporal differences, for instance, between the Iberian peninsula and the Iberian colonies, and between the sixteenth and eighteenth centuries. This may seem cavalier or methodologically unsound, but local factors notwithstanding, discourse about race and ethnicity was remarkably global and fluid. Obviously, differences can be found in, say, attitudes toward master-slave relations between Iberian metropole and colony, and demographic concentrations of slaves or New Christians created loci of particular legislative or inquisitorial concern. Yet in many ways daily life in Lima was not very dissimilar to life in the Castilian town of Cuenca, while life in villages or in the countryside was even more alike. It is telling that many of the Franciscans who went to missionize in the New World got training in the isolated rural precincts of Spain. Some Jesuits were even known to refer to the backwaters of Europe as "los Indies de por acá / the Indies here."[19] Many of the incidents of conflict between Judeoconverso masters and Afroiberian slaves bear a remarkable similarity to those that transpired in Protestant or Muslim households, at least according to Inquisition documents.[20] The reason for this similarity is the almost structural, overdetermined nature of religious and caste tensions that unfold simultaneously in the private domestic and public institutional spheres. I argue that from the perspective of some kinds of relations, a vertical overview reveals as much as highly local ground-level studies. I also tack back and forth between social and literary sources. The use of two methodological approaches helps prevent the kind of one-dimensional perspective that I feel results from an exclusive focus on *either* source type. I take the above approaches because

I am interested in the confluence and mutual vexations of personal subjectivities with the objective structures of the world; of intimate experience with solid, stolid law; of the emotional life with the logic of systems. These approaches entail my methodological response to some of the interpretative challenges in doing history as laid out by Catherine Gallagher and Stephen Greenblatt — defining scales and units of analysis, identifying relevant textual records, defining and treating facts while interpreting the frames that determine their very constitution.[21]

Partly responsible for the homogeneity of caste and religion as factors in social interaction was the global surveillance apparatus of the Inquisitions of Spain and Portugal, encouraged by the leadership of the Catholic Church, serving the political aims of a monarchy and a culture seeking uniformity. Some recent scholars emphasize the Inquisition's existence as part of the machinery of state rather than of the church bureaucracy, though to the victims the difference may have been relatively unimportant.[22] What is more important is the very nature of the Inquisitions as an institution for the policing of political-theology. In a theistic society, heresy, because it violates divine law, also violates civil law. Religious dissent is therefore both a sin and a crime. Irene Silverblatt nicely sums up the purpose of the Inquisitions: "to clarify cultural blame: to specify and bring to judgment those among the [...] inhabitants who held contrary beliefs or engaged in life practices perceived to threaten the [...] state."[23] Through the lens of documents produced by the machinations of the various early modern Inquisitions, particularly those of Spain and Portugal, one can illuminate the lives and thought of New Christians of Jewish and African origin in the Iberian homelands and colonies as they interacted with one another or merely regarded one another.

Inquisition trial records yield a plethora of information about how Judaism and Christianity intersected with caste to shape the interactions and mutual understandings, or misunderstandings, of Judeoconversos and Afroiberians within the orbit of the Iberian empires, and sometimes beyond. I first became inspired to search through Inquisition materials for information on these themes due to the work of Solange Alberro, who uncovered and analyzed such information in the course of a study about Blacks and Mulatos in Mexican Inquisition documents and in slightly modified form as part of her general exposition on the Inquisition in Mexico.[24] In many respects the first half of this study could be considered an expansion and adjustment of her intriguing findings. Inquisition documents, read properly, can tell us a great deal about relations between the subaltern groups of the Iberian Atlantic.

As groups, Judeoconversos and Afroiberians shared relatively similar experiences under the Catholicism imposed upon them and thus somewhat parallel subject positions in the Spanish and Portuguese empires. At the same time, the ethnically oriented policy of the crown and local elites frequently arrayed these various New Christian groups against each other. Individual Judeoconversos and Afroiberians thus found themselves facing a range of possible stances toward one another which revolved around accepting or rejecting dominant constructions of 'Judaism' or 'Judeoconversos,' 'Africans' or 'Blackness' and 'primitivity.' The chapters here lay out the theo-political patterning of these intergroup relations as manifested in numerous cases of day-to-day interaction and textual projection. Members of these subaltern groups wielded dominant stereotypes about Others in order to establish their own identities, in order to position themselves to best advantage, in order to assert control over the parameters of the relationships in which they found themselves with members of the other groups. It must be remembered that the stereotypes in question often were manufactured and disseminated by elites whose interest lay precisely in ensuring the marginalization and disempowering of subalterns. Hence the uniqueness of subaltern mimicry of elite prejudice, which complicated this prejudice by altering it while wielding it from the vantage point of the Others' relatively weak subject position and which at times resisted it through a pragmatic or even empathetic recognition of mirrored suffering.

Much of the following material was originally formulated in the 1990s, as part of my dissertation, which became my first book, *Jews and Blacks in the Early Modern World* (New York: Cambridge University Press, 2004). For methodological reasons, I decided to jettison everything pertaining to conversos in the dissertation, limiting my treatment and book to open Jews. Having returned to these chapters a decade or so later, I am gratified to find that in at least some respects I was on the right track, as corroborated by various works published in the meantime by others. In particular, I see my study as a complement to the recent work done by scholars such as Diana Luz Ceballos Gómez, Barbara Fuchs, Luz Adriana Maya Restrepo, and Irene Silverblatt. If, on the other hand, anything here has been said already, please forgive me for repeating it.

The text unfolds as follows, in chapter 1, I set out some of the religious, political and ethnic configurations that help forge the identities of Judeoconversos and Afroiberians and that lead to the complex, almost necessarily ambivalent relations between the various newly Christian populations under discussion. Finally, I give a brief history and contextualization of the Spanish and Portuguese Inquisitions whose paper trail informs so much of this study.

Chapters 2 through 7 constitute a series of explorations of day-to-day ethnology, describing interactions between Judeoconversos and Afroiberians from a variety of angles. These chapters alternate between thematic analyses and microhistorical studies but share a strong reliance on Inquisition records as source material. Chapter 2 entails a look at relations between Judeoconversos and free Afroiberians, often determined by the contradictory socio-economic and religious trajectories of members of the two groups and the tensions and hostilities that resulted. Free Afroiberians often expressed interest in becoming Catholic but, more importantly, were assimilated in ways into the Catholic organization of society, both conceptually and in practice. This included the adoption of or coming to share perceptions of Judeoconversos and (crypto-)Judaism. For their part, despite their persecution, Judeoconversos saw themselves as White and at times wielded anti-Blackness as a means of maintaining their own sense of honor. On the other hand, members of each group might recognize the parallel outsiderness they shared and evoke it in order to build common ground.

In chapter 3, I offer a case study exploring the parallels and explosive contacts that unfolded between a pair of Mulatos, a Judeoconverso and the local Inquisition of Cartagena de las Indias in the 1620s and 1630s. The two Mulatos, the free Diego Lopez and the slave Rufina, discussed and spied on those they suspected of being marranos (crypto-Jews). They were also both involved in circles of magical practitioners. Arrested by the Cartagena tribunal of the Inquisition, Lopez offered denunciations of numerous Judeoconversos, particularly Blas de Paz Pinto, a fellow surgeon. The colorful events that link Rufina, Lopez, and Pinto offer further evidence of how members of these different subaltern groups sought to survive and thrive despite the theo-political web that attempted to keep them in their societally assigned places and that also often brought them into direct confrontation with one another.

In chapter 4 the focus on difference narrows to a discussion of the not infrequent conflicts that arose between Judeoconverso masters and their Afroiberian slaves. Here the theo-politics of empire coalesced within numerous private domestic spheres, in a nearly structural manner that operated similarly on the Iberian Peninsula or in obscure corners of the empire. Slaves seeking their freedom, to improve their servile conditions, or to harm or antagonize their masters often resorted to the Inquisition as a lever, charging their masters as judaizers. Some of these denunciations stemmed from the sincere Christianity of the slave, others from the calculated manipulation of Christian values and dictates. Slaves performed unofficial surveillance for the Inquisitions, producing evidence that might prove useful should the slave or local inquisitors need it. From the vantage point of the masters, their suspect identity as New Christians or illicit and often oppositional Marranism engendered certain pressures regarding those who worked in their households. Slaves were greatly feared for the potential power they could unleash from church-state authorities onto the lives of the masters.

Chapter 5 provides a glimpse into relations of an opposite order. Here bonds of pragmatism or affection brought Afroiberian slaves and their Judeoconverso mistresses into various kinds of unity, however tenuous and tentative. Some Judeoconverso masters entrusted their slaves with knowledge of their crypto-Jewish practices, some even invited their participation in them. Some slaves also evinced strong loyalty to their masters, defending them against accusations of judaizing, serving them in the face of inquisitional persecution, aiding them in contravention of inquisitional dictates.

Following on this theme, in chapter 6 I address some episodes in which Judeoconversos imprisoned by the Inquisitions and Afroiberian slaves who worked either for the Inquisitions or for the prisoners themselves collaborated to transmit messages to and from jail, subverting the inquisitional drive for secret proceedings. In this context Judeoconversos and Afroiberians seem to have collaborated as subalterns resisting their common oppressor. Yet, as always, these cases reveal the ambivalence and ambiguity of motivation, desire and manipulation, the difficulty of trust that characterized both masters and slaves in their relations with one another.

In chapter 7, I focus on the life of Esperanza Rodriguez, born in Seville toward the end of the sixteenth century, the daughter of a Judeoconverso father and an

African slave mother. In the Judeoconverso household where she herself served as a slave, the young Rodriguez learned about crypto-Jewish beliefs and practices. She later moved to the Americas, eventually settling in Mexico City. There, she circulated among the city's crypto-Jews, many of them her relatives. When the inquisitional authorities cracked down on alleged marranos in the early 1640s, Rodriguez found herself arrested, along with her three daughters. Based on the Inquisition record of her trial, among other documents, I explore Rodriguez's experiences within the Mexico City crypto-Jewish community and the significance of her newfound religion and kin network. The riveting, troubled life of this vibrant and ambitious woman of color is set amid the context of colonial Iberian theo-politics, in order to evoke the manifold meanings 'Jewishness' held for many Afroiberians oppressed by the Atlantic slave system.

Some terminological remarks: I use the term Afroamerican in the hemispheric sense. I often use the term Afroiberian, but in truth the degree to which an individual or a particular historical collective was more African than Iberian or the specificities of being Afro-Mexican rather than Afro-Brazilian, for instance, is the kind of unpacking that I don't supply. I touch on some of these matters in chapter 1. Briefly, however clumsily, it can be assumed that the more recently individuals arrived in the Americas from Africa or the more refreshed collectives were with newly arrived slaves or the more intent or resistance/escape individuals or collectives were, the more African we can say they were, or rather, the more Congolese, Yoruban, Fon, Angolan and the like. Because I am dealing with the Iberian world, I have chosen to use the Spanish/Portuguese *mulato/mulata* rather than the English mulatto.

When it comes to conversos of Jewish Descent, I follow Yosef Hayim Yerushalmi's sensible and oft-quoted distinction between, New Christians and marranos.[25] Those who maintained Jewish beliefs and practices — keeping in mind the wide range that these took after decades and centuries without much if any refreshment from living normative Jewish communities — comprised a subset of the New Christian population. Sometimes this subset was stronger and more numerous as a percentage of the entire New Christian population; often it was rather miniscule. While I touch on some of these issues in the first chapter, I refer readers to Yerushalmi's still unsurpassed relevant methodological meditations.[26] I am very careful to distinguish Jews from Judeoconversos. When I use the former term it never refers to Judeoconversos who are living, regardless of their inner feelings, outwardly as Catholics. When I use the term Judeoconverso it is as a synonym for New Christian, meaning there is no implication regarding religious loyalty; it is a purely sociological category. When discussing an individual converso or group of conversos still loyal to Judaism, I use the terms marrano or crypto-Jew as synonyms.

Unless otherwise noted, all translations from languages other than English are my own. When I quote primary material that has been directly quoted in secondary sources, I note as much: "cited in Medina, *Inquisición en Cartagena*, 23" or "quoted in Baião, *Inquisición em Portugal e Brasil*, 85."

Inquisition sources contain all the orthographic inconsistencies of writing in an age before standardization. Within quotes, generally I have kept this non-standardized spelling, even of proper and place names, as it appears in the original Spanish or Portuguese. Frequently, then, I have chosen to leave all spellings and capitalization, or lack thereof, as they appear in the original. Readers are forewarnedersothat proper names may appear in different spellings and may not correspond to their modern manifestations. Unless otherwise noted, comments or clarifications that appear amid quoted material within square brackets are mine. When relating what is said to have occurred within such documents, I use the present tense, the mode of conveying that which must remain eternally textual. I have maintained the flavor (or lack thereof) of the original 'legalese' to be found in Inquisition documents and have not 'improved' the language or style. Since such was the stylistic choice of the Inquisition functionaries, I thought it worth retaining. I do not try to reconstruct scenarios in 'the real world' that are known to us only through depositions given by numerous, often contradictory witnesses in theo-judicial chambers.

For the sake of space, I do not provide the original Spanish or Portuguese of Inquisition documents that I cite, unless there is some specific confusion or reason to highlight an aspect of the original formulation. For the sake of readers familiar with these languages, however, I provide the original when citing the more ornate and often obscure language of literary sources.

I capitalize ethnic, caste and/or racial markers, such as Mulato, Judeoconverso, etc. However, distasteful or ridiculous they may seem to us now (though perhaps not to enough of 'us'), these were categories constructing reality. Though the monikers originated by outsiders seeking to describe — or insult — another group, the latter often then picked up the terminology as a means of self-description. My capitalizing them aims to remind us of their status as proper nouns, where not capitalizing them — mulato, mestizo, black — strikes me as not allowing them to seem natural, while also not granting them the same kind of legitimacy as terms such as French, Catholic, or Jewish.

Earlier versions of some of the following chapters appeared in print prior to the Brill book. Material from several chapters originally appeared in "Cristãos-novos, judaísmo, negros e cristianismo nos primórdios do mundo atlântico moderno: uma visão segundo fontes inquisitoriais," in *Diálogos da conversão: missionários, índios, negros e judeus no contexto ibero-americano do período barroco*, ed. Lúcia Helena Costigan (Campinas, SP [Brazil]: Unicamp, 2005), 155-84. An earlier version of chapter 8 was published as "Blacks, Jews and the Racial Imagination in the Writings of Sephardim in the Long Seventeenth Century," *Jewish History* (Haifa University) 19,1 (Winter 2005): 109-35.

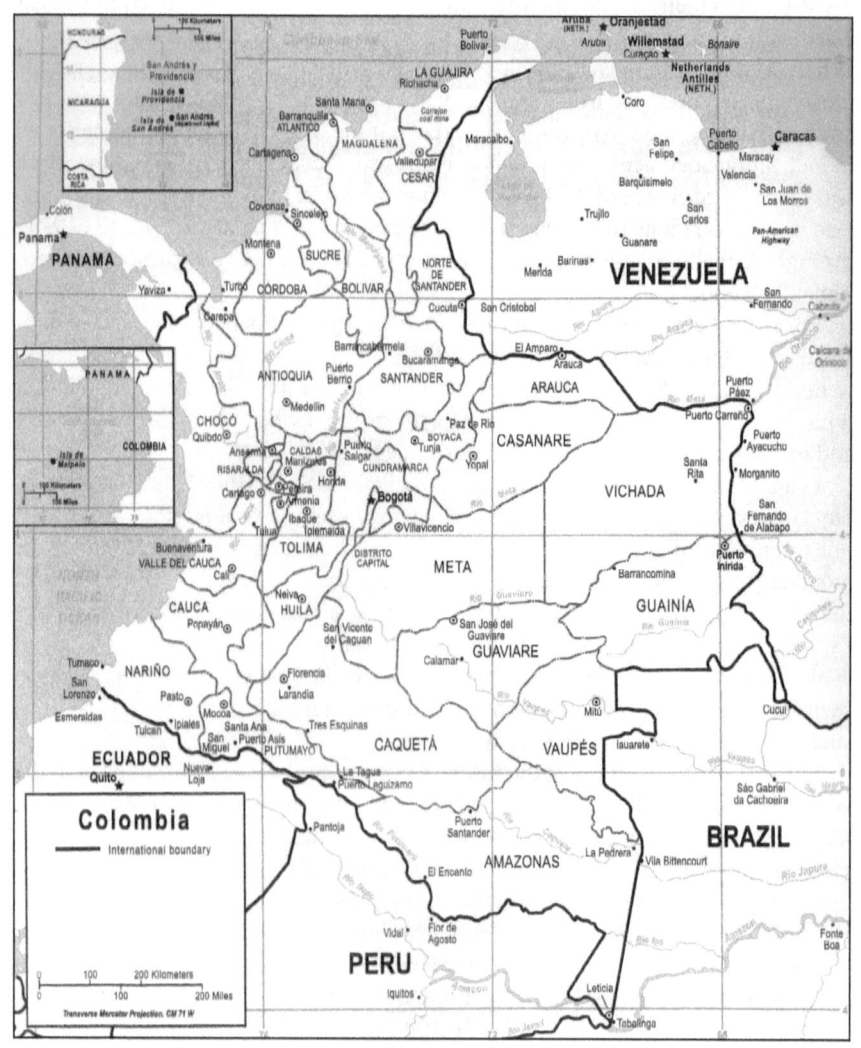

Map of Columbia

CHAPTER 1

The Whirlpool of Otherness: Judeoconversos, Judaism, Afroiberians and Christianity

An adequate synopsis of the diaspora of Africans outside of Africa, as well as those within Africa involved with the Portuguese, or of the diaspora of Jews expelled or fled from Spain and Portugal, plus the spread of Judeoconversos still within Iberian territories is beyond the scope of this book. In this chapter I seek merely to provide some discussion of the kinds of identity, the variety of subject positions that might have been held by Afroiberians and Judeoconversos, in order to provide some contours to the interactions between members of these groups that will constitute the bulk of the treatment in the following chapters. Even this discussion will be hardly definitive or thorough. As a good deal of our knowledge regarding these personal and collective identities derives from sources from the Spanish and Portuguese Inquisitions, in the second half of this chapter I offer some meditations on these institutions and the hermeneutical challenges of relying on their documentation.

Identifying Afroiberian Identity

The degree to which 'identity' stands as a central question needs to be noted at the outset. The very possibility of studying crypto-Jews, Blacks or Mulatos through documents from the sixteenth through eighteenth centuries depends on the ethnic, religious and caste categories that both caused and resulted from the machinery — social, institutional and textual — that produced the documents. Often no way would exist to identify 'Blacks,' 'Mulatos,' 'judaizers,' or 'descendants of Jews' in these materials other than the fact that the individuals are throughout identified as such by lettered official functionaries themselves.[1] Officials wanted to know how to categorize individuals and the groups to which they belonged because the caste system and the laws concerning blood purity determined to a great extent how Spanish and Portuguese society functioned, who was permitted to do or be certain things and who was not. The two systems — blood purity and caste — originally stood as separate taxonomies, though by the seventeenth century, perhaps slightly earlier, they began to merge. How the former, earlier peninsular system of excluding believers of problematic religions (Judaism and Islam) morphed into the latter and slightly later colonial system of controlling and excluding members of problematic races (Africans, Amerindians, racial mixtures) is still not fully clear, though recent studies have begun delineating the process. I treat this matter where appropriate in the ensuing pages. Of course, "race" itself is a constructed matter and therefore bears a history. "Blackness" or "Jewishness" meant different things to different people depending on time, place and other factors such as gender and class. In the limited space available, I try to attend to these variations.

Without entering the complex details of the unfolding of colonial society and culture, it can be stated that while African elites in Africa might have been treated with some degree of respect and equality because they managed to wrest such from those, like the Portuguese, who sought to trade with them, the increasing numbers of Africans bought or stolen into slavery and sent to Europe and then the Americas found themselves in quite another predicament. In these locales Africans became, with rare exceptions, slaves put to the most lowly, arduous and dangerous tasks. Despite their frequent use as brute labor in mines and plantations, African slaves were needed for the skills they brought with them and for the skilled work they contributed to the building of the Spanish and Portuguese colonial societies. Gwendolyn Midlo Hall reminds us that:

> Enslaved Africans were blacksmiths, metallurgists, toolmakers, sculptors and engravers, silversmiths and goldsmiths, tanners, shoemakers, and saddle-makers. They were designers and builders of warehouses and docks, barracks and homes, public buildings, churches, canals, and dams. They were coopers, draymen, and coach drivers; breeders, groomers and trainers of horses; and cowboys skilled in cattle rearing and herding. They were hunters and fishermen, as well as pearl divers. They were ship builders, navigators, sounders, caulkers, sailmakers, ship carpenters, sailors, and rowers. They were indigo-makers, weavers and dyers of cloth, tailors and seamstresses. They were basket weavers, potters, and salt-makers. They were cooks, bakers, pastry chefs, candy-makers, street vendors, innkeepers, personal servants, housekeepers, laundresses, domestics, doctors or surgeons, and nurses. They cultivated corn, rice, garden crops, tobacco, poultry, pigs, sheep, and goats.[2]

By the middle of the seventeenth century, perhaps some 15 percent had escaped their slave status by one means or another to become free. Female slaves, who often served their masters romantically or sexually, whether voluntarily or not, were manumitted more readily than male slaves. Whatever ethnic or national identities these men and women may have had back home — Fon, Mandinka, Ewe, Bantu, Mozambique, among others — in their new settings they became simply Africans, but more ubiquitously, *negros*, Blacks to their overlords. Their generally darker skin color may or may not have served as an excuse or cover for other already traditional European denigrations of their culture, seen as primitive and barbaric, but in any case, skin color quickly came to serve as a metonym for their status as natural born slaves for the 'higher' and lighter skinned Iberians. In the early seventeenth century the Portuguese Jesuit Antonio Vieira preached to slaves in Brazil that they should "thank God for having removed them 'from the country where [they] and [their] ancestors lived like savages,'" who would "burn in Hell," while they, now living among Christians "would go to heaven instead."[3] Slave or free, Africans and their descendants were subject to persistent and widespread dehumanization, denigration, marginalization and cruelty.

Beyond 'pure' Blacks, many of the Iberian terms denoted, as Douglas Cope reminds us, the "products of miscegenation, new kinds of people for whom new names had to be invented: *mestizos* (children of a Spaniard and an Amerindian), *castizos* (children of a Spaniard and a mestizo), *zambos* (children of an African and an Amerindian), and many others."[4] Mulatos can be added to the list, a term having been coined only in the late middle ages in light of increasing European contact with West and sub-Saharan Africa, along with conversos, marranos and 'New' Christians, identities resulting from the numerous conversions, forced or otherwise, of Jews from 1391 onward.[5] Though this contemporary identification must be taken seriously as the governmental and, to some degree, social perspective that constructed ethno-racial identity, it also comprised something that was questioned and modified, where possible, by the individuals living 'under' the designated categories. Approaching this multicultural, polyglot yet strictly hierarchical Iberian Atlantic world, Stuart Hall's discussion of hegemony is useful. He argues that the "cohesion and stability of [the] social order" is achieved "in and through (not despite) its 'differences,'" and that "what matters is not simply the plurality of their internal structures, but the articulated relation between their differences."[6]

So much for the top-down view. Uncovering identity as voiced by the dominated actors themselves can be difficult. A phenomenon that historian Murdo MacLeod points out regarding Afroiberians seems eminently true regarding Judeoconversos as well. In both cases personal identity was itself contradictory. On the one hand racial/ethnic categories were useful as a way to distinguish oneself from others in "lower" categories. On the other hand, one's own racial/ethnic identity was precisely something one hid in order to avoid notice or arrest by various authorities, especially given that many activities were prohibited to members of these categories; that is, people hid their identity in order to survive.[7] To some degree, therefore, racial or ethnic consciousness does not readily surface in personal or public interactions or personal correspondence, despite the increasing paper trail of the early modern period. For one thing, most Afroiberians could not write. Self-revelation was also not as casual or guaranteed as it is today. Possibly the absence is a result of the limited types of sources at our disposal. Written 'high-culture' sources — laws, literature, governmental decrees, correspondence between officials — provide access to certain kinds of reflection on and speculation about matters of caste, race, ethnicity, religion, morality, national characteristics and destinies, personal belonging and loyalties, but capture the subaltern perspective only indirectly, if at all. Most daily interaction, however, fell under the horizon of the written and printed discourse of the day. It is rare that personal letters contain anything, certainly anything extended, regarding questions of race and caste. Most people did not write letters in any case. Here are just a few examples, though still from the hands of Whites. In her racy memoirs (written between 1626 and 1630) of her days passing as a man, Catalina de Erauso relates that a mestiza lady wanted to marry her daughter to her, thinking that Erauso was a White Spaniard. The daughter in question was "a girl as black and ugly as the devil himself, quite the opposite of my taste, which has always run to pretty faces."[8] One New World Inquisition functionary complains by letter regarding a second, delinquent one: "Ah! sir, such are the things of the Indies! [...] This friar is the son of a *barbero* [Berber? barbarian? barber?] and a Berber woman, grandson of a moor and a black woman."[9] The letters of the famous dramatist Lope de Vega (1562-1635), a friar, priest, commissioner and employee of the Holy Office of the Inquisition who appreciated a good *auto de fé*, show that "when sodomites and blacks died, no great compassion for the accused is felt."[10] The mystically inclined (and possibly mentally imbalanced) Dominican friar Francisco de la Cruz, living in Peru in the 1560s, relates that an angel told him to absolve those who possessed (Black) slaves.[11]

Cope argues that categorization by race was imposed by governing authorities through the caste system. Only when individuals got caught up in this bureaucratic machinery did they resort to knowledge of this system. Some scholars, such as Stuart Schwartz, Cope and others, argue that the newly invented racial terms — *negro, mulato, mestizo, pardo* and the like — represented little more than legal-administrative attempts to create difference and identity where none existed.[12] Herman Bennett notes that in both rural and urban "areas [in New Spain] with a small African population liberally dispersed, the descendants of Africans tended to blend physically and culturally, eventually acquiring identities as Indians or Spaniards but most likely as mestizos."[13] Yet a clean segmentation of political racial categorization from daily use seems artificial. The origin of racial categories in governmentally instigated social engineering did not prevent their use for various purposes by individuals of all kinds, already in the sixteenth century and in some places even earlier. Category *produced* identity fairly quickly, certainly from the outside, but also from the subject positions of those within the administered categories. Constructed administrative categories eventually did produce particular collective subject positions, though, of course, individual stances varied widely. When caste or race — or the caste or race of others — arose, in subaltern conversation, behavior and actions stemming from the everyday, which was all too extraordinarily trying, they were usually matters wielded strategically, from a speaker's assumption as "a place that can be circumscribed as *proper* (*propre*) and thus serve as the basis for generating relations with an exterior distinct from it (competitors, adversaries, 'clientèles,' 'targets,' or 'objects'" of research)." Often, such matters served to disarm or defeat "the 'strong' (whether the strength be that of powerful people or the violence of things or of an imposed order, etc.)."[14]

One of the clearest indications that consciousness of caste discourse, racialist assertions and rebuttal to them circulated among the populace is the proverb entered into peninsular Spanish written discourse in different versions by the early seventeenth century: "Though we are black, we are people."[15] The second person voice explicitly marks this statement as a retort to racism made by Afroiberians themselves, enunciated enough to make it a proverb, that is, a collective sentiment, even if it was at some historical or discursive point picked up by non-Africans and in this guise ventriloquizes a hypothetical response. In a typical case, one Mulato, testifying in 1630s Cartagena de las Indias to his inquisitors, appears quite conversant with who is a *quarteron* (someone with a single Black grandparent), who a *zamba*, who a *mestizo*, all terms that arise unprompted in his rambling confessions and denunciations. Though it may true that such categorization arises instrumentally, in order to identify the persons in question to the authorities, it seems unlikely that such terminology would not influence choices made by individuals or shade mundane conversation between peers. The patterns of marriage for urban Afroiberians, at least in Mexico, indicate a high degree of endogamy, showing that individuals within certain categories were conscious of the choices they made, even if these might be constrained by demographic, socio-economic or linguistic conditions. Within very real constrictions, Blacks *chose* to enter certain kinds of marriages; they were not legally prohibited from marrying Amerindians or Mulatos or Mestizos. Indeed, their choice of partners of similar background stands out against the reality of their residence in neighborhoods hosting free and slave Blacks and Mulatos, Mestizos and any number of other combinations.[16] Bennett, here referring to church-sanctioned marriages between people of varied African descent in New Spain, states that:

> even as "Angolans" formed communities with individuals from "Lamba Land," for example, they retained their newly imposed ethnic identities. What was once simply a European-imposed label acquired meaning for individual Africans in New Spain as specific cultural experiences in the Americas — experiences that they chose and sought out — shaped their memories and the course of their lives.[17]

Friendship is another arena from which we might infer identification. In Inquisition testimony, slaves seem to reserve the term *compadre* for other slaves or free Mulatos/Mulatas. In 1660s Callao, near Lima, a Mestiza and a Black slave met at a corn-beer tavern to chew coca and ponder matters of romance, while an AfroPeruvian tavern keeper hosted a group of three Spanish creoles and another Black woman to chew coca together.[18] Here, socializing over, through certain rituals crosses caste distinctions. Identity was not solely negative, but also positive.

Scholars have still only begun to scratch the surface of the question of colonial subaltern identity as a subject position. What kind of identity does a *negro* or *negra* of this period have? In what ways is she 'African' because her mother or grandfather is cited as having been born in Guinea? What would she consider herself? One answer, of course, is readily available from mass behavior. Many slaves sought to escape their miserable condition; runaways constituted a problem from the beginning, so much so that by 1532 the Spanish Crown created a special police force in the Indies for capturing the fugitives.[19] Within the last few decades a number of scholars have begun to open up the subject of Afroiberian identity from a variety of perspectives such as ethnicity, religiosity, gender or organizational affiliation, in both English, French and Dutch colonies[20] as well as Iberian ones.[21] For the Iberian world, much work also has been done on organizational developments among slaves and freed Afroiberians, such as religious confraternities or brotherhoods.[22] Evidently, some slave rebellions were planned by the membership of one or another of these church-sponsored organizations. In some colonies, free men of color served in mixed-caste or special militia units for Mulatos or the like.[23] Real differences also existed between the peninsular metropole and the overseas colonies in terms of availability and type of opportunities, among other factors. As some few Afroiberians rose through the social hierarchy, class also became an element of identity.[24] Further nuances of identity-construction within the Iberian world were quickly picked up and wielded by Afroiberians. Baltasar Fra Molinero offers an analysis of the way the former slave, poet and professor Juan Latino (1518-ca. 1596) distinguished himself in his writings after the Morisco insurrection in Granada from the Morisco rebels, many of whom were Black. According to Latino, his enslavement had been accidental and now he was a Christian, even if Black; the rebels' enslavement during and in the wake of the conflict was just, a consequence of their Morisco religious heresies.[25] Court records from colonial Mexico reveal further examples of such self-presentation. One free Black woman arrested in 1655 for witchcraft, Adriana Ruíz de Cabrera, protested that she "had grown up in the 'unblemished' house of a Spanish lieutenant and his wife" and characterized the accusations she was sure derived from another free Black woman as the fabrications of a "lying cheat" who could not be believed because she "is a *negra*." In contrast, Cabrera, according to her lawyer, was "a *clean-living* black woman," while Cabrera defended herself by saying that she owned slaves.[26] These depictions of course bear a strong instrumental motivation, but also clarity about Spanish values and their importance. Place of birth also might bear social significance. Archival records from 1565 Cartagena de las Indias offer a portrait of one Black woman slave, Catalina, who was "apparently much detested by the [other] black slaves, though she did not have anything to do with them 'because she is a creole [*criolla*] of Seville,'" according to one witness, meaning that she felt superior because she had born in the Spanish world and not in Africa like them.[27]

For the most part, Portuguese and Spanish discourse fails to specify, probably due to ignorance, what behavioral or ideational characteristics Blacks or Mulatos, slave or free, retained from their African backgrounds. Most Afroiberians were not able to produce and leave the kind of paper trail that the educated and socially ascendant Latino did. Hence the increasing attraction of Inquisition trials and records for scholars of Afroiberian history, culture and religion, which afford an invaluable window. Yet, unlike the extremely familiar and well-documented '*judaísmo*' known by the Inquisition machinery (accurately or not), the nature and even names of the 'pagan' religions of the Africans remained unknown to the overwhelming majority of government and church functionaries. Occasional efforts at such understanding did spring forth, such as *Naturaleza, historia sagrada y profana, costumbres y ritos, disciplina y catecismo evangélico de todos etíopes* (Seville, 1627), a thick description produced by P. Alonso de Sandoval, rector of the Jesuit college at Cartagena de Indias and experienced preacher to the area's African slaves. In terms of the most basic level of self-location, one that was particularly important to Iberians, most Afroiberians who had been born in Africa could not trace their genealogy beyond their parents. Inquisition officials thus often simply assumed that Blacks were bereft of any proper lineage.[28]

Explicit statements of group or national awareness or allegiance by slaves or even free Afroiberians are not rare, though with some exceptions they were generally ignored by the Spanish and Portuguese (and, until recently, by many scholars), while actions often reveal them as well. According to the early seventeenth-century Jesuit Sandoval, in and around Cartagena one could find more than seventy African languages spoken.[29] Regarding relations among Blacks or among slaves, hints arise here and there. In Lima, for example, but also elsewhere, confraternities were organized according to different place of origin or nation in Africa, as well as by caste, that is, freedmen or Mulatos.[30] Evidence from Cartagena refers to religious chapters of various African nations in the city, such as Arara and Mina, that is, to associations organized to celebrate traditional African rites and festivities under the guise of Catholicism, though by law such associations were forbidden as of 1610.[31] In the Inquisition testimony of a Mulato in 1630s Cartagena, we find a Black slave whom another slave paid to help kill by magical means yet another Black. The first slave did not, however; he ultimately "had not wanted to do her [Juana] harm, being a daughter of Dominga Arara, of his own nation," that is, Arara.[32] On the other hand, according to the anonymous Description of the Viceroyalty of Peru (ca. 1615), "That which most assures the city [of Lima] that the blacks do not rise up is there being among them many nations and castes and thus nearly all are enemies one of another."[33] Though this is a report by a White it should not be discounted completely. Sometime during the same decade, a slave from the Barenba nation (in present-day Gabon) responded to inquisitional querying regarding the accusations made by another slave, from Mozambique, about their mutual master, a slave dealer of Zacatecas. Whereas the Mozambican slave reported seeing their master kick, drag and whip a crucifix, among other heretical actions, the Barenba slave stated that the two slaves had never communicated because the other slave "was not of his *nación* or his language."[34]

The same questions of class, nation or subculture can be asked about Mulatos. Should Mulatos be considered more Black than White? Is their identity that of being neither, of being a mixture? Are Mulatos (or for that matter *ladino* Blacks, i.e., those assimilated enough to speak Spanish or Portuguese) crypto-Africans in the way that New Christians of Jewish descent are considered crypto-Jews?[35] We know from myriad sources that Mulato slaves had higher manumission rates and as free individuals were offered more opportunities for participation and advancement by White society in Catholic, Protestant and Jewish environments, but we know precious little about their subjective perspective on their own identity before the eighteenth century. According to Lutz, Mulato slaves in Santiago de Guatemala seem to have married most frequently with other Mulato slaves, while free Mulatos chose to marry predominantly slave Mulatos, possibly indicating some degree of collective self-awareness.[36] Writing of Brazil, and probably of the eighteenth and nineteenth centuries, Stuart Schwartz argues that "unlike the colonial elite that was composed of immigrants and the white American-born children of European parents, [the *mestiço* and mulatto populations] had no particular attachment to Portugal, nor did they feel the pull of sentiments in conflicting directions."[37] There is no doubt truth in recording this turning of the back on the dominant culture, but I suspect such a view oversimplifies the ramifications of mixed heritage and in-betweenness. Gender, for instance, determined that the slave status of an individual followed that of the mother, while caste might follow that of the mother or father, depending on a variety of circumstances. This meant that individuals of partial African or Amerindian descent might claim a variety of statuses and that non-Spanish women might understand the opportunities and limits of racial status for themselves and their children differently than men. Throughout the empires, for a variety of social and legal reasons, such as the right to bear arms, Mulatos claimed forms of Whiteness by dint of marriage to a Spanish partner, and/or having Spanish children, descent from a Spanish parent — a Mulato born of a Spanish father was often called a White Mulato *mulato blanco* — or through characterological qualities: being "quiet and calm," "not noisy and virtuous," "well-liked and loved," gainfully employed. Caste, particularly of the mixed sort, was often negotiated, at times through formal litigation, between the individual and a variety of authorities.[38] Thus the panoply of caste categories, particularly those of intermediate or mixed status, remained more ideal than real, as the amount of mixture often made accurate categorization of others "at best a speculative art in Spanish America," while self-identification was often situational.[39]

Afroiberian religiosity provides an opportunity for further contemplation of identity. Other than Ethiopian Christianity, which faced certain objections from the Catholic Church, all African religions were viewed as false or heretical, if they were even taken seriously as 'religion.' While this was true in a theoretical manner in the discourse of medieval theology and philosophy, such rejection became all too concrete with the arrival of Europeans in Africa. There, Catholic priests "burned 'idol houses' and 'fetish objects' in grand displays meant to demonstrate the impotence of African spirits and religious leaders," while "the burning of African sacred objects continued in Brazil."[40] The idea of continuing revelation, of open-ended communication between ordinary individuals and other-worldly beings, increasingly suppressed in European Catholicism after the Council of Trent (1545-63), occupied a central position in African (and Amerindian) religions. With contact and conquest, African and Afroiberian attempts to maintain such an approach within Christianity faced severe condemnation and punishment. Yet, intriguingly, of the 102 people accused by the Inquisition in New Spain between 1593 and 1801 for being 'false mystics,' *ilusos* or *alumbrados*, some 12 percent were "of mixed, Spanish, African, and indigenous (American) ancestry."[41] In addition, Nora Jaffary and others argue that the New World Inquisitions, unlike their Old World counterparts, were "more concerned with maintaining the population's practice of orthodox Counter-Reformation Catholicism uncorrupted by Indian and African influences."[42] In some respects, however, to varying degrees, depending on time and place, the missionary project tolerated certain aspects of indigenous religiosity in Africa, Europe and the Americas to color local Christianity.[43]

While Afroiberians were not technically New Christians, a term invented for Judeoconversos and then applied to Moriscos and Amerindians, they were similarly "newly transplanted to the faith," as wrote the biographer of Father Pedro Claver, missionizer to Blacks around Cartagena de Indias.[44] Frederick Bowser claims that in the Americas "the African, unlike the Indian, was not granted the status of neophyte in the Faith," though Jonathan Israel writes that in the Jesuit view Blacks, Mulatos as well as Mestizos were considered "neophytes of the Church."[45] Agostinho Marques Perdigão Malheiros notes that "In a Bull of October 7, 1462, Pope Pious II censured the slave trade, especially the reduction of the neophytes of Africa to slavery."[46] It is unclear whether these authors use the term 'neophytes' technically or figuratively. While in the Americas Blacks were forbidden to receive holy orders (along with Amerindians), Africans had not been forbidden to do so in Africa or in Portugal. No debate accompanied the training of Africans for the priesthood already from early on, while a debate festered for years regarding the ordaining of Amerindians. Some jurists, such as Juan de Solórzano Pereira, author of the most important collection of laws covering American Spanish territories, distinguished the less problematic background and coming-to-Christianity of Africans and Amerindians from the more problematic 'race / raza' of Judeoconversos. Amerindians, in his view, should not necessarily be denied the holding of governmental office, certain professions or the nobility.[47] At the same time, Judeoconversos of Cabo Verde argued, in 1627, that they should be known as Old Christians, since it was those with African blood who were 'really' New Christians.[48] Views regarding the variety of new Christians were not at all consistent, however. By the seventeenth century, various guilds in fact excluded full Blacks, others full Blacks as well as Mulatos; soldiers of African descent had a difficult time claiming the military honors awarded them.[49] Yet by the seventeenth century one finds repeated references to Blacks and Mulatos who presented themselves to inquisitional authorities as Old Christians. María Elena Martínez López offers an important discussion of the late seventeenth-century evaluation by the Supreme Council of the Inquisition in Madrid (the *Suprema*) of the question of whether descendants of Amerindians and/or Africans needed to be subjected to the regime of the purity of blood laws, as well as whether they could be considered Old Christians. Basing itself on numerous sources, the *Suprema* accepted Amerindians as both pure of blood and Old Christians, while Afroiberians "gradually drop out of the discussion and toward the end are hardly mentioned at all."[50] All this yields a rather ambiguous and fluid attitude, in which concern for caste began to impede religious inclusivism.[51]

A more ground-level survey helps determine specifics. Like many groups of medieval Jews, most Africans came to baptism en masse, either at their departure as slaves from Africa or on arrival at a port of entry in the Americas.[52] Active steps to ensure the baptism of incoming slaves to Portugal were taken only after 1514, while in 1513 the Spanish Council of the Indies, in order to supply African slaves to the New World colonies in sufficient numbers to satisfy the demand, authorized that they be sent directly from Africa without the previously required period of catechization in Spain.[53] In 1620 a Portuguese resolution insist that a chaplain accompany each transatlantic slave journey in order to catechize the captive audience, though this may not have been the first such legislation.[54] In any event, actual familiarity with Catholic doctrines and practices remained minimal. Strong resistance to Christianization of slaves came, not surprisingly, from those who owned slaves and plantations. A 1525 Inquisition census from the Canary Islands showed that fully 40 percent of the Black slaves over the age of 12 in the sample did not know how to cross themselves (*persignarse*), 44 percent could not recite the *Padre Nuestro*, 83 percent could not say the *Credo* and 92 percent did not know the *Salve*.[55] Therefore, in 1537 Carlos V of Castile decreed that all slaves be released each day at a certain hour for religious instruction and, in 1541, that they may not work on holidays or feast days, but should attend mass.[56] Writing about Cartagena de Indias in the 1560s, Diana Luz Ceballos Gómez finds that notwithstanding the royal legislation slaves were not accustomed to attend mass "and, it seems, their masters did not force them."[57] One Dominican friar in 1570s Perú, Francisco de la Cruz, was said to have preached that when it came to the things that all Christians needed to believe in order to be saved, "those who are very uncultured and ignorant (and he gave the example of blacks and Indians), for them it would suffice to believe in order to be saved that there was a God and that the law of the Christians is the true one and to believe in the mystery of the Trinity, even if they should not perceive it, and in Jesus Christ."[58] None of this means that African slaves did not resort to Christianity for spiritual needs. To defend the honor of an accused slave woman in 1560s Cartagena, one witness reported how "last Sunday the said Catalina sent to San Francisco [Cathedral] four *reales* and a wax candle in order that they say a mass for her, that God should free her from that which they have raised [against her]."[59] Larger questions remain, however, regarding the kind of Catholicism that Afroiberian slaves practiced; the ways they modified it, if at all; the different varieties of Afroiberian Catholicism or syncretic religiosity; who practiced what kind and why.

The Spanish ideal regarding African slaves aimed at their becoming *ladinos*, that is, becoming fluent in the Latinate language and hence culture of the Iberian motherland (*ladino = Latin*).[60] According to the *Concilios* of Mexico and Peru (1585 and 1583, respectively), in the New World territories Afroiberian slaves, even if considered 'colored' through only one parent, the children of Spaniards and the Chichimec were to be taught Christian doctrine in Castilian, unlike the Quechua- and Nahuatl-speaking peoples, who were indoctrinated in their own languages.[61] Indoctrination in Christianity did not always come for free. In the mid-seventeenth-century Popayán province of Nueva Granada (in present-day

Colombia), every Black slave between the ages of 18 and 50 who worked the sugar plantations and cattle ranches had to pay the local priest 10 1/2 *reales* annually.[62] The Iberian ambivalence regarding bringing slaves into Catholicism led one scholar, Luis Felipe de Alencastro, to characterize the results as bipolar slavery.[63]

Furthermore, according to some recent scholars taking an Africanist perspective, the cultural lives of even Christianized Afroiberian slaves remained something apart. The religions of Afroiberians in the seventeenth century, particularly in Brazil, "were not synthetic or creolized but were independent systems of thought, practiced in parallel to Catholicism," argues James Sweet.[64] Therefore, due to Afroiberian ignorance of the details of Catholic doctrine, their intentional adapting of it for their own needs and their continued involvement in the religious ways of their homeland, Afroiberians often found themselves victims of inquisitional jurisprudence. In southern Spain and Portugal in the fifteenth and sixteenth centuries, for instance, many slaves of African origin were punished for attempting to flee to Muslim North Africa. Blasphemy, especially in response to mistreatment by their mistresses or masters, constituted one of the most prevalent of slave offenses punished by the Inquisitions, though, ironically, many of the slaves might well have blasphemed in order to beseech the Inquisition to intervene in their case against their owner.[65] "Idolatrous" practices of slaves or free Afroiberians, in many cases rituals from their homeland or some adaptation of them, often subsumed by inquisitors under the label of witchcraft, were another often-punished "heresy."[66] Though seemingly exaggerated, Herman Bennett cites Solange Alberro for the assertion that "nearly 50 percent of the [Mexican] inquisition proceedings involved Africans and their American-born descendants."[67] Afroiberians who succeeded in wresting for themselves some autonomy made use of it to live as they saw fit. A community of runaway (*cimarrón*) slaves on the coast of the Gulf of Mexico was said in 1609 to "defiantly eat on Fridays, Saturdays, and holy days" and to have rejected a priest's offer to sanction their unofficial marriages.[68]

The Converso/Sephardic Atlantic

From the Jewish perspective there existed not one but two Atlantic worlds. The orbit of the Iberian, Catholic mainland (Spain and Portugal) and colonies constituted a sphere forbidden to Jews as Jews.[69] The tragic end of medieval Spanish and Portuguese Jewry, a history filled with long moments of coexistence and rich accomplishment, is well known: a 1492 royal edict ordering the expulsion from Castilian territories of all Jews who did not convert to Catholicism; the many thousands who fled to Portugal, together with the Jews already residing there, faced another royal edict in 1497 commanding the forced conversion of every Jew in Portugal, this time without the option of leaving. According to many sources, both contemporary and modern, the manner of the sudden, collective conversion in Portugal generated a community far more knowledgeable in and committed to Judaism, as least for the next few generations.[70] The problem of so-called *cristianos nuevos* or *cristãos novos*, of Jews who had been forced to or chose to become Christians, that began in earnest with anti-Jewish persecutions and massacres in Spain toward the end of the fourteenth century (mainly 1391), and that had led to the re-establishment of the medieval Inquisition there in 1478 (ostensibly in order to protect the religious integrity of the New Christians), now swelled to institutionalized, national proportions and became endemic to Spanish and Portuguese existence for the next few centuries.[71] Despite various institutional desires to assimilate the population of New Christians into the Catholic body politic, they faced persistent and widespread denigration, exclusion and persecution because of suspicions that, intentionally or not, they perpetuated 'Jewish' beliefs, practices or characteristics.

In what we might call the Protestant Atlantic, on the other hand, Sephardic Jews who had fled Iberian territories not only found an increasingly tolerant welcome (not without difficulties and in the face of exclusions, at times severe) and gained previously unheard of privileges and rights as useful instruments of colonialist reasons of state. This trend seems to have reached its zenith in the Dutch colonies, where Jews constituted roughly a third of the European population. Catholic France provided an environment less xenophobic than Catholic Spain and Portugal, but its welcome of Jews in its colonies proved more complicated. Sephardim played an important role, even a dominant one, in various aspects of Atlantic and general international commerce. In family-based networks that spanned European motherlands and their colonies, Crypto-Jews and Sephardim at various times were active in trading and/or processing pepper and spices, sugar, indigo, chocolate, slaves, coral and diamonds, not to mention more mundane goods such as wool, civet cats and wine. Sephardim participated as well, insofar as they were able, in the more colorful and exploitative aspects of colonialism, though they are underrepresented, often significantly, in the more directly dominating, martial or violent activities.[72]

Many Sephardim and Judeoconversos referred to themselves, and were referred to by others as members of *O Nação* / The Nation, by which they meant something like "those of Spanish and Portuguese Jews and their descendants."[73] Even so, the far-flung communities of the Sephardic diaspora — from Paramaribo to Izmir, Hamburg to Sale, Morocco — can hardly be said to constitute a nation-state, though individually and to some degree in concert they exercised varying degrees of political power, self-organization, autonomy from the nation-states in which they resided and coordinated policy-making. On the other hand, the centrality of kin network-based merchant capitalism to the basic survival, economic success and political robustness of this trans-continental Jewish archipelago, as well as its prominent intertwining with Sephardic political ruling structures, strikingly parallel the same formations in what sociologist Julia Adams calls the "familial states" of the colonial powers of western Europe.[74] Judeoconversos, on the other hand, were neither a typical diasporic community, merchant or otherwise, nor an organized entity. Other than a few exceptions on the peninsula in the early sixteenth century, Judeoconversos had no recognized physical public sphere, no gathering points. They comprised an ethnicity that could not really celebrate itself openly, not to mention identify explicitly in positive ways (though sometimes New Christian individuals expressed great pride in their Jewish origins). Some forms of internal communal organization can be found: especially before the seventeenth century, the peninsular Judeoconverso population showed some signs of coordinated leadership; endogamous marriage was often prioritized by New Christian heads of households regardless of geography. Few of these phenomena derived from centralized authority.

If the Iberian Atlantic can be called Sephardic, this resolves nothing about the question of Jewishness there. The most basic questions of Jewish identity seem vertiginous in the early modern Iberian Atlantic world. Was a person Jewish? In what ways? When? Where? To whom? Neither Jewishness nor New Christian identity were visually recognizable, as the persistent inquisitorial obsession with genealogy makes abundantly clear, even if various figures tried to identify visible signs (discussed in the chapters to come). Even given the "other nations of white men" besides Spaniards that the 17th-century Father Francisco de Avila spoke about in his sermons to his Native American audiences around Lima when he discussed Europeans, Judeoconversos were considered by everyone in the Spanish and Portuguese colonial orbits as (white) Iberians, though with a (hidden) difference.[75] It strikes me as most appropriate that the first 'Jew' to walk the shores of the New World, Columbus's translator Luís Torres, who was to greet the natives in their native Aramaic or Chaldean, was a non-Jew, a descendant of New Christians (a euphemistic name masking the violence of coerced conformity by means of magical spiritual-legal acts) whose religious loyalties remain known only to him and God. This aspect of hiddenness also points to another unique facet of the converso diaspora. Crypto-Judaism's unauthorized status (from the perspective of the Catholic state) and therefore clandestine organizing principles meant that in many respects it differed little between the Iberian Old and New Worlds, unlike Catholicism and American African religiosity, which both reflected novel formations influenced by the demographic and ethnographic specificities of the Americas.

Despite, perhaps because of the official enforced non-existence of Judaism and Jews, the Iberian Atlantic world experienced its own persistent 'Jewish question.' New Christians, though ever suspected of judaizing tendencies and excluded from certain institutions and honors, were purposefully integrated into society; after all, they were now Catholics. They were thus active throughout the empire. It has been estimated that in 1593, New Christians comprised 14 percent of the population of Pernambuco.[76] Seymour Liebman estimates that conversos constituted some 10 percent of the total non-Indian population of early New Spain.[77] A French traveler passing through Rio de Janeiro in 1695 calculates that three fourths of the city's White population possessed Jewish roots, surely an exaggeration, though no fewer than 1116 New Christians were either imprisoned or denounced to the local Inquisition during the eighteenth century (the total population in 1750 stood at around 20,000).[78] One historian of the northern Mexican province of Nuevo León, Eugenio del Hoyo, claims that some 68 percent of the original sixteenth-century settlers were New Christians.[79] Since Jews had constituted the major commercial sector of medieval Iberian society, Judeoconversos, now freed from anti-Jewish legislation, achieved even greater mercantile domination, occupying, if not controlling, significant branches of commerce both within the empire and between it and other powers in Europe and beyond. One survey of Judeoconversos who had been tried by the Castilian Inquisition and then rehabilitated between 1535 and 1575 found 49 percent involved in commerce and 21 percent in finance.[80] In the seventeenth century Judeoconversos made up some 65 to 75 percent "of the total Portuguese mercantile community while hardly totaling more than 10 percent of the population."[81] An important recent dissertation argues that New Christians comprised "*the* predominant European social group in Cabo Verde and Guiné" between colonization by the Portuguese and the late seventeenth century.[82]

Between 1580 and 1640 Portuguese New Christians flourished in the trade, licit and often illicit, linking Potosí (the silver center and hence economic engine of the Spanish Americas), Tucumán, Buenos Aires and the Río de la Plata with Europe, frequently via Brazil, frequently in partnership with Dutch interlopers and Sephardim in Amsterdam. In seventeenth-century New Spain, Portuguese New Christians established a flourishing trade network between Mexico City, Veracruz, Guadalajara, Puebla and Zacatecas, trading goods from and to places as far away as Seville, Central America, Cuba, Brazil, Peru, Buenos Aires, the Canaries, and the Philippines. This network, dealing in both legal and contraband items such as textiles (linens, woolens, Chinese silks), cacao, slaves, collapsed with the inquisitorial persecutions of the middle of the century. Perhaps most surprising, in the same first decades of the seventeenth century, Portuguese New Christians attained a significant and much noticed position as bankers and international merchants servicing the needs of the Spanish empire. Study of the mostly familial networks of converso/Sephardic traders has flourished, providing an increasingly clear picture of their methods, extent and success.[83]

Beginning in 1595, Spain outsourced the supply of its slaves to Portuguese slave traders in a mutually beneficial arrangement that lasted, despite official interruptions, for well over a hundred years.[84] Many of the slavers were New Christians.[85] New Christians also occupied a solid position among the population of those who depended on slaves, whose agricultural productivity instigated slavery for many. Of those 41 sugar mills (*engenhos*) in Bahia and Pernambuco whose owners could be identified between 1587 and 1592, Stuart Schwartz finds 12 that belonged to New Christians.[86] According to a contemporary chronicler, among the 101 mill-plantations around Rio de Janeiro in the seventeenth century, some of which employed over 100 slaves, 21 belonged to New Christians, about 20 percent of the total.[87]

Conversos in commerce took advantage of the fact that in order to facilitate and encourage trade the crown exempted merchants from the need to prove their purity of blood.[88] Many of the commercial activities of conversos also took advantage of the limits of imperial Spanish power, perhaps even aimed to undermine it. Perhaps there is a specific Portuguese converso 'attitude' at work here, a kind of counter-culture that may not have been unique to conversos, but that they frequently exhibited. The Portuguese Judeoconversos who returned to

Spain with the unification of the two countries in 1580 in order to escape the far more virulent Portuguese Inquisition were "notoriously active in the illegal export of Spanish silver to northern Europe and in evading the crown's numerous restrictions on trade with the Spanish Indies."[89] Conversos and former conversos spied for powers hostile to Spain and Portugal. The Portuguese friar Pantaleão d'Aveiro discovered on his journey to the Holy Land in the 1580s that the Portuguese Jews, "having formerly been Christians themselves, were the most vehement critics of and — to his horror — scoffers at Christianity in the Levant."[90] Rodrigo Pereira de Castro, a Portuguese from Zaragoza, was prosecuted by the Cartagena inquisitional tribunal sometime between 1618 and 1620 for refusing to remove his hat when passing a Corpus Christi procession.[91] This contemptuous attitude no doubt entailed a weapon of the weak for those still living under Catholic domination, while helping justify actions committed at the expense of their former oppressors by those who escaped elsewhere. Such behaviors hardly belonged only to Portuguese conversos. By the early seventeenth century, many local Muslims on the Mozambique coast did all they could to resist or subvert Portuguese efforts to control long-standing local trade arrangements. Returning Portuguese racist attitudes with sarcasm, a member of a group of Bantu watching a *fidalgo* strum his guitar in the 1630s exclaimed, "You see, these savages have musical instruments just like we do."[92]

The cultural commuting and worldliness of many Judeoconversos and those who became open Jews stemmed from a combination of factors, not all donned voluntarily. Furthermore, not all saw cosmopolitan worldliness in a positive light. Rabbi of the Spanish and Portuguese community of Amsterdam Saul Levi Morteira, in a 1635 sermon on Gen. 37:14, based a lament against wealth on the ancient midrashic collection Genesis Rabbah (50:11). Marc Saperstein summarizes Morteira's text, still in manuscript:

> Korah represents those whose economic security leads them to think they can sin with impunity. Haman is "the prototype of men who involve themselves in great and dangerous business affairs, crossing seas and wildernesses to fulfil their desires." The tribes of Gad and Reuben represent yet another group: "those who, because of money, do not rest or repose; they find no respite for their feet or slumber for their eyes. Because of their business affairs they live a life of sorrow, toiling hard, running around and exhausting themselves until they bring death near."[93]

Morteira's moral qualms echo similar exhortations by Catholic Iberians. Current events led many converso writers, like their Catholic counterparts, to hark to the biblical trope of Babylonia and its condemned tower when considering the new worlds of colonialism. Moseh Belmonte (Amsterdam; 17th-18th centuries?) critiques the new ethnographically inspired relativism in the course of an anti-Christian poem: "The world with diverse opinions / all is Babel, all is confusions."⁹⁴ The Judeoconverso and possibly crypto-Jewish Antonio Enríquez Gómez repeatedly attacks Spain and Iberian imperialism by wielding the term Babylon. The Judeoconverso and later open Jew Miguel Daniel (Levi) de Barrios writes ambiguously that "Lisbon is the greatest Babylon in the world."⁹⁵ The recognition of Babel in the feverish contemporary overseas expansion, mercantile feeding frenzy, racial confrontation and demographic earthquakes also stands behind the title of Joseph Penso de la Vega's description, the first ever, of a stock exchange, the world's first, in Amsterdam: *Confusion of Confusions* (1688).⁹⁶ The stock exchange serves Vega merely as a metonym for the regnant world system of monarchic capitalism and its magical, illusory, yet utterly disruptive effects. Spinoza, in the Preface to his *Theologico-Political Treatise*, seems to lament the homogenization of his day: "you almost cannot recognize who anyone is — whether Christian, Turk, Jew, or Heathen — unless by the outward habit and worship of his body, or because he frequents this or that Church, or, lastly, because he is addicted to this or that opinion and is accustomed to swearing in the words of some master or other. Otherwise life is the same for all."⁹⁷ This complaint comes across as somewhat amusing, as if the medieval world were hundreds of years gone, and even fails to mention the Americas and the more recent forms of European overseas colonialism, though elsewhere in the text Spinoza raises the Chinese and Japanese.

It should be noted that though many Judeoconversos were merchants, even phenomenally wealthy ones, Judeoconversos could be found in all of the classes.⁹⁸ They were also not by any means exempt from the kinds of collective mistreatment we usually associate with other groups. Toward the end of the fifteenth century, King Manoel of Portugal pressed possibly two thousand Jewish youths into service and sent them as forced settlers to the island of São Tomé off of the Atlantic coast of southern Africa. In the mid-seventeenth century an Italian Capuchin priest described how the Portuguese in Luanda, Angola, made enormous use of forced labor, by which he meant not African slaves but Judeoconversos banished for some (alleged) crime or other.⁹⁹

What about the identity of New Christians? In a seminal article, Miriam Bodian correctly notes how until recently most analyses of Judeoconverso identity focused on *religious* identity, though this propensity in fact continues.¹⁰⁰ Let us not start there. Thomas F. Glick, taking up sociological methodology, cuts through the ideological knots of these identity questions in a fresh and useful manner. "Marrano" identity, for Glick, entailed cultural commuting between 'Jewish' and 'Catholic' lifestyles, as "a way of dealing with or acting out ambivalence" regarding two religious systems, two ethnicities regarding which 'the marrano' felt both inside and outside. Glick is worth quoting at length:

> Essentialist definitions of ethnic identity are conducive ultimately to ideologized and misleading conceptions of true and false identities. Ethnicity is a collection of traits, traditions, values, and symbols that situate a group with respect to its ancestors and to other ethnic groups, and a single individual can

easily partake of or draw upon more than one such collection. Thus [anthropologist] F. K. Lehman concludes, with regard to the Karen [of Burma]: "The whole business of insisting that there must be an objectively unique definition for a true ethnic category is vain. It is grounded in the romanticist tradition of associating a cultural inventory with something vaguely and mystically thought of as a unique historical experience, properly attached to racelike populations." The point is important because the notion of "true Jew"/"false Jew" turns up too often in the historiography of crypto-Jews. It is legitimate to specify the "core" identity of a carefully defined group but not to posit a "true" or "false" one. The identity of the cultural commuter is a real one and we should validate it as such.[101]

Though still a model and an abstraction, Glick's approach at least leaves us with an appreciation that marrano identity yields not 'false' Christians or Jews but individuals whose identity may have been rather more complex. The reason such models fail methodologically is that not all Judeoconversos were cultural commuters, in other words, not all New Christians were marranos of Glick's type; some indeed chose one option or neither option. Glick, like Yirmiyahu Yovel after him, tries to erect a typological understanding of Marranism that, by definition, must be false for exactly the reasons Glick lays out at the beginning of the above passage. In an attempt to escape such a conundrum, José Faur argues that, ideologically speaking, there are four types of Judeoconversos: "[T]hose who wanted to be Christians and have nothing to do with Judaism, those who wanted to be Jewish and have nothing to do with Christianity, those who wanted to be both, and those who wanted to be neither."[102]

Faur offers a sociological neatness that avoids establishing and then favoring a 'core' essence of marrano traits, but his schema also suffers from its own neatness. For one thing, it understands converso identity solely in a religious manner, as Bodian complains, and does not allow for a New Christian identity that revolves around itself as ethnicity, demographic unit or subculture. In addition, it fails to appreciate that individual Judeoconversos may have felt drawn to or by more than one ideological pole or may have gone back and forth between them.

Though messier and less reducible to generalization, attempts to approach Judeoconverso identity through concrete historical examples affords us another path. As mentioned, it is generally accepted by scholars, and was a widespread sentiment at the time, that the Portuguese conversos maintained a far higher loyalty to Judaism as a result of the sudden and collective conversion of the entire Portuguese Jewish population at one time. The closer one stands to 1492 and 1497 the more likely it is that self-awareness of Jewish identity will be present and meaningful among both Spanish and Portuguese Judeoconversos. This does not necessarily have to do with judaizing, but merely pride in and insistence on maintaining the meaning of ethno-religious origins and unity. Hence in 1512, a law was passed on the island of São Tomé, settled in part by possibly two thousand

Jewish youths forcibly removed there by the Portuguese king, that of the four aldermen sitting on the municipal council, at least one had to be a New Christian, a sign of successful New Christian political pressure.[103] Even in-group behavior, such as insularity or endogamous marriage, whose rates varied considerably (and whose statistics must be taken with a grain of salt for methodological reasons), do not necessarily translate into marrano leanings, but possibly only ethnic self-consciousness. Solange Alberro reports that among Mexican Judeoconversos, many of them originally Portuguese, 96 percent married endogamously.[104] Looking at records produced by the 1591 and 1593 inquisitorial visitations to Brazil, Stuart Schwartz found that 59 percent of the New Christian men and 56 percent of the women were married to Old Christians.[105] Among the New Christians of seventeenth- and eighteenth-century Rio de Janeiro province, finds Lina Gorenstein, some 66 percent of the marriages are with other New Christians.[106] One Judeoconverso from the mid-seventeenth century attests to these tribal feelings when he testifies that "'judaizers' had a common style of letting themselves be known amongst" themselves. They "would ask each other about their places of birth and about their parents and grandparents, and upon knowing that they were of the nation, they would say [of each other] '*és dos nossos*' [in Portuguese: 'He/she is one of ours']."[107] Whether non-judaizing conversos also behaved in this manner needs to be determined.

Many scholars suggest that Judeoconversos manifested certain ideational characteristics that reflected their difficult situation. Judeoconversos, according to Inquisition and other sources, expressed great pride in their origins, their religion (the so-called Law of Moses), both because from them Christianity had sprung, even their Jewish nicknames. Many of them married only other Judeoconversos and, especially early on, attempted to maintain some forms of separateness. For instance, in the Castilian town of Guadalupe, Judeoconverso men "congregated apart from Old Christians both during and after mass" at the church known as St. Gregory's Nave.[108] (The women apparently did not self-segregate in this manner. This example brings up once again the likelihood that identity was inflected by gender.) Judeoconversos lamented the innocence of those martyred by the Inquisitions and the cruelty with which they were dispatched. They saw themselves as embodying all the highest virtues and traits: honor, nobility of spirit, greatness. Caught between warring religious systems and seemingly entirely antagonistic symbolic universes, Judeoconversos are said to have been prone to skepticism, doubt, disaffection, irreverence.[109] They were frequently accused of disbelieving the claims of the Catholic church, its institutions and rituals, priests, saints, eating of the host, baptism and the Inquisition (as open Jews they not infrequently had difficulty with the claims of the rabbinic establishment). Even more problematic, Judeoconversos were often charged with mocking and blaspheming against all the above. In some sense, Judeoconversos are often seen as expressing modern outlooks, for instance in 'inventing' the picaresque novel or adopting philosophical positions of extreme rationalism. At the same time, many conversos, intellectuals and lay people alike, saw their group as being made up of devoted Catholics who were victims of inquisitors and other Catholics who were the actual religious hypocrites.

One crucial aspect of Judeoconverso identity is the peculiar position of Jews in European society, where they often found themselves between the colonizers and the colonized.[110] Just as in England after the Norman invasion, where Jews were used by the conquerors as tax collectors, Jews made up the majority of tax farmers in many of the kingdoms in Moslem and Christian Spain, serving the interests of the monarchy and nobility 'against' the internally colonized peasants. Hence after the Reconquista Jews made convenient new settlers for towns emptied of their Muslim populations.[111] It was convenient and for the most part effective for medieval Christian Europe, a cluster of societies that for the most part despised, shunned and even demonized physical and cultural mobility, curiosity and multiplicity, to have Jews and later conversos serve as commercial intermediaries.[112] All this helped create the position of conversos and Sephardim in the Atlantic world. Jonathan Israel hints at the economic uses to which Jews were often put by colonizing European countries (his examples are all from the mid-seventeenth century):

> At Hamburg, the rules imposed by the Senate excluded the Jews from practically every form of activity other than overseas trade [...] Even at Amsterdam, guild restrictions excluded Jews from most crafts and forms of shop-keeping and those crafts they were allowed to practice, such as diamond-processing, tobacco-spinning, and chocolate-making, were, generally speaking, closely connected with colonial trade.[113]

In light of the difficulties of attracting Europeans to settle in the new-found overseas colonies, Jews were offered rights and privileges if they would settle, for example, in early Dutch Surinam, rights and privileges which were reaffirmed by later conquerors who wanted to keep the Jews there. Conversos fulfilled similar commercial functions in the Iberian empires. From the beginning, Spain and Portugal forbade Jews and conversos to emigrate to the New World.[114] Yet even in the Iberian backyard of the Inquisitions the economic benefits of tolerating not only 'New Christians' but even Jews swayed some to seek to rein in theological zealotry for 'reasons of state.' So the Portuguese mercantilist Duarte Gomes Solís, himself a New Christian, "urged Philip III not just to restrain persecution of New Christians but to allow professing Jews to settle in the Portuguese colonies in Asia and have ghettos there 'as they do in Rome and other parts of Italy' as a means of defeating Dutch and English commercial rivalry in the east."[115]

This is not to imply that Jews/conversos were solely abject victims of Christian regimes, unwilling converts to colonialism. Where possible, they were seeking their own survival and gain like everybody else. (It needs to be kept in mind that the majority of Jews in *every* early modern city in both the old and new worlds was poor.) Like so many Europeans, conversos flocked to the Americas in the hope of obtaining the privileges that in Europe remained the prerogative of the nobility. Many conversos also fled to the Americas in order to escape the tyranny of the motherlands' Inquisitions which hovered over them regardless of their religious orientation. It was precisely the confluence of Jewish self-interest and European colonial desires that put Jews and conversos into often problematic situations vis-à-vis other colonized peoples. Conversos or Jews were but a minority of the actual colonialists but carried out much of the trading. Just as lower-class Europeans found an elevated status in the Americas — as Whites living above Amerindians and Blacks — so did Judeoconversos.[116] Nonetheless, the New World was not necessarily a paradise for Judeoconversos, particularly as their commercial success only attracted greater inquisitional interest. The Inquisition followed these refugee colonialists there, where 'Jews and heretics' were hunted out beginning in 1570 in Peru, 1571 in Mexico, and 1579 in Brazil, as the Inquisition in Portuguese Goa (India) had begun in 1561. The few Judeoconversos who made their way to Portuguese Angola were likewise followed by an Inquisitorial visitation in 1626.

The peculiar status of European Jews engendered a peculiar logic for some Jews and conversos, since they were dependent for their privileges and often their lives on Christian rulers whose success was more and more achieved at the expense of other peoples. Jews and conversos were, of course, expected to contribute to the attainment of this national success, but in any case it is difficult to cut the circle between the external coercion to perform any and all tasks and the internal desire to stay on the master's good side for one's own benefit.[117] The poet and physician Yehudah ha-Levi captured beautifully the angst of this dialectic when in the twelfth century he described in a letter to Rabbi David of Narbonne the difficulty of medically treating the "giant" inhabitants of Toledo, those "hard masters." "[A]nd how can a slave please his masters other than by spending his days fulfilling their desires...we heal Babylon, but it is beyond healing."[118]

The same dialectic is differently thematized, though without rationalization or even comment, in a recent description of the Barcelona scholar Abraham bar Ḥiyya (b. 1070): "In his work *Megillat ha-Megalleh* he attacked the opinions of the church fathers which were prevalent at the time. He considered the crusades as signifying the end of days and poured out his wrath against the Crusader kingdom in the Land of Israel, also opposing Islam and even more, Christianity. While in the [Catalonian] prince's service, he wrote *Ḥibbur ha-Meshikhah ve-ha-Tishboret*, a geometrical work for the measurement of land and its allotment during the *Reconquista*."[119] Here the question is not healing Babylon, but aiding and abetting the expansion of its empire, a process to which this resister-at-heart in the heart of the state seems to offer no resistance. Though on the one hand many scholars point to widespread 'Portuguese,' i.e., Judeoconverso skepticism, distance, even mockery toward Catholicism, as discussed above, most Judeoconverso authors from the sixteenth and seventeenth centuries failed to critique the colonial practices of Portugal or Spain. Insistence on tolerance concerning themselves did not necessarily translate into empathetic tolerance for victim groups. On a related note, some scholars, such as Tobias Green, argue that the groups of Judeoconversos who migrated to imperial outposts — Cabo Verde, for instance — helped forge the specific creole identities of these places.[120] This is an avenue worthy of further study.

When it comes to religiosity, within the Iberian world it is notoriously difficult to tell who is a secret Jew and, if so, what kind. I will not enter here into the nature of marrano religiosity, as it is discussed by many other authors and to a certain degree it will come up in the course of the chapters to come. Judeoconversos obviously ran the gamut from sincere Catholics to sincere marranos to sincere unbelievers. The kind of systematizing of 'marrano religiosity' done by David Gitlitz, in an otherwise useful survey, deceptively erases the very extreme variability that of necessity characterized a forbidden religion.[121] Many of the figures in question do not necessarily maintain an identity over time or space, despite the fact that most researchers remain mired in reproducing the racialist assumptions of Iberian antisemitism by resorting to genealogical 'proof' of Jewish descent, that is, arguing from biology as much as or instead of from belief or action. That a particular New Christian bore one or more Jewish ancestors only opens up the possibility that he or she might have been instructed, in some more or less tenuous form, in Jewish law or customs, but it certainly does not guarantee such a circumstance. It is known that surviving members of the prominent Carvajal family, persecuted as judaizers in sixteenth-century Mexico, and their descendants changed their names to avoid further trouble with the Inquisition, while some scholars write of members of other families with names 'known' to betray converso origin who took on new names.[122] Anyone caught passing as an Old Christian was punished and declared a Jew (and how many escaped notice?), though of course religiosity may have had nothing to do with their attempt to avoid their stigmatized New Christian status. Often families had openly Jewish members in the Netherlands or Italy, for instance, and Catholic members in parts of the Iberian empires. Sometimes a person might follow a combination of Christian and Jewish beliefs or practices, as did Diego de Padilla of Córdoba, of the Río de la Plata province of the Viceroyalty of Perú, tried in 1579 for believing in God, Mary, Abraham and Moses.[123] María de San Juan confessed to the inquisitors of peninsular Córdoba that she "inclined to the law of the Christians, though sometimes she made fasts of the law of Moses when she was with her sisters and saw them fast; and it had been four years since she had completely departed from the said law and never performed any more ceremonies, because in that time she had not been with her sisters, nor had dealings with them."[124] A descendant of the prominent New York Jewish Phillips family wrote in 1894 that he heard his father, "the late Isaac Phillips, say that for years after their arrival in this country the female members of the family were unable to repeat their prayers without the assistance of the Catholic rosary, by reason of the habit acquired in Portugal for the purpose of lending the appearance of Catholic form should they be surprised at their devotions."[125]

Many New Christians may have practiced 'Jewish' customs without knowing that they were such, or with only the most minimal understanding of their meaning and origin. Scholar Juan Blázquez Miguel calls this phenomenon "residual crypto-Judaism."[126] Does this make these individuals judaizers? In 1593 Pernambuco, Pedro Bastardo, a *mameluco*, that is, a Brazilian Mestizo and/or slave-hunter, confessed to the visiting inquisitor that "he spent seven years in the bush among pagans (*gentios*), living by gentile customs and did not know whether he was New Christian or Old." Accused of conducting Jewish rites, he stated that "he did not know that [a certain] ceremony was Jewish."¹²⁷ As hinted in Bastardo's testimony, some scholars conclude that by the sixteenth century 'vibrant' Marranism survived only in smaller towns and rural villages, where strong family alliances countered official destructive pressures. Of course, it is possible that Bastardo simply sought to avoid charges and punishment, but this cannot be assumed. Juan de León, alias Salomón Machorro, born in Pisa, raised as a Jew in Livorno and arrested by the Mexican Inquisition as a judaizer in May 1642, told his inquisitors during the course of his trial that one Portuguese Jew he knew "had not been in Ferrara with the Jews because the Jews from there feel maliciously toward the Portuguese judaizers who go and come from Spain, and denounce them before the Bishop, because they don't know the Law in Hebrew."¹²⁸ These examples — and many, many more could be brought — only hint at the complex variety of possible stances forged by and circumstances forging Judeoconverso religiosity.

The 'in-betweenness' of many types of New Christians is frequently noted and bespeaks a more general cultural predicament. In the first centuries of colonization, children of mixed Spanish and Amerindian parentage were considered either Spanish or Amerindian according to which cultural norms they followed. This relative acceptance disappeared by the seventeenth century, as was true regarding Mulatos and Judeoconversos. The distrust and enmity shown toward the last category of 'mixed-breeds' by both 'normative' Christians and Jews directly parallels the definition for *mulato* offered by the contemporary Sebastían de Covarrubias Orozco in his famous *Tesoro de la Lengua Castellana o Española* (Madrid, 1611): "One who is the son of a black woman and a white man, or the reverse: and *due to being an extraordinary mixture* he is compared to the nature of a mule" (my emphasis).¹²⁹ Mixed-breeds, Mestizos, were ostracized by certain Amerindian elites, as represented by figures such as Guaman Poma, just as were Luso-Africans by the Wolof, Serer and Mandinka of West Africa.¹³⁰ At the same time, gender assumptions often led Spanish male elites to seek the assimilation of mestizas and mulatas as servants, tutors or wives, as auxiliaries in the reproduction and dissemination of Spanish "Christian" society.¹³¹ Though initially racial miscegenation did not seem to represent a policy issue in western Africa, by 1620, King Felipe III of united Spain and Portugal ordered that Portuguese prostitutes, formerly punished with exile to Brazil, be sent instead to Cabo Verde "with the objective of extinguishing, insofar as possible, the race of mulattos;" in other words, Whitening the population through a breeding program.¹³² The confused and often syncretistic nature of the religion of many of the descendants of Judeoconversos, was astutely described by the Inquisition tribunal of the Spanish city of Llerena, despite the depiction's inherent bias:

> Evidence deposed in this inquisition by the prisoner Manuel de Silva, against various persons in Arroyuelos, a village in which all the inhabitants are observers of the Law of Moses, but who observe it just as badly as they observe the Law of Christ, for they know neither the rites nor the ceremonies, as there is no Jewish priest. They live only with the consciousness that they

are Jews, and they do no more than declare themselves to be adherents of the Jewish religion and pray to Moses with the prayers of Our Holy Mother, which they direct to him, for they say that he is another God to whose care they commend themselves.[133]

In a society obsessed with the eradication of religious difference, with conformity to traditional and honorable mores, in-betweenness evinced an intolerable threat.

Besides the problem of ignorant syncretism there exists much evidence for persistent shuttling between faiths. Giorgio Rota cites from the archives of the Venetian Inquisition the story of Giovanni or Abran Battista. Born Jewish to Portuguese parents in Salonika, he was baptized in Rome at the age of thirteen. His parents returned him to Judaism but four years later he turned Muslim in Constantinople. Sometime later, in 1583, Battista showed up in Venice and presented himself to the Holy Office there, stating that he wanted to become a priest.[134] The case of Daniel Gabilho or Habilho, also known as Bento Jorge Borges, serves as another example of these difficulties. Living in Recife, he began in 1641 to buy and sell slaves from Angola, among other goods. Throughout his stay in Brazil he faced judicial problems: in the beginning of 1642 he found himself condemned to the gallows for debts and other larger faults, from which he was spared by the intervention of the Recife Jewish community and a fine of 15,000 florins, to pay for his ten-year deportation to the island penal colony of São Tomé — a punishment never carried out; in July of the same year, again condemned, this time for blasphemy, he handed over a 4,000 florin penalty. In 1645 he returned to Lisbon, whence he embarked for Amsterdam. Here he had to make public penitence for "having abandoned the Law of God and having converted to Christianity."[135] Clearly, he had been living in Brazil apart from the Jewish community, though he ultimately joined the one in Amsterdam. Was he a Jew in Brazil? a Christian in Amsterdam? He left Brazil (in 1645) nearly a decade before the Catholic Portuguese reconquered what the Protestant Dutch had occupied — when he also happened to be denounced to the Inquisition in Lisbon — though that same year the Portuguese Brazilians began their campaign to reconquer those parts dominated by the Dutch. Did he leave to pursue his religious beliefs? Did he move because of judicial or even financial difficulties or merely fear of the Inquisition? Manoel da Costa, a Frenchman of Portuguese descent, constitutes a similar case. He told Jews that he came out as an open Jew in Holland but told Christians that he was Christian. When he spoke with Dutch individuals, he said he was Calvinist, read their books and attended the Dutch Reformed churches in Paraíba, when the Dutch conquered it.[136]

Precisely because of such cultural commuting, the Spanish-Portuguese community in Amsterdam forbade 'passing' as a Christian in the Iberian Catholic 'lands of idolatry / *tierras de idolatría*' in 1644. Any Jew, who in order to do business or the like, 'passed' as a Christian for a time, could not, upon returning, be received by the community or be a member of a minyan, without a public apology; thereafter for four years he was not allowed to be called to the Torah, to be honored by any mitzvah in the synagogue (excepting his own family celebrations), to discharge any community function. Between 1645 and 1725, 80 persons were so punished for these transgressions.[137] The existence of this policy points to the very problem under discussion, i.e., the prevalence of moving back and forth between religious, social and cultural orbits. Were those who lived as Catholics in Catholic Brazil, then as Jews in Dutch Brazil and then again as Catholics after the ouster of the Dutch — Jews or Catholics? Such cases recurred even without the exchange of ruling powers in a territory. David Graizbord's important recent study shows that former émigré conversos who opted not to join a Jewish community or who chose to return to Spain or even to become Catholic again were not negligible numerically or culturally.[138] Given the fragmented state of the documentation, none of these questions can be answered with certainty. The more important point is that the questions are as much philosophical as epistemological. In the case of each historical figure, the researcher needs to attempt to determine just what makes her subject Jewish or not, something that cannot always be accomplished.

The assimilation of the Judeoconverso minority into the general population certainly only increased with the passing of the centuries, even if pockets of Marranism persisted. The descendants of Rabbi Salomón Ha-Leví of Burgos, who converted in 1391, becoming Pablo de Santa María, "became so widespread and so interrelated with Castilian nobility that a royal decree was issued by King Felipe III [...] accepting their *limpieza de sangre*, or purity of bloodline, and officially recognizing the Ha-Leví family as an honorable and noble family of Christian blood and faith."[139] Interests of state also motivated the assimilation of Judeoconversos. In addition, in certain periods, such as the debt-ridden reign of Felipe II, money from conversos was accepted by the crown in return for 'favors,' such as the granting of titles of nobility, territory and certificates of 'pure blood' that allowed their converso bearers to emigrate to the Americas. Felipe II even granted the Portuguese New Christian conquistador Luis de Carvajal y de la Cueva a territory of some 700,000 square miles in the north of New Spain, which was to be completely independent, of which Carvajal would serve as governor, and permitted Carvajal to bring 100 settlers without need for certificates of *limpieza de sangre*. As with all of the colonial territories, Carvajal's territory was given the title of kingdom / *reino* and its first governor was assigned rights to have his heir succeed him. Pragmatism, of course, generated Felipe's beneficence: the territory granted Carvajal, already a heroic figure, entailed an isolated frontier of the empire populated by hostile Amerindians that the king wanted conquered and pacified; allegedly, Carvajal's apotropaic service to empire was offered to Felipe for the price of two million ducats.

Scholars like Anita Novinsky and Angela Maria Vieira Maia argue that in Brazil the necessities of colonial living facilitated socialization and the mitigation of discriminatory barriers between New and Old Christians.[140] Maia finds endogamous New Christian marriages fairly low in the late-sixteenth century sugar-producing captaincies of Brazil: 27 marriages with Old Christians out of 55 mentioned in Bahia, 43 mixed marriages out of 69 in Pernambuco, 14 out of 26 in Itamaracá.[141] Novinsky cautions us to recall that many of Brazil's New Christians, perhaps even most of them, opposed or fought against Dutch attempts to take territory from the Portuguese in the early and mid-seventeenth century.[142] Lina Gorenstein cogently summarizes the assimilation of New Christians into the life of Rio de Janeiro in the seventeenth and eighteenth centuries:

> [T]hey lived like [the Old Christians], dressed and conducted themselves in the same manner. They lived together with them, were godparents of their children, did business, frequented their houses. [....] the New Christians had been baptized at birth and educated as Catholics. They frequented the churches, attended masses, took communion and confessed. The majority of them were christened, knew all the Catholic prayers, made the sign of the cross, kneeled and clamored for the saints.[143]

Yet, given the prejudices against New Christians and the pressures for keeping such an identity hidden, many Judeoconversos may not have known who else shared their background and even when they knew, their knowledge may have been purely formal. After having related a great deal of information about her own Jewish practices and those of her family, after having denounced numerous people in the course of nearly two years in an inquisition jail in Mexico in the 1640s, Beatriz Enriquez denounces yet one more individual. She claims that another New Christian, named Ysauel Duarte told her that Luis de Olivera "was of a good heart," i.e., that he was a crypto-Jew. But, says Beatriz to the inquisitors, "even though he sold to this confessant [i.e., herself] a black woman, named Magdalena, she [Beatriz] never has interacted nor communicated with him."[144] During her 1590 Inquisition trial in Toledo, Catalina de Moya (Quintanar, Castile) states that whether she descends "from Old Christians or New Christians she is not able to determine."[145] Sergeant of the auxiliary militia Adrião Pereira de Faria, of the state of Pará, Brazil, imprisoned on charges of witchcraft (feitiçaria) in 1756, did not know whether he was Old Christian or New Christian.[146] One Conversa told her Coimbran inquisitors in 1583 that "she did not know whether her father and mother were New or Old Christians and she did not comprehend this [question] nor did it ever cross her mind to ask her mother whether she was a New Christian or an Old Christian, and in this she persisted in spite of being much admonished" by her interrogators.[147] Of course, whether these protestations should be believed is another story.

Discussing the late twentieth century "cultural remnant" of early modern crypto-Jews in the area of New Mexico, Stanley Hordes summarizes his findings:

> At one extreme are individuals who are biological descendants of the original fifteenth-century *conversos* but retain neither an awareness of their ancestral faith nor any vestigial Jewish customs. The other extreme, very few in number, encompasses

those who profess a retention of a consciousness of the family's Judaism and continue to observe Jewish practices, either openly as Jews or in secret under the cover of Catholicism or Protestantism. The majority, however, fall in a middle category: those Catholics or Protestants whose families display observances suggestive of Judaism, but without any specific knowledge about why they do so.[148]

Though this summary in fact goes against the argument of his own book, it is one of the most concise and excellent statements in favor of the skeptical position. By our own times, the number of crypto-Jews entails "very few" individuals. Many descendants of conversos, on the other hand, might well know of or maintain retentions of Jewish customs or beliefs but without any understanding or intention. These sociological conclusions reflect a period of over a century in which this population lived with legal freedom of religion, though of course social pressures continued, which can be more conservative than legislative decree.

There is no reason to believe that during the sixteenth to eighteenth centuries — at least from the time when conversos were personally disconnected from a Jewish past for one or more generations (except in exceptional cases of having lived in open Jewish communities abroad), when legal and social pressure to live as Catholics ran extremely and explicitly high — the number of crypto-Jews comprised anything more than a "very few" individuals relative to the total number of New Christians. This would certainly have been true for Spanish Judeoconversos. As Glick and others point out, those who wanted to flee Spain and could do so left in 1492. But it may even be likely that among Portuguese New Christians, Jewish practices faded away relatively quickly among the majority of the population. Though I have seen no attempt to quantify this and the necessary documentation simply may not exist, I suspect that the numbers of Portuguese New Christians who fled Iberian territories, even when they could do so, is smaller than the number of those who remained. Was this only because of the very real difficulties in obtaining permission to leave or fleeing without such permission? When such permission was granted as a matter of general policy, most Judeoconversos chose to stay. The number of those who assimilated into Jewish communities abroad is no doubt far smaller still. Anita Novinsky notes that "It is a striking fact that the number of New Christians residing in several Brazilian cities exceeded the total number of Jews living in Amsterdam when the Sephardic community there reached its height."[149] This might be because, whether they judaized or not, New Christians who sought to escape the ever-present possibility of inquisitional trouble saw Brazil as a place of relative refuge. To speak of judaizing 'tendencies' in extended families is to assume a transmission that by definition can never be disproved. It is obvious from many cases, however, that even in marrano families some individuals were not included in judaizing practices or opted not to engage in them. Therefore, family connections to judaizers can never prove anything about another individual. Business connections with those later accused, arrested or sentenced for judaizing prove even less. It is not even clear that business connections with individuals in open Jewish communities proves judaizing on the part of a New Christian, as many such connections spanned religious difference.

This is not the place to rehearse the dark history of Iberian Catholic anti-Judaism. A combination of religious politics and economic motivations drove those forces that opposed the assimilation of Judeoconversos into Iberian society and that argued that the Judeoconverso population was riddled with secret Jews. Ironically, the problem was of their own making. Since at least the twelfth century, inspired by an increasingly militant Christianity led by mendicant preachers, Spanish clergy and crown insisted on forcible conversions of Jews, notwithstanding papal non-recognition of such methods. The 1497 mass conversion of the entirety of Portuguese Jewry in one fell swoop by King Manoel III stands as the peak of this tragically farcical practice, which could only backfire, leading to what is called in today's geopolitical game-playing 'blowback.' Having demanded loyalty to a religion many Jews neither sought nor liked, perhaps true of all of the Jews of Portugal in 1497, this same clergy and crown, each for its own reasons, quickly erected an enormous institutional machinery to prevent 'backsliding' from an identity most of the targeted population had no desire to maintain. Many who were not even Judeoconversos would have agreed with the imprisoned woman in 1640s Mexico who said that "these señores [inquisitors] wish to have more power than God."[150] Adding perversity to absurdity, it is the very victims of such mendacious and hypocritical religious oppression who become targeted as traitors and punished, even posthumously, with rhetoric about innate deceitful Jewish traits and labeled, as was one victim of the inquisition, "ungrateful for so much good as he has received from the hand of God, making him a Christian."[151] Hence the hypocrisy and tragic irony with which triumphalist Iberian Catholicism and imperialist Iberian expansionism of the "Golden Age / Siglo de Oro" turned around to accuse "the Jews" of arrogance and haughtiness, as in Quevedo's work, *Virtud militante contra las cuatro pestes del mundo*.[152] In other words, Jews/Judaism were obstacles preventing Iberians from making the world safe for Christianity (and for Iberians).

The truth is neither with those who see in every New Christian of Jewish background a fervent marrano, nor with those who imagine that there never existed such a thing as a fervent marrano. The truth seems eminently sociological and deflating to heart-throbbing or heartrending narratives pushed for ideological reasons. As Faur and Glick argue cogently, though differently, it is impossible to generalize about the Judeoconverso population. Much evidence confirms their abstract reasoning. The narratives at work here may have been far more private than collective. They repeatedly confirm Ellis Rivkin's thesis that the "negotiable" religious identity of most of the New Christians shows that they were "crypto-individualists" more than anything else. To paraphrase Graizbord, many Judeoconversos "created their respective religious self-identities as a contingent basis by emplotting (or reemplotting) their individual lives as meaningful narratives." Elsewhere, Graizbord suggests that "the notion of a perfectly hermetic, 'real' identity totally distinct from self-perception and self-revelation is illusory, inasmuch as selfhood is not a fixed fact *entirely distinct from the subject's point of view*, namely that person's unique and evolving perspective of life given his or her changing circumstances."[153] The problem, as with the observer effect known in quantum physics, is that the object — the identity of a particular Judeoconverso — can be known for the most part only by means of a system that seemingly determines the way the object constructs itself, thereby making knowledge of the object's 'true' state nearly impossible. Despite this, too many scholars even today reiterate the inquisitorial obsession with bio-physical identity. Generalizations will not do. Only a case-by-case analysis can avoid leaping to conclusions. Yet the evidence at our disposal comes overwhelmingly from the Inquisitions themselves. What kind of evidence did they produce?

Inquisition Matters

The self-proclaimed Holy Office served as *the* "instrument for ideological regulation, [...] one of the tools for [the] 'homogenization'" of Catholic society attempted by "the state, the Church, and the ruling classes," under whose stern gaze fell Judeoconversos and Afroiberians, among others.[154] Appropriately enough, the Spanish Inquisition, stood as "the only agency of government whose jurisdiction extended throughout all of the [...] empire."[155] The Inquisitions' intimate concern with the ideational and behavioral components of its subject populations' lives, combined with their early modern bureaucratic mode of operation, led to the creation of enormous archives of documents which record the processes and results of the Inquisitions' essentially ethnographic surveillance. There were far more than the 44,000 or so cases now extant which had been prosecuted to some degree by the Portuguese Inquisition. The larger Spanish Inquisition generated over 150,000 cases.

Inquisition documentation begins with the institution's early modern re-establishment in Castile in 1478 (and the many local tribunals which sprouted in its wake: Seville, 1480; Cordoba, Valencia and Zaragoza, 1482; Toledo, 1483; Barcelona, 1484; Palermo, Sicily, 1487; Las Palmas, the Canary Islands, 1507; Granada, 1526, and so on). Portugal received an Inquisition of its own in 1536, though it began operating only in 1540. In 1542 the Roman Inquisition was reconstituted. A tribunal of the Portuguese Inquisition in Goa, India, commenced operation in 1560, having jurisdiction over all of Portugal's Asian and East African territories. Lisbon's tribunal dealt with colonies in and on the Atlantic: the Azores, Madeira, Cape Verde, Guinea, São Tomé, Angola. For various reasons Brazil never hosted its own tribunal, remaining instead under the eye of local commissioners and familiars of the Lisbon Inquisition and occasional visitations by Inquisitors sent from the homeland. In 1570 or 1571, the Spanish Inquisition opened a tribunal in Mexico City, whose jurisdiction included the Spanish colonies north of Panama, as well as the Philippines. Tribunals in Lima and Cartagena de Indias were established in 1570 and 1610, respectively. The former's surveillance covered the viceroyalty of Peru, which included what is now Bolivia, Ecuador, Chile and

Argentina; the Cartagena tribunal presided over Nueva Granada, what is now Colombia and Venezuela and the islands of the Caribbean. The end of the various Inquisitions began in the early nineteenth century, but their usefulness for the purposes of this study predates this period by perhaps a century, if not more. By this time, they tended to focus on forbidden books, minor heresies within Christianity and the like.

King Ferdinando and Queen Isabella of Castile re-established the Inquisition at the behest of the leadership of the Dominican order, in particular the queen's confessor, friar Tomás de Torquemada. The initial worry was Judeoconversos who may not have been living up to their professed Christianity. The inquisitors quickly expanded their targets to include moriscos, Muslims who had likewise been for the most part forcibly converted to Catholicism during and after the Reconquista, the growing number of Protestants, at first foreigners and then even Spaniards, and other religious deviancies such as witchcraft, self-proclaimed mystics, transgressive priests, blasphemers, those who engaged in sex deemed sinful by the church, those who made heretical statements, and so on. Originally, the Franciscans who ran the early Inquisition in New Spain had jurisdiction over Amerindian spiritual matters, but because of their extreme harshness in seeking to eradicate indigenous religious practices, Felipe II removed this power when he ordered the establishment of an official tribunal in Mexico City in 1571. Nonetheless, Mexican inquisitors continued to interest themselves in Amerindian influences on the colony's Catholicism.

On the one hand scholars must ask themselves concerning the ostensibly objective identities that might lay 'behind' the inquisitional documentation. Additionally, standing in need of scholarly interrogation is the production of the documentation itself. How does one approach the mass of proto-ethnographic documentation produced by the Inquisitions, so rich for scholars? Scholars are divided. Let us start with the question from the perspective of Jews/conversos, the original targets of inquisitorial activity. On the one hand is an odd assortment of Iberian scholars, some even defenders of or apologists for the Inquisition, and Jewish historians, some of whom could be called romantic, who agree at least on the fact that the population of Judeoconversos contained many, perhaps mostly, individuals who were devoted to maintaining their Jewish religiosity. Into these groups fall researchers such as Amador de los Rios, Yitzhak Baer, Cecil Roth, Israel Salvator Révah, J. Lúcio de Azevedo, Haim Beinart (a student of Baer's). On the other hand stand skeptics, such as Benzion Netanyahu, Francisco Márquez Villanueva, Ellis Rivkin, Herman P. Salomon, Norman Roth and, perhaps most forcefully, António José Saraiva, who feel that crypto-Judaism was minimal, limited to a few times and places, and mostly generated by the Inquisitions themselves.[156] Saraiva, among others, believes that the Inquisition in Portugal, at least, used the issue of alleged judaizing as a cover for a socio-economic war that sought to keep the commercial class of New Christians from intruding on the turf of the nobility (from which class practically all of the inquisitors derived), that the Inquisition's procedures themselves created judaizers out of good or indifferent New Christians and that the Inquisition had an institutional interest in convincing the Crown and public of the reality, enormity and threat of rampant judaizing.[157] The same could easily be said about the Spanish Inquisition.[158] Scholars such as Salomon point to the abysmal lack of judicial protocol in the earliest trials by the Spanish Inquisition, which acted on little more than the denunciations it received.[159] A third, mostly younger set of scholars such as Anita Novinsky accepts some conclusions from both divisions of scholars, arguing both that crypto-Judaism was real but that the Inquisitions understood and constructed it and put it to use in a particular manner for particular purposes. I would place myself in this third category.

In recent years, scholars from other fields have come to appreciate and make great use of inquisitorial records in order to explore early Afroiberian history and culture. In the second half of the twentieth century perhaps the first to mine inquisition sources for information about the material and spiritual lives of Blacks in the Spanish and Portuguese empires were Solange Alberro and Colin Palmer.[160] More recent studies have made important use of Inquisition sources, among them those of Herman Bennett, *Africans in Colonial Mexico* (2003), James Sweet, *Recreating Africa* (2003) and Luz Adriana Maya Restrepo, *Brujería y reconstrucción de identidades entre los africanos y sus descendientes en la Nueva Granada, siglo XVII* (2005).[161] Works by Ruth Behar, Diana Luz Ceballos Gómez, Martha Few, Laura Lewis and Irene Silverblatt, among others, have greatly contributed to our knowledge of caste women in particular through their reliance on Inquisition records.[162]

Interestingly (ironically?), scholars of Afroiberian studies tend to parallel the more romantic and nationalist Jewish scholars of the Inquisition, also seeking in the trial records a maximal and oppositional 'African' culture, also minimizing the political gamesmanship of the inquisitors. Sweet asserts, for instance, that "[t]orture and coercion were rarely a part of the equation in Inquisition cases in which Africans were named."[163] This seems to me to vastly downplay the intensity of the inquisitional reality for Afroiberians, who remained subject to the institution's psychological terror and were frequently sentenced to harsh physical punishment or time in the galleys, even if it is true that the Inquisitions focused far more energy on judaizing New Christians. The less methodologically fraught views of scholars of Afroiberian history point up what might be very real distinctions in subject position between Judeoconversos and Afroiberians. For many of the latter group, the Inquisitions could serve as protection from masters or as an institution (at times and to varying degrees) concerned with the implementation of law regarding (mis)treatment of slaves.

The vision of Jean Pierre Dedieu tempts the historian with unexamined transparency: "the documents offer us direct testimony from the 'players'' mouths."[164] But what kind of "players" were these? To say that they had various vested interests flirts with understatement. And was the testimony really so direct? Dedieu himself notes that "the material which [the Inquisition] offers may well have been heavily biased."[165] Discerning the degree of sincerity in the acts of those who testified to and worked for the Inquisitions (even those defending themselves) remains elusive. Are they being honest? Are the facts invented? Are the facts essentially true but couched to make the witness conveying them look as good as possible and everyone else as guilty as possible? That many of the witnesses and informers thought to do their Christian duty in identifying 'unorthodox' strangers, neighbors or relatives seems clear. It must be remembered that "the denunciation was the foundation of the trial's organization and was obligatory, under penalty of excommunication" for the inquisitional judges.[166] That is, without a denunciation there was no trial, unlike the procedure in secular jurisprudence. Were the charges of the denouncers and the inquisitions, on the other hand, mere invention? This seems as ludicrous as believing that all Inquisition charges and testimony are accurate and true.

What about the defendants? Are their confessions proof of their judaizing? What is one to make of defendants who confess under torture, then recant afterward, confess when tortured again, later recant? Is it relevant that defendants accused of judaizing who refused to identify and denounce others were practically guaranteed the death sentence? Along other lines, H. P. Salomon and I. S. D. Sassoon point out that already in 1735, the Portuguese Enlightened critic António Nunes Ribeiro Sanches suspected that

> generations of prisoners who had gone through the interrogations and confessions, though sworn to secrecy and without access to the rule book, must have rehearsed their relatives and friends about "Jewish actions" [...] expected in their confessions [...] The more Jewish prayers and practices "spontaneously" confessed and the more "accomplices" denounced, preferably close relatives, the greater one's chance for rapid reconciliation and a light penance. Original "Jewish" rites (especially prayers cracked up to be "crypto-Judaic," more often than not essentially non-Jewish in nature) were devised *ad hoc* in view of an imminent trial, learned by rote, and opportunely "confessed." The sporadic authentically Jewish prayers (frequently in Spanish translation or in macaronic Spanish-Portuguese) and practices registered in confessions may well derive from contacts of New Christians with the Sephardic communities of Italy and, at a later Inquisitorial period, with those of Hamburg and Amsterdam and demonstrate a strategic adoption, rather than any clandestine retention of traditions.[167]

Novinsky cites an eighteenth-century anecdote from the Inquisition archives: "Upon leaving prison, one New Christian encounters a friend who asks him, 'So, how did you escape death?' And he responds, 'As all others do, by telling them I was a Jew.'"[168] While Saraiva's argument is hyperbolic, parallels existed beyond the world of Judeoconversos. We know that in the seventeenth century "blasphemy was taught and transmitted among Afro-Mexican slaves as a strategy to prevent bodily harm" from masters.[169] Graizbord offers yet another interpretation, a more constructivist one, which I paraphrase: defendants were not "lying" per se, only fashioning their narratives "under the extreme stress of inquisitorial questioning" and therefore not in "logical and rational ways; they were neither "calculating cynic[s]" nor "spewing forth an ideal and obvious 'truth'" about themselves; they were "complex [individuals] laboring under the burden of [their] circumstances who made sense of [their lives] by selecting, organizing, and molding [their] memories and wishes into a self-portrait. Again, the sheer depth and complexity of that portrait prohibits that we dismiss it as simply 'perjury.'"[170]

In any case, this discourse still demands interpretation: why did charges take *this* form and not another? Why was so-and-so accused of *that* crime and not another? Recent statistical surveys of trials and sentences make abundantly clear the ebb and flow of persecution of particular crimes such as judaizing, witchcraft, Protestantism, and the like. Is it possible that the inquisitional machinery could be biased, predisposed to find guilt or processurally tainted when it came to alleged judaizers but not when it came to, say, African slaves suspected of blasphemy? Torture, for example, was most readily applied to suspected judaizers, 75 percent of them in late seventeenth-century Spain, according to Henry Kamen.[171] It is quite possible that the inquisitional tribunals at different times and in different places indeed differed in the manner in which they assized the individual and collective human objects of their pursuit. That is, depending on specific local conditions and fears, Judeoconversos might well have been perceived as inherently suspicious enough to be silently declared guilty, while elsewhere the same could be said for Amerindian magical practitioners or shamans (despite the fact that the native Americans stood supposedly beyond the inquisitional jurisdiction).[172] The fact that the Supreme Council of the Spanish Inquisition in Madrid (the *Suprema*) repeatedly castigated the tribunals of Lima and Cartagena for flawed trial procedures during their pursuit of the so-called Great Conspiracy of judaizers in the 1630s could be taken to indicate that many of these cases in one way or another had been fixed. On the other hand, the *Suprema* never demanded the dismissal of the responsible officials nor the closure of the clearly problematic tribunals and it insisted on the release or retrial of the prisoners in question in only a few rare cases.

Ultimately, it should be kept in mind that, according to the first systematic statistical analysis of all of the cases of the Spanish Inquisition worldwide that unfolded until their conclusion, between 1540 and 1700 some 4,397 cases against judaizers occurred.[173] Even knowing that the overwhelming majority of cases held between 1480 and 1540 involved judaizers, even assuming that the number of cases that were dismissed was three times this number, we would come to around 20,000 cases over the course of three centuries.[174] While the psychological and physical torment of the accused and punished remains unforgivable, this number comprises, at most, a very small percentage of the total number of conversos within the Spanish imperial orbit. For an institution as thorough and effective as the Inquisition was according to its reputation, this number is astonishingly small. If the Inquisition invented cases of judaizing at its pleasure, wouldn't the number of cases have been far higher? The only possible explanation for the relatively small number of cases is either that the Inquisition succeeded in identifying and trying only a small percentage of actual incidents of judaizing or that actual judaizing constituted an activity of a small proportion of Judeoconversos. The latter strikes me as a more plausible and supportable conclusion.

If the Inquisition reflects mass hypnosis by extreme Catholic theology, the forms it took in specific instances nonetheless require explanation, perhaps even a reading, à la Franz Fanon, of the interpretation of the inquisitional dreams (or nightmares) enscripted in flesh and blood. Pierre Chaunu, as early as 1956, foresaw such an approach to the use of inquisitorial documentation "for a global psychoanalysis of society" when noting that the inquisitions' "probes entered between marrow and nerve into the deepest secrets of the conscious and unconscious."[175] Carlo Ginzburg suggests a cautious but optimistic approach for steering through these inquisitional documents' dialogic structure that weaves between the inquisitors' voices and those voices extracted and/or appropriated from the inquisited, in his thought-provoking essay, "The Inquisitor as Anthropologist."[176]

Ultimately, in my opinion, researchers are confounded by a number of circular problems. The fact that Marranism existed cannot prove crypto-Jewishness in any particular case, yet the fact that most Judeoconversos may have been innocent of judaizing cannot prove innocence in any particular case. The same can be said for heretical African or Amerindian practices. On the one hand, it seems obvious that a case-by-case approach sensitive to the various hermeneutical and epistemological difficulties affords the most fruitful methodology, avoiding generalizations of either extreme regarding the behavior of the accused as well as the accusers. At the same time, as Rivkin and Saraiva argue cogently, the Inquisitions' documents "must be considered, to use Rivkin's term, structurally, in light of the entire mechanism of this massive system."[177] In other words, to understand any particular case, its context and details, one must possess a theory about the Inquisitions' purpose and methods; to construct a theory of the Inquisitions' purpose and methods, one must possess a knowledge of the workings of many particular cases, as well as of a vast documentary trail of institutional negotiations, disputes and procedures. However, and here is the final hermeneutical circle, a theory that holds the Inquisitions to have been the producers of the majority of cases of crypto-Judaism still cannot account for the possibility that any particular case might reflect authentic crypto-Judaism, while a theory positing that Marranism was real and widespread still cannot discount the possibility that in any given case the Inquisition artificially and unjustly produced the results it desired.

As I will proceed to investigate cases tried by the Inquisitions, despite my admitted skepticism, I followed some very rough guidelines. If some of the following questions bore affirmative answers, I was more inclined to accept all or part of the judaizing activities alleged: Can we tell whether the charges from denouncers are run-of-the-mill, vague or mere repetitions of the items listed in the Edicts of Faith? Does the evidence present significant and concrete details that reflect specific activities or beliefs? Do depositions from multiple witnesses corroborate one another on specific details and not just general charges?

At any rate, I confess that my use of Inquisition records is somewhat sly. For the most part I am not interested in the obvious surface goals of the inquisitions, the religious lives of Judeoconversos or slave or free Afroiberians. Rather, I am using this enormous body of sources mostly in order to access something seemingly irrelevant to the inquisitors themselves, something contained within the voluminous paper trail they produced but only by accident: material that touches on relations between individuals of different castes, racial attitudes held by individuals, institutional events or behavior from which one can infer racial attitudes. In a way, I am actually reading Inquisition texts against the grain. The kind of statements I draw from these sources mostly (though not always) arose in passing in the course of testimony by witnesses or comments by inquisitors, as local color, mere details, bits of conversation. Many of the methodological concerns noted above would not seem to apply; after all, caste and ethnicity was not necessarily germane to the inquisitors and often to the witnesses themselves in an explicit manner, fixated as they both were, from opposing directions, on a particular set of theological and theo-sociological battles. On the one hand, caste and ethnicity exist as a subterranean discourse in inquisitional records. Yet the power of this discourse comprises both less and more than might be expected by today's scholars because in actuality caste, ethnicity and blood purity were intimately, inextricably linked for the accused, accusers and inquisitors alike.

CHAPTER 2

The Free and Not so Free, the Christian and Not so Christian

Afroiberians and Judeoconversos came into contact throughout the Portuguese and Spanish empires. In these next chapters I explore a multitude of interactions between members of these two groups. Tensions as well as attractions often derived from the Judaism (real or imagined) of Judeoconversos and the Christianity (authentic or feigned) of Black New Christians. Though racial attitudes came into play at times, as well as matters of class, many interactions, at least through the lens of documentation from the Inquisitions, reflected the generally opposed trajectories of Afroiberians and Judeoconversos vis-à-vis Christianity. Individuals from both groups seem to have been aware of these differences, some even self-conscious about them. In the early colonial era, then, some Christian Blacks, slave and free, enhanced their Christianity by demonizing New Christians or alleged crypto-Jews, while others found judaizing an attractive antidote to their own denigration and oppression (the latter the subject of chapters 5 and 7). Some New Christians of Jewish descent bolstered their sense of self-identity and social status through denigration of Blacks. Members of both groups, marginalized and persecuted, though differently from one another, still resorted to a hegemonic discourse through which they could construct their own identity over against another outsider group, often even when expressing positive feelings.

    The examples I present reflect the perceived usefulness of Othering discourse in certain 'ordinary life' situations created by the often life-threatening institutions of Iberian religious nationalism and colonialism. When caste or race — or the caste or race of others — arose in conversation, in behavior, in actions stemming from the everyday, which was often all too extraordinarily trying, they were usually matters wielded strategically, from a speaker's assumption of "a place that can be circumscribed as proper (propre) and thus serve as the basis for generating relations with an exterior distinct from it (competitors, adversaries, 'clientèles,' 'targets,' or 'objects'" of research)." Often, such topics served to disarm or defeat "the 'strong' (whether the strength be that of powerful people or the violence of things or of an imposed order, etc.)."[1] This first chapter concentrates on Judeoconversos and Afroiberians who were not slaves, though, in truth, this does not mean that they were particularly free. Most of the material quoted derives from Inquisition sources, whether primary documents or secondary sources that cite original records. I suspect that a great deal more material awaits discovery and, more importantly, investigation in the various Inquisitional archives.

White but "Jewish"

Many contestatory evocations of religious and racial loyalties between Black and Jewish New Christians came in a context brought into being by Iberian imperial expansionism. The context included the ubiquitous Inquisition, itself a result of the politics decided upon in the fifteenth century of conversion/exclusion of the converted Jews. The inquisitorial atmosphere itself inspired and exacerbated personal feelings, such as defensiveness or ethnocentrism, but to some degree these social tensions also existed as a result of the larger politics of conversion/exclusion of the Jews. Still it seems that only in rare cases did ethnic-racial identity itself seems to generate the denunciations.[2] The triumphal Catholicism of the Portuguese and Spanish empires wielded the power to determine which groups, which beliefs, would merit entry into the chosen circle. Many supplicants arrived proclaiming their devotion, some to share in the advantages of conquest, some the very result of these conquests: monophysite Ethiopians, Jewish conversos, Kongolese neophytes, converts from the East and West Indies, etc. Difference itself became, as in the early days of the Church, a theological issue. Alfonso Salmerón, a close associate of Ignatius Loyola and one of the earliest members of Loyola's Society of Jesus, a defender of the rights of conversos and possibly of converso background himself, wrote to a fellow Jesuit in 1553 insisting that "Superiors of religious orders must be warned that no greater pestilence can spread among religious men than the creation of distinctions between races."[3] A 1586 tract by Franciscan theologian Gaspar de Uceda's notes the tensions to arise in the metropole as a result of competition between what might be seen as ethnic groups in the contest for advancement within Iberian Catholicism. The frequently intolerant welcome proffered by Catholicism, especially of the Iberian variety, wittingly or not seemed to pit one aspiring group against another.

> [I]n the primitive church there arose among the Romans this same schism which at present occurs in Spain, because those newly converted from paganism wish to be preferred over those converted from Judaism, saying that [the Jews] had been unbelieving and had crucified the Son of God, and for this should not be admitted to public offices. And contrariwise, the descendants of the circumcision [i.e., Judeoconversos] exclude those baptized from paganism, for having been idolaters.[4]

Judeoconversos shared in the culture's generally negative perceptions about Blacks. Rhetorically, New Christians, like the rest of the White population, valorized Whiteness. The supposedly "Jewish" formula for parting from someone consisted of a blessing for being surrounded by goodness, "May you be covered in white."[5] Blackness, then, signified something problematic, disturbing, abnormal.

This attitude derived from medieval Jewish discourse. I invoke this less because of its influence as a continuity in the lives of most conversos than because of its strong similarity to Muslim and Christian discourse regarding Africans and pagans, despite the fact that rabbinic and biblical Judaism on the whole evince no particular animus against Ethiopians, Blacks or human blackness. One particularly critical text about pagans for early modern Jews might have been a passage from the work of Moses Maimonides (1135-1204), who presents one view of the 'civilized' gazing upon the 'barbaric' during the medieval period. In his Guide to the Perplexed (bk. 3, ch. 51), the eminently Aristotelian Maimonides provides a parable for the reader about a ruler in his palace and all his subjects, partly within the city and partly outside, some with their back toward the king, others facing him. Maimonides proceeds to interpret his own parable:

> Those [in the parable] who are outside the city [i.e., most distant from the ruler, God] are all human individuals who have no doctrinal belief, neither one based on speculation nor one that accepts the authority of tradition: such individuals as the furthermost Turks found in the remote North, the Negroes found in the remote South, and those who resemble them from among them that are with us in these climes. The status of those is like that of irrational animals. To my mind they do not have the rank of men but have among the beings a rank lower than the rank of man but higher than the rank of the apes. For they have the external shape and lineaments of a man and a faculty of discernment that is superior to that of the apes.[6]

Like Maimonides, most Jewish thinkers distinguished between monotheists (Jews, Christians and Muslims) and pagans without true religion. Though enmities between Jews and Christians or Jews and Muslims existed, the three monotheisms nonetheless proclaimed that they shared a higher status than all other lesser religions.

General Iberian attitudes toward Blacks and Blackness remained negative. It is no surprise, therefore, to find Judeoconversos in Iberian territories wielding Blacks as a contrastive example, seeing in them a lower group accorded (in some ways) higher status. In some cases, it is merely a question of the starkly differing trajectories of Judeoconversos and Afroiberians, many of the former resenting, even avoiding Christianity, many of the latter seeking it. By the seventeenth century one finds repeated references to Afroiberians who presented themselves to inquisitional authorities as Old Christians.[7] Gracea Rodrigues, a Conversa in Portugal accused by the Inquisition in 1543, sees two Black women in the street praying their rosaries to which she supposedly remarks mockingly, "Beads, beads; bunk, bunk."[8] But mutual animosity often based itself on prevailing religious and racial stereotypes, especially since Judeoconversos shared in the general discourse's negative perceptions about the other group. Watching the 26 September 1540 Lisbon auto da fé in which the alleged crypto-Jew and messianic pretender Diogo de Montenegro is burned alive at the stake, one Conversa reacts with visible rage — at least according to one of her denouncers to the local Inquisition. Furthermore, testifies another neighbor, some neighbors told the accused judaizer "how a black looked with evil intention at Montenegro, and [the accused judaizer] responded that in the same way would she watch the black dragged [through the streets]."⁹ The "evil" look of a Black in the crowd, whether it happened or was invented by the neighbors, proved to be an effective taunt, likely because of the racial makeup of the look's giver.

In the 1550s, an older Jewish widow who converted in Italy to Christianity in order to maintain contact with her sons, who had both previously converted, nonetheless has difficulties with her new pragmatically acquired Christianity. At one point she blasphemes publicly in church, shouting, among other things: "That mulatto bastard, he's out of his mind, because I don't want him for a spouse."¹⁰ Her explanation to the Inquisition purposefully reduces the multiple meanings readily apparent in her statement: she says "she had been praying to the Madonna to deliver her from the importunities of a servant who wanted to marry her, and he was the lying bastard to whom she had referred." But, as the context of the accusation hints, might she have been deftly insulting Christ (so frequently called a Christian's spouse) as a Mulato, conflating anti-Christian and anti-Black feelings? Such ornate blasphemies, stemming from disenchantment widely expressed in urban and market culture, were popular in the seventeenth century. In rural Galicia, for example, people would use expressions such as "Christo bellaco y cornudo / the scoundrel and cuckold Christ," "Virgen, mala puta / the Virgin, an evil whore" and "el trasero de Dios / God's buttocks."¹¹ One sixteenth-century Brazilian man was denounced for swearing "by the private parts of Our Lady" or the "holy pubic hair of the Virgin Mary."¹² Perhaps similarly, a woman accused of judaizing in Mexico appeared fond of an insulting blasphemy that links Black inferiority to that of Christianity. Her denouncer relates to the inquisitors how "many times, María was in the habit of speaking badly about the saints whom the Church has canonized and beatified, she not believing that there could be saints in the evangelical Law, and in particular she said of Saint Benito of Palermo, the black, that 'how could a black be a saint?'"¹³

More pointedly, perhaps, the New Christian Alvares Calcaterra, arrested by the Portuguese Inquisition, ca. 1594, said in the midst of a long diatribe against the Inquisition that "the inquisitors of Évora are low persons who live badly and are amancebados [cohabiters, that is, they live with women outside of marriage - js], and that the blacks [slaves - ss] of his parents are better than them..."¹⁴ It is clear that anti-Black attitudes could well serve Whites persecuted for allegedly believing in Judaism as a component of insults to be slung against the "Christian Empire." Hence the particular gall in one imprisoned crypto-Jew's comment that he regrets having come "to this awful land," Mexico, and wishes "not to live where there are [...] the type of people who treat honorable men worse than blacks."¹⁵ In this view, persecuted Jewish New Christians possess an inner "honor" or "nobility," though their outward circumstances appear worse than those of the lowliest Black slaves, who by implication lack the "honor" that would make their fate undeserved. It must be recalled that Afroiberians outside of Africa, where some managed to achieve economic independence, for the most part remained untouched by the commercial success that raised up and carried so many Judeoconverso merchants.

Those of Judeoconverso background could also find Blackness to be consistent with or useful within their religious imaginary. María López, a resident of Castile convicted of judaizing in 1518, cried out during a session of torture by her inquisitors to the "Holy Mary of Monserrate," that is, to the beloved Black Madonna of Montserrat.[16] A Mexican judaizer sentenced in 1649, Leonor Vaez Sevilla, experienced visions after contracting the illness that eventually ended her life:

> Throughout the illness she showed signs of her obstinacy, taking advantage of the circumstances by saying (on an occasion when they wanted to play some music in order to cheer her up) that it had been three days that she enjoyed being regaled by Angels, in the company of her great-grandmother Iuana Rodriguez; and not long after, when a little black girl [negrilla] was at the foot of the bed [...], which filled everyone with admiration, as there was no one then in the chamber.[17]

Ana de Leon Carvajal, tried by the Mexican Inquisition for judaizing and sentenced in 1649, was visited one time by a demon, who appeared in the proverbial guise, "in the figure of a little black and sat himself down with much familiarity on her bed."[18] Black demons and a black devil constituted long-standing Christian tropes, but Carvajal's demon reminds us that, perhaps influenced by African and Amerindian religiosity, "many colonial Mexicans" viewed the devil "not so much as a horrible and frightening creature, but as a figure who in times of crisis offered solace, conversation, and the illusion of hope[, ...] listened and responded to their problems more directly and quickly than God."[19] The same would obviously be true of lesser demonic figures. New Christians, that is, often saw saints, angels and demons in the same variety of possible forms as did most Catholics.

Judeoconversos could find useful the manipulation of anti-Black prejudices for their own ends. Some alleged judaizers in seventeenth-century Brazil, in order to send one of their own to teach and missionize in Dutch-controlled Pernambuco, "a center of public Judaism,"[20] concocted the following tale, related to the Inquisition by an associate of the institution, known as a familiar: "The witness being with the governor, Matheus Lopes Franco entered and requested of him that he help him with an affront into which he had fallen, that a nephew of his, a bachelor, was going to marry a mulata prostitute, and he asked the governor if he [Bacharel] could embark for Pernambuco, in the caravels which were to leave with as much speed as possible."[21]

Whether or not the nephew was really marrying a Mulata remains unclear, although surely the governor or the Inquisition could have ascertained the veracity of the story. What seems clear is that such a marriage with a Mulata of ill-repute constituted enough of a disgrace to make the teller's tale convincing and provide him an excuse to get to Pernambuco.

At times a Judeoconverso might see fit to make rhetorical use of the similarity between non-Christian Blacks and Jews. In 1649, Juan de León, alias Salomón Machorro, had been a prisoner of the Mexican Inquisition for some seven years. He tried denying the accusations of his judaizing. He tried to evade inquisitional jurisdiction by claiming never to have been baptized. In short, he tried several tactics without successfully slowing or stopping the forward motion of his prosecution. Juan de León then decided to beg mercy and offer himself to the inquisitors as a willing Christian. After he showed the requisite penitence to gain mercy and clemency, he told his judges, "they should baptize him out of his condition the way some uncivilized Black who comes from Angola is baptized," in order "to make the holy tribunal see that he is well and firmly converted to our holy Catholic faith by one or another path, and that he wishes to live and die in it."[22] Unfortunately for León, his ploy, sincere or not, failed. In early modern Christian schemes, derived from Pauline theological ethnography, pagans such as Amerindians lived innocent of God's revelation at Mt. Sinai, which had never reached the Americas, and were therefore blameless for maintaining 'heretical' practices. Depending on the specific theo-political situation, Africans might be seen as innocent pagans who never had been exposed to Christ's message or, contrarily, as Ethiopians who had been made aware of Christianity already in ancient times but who nonetheless had degenerated into paganism. A crypto-Jew such as León could never claim the innocence of living ante legem, before the giving of the law, since Jews were privy to the Revelation and should have recognized the true and correct Christian understanding of the Jewish law. As far as the inquisitors were concerned, Jews and their descendants were imprisoned sub lege, under the law.[23]

For a reason left unclear by the documentation, Manuel Nunes, a Portuguese merchant of Amsterdam, required in 1610 corroboration of his social stature. Perhaps some questions about his genealogy threatened his status in or entry into the 'Portuguese nation' in Amsterdam. Financial difficulties may have stood behind his need. So, one day that year no fewer than six other Sefardim, friends or associates acting on Nunes' initiative, appear before a notary public.[24] They declare "that Manuel Nunes is the son of Fernão Rodrigues and Leonor Nunes [...] in Lisbon and that he is the son of a white father and mother and that neither of them have any part Morisco [blood] nor [the blood] of Blacks."[25]

In order to assuage his doubters or debtors, Nunes has some associates record an official statement of his 'quality,' which, not coincidentally, emphasizes his social and inherited 'purity.' But one wonders about the exact formulation. The general source of the terminology existed in the standard contemporary Portuguese discourse about 'purity of blood.' Perhaps the intended audience of this declaration resided in Iberian Catholic territories and worried about Nunes' blood lines. But why bring up his lack of Black blood? The inclusion of African descent as a source of 'impure' blood can be found in colonial probanzas de limpieza and other investigations already toward the end of the sixteenth century.[26] The terminological evocation of Nunes' friends neglects, obviously, his Jewish blood; in other words, it specifies just which elements of the blood-purity discourse some Sephardim found useful in this Amsterdam outpost of the Iberian commercial empire and Sistema de castas.

Catholic but Black

Afroiberians stood both outside and inside respectable Catholic society; outside by dint of their color, inside due to their religion. As Catholic residents, whether slave or free, for the most part they lived and circulated within the ranks of the plebian population. Still, in some ways they could claim an advantage over New Christians of Jewish descent, who were persistently suspected of religious deviance.

Anti-Jewish prejudices served some Afroiberians well. In a recent essay, T. F. Earle provides an analysis of a saint's play, Auto de São Vicente, penned by a Mulato author, Afonso Álvares, in 1532. Possibly born to the aristocratic bishop of Évora and raised in his house, Álvares seems to have internalized a sincere and intense Catholicism — his four known dramatic works are all saints' plays. Though never mentioning them by name, the Auto de São Vicente presents an extended critique of New Christians: their poor or false religiosity, their vain hopes for a national messiah who is not Christ, their inherent fraudulence in business. In the play Álvares repeatedly names as Pharisees those who interrogate St. Vincent, a Christian missionary to pagan Spain around the fourth century, who has been arrested by the authorities.[27]

From the perspective of Afroiberian attitudes toward Jews one is struck by the paradoxical fact that Blacks and Mulatos, though severely denigrated in so many ways, often claimed a Christian identity — even, on occasions, an identity as Old Christians — that made them 'insiders' in a way New Christians often could not. What, in general, did 'Jewish' even mean to people within the Atlantic world? One could reply with a litany of prejudices that long have been treated by scholarship. One feature worth mentioning is that in sixteenth- and seventeenth-century Spain, the colonies and perhaps much of Europe, 'Portuguese' was considered a synonym for 'Jew.' This notion based itself on the perception, largely accurate, according to scholars such as Yosef Hayim Yerushalmi, that the Portuguese conversos maintained their Judaism with much vigor and stamina. The large population of Iberian New Christian merchants in the late-fifteenth and sixteenth centuries suffered, in addition to ethno-religious prejudice, from the Spanish dislike of sailors, with whom early merchants were closely allied, for obvious reasons.[28] Iberian Christians, in particular, saw Jews everywhere and it is difficult for us to tell whether they distinguished between 'real' and figurative Jews. It is probable that Afroiberians participated in the Corpus Christi processions in Portuguese cities, which featured judangas, satiric recreations of Judaism where masked paraders conducted a live she-goat and pretended to read sacred texts, in the midst of jeering and name-calling at notorious New Christians.[29] That Afroiberians might therefore share in anti-Jewish prejudices, as numerous examples show they did, should not surprise. During the processions of the religious brotherhood for Blacks in Seville, as reported some years before 1604, White spectators delighted in antagonizing and mocking the marchers in a denigrating, racialized manner that provoked an equal and opposite reaction, calling the marchers "drunks and blacks," "speaking Guinean to them and offending them," "poking them with pins, which angers them and they call the whites Jews [i.e., conversos], which the Black women who accompany them do likewise."[30] Similarly, in one short theatrical farce called Los negros a master makes fun of his slave woman because of her color, causing her to respond spontaneously with a contrast-making attack on alleged New Christian hypocrisy that "at least we are not of those Jews who carry the floats [in religious processions] / no somos a lo menos de los judíos que llevan los pasos."[31] In a statement from the 1730s, a Black who was born in Mina and spent time in Brazil was arrested for sorcery in Lisbon by the Inquisition. Among other heterodox guidance he received from his 'devil' or spirit guide (discussed in the next chapter), he was warned not to stay long in church, "for only Jews sought the Church and had the habit of staying there for very long," a hint at the still common perception that New Christians dissembled great piety in order to preempt suspicion that they were not sincere Catholics.[32]

Carlos de Bayén, a Mulato tailor in Campeche, Mexico, claimed that the Portuguese merchant Antonio Fernández Ferrer sold him bad quality fabric. The tailor

> hid in the fabric's folds wafers of the kind of the host, and when the Portuguese extended the fabric to measure the quantity ordered by the mulatto, who declares himself finally ready to buy it, the pieces fell to the ground. The tailor then made "many acts of admiration, saying: 'how does Your Grace have these pieces of the host amidst the cloth?'" hoping in this manner to terrify the merchant and obligate him, through fear of the Holy Office, to give him the fabric for nothing.[33]

Desecration of the host, a crime often leveled at Jews, was not something for which a merchant, especially a Portuguese, would want to become incriminated by the Spanish Inquisition in Mexico. The Mulato tailor De Bayén ingeniously played with this fear to get what he thought he deserved out of the situation.

Gossip, a form of unofficial social regulation, targeted Others and circulated without regard to racial or caste divisions. Two examples will have to suffice for now. In 1541, the New Christian Catharina Fernandes (mentioned above) was denounced to the Lisbon inquisitors for having told an Old Christian youth that he was no longer welcome in her house and that he had no right to accuse her of judaizing her Black woman or man slave.[34] Pero Cardigo was denounced to the inquisitional visitor in Salvador, Brazil, for the following reason: one day in Olinda, Pernambuco, around 1591, he had been engaged in conversation in front of the Church of Our Lady of Conceição with Afonso Duarte, a Portuguese from the Island of Terceira, Diogo Martins, a Spanish Mulato, Álvaro Fernandes, a local resident, and his (Pero's) nephew. When a disagreement arose between Pero and his nephew, the former, aghast, uttered a blasphemous swear and "everyone was scandalized."[35] These men conversed and reacted as Christians among Christians, though one was a Mulato and the others Whites. (Of course, in many cases, Old and New Christians also conversed as equals, neighbors and friends.) Growing polyglot urban populations made such intermingling inevitable, as Whites, freed Afroiberians, Amerindian servants and slaves often inhabited the same neighborhoods and mixed in the streets and plazas, at the markets, at events and even in church, all of which in the course of the seventeenth century produced much alarm for the governing elites. "Broad interaction across ethnic and status lines," in the words of Martha Few, is evident from a variety of types of archival records and readings-against-the-grain of elite sources.[36]

In many cases, gossip about who was "Jewish" turned into denunciations. The denouncers often claimed to be acting out of Christian duty. On 14 April 1526, Maestre Juan de Leon, a surgeon in the Canary Islands, deposes as follows:

> having enquired of Bartolome, a black labourer, for news of Yñes Tristan, mother-in-law of Pedro de Lugo, the said Bartolome replied that he believed Juan de Vergara had given information against her to the Holy Office, because she had told the said Vergara and himself that she would pay fifty doblas yearly to be exempt from confession, as she wished to have peace in this world, for as to the next [world] it was all nonsense.
>
> That the said Bartolome further told this deponent that the daughter of the said Yñes Tristan used to read a certain book which they called "La Bribia" [Dialect name for the Bible - lw] and that he has heard the said Yñes telling her daughter that the book was a good book and gave good counsel, that one day Pedro de Lugo coming in while they were reading this book said "I do not wish to see it, it is 'La Bribia' or some such diabolical work."
>
> That the said Bartolome told deponent that the book was written in Hebrew, and further said that he was amazed that the said Yñes had not been arrested by the Inquisition upon the information given by Juan de Vergara, and that it was well known in Teneriffe that she was a Jewess.[37]

One free Mulata deposes against a family of alleged judaizers in 1630s Mexico City, claiming that she came before the inquisitors "for the discharge of her conscience and [because the matters to be discussed] had seemed bad to her."[38] In the next decade, a free Mulata of Mexico City comes to testify before the local inquisitors "for the discharge of her conscience and due to having heard the edicts of the faith which were read the past Sundays."[39]

The two just-mentioned Mulatas, Mariana de Guzman and Maria de la Conçepçion, shared an experience with the extended Enriquez family of alleged judaizers. The first was asked, along with her mother and two sisters, to help for eight days with the preparations for a wedding being celebrated by an allegedly judaizing family. Though they cooked "more than a hundred birds, of this land and [also of] Castille," not once did they ever see one of their heads (nor any blood in the meat). Though they even asked for the heads, the family members "did not want to give them." Obviously, if these declarations are accurate, the birds had been slaughtered according to the method of slitting the throat required by the rabbinic laws of kashrut. Another woman who helped with the wedding preparations, Sebastiana de Ortega, a slave of someone not connected to the Enriquez family, testified that the chickens "were brought to the kitchen decapitated with a knife."[40] "[T]he black women Boçales told [the Mulata Mariana de Guzman and her group] that their mistress doña Rafaela wanted them thus without the heads." During this same period, the Mulata brought a thigh from the butcher and added it to the other meat. "A black woman named Ynes, a boçal, cook of the said house, told her that she should take the said meat [out] because her mistress did not want that it should stay and that they never eat thigh meat in their house, except for the front quarter."[41] It is doubtful that these slave women understood their mistress' reasoning. Guzman's suspicions grew out of her having heard a description of the Jewish practice of slaughtering and preparing animals at the auto de fé celebrated at the city's Santo Domingo cathedral. Another Mulata who worked at the house in preparation for the wedding, Maria de la Conçepçion, who usually washed the clothes of the household, testifies that when she complained regarding the headless fowl, Blanca Enriquez told her that "they were more tasty decapitated [and] not killed in another manner."[42]

Often, an Afroiberian already caught up in an inquisition's net might attempt to turn her situation around by denouncing someone as a judaizer. On 29 July 1627, the free Mulata María Martínez testified to the Inquisition in Lima against Francisco Maldonado de Silva, an unabashed Jew who made no effort to hide his beliefs from the inquisitors.[43] Martínez, originally from Portugal, was staunch enough a Christian to wear rosary beads around her neck. Her detailed denunciation, which can be corroborated by the testimony of other witnesses as well as Silva's own confession, stemmed entirely from a two-hour meeting she had with the accused when he had first been brought from Chile as a prisoner of the Inquisition only the week before. Here is an excerpt:

> María Martínez, free mulata, born in Vega in the Kingdom of Portugal, 36 years old, detained for witchcraft at the house of the jailer where she lived. She declared against the accused [...], who said that [...] in the two hours in which the witness was with him [...] he said to her that he did not believe in Christ our Good, that it was idolatry and idols to adore the images, and seeing a cross that the witness had around her neck on a rosary, he said that he did not believe in it, and that Christ was [made] of wood and if he were what the Christians said, he would shine; and that the accused was from those two tribes of Israel who are preserved/protected in the terrestrial paradise awaiting the end of the world, [...] and that the father of the accused had left this Inquisition with a sambenito,[44] because of which he left his children poor, [...] and that the accused was a Jew to the point of anathema, [...] that they would burn him, that those who

would die burned would not die, rather their God would let them live eternally, and that such he had to say in this holy tribunal when they call him.⁴⁵

Martínez lived at the house of the jailer, where Silva was taken en route to the secret prisons. Was Maria the jailer's servant or mistress? María had been arrested earlier by the Inquisition, for witchcraft, and had been a prisoner already when Silva arrived. Why he confided in this mixed-race stranger cannot be said.⁴⁶ It is unlikely that he knew anything about her. (If she revealed anything about herself to Silva, she refrained from telling the inquisitors so.) He might have discovered enough to trust her. He might have suspected that they shared a similar fate. He might have been temporarily mentally unstable or so insistent on his religious self-vindication that he lacked discretion.⁴⁷ She decided to denounce him, she claims, because he mocked the cross she wore around her neck. She knew that he was already a prisoner, just as she might already have known that it would be helpful to her own case to have others to denounce. Whether accurate or not, Martínez's testimony as the prosecution's fifth witness implies that Silva had confessed a great deal to her in that one chance encounter. Silva seems to have been unusually open about his religious propensities. Perhaps her skills in reading people, attested by many witnesses, helped her draw him out. Perhaps, already on the way to the Inquisition jails, he sensed that the time for secrecy had long passed. Or perhaps his openness entailed part of his pride in his judaizing.

In a case from mid-sixteenth-century Portugal, the inquisitors in Évora placed a Mulata named Guiomar in the cell of a New Christian woman accused of judaizing, Lucrécia Nunez, in order to ferret out and report confessions relating to her practices and beliefs.⁴⁸ Both the accused woman and the Mulata informant came from the town of Trancoso. Guiomar feigned being the daughter and granddaughter of New Christians who had died in Inquisition jails. Guiomar related to her 'handlers' that Lucrécia disclosed to her that she was a New Christian and practicing Jewess and said "various things in praise of the Law of Moses and [things] blasphemous and harmful to the Catholic faith." Not satisfied with this, the jailer, who operated ostensibly at the behest of the inquisitors, instructed Guiomar to tell Lucrécia that he himself was also a New Christian. She did so. The following day, Lucrécia called him and, confirming that he was a New Christian, "she blessed him" and confessed to being "a Jew and an enemy of the Christian faith, whose dogmas and principles she ridiculed." She counselled the jailer to reveal himself as a New Christian to her husband, who was very knowledgeable in Jewish law and in whom he could trust, and that, for more security, the jailer should request that her husband swear on a set of tefilin.⁴⁹ The remainder of the intriguing information extracted fraudulently from the accused Lucrécia by Guiomar and another planted informant, a cousin of the jailer, remains beyond the scope of this summary.⁵⁰ Interestingly, Lucrécia seems to have revealed far more to the (White) cousin of the jailer than to (the Mulata) Guiomar. This could have been because the former's skills as a dissembling compatriot exceeded those of the latter. Racial factors could have been involved; Lucrécia might have found it easier to confide in a White coreligionist than one of Black descent. At the same time, that Lucrécia found it credible that a Mulata was a New Christian testifies to the fact that New Christian men having children with Black women was not surprising. One wants to know more about what led Guiomar to seek (?) or accept the task of informing for the Inquisition on an accused judaizer. She does not seem to have been a prisoner of the Inquisition herself. It is not clear whether she was a particularly devoted Christian or wanted to seem so. In this case we will have to accept few answers.

Denouncing Others

All in all, the motivations or pressures that forged Afroiberian denunciations of alleged judaizers did not differ significantly from those that led them to denounce other Afroiberians, or that led Judeoconversos to inform on other Judeoconversos, judaizing or not, including relatives and even family members. Judeoconversos may have denounced other Judeoconversos because they had internalized Catholicism and resented or feared judaizers, because they sought advantage over competitors, because they sought to get back at or harm someone, or because once already within the Inquisition's net they feared for their own safety and wanted to 'behave well' and earn their own release or acquittal. Afroiberians operated from the same set of motivations.[51]

Inquisitional documentation evinces a general absence of Judeoconversos denouncing Afroiberians. This might indicate that the class and religious prejudices against Judeoconversos which informed White Spaniards and Portuguese drew Afroiberians into inquisitional proceedings more than anti-Black prejudices provided Judeoconversos a reason to resort to the Inquisitions. For example, Gabriel de Granada, accused of judaizing by the Inquisition in New Spain, denounced, among many others, "Elvira, a Negress who served in these prisons. She died."[52] I will explore this case further in chapter 4. Another case is the testimony of one alleged Pernambucan judaizing woman. Called back in 1602 by the inquisitors to ratify earlier testimony, she declared "that everything that she had said in the said session she had heard said to her spouse [...], who will say that he heard it thus said to Antônio Vaz, mulato, of whom she knows not where he lives, nor who he is, nor where he is."[53] It is impossible to verify the accuracy of this woman's statement, and perhaps that was the point, but one way or another it seems an obscure Mulato served perfectly as a convenient evidentiary prop. Another case is fictional: the confession of Lazarillo de Tormes which convicts his mother and "stepfather," that is, her Black lover, a Moorish stable boy.[54] The charges here might stem from emotions generated by this lover: jealousy, condescension and/or anxieties regarding class and/or race. Given the probable Judeoconverso origin of this text, and the protagonist's arguable Judeoconverso sympathies (and certainly parallels), Lazarillo's confession presents an instance of the kinds of class and racial hostilities that might have caused a White New

Christian to denounce a Black. Whether the author sympathizes with or critiques Lazarillo's denunciation is another matter.

Given the ways in which both Judeoconversos and Afroiberians faced denigration and suspicion, it is not surprising to find allegations of Jewishness and accusations of judaizing connected to other forms of racially tinged signification in the popular imagination. Depending on the situational needs of the accuser, the descendants of Jews could be considered either overly haughty or tainted by too intimate a connection to other debased races. María de Encío of Santiago de Chile, arrested in 1579, was charged with a variety of transgressions:

> [Others] telling her not to whip the Indians, she said: "God lives, that even if St. Francis came down from heaven, or if St. Francis commanded me to stop whipping, I do not have to stop whipping them;" and that she performed work with the Indians and Blacks on holidays on a sugar plantation which she owned, and ate meat on Fridays and Saturdays and impeded marriages, and was married two times, and read the lines of hands, and believed in dreams and other superstitions and consulted Indian women taken to be witches.[55]

Part of Encío's suspect behavior lay in the mistreatment of innocent Amerindians, powerless and vulnerable slaves, who should attract Christian mercy, not unwarranted cruelty. She also supposedly used these human instruments, who were enslaved ostensibly for their Christianization, intentionally to transgress religious and civil law. One slave in 1635 Mexico City testifies that she heard her mother told many times regarding a family of alleged judaizers that "they washed the [floors of their] house on Holy Thursday and Friday [i.e., the days leading up to Easter, Maundy Thursday and Good Friday] and whipped their blacks on said days."[56] Perhaps it is not a coincidence that both of these accusations were formulated by slaves and servants. In Bahia, in 1591, the New Christian Diego Castanho was denounced for having "carnal relations with a black slave who was lying on a crucifix."[57] Here, as well, two different acts, one an outright heretical desecration of the central Christian object, the other an act of extra-marital fornication with an "unworthy" partner (many colonial men rationalized such sex as not going against Church law, a rationalization considered heretical), serve to fortify each other's subversiveness.

The last charge hints that interracial sex constituted a problem of unsuitable intimacy. Many similar cases could be adduced. I will focus briefly on one involving the famous then infamous Antonio José da Silva (1705-1739), New Christian, poet, dramatist, student of canon law, lawyer. The day of his arrival at the Inquisition's secret jails in Lisbon (8 August 1726) he related the following tale involving his widowed aunt Dona Esperança, with whom he stayed when he had been in the city already some four or five years (in other words thirteen years previously, when he was aged twelve or so).[58] Being attracted to one of his aunt's maids, he and his aunt were alone for the purpose of the confessant having an illicit affair, and procuring for vile ends a maidservant of the aforementioned aunt, whose name he doesn't know, and his aforementioned aunt, having notice of the depraved intentions of the confessant [which he told her] so that she will help, and manage things for him with the same girl, she inducing the confessant that he should make an attempt, [saying] after all simple fornication was not a sin in the law of Moses, and the confessant responding to her that he lived in the law of Christ, in which such a base act was a sin, his aforementioned aunt says to him, that he should live in the law of Moses, which was better and greater, and in which, as had been said, simple fornication was not a sin, and for which he should hope for the salvation of his soul, [....] and what his aforementioned aunt told him and taught him seeming good to the confessant, and carried away by the appetite which he had for pursuing the vile acts which he intended with the said girl, in order that remorse would not remain in his conscience, he then and there abandoned the law of Christ, our Lord, of which he already had enough information and instruction, and went over to belief in the law of Moses, hoping to save himself through it.[59]

Da Silva, soon overcome with remorse, returned to Christ's law — or so he claimed.[60] This tale stands in need of more unpacking than I can here devote to it. In any case, it is a rather cynical rendering of Judaism and its import for New Christians. It might have been so purposefully. He might have been giving the Inquisition what he thought was wanted. The statement is equally cynical about servants and projects onto them an all-too-prevalent fantasy of sexual availability. (It should be noted that here the race of the maidservant remains unmentioned; this was not Leonor, his Black slave.) Regardless, Da Silva was soon released after abjuring his errors of faith.

This little text offers a liberal understanding of sexuality that overlapped with certain trans-racial and inter-class desires. The same reasoning played a role in condoning sex with non-White women, especially in colonies lacking normal numbers of White women. Such sex, if not interdicted by the Spanish and Portuguese authorities, certainly stood under severe social discouragement.[61] Nonetheless, based on numerous examples, it can be assumed that some European men saw no reason not to enter into relations, whether sexual or romantic, with non-Whites. Nun Frances da Costa, a New Christian residing as the royal factor among the Biafada on the West African coast in the 1590s, was denounced to the Lisbon Inquisition for allegedly boasting that "He cared more for the finger-nail of his African wife than 'all the confessions and masses.'"[62] His wife's ethnicity likely added to the contrast he was accused of drawing. The newly appointed Inquisitor in Lima, Antonio Ordóñez, wrote in a worried letter to the Inquisition Council about the alarming number of priests soliciting Amerindian (and other) women in the confessional: "and what is worse is that there are some giving depositions who said to the Indian women that the sin with them was not a sin, and were with them carnally in the church."[63] The Castile-born Gaspar de la Plaza was tried in 1538 in Mexico even before the formal establishment of the Inquisition there for "assuring that it was not a sin to be with an Indian woman," while the more explicit Andrés Monje was accused in 1544 in Mexico for saying "that it was not a sin to fornicate with an Indian woman."[64] The Lima Inquisition arrested a blacksmith, the Spanish-born Diego Hernandez, in the 1580s for "having said before many people that it was not a sin to have sex with a Black woman, nor to be in love with her, for God had commanded that man should fornicate."[65] In Spain itself such ideas also found expression. In the 24 November 1566 auto de fé in Córdoba, the mayor of Aguilar, Gil Gómez del Lagar, found himself fined 4,500 pesos and forced to make a light abjuration for saying that "it was not a sin to be in love with a mulata."[66] Apparently even some women voiced opinions of this kind. Among those punished in the Lima auto de fé of 30 November 1587 with a light abjuration and banishment from the city was "María, a Black woman born in the Indies," for holding that sex constituted a venial sin, not a mortal one.[67] Such "heretical" propositions served to permit other types of relationships frowned upon under official Iberian social control. In 1570, Catalina, a slave of Juan de Jerez of Priego, said, when reprimanded by her mistress for going out with men, that "it was no sin to have relations with a man who was her boy-friend."[68]

Some of these examples indicate that it was likely not only individuals desperate for human intimacy who rationalized (away) the sin of simple fornication, but those from non-Catholic backgrounds for whom such strictures seemed foreign. Was Antonio Silva's aunt correct that Judaism did not consider "simple fornication" to be sinful? Had she taught the young Silva that "the Law of Moses is more tolerant in matters of a sexual nature"?[69] I cannot recall any case of a New Christian being charged with holding or expressing any of the above "propositions" as a component of her judaizing. Still, it is true that much of Iberian Jewish thinking on sexual issues evinced "a sober realism and a pragmatic approach," often recognizing concubinage, for instance, in preference to indiscriminate sexual affairs.[70] Furthermore, writes Yom-Tov Assis, according to Jewish law, "sexual relations between mutually consenting unmarried Jews (or even if the man involved is married) are not punishable although they are condemned by the halakhists on moral grounds."[71]

Alternative views of sexuality were but one of the ways in which Jews or conversos were sometimes linked or "confused" in the Iberian imagination with other Others. It goes without saying that in the eyes of many inquisitors and proponents of "blood purity" statutes Jews and Muslims, or, more accurately, their converted descendants, occupied similar positions as disloyal Christians and citizens and as eternally potential heretics. Members of all of these groups were routinely insulted as "dogs" by Spaniards and Portuguese.[72] "Jews" were also seen as bearing a certain kinship with decidedly "primitive" peoples. Padre Mestre Gaspar dos Reis, designated by the Portuguese Inquisition in the 1640s to engage the accused judaizer Isaac de Castro in theological debate and convince him to renounce Judaism, gets nowhere with the youth, as is true of all the others appointed for the same end. With frustration the priest concludes, citing Jeremiah (13:23), that "it seemed to him that it is impossible for the Jews to repent of their errors, as it is impossible for the Black to change his skin or the leopard to change his spots, and thus he judged the youth [Isaac de Castro] obstinate and pertinacious."[73] The writer André de Resende complains about the influx of foreigners to Lisbon: "Over there you will encounter the Indian, the Japanese, the Persian, the Chinese, the Turk, the Moor, the 'Marrano', the Muscovite [...]."[74]

The Ethiopian Christians, for instance, failed to gain acceptance from the papacy or the Portuguese Church, which rejected them as monophysites and followers of many Old Testament practices (on which more below). The Portuguese humanist Damião de Gois asked the envoy of the Ethiopian Negus to write up the articles of faith of Ethiopian Christianity, which he translated into Latin and produced in a book pleading for religious tolerance for all manner of Christians, "Fides, Religio, Moresque Aethiopum sub Imperio Preciosi Joannis," (1540), but the Portuguese Crown did not allow the book to circulate in Portugal. Part of the complaint against the Ethiopian rites was their closeness to Judaism and the fear that New Christians would learn to judaize from them.[75] Writing against the New Christians around 1541, Francisco Machado wistfully imagines "Portugal [...] cleansed of heresies and of Jewish ceremonies, and of Moors and Blacks."[76] To Machado it is clear that the constant shaming and humiliation of Jesus in Portugal stems directly from the fact that "where there are Moors, Blacks, Indians, Jews, it is inevitable that each one follows his own path and sect."[77]

Hence the perception or accusation of being too close or sympathetic to Blacks could also structure useful narratives regarding conversos. In 1607, a White in Santiago de Chile denounced a Portuguese New Christian merchant named Diego López; the witness had heard someone say that López was "the son of a Jewish converso and a half mulato."[78] When the prominent merchant Manuel Bautista Peres was arrested by the Inquisition in Lima, he warned the inquisitors that many individuals might well have sought to harm him through false denunciation. One example he provided consisted of one of his mayordomos (a steward, foremen or aide), who "'went around telling everyone that [Pérez and his brother-in-law] were Jew-dogs' because they threatened to have him punished for beating an African slave to death."[79] Judaizing was seen as infecting, either in potential or in fact, the beliefs and practices of Africans, Afroiberians and Amerindians. In 1702 Bahia, the missionary Francisco de Lima expressed outrage that the leader of a feast celebrated by a Mulato brotherhood in honor of Our Lady of the Assumption was a colored woman named Rosa who just happened to be the mistress of the brother of the local priest. These two brothers, New Christians, protected Rosa, despite her being known for uttering various heretical propositions. Referring to the rampant African ceremonies, joined even by Whites, the Commissioner of the Inquisition, friar Rodrigo de São Pedro, saw Bahia at this time as the site of so much spiritual turbulence, if not turbidity, precisely because of the "multitude of New Christians that live in this land," who had fostered an atmosphere of disrespect for orthodoxy and authority.[80] The gatherings of an all-African congregation of Mina Catholics in Itaubira, Minas Gerais, Brazil, were called by those who denounced them to the Inquisition a "synagogue."[81] Here it is doubtful that anyone thought the offending Afroiberians, slave or free, were actually Jews or practicing Judaism; the name merely indicated the heretical nature of what was going on by means of a familiar theological lens — and this was in 1754.

The West African Coast and Coastal Islands: A Special Case?

In African regions confusions of the kind just discussed may have been influenced by perhaps the most persistent and aggravating appearance of 'Jewish' practices in Africa, from the Portuguese perspective, which took place in Ethiopia. Many followers of the monophysite Ethiopian Church observed Sabbath on Saturday, not Sunday, practiced circumcision, and ended their Lent abstention from meat or dairy products at sundown. Hence Jesuits and Catholics alike accused the Ethiopians of maintaining "a thousand ceremonies of Jewish Law," as the French physician Charles Jacques Poncet put it in his account of his travels there from 1698 to 1700.[82] In West Angola, Portuguese officials, as late as the seventeenth century, often believed that the indigenous circumcised male children and youths because they were Jews.[83] It is unclear whether this meant that the African Other was being conflated with Jews as the primitive "bad" cultural self or whether the connection was historical, that "some Portuguese New Christians had reportedly taught Jewish rites and notions to blacks in 'Guinea,'" a view frequently held and disseminated by those associated with the Inquisition.[84] Thus, an anonymous legal opinion from around 1620 warned against letting New Christians reach Perú from Buenos Aires due to fears of their judaizing among the 'natives': "as experience has shown that they have done in some parts of Guiné, where they have managed to teach Judaic ceremonies and rites to the gentiles."[85] Similar allegations were raised in connection with the two thousand or so Jewish youths who had been forcibly taken by the Portuguese King Manoel I in 1493 and sent to help colonize São Tomé.[86] Some European visitors had the perception that New Christian traders in western Africa were able to live as open Jews, citing, for instance, the example of Amari Ngone, the Wolof ruler of Cayor and Baol in the late sixteenth century, who permitted both "Portuguese Jews and Portuguese Christians" in his realm, but forbade them "to dispute about which religion is best," allowing each to "live as he wishes in the religion he accepts."[87] New Christians were also accused of (re)turning to open Judaism in Morocco, which, like western Africa, comprised a marginal space in the Portuguese imperial orbit, both heavily involved in trade and political alliances with the Portuguese, yet ultimately beyond the latter's full control. In these regions, including the Cabo Verde islands, therefore, New Christian traders faced constant complaints and accusations of judaizing even before the establishment of the Portuguese Inquisition in 1536.[88]

Malyn Newitt provides one explanation for the charges of judaizing raised against various Luso-Africans (she terms them Afro-Portuguese) along the western coast of Africa: "Catholic when in a Portuguese settlement, their religious practices when at home in Africa conformed to local ideas and led to the accusation [...] that they were Jews." These traders, that is, observed "local religious rites appropriate to their standing within the African community."[89] Some of the Portuguese lançados and tangomaos, that is, those traders who assimilated into the local West African societies "wore African garments and protective amulets, underwent circumcision and scarification."[90] The New Christians of São Tomé were accused of practicing "thousands of gentilic rites in opposition to our faith, like offering gifts to the Gods of the blacks, which are demons with whom they deal and talk quite naturally; without doing this they are unable to trade."[91] They were Jews by analogy as much as by practice or belief, both for having voluntarily abandoned the graces and benefits of the Church as well as for having adopted practices that shared with Judaism the status of idolatry and heresy. Hence a 1546 petition by prominent local Old Christian citizens to the Portuguese king to establish an Inquisition in the Cabo Verde islands claims that some 200 New Christian lançados of the coasts celebrated "Mosaic ceremonies," participated in African religious ceremonies and contracted polygamous marriages.[92] Another explanation for some of the allegations of judaizing resides in the economic, social and political war being waged by Old Christians, particularly merchants, against opponents, New Christians in fact or rhetorically.[93] This competition was exacerbated with the arrival of the Dutch in the seventeenth century, which generated accusations that the local New Christian merchants were in league with their Dutch Jewish kin.[94] Various sources, as well as Inquisitional denunciations and trials from Cabo Verde, the Senegambian coast, and São Tomé, offer evidence — much of it admittedly circumstantial, much of it of dubious merit — for some open Judaism and crypto-Judaism in these areas in the sixteenth and seventeenth centuries. Two of the coastal port towns, Portudal and Joal, were said to have hosted open communities of Sephardic traders who operated a synagogue, had books of the Jewish Bible, ritual objects, and conducted circumcisions. Still, most of the Inquisition records concern little more than run-of-the-mill immorality, religious laxity, skepticism, and doubt.[95] At times it seems that scholars cannot accept the idea that New Christians were not the only ones to feel and express "brusque irreverence toward the external authority of the church," and must make 'Jews' of all doubters and rebels.[96] All of this does not negate the possibility that Jewish populations trickled into the area over the course of time and even spread their beliefs and practices, but firmer evidence would be nice.

Knowing Where One Stands

The opposing Christianity and Judaism that informed much of the way in which Afroiberians and Judeoconversos saw one another even became on occasion the explicit content of interchanges. The Portuguese Maria Rodrigues was imprisoned in 1541 for having cursed King Dom Manuel and those who tried to force the Jews to become Christians. The high number of denunciations and arrests from 1541 stems from the fact that the previous year the Portuguese Inquisition opened its doors. Additional charges accrued against Rodrigues, such that she also judaized. On 23 March of that year, a Mulata informer denounced Rodrigues, saying that she had been telling her about the case of a Jew who was burned at the stake and did not want to die as a good Christian (likely the same Diogo de Montenegro mentioned above). Rodrigues had retorted: "And if they told you that should turn Moor [Muslim], would you?" The Mulata witness responding in the negative, Rodrigues said to her: "Well, we are the same!" Rodrigues went on to ask the witness: "After you are satiated, if they give you bread, would you eat it?" and as the witness answered in the negative, Rodrigues exclaimed: "We are the same; after we are in our law, we are not allowed to throw it away!"[97] In this spontaneous religious disputation in the street, Rodrigues made deft use of ethnic and religious sensitivities — notably drawing on shared anti-Muslim sentiment — to arouse empathy from an Afroiberian to her own and the general New Christian predicament as Others pressured to abandon their culture.[98] The simile Rodrigues employs regarding bread and satiation asserts that religiosity does not fall under the standard scarcity model (whereby outsiders are starving for the lack of 'our' 'true' religion) but quite the contrary: all can be nourished within their own tradition. The degree of self-consciousness displayed regarding racial and religious status and their intersection is noteworthy.

A different Black woman of Lisbon testifies against the same Maria Rodrigues, who already had been imprisoned for several months on charges of judaizing. This Black woman claims that the two are (or were) friends. According to her statement, this woman had invited Rodrigues to go see an auto da fé by the Teja riverside in Lisbon.

> She responded, "God's evil inferno for King Dom Manuel who made us Christians by force!" She further asked the witness if she would like it if she were turned white, to which she responded that yes, she would like it, Maria Rodrigues retorted: "Well, so we will turn ourselves into good Christians like you will yourself turn white!"[99]

This Black Christian expresses the desire to turn White as a means of convincing the inquisitors that she sought "conversion" in a manner directly opposite the stubborn refusal of the accused judaizer. Such a desire manifests a distinct similarity to her interest in watching an auto da fé to begin with, and her later denunciation of a friend formerly but mistakenly thought to share her Christian desires, ocular and otherwise. She equates turning White with turning Christian and equates the judaizer's emphasis on the inability of Blacks to turn White into a denial of the potency of the universalizing Christian mission. Once again Rodrigues turned to racial and religious argumentation to try to make her Afroiberian friend understand her position. Whether Rodrigues constituted a particularly articulate Judeoconverso spokesperson is beside the point, as is the historical fact that Lisbon then hosted the largest population of Africans, slave or free, in all of Europe. Whether these are accurate depictions of Afroiberians' reactions or not, these testimonies deftly and perhaps even inadvertently assize the contestatory group dynamics that could be so overheated in the crucible of a mass exorcism of 'heresy.'

The differing subject positions of Afroiberians and Judeoconversos vis-à-vis the Inquisitions, a combination of their religious, racial and class differences, also surfaced on occasion. Duarte da Sá was a New Christian plantation/mill owner and member of the governing elite of Olinda, Brazil. In the early 1590s he was denounced for, among other things, having said to an allegedly decadent Black slave who had been threatened by his master with the fact that an inquisitorial visitor was present: "talk Jorge, talk, because if you have a hundred or two hundred thousand cruzados you will hold your tongue, but as you don't have anything you can speak."[100] Sá alludes to the fact that New Christians comprised a perennial target for inquisitorial greed or pecuniary self-sustenance and therefore stayed as far away from inquisitors as possible. Afroiberians, on the other hand, with little or nothing monetarily valuable to lose, could afford to approach the Inquisition in order to right wrongs. Sá's statement was deemed dangerous, even blasphemous, because it implied that the Inquisitions operated based on mundane economic motivations rather than holy considerations. Of course, the unfree and poor slave Jorge may well have perceived Sá's observation, ostensibly correct when it came to inquisitorial hypocrisy, as bearing its own form of willful blindness, coming as it did from the mouth of a wealthy White, however persecuted as a subaltern in his own right. Once again, race and socio-economic status become explicitly thematized in daily conversation among subalterns.

Other cases show, however, that even members of the lower classes and 'despised races' might take a strong stand despite their seeming powerlessness. In Portugal, one Black former slave, Gaspar de Colonia, refused to testify against someone accused of uttering heretical statements, ca. 1651.[101] This shows that even those low on the socioeconomic scale sometimes chose to resist the Inquisition in the name of truth.

CHAPTER 3

Some Incidents in Cartagena de las Indias

In early seventeenth-century Cartagena de las Indias two men, both surgeons, came to know one another, though one was a Judeoconverso and the other a Mulato ex-slave. This inter-racial acquaintanceship, probably fairly typical for urban milieus of the time, evolved into a rather complicated relationship. Both converso merchants and Mulatos embodied cultural miscegenation and mobility, though in different ways, and both parties in this relationship suffered as a result. Each party in this relationship found himself accused by the city's inquisitional tribunal, a tribunal increasingly zealous to arrest the perceived threat the colony faced from multicultural witchcraft and sorcery as well as from wealthy merchants who were allegedly secret Jews. Within the space of a few years, the tribunal seized and charged the Mulato as a brujo or practitioner of improper magic and he, for one reason or another, denounced his converso colleague as a secret Jew. One of the Mulato's lovers, also a Mulata, had involved herself in the same circle of magical practitioners and had expended much energy gathering information about the city's alleged crypto-Jews, sometimes in cooperation with her lover. Three interlocking cases, ordinary yet extraordinary, which left behind a documentary record whose unexpected richness allows us to further limn the fragile coexistence and differing trajectories of minority groups in the Spanish Indies.

The port city of Cartagena served as one of the main gateways to the Spanish Indies, both physically and commercially, as the beginning of one of the land routes to the thriving city of Lima and the silver mines of Potosí. The anonymous author of the Description of the Viceroyalty of Peru, written around 1615, says that Cartagena "is better and bigger than Panama City, has very good houses of stone and very good streets, very rich churches and monasteries, stores or merchandise."[1] A 1629 description declares that the city hosts "more than 1,500 Spanish residents."[2] Because of its commercial importance, Cartagena also attracted many non-Spanish Europeans interested in taking advantage of colonial possibilities. One of the city's booming socio-economic features consisted of the transshipment of enslaved Africans and a dependence on African domestic slaves, which, together with the inconsistent acculturation of Amerindians, produced in the population an entire range of Mestizos, Mulatos and other "racial mixtures."

The city's demographic variety obviously was not entirely the result of voluntary immigration. The above-quoted anonymous Descripción nodded to the polyglot nature of the city, containing as it did "many settlements [rancheríos] of Blacks," since "here many ships arrive which the merchants of Guinea bring, loaded with Blacks."[3] According to historian Charles R. Boxer, Cartagena "was the principle depot for the Portuguese slave-traders," a precedent established already with their first Spanish slave asiento or contract in 1595, which designated Cartagena as the port of primary entry for the Viceroyalties of New Granada and Peru because it was so well situated for the further distribution of slaves into those territories.[4] With the gradual decimation of the Native American population, African slaves became increasingly important as laborers in the colonies' mines and plantations and as servants tending to the needs of the cities' elites.[5] The anonymous seventeenth-century description of Peru continues by relating how "here [in Cartagena] arrive merchants from Peru to buy" slaves.[6] The chronicler Pedro Simón, writing in the 1620s, describes how "that which most increases the volume [of the Magdalena River] is the rowing of the canoes with black slaves until the port of Honda," far inland.[7] The Cartagena customs house reported 6,884 slaves imported between 1585 and 1590.[8] Official letters detail the arrival of 4,810 slaves between May 1615 and April 1619, and over 6,000 between May 1619 and December 1620.[9] These constitute only the official tallies, numbers probably far exceeded by the actual total of arriving slaves. According to the biographer of Father Pedro Claver, who devoted his life to Christianizing the Blacks in and around Cartagena, "In the course of every year, from ten to twelve thousand [blacks] are brought. And in [16]33, fourteen ships were seen in the port together, without any merchandise other than blacks, with 800 to 900 on each one."[10]

According to this estimate, the minimum total for 1633 would have surpassed 11,000 incoming slaves. Most of the slaves were sold or shipped off to other locations, but no small amount remained to serve individual or institutional masters in the immediate area. A letter of 1619 from a local Franciscan friar, Sebastián de Chumillas, estimates that "there are in [Cartagena] and its district from twelve to fourteen thousand blacks in domestic service."[11]

While Africans came to Cartagena against their will, others sought out the city. Gaspar Rodrigues Nunes, the father of the Amsterdam rabbi Menasseh ben Israel, described in one of the audiences during his Inquisition trial in Lisbon how his first cousin, Manuel Dias, urged him and others to flee Portugal with him for Cartagena, "because there everyone lived the way he wanted and one was not observed to find out how one was living."[12] Dias' perception had a basis in reality; in 1630 Portuguese, many of them no doubt New Christians, comprised no fewer than 154 of the city's 184 registered foreigners and made up some 10 percent of its White male citizens. Portuguese New Christian merchants indeed dominated the commerce of the region, Nueva Granada.[13]

Contrary to Manuel Dias' notions, however, by the seventeenth century Cartagena had become all too Spanish. In 1610 the Inquisition opened a tribunal in the city, a tribunal that ended up overseeing an enormous physical terrain. In the relatively small city itself, "where almost everybody seems to know each other," it had become all too tempting to gather and use knowledge of other people's lives.[14] This explains the interests of two local Mulatos in observing and uncovering the private behavior of other local, mostly Portuguese, residents, whom they suspected of being Jews.

Swimming in the Catholic Atlantic

The alleged marrano on whom this chapter focuses is Blas (or Bras) de Paz Pinto, a Portuguese surgeon, born in Évora in or around 1590.[15] Until roughly the age of thirty he lived in Lisbon. He is called a licenciado in one letter between some of his commercial associates, meaning that he was university trained and passed a medical exam.[16] Arriving in Cartagena from Angola in 1622, Pinto treated sick slaves in the process of being sold by Portuguese slavers. His medical practice operated out of the Franciscan convent of San Diego.[17] On his farm or ranch (estancia) at the edge of the city, he "dedicated himself to the cultivation of medical plants," while also investing in "inter-regional commerce, turning himself into an indispensable partner" and intermediary of merchants from both Lima and Cartagena, including some of the most prominent, Sebastian Duarte, António Nunes Gramaxo, João Rodrigues Mesa (or Juan Rodriguez Messa) and Manuel Bautista Peres (or Baptista Pérez), all Portuguese.[18] Pinto also traded in slaves, in this connection even working with slave traders of Lisbon.[19]

The Colombian scholar Iţic Croitoru Rotbaum published a photo of Pinto's house, which, according to his book's Index of Illustrations, the author "recently identified" (at Plaza Fernández Madrid, No. 37-14).[20] Pinto considers himself "quiet and pacific," according to the official who compiled and submitted the list of the city's foreigners in 1630, who adds a mention of the surgeon's "useful [menesteroso] occupation," his being "without suspicion" and the fact that he dutifully pays what he owes the government. For these reasons, and the fact that he paid 350 pesos, it was ordered that he receive a letter of naturalization.[21] None of the documents relating to Pinto make clear whether or not he was married. In 1633 he sought help obtaining the certification of naturalization that had still not arrived, turning to the local prominent Portuguese merchant Antonio Nunes Gramaxo, who tried, unsuccessfully, to purchase it for 300 ducats.[22]

When the inquisitional tribunals of Lima and Cartagena became active in fomenting anti-Portuguese hysteria around 1634, Pinto fell into the latter's hands, through the usual web of denunciations targeting outsiders, in this case Portuguese, suspected Jews, merchants, the wealthy.[23] Of the 81 alleged judaizers sentenced by the Cartagena tribunal in the seventeenth century, 57 were Portuguese and 38 were merchants.[24] The tribunal arrested Pinto on 22 July 1636, the same day it arrested four other Portuguese New Christians. After being reconciled to the church on his deathbed while still imprisoned by the Inquisition, in other words, once the inquisitors satisfied themselves that Pinto had died a good Christian, he was described in the report of the auto de fé at which he was posthumously displayed in state as having been "esteemed and beloved by all for being very interested in and enthusiastic for repairing altars and decorating churches." He served as the majordomo of the confraternities of Saint Antonio and of the Immaculate Conception, yet the inquisitors could only see this as a calculating show: "to have it understood that he was a Catholic Christian, being a descendent of Hebrews."[25]

Pinto was denounced to the Inquisition by a number of people, accused by various witnesses of hosting gatherings of Portuguese conversos in his house, which one witness calls a synagogue.²⁶ This same witness testifies that Pinto acknowledged that he was Jewish and that a sister of his was 'penitenced' by the Inquisition in Portugal. It is said that he verbally denigrated the holy images in one of the city's churches and even spat on one such image. The rest of the accusations against Pinto come from other Portuguese New Christian merchants already imprisoned by the same tribunal as suspected judaizers: Manuel Álvarez Prieto, Juan Rodríguez Mesa and Francisco Piñero. Rodríguez Mesa says that Pinto "was a Jewish judaizer, observer of the law of Moses" and was known as such. He supposedly didn't eat pig (tocino, bacon); kept fasts, including "the fast of the month of September," i.e., Yom Kippur, when he would not eat "until the night emergence of the star;" kept the sabbath as a festival, for which he wore new clothes and used fresh linens and tablecloths; and ate fish with scales (one of the requirements for fish to be considered kosher, the other being the presence of fins).²⁷ According to Francisco Piñero, Pinto participated with the other Portuguese in various "ceremonies and fasts" and "was held to be a man learned and capable among the Jews."²⁸ Based on the above information, the Cartagena tribunal imprisoned Pinto and sequestered all of his goods. One accused judaizer, Manuel de Fonseca Enríquez, later claims under torture that it was Pinto who had taught him the law of Moses, beginning in 1632.²⁹ Another, Francisco Rodríguez de Solís, states that Pinto "gave some talks [pláticas] regarding the observance of the [...] law."³⁰

It is difficult to know what to make of the charges against Pinto. Some of the detailed allegations evince familiarity with marrano practices that go beyond the usual litany given in the edictos de fé that were read in the churches and posted on church doors, as had been done in Cartagena in 1610 with the opening of the local tribunal.³¹ These details may reflect more on the knowledge of the witnesses than on Pinto, of course. Some of the purported crimes seem strange, to say the least. For instance, Rodríguez Mesa alleges that Pinto "put his hands behind him above his belt (que ponía las manos por detrás sobre la cintura), as a rite and ceremony of the law of Moses and as his own observance," a ritual of which I have never heard nor found documentation.³² On the other hand, keeping in mind the usual inquisitorial context, all of those who denounced Pinto were themselves under suspicion by the local tribunal for one reason or another. Protesting that they knew nothing did not spare them in the least. One Portuguese merchant in Cartagena, Luis Gomes Barreto, tried in 1636 by the local inquisitorial tribunal, includes Pinto among the group of Portuguese merchants who got together to conduct business — they were all involved with one or another aspect of the slave trade — though he denies that any discussions of or observance of things Jewish took place.³³ Barreto relates that the group met at Pinto's ranch (estancia) around 1630, on which occasion the Archdeacon and Senior Inquisitor were among those present (making it hard to believe anything unsuitable happened).³⁴ Another Portuguese merchant, Manuel Álvarez Prieto, arrested in April 1636, names Pinto as "his capital enemy" as the rack on which he was strapped was given a second, more excruciating tightening. As the rack tightened, Álvarez Prieto accuses Pinto of accusing him falsely and insists that he knows nothing of any Fraternity of Holland (a nation comprising Spain's own capital enemy; the fraternity is discussed below). Through seven turns of the rack's wheel (his screams duly recorded by the scribe) Álvarez Prieto offers nothing more substantive, though the Inquisition surgeons confirm that both arms have been broken (by July he is dead).[35] According to the tribunal's summary, Álvarez Prieto called Pinto a Jewish judaizer, but later retracted his accusation.[36] Finally, it is odd that Pinto is considered by some of his denouncers to be the group's 'rabbi,' since it seems from the documentation that others knew and practiced much more than he. Still, enough of the Portuguese conversos confirm the gatherings at Pinto's house that it seems likely that they indeed occurred, though whether they were social affairs or ritual events remains murky. Tobias Green finds that "one of the formulations of Blas de Paz Pinto in his letter to Tomás Rodriguez Barassa of October 12th 1635 — "Alavo a Dios" — was a variant of a prayer which had been recited by converted Jews in Spain in the 15th century, and also of a favored prayer of Tomás Treviño de Sobremonte, the famous crypto-Jew of Mexico who declared his Judaism as he marched to the stake and was burnt in the great Auto of 1649."[37]

At first Pinto claims not to know "what caste he was," i.e., whether any of his parents or grandparents were conversos, and he denies, through all of eight audiences, being anything other than a good Catholic. Submitting challenges to the witnesses for the prosecution, all unknown to him, the results, according to the inquisitors, yield "nothing in his favor."[38] Continuing to deny all of the charges, the inquisitors and four consultants voted to apply torture in the hope of extracting a confession corroborating the charges they take as truth.[39] After two turns of the rack's belts — or three quarters of an hour — Pinto "wished to confess the truth entirely," stating that he has been "judaizing" for thirty years, since his time in Lisbon, where he was taught by a woman named Violante Duarte.[40] He says that "he had fasted Wednesdays and Fridays of some weeks," kept Saturday sabbaths as a festival, putting on new clothes, and avoided eating pig whenever possible.[41] He names many of the group of Portuguese merchants with whom he would gather to perform rites and "to confess the fast days that they kept:" Juan Rodríguez Mesa, Francisco Rodríguez de Solís, Manuel de Fonseca, Manuel Álvarez Prieto, Manuel de Acosta, Alvaro de Silvera, Francisco Piñero, Luis Gómez Barreto, Francisco de Heredia, Antonio Rodríguez Ferrerín and Antonio de Acosta. He also denounces as judaizers Amaro Denis, already imprisoned by the Lima tribunal, and the slave traders and brothers Juan Rodríguez de Silva and Jorge de Silva. He claims that it was Álvarez Prieto, whom he met in Angola, who convinced him to keep the law of Moses, "which was the good one for saving oneself in it," and who taught it to him again. This odd formulation could mean that Álvarez Prieto refreshed his knowledge or taught him more than he knew previously or that Pinto was merely spinning tales for the inquisitors. He implies that Rodríguez Mesa's house served as the main gathering place for this group, that Rodríguez Mesa would often conduct ceremonies in which scriptural passages were read and said that "the promised messiah has not come."[42] Despite being tortured, it seems Pinto gave his inquisitors only bits of information regarding others.[43]

Some of the details of Pinto's confession make it appear convincing that he knew something about marrano beliefs and practices. The confession of the fast days to one another was not an element of the edictos de fé and would not likely have been known by non-conversos. In addition, the charges against the other sentenced Portuguese conversos show impressive variation.[44] Most of the components of Pinto's admission were standard fare, however, and would have been known by most Iberians. Of course, just because Pinto knew these details does not mean he observed them, nor can one jump to conclusions because of the knowledge or activities of others in his sphere. It could well have been the accumulated pressure of his imprisonment and trial, and, finally, his torture, that brought forth this gush of information. He could well have learned in the Inquisition jail just which Portuguese New Christians had been arrested and, possibly, even who had denounced him.

A Mulato in the White Atlantic

The only non-Portuguese who denounced Blas de Paz Pinto seems to have been the Mulato Diego López, who had been arrested by the same tribunal for alleged crimes of his own. Almost all of our information regarding him comes from Inquisition sources. He informs his inquisitors that he is a surgeon.[45] He was born in Cartagena in 1591 or 1592. As a slave he served in one of the city's hospitals, either San Sebastián, then known also as San Juan de Dios, after the religious order that operated it, Espíritu Santo, founded in 1613, or San Lázaro, ordered founded in 1598. Espíritu Santo treated and housed incurables, the chronically ill and convalescent, while San Lázaro received lepers and those suffering from sores/ulcers.[46] López took advantage of this opportunity to enter the medical profession, which he practiced for his income once he obtained his liberty. It was not infrequent that Blacks and Mulatos acquired European medical skills through such servitude.[47]

Surgeons comprised a mixed lot, some considered mere bloodletters, others 'full' physicians. Still, all had only to obtain the license of a 'simple' protomédico, along with druggists and barbers. According to colonial legislation from 1605, their exam consisted of relevant questions concerning human anatomy, the variety of sores, head wounds and other serious sicknesses. If the questions were satisfactorily answered, the applicant had in addition to agree to cure the poor pro bono.[48] Hence both Diego López and Blas de Paz Pinto ministered to slaves and the non-White population, though not always for similar motivations. The primary function of surgeons was to treat the blood and/or humors and to prescribe medications. Given the frequent lack of doctors, they often fulfilled the complete range of physicians' functions.[49]

On 8 January 1633, López was incarcerated by the Holy Office on the testimony of nine witnesses, all women over twenty-five, who provided concrete accusations depicting him as a "heretical apostate witch [brujo]." In his first three meetings with his inquisitors he denied absolutely everything. On 7 April 1634, more than a year after having been imprisoned, López began to confess his crimes and to name accomplices.[50] In the course of these confessions a number of local "Jews" make an appearance, including Pinto.

A close friend of López's and a lover of his beginning in 1627, if not earlier, despite his being married, was the Mulata Rufina. Rufina, a slave of Clara Núñez and her husband, Rafael Gómez, not only participated in the magical practices that claimed the involvement of a good number of the city's women and men but stood as the only non-White permitted to participate in a select group of White practitioners of magic (brujas), all of whom had supposedly learned their skills from a Black woman named Paula de Eguiluz. Rufina even served as a kind of aide to this famous Eguiluz.[51] As Mulatos in an urban setting, López and Rufina represented and enjoyed a cultural integration, social mobility and economic opportunity that, while limited by factors of race, went far beyond the world of bozal slaves trapped amid mines or plantations.[52]

López and Rufina had a tempestuous relationship. Imprisoned, he denounces her as one of the "enemies" whose testimony had landed him in trouble.[53] She had attempted to wreak vengeance on a new lover he had taken. And in a fit of anger and jealousy when his wife delivered a baby, causing a temporary separation between the former lovers, she used her magical powers to threaten him that the baby would die shortly, which it did.[54] (The married López's lovers are listed in one of his audiences: first Juana Hortensio, then Rufina, slave of Amador Pérez, later 'our' Rufina, slave of Rafael Gómez, and finally Ana María of Jamaica, against whom Rufina sought vengeance.)[55] Still, López and 'our' Rufina seemed to be constant companions.

Fascinating Jews

One mutual interest of Rufina and López, mostly instigated by Rufina's determined curiosity, at least according to López's narration, consisted of spying on the city's suspected crypto-Jews. Rufina appears to have delighted in spreading gossip about who might be a Jew (and acting on it), telling Diego, for instance,

> that an old woman who is Portuguese and who lives in the street with the rest [of the Portuguese (?)], in some low houses of Juana Colón, also Portuguese, mother-in-law of Miguel de Chabes, is a Jew and communicates with the mother-in-law of Rafael Gómez, whom he now remembers is called Beatriz López and similarly that the mother-in-law of doctor Báez was a Jewess and all three communicated in secret.[56]

The self-interest motivating at least part of Rufina's curiosity can be gleaned from the appearance of the mother-in-law of her master, Rafael Gómez, and mother of her mistress, Clara Núñez, in this listing of alleged secret Jews, a miniscule portion of the detailed and colorful gossip about secret Jews (among other things) that Rufina shared with Diego. It should be recalled that even as mere Portuguese, these individuals were considered outsiders and suspect, especially as Portuguese hostility to the union of Spain and Portugal (1580-1640) grew. Other episodes of spying on her mistress and master and their local relatives suggest that her interests in the religious life of her neighbors had roots in possibilities for improving her situation. But her persistent curiosity, stemming perhaps as much from ethnological interests as from ulterior motives, led her to understand the importance of "knowing other people's lives," an importance encouraged by the Inquisitions and reflecting precisely the inquisitionally sponsored confluence of 'neutral' ethnology and self-interested ideology.[57]

> Rufina's interest in discovering and uncovering the goings-on of those she thought might be Jews spread outward and enveloped López in ways beyond sharing rumors. The Évora-born Blas de Paz Pinto, whom Rufina calls on one occasion, perhaps sarcastically, her or Diego's friend, became a focal point of her interest. She told Diego that the Portuguese have a synagogue at his house and that desirous that this one [Diego] see something of what they read at the gatherings which she knew they secretly had [...] sometimes at night and others at midday, she went up to call the accused [Diego] [...] and, accompanying the accused, the said mulata went ahead and entered and then came out and said to this one [Diego]: "now is a good time, go in and see what they are doing."[58]

From the way Rufina went into the house or was said to have gone in it would appear that she had entry, that is, that she was familiar to either Pinto himself or, more likely, a member or members of his household staff. These situations remind us of the relative freedom of mobility possessed by those who lived on the margins of respectable society. As Diana Luz Ceballos Gómez writes, "certain service slaves, for example, visit the world of the blacks, that of their own masters and that of the masters of other blacks; they enter the houses, bearing messages and orders, go to the market to shop and enter into contact with the merchants, go freely about the city."[59] Diego, finding the door closed, had to go around to the house of Martín Sánchez in front, where he remained until five in the afternoon.[60] But the street windows of the Pinto house stayed shut the whole time "and the slaves of the above-mentioned [Pinto] were posted at attention in places, in order not to allow entry to anyone who came to do business with him." Eventually, around five o'clock, Diego saw "ten men, more or less," exit the house, among them some he knew.[61]

Around 1629, perhaps when the two were still lovers, Rufina told Diego that he should go visit Paz Pinto,

> who was ill and that [Diego] said to her, "what sickness does he have?" and she responded that he was like her, he was menstruating and not understanding what the said mulata had told him, he went to the house of the said Blas de Paz and, asking him about his sickness, he told him the cause and that he was

bleeding, and that he [Diego] should see whether he [Blas] had some hemorrhoids or some inflammation in the rear and this one [Diego] looked at him and told him that he had no inflammation, with which he ordered this accused [Diego] to go look at the blood, which was in a silver basin and before he did the abovementioned, the said mulata Rufina had said to this accused [Diego] that the said Blas de Paz had covered his toilet with a linen on which was an image of a saint with a diadem and [with] the cloth of the toilet over the said image and that he would sit on it when he went.[62]

Given the opportunity, López says he looked at the toilet, finding exactly what Rufina had predicted. Though he claims he could not identify the particular saint, he saw that the figure in the image wore the habit of Saint Francis and was a youth. The inquisitors' report about the auto de fé in which the late Pinto appeared speculated that "according to everyone it was understood that it was Saint Antonio, of whose confraternity [Pinto] was superintendent [majordomo]."[63] Saint Anthony, patron saint of travelers and seafarers, served logically as the patron saint of diasporic Portuguese communities, which set up many chapels in his honor.[64] In other words, Pinto's existence was taken to be not only schizoid — a Jew pretending to be Christian, the inner life differing from the outer — but to comprise a complete and absolute self-negation, intent on destroying precisely that which it upheld, on upholding exactly that which it despised.

Rufina's description of Blas de Paz Pinto's sickness draws on two related, often conflated traditions in Christian discourse. The first and earlier one held that Jews experienced hemorrhoids, bleeding from the anus, as a result of their denial of Christ, either permanently, or every Easter or Good Friday. The second posited that Jewish men menstruated, a theory going back at least as far as the thirteenth-century anatomist Thomas de Cantimpré and recurring among Christian thinkers into the seventeenth century, if not later.[65] The former tradition was "imputed to the paradigmatic enemies of God" from late antiquity through the middle ages: Judas, Arians/heretics, and Jews."[66] Continues scholar Willis Johnson:

> This idea may well have originated when the heresiarch Arius died by prolapse — the herniated extrusion of the intestines — in a public toilet in Alexandria. This death was interpreted by his contemporaries as a divine condemnation of Arius's teachings regarding the physical body of Christ, and exegetically equated with the mysterious bursting of Judas's belly (Acts 1:18) when he hanged himself. As symbolic betrayers of Christ, Jews were exegetically linked with Judas and Arius in many texts through the middle ages. In the twelfth century, a consolidation of Church power that led to the eventual demonization of the Jews coincided with the arrival in the West of the elaborately theorized humoral medicine of the Arabs. Numerous sources

from this period reflect a rationalization and medicalization of the formerly religious symbolism of Jewish bleeding. By the thirteenth century, these traditional associations had evolved into a belief in the annual bleeding of Jews at Easter. For more than a century these two ways of understanding the Jewish flux coincided and occasionally reinforced each other. Jews were thought to suffer a disabling bloody flux from their anuses in annual commemoration of the killing of Christ.[67]

These theories witnessed a revival in seventeenth-century Spain and Portugal, where Old Christians wielded them against suspected crypto-Jews, whose increasing invisibility heightened fears of their invidiousness. In early 1632, the Spanish court official Juan Quiñones submitted a memorandum to the Inquisitor General Antonio de Sotomayor, suggesting methods for discovering whether a New Christian was a judaizer:

> [...] every month many of them suffer a flowing of the blood from their posterior parts, as a perpetual sign of infamy and shame... Many authors say therefore that when Pilate said, as Saint Matthew relates, that he was innocent of the Just One's blood, all those Jews who shouted and said let his blood be on them and their children, they and all their descendants remained with the blemish, plague, and perpetual sign so that every month they suffer a flow of blood like women... The sign is nothing more than making a mark (on something) so that it is different from others, so that it is not confused with them... and when recognition is difficult from the look of the face, one should resort to the hidden signs that are on the body.[68]

Quiñones had composed his treatise attempting to prove the myth of Jewish male menstruation as an intervention into a particular Inquisition trial. Quiñones's allegation accompanied a wave of similar insults against 'Jews' and 'Jewish' doctors in the course of the movement for strengthening purity of blood statutes.[69] The year before, a translation of a Portuguese anti-Jewish tract announced that some "say that on holy [i.e., Good] Friday all the Jews, male and female, have that day a flux of blood, and for that reason almost all are of a pallid color."[70] Similar charges had been raised already in a 1604 text: "[T]he Jews suffer permanently from hemorrhoids and from 'an anal flux of blood and they are called circumcised because they clean their anus with their fingers."[71] Gerónimo de la Huarta (or Gómez de Huarta; 1573-1643), personal physician of King Felipe IV (reigned 1621-1665), proposed applying purity of blood statutes in the medical profession, a field often seen as monopolized by Jews, a proposal not unconnected to his scientific opinion about "the putrid odor of the Jewish physician caused by his murder of Christ, his permanent condition of hemorrhoids, and the flux of anal blood on his bare fingers."[72] In Portugal, in particular, Old Christians were said to prefer disease or even death to treatment at the hands of a converso doctor. In short, we have here a discourse constructing Judaism as "one of the incurable diseases," in the early sixteenth-century words of the exiled Spanish-Jewish author Solomon ibn Verga.[73] Perhaps we should not be surprised, then, by the fact that when the charges against Blas de Paz Pinto are drawn up by the tribunal, both in 1636 and when re-presented in 1651, the one regarding male menstruation heads up the list.[74] It is as if the inquisitors find this "condition" the strongest proof of Pinto's Jewishness.

Rufina, an illiterate slave in Cartagena de Indias might well have picked up the rumor of Jewish flux somewhere, which would indicate that the pseudo-scientific myth had a life beyond 'elite' thinkers in Europe.[75] The notion probably did not come from a book produced in Cartagena, as the city possessed no printing press for most of its history before the nineteenth century.[76] In this case, Rufina's magico-medical knowledge would have derived from acquaintances or even her mentor Paula de Eguiluz, who might have learned of these notions about Jews from someone in the medical field. Indeed, Eguiluz, who had been arrested twice by the Cartagena Inquisition, in 1624 and 1632, was sentenced at her first trial, among other penalties, to work in the city's hospital, where she would also live.[77]

In fact, given the medical provenance of much of this discourse regarding Jewish male menstruation, it is just as likely that Diego López himself applied the theory to Blas de Paz Pinto on his own, perhaps even more likely, and simply blamed Rufina when standing before the inquisitors. López, after all, was trained as a surgeon and had worked in one of the city's hospitals, a site where continental "medical" theories regarding Jewish male menstruation might well have been discussed. Though Cartagena does not seem to have had a facility teaching medicine, it hosted one of the era's most innovative surgeons, Pedro López de León, of Seville, for twenty four years. In 1628 he published the book he wrote while in Cartagena, Theory and Practice of Abscesses.[78] Ceballos Gómez points to our Diego López as an example of an individual who is both a cultural intermediary as well as himself a bearer of several biological/cultural traditions, who even comes to learn his practice "alongside a doctor instructed in the Mediterranean tradition" of medicine.[79] The local mistress of magic, Paula de Eguiluz, could be characterized similarly. Though clearly working with African and Amerindian knowledge and practices, as shown by Maya Restrepo, according to Ceballos Gómez,

> If at first [Eguiluz] did not know the details and twists and turns of the imaginary of European diabolical witchcraft, by the end of her first trial she will know the basics and, by the conclusion of the third she will be the greatest expert, "educating" in these matters her acquaintances [...] between [her] trials, but also conducting an exchange of magical recipes and love potions with other people in Cartagena [...] or instructing her alleged accomplices in what they should declare before the inquisitors.[80]

It is very likely that López and Eguiluz had come to know one another while each worked at the hospital, though López blames Rufina for introducing him (earlier?) to Eguiluz's circle of magical practitioners.

Sharing this knowledge between them, or perhaps acting on his own, the interest of the 'scientifically'-oriented López was piqued enough to spur him to take advantage of a chance to investigate its truth. Without mentioning Rufina's mandate, López examines Paz Pinto and tells him that he has no inflammation. His bleeding comes from another cause, says López, implicitly supporting the notion that he is menstruating due to supernatural reasons.[81] Indeed, López's diagnosis that Pinto lacked any medically observable ailment became the basis for the first of the Inquisition's sixteen charges against the alleged judaizer:

> a certain person urging another to go visit Blas de Paz, who was sick, [...] and examining him with care, the said person found that he had no sort of inflammation, because of which it is to be believed that the said Blas de Paz is a descendant of those who, with shouts, said "crucify [him], let his blood be upon us and upon our children [Matt. 27: 23, 25]," and because of which blood goes over him [probably alluding to Matt. 23:35].[82]

These words of the inquisitors resemble the framing of this whole issue in Quiñones and earlier authorities suspiciously closely, down to the invocation of the verses from Matthew. It seems difficult to believe that the illiterate Rufina or even López would have been aware of such theological contexts and connections. The allusion to the Christological punishment of Jewish men for their alleged deicide comes in Latin, but the framing of the episode would appear to point right to López as the author of this charge against Pinto and its formulation. Yet it is not just the formulation of the quoted or paraphrased learned officials which should rouse curiosity. The structure of the entire investigation conducted by López and Rufina appears to be a concrete application of the hermeneutic suggestion proposed by Quiñones: "when recognition is difficult from the look of the face, one should resort to the hidden signs that are on the body."

Knowledge is Power, Especially Through the Gaze of the Invisible

Rufina's hand should not be dismissed too quickly, however. Like the later fairly well-known Marie Laveaux of New Orleans, Rufina, though still a slave, reigned over a kind of fiefdom.[83] Rufina held a prominent place in the quasi-African magical gatherings headed up by Paula Eguiluz. Like Marie Laveaux, Rufina, too, was highly attentive to gossip, encouraging it, cultivating it, controlling it. Both women understood that knowledge is power and put this understanding into practice. Discussing other cases in Cartagena, Ceballos Gómez calls attention to the way

> blacks testify in the trials against white women and fabricate rumors against them; contrary to Indians, who have keeping quiet as a virtue, they are talkers, prone to gossip and appear

with too much frequency as witnesses in the criminal trials, with their world populated by spirits and curses, intriguing against the rest. The slaves talk, comment and return the vox populi that certain whites are brujas."[84]

When Rufina tells López that Pinto's house serves as a synagogue, he asks her how she knows this. She "responded that every day she hears many things about this in her house [that is, the house of her Portuguese masters Rafael Gomez and Clara Nuñez] and through this she knows."[85] According to López, Rufina had told him that one older Portuguese woman had "gone out in an auto de fé" and that Rufina's master's mother-in-law, also Portuguese, "was a descendent of Hebrews."[86] After detailing one episode of spying with Rufina on her master's mother-in-law, who was supposedly abusing a small Christ on a crucifix, an accusation commonly lodged against New Christians, López informs the inquisitors that "Rufina always said with admiration that were one to touch this material it would certainly bring ruin," an allusion to the potential harm such knowledge of others' behavior could wreak, as well as Rufina's seeming enjoyment of this power.[87]

Diego López seems to have been just as curious to know about other people's lives and just as active in gathering information, if his confessions to the inquisitors have any truth in them. Passing the house of one Portuguese whom Rufina has told him "was a Jew when he came from Spain," López supposedly sees him or his young son urinating on an image of the Virgin. López investigates, "in order to better satisfy myself."[88] It appears that he was even caught several times nosing into the business of others. One time, for instance, he comes across one of the men he suspects to be a judaizer sitting in the house of another suspected judaizer, reading a book. Seeing López enter, the man quickly hides the book under folds of cloth or curtain. Recalling Rufina's allegations that this man was a Jew, López imagines

> that that must be some book of his Law and the said man who reads in the book having been called upstairs, [López] remained in the corridor that goes down to the patio where he had to stay until they advised him that he could come, and as he had the suspicion that he related, he took the book with one hand and opened it with it and saw that the beginning of it said "Compilation of the Bible."[89]

Perhaps because López was an ex-slave, perhaps because he was not White, it seems that the Portuguese whom he was surveilling either did not take the threat seriously or could do nothing about it given the necessity for him to carry out his tasks. In many instances, including this one, those being investigated make efforts to explain away things. The brother of João Rodrigues Mesa, finding López looking at the book, took the book with great speed and anger and put it under his arm, smiling with the said youth with the large nose, their voices all nervous/agitated, and J[oã]o Rodriguez Messa came out, saying that people came to other people's houses not to conduct business but to see what was up, and [he said] this with much annoyance [...] and then Blas de Paz came to speak with [López] and made particular effort to ascertain whether he had seen what the said book contained.[90]

Pragmatically, López simply lies to him, pretending that he saw nothing, while Pinto tries to make it seem that the privacy of business accounts are what is at stake, in what can be read as a kind of patronizing effort at manipulation. It seems to have been quite clear to López at least what he had done.[91] A long time after an incident in which López claims to have rebutted some anti-Christian remarks by the father of Rufina's mistress, the man (whose name López cannot recall) asks López if he remembers their exchange; again, López simply lies and says he remembers nothing.[92]

The Inquisition as an institution thus did not merely function as a neutral observer. As in quantum physics, the presence of an observing entity actually determined matters to some degree, fanning personal inquisitiveness, producing new opportunities, within the context of the very structure of the socio-economic hierarchy to produce a war of all against all. Again Ceballos Gómez excellently captures the way pressures led people to "unburden their emotions/grudges in gossip and slanders, among whites to stand out in order to win the favor of the king or of the officials — in order to improve one's position, to obtain mercy or expediting — and among blacks procuring the appreciation of the masters — in order to get better work and be assigned less arduous labor, [all this] had to have created a conflictual environment."[93]

A case of feared witchcraft that exercised the authorities of Cartagena in 1565 serves as an excellent model for understanding the gathering of information by Rufina and the denunciations made by López. A 25-year-old Black slave woman, Guiomar, taken from Africa at the age of 10 or 12, seems to have suffocated or drowned various children of the household in which she served, as well as committing other acts of magical terrorism, in order that her master sell her. Ceballos Gómez, who studied the case of Guiomar and her accomplice, an older Black slave named Bartolomé, finds that throughout the trial Guiomar manifests "a profound hatred toward whites, justifying her acts and her accusations against other blacks by the harmful actions of the masters: the mistreatment, the excessive work to which they were subject, having to raise the masters' children and look after their sustenance, the fact that they would have slaves or, simply, the fact that someone would not want to liberate a slave." Other Blacks who were interrogated (many by the province's Governor, no less) confirmed the sentiments, hoping to "improve their situation [by] giving to their masters herbs so that they would wish them well, others working sensibly so that their master would liberate a child or in order to win his appreciation."[94] Both Bartolomé and Guiomar confess their having gone out to kill "all the people of Cartagena."⁹⁵ Other slaves recognized Guiomar's uniquely deep hatred, having heard her say things such as that she "would eat all [her master's] blacks."⁹⁶ Sweet discusses an early eighteenth-century Brazilian-Portuguese case in which a slave woman used incantations "to attack rival servants" and reads such attacks as "always more than a personal attack; it was also a strike against the master's economic and social well-being."⁹⁷

The Meaning-Making of Afroiberian Magic

Similar motivations seem to have pushed Rufina and Diego. Their participation in the local circles of brujería — López only from 1628 or so, according to his own testimony⁹⁸ — reflect their anti-establishment sentiments and acts of counter-hegemonic disobedience, grounded on their understanding that the law and establishment entailed a fundamentally xenophobic and slave-based system. Through a thoroughly Africanist or Afroamericanist reading of seventeenth-century Nueva Granadan culture, Maya Restrepo characterizes these groups of magical practitioners, which included non-Whites of all kinds and sometimes Whites as well, as engaging in "symbolic marronage."⁹⁹ Irene Silverblatt notes how the perceived 'political' threat of multicultural magic in Peru increased as the seventeenth century went on; "it was said that [witches] could stop royal officers from carrying out a sentence, or even inquisitors from pursuing a case."¹⁰⁰ The threat may well have been perceived accurately. Michael Taussig asserts that the "leaders of the palenques or runaway slave settlements were as likely as not to be wizards and witches, according to the official texts."¹⁰¹ At the same time, African knowledge, herbal or pharmacological, for instance, served as a means by which the enslaved and the 'colored' could sell their expertise, mostly to White Spaniards, and thereby reaffirm their personhood and escape to some degree the condition of objectification imposed on them.¹⁰²

Both Diego and Rufina participated in Eguiluz's circle, which met on the beaches and fields of Ciénaga de los Manzanillos / Swamp of the Manzanillos (a South American tree with fruit like an apple), near the city, as well as at the house of Elena de Viloria, in the city itself. One of the major, and first, charges against this group of non-Whites mentioned in the audiences of López is the "crimes, damages [...] which are notorious [...] which they [i.e., the entire group] have caused to many important persons in this Republic."¹⁰³ Even before joining these circles, claims López, Rufina had told him with seeming pride who the local brujas and brujos were, "some [of whom] were referring to the harmful acts that they had done."¹⁰⁴ Many of the murders and casting of spells attributed by López to this circle relate to romantic interests, which James Sweet interprets as efforts to gain "access to members of the opposite sex" by a population suffering from "the void in human contact and affection that was created by slavery."¹⁰⁵ But the group's alleged crimes went far beyond this. Eguiluz allegedly had one of her minions kill a merchant named Hernando Godo Mexia for reasons left unstated.¹⁰⁶ Some of the acts supposedly perpetrated by Eguiluz herself and others within her circles include mockeries of or attacks on representations of Catholicism in various local churches. Charges from the 1630s as well as from her first trial in 1624 point to other classic forms of satire or rebellion, that is, acts of symbolic or real subversion.[107] Supposedly finding out that Rufina disinterred a recently buried infant girl for nefarious purposes, López accuses her of carrying out acts of horrifying audacity. She, in turn, lays all the blame on her superior in magic, Paula de Eguiluz: "who inspires us to [do it] all, as with [other] similar cases."[108] In what might be an indication of the sway Eguiluz held over her followers, when in front of the inquisitors López seems afraid or unwilling to "believe the said Paula [is behind] any evil [deed] but rather her zamba," whom he doesn't name.[109]

At one of his first gatherings with Eguiluz's junta, López is assigned, "as a companion" a "devil named Taravira, who appeared in the figure of a man dressed like an Indian," to whom López pledges allegiance and whom he penetrates in anal sex, later confessing to bearing a mark on his left rear thigh, made as a demonstration of his loyalty to this "devil," in the inquisitors' terms.[110] The fact that López's spirit guardian was Amerindian points to the increasingly syncretic nature of the magical practices wielded by these Afroamericans as time went on and as they went from being bozales to becoming part of the cultural mix of their new setting. Things Amerindian possessed enormous potency for many non-Whites of Nueva Granada as a component of their symbolic marronage, subconscious or otherwise.[111] López tells the inquisitors that "when he coupled with his devil Taravira and knew him from behind he had more pleasure with him than as if he were with a woman"[112] López's statement might allude to the kind of proclivities, repressed in upstanding Catholic society, that were allowed, even encouraged to surface in such counter-cultural fora, but also to the intentionally contrarian nature of the acts embodying efforts to challenge or overturn, in whatever manner, an unjust socio-politico-economic system. It is telling that Rufina's spirit companion is named Rompe sanctos / Breaks Saints.[113] In the words of Maya Restrepo,

> [T]he Africans and their descendants rapidly understood the power that being the representation and incarnation of the devil in the land of the Christians conferred on them. In this mode, the image of the black soul, demonized by the masters, was utilized by the captives as a strategic apparatus in the context of Catholic colonial society. Paradoxically, the demonization constructed by the theologians and men of science of the epoch was converted into an implicit weapon most subversive of the imperial system.[114]

Denouncing Injustice?

The interest of Rufina and Diego in Blas de Paz Pinto thus may have stemmed from more than the latter's allegedly prominent role in the Cartagena crypto-Jewish community. Though a surgeon by profession, the licenciado Pinto dealt in merchandise such as slaves. Many Portuguese in the Spanish Indies engaged in trading slaves, some as a lucrative supplement to their principle occupations.[115] Pinto was part of the commercial network of Manuel Bautista Peres and his partner Sebastião Duarte, of Lima, whose firm was involved in transshipping slaves, silver mining in the Andean mountains, as well as the trade route between Acapulco and Manila.[116] By no means, though, can Pinto be included among the most prominent slave traders, even within Cartagena. Perhaps he picked up this business while in Angola, where he resided after leaving Lisbon. Tobias Green states that Pinto "was so well known in Guiné that on March 4th 1637 4 people testified in Cacheu that they recognized his handwriting."[117] According to one witness, testifying to an inquisitorial visitor in 1635, a 13-year scheme to bribe officials in Cartagena to ignore their illegal importation of slaves was arranged by Pinto.[118]

Scholars suggest that New Christians, who were not allowed in the Americas by law, often took a circuitous route via Guinea or Angola, finding entry in the western hemisphere through Buenos Aires or elsewhere "under the guise of bringing along slaves."[119] Jonathan Israel suggests that Portuguese New Christians served as "agents of Lisbon contractors handling the slave trade" in order "both to emigrate and make money."[120] According to Israel, "most of the leading and middling Portuguese crypto-Jewish merchants of New Spain seem to have got started in trans-Atlantic commerce in this particular way."[121] A glance through the 1630 list of foreigners in Cartagena reveals that a high number of the Portuguese there came by way of Guinea or Angola, many having served in one capacity or another on slave ships.[122]

Portuguese New Christians testifying (under one or another form of duress) to various inquisitional authorities in the Americas often cite Angola as a place where they were introduced to judaizing practices by a family member or friend.[123] For instance, the 1641 confession of Gaspar de Robles to the Inquisition in Mexico City: as an adolescent, two uncles convinced him to sail with them in the slave trade to Angola, persuading him en route to believe in the Law of Moses. In Luanda, where they lived, their proselytization continued.[124] Manuel Álvarez Prieto, a slave trader living in Cartagena, confessed in 1636 to the Inquisition there that some twenty years earlier, "being in Angola," a business associate (now deceased) "taught him the Law of Moses." He also mentioned as judaizing mentors "a scribe of the Angola contract, about whom they told him he left for The Hague" and "some priest..., who is in Guinea."[125] The Portuguese converso Garci Méndez de Dueñas left Portugal around 1590 on a slaving ship to West Africa, "in the company of a certain Ruy Méndez" — a relative? — who, he later stated, had induced him, "in the sweltering heat of Guinea, to forsake Christianity and embrace Judaism."[126] Such allegations were easy to make, of course; West Africa was far away and often those featured in the accusations were already deceased. One corroborating allegation comes from a Portuguese Jesuit visiting Angola in 1593, Pero Rodrigues, who reports the existence of a Torah in Luanda and the celebration of a Passover.[127] Intriguingly, counter to the Inquisitions' view, one Conversa of Mexico City complains about the disinterest of New Christian slave traders in preserving their tradition. Rafaela Enríquez, part of an extended family of judaizers (treated at length in later chapters), is accused of criticizing

> certain Portuguese masters/skippers of blacks who are carrying on romances with Old Christian women, not marrying with girls of the Law [of Moses]. [Rafaela,] Inveighing [against them] that they were in a bad state and that they rendered the children that they had with their girlfriends lost, without teaching them the law, which is the goal for which observers [of the law] are married to each other.[128]

Though never making explicit reference to race or slavery as a motivation for surveilling or denouncing Blas de Paz Pinto, López and Rufina seem to have been well aware of the centrality of race in their own lives as well as of the racial and thus 'political' context of Paz Pinto's activities. At one point in 1629, Rufina's masters beat or whipped another of their slaves, a Black named Pablos, to extract a confession that Rufina on occasion left the house at night to go sleep with López. As a consequence, Rufina fled the house, not returning for five or six days and the two lovers rendezvoused at night less frequently after this incident.[129] In the wake of this, claims López, Rufina came up with a magical means of "taming" her masters.[130] Along more mundane lines, López also claims to have given Rufina four hundred pesos to buy her own liberty.[131] Afterwards, she tried another magical means of "being able to leave her house more freely," through an accord with the spirit Huebo (called a demon in the testimony) arranged for her by Eguiluz. The spirit was to assume her form and take responsibility for her tasks. In addition, the spirit would help her ward off the unwanted advances of a White Spaniard, Diego López Arias, which, as a slave, she could not resist without negative consequences.[132] The Black slave whom Rufina paid to help her kill another Black, Juana de Hortensia, ultimately "had not wanted to do her [Juana] harm, being a daughter of Dominga Arara, of his own nation," that is, Arara.[133] Though López leaves the fact out from his own description of one of the magical gatherings where some of the participants were turned into pigs, the gathering had been called for the purpose of "mourning an old Black who died."[134] This eulogizing ceremony, known as a lloro, lends yet another communal tint to the group's activities. Maya Restrepo convincingly argues that the juntas of mixed-race individuals comprised "the new spaces and social administration of the captivity."[135] The possibility of socializing — socializing, dancing, eating, frolicking together — was not an insignificant attraction as well; Diego and Juana de Ortensio each mention the tables laden with food and the fried fish consumed at the gatherings.[136]

Regarding Blas de Paz Pinto, it is difficult to believe that Rufina and López were not aware of the ethnopolitical components of his commercial activities, even if they might not have known the details. In one audience López claims a visiting Portuguese youth had told him that Pinto had come to the Indies "via the Kingdom of Angola" because various family members had been hounded and punished by the Inquisition.[137] Pinto himself had arrived from Angola, as a surgeon on a slave ship, bringing with him several slaves of his own, who evidently died of smallpox.[138] According to López, Rufina had also told him that at one point there arrived in Cartagena "an important Jew / un gran Judio," whom Pinto and "all the Portuguese" went to visit. He had come "on a ship of slaves."[139] Beyond a merely biographical link to Angola, Pinto negotiated the sale of slaves who arrived from Guinea, among other goods.[140] He served as a physician to Blacks, but perhaps mostly in connection to his trade in sick slaves as an agent of Sebastião Duarte, partner and brother-in-law of Manuel Bautista Peres, one of the most active slave traders in the region.[141] From around 1628 on, it seems Pinto became more directly incorporated into the commercial network of Bautista Peres.[142] Pinto probably inspected the incoming slaves to determine which were healthy enough to be sold or distributed to their owners. In 1630 he tells the authorities that his work consists of "buying sick blacks and [those who are] rejected and that curing [them] he turns them over for sale." At this point he himself owned five slaves.[143] His work with non-Whites led to other forms of relationship. One Black woman named Ysabel de Ortega came to the authorities in 1636 to pay 90 pesos of 8 reales that she owed to Pinto.[144] Another alleged judaizer whom López denounced to the tribunal was João Rodrigues Mesa, like Pinto a principal correspondent and factor of some of the Portuguese bankers in Seville.[145]

Ventura, basing herself on Bautista Peres' business letters, estimates that Bautista Peres treated his human merchandise relatively well (primarily for financial reasons?) and cites communications to Pinto in which he informs him of illnesses among the slaves in his charge, as well as of the diligence with which he cares for their well-being.[146] In his own, frequent letters to Sebastião Duarte, Pinto gives detailed updates on the health of the slaves in his own charge.[147] None of this alters the miserable conditions of the slaves' transshipment, which necessitated such medical care in the first place. In a letter to Duarte, Pinto celebrates Duarte's news in a previous letter regarding the good health of Bautista Peres and his household, mentioning in passing some deaths among the slaves: "even though I feel the death of [the] blacks, certainly much less lamentable than [the death of] others / aunque siento la mortadad de negros si bien menos lastimado que otros." Pinto refers to the death of a slave either named Brame or from the Bran nation (or both),[148] which, he writes, "I feel as my own, as sir captain Pedro Duarte [feels] that of the black girl but they are goods that have life and I beg God for life in order to serve it [Him?] / Siento como mio la muerte del negro brame y como del señor capitan Pedro Duarte la negrita pero son bienes que tienen vida yo la pido a Dios para servirlo."[149] Pinto's sentiments here hover between dismissal of the value of this human merchandise — better their death than one of 'ours' — and recognition of their kinship as mortal beings, 'goods' to be bought and sold but also people. The last phrase is obscure and could mean that Pinto prays to be able to make morally good use of his own life, the death of these slaves presenting him a kind of momento mori, or perhaps, less likely, even prays on behalf of the dead negrita that God should look out for her.

Pinto would seem to have been among the city's wealthier residents, though he claims to have arrived from Angola poor, with only two of his slaves surviving the transoceanic passage.[150] Among the goods deposited in his account after his arrest, either sequestered by the Inquisition from the inventory of his house or owed to him by others, were at least eight bars of gold and three of silver; a goblet, cruet and shaker of silver; a hair band of pearls; a smelted gold cross; some avocados of minute crystal with small shields each featuring an emerald; an avocado of crystal with a gold mount; a gold cross with white stones; gold shields, each featuring nine emeralds; a lamb of smelted gold with an image of Our Lady of the Rosary and Lady Saint Ana; three gold rings; a very small gold image of Our Lady and a green cross with an emerald back; three strings of pearls.[151] The Inquisition also confiscated fourteen personal slaves.[152] According to the Cartagena tribunal's tabulations, Pinto's sequestered goods valued almost 22,000 pesos, while a 1638 letter from the tribunal's official receiver to the Suprema cites the confiscation of 50,000 pesos from the Portuguese surgeon/merchant.[153] Yet he clearly lived within physical proximity to the Mulata slave Rufina and the free Mulato López. Did they feel they could indulge desires for revenge against someone who had helped enslave their people? A murder that López attributes to one of Paula de Eguiluz's disciples, Maria Romero, had to do with "a Portuguese whose name he does not know because of jealousies she had regarding a mulata who lived in front of the house of the said Doña Maria Romero and the said mulata is Portuguese and has gone to and returned from Guinea."[154] Did this act evince an undertaking aimed at harming someone from a perceived higher social station?

Though Rufina and Diego were allowed to participate in Eguiluz' 'Whites-only' magical gatherings, both she and López seem aware of the exclusive nature of the White privilege operating there; the topic came up frequently enough, and they probably resented it. On one occasion another Mulata slave challenges how Rufina can attend if, as was rumored, Eguiluz admits "neither blacks nor mulatas" and Rufina and Diego offer to provide her a secret glimpse of the goings on. Similarly, a free Mulata and friend of Rufina's, conversing with her and López, relates how she stopped being a bruja, explaining how one time "my friend Rufina [a different woman] brought me in to [a gathering] and Paula says that she can't go with me because she goes with whites and Elena de Vitoria says that she can't admit me."[155]

Interestingly enough, Rufina never went to the Cartagena Inquisition with her painstakingly gathered information. Perhaps her store of data was to be put to use only in the event of need. However, unlike López or even Eguiluz, Rufina was never bothered by the local inquisitors, despite her serving, according to López, as Eguiluz's 'aide.' In his thirty-ninth audiencia (!) López recants what he has said against "a certain mulata," who must be our Rufina, "whom he named in order to avenge himself on her and have her brought a prisoner to this Holy Office."[156] The fact that Rufina was not tried makes it highly probable that López invented many of his charges against her and that it was actually López who instigated most, if not all of the activities he attributes to her inspiration. Douglas Cope, among other scholars, has noted the general reluctance of those from the plebian classes to inform on one another. Yet López also withheld his knowledge of people such as Pinto until he found himself a prisoner of the Inquisition.

Spilling One's Guts

It is readily noticeable that the accusations of López against Pinto differ in quality from anything divulged by the other witnesses, all Portuguese merchants and acquaintances, if not partners of Pinto's. From the similarities in content and wording, it seems clear that the unnamed witness whose charges are reiterated in August 1651 against a handful of Portuguese in Cartagena (João Rodrigues Mesa, Blas de Paz Pinto, Francisco Pineiro), is none other than our Diego López.[157] These charges seem to merely rehash the information López delivered years earlier. Hence it states at the end of each set of charges that they accord with those of the original trials.[158] Yet these accusations — each set relating to each converso stem from a single, unnamed witness — bring a great amount of detail regarding Jewish practices not to be found in the Testimony of Diego López recorded for his own trial. Below I deal with whether it is possible that by 1651 López had learned enough from the Inquisition to deliver precisely what he thought his inquisitors wanted to hear or whether these charges were "polished" by one of the inquisitors.

If race was not a factor, the motivations of Diego López remain obscure. In truth, specific motivations may have been of secondary importance when one was facing inquisitors and possible torture, knowing that one of the things they most wanted from you was the names of other sinners/criminals. López was supposed to be a friend of Pinto and both men were surgeons. As we have seen, the lives of López and Rufina were thoroughly intertwined with those on whom they spied, who were mostly their social superiors. López relates that the father of Rufina's mistress, Clara Nuñez, also a surgeon, "knows him from the time he was a slave at the hospital" as well as "after his liberty [sic]."[159] López claims that he never informed on yet another surgeon, Martín Sánchez, because "at the time he was his friend and was very poor and needy."[160] López himself was fairly well off for an ex-slave. Before his arrest, according to his own testimony, he possessed a Black slave named Luisa Dominguez.[161] In actuality, he owned several slaves, since during his imprisonment four were sold at auction (along with eight mules) in order to pay off his debts, which included 2,200 pesos that he owed to Maria de Esquivel, wife of the infantry captain Diego de la Torre.[162] Ceballos Gómez even cites our López as an example of the ambition and skill for economic ascent that characterizes many of the magical practitioners who found themselves in the Inquisitions' web.[163]

When asked by his inquisitors why he never came forward with the information regarding Pinto, López tells them that he feared doing so while being at the same time involved with the above-mentioned magical circles and conducting illicit relations with Rufina.[164] López may well have been telling the truth here. Perhaps López and Pinto shared a friendship, one not strong enough, obviously, to withstand the Inquisition that eventually came between them. Perhaps professional competitiveness or other more specific matters arose between them. Pinto, as was mentioned, dabbled in raising medicinal plants. His older colleague and fellow Portuguese, João Mendes Neto, a physician, treated individuals of all races with native medicines, which he describes in his Discursos Medicinales (1608).[165] As has been documented in recent studies, some of the botanical and medical knowledge used by European physicians in the Americas was gleaned from Amerindians and Afroamerican slaves, the latter often versed in African expertise, though often uncredited as sources.[166] Given López's involvement in magical circles as well as in medicine, perhaps he and Pinto discussed or shared professional knowledge. Finally, it is illuminating that Pinto faced feminizing charges from an anti-Jewish discourse that feminized Jewish men, while López seems to have been not only a womanizer but a man who enjoyed penetrating his masculine spirit companion. The two men, each from a marginalized and denigrated group, operated in different subject positions in relation to the dominant culture. Is it possible that the tensions between the psychological set of Pinto, declared 'womanly' as a descendant of Jews, and that of López, opting for phallic dominance of others, might have contributed to López's willingness to inform on Pinto? Yet Pinto's entire career depended on the kind of dominance that his race and class made possible. It is easy to imagine between López and Pinto multiple relations of camaraderie and competition.

López may have been goaded into action by Rufina, though he never resisted or refused, indeed, he seems to have been as intrigued as she by these investigations. It could well be that he feared her. After all, it had been she who introduced him to her 'devil-worshipping' magical circle. In 1627, she had allegedly killed, through magical means, the newborn daughter of López and his wife, or at least so he believed.[167] Two years later, he claims to have told her not to come back to his house and to have given her the money to purchase her liberty (in an effort to buy her off?).[168] López also accuses her of killing a free Mulata in whom he took an interest, and of whom Rufina became jealous, by magical means given her by Paula de Eguiluz.[169] He claims to have broken off their affair in July 1631, after he became ill, though he claims that even after this Rufina and Eguiluz beat his new lover, a Mulata from Jamaica, with clubs.[170]

López certainly makes efforts to convince his inquisitors that his denunciations, however belated, derived from sincere Christian piety. Even some of the witnesses who testify against him say that they "took him to be a good Christian and had seen him do works of charity."[171] He claims to have attended mass at the Convent of San Augustin one time, when the father of Rufina's mistress pointed with a candle toward the Christ on the altar, saying "Doesn't this Christ have an evil face?" To which López responds, "He has nothing but a good face." The unnamed Nuñez goes on to say, "By God, he has such a villainous face." More explicitly defending the faith, or so he states, López retorts, "It is a great crime and sin to say this."[172] López claims to have been "scandalized" when he witnessed a Portuguese youth "gargle and spit" on an image of the Virgin and the infant Jesus in the Convent of San Augustin.[173] Suspiciously, all of these declarations come minutes after a few leading questions from his inquisitors, in which they explicitly challenge him on why he held back this information until now. In addition, as discussed above, López himself mentions conversations he has had while in prison with Juana Zamba and Rufina, among others, making it likely that he is being fed certain information. It does seem that he knows too concretely the terminology that the inquisitors want to hear, for instance that so-and-so is a "judaizer, observer of the Law of Moses," that so-and-so made a "reniego ordinario" at one of the magical gatherings, or that so-and-so adopted such-and-such an individual as her magical godmother (amadrinarle) "in order that she should become a bruja." Of course, it is quite possible that these terms are insertions of the inquisitorial scribe, seeking to 'clarify' the testimony of the person deposing. López knows that Paula de Eguiluz and her alleged disciple Juana Zamba have already been arrested by the local inquisition.[174] Indeed, after investigation by the inquisitors, no fewer than eight prisoners confess to having "communicated under the doors of their cells."[175] It could thus well be that by this time López knows just what kind of things his inquisitors want to hear. The key question remains, obviously, whether he is inventing the contents of the various accusations he raises. It is hard to resist applying to López the general characterization formulated by Ceballos Gómez regarding the kinds of magical practitioners so frequently tried by the Inquisitions: "talkers, vivacious, often social climbers, capable and intelligent and astute;" "mulatos, zambos and mestizos, but above all most of them are free, for which reason they are not under the direct control of micropowers, which allows them more freedom of action; people "who fully believe that it is possible to modify destiny and the circumstances of life through extraordinary means."[176]

Trials and Errors

Over the course of his trial, it turns out, López met with his inquisitors an astounding forty times.[177] Despite providing a plethora of evidence against others, he denied the charges against him through the thirty-ninth audiencia. A single turn on the rack at that point prompted him to admit his life as a brujo, that is, not merely a practitioner of herbalism or magic, but a practitioner of witchcraft, of the diabolical sort.[178] Evidently, various witnesses were interrogated regarding the seeming epidemic of magic that plagued Cartagena and often confirmed López's narratives of magically caused deaths around town.[179] After a three-year imprisonment, López appeared as a penitent in the auto de fé celebrated at the cathedral of Cartagena on 1 June 1636, wearing the special punitive emblem identifying him as a brujo and the required penitential habit, the sambenito, to receive a punishment of perpetual imprisonment and, on another day, two hundred lashes to be administered as he is led through the streets.[180]

About a month later, on 22 July, Blas de Paz Pinto was arrested by the Cartagena Inquisition. Of course, like most of the alleged judaizers, his heresy consisted of believing, despite being a Christian, that Judaism, the so-called law of Moses, was better for his own salvation, perhaps even better in general, than Christianity and of acting on this belief. Beyond the Jewish practices Pinto supposedly carried out, that is, crimes of domestic cultural treason, the tribunal raised hints of crimes of political treason stemming from foreign provocation. Several of the local Portuguese merchants sentenced in 1638 — Juan Rodríguez Mesa, Manuel Álvarez Prieto, Manuel de Fonseca Enríquez, Fernando Suárez and others — were accused of having contacts with Holland, as members of the so-called Fraternity of Holland.[181] Fonseca Enríquez mentions seeing Pinto's firm mentioned in the group's logbook.[182] The members of this body are said to have contributed a great deal of silver in order to fund a Dutch fleet that would attack Pernambuco or even Cartagena itself.[183] Enriqueta Vila Vilar thinks the above-mentioned fleet consisted of the one formed by the Dutch West India Company (WIC) which attacked and conquered Pernambuco in 1630.[184] According to Ventura, the fleet the members of the fraternity were alleged to be supporting might have entailed one mentioned by a Portuguese captain tried by the inquisition of Toledo, a "Company which the Portuguese Jews of there [Amsterdam] raised in order to go to Pernambuco against his Majesty and the Catholics who reside there," a group created in 1634.[185] Though the group's purpose and history shift from prisoner to prisoner, the alleged members supposedly considered it a vehicle for getting back at Spain and imagined this with relish, if not full accuracy. Duarte López Mesa, one of the Portuguese conversos accused in Cartagena in 1636, claims that Manuel Álvarez Prieto once described being in the Netherlands and learning the methods of the WIC: twenty four powerful and wealthy directors gathered daily, with five Portuguese (i.e., Sephardim) joining the Dutch, English, Danes, French and other directors, sitting on a fund of 1,800,000 ducats for the purpose of making war against Spain. López Mesa himself testifies that a Portuguese youth in the Canaries told him that in the WIC's first five years its directors earned enough money, not even counting what had been robbed and pillaged by Dutch soldiers, "that they would be able to set up forty thousand paid men in the Indies."[186] These statements constitute much wishful thinking. The first only loosely resembles what is known of the organizational structure of the WIC, which in fact was run by nineteen directors, none of whom was ever a Sephardic Jew, though some Sephardim became prominent investors in the company.

In addition, among the allegations against Pinto listed in 1651 is the following:

> And as a Jewish judaizer, observer of the Law of Moses, following the counsels contained in the letter of the Jews of Constantinople, [that they] wrote to those of Toledo, in which they say to profane the temples, and their images, a certain monk, from the convent of the discalced Carmelites of this city, making a profession that a certain person went to speak to the said Blas de Paz, who assisted in the hanging [of icons and art] and adorning of the church.[187]

While the monk's accusation that Pinto purposefully spat on the face of an image of Our Lady of the Conception comes straight out of López's testimony from 1634,[188] the matter of a letter from Turkish Jews that prompts attacks on Catholic property and sacred items is totally new. It is not clear whether Pinto's actions merely paralleled those called for in this letter or whether he was actually following its suggestions, but in any case, I have not seen any other reference to this letter in the records of the Cartagena tribunal. Somewhat surprisingly, the letter in question refers to a forged correspondence dating from the time of the expulsion of the Jews from Spain. The afflicted Toledan Jews supposedly wrote to their coreligionists in Constantinople, asking for advice. The response, from the "Chief of the Jews of Constantinople," urges the Spanish Jews to wreak revenge through a variety of patiently devious means: they should have their children become merchants, to slowly pilfer the goods of Spanish Christians, physicians, in order to take their lives, clerics and theologians, to destroy their churches from within, etc. Though not the last time the letter would be wielded by Iberian anti-Semites, it had been discussed and reprinted in an anti-Jewish work published in Madrid in 1614.[189] Daviken Studnicki-Gizbert suggests that the accusations of Jewish coordination with their Turkish leaders may be drawn from Quevedo's 1633 play, Execración por la fe Católica, which accused the Jewish Portuguese asentistas (contract holders) of "greater revenge than any of the machinations of the detestable rabbis of Constantinople."[190]

It seems improbably that Diego López would have been aware of the tradition regarding these letters. It must be that it was Juan Ortiz, formerly the local tribunal's fiscal and now inquisitor, who 'improved' the formulation of López's charges with such material, buttressing the case against this alleged marrano long after his death. This might have been done as a response to the Suprema's criticisms leveled against the local tribunal for the flaws in several of their trials from the late 1620s and 1630s, criticism that led to a new trial for Luis Gomes Barreto, begun in 1652. Already in 1645, an investigative visit was conducted, under which numerous interviews turned up a great deal of inquisitorial abuse.[191] In 1648 a long list of accusations of irregularities by the Cartagena inquisitor and the fiscal Juan Ortiz, among others, were conveyed to the Suprema. Many of these transgressions revolve around favors that seemed to pass between Barreto and the inquisitor Juan de Uriarte, that is, around close relations between the commercial and religious elites, where the latter should have superior to, supervising and guiding the former.[192] (Recall that Barreto told his inquisitors during his first trial that among those hosted by Blas de Paz Pinto on his ranch were the town's archdeacon and senior inquisitor.) The cultivation of such relations did not always help the Portuguese converso merchants. The inquisitor Uriarte was accused by Don Joseph de Bolibar, knight of the Order of Santiago and bailiff of the Cartagena tribunal, of receiving the payments owed to Pinto by other Portuguese merchants of Angola or Lisbon, not giving them any receipts that they had paid and, obviously, never remitting the payments to the rightful recipient.[193] It should be pointed out that nowhere does the Suprema seem to have been bothered by the fact that much of the testimony regarding the judaizing alleged against various Portuguese New Christians came from the mouth of a former slave who confessed to brujería and whom the inquisitors themselves call a "heretic and apostate."[194]

Beyond hoping to distract attention from his own misdeeds, Ortiz no doubt wished to correct the bad impression of an incompetent and morally lax tribunal by emphasizing the prescience and sagacity of its sweeping and harsh treatment of the Portuguese New Christian merchants.[195] Several of the charges against Pinto from 1651 feature the kind of "improvements" that have been mentioned previously, mostly the addition of technical theological terms. Thus where López merely describes the gatherings at Pinto's house, with slaves posted to keep out visitors, the new charges tack on "with which it is an evident thing that they have gatherings, of synagogues in contempt of the evangelical Law of our redeemer and savior Jesus Christ and falsely in their expired, condemned and dead law of Moses."[196] Where López merely depicts the low voices, pauses and seeming sighing of lamentation that lead him to believe that prayers are being conducted in Pinto's house, the later charges clarify that "without doubt [this] would be because they had neither temple nor King of the tribe of Judah, and because they did not sanctify and adore in excelsis [in the highest], as they have by custom, as obstinate and pertinacious, in their expired law."[197] It is here in the 1651 charges, more than a decade after his death, that Pinto is called "Rabbi of the said Law of Moses," and is considered by the other "Jews" "as a man learned and expert in the Law of Moses, and that he was a teacher of its ceremonies," is said to have observed various fasts "so that God should give them success and save their souls."[198]

The torture Blas de Paz Pinto underwent on 9 February 1637 produced contusions in his toes, nerve damage and caused him to go into shock. His right foot required amputation. He asked for a confessor, to whom he confessed, as well as for the administration of all the sacraments. Despite the attention of two surgeons, Pinto's condition worsened. The inquisitors gathered with their consultants, deciding that if the prisoner should live, he would go out in the next auto de fé, to be reconciled to the Church. His punishment would entail confiscation of all his goods, the wearing of the penitential habit and perpetual imprisonment. Given his state, however, the inquisitors saw fit to conduct a private ceremony of reconciliation in the jail, as Pinto himself desired. As the prisoner's condition deteriorated, his confessor, a priest serving as an officer of the Inquisition, was sent in to console him and offer him the last rites. In a fitting if unintended irony, the inquisitors asked that the priest be accompanied by Father Pedro Claver, whose ministrations to slaves and non-Whites would eventually earn him sainthood in the nineteenth century. Perhaps Claver and Pinto knew each other, had even been brought together by their different functions having to do with slaves. Pinto died on 20 February 1637, without ever leaving the Inquisition jail.[199] Testifying in 1648, Gabriel de Uria Munguia, treasurer and judge of the royal court in Cartagena, recalls having heard that when Pinto died "they took him out [in the auto de fé] in state with a sambenito."[200] This would have been on 25 March 1638.[201] Because he died before the formal completion of his trial, Pinto was buried in a secret location, which would be revealed to his family only after the closure of the legalities. Hence those involved in his interment were sworn to secrecy, the sacristan, the gravedigger and the Blacks who carried his body.[202]

Appearing at the same auto de fé as the effigy of the defunct Blas de Paz Pinto was Paula de Eguiluz. She had evidently confessed to the accusations of her sorcery in her very first audiencia. She, too, was reconciled to the Church, and received as punishment the confiscation of her goods, two hundred lashes and perpetual incarceration. The causa or summation of her crimes and punishment could not be read aloud to the assembled crowd, because of the great noise into which it erupted.[203] It is not clear whether the murmuring of the crowd signified an outcry against a detested and feared bruja or a protest by a mixed-race crowd against an unjust sentence. At any rate, the imprisoned Eguiluz continued to be a requested healer in Cartagena, receiving permission to leave the inquisition jail in order to treat patients, who included local inquisitors and the city's bishop. On these occasions she went out carried by slaves "in a sedan chair, without her penitential habit, wearing a little cloth with a gold border, and earned much money, part of which she distributed as alms between the rest of her prisoner companions."[204]

We do not know how many of the city's residents noticed the tragi-comic ramifications of Spanish racial politics. In the case of the individuals treated in this chapter, we ultimately know too little about their lives to fully explain the way their physical and social coexistence in the terrain of colonial Cartagena led them to get along, to understand one another or not. While the urban sphere and its daily exigencies in many respects led people of different classes to come together in an irenic manner, the inquisitorial mentality, class differences and the racial caste system that seeped into the consciousness of those high and low all too often generated quite contrary, agonistic results. In 1675, the Rev. Elias al-Mûsili, an Arab Christian from Baghdad, visited Cartagena for forty days. With himself in mind as a tourist, he described the city's inhabitants as "Catholic, true Spaniards who love foreigners."[205]

CHAPTER 4

Masters and Slaves Under the Stare of the Cross

In this chapter I turn to relations between Afroiberian slaves and Judeoconverso masters, in particular insofar as they were influenced by the theopolitics of the Iberian caste system and system of blood purity. Though often the Afroiberians involved were not directly owned by Judeoconversos, religious differences between members of the two groups were impacted by the even more overt tensions of caste subject position. Before getting to the complex master-slave interactions documented in the households of Judeoconversos in inquisitional records, I look at the sphere of the Inquisitions themselves, where Afroiberian slaves found themselves in some ways in positions of power and cultural belonging over against imprisoned Judeoconversos.

Slaves of the Inquisition

Some of the Inquisition tribunals themselves served as one of the most fascinating and well-reported points of intersection between Judeoconversos and Afroiberians in the Iberian empires. For one thing, despite the fact that many Afroiberians found themselves victims of inquisitional surveillance and litigation, most of the slaves and servants of the local Inquisition bodies were also Afroiberian. Afroiberians carried out some of the Inquisitions' 'dirty work,' mostly without a choice. The structure of such situations often made these slaves spectators and collaborators in the persecution of conversos, on the one hand, and aiders and abettors of the converso victims, on the other (the latter to be treated in chapter 6).

How might slaves come to work for the Inquisition? Those who worked for the institution on contract, as jailers, for instance, would bring to their service their personal slaves. Inquisitors themselves frequently owned personal slaves. When in 1636 the goods of the accused judaizer Manuel Alvares Prieto were sequestered by the Cartagena tribunal, "they brought to the house of [the señor liçenciado (attorney) Juan Ortiz, fiscal (prosecutor) of the holy Inquisition of this city] two blacks who they said belonged to said Manuel Albarez Prieto, being bozales from the Rivers [da escravos, a region of Guinea, now Benin]."[1] What Ortiz did with the two slaves is unclear, though it is likely they ended up in his employ, a perk of his position. In this case, the two slaves probably served Ortiz's personal needs rather than the institution for which he worked, though the line between the two was often blurred. A Black slave arrested and imprisoned by the Mexico City tribunal in 1642 for having two wives was pressed into service as an assistant to the tribunal's jailer "due to the present necessity of there being so many prisoners in the secret jails."[2] Indeed, of the 53 slaves who had belonged to the alleged marranos arrested in Mexico in 1642 and 1643, all who had not died or escaped were sold at auction or put to work by the Inquisition "warden and jail staff."[3] Such a functional arrangement was typical of the way slaves were distributed by the managerial class. The bakers of Potosí, who desired but could not generally afford the expensive advantage of slave labor, won a compromise from the authorities whereby slaves of local slaveholders who merited punishment were imprisoned in bakeries (only those run by Spaniards, of course) and forced to work.[4]

What might it mean to work as a slave for the Inquisition? In 1621, two Blacks acted as town criers for the Inquisition in the province of Paraguay, carrying out the public readings of announcements: "the two Blacks should announce publicly in the voice of the town crier, being present all the neighbors and residents of the royal city."[5] Afroiberian slaves often served in Inquisition jails in various capacities. As Manuel Tejado Fernandez writes,

> among the functionaries on whom the inquisition relied for the supervision and care of the prisoners are [...] the jailer, his assistant, who was sometimes one of the jailer's own slaves, and a pantry officer. [....] Even if auxiliary functionaries are not spoken of, however, we believe it not venturesome the supposition that there existed men or women in charge of the kitchen, slave women for the cleaning and night watchmen. Without doubt, as much as the jailer's assistant, all of these or most of them would be from the "family" of the jailer or the pantry officer.[6]

The actual tasks done by such slaves varied widely. The Congolese slave Sebastian/Mungia, mentioned above, cleaned the prison's cells and removed the prisoners' bodily wastes.[7] The accused judaizer Francisco Botello complained (ca. 1645) from his jail cell in Mexico City to his neighbor in prison "that the black [slave who worked for the Inquisition] put very little water in the [large earthenware] jar" in his cell when he was supposed to fill it up.[8] This same Botello, however, also seems to have related to his nephew experiences of another sort. After he had been tortured in the course of his trial, he was moved to a new cell without light, "where they treated him [medically] from afternoon to afternoon, and badly, and because of that he had remained without the use of his hands, [...] and that a Black who did not say who he was attended him, that he fed him because he could not eat."[9]

More removed from the quotidian are the following two cases. In 1736, two Black slaves working for the secret Inquisition jails in Lima helped retrieve the corpse of an Inquisition prisoner whose bad health forced his transfer to a hospital.

Having died there, an Inquisition official stumbled across him, recognized him, and had the slaves bring him back to the secret jails for burial.[10] Around 1577, two Santiago de Chile residents,

> two blacks and a morisco [descendant of Muslim conversos], who was here as a slave and sold, were commanded to take from the church the said Pero López, cleric, the blacks and morisco being persons who did not have to have respect or reverence or fear for the most Holy Sacrament, as in fact they did not have, and with violence they took from the Great Church the said Pero López and brought him to the house of Teniente and from there to the jail.[11]

What White Christian would drag a priest, even a deviant one, from a church to the Inquisition? Though technically Christians, a Black and Morisco, in this view, did not have to think or feel Christian. The very split between inner belief and outer action so often seized upon by the Inquisition in attacks on 'judaizing' New Christians was encouraged here in order to further Inquisition ends. There are also cases in which those working for the Inquisitions served what might be seen as above and beyond their routine tasks, though it is doubtful they could refuse. One Mexican Conversa sitting in jail in the 1640s relates to her inquisitors that she heard from a cleric sitting in another cell "that Catana the mestiza who serves in the said jail should feign being a prisoner, and from that which she should say and counsel to the rest [of the prisoners], that they should beg mercy, and this they did."[12]

Working as a slave for an inquisitional tribunal often brought Blacks and Mulatos into the orbit of imprisoned real or alleged crypto-Jews in ways beyond that of providing service. Juliana, "a Negress (a slave)," testified in 1646 against Gabriel de Granada, among the many other witnesses who deposed against him. Granada in turn denounced, among many others, "Elvira, a Negress who served in these prisons. She died."[13] Perhaps Elvira was named as a judaizer merely in order to give the Inquisitors what they wanted, more names. Perhaps she had been a cruel jailer's accomplice, thereby drawing the wrath of the prisoner Granada. While we may never know in this case, it illustrates the randomness and pettiness of power: a slave of African origin who, as an employee in an Inquisition jail, happened to stand over a prisoner accused of being a Jew; an impoverished quasi-Jew languishing in the Inquisition's prison lashing out at a peon employed at the facility. In short, the jails of the Inquisitions may have been a site whose social structure generated for a Judeoconverso the kind of emotional opening to denounce an Afroiberian.

Slaves helped in the construction necessary for celebration of the autos de fe, the public celebrations at which those tried by the Inquisition were punished, for instance converting a city's plaza into an appropriate setting for a solemn yet 'festive' and instructive spectacle. Slaves also participated in the events in various ways. As will be seen from even the select aspects I will mention, such autos de fe constituted anything but a spontaneous outburst of religious violence: "Around a precise objective were structured a successive series of programmed acts with the express goal of impressing the public sense with the emphatic example of punishment. Nothing was abandoned to improvisation, every detail that would appear, no matter how small, was conscientiously studied."[14]

The decision to hold a public 'act of faith' rested with the inquisitors, who made use of these staged events when 'sin' appeared too widespread, as José Toribio Medina implies about the inquisitor Ulloa, who planned the 30 November 1587 auto de fé in Lima because of "the accused tried [by the Inquisition] for reasons of faith, whose number then was so considerable that he [the Inquisitor] resolved to celebrate a new public auto."[15]

The list of expenses for the auto de fe held on 2 February 1614 in Cartagena shows that convicts doing forced labor and slaves installed trees and raised tarps (velas, literally sails) for a tent in the town square, for which they were given a lunch worth 18.5 pesos.[16] Like the trees installed for the 23 January 1639 auto de fé in Lima, at which the well-known marrano Francisco Maldonado de Silva was burned at the stake, these trees served to hold up the tent and to protect the distinguished members of the crowd from the hot summer sun.

> For the shade of the principal stage and the others, 22 trees were installed, each one 24 varas [a measure approximately equivalent to one yard] in height, and on these they made firm the tarps, which occupied 100 varas in length and 70 in width, tied with many threads of hemp, with their blocks, pulleys and ribs, with which the sail remained so smooth and firm, being so large, as if it were made with a frame: it came to be twenty varas from the ground, causing peaceful shade.[17]

The completion of the stage for this occasion was 50 days late, despite the fact that the 16 Blacks who built it worked continuously, not even resting for sacred holidays.

Blacks and Mulatos made up an important part of the crowd and its activities orchestrated by the Inquisition authorities for these events. Describing the same 1614 auto de fe in Cartagena, one Inquisition official produced the following summary of the opening events:

> The order was given that the accompaniment of the execution of the sentences was to be at four in the afternoon until twelve thirty, and aside from the officials and familiars of the Inquisition, [there were] eighteen of those [slaves] who the day before had brought sticks [firewood] on horseback, and the gentlemen Inquisitors seeing that in the plaza and streets there were more than four thousand souls, Blacks, mulatos, mestizos, and Spaniards, loaded up with oranges and other fruits to throw at those being whipped, and that those who had been called for

the accompaniment [of those to be sentenced?] did not dare to go out with them for fear of some disgrace [i.e., having fruit thrown at them], such that at first the complement hesitated by the barbarous rabble which was waiting, they [the inquisitors] agreed that an announcement would be given with a penalty of a hundred lashes, that no one throw oranges or any other thing. No sooner had it been given, when young and old, all held back their hands, a thing which those who know the liberty of the ones and the incapacity of the others took as a miracle, and thus all was executed without anyone doing anything but watch.[18]

The Inquisition official who wrote this summary chose to list the mob's constituent elements in ascending order from the point of view of caste classification. Not coincidentally, from the point of view of the importance attached by the Inquisition to each group's moral/pedagogical improvement from these spectacles, the list appears to be in descending order. The author's impression might have been that the 'lower classes' threw fruit more often or readily, were more unruly, though their enthusiasm for thus disrespecting the Inquisitions' intended scapegoats may or may not have translated into the intended internalization of the moral lessons involved. A similar schematic can be found in a later description of the 1649 auto in Mexico City: "Fervor and Christian piety without doubt abounded on this occasion, which made the men, and women, children, slaves, indians, and rude people break out in voices, and shouts, with which they professed our holy Catholic Faith, speaking from the fence, stages, carriages, and balconies with the Hebrews, and persuading them, not without tears, that they should repent, and confess."[19]

One gets a visceral sense from this depiction of the mob dynamics that must have made these events frenzied instantiations of "communitas," extraordinary moments that temporarily forge a utopian community. As suggested in the inquisitors' manual composed by Nicolas Eimerich, these events served as an imitation or foreshadowing of the Last Judgment.[20] Describing the public whippings for those sentenced at the 23 January 1639 Cartagena auto that took place after the main event, the Presbyterian Fernando Montesinos reprinted the announcement that was made that "no one should throw mud, stone or any other thing at those penitenced." For "Spaniards [who violate this prohibition:] banishment to Chile, for the Mulato, Mestizo, Indio or Black, 100 lashes."[21] From the perspective of the New Christians punished at these spectacles, the enthusiasm of the lower classes comprised an especial insult to their sense of honor. A 1561 letter to the Portuguese king from a New Christian spokesman complains that "it was particularly the 'rabble' which rejoiced at the sight of the auto da fé executions," where "all and sundry join in persecuting them."[22]

Some privileged servants of the Inquisitors also participated, voluntarily or not, in the processions of the autos de fe, at least as reported from the Lima auto of 1 June 1608: "and behind went the principal mayordomo [Keeper of the Keys] captain Jara, the principal caballerizo [Keeper of the Horses] don Joseph de Castilla

Altamirano, the secretaries and other servants and gentlemen of his Excellency and of the chamber, and the servant pages of the lords Inquisitors."[23] In other cases, certain privileged servants sat along with their employers or masters in what must have been considered the best seats from which to view the proceedings, regardless of whether the servants relished witnessing the events as much as their royal or ecclesiastical superiors. The following description, written by an Augustinian monk, concerns the Lima auto of 21 December 1625: "On the main stage was a round dais, preeminent to the rest, covered with silk and with raised latticework, for my lords doña Mariana de Córdova and doña Brianda de Córdova, daughters of his Excellency, his governess and his servants, and behind, the servants of his Excellency."[24]

From the perspective of the Inquisition, the servile classes formed a necessary part of the collective confronting heresy, as can be seen by the treatment accorded to the spectating crowd in the anonymous chronicle of the 1672 auto de fe in Málaga, on the peninsula:

> Filled, finally, that rare map, with such perfect placement that, in the combined variety of classes that occupied it, it made compatible the difference and the consent and, its admirable body animated by the great soul of such circles, estates and hierarchies, it formed out of itself an object so immense, that seeing it, no matter how expanded the view in the breadths of the imagination, it was not possible at one time to embrace in the sphere of the eyes.[25]

Unrecorded went whatever ran through the minds of the servants and slaves as various Afroiberians received punishments and 'judaizers' burned to death for their 'crimes.' According to the Portuguese humanist Damião de Góis, "some of the fires for the burning of the cristãos novos in Lisbon were themselves stoked by African slaves."[26]

Two incidents from Portugal, though perhaps not fully elucidating the feelings of Afroiberian spectators, hint at the heterogeneous context in which such spectating might have occurred. As mentioned in chapter 2, watching the 26 September 1540, Lisbon auto da fé in which the judaizer and messianic pretender Diogo de Montenegro was burned alive at the stake, Catarina Fernandes, herself already imprisoned as a judaizer, reacts with visible rage — at least according to one of her denouncers from 3 February of the following year.[27] Furthermore, testifies another neighbor on 14 March 1541, some neighbors told Catarina "how a Black looked with evil intention at Montenegro, and Catarina Fernandes responded that in the same way would she watch the Black dragged [through the streets?]; and the neighbors said further about Montenegro that he didn't want to look at the cross, and Catarina Fernandes responded that God knew where each one would be [after death]."[28]

The "evil" look of the Black in the crowd, whether it happened or was invented by Catarina's neighbors, seems to have proven an effective taunt.[29] Also in 1541

Lisbon, as discussed in chapter 2, a Black woman testifies against Maria Rodrigues, already imprisoned several months for judaizing and cursing the Portuguese King for the forcible conversions of Jews. According to her statement, this Black woman had invited Maria to go see the auto, probably the same one of 26 September just discussed, by the Tejo River in Lisbon — which provides another glimpse of the social nature of the event — clearly not knowing Maria's loyalties.[30]

Denouncing Slaves

Contestatory dynamics generated equally tumultuous consequences in the supposedly private sphere, where Black and Mulato slaves and servants turned to the Inquisitions for protection against, leverage or revenge against, liberation from their masters. Following David Nirenberg's characterization of inter-minority violence in medieval Spain, such rhetorical violence "could be classified as 'situational' in that it sprang from specific relationships between individual [Afroiberians] and Judeoconversos, and not from ascriptive 'religious identity,'" though the influence of the latter on the former should not be totally dismissed in the cases we will examine.[31] In a study of the accused marranos of Badajoz from the 1630s, Pilar Huerga Criado characterizes the master-slave relation as bearing more significance than the clash between Old Christians and New Christians.[32]

As Renée Levine Melammed notes, the "average home had numerous servants whose turnover rate as employees was considerable."[33] In Jewish homes in pre-expulsion Spain, at least, "most household servants were not Jewish."[34] Defending themselves against accusations of judaizing, one not particularly elite family from the Spanish village of Cogolludo in the early seventeenth century identified over 30 former servants who could have acted as hostile witnesses for the inquisitorial prosecution.[35] What was stated by María de Encío, arrested in Santiago de Chile in 1579, no doubt often held true: Many of the trial witnesses against her "were her servants, and she had disputes with them and they left her house discontented."[36] In the early 16th century, a list of all New Christians of Segovia was compiled, "listed by parish, together with particulars concerning their families and other members of their households."[37] The last element possibly related to Old Christian servants or slaves, either because their presence in the households of Judeoconversos worried officials and clergymen that they would be judaized or in order to build a stable of potential witnesses. Moriscos generated similar worries. A 1548 edict of grace issued by the archbishop of Seville ordered that Moriscos live among Old Christians and that their servants be Old Christians. The wording of the decree and its context suggest that the servants were utilized as an instrument of Christianization.[38]

Some families likely tried to avoid just this situation. Andrée Aelion Brooks writes that converso "families were exceedingly cautious concerning the loyalties of the servants they hired, tending to choose from among their own. Providing employment to conversos in need was also a way to fulfill the family's commitment towards their less fortunate brethren. This becomes clear from testimony given [...] in Antwerp by a 75-year old conversa refugee who had served as a wet nurse."[39] It is difficult to say whether or not this was true. In Mexico City, a neighbor of a family of alleged crypto-Jews, the Blancas de Rivera, claims that they "must be Jews or at least not good Catholics[,] because during the time they lived in the house across the street from his they never had a servant nor did anyone ever come into their house from the outside to work for them."[40] Sandoval's testimony may have been accurate for the time he described; we know that at least one of the women in the family, María de Rivera, at some point owned an Angolan woman named Juliana and her small son Pedro, who did her cooking and sold embroidery in the streets of Mexico City. Likewise, Herman Salomon notes the accusation made by an otherwise benign employee of the Inquisition in Quintanar, Castile, against a family of Judeoconversos there. "The Moras took nobody into their employ who was not a relative," he claims, though the fact that the family is also denounced by two unrelated former servants (with totally different last names) makes his allegation a "patent fib."[41] In other words, allegations of insularity in hiring might have entailed merely another means by which Old Christians accused New Christians of 'Jewish' clannishness. Even if such self-reliance was sought, it certainly was not always achievable and in might have been a priority only of actively judaizing families. Luis Henriques, an early 16th-century New Christian of the Trás-os-Montes region of Portugal, manifested such good Christian behavior that, unusually, he always had "old Christian manservants and maidservants and he married them [off?] and honored them and gave many alms and did pious works."[42]

At any rate, numerous bits of evidence point to New Christians hiring servants who were neither family members nor even New Christian themselves. Typical of the general urban milieu, certainly for the Americas, are the details coming out of the trial of one New Christian accused as a judaizer, Sebastian Rodriguez of Panama City. He employed a free Black woman, Juana Cassanga, also of the city, as a domestic servant. The young son of Juana Cassanga apparently also worked for Rodriguez, probably so that she could earn money and continue to keep an eye on him.[43] The New Christian Anrique Dias Milão was arrested by the Lisbon tribunal in 1606, along with his household staff, which included an Old Christian servant who refused to renounce his master's "Judaism" and was executed along with him. Paulo de Milão, Anrique's son, also arrested, retained a servant, António Barbosa, who was a partial Old Christian. Barbosa's sister, Violante, served as the maidservant of Beatriz Henriques Milão, Paulo's wife.[44]

Servile loose talk or denunciation is a trope already in Patristic literature and a mainstay of classical and medieval discourse.[45] It stems from the structural determinants of a situation, often miserable, over which servants and slaves had little or no control yet from which they often accumulated great information about the very ones who did control their situation (and them). As was discussed in the previous chapter, among those whom slaves had the most motivation to oppose, disarm or even kill were their masters, and in Inquisition trial records from the Americas they frequently confess to "having intended to assassinate, and not always as magical practitioners, their masters, other whites, other slaves; having given powder or herbs or poisons and prayers/spells."⁴⁶ One former slave woman declared to her inquisitors at Cartagena, after having spoken about gatherings of magical practitioners, that she killed "her master Juan Hortensio with some colored powders that her devil Ñagá had given her, because he [the master] did not want to give her freedom, they being put twice in his soup/broth, from which he died."⁴⁷

Conflict often derived from or was exacerbated by the real or imagined Marranism of Judeoconversos and the authentic or feigned Christianity of Blacks. Black and Mulato servants and slaves did not denounce their employers or masters and mistresses only of judaizing, of course, and the reasoning behind the choice of allegation remains to be deciphered in each case. For instance, a Black woman was burned in Seville on Monday, 18 August 1631, for having "accused her master of an unmentionable sin [usually referring to sodomy] with a child of his; he lost the judgment and died from the penalty, and having verified it [the accusation] being false, they carried her in a boat and burned her."⁴⁸ On the one hand it could be assumed that the charges raised by slaves are transparent, that is, generally accurate; on the other hand, one might infer certain 'narrative' choices on the part of the denouncing servant. These narrative choices might reflect merely the imagination of the servant in question, the particular set of possible examples to which the servant had been exposed, or the specific character and situation of the master's household, lifestyle, etc. For instance, though Afroiberians accused one another of various crimes and heresies such as adultery, bigamy or blasphemy, I have seen no cases of one Afroiberian accusing another of judaizing, probably because the charge would not have appeared convincing; very few Blacks and Mulatos were judaizers.

As occurred in some of the cases investigated below, slaves, like other witnesses, cited as their source of knowledge about their masters' practices the publicly read Edicts of Faith, which, beginning with the Seville Inquisition in 1481, detailed the practices and beliefs of Jews, Muslims or Lutherans for which people should be on the lookout.⁴⁹ Thus on 21 August 1512, Pedro de Villarreal's Black slave Catalina testified against his wife María González, accused of judaizing, buttressing her deposition with the following summation: "it seemed to this witness that the above-mentioned was a heretical thing because she had heard it read in the things of the inquisition, which were heard by her when the lord Inquisitor Mariana was in Ciudad Real."⁵⁰ Accusations by servants could also be preposterously vague, based on the kind of anti-Jewish notions that circulated throughout Iberian society. The reported findings of two Spanish servants who worked for Portuguese families, the latter by popular reputation in the seventeenth century almost all secret Jews, serve as typical examples: the first declared how strange she found it that her mistress "washed her hands every time she attended her bodily needs [...] even if it were very late at night," while the second merely suspected that the acts of her masters "would be some kind of Jew thing (será alguna judiada)" and denounced them.⁵¹ Irene Silverblatt brings the example of one slave in Lima who swore before the local inquisitional tribunal that his Portuguese master, Jorge Paz, must be a judaizer because "whenever a Portuguese came to talk to [Paz], he would close the door."⁵²

Despite its problems, many within the Inquisitions' administration might have been ideologically disposed to accept testimony from servants or slaves, a feature already of the medieval Inquisitions, as described in the fourteenth-century Aragonese inquisitor Nicolau Eimeric's foundational text, Directorium Inquisitorum. Though denied many, if not most rights in societies from ancient Greece to Renaissance Europe because of the circular reasoning that saw slaves as suited for their condition, slaves could still serve the interests of the ruling classes when convenient for the latter.[53] This is precisely the motivation cited by Eimeric, who states that it is the terrible gravity of heresy that permits the acceptance of testimony from servants or slaves "with circumspection, as in general they bear extreme malevolence against their masters. Contrarily, it is licit to torture a servant/slave who shows himself reluctant to denounce his master."[54] John Leddy Phelan summarizes this from the perspective of social responsibility:

> In matters of morality and purity of faith, the privileges of class and caste disappeared. The evidence of one man, no matter what his social background might be, was as good as another man's. Servants could testify against employers, social inferiors against social superiors, and slaves against masters. Like most authoritarian organizations, the Holy Office was equalitarian, certainly much more so than the corporate society in which it functioned.[55]

In contrast, Carole Myscofski reads this quality of the Inquisitions as the "encouraging [...] of hostilities between social ranks and sexes."[56] Yet some officials of the Inquisitions that used servants and slaves as witnesses acknowledged the particular difficulties of accepting their testimony. The Supreme Council of the Spanish Inquisition, the Suprema, which "addressed itself to the question of the character of witnesses" in 1509, decreed that "witnesses who testified against their masters should be examined, and that if there was any suspicion concerning their character they should even be tortured."[57] It could be that this revision came as a consequence of excesses committed by the controversial inquisitor of Córdoba, Diego Rodríguez Lucero, who was appointed in 1499. Among other problems which caused outrage in the populace and which were reviewed in a 1508 commission, Lucero had arrested the archbishop of Granada, Hernando de Talavera, a respected and admired individual (of Jewish background), who had treated the Muslims under his jurisdiction kindly, and charged him with judaizing and maintaining a synagogue in his palace "on the strength of a denunciation obtained from a servant under torture."[58] When the Portuguese king João III, under pressure from Spain and the Papacy, considered establishing the Inquisition in his country, he secretly consulted four prominent conversos, as he worried that the Inquisition would only further drive the New Christian population to flee. The committee of New Christians suggested that negative consequences would be minimized were the new Inquisition, in contrast to that of Spain, to operate within the guidelines of Common Law, which included declaring testimony from slaves and 'vile persons' invalid.[59] The suggestion went neglected. The record of the first trial against alleged judaizer Luis Gomez Barreto (1636) was reviewed by the Suprema in Madrid, which sent the inquisitors in Cartagena a list of the flaws found therein. Among them were the following:

> If some witness in favor of or against the accused is examined his quality must be put [in writing], and if he was a prisoner of the Holy Office and the cause and how it ended up being dispatched; and such was not done in the examination of Isabel Lopez, black slave, of Doña Gracia Pereyra sister-in-law of the accused, it being said that the witness was a prisoner for 22 months as a witch (bruja), it needed to be stated whether she came out penitenced, and this not having been done it is necessary to see her trial and to insert in [the trial record] of this accused [i.e., Gomez Barreto] testimony regarding her sentence.[60]

These punctiliousness corrections fail to note whether this means such testimony was to be rejected. Their motivation would seem to be to provide the inquisitors with enough information to render a decision about the witness's 'quality' and, therefore, to help produce a fair trial.

It should be kept in mind that false testimony itself constituted a crime punishable by the inquisitional authorities. False denouncers could find themselves punished before or instead of the denounced master.[61] A penitent punished in a 1643 Seville auto de fé had brought false testimony against a Portuguese and his wife. This former servant, it seems, had inserted a crucifix in one of several cushions that her employers had borrowed, and denounced her mistress for sitting on it.[62] No mention is made of any trial of the master or mistress. At least one Black slave, a zambo (someone of mixed African and Amerindian blood) named Francisco del Rosario, found himself arrested in the 1740s by the Inquisition in Chile for "being an inventor, promoter and director of the false calumny of [being] a Jewish judaizer" against his master Juan de Loyola. His punishment included receiving 200 lashes, perpetual servitude (without salary) on the staff of the Valdivia prison, and the recitation every Friday of part of the rosary to the Most Holy Mary.[63]

Both of these theoretical factors — the strictures against carelessly using the testimony of slaves or servants and against providing false testimony — seemed to do little to curb the Inquisitions' inclination to use and accept the testimony of servants and slaves against their masters and mistresses, even if in some few cases the inquisitors acted with caution. In the case of Sebastián Rodríguez of Panamá, a Portuguese New Christian arrested in Cartagena in 1642, the accused denied all the charges. The inquisitors, unable to reach a decision, contacted the Suprema, which finally responded in 1645 (Rodríguez sitting in jail the entire time). It was ordered that a witness from Panamá, Juana Casanga, a free Black who had worked for Rodríguez, be interrogated again. If no flaw should be found in her testimony, the accused should be tortured in order to extract a confession.[64] In response to the extensive depositions of a Black slave woman to the Mexico City tribunal in the early 1640s, the inquisitors state that "without another procedure that will give her complete faith, and credit, being a slave, vile person [...] of bad habits, [...] and that realistically it is possible to believe that she lies against her said masters and other persons against whom she deposes [...] that the said black woman [...] should be faced with torture," to see whether or not she changes her testimony.[65] This step was not, of course, taken with all slaves or non-Whites. Something about her character or testimony must have made the inquisitors suspicious in this case. The testimony of another of the slaves caught up in helping prisoners communicate in the jails of the Mexico City tribunal was also doubted by the inquisitors, and this Black slave man was also sent to the torture chamber. In his case, the inquisitors contented themselves in describing him with the stock phrase, "being a slave [and] vile person."[66] So too another female Black slave caught up in the same episodes.[67] On 6 March 1526, in Galdar, the Canary Islands, Friar Alonso de Carmona deposed to "having heard Arias Varela say that Silvestre Gonçales had been burnt on the false testimony of a slave and others, who bore ill will to the said Silvestre, and to his father Alvaro Gonçales, and that the said slave had been told to give this information against her master."[68] As late as 1683, a Spaniard who had fled the Spanish Inquisition for Holland and later became an open Jew, Abraham Ydaña alias Gaspar Méndez del Arroyo, complained in a letter to an Inquisition official that the Inquisition apprehended suspected judaizers "even on the mere word of a servant or slave, without knowing a thing about Judaism."[69] According to Jonathan Israel, Catholic officials at Oran, "made much of adverse reports collected from former slaves of Jews who had converted and been freed." Thus, Luis Joseph de Sotomayor y Valenzuela, in his chronicle of the 1669 expulsion of Jews from Oran, writes that it "is known from some Moors, former slaves of Jews [...] that they mock our true faith and utter curses when they pass by churches."[70]

Masters certainly had ways to try to prevent or react to slave denunciations or the threat of making them. One cannot discount the avenues of pressure and coercion available to masters, especially in more isolated 'plantation' settings. One Bahian master took revenge on two of his privileged domestic slaves who testified against him (1613-1614) by ordering them to be transferred "as field hands to his sugar estate" inland, where they were quickly killed by "many whippings and bad life and labor."[71] An Inquisition trial in Covilhã, Portugal, begun in 1575, shows that in some cases slave testimony was evaluated against other social and class factors. When there existed concern with "avoiding public scandal and sustaining the social order," the testimony of slaves might not carry weight. Historian E. R. Samuel remarks about this trial of Maria da Fonseca: "hearsay evidence from gentlemen was given much greater weight than direct evidence from servants against their mistresses" that "the family ate apart from their servants and did no work on Saturdays," among other charges. Here the social pressure to acquit probably stemmed from the fact that Maria da Fonseca's husband, Jeronimo Nunes Ramires, "seems to have had the most fashionable medical practice in the country town" and that Maria's father had been sometime physician to Queen Catherine of Portugal. Asking his "more important patients among the local gentry" to testify on behalf of his wife, Dr. Ramires was able to secure as character witnesses "three gentlemen and nine ladies of the Old Christian nobility, three neighbors and two priests."[72]

At Home (?)

The inquisitionally sponsored discourse that encouraged and emphasized the centrality of "knowing other people's lives" began at home. Not for nothing, then, does Encarnación Marín Padilla warn that "the thoroughness with which some servants laid out the details of what they saw and heard turns out to be suspect."[73] Slaves essentially performed surveillance for the Inquisitions within the homes of their owners, alert to domestic practices which deviated from Iberian Christian norms or keen to invent such deviations. Slaves did this without formal instruction by or arrangement with inquisitors (in chapters 2 and 6 I discuss cases in which slaves who worked for the Inquisition were asked to conduct surveillance within the jails). Slaves and masters, servants and employers lived in tremendous intimacy with one another, differences notwithstanding, so while the charges raised by servants or slaves may often reflect more or less than 'the facts,' the structure of their living situation combined with social obsessions regarding Catholic orthodoxy generated the desire and means for surveillance from 'under the stairs.' As expressed by Ceballos Gómez, who also discusses such phenomena, domestic slaves "see their masters eating, sleeping, dressing, loving, defecating, renouncing [the faith], raging; they hear all the conversations; they see all the visits; they know all the secrets."[74] One witness testified to the visiting inquisitor in Bahia in 1591 about how a master had "requested a candle at night from his black women [servants], and they, wanting to see through a hole what he did, saw him take [....]."[75] The specific charge is irrelevant. The point is that the curiosity of slaves had ample opportunity to roam over the daily life of their mistresses and masters. A servant who cooked for a family obviously stood in a position of great knowledge about that family's eating habits, especially if they betrayed any signs of 'deviance.' Hence the statement of one witness testifying against a family of alleged judaizers: "and the said mulatas and a Chinese woman named Jacinta, slaves of the said doña Ana Alferez know very well other things because they saw them."[76] Trying to defend himself, the accused judaizer Manuel Bautista Peres, arrested in Lima in the 1630s, urged his inquisitors "to interrogate the cooks in order to find out about the meals he and his family consumed."[77] Again, Ceballos Gómez: "The kitchen is the place of gossip and the majority of the people who work there play the role of cultural intermediaries," acting as a "springboard between the world of the Whites and that of the others, the Indians, the Blacks, and they have interests to defend."[78]

Servants and slaves clearly gossiped about their masters and discussed these matters among one another and with those outside the household. One witness testified that another person's slave "said to him many times that his master had a room filled with silver."[79] Bento Rodrigues Chamusqua, a Brazilian who was carrying on an affair with a mulata servant or slave on a plantation, reported in the mid-1640s that the plantation owners (at least the women) were Judaizers, in view of certain "occurrences, and also because the mulatto woman he used to see had told him they were Jewesses."[80] A former servant, who stated in an English court about his former employers that "their superstitious ceremonyes they kept as secretly as they could from me and others who were not of their religion," nonetheless provided testimony on them based on the "observations" of "Blackamoor" slaves among the "entourage [...] of servants, clerks, a butler, and two negresses."[81] Some servants went so far as to mock the Jewish practices of their masters, a dangerous game to play against their social superiors. The (non-Black) servant of one alleged marrano, on his master's becoming circumcised in London and burying the foreskin, a traditional Jewish custom, "dug it up publicly, to make jest of it with some others; which having come to the ears of the [master] he was much vexed and turned the said [servant] out of his house."[82] In 1541, a neighbor of a New Christian woman of Lisbon reported to the local inquisitors that her brother told her that a slave of their New Christian neighbor confirmed to him that his mistress ate meat at vespers of the Day of the Ascension.[83] In October 1591, Caterina Fernandes related to the visiting inquisitor in Salvador, Bahia, what she had heard about a neighbor's honoring of the Jewish sabbath: "Izabel Pesqueira [...] told her a year and a half ago in the house of her mother in Perabasu that a Black cook of Diogo Lopez Ilhoa, New Christian, told her that the said Diogo Lopes ate chicken on Saturdays."[84]

In these cases one gets a glimpse of the chain of personal communication, gossip and rumor that, often crossing lines of class and race, contributed to the construction of the surveillance on which the Inquisitions fed.[85] Francisco de la Cruz, a Dominican friar in Peru, tells his inquisitors in 1571, in passing, while discussing some episode involving slaves, "And as blacks, insofar as they intended to lend color to their lies, they gave occasion for the truth to be known."[86] Referring to Pernambuco, where he lived, one witness reporting to the visiting inquisitor in 1601 lamented that "the land is one of little secrecy, [the colonists] being served by blacks, therefore everything is publicized."[87] This situation, universal in societies dependent on domestic slaves or servants, makes comprehensible, though no less tragically absurd, the tearful outburst of Juana Enríquez, wife of Simón Váez Sevilla, whose husband and many friends had just been arrested by the Mexican Inquisition on charges of judaizing: "She retired, a prisoner of desperation, to the kitchen; there, seated on a box in which the pots and pans were kept, she addressed the Black women who serve her, crying: 'look, don't we eat stew and chickens like everybody? and if I don't eat lard and bacon, it is because I have a sore throat.'"[88]

In the crisis provoked by the implementation of inquisitional knowledge, this woman spontaneously confessed to her own servants, not coincidentally at the very site where such knowledge was produced, a site for possession of which servant and mistress contested.[89] This mistress confessed with the most sincere emotions, yet unable to reveal the real rationale behind her agony, a rationale the servants very likely already understood: she maintained Jewish practices. Many such denunciations could be cited.[90]

A slave stood as a possession of her master and her religious life was often determined by him against her will. Several masters accused of judaizing were charged with not permitting their slaves to be baptized.[91] A variety of early Inquisition cases from the Canary Islands sheds light on the ways interreligious dynamics played themselves out in the homes and lives of alleged judaizers and Black slaves. That these tensions surface to such a degree reflects the early date: many of these Canariote New Christians possessed actual past connections to functioning Jewish communities, while many of the slaves can be presumed to have been thinly Christianized, if at all. One black slave testified that "her master told her that she was to be called Penda and not Beatriz," a name that she implied struck her allegedly crypto-Jewish master as too Christian.[92] This was an effort to undo the slave's Christianity through the power of naming. Religious tensions combined with the already intimate, messy and often violent situation of a slaveholding house to create a potent brew of complications. One servant testified that his master hit another of his maidservants "for her having gone to Mass."[93] When a Black slave of Alvar Gonçáles went to hear the Easter sermon one year, the master inquired afterward into "what he saw there, and the witness responded that he saw how the people wept because the Jews killed Christ. And that the said Alvar Gonçáles said: 'All of that is wind and all is nothing.'"[94] One gets the sense that the scene is almost as novel to the slave as it is repulsive to the master, even if the slave's summary is barbed. The plight of the Black slave Antonio Martinez, conveyed by a third party to the Inquisition on the Canary Islands, resonates with the religious tensions that might have exacerbated the already-difficult situation of slave and master:

> In the year 1500 Antonio Martinez, a negro, owed a certain sum of money which he was unable to pay, whereupon Luis de Niebla volunteered to pay the money on the understanding that the negro should serve him for a certain period. That during the time of his service the said negro came to this deponent and begged him to help him get free from serving the said Luis de Niebla, as life in his house was unbearable.
> That upon deponent endeavoring to induce him to fulfil his contract, the said negro exclaimed: "Do not compel me, Sir, to serve that man. I shall kill him, or he will kill me, neither I nor my wife can bear the life he leads us; he keeps my wife up until midnight on Fridays and during Lent roasting fowls, cooking meat, and other things.
> That deponent told the negro to come back another time, and meanwhile begged Pedro de Herbas to endeavor to reconcile the parties, but that the said Herbas returned with the negro some days later, and said that it was impossible to persuade him to fulfil his contract, as he declared that the life at Niebla's house

was unbearable, his wife being compelled to cook fowls etc. until midnight on Fridays and certain days in Lent, for the people who came to supper on those days.[95]

Lucien Wolf insists in a defensive footnote that the wife's cooking as described "would have been impossible if Niebla was a Jew, as the Jewish Sabbath begins at sundown on Friday." He misses the point that often slaves were not converted precisely so that they could attend to the family's needs at times when family members could not cook themselves (because it involves using fire, forbidden on sabbath and other holidays). Not converting slaves, especially female ones, has a long and respected pedigree, codified in the Shulkhan Arukh (completed in 1555, first edition in Venice, 1565), the legal code that became canonical among Jews. One section explicitly forbids someone other than the master to immerse a non-Jewish woman or girl for the sake of slavery, which would make the slave subject to certain minimal ritual requirements. Why? "Lest the master does not wish to immerse her for the sake of slavery, for it is preferable to him that she is a non-Jew, for she can serve his needs on the Sabbath."[96] At any rate, since this case concerns a family of alleged crypto-Jews to begin with, such halakhic scruples may not have been known or shared by Niebla or his family.

Beatriz, a Black slave of Francisco del Castillo, from the same island as the previously mentioned slave Antonio Martinez, provided testimony, in 1520, about a miserable slave existence in a 'Jewish' household, or at least one she claimed to be such. Here as well we see the religious pressures that devoted crypto-Jews might have exerted on their non-Jewish slaves. After listing some of the suspicious practices in which her master and mistress engaged,

> The deponent further says that her employers tried to terrify her into adopting their customs, but she would not, for which reason, being frightened that she would denounce them, they put her in irons for three months, and only took them off to take her to the fair at Guadajoz.
>
> And that two or three times Castillo has made her carry a bench on her shoulders, saying "Carry the cross as Christ carried it," and had beaten her while she did so.
>
> And that they have terrified their black slave Philippa into adopting their customs, and the said Philippa said to deponent: "You pray to Mary, and they say their Jewish prayers."
>
> And that they frequently told her that if she would do as they did, and hold her tongue about the things she had seen, they would treat her as a daughter and clothe her well, and the said Castillo told her when putting her in irons that there was no other creed than that of Moses, and that the Messiah would come who was to save them
>
> That one day deponent escaped and went to the church of St. Augustin, where she heard a very good sermon, and on that same

day the old people also went there, and on their return, deponent heard the old woman say to her husband "Did you hear the things that devil [the preacher] said?"[97]

The scenario Beatriz depicts intriguingly parallels the forced Christianization of Jews, though it is unclear whether this reflected the (un)conscious displaced anger of the masters or the (un)conscious recreation of the original coercion by the slave in her testimony. Similar situations arose not just on the Canary Islands, of course. In 1541 in Lisbon, a woman denounced Francisco Fernandes of having pointed out a crucifix to his slave woman, saying in a double entendre that this "was a man who hanged himself/was worthless (que era um homem enforcado)."[98] "The hanged one" was a traditional Jewish way of disparaging Christ and his crucifixion.

Together, religious tensions, unjust power dynamics and poor conditions in the household often generated denunciations to the Inquisitions of judaizing by the mistresses or masters. Slave or servant conditions were usually miserable to begin with in any family, not only physically but emotionally. The defense testimony of one eighteenth-century master in Lisbon illustrates this situation from the perspective of the master. A woman servant of his

> had many bad manners and vices, and carried on an affair with a black, to whom she gave entrance to the house, by day and by night, and sent word to him by means of youths belonging to the accused [...] having information about the said illicit affair of the said slave, [the master] censured and castigated her on many occasions; as he also censured the [nursemaid] Maria Thereza for collaborating in similar folly; but instead of making amends they did worse, for the slave, through her bad quality, was often disobedient, gave many bad retorts, treated the accused and the mistress without respect, agitating the neighborhood with her wrath, and saying she doesn't want to be in said house, and that they should try to sell her; and in the absence of the accused and of his mother she railed and murmured about them, calling them Jews [....].[99]

Seen from the servant's or slave's perspective, the almost total lack of control over her own life must have been unbearable. Her eventual denunciation in this case might have stemmed from goals more strategic than spiritual, but it is obvious that the denunciations of some servants had sincere psychological roots.

Many of the Blacks coming before the Inquisitions acted out of a desire to do their Christian duty (or at least made it appear so to the inquisitors). As aspiring Catholics, they internalized the dictates of the Christianity into which they sought entry. In ways both social and ideational, many Blacks participated in the culture that created and fueled the Inquisitions. One servant who worked in the home of a family accused of judaizing testified that her co-worker, a black woman slave, "said many times and told this witness that her mistresses were some great heretics, and that she showed this witness some sheaves of grapevine shoots and [...] said that they must be kept in order to burn her said mistresses."[100] Conceptually, the Inquisitions even may have helped shape their world view. Many of these accusations constitute a form of resistance among Black New Christians, using the 'judaizer' card against the master if there arose the honest perception or even the reality of judaizing in the household, or the invention of such charges. The denunciations might also stand as an effort to demonstrate loyalty to the denouncers' new Christian religion, to show that Catholicism's dictates have been fully integrated into the aspiring newcomer's psyche. They might also be an honest or strategic wielding of the claims of Christianity against the cruelty of a master who was supposed to behave in a 'Christian' manner.[101] Cut off, most probably, from the kind of family and communal ties their masters could claim even as crypto-Jews, many slaves very much wished to enter the regnant community. According to his testimony of 1519, when Fernando, the Black slave of Alvaro Gonçales, La Palma, the Canaries, would ask his master "to allow him to become a Christian," Gonçales "always replied: 'Why do you wish to become a Christian, there are no Christians in your land [of origin]?' to which deponent would answer: 'Because I live [now] in a Christian land, and if I die [as a 'pagan'] they will not bury me, but throw me into a field.'"[102] Fernando's complaint constituted more than mere rhetoric. Though most sixteenth- and seventeenth-century evidence points to the Christian burial of blacks in the Iberian world, exceptions may not have been rare.[103] The seemingly crypto-Jewish Gonçales, who supposedly strenuously attempted to avoid and defy the dominant Christianity, evidently pressured his slave to follow his path, whether or not his assumption that the slave's pagan origin meant that he shared his master's anti-Christian leanings was ironic or sincere. The assumption seems to have been false. It is obvious that on both sides of the Atlantic many Afroiberians came to live under the umbrella of the Catholic church, became familiar with Christian tropes, institutions and dictates, and wielded them for their own ends.[104]

It remains unclear whether these tales reflect merely the manipulation (and thus not necessarily the acceptance) of the cultural demarcations and stereotypes involved. The authenticity of the denouncing servants' Christianity therefore often stands as much in question as the Judaism of the denounced masters or mistresses. Nonetheless, Inquisition officials often intervened when masters were accused of failing to treat their slaves in a 'Christian' manner. In the case of the slave Beatriz, she had been told by the abbess of the local St. Andrew's church "that she could not receive absolution without making this deposition."[105] Hearing this, the Inquisition notary went to the abbess, who confirmed

> that this Lent a negress, having a chain on her leg, came to the nunnery and told her that she had belonged to Dona Beatriz, wife of Martin Fernandez Galindo, and that for the half they had sold her to a convert whose name she could not say, and that he was a Jew, who did not allow her to pray, and he had taken away her

rosary, and had beaten and ill-treated her, and that he had said many things to her like to a bad Christian.[106]

When, in 1673, a Black slave-boy of Alvaro Rodríguez de Acevedo in Tucumán in the Río de la Plata province "went to complain to the Bishop that his master did not teach him the prayers or allow him to go to mass," did he complain sincerely or strategically? The young slave further informed the Bishop that another Black slave-boy sold by his master had told him that their master whipped a Christ every Sabbath at night, a more dubious though oft-repeated charge. Yet in his first inquisitional audience, Acevedo "gave satisfaction to all the questions they put to him," and "prayed the prayers perfectly." Indeed, the case itself seems not to have been resolved, while the gout-stricken master languished in prison for over a year.[107]

The presence of religious hostilities certainly exacerbated servitude. But desires to escape a servile condition contributed to the making of slave denunciations even without religious conflict. One mistress from Pernambuco, Catharine Mendes, was denounced as follows: when some Mulato soldiers returned with one of her Black women slaves who had fled, they requested some compensation for their trouble, "asking as well that she not whip her [the runaway slave], and she responded to them, aghast, 'that even if God should come to the world I would not refrain from giving it to her.'" For obvious reasons, this kind of attitude and treatment often generated retribution from slaves.[108] Another Pernambucan New Christian was denounced by the mistress of a Black woman slave newly imported from Angola (who deposed through an interpreter) for having forcibly sodomized her.[109] The son of the mistress of one disgruntled Black slave woman in eighteenth-century Lisbon testified that the slave had been aided in her general rebelliousness against the family by the wet nurse also working in the household, who advised her colleague "that she should raise false testimony against the accused and all the people of the house, for thus she would see herself free to marry a black man, with whom she was involved, the black woman also saying many times, when they castigated her, that she had to go to the Holy Office and raise testimony against herself of being a witch, thus finally would she see herself free of servitude and of that house."[110] Certainly this slave was not alone in believing denunciations to the Inquisition could extricate her from her condition.

It is possible that in cases like the above slaves or servants brought denunciations on the order of their current mistresses, who might have had one reason or another to seek the harm of a neighbor, competitor or enemy. As "living tools," in the Aristotelian vocabulary, slaves were frequently used as go-betweens or emissaries of their mistresses' will. The denunciations of these slaves or servants may also have represented their having maintained animosity against their former owners/employers or internalized the perspective of their new masters/employers. Pilar Huerga Criado comes to this conclusion from her study of the Judeoconverso community of Badajoz in the 1630s, where, she says, denouncing slaves almost always had served those they denounced in the past and now belonged to other households.[111]

Mistresses of Fear

Regardless of the sincerity or insincerity of the denouncing servants, these cases help explain Judeoconversos' recurring fear of Black and Mulato servants which appears in trial and other documents. The variety of precautionary measures taken by Judeoconverso masters clearly reflects this fear of the surveillance being carried out in their own homes by their underlings. After the arrest of some of their comrades in 1642 Mexico City, some New Christian women sitting at a window of one of their houses called to a passing friend, to discuss with her the important news. Entering the house, the friend was told that "they had to speak alone because the black men who carried the sedan [silla] were there."[112] Particularly when it came to their judaizing practices, masters took extra caution. In the 1590s, Luis de Carvajal's family in Mexico was warned not to recite prayers in front of their Indian slave woman.[113] According to the testimony of Bento Teixeira (given in 1597), many New Christians in Bahia and Pernambuco had returned to Judaism. Some of these well-educated marranos "acted as rabbis and [...] spoke Latin during their secret gatherings to prevent being understood by their slaves and servants."[114] When Maria de Rivera kept an ordinary fast (ayuno ordinario) with another alleged judaizer at the latter's house, the hostess "burned two wax candles in a pantry where they were reciting prayers of the said law, and the said Doña Maria guarded the door so that no slave woman should enter."[115] Juan de León, alias Salomón Machorro, confessed in 1644 to his Mexican Inquisitors that on some Friday nights he and Gaspar Váez "used to light a torch in a bowl with oil and putting over it an empty barrel so that the Black maidservants shouldn't see it."[116] In 1642 León/Machorro informed the inquisitors that three years earlier the Rivera family, with whom he would celebrate Yom Kippur, did not light candles for the holiday, "so that a Black woman who served them would not start to see."[117] Blanca Enriquez, "out of fear of the slave women, that they shouldn't see it, did not dare light candles. As [Beatriz Enriquez's] said mother [Blanca] told her, it was enough to have the said law of Moses in the heart."[118]

The number of such examples, from many individuals and different locales, testifies to the reality of these fears. Asked in an audience of 12 August 1589 who else was present when the family gathered in Pánuco, Mexico City and Taxco "to communicate the things of the Law of Moses which have been declared, to celebrate Passover, keep the Sabbaths and fast on the Great Day around September," Luis de Carvajal the younger listed, among others: "the two Black women Catalina and Clara, that Catalina was in Tasco with Felipe de Fonseca, and Clara in Huaxutla with Joanes de Urríbarri, dead, and some ever-changing Indian serving women." Yet it seems these servants were excluded from any knowledge of the proceedings, since Carvajal tells the inquisitors that the family "hid and shied away from everyone, and ceased whenever they noticed that some people entered, lest they say 'why are they [the masters] shying away from us?'"[119]

In the 1520s, Francisco Mendes, physician to the Portuguese king Afonso, began keeping Jewish practices with his wife and mother. The wife observed sabbaths and they celebrated the various Jewish fasts and holidays, including

Passover. They later confessed during the trial of a companion, the Old Christian High Court judge Gil Vaz Bugalho, that at Passover they received from the house of Francisco's mother the matza or unleavened bread which "they did not cook in [their] house so that a Black [serving-]woman and others of their house would not know of it."[120] Though Blanca Enriquez, alleged leader of an extended family of crypto-Jews in Mexico City until the 1640s, prepared matzah on occasion with her daughter Beatriz, "they did not make it more than the said three times due to the wariness they had that the slave women of the house might see them." Even so, the preparations took place only when she "sent the men and women slaves to watch the [Easter] processions."[121]

Not only did masters hide actions from their slaves, they also sometimes dissembled in rather extraordinary ways, considering their supposed dominant status. Ysavel de Silva, testifying against this same Beatriz Enriquez in 1643 Mexico City, relates how the latter acted out normalcy for her slaves. Once she visited her friend Beatriz, Ysavel tells her inquisitors, on a day when the latter's husband was out of town on business.

> Having taken out a first chocolate [drink] for this confessant, in order to hide her fast, doña Beatriz, who was fasting that day, took the chocolate that they bring to this confessant and threw it under the platform of the dais [porch?]. She ordered another chocolate for this confessant, saying that between the two of them they had already drank the first, with which the black women brought another calabash [drinking bowl] of chocolate.[122]

During the trial of Juan de León/Salomón Machorro, Catalina de Rivera testified that when Juana Enríquez and her husband Simón Váez Sevilla "made the fast of the Law of Moses, which was only that of the Great Day [Yom Kippur], [...] they carefully feigned a fight in order not to eat that day, and that the servants and slaves would not know that they fasted, but rather that they didn't eat because they were angry."[123] Similarly, on one fast Blanca Enriquez, matriarch of the same extended family, "sat all day by the window, and feigned that she cried because of the absence of her husband [who was away], and with this ailment she could hide from the black women her not having eaten that day."[124] When members of the same extended family held a supper on the third day of their mother's death, while abstaining from meat due to their mourning, one participant brought pig's feet "so that it should not seem to the domestics and other mulatas and black women who were in the said house that they do not eat meat."[125] Her daughter Beatriz recalls an evening supper, possibly on a day such as Sunday, a "meat day," when meat was traditional, when "they put meat on the table in order to entertain the serving women."[126] Juan Rodrigues Mesa, a Portuguese merchant in Cartagena, was accused in 1641 by one witness of eating neither pig nor fish without scales, "and if he did on occasion it was so that his people [i.e., domestic help] wouldn't know that he was a Jew and observed the Law of Moses."[127] According to one witness, when Maria de Rivera and a friend once fasted, at mid-day "they brought the slave women of the said person to eat at the table, and the said Doña Maria and the said person made as if they ate, but in truth they didn't eat, because the said doña Maria, excusing the servants, threw the food to the cats through a window."[128] When about to die, Leonor Vaez, an alleged crypto-Jew in Mexico City, is said to have ordered a crucifix to be placed on her corpse and not to be taken off, so that "the black women and other persons will be able to see it."[129] The accused judaizer Gabriel de Granada, a young teenager, told the Mexican Inquisition during his trial (1642-1645) how doña Juana Enriquez told "his said uncle [Diego Correa] to change his name and call himself Don Pedro so as not to be recognized by the negroes and also to change his voice as he did sometimes."[130]

Though some masters assigned their slaves intimate tasks, functions involving their religious life remained off limits. The early case of María González (ca. 1512 in Ciudad Real), who probably lived as a Jew before the expulsion from Spain, shows a distancing stemming from religious scruples. "They did not want this witness [a maidservant] or the said [black slave] Francisca to scrub the plates and bowl in which the said masters ate with the [same] dishcloth with which this witness and the said slave scrubbed the platters and bowls in which they [the servants and slave] ate."[131] Since the family itself observed the laws of kashrut, while the servants and slaves did not, the mistress did not want the same dishcloths used on the family's dishes. The Mexican converso Antonio Méndez would allegedly bathe intensely in preparation for the sabbath. While on all other occasions his Black slave, Juan Angola, bathed him, for his Friday purifications he would not let his slave wash him.[132] Beatriz Enriquez, also of Mexico, relates in her testimony that while it is true that after her mother's death she sent alms to various members of her extended family by means of her Black slave Ysavel, she did not, as was alleged by a certain witness, "send her to say that they should fast [for the soul of her deceased mother, a marrano custom], because this was not something to entrust to a black woman."[133]

Some masters whose practices drew notice may have promised a slave liberty if she would not betray them to the Inquisition.[134] Antonia de la Cruz, slave of Simón Váez Sevilla's brother-in-law Thomas Nuñez de Peralta, related that Váez Sevilla and his wife Juana Enriquez gathered their many slaves and told them that if they were brought into the Inquisition to testify "we were [told] to be good slaves."[135] Antonia also testifies that Váez Sevilla warned his slaves that if they gave information to the Inquisition, "his compadre, Garcia de Valdés Osorio, an Old Christian, would purchase them and force them to work in his sugar mill. If they remained loyal, however, they would be rewarded with emancipation."[136] More extreme reactions to the threat that slaves' knowledge might serve the Inquisitions ensued as well. In Mexico, during the 1590s, Jorge de Almeida was accused of helping to strangle a Black woman who called her master, Christoval Gomez, a Jew, fearful of the consequences.[137] More reasonable was the approach of León/Machorro to the threat posed by a slave who might denounce. A family with whom León/Machorro often celebrated Jewish occasions — the family of Blanca de Rivera — closed the doors to the street at such times, for obvious reasons. Nonetheless, from his jail cell he later told Francisco Botello, in a neighboring cell (ca. 1645), "there was an enemy behind closed doors, a black woman belonging to the said person, who, when her mistress beat her, she [the slave] then threatened to accuse her and all those that they had [i.e., friends and relatives], and that the said León told her [the mistress]: either sell this black woman far away from here or stop beating, for she will wring all our necks."[138]

Unfortunately, the imprisoned León/Machorro continued, his reveries of the beauty and purity of their former celebrations turning bitter, "as I understand, she did just this and was the cause of our destruction."[139] Ignorant of why he was imprisoned in 1642, Thomas Nuñez de Peralta was able to communicate from his cell with his wife Beatriz Enriquez by means of messages carried by intermediaries. In his response to a note of hers, he assures her that "no black woman could have done this damage to him" and names instead a relative. His wife's first impulse, then, had been to suspect one of their slaves.[140] Blanca de Rivera and her daughter Ysabel, alleged judaizers sitting in the Mexico City inquisition jail in the early 1640s, tried to figure out who might have accused them, lingering on the Angolan slave Juliana.[141]

Francisco Botello remained in prison through 1649, when he was penitenced in that year's auto de fé.[142] In January of that year he related to his comrade in jail, León/Machorro, a dream that he had just had. He said

> that he had dreamed that having escaped he walked through the street eating and always found himself in a stall [at the market], and saw many people coming, and having dropped himself to the irrigation channel of the Palace he hid under the bridge, and that hearing that the people said that a sack had dropped over there he tried to escape from there and returned to find himself in the same place, and that he heard a Black who said: here is the man, and that having come to Santo Domingo [Cathedral], the people grabbed him and put him in a very dark and gloomy room, with many niches.[143]

Without wanting to overinterpret, it can be said that Botello fears being turned by his persecution into something lifeless and inhuman (being mistaken for a falling sack); he is trapped in his role as a merchant (he "always found himself...") by anti-Jewish/anti-Judeoconverso prejudice; he attempts to prove that he is a good Christian (he tries to get to the cathedral); the church (hope, eternal life, light) turns into its opposite, a jail (dark, very gloomy, labyrinthine). The fearful content of the dream should come as no surprise. Neither should the role of the Black man who points out the dreamer. Whether or not one agrees with Leon/Machorro's interpretation of Botello's dream, in particular that the Black represents the executioner, one readily understands why the imprisoned Francisco Botello "had awakened crying."

To conclude, I am not at all sure that "slave-owning crypto-Jews controlled their domestic space well enough to allow them, with some caution, to practice

[...] with a fair degree of security that they would not be discovered," as Robert Ferry suggests.[144] Quite the contrary. Though some masters or mistresses might have been able to or felt able to trust their slaves, or some of them, it appears that despite their subaltern status slaves often exercised disproportionate influence on their owners' behavior. Why so many of these worries surfaced amidst the New Christians of Mexico and not elsewhere is not quite clear. Many slave denunciations from the Canary Islands can be found in Inquisition records, for example. Writing of Peru, Jean-Pierre Tardieu notes that the African servants or slaves of Judeoconversos "on occasion revealed the customs which made manifest the religious affiliation of their owners."[145] Perhaps the likelihood that the Mexico City group of crypto-Jews was large, active spiritually and self-aware lent more danger to the power of slave and servant knowledge. It seems doubtful that only this group would be impacted by the surrounding environment's racial-religious politics. Again, I suspect that Inquisition archives hold many more such cases of servile denunciations. It is likely that the more extreme and harsher racial conditions of the American slave societies distorted, if not sundered the loyalties that slaves and servants might have internalized and upheld in Europe.[146] Even if limited, the more global investigation I have tried to carry out shows that such denunciations were not so rare and that masters indeed feared them. Ultimately, mistresses and masters had no way of knowing whether slaves, even seemingly loyal ones, could be trusted under the stare of the inquisitorial gaze.

CHAPTER 5

Slaves and the Downtrodden Religion of Their Masters

> "Various people denounced the shoemaker Alvaro Gonçales in 1524 for having 'employed a negro to cast spells to discover whether the Inquisition would be established in the [Canary] islands.'"[1]

This chapter explores further aspects of the relations between early modern Afroiberians and Judeoconversos. For the most part, it covers relations of an opposite order from those of the previous chapters, relations of mutuality, sharing and collaboration, though such siding together did not always come voluntarily to those Afroiberians who still served as slaves.

The example from the Canaries cited in the above epigraph is one sign that in some ways Judeoconverso masters were open to the culture of their African slaves. As was mentioned in preceding chapters, many Whites found African or Amerindian religious and magical practices useful or attractive in the Americas. Here as well, a New Christian saw fit to turn to an Afro-Canariote, whether free or slave (perhaps even his own slave), with skills in divination in order to interpret events, in this case events that might not have yet happened.[2] How appropriate that a man who might well have been living an alternative life to the regnant Catholicism, one that he may have wanted to continue protecting and hiding, would seek information from another alternative knowledge system. In this case, both men had been dislocated, differently, from their homelands. Whether this means that Gonçales approved of or respected the African knowledge system grounding such acts of divination, whether such recourse to African divination entailed something common among Canariote Whites or whether this constituted a move of pragmatism, even desperation, on his part, remains more difficult to answer. The work of Peter Mark, José da Silva Horta and Toby Green, cited in chapter 2, has provided examples from the western African coast and coastal islands of New Christians (and Sephardic Jews) adapting themselves to the ways of their African surroundings, going "native" to some degree in order to survive and succeed in trade.[3] Similar questions need to be asked regarding Afroiberians who adapted themselves to the Marranism of their mistresses.

Belonging to One's Master

If the above event indeed took place, Gonçales obviously entrusted the matter regarding which he sought information — the coming of the Inquisition — to the man performing the ritual of divining. Some masters and mistresses certainly at times brought their own slaves into their most intimate circle of trust. Such trust might stem from lack of other or better options but might also evince true feelings of comradeship, alliance or affection. Rafaela Enriquez, accused of judaizing by the Mexico City Inquisition in the early 1640s, testifies that on the evening of a recent Fast of the Great Day (Yom Kippur), an acquaintance came over to see her. He greeted her with a typical blessing, "that she should have many such days and that God should grant this." Enriquez responded "that they couldn't be good because that day a black woman [slave] had died on her."[4] The mistress's sense of loss appears real enough, though without more knowledge it is difficult to say whether it derived from bereavement over a personal loss or anxieties over the disruption and inconvenience caused by the slave's passing. Several instances exist in which New Christians who feared they might be arrested by the Inquisition ordered their slaves to hide their valuables. When arrested by the same tribunal in June 1642, the wealthy Matias Rodrigues de Olivera entrusted his money and valuables to one of his slaves, promising him his freedom if he guards them punctiliously until Olivera should leave prison.[5] Here, too, the emotional context needs to be ferreted out from the records, if possible. Isabel de Esperanza had allegedly helped her owners Simón Váez Sevilla and Juana Enriquez hide "jewels and cash in a secret room in their house."[6] In cases such as these, the underlings' unfree status and dependence on the mistress makes their loyalty coincide with their self-interest.

Sources do not reveal that New Christians employed their own slaves or the slaves of others in a manner any different from Old Christians. In 1625, one allegedly judaizing Portuguese New Christian of Madrid who became annoyed with another begged him not to acknowledge their acquaintance, threatening to hire a slave to kill him if he did. The use or hire of slaves to perform such functions was common among Spaniards.[7] In 1541 Lisbon, a man insulted a New Christian woman's husband, whom he had previously reported to a priest for ordering "his Blacks" to dig on Sunday. This new insult drew a curse from the wife, as well as a drawn knife from the slave accompanying her, ready, obviously, to defend the honor of his masters.[8] Adversity or crisis could put master and slave together on the same side, could cause the temporary erasure of that which might distinguish them.[9]

Loyalty to the master did not stem only from circumstances of immediate self-interest. As possessions of their masters and mistresses, slaves often had little choice but to tolerate or follow their religious paths, though as the previous chapter shows, opportunity for protest or subversion existed. Gretchen Starr-LeBeau reports, from late fifteenth-century Guadalupe, Castile, accusations that various New Christian masters made their servants work on Sunday.[10] Though one's place in the system that supported one's servitude might be lowly and miserable, it had its security, order and comforts. Doing what one was commanded to do could bring rewards. Beatriz, who belonged to the above-mentioned Alvaro Gonçales, of the Canaries, was more than likely not the only slave whose master "told her that she was never to speak of anything that she saw done in the house, and that he would reward her."[11] Blanca Enriquez, matriarch of a family of alleged judaizers arrested in 1640s Mexico City, gave out alms before she died, entrusting a slave woman to deliver them to the poor patients in the hospital of Our Lady as well as to the poor who sat in jail.[12] Blanca's daughter, Beatriz, referring after her imprisonment by the Inquisition to the above-mentioned hiding of jewels by Juana Enriquez's slave(s), though with a different perspective, offers testimony that illuminates several aspects of the master-slave relationship:

> she knew in the prison of Picayo, that her slave Antonia told her, through a window, that she and another black woman, her companion, slaves of this confessant [Beatriz] had hidden some pearls and jewels from those that were in the said little chest, and that a black woman called lucia, slave of her sister doña Juana enriquez, had discovered them and given them away because they had not wanted to give her some earrings, and that the señores [inquisitors?] had taken from them that which they had hidden, if indeed the said black woman Madalena said honestly to her that she had guarded some things, for when this confessant should go free, and that therefore she would not request anything.[13]

Beatriz's description attests to the loyalty of some of her slaves and disloyalty of others, raises the competing interests that might motivate members of the servile class, as well as the possibility of gendered bonding across the master-slave divide. Despite very real issues of status and race, it is not so clear that "in no case can servants [and slaves - JS] be considered as members of the family," as Pilar Huerga Criado states when discussing some Old World examples.[14] Robert Ferry claims that only one of the alleged judaizers arrested in Mexico in the 1640s was denounced by slaves for 'heretical behavior,' the slave trader Agustín de Rojas, accused by the Mozambican Diego de Sevilla.[15] The rest of the slaves, Ferry argues, never made denunciations, or at least not voluntarily. Huerga Criado comes to a similar conclusion when treating the Inquisition's pursuit of judaizing in the New Christian community of Badajoz in the 1630s. There, slaves or servants showed absolute loyalty to the mistress or master whom they presently serve, affirming the latters' statements and denying their supposedly judaizing tendencies, while former slaves/servants often take an opposite perspective, turning against former owners/employers. In naming witnesses, the mistresses assume the loyalty and submissiveness (not always the same thing, of course) of their present domestic staff, naming them as defense witnesses, while identifying former staff as those who might have had reason to denounce them.[16]

As I have shown, while such loyalty and/or deference did help structure some master-slave relationships, it was by no means guaranteed, particularly in the harsher industrial slavery environment of the Americas. An excellent sense of the emotional complexities and competing desires or interests at work within the master-slave relationship appear in two incidents related in the Dialogues of the Great Things of Brazil (1618), an extended advertisement for Brazil written by the New Christian Ambrósio Fernandes Brandão. The author, a retired Pernambucan sugar planter of some prominence, puts the tales into the mouth of a character named Brandônio, likely an autobiographical projection. The first incident:

> [T]here was living in my house a little mulatto girl of tender age, who was born there and whom I loved dearly, for I had reared her. A slave of mine, with diabolic intent, spurred on to this by the girl's having told me of a theft he had committed, gave her poison, so that in a very short time [she] showed all the signs of being at death's door. Seeing the girl in such a state, not only was I extremely sorrowful, but I had a firm suspicion that poison had brought this about and that the guilty person must have been the very slave who had, in fact, given it to her, for he had among his fellows the reputation of being a sorcerer and herbalist. Hence, I had him seized, assuring him that he would live no longer than the girl did, because I knew for a certainty that he had given her the poison. I said some other things to him and even showed him what I intended to do, which was to run him through the cane press; therefore, he should try quickly to find a remedy for the evil he had done. [...] he undertook to cure the sick girl on condition that he might have leave to go to the woods to pick some herbs for this purpose. I consented to what he asked of me, but I had him shackled to another house slave, whom I secretly charged to note carefully the herb that was picked so that we might recognize it later. But the first slave was so crafty that, to keep from revealing it, he picked many different herbs, among which was the one he had need of, but in such a way that the slave who was shackled to him could not tell which one was the herb he was going to use. [...]
>
> [The girl was cured, but] I was most woefully upset because I did not know what the herb was, but I was never able to get that slave, either by threatening him or by offering him presents, to show me what it was.[17]

The second incident:

> The other case was that of a slave of little value, one of those from Angola. I have seen him pick up the most poisonous snakes and wrap them around himself. Although they bit him in many places, their bites did him no harm. [...] I marveled at this and

thought that it must be the work of magic words or the power of some kind of spell. But in the end, I found out that it wasn't either one.

When I had won the black's good will by means of presents, he finally showed me some roots and another herb, telling me that whoever rubbed his joints with the juice of that root, after chewing it well in his mouth, could in all safety pick up as many snakes as he wanted to, without fear of their bites' doing him harm, no matter how poisonous the snakes might be. I tried it myself and had experiments made, and it is still used by my slaves today.[18]

Many of the themes raised in previous chapters and to recur below course through these brief narratives. Unfortunately, space does not permit the full unpacking they deserve. For my purposes here I merely note the variety of relations possible with different slaves at the same time; the means, positive and negative, by which a master might try to gain the good will or cooperation of slaves; the relative degree of autonomy and agency possessed by slaves; the possibility of cooperation if not affection between master and slave, between slave and master; and the fact that often masters and slaves shared the same environment, faced the same dangers.

The intrusion of the Inquisition into the life of a slave's owner often bore consequences equally as intrusive for the slave. Slaves were called upon to come to the aid of their masters and mistresses. When Raphaela Enriquez was arrested by the Mexico City tribunal in 1642, "speaking with her black women, the mulata who raised the baby boy went to the house of [Raphaela's sister] Micaela and advised her regarding what had happened."[19] Juan Bautista Corvera, accused in 1564 in Guadalajara, Mexico, of being a follower of the law of Moses, attempted to flee before his imprisonment, advised to do so by various neighbors, who helped him hide in a local house. So that Corvera could escape, one neighbor, Bernardino Vázquez del Mercado, brought the fugitive his (Corvera's) horses, saddled and with the bit prepared, with his (Corvera's) one Black slave, already embargoed by the ecclesiastical authorities. But all to no avail, as the plot was discovered and the accomplices arrested.[20] Without documentation, one can only speculate on the slave's thoughts during all this; whether he wanted to remain with his fugitive master, to challenge the Inquisition's embargo of his person, whether he surmised that the authorities might have charged Corvera, the master, rather than himself, the slave, with the inspiration and consequences of such a challenge. Sometimes the intrusion of the Inquisition pointed up certain ironies, as when an indicted New Christian, Felipa Rodrigues, first wife of Gaspar Rodrigues Nunes (Menasseh ben Israel's father), cited as character witnesses for her defense two of her former maids, Maria Antunes and Antónia, because, among other things, they happened to be Old Christians.[21]

Since prisoners had to pay for their own imprisonment, slaves of individuals arrested by the Inquisition might end up working at the inquisition jails. Francisco de la Cruz, also known as Queretano, a Black Angolan slave of Simon Vaez Sevilla of Mexico City, wound up serving in the local tribunal's jail, bringing food to the prisoners, including his arrested master.[22] Two other slaves belonging to Vaez, Ysavelilla, a Creole, and Francisco, a bozal, found themselves working in the jail kitchen.[23] If a master was arrested by the Inquisition and could not afford to pay the expenses of his own trial, as required, confiscated goods, including slaves, would be sold to raise the necessary funds.[24] This happened in the case of Francisco Maldonado de Silva, whose lack of available money caused Friar Martín de Salvatierra to counsel the sale of Silva's goods, such as "the little Black," one of Silva's four slaves, probably "a little Black called Francisco from Angola of twelve years more or less."[25] Somewhat later, Silva's wife, doña Isabel de Otáñez, petitioned the tribunal to allow her to sell two other Black slaves, who had been part of her dowry for her husband, but who had been embargoed along with his goods (even though she was not being accused of anything), so that she could raise enough money to recoup at least some portion of her dowry's value.[26] The slaves were finally sold the next November, at a greatly reduced price because of various problems, as the Inquisition notary put it: "darkies [morenaos] so worthless and with such ailments and faults, the one suffered from a leg with sciatica, the other with a bad heart and [is] a big drunkard with other flaws."[27] Whether these Afroiberians preferred being sold to new owners we do not know and it may not have made a difference to them that the decision to sell them derived not from the volition of their master, but of the Inquisition. In one case from Cartagena, mentioned in chapter 3, an Inquisition official was accused of failing to include Black slaves (among other confiscated goods) belonging to a suspect on the inventory, no doubt in order to abscond with them for his own use or profit.[28]

Making Their Slaves "Jewish"?

I now consider the ways in which the persecuted religious beliefs and/or practices of Judeoconverso or crypto-Jewish masters shaped the nature of relationships with their Afroiberian slaves. The question is not merely about internal matters — how the masters and slaves interacted — but how the structure of the intersection of the domestic and external socio-religious environments constructed possibilities for slave-master relations.

In 1579, the Portuguese New Christian Antonio Saldanha told the inquisitors in Venice, where he lived among the Portuguese New Christians, that three years earlier he had heard from "the Jew David Pas," at whose house in the Ghetto Saldanha had been a frequent house guest, how "Portuguese New Christians, both in Portugal itself and in Venice, habitually judaized the slaves in their own households and gave them gentle and loving treatment."[29] One such might have been Gaspar Ribeiro, who was accused in Italy, toward the end of the sixteenth century, of "enticing his sister and some of his Christian servants to become Jewish."[30] Saldanha, an ex-Franciscan who had abandoned the cloth and now led a dissolute life and who "had never avoided Jewish company himself," seems, as the result of a quarrel in which he had become unwillingly involved, to have then been in a mood "to unmask those Portuguese who did not live according to Christianity."[31] Whether his testimony was as accurate as it was self-serving and purposely provocative to Christian sensitivities is thus difficult to know. The statement transmitted by Saldanha implies — as does the context of its double transmission — that such "gentle and loving" treatment constituted part of the wooing of slaves toward Judaism, a wooing encouraged by Jewish law, but also by a form of cultural defiance on the part of believers in this persecuted religion. A similar allegation was raised by another fascinating double figure, Abraham Bendana Sarfatim, who as a Catholic polemicized harshly against Jews. In 1599 he testified that in Pisa he had lived with some 90 other New Christians. One of these was "Simão Fernandez Sam Thome, a man thirty five years old, with a small black bear, and he doesn't know where he was born. This one remained also in Piza with his mother-in-law, his wife, and a black woman, also Jews, and he knew them as Jews, and saw them going to the synagogues, and that the black woman was also a Jew, and he knew her as a Jew, and he knows that it is very common among Jews to buy Black men and women, and make them Jews, and he has seen in Piza some of those Black Jews, both men and women."[32] Moriscos, who were also for the most part forcibly Christianized, were accused of similar missionizing of their slaves. Morisco ownership of African slaves concerned members of the Cortes that met in Toledo in 1560, whose members asserted that Moriscos taught Islam to these slaves.[33]

Thus around the Spanish North African enclave of Oran "Jews were thought to be determined to dissuade their Moorish slaves from converting to Christianity, in which, admittedly, they had an interest but which was also a remarkable feat, since slaves of Jews, once baptized, were immediately set free."[34] The Vicar General of Oran, Fernández de Humada, complained in 1661 that "no Moor living among them ever became Christian, while those who live among Catholics ask daily for baptism."[35] Continues Jonathan Israel, this "lack of conversion among the slaves of Jews was indeed one of the most persistent allegations made by those who pressed for the expulsion of the Jews from the fronteras." Similar allegations were made against the Sephardic Africa merchants operating from and residing in some of the port towns on the Senegambian coast. A document of 1623 recommends that slaves being sent to the Americas from Cacheu, on the West African coast, first be instructed in Christianity, "owing to the levels of Judaism in Guiné."[36] These examples refer to open Jewish communities and even there it is clear that some opposed the conversion of non-Whites to Judaism, especially the communal leadership.[37]

Internal relations within a Judeoconverso household often fell under the sway of external relations between the alleged religion of the masters and that of the state. The accumulated bits of data about domestic affairs in Judeoconverso homes that lies scattered in the various inquisitional archives will be more useful as evidence than the kind of overt but general propaganda conveyed by the apologetic Pas and the antagonistic Saldanha. Claims of Judeoconversos judaizing among their slaves remain difficult to corroborate, though I will endeavor to do so to the extent possible. Jean-Pierre Tardieu, who devoted much effort to investigating the religious history of Afroiberian Peru, concludes that "The 'followers of the law of Moses' had no interest in converting their black servants."[38] Based on the evidence with which I am familiar, I tend to agree. That a program of winning slave souls for (crypto-) Judaism existed among marranos can be rightfully doubted. Exceptions can be found, of course, among New Christians who were pious and/or opposed to Christianity. As we shall see, some Afroiberians, slave and free, came to ally themselves to differing degrees with crypto-Judaism and even to value it for a variety of reasons. In chapter 7, I discuss the handful of Afroiberians who did, indeed, adopt crypto-Judaism.

Slaves were by definition possessions of their masters. Though slaves by duress, slaves of Judeoconversos or crypto-Jews often became entangled in the state of affairs both producing and produced by their masters' alleged Jewishness — willingly or not. Servants, although not as thoroughly dependent on their masters' will, nonetheless also lived subject to many of the same pressures from within Judeoconverso homes and from without because they served in the homes of alleged marranos. The Jewishness or alleged Jewishness of a slave's owners carried inescapable ramifications for a slave, even if she was not herself crypto-Jewish, both subjectively in the eyes of her Catholic peers and often objectively, through the institutional repercussions of Iberian society's deep religious nationalism.

According to one seventeenth-century denunciation given to the Portuguese Inquisition in Brazil, the 'judaizers' of Bahia could practice their illicit rites without fear of discovery because they "live in their ranches, separated from communication, served by brute negros who don't have anything Christian but the water of baptism."[39] This charge alleges that Judeoconversos neglected to see to the Christianization of their slaves, which will be discussed further. Perhaps one aspect of this service was protection against the intrusion of unwanted Christians, an extension of the "private police force[s], which the masters needed to maintain because the authorities were so far away," made up of manumitted slaves, poor whites or free coloreds, who would attach themselves to plantation-owners.[40] As was said of Blas de Paz Pinto, the wealthy Mexico City merchant Simón Váez Sevilla was alleged to have "[n]ight and day a slave in a sentinel's room (postal) guard[ing] the entryway (zaguán) of the house."[41] Some sincere crypto-Jewish masters may have baptized their slaves for the sake of appearances, but, newly arrived from Africa, their slaves often were alleged to have received little further Christian edification, whether or not they desired it.[42] Diogo Nunes Henriques, who had lived in Minas Gerais for some 30 years, was arrested in Ouro Preto in 1728 and accused of practicing Judaism. One of the charges against him held that he taught his slaves to disobey Christian dogma.[43]

The actions of slaves and masters reflected on one another, since the former were understood to follow the commands of the latter. Thus, Branca Dias stated in her defense to the Inquisition that

> she had in her house Old Christian serving women and that she made them eat pork fat that she made and killed all these years

in her house, and the said servants kneaded the bread for her and made the beds for her, putting out only washed sheets Saturday nights, in honor and veneration of the sacred day of sunday, and sundays she wore her cleaned shirts, without ever using or doing Jewish ceremonies.[44]

According to the testimony of one stone mason who used to visit the house of the wealthy New Christian merchant and sugar plantation owner João Nunes Correia,

> going and setting in order some houses for the said João Nunes he comes across a servant, filthy drunk and covered with a cap of old flannel and that by the house [that is, by the apartment] were some panels from Flanders and that arriving there there was the said João Nunes, he tells him this and wonders greatly, saying to him that being that there was a chapel there it was not good and he would say to him that they were overlooked by the blacks.[45]

As comes across from other testimony regarding him, Correia, was not having his engenho chapel properly maintained and it was being used for unseemly purposes. Master and servant stood complicit in the neglect of good Christian comportment. None of this of course proves that the slaves or servants in these cases knew anything about Jewish practices or had been indoctrinated in crypto-Judaism.

In 1640s Mexico City, the slaves belonging to an extended family of alleged judaizers would confer with their masters each time they went to participate in the processions of Holy Week, which the masters seemingly did not attend.

> During Holy Week just past every time that the black women went up to do the processions, they spoke with their mistresses who are Doña Beatriz [Enriquez and her husband] Thomas nuñez, Doña Rafaela and her daughters Ana and Blanca in the Angolan language which the said Doña Beatriz speaks very well. That which I could hear was the said black woman Antonia saying in Romance [i.e., Spanish] that the said Doña Beatriz will send her the measurement and would send her some shoes in the clothing. And she had not sent the melon in the clothing because it smelled much [and] that the little mulato would bring it. And she told them not to speak because many spies were about. And she [Antonia?] would sell them [the melons and/or clothes?] to give a reason for what would be.[46]

The conversations evince a certain complicity between masters and slaves, as they are discussing bringing things to imprisoned relatives or friends. (Below I discuss the matter of the shared African language.) The mistress Beatriz Enriquez warns the slaves against mistakenly informing on their owners (who are themselves seemingly absent from the festivities) while in public and even to be providing an alibi of sorts, seemingly that the slave woman Antonia should pretend to be selling the things that are actually being brought into the prison to arrested family members. It should be recalled from the previous chapter, however, that this same Beatriz Enriquez would pretend to drink chocolate on days that she fasted, in order to keep up pretenses before her slaves. Such conflicting testimony raises many issues that are difficult to resolve. These might not have been the same slaves. Enriquez might have behaved differently with different slaves. The testimony of this witness might not be credible. Enriquez may have behaved inconsistently.

The attitude and behavior of crypto-Jewish owners regarding a Catholic sacrament and rite such as baptism offers further evidence of the crossed theopolitical vectors marking domestic situations. The behavior and life, if not always the belief, of the slave might have been significantly altered depending on the attitude of the owner toward baptism. One of those accused of judaizing by the Mexican Inquisition in 1643 was Captain Matias Rodriguez de Olivera, at the time a 51-year-old bachelor from Portugal, involved in the slave trade.[47] One slave formerly in his service, an Angolan named Baltazar, testifies that Olivera never permitted him or other slaves to receive baptism, something most Judeoconversos living in the Spanish-Portuguese orbit probably did at least for appearances' sake. Olivera supposedly argued that they had already been baptized in Angola, which was not always the case, though by law they should not have arrived in Spanish territories unbaptized. Baltazar says that he and a companion named Christoval eventually had themselves baptized at church surreptitiously, something they never revealed to their master.[48] Other Judeoconversos were also accused of not allowing the baptism of their slaves, such as the above-mentioned Alvaro Gonçales of La Palma, the Canaries, sentenced in 1526. As an example of what was probably more typical behavior, Filipe de Nis (a.k.a. Solomon Marcos) bought a Black slave, Luna Maura, when he was a trader on the island of São Tomé around 1566-67 and had her baptized. The family was then living a Christian life. They later moved to Venice, where in 1586 Luna Maura "admitted" to the Venetian Inquisition "having lived with the family as a Jewess in Venice when they subsequently judaized outside the Ghetto, but not to having attended any synagogue there."[49] The New Christian Jorge Thomas was denounced to the inquisitor Marcos Teixeira when the latter visited the Azores between August 1575 and July 1576 because Thomas allegedly "discredited the effect of the baptism administered to a Black slave at the hour of death."[50] His doubts notwithstanding, however, the master Jorge Thomas did not forbid his slave to receive this component of the last rites. Finally, the well-known judaizing martyr Izaque de Castro claimed that a servant's infant had been surreptitiously baptized in his stead by his family:

> they commanded a search [be made] from the town of Tartas [in France], where they lived, to the [nearby] place of Odon, for an infant who at the same time had been born to the mother of a

maidservant of theirs, and putting the said infant in place of the accused, they baptized it in his name, without telling anyone about it other than his said father and mother who on many occasions told this to the accused.[51]

Castro's story constituted part of his effort to convince his persecutors that, having never been baptized, he did not fall under inquisitorial jurisdiction as a lapsed Christian. Such ulterior motives notwithstanding, the story's scenario, real or imaginary, depicts a usage of a member of the serving class well within the hierarchical social reasoning of the times. It is not difficult to imagine that a bribe or threat would have helped persuade the servant's family to refrain from reporting such a transgression to the authorities.

While baptism left documentary evidence, circumcision left permanent and dangerous physical traces. Devoted crypto-Jews continued to circumcise themselves even in the absence of the trained mohel, ritual circumciser, who would readily have been available in an open Jewish community. According to a study by Seymour B. Liebman, in "50 cases where the inquisitors ordered a physical examination of the accused to ascertain circumcision, it was found that 48 bore the mark of the covenant."[52] I know of no cases that reveal the circumcision of slaves in regions under the watch of the Inquisitions.[53] One related case is that of the Mexican Francisco Lopez Blandón, alias Ferrasas, born in 1619, who was accused of having circumcised his illegitimate son born of his Mulata lover, Agustina de la Cruz, who herself allegedly 'converted' to crypto-Judaism.[54]

Black and Mulato slaves sometimes participated, though often in ways limited by their ambivalently adoptive families and communities, in the crypto-Jewish life of those families and communities. Slaves might be included in the Jewish practices of their masters and mistresses whether the slaves knew it or not. In some cases, even the masters might not have been aware of the real significance of the practices. Sometimes, it can be inferred that slaves had guessed the true significance of the tasks with which they were charged. Non-ritual functions devolved onto the slaves of Judeoconversos. One woman accused of judaizing by the Mexican Inquisition in the 1640s, Margarita de Morera, allegedly told an Old Christian that when the crypto-Jews were to gather she "dressed up a little black [boy] in colors, who with dissembling they put out on the streets, in order that he should play a tabor [a kind of drum], this being the signal by which it was understood to get together to judaize."[55] More substantively, one servant in Ciudad Real, in 1511, testified that not only did her employers not cook anything to eat on the Jewish sabbath, but also forbade her and a black slave woman from even making a fire in the house.[56] Baltazar, the former slave of Matias Rodriguez de Olivera, claims that his master "taught this declarant and his said companions to pray the four prayers through a Portuguese youth called Manuel Freile who served" Rodrigues de Oliveira. What these "four prayers" are in a marrano context I have no idea. According to Baltazar, when the slaves' prayers in the salon made too much noise, they were ordered to go pray in the kitchen.[57] One witness who went to the Mexico City tribunal to depose voluntarily against Olivera recounts a conversation he conducted with one of Olivera's slaves. The witness had noticed various errors in the slave's religious behavior and approached him, asking

> "don't you believe that there is a God?" The said black responded to him: "what God is there? He is only in the heavens, for on earth there is none." And the said person replied to him: "Look, he is on earth." Said the said black, "no, no, in the heavens." And the said black said, "what did it matter if the water of Baptism was thrown on one's head if the heart did not conform or if one did not want it?"[58]

This slave of Olivera's appears to the Catholic witness to be spouting a "Jewish" understanding of a single, incorporeal God, in opposition to the view that God was/is (partially) embodied in Christ, as well as a 'Jewish' critique of baptism (the same one proffered by Protestants, by the way). The witness went to Olivera to alert him regarding his heretical slave, whom he suggested should be denounced to the Inquisition. The unspoken implication of the witnesses' own deposition is that the slave's heterodox religiosity might have been influenced by that of his master. If indeed such influence existed in this case, it could have been the result of mere imitation of the master's attitudes. Or was there actual, explicit conversation regarding religious matters?

According to Jewish law, only a slave ritually immersed in water becomes obligated to observe a certain minimum number of biblical commandments. This ritual immersion, 'for the sake of enslavement,' in other words, to make someone ritually fit to be a slave, bore many similarities to immersion 'for the sake of conversion,' since the former constituted a partial step toward full conversion to Judaism. It differed in both form and result from immersion 'for the sake of freedom.' Immersion for the sake of slavery, obviously, took place at the acquisition of a slave, immersion for the sake of freedom at his or her manumission. Both were to be performed in a mikva, a pool of prescribed dimensions and construction, or, in the absence of a mikva, in a stream or river. According to halakhah, a slave immersed for slavery cannot be sold to a non-Jew (Shulkhan Arukh, section 267, law 11, note). See, for instance, the Shulkhan Arukh, section 267, law 3: "The slave taken from a non-Jew, one says to him, 'is it your will to enter the group of the slaves of Israel and become one of the kosher ones or not?'; if he wishes to, one conveys to him the principles of the faith and a bit about the commandments, simple and difficult, and their punishment and reward, as one informs the convert." Also law 267:17: "as long as he is not immersed for slavery he is legally treated as a non-Jew in all things, and after he is immersed for slavery he is a slave and is obligated in the commandments in which women are obligated."[59] Yet repeated mentions of slaves performing certain ritual commandments appear in Inquisition documents in situations where their immersion or conversion seems far-fetched for a variety of reasons and is not once mentioned in the course of any trial record I have seen.

In the 1511-1513 Inquisition trial of a Castilian woman accused of judaizing,

María González, wife of Pedro de Villarreal, she testifies that her Black slave Catalina not only swept and cleaned the house in preparation for sabbath, but also sometimes lit the sabbath candles for her on Friday nights, at her command.[60] Another of the González women would tell Francisca, another black slave, "to clean three lamps they had, and after cleaning, when the sun was setting, the said wife of Juan de la Sierra said to the said slave: 'See if the sun has set, light these lamps.'"[61] Technically, she could only do this had she been ritually immersed, becoming thereby a partial Jew or beginning the path to becoming Jewish. On the one hand, González comes across as being quite fervent in her Judaism. One witness claimed that she "would never let her maidservants work on Saturdays but that they would do the housework on Sundays."[62] It is likely that she was familiar with living Judaism from before the expulsion. Haim Beinart reports that Judeoconversas in Ciudad Real frequently maintained the precepts involving ritual immersion after menstruation, using pools which apparently existed at several Judeoconverso houses or nearby streams.[63] All this makes it possible that González might have immersed a slave on newly acquiring her. On the other hand, going so far as to immerse a maidservant in such a dangerous situation would imply an enormous devotion to Judaism (if González even knew about such requirements) and an equally large trust in someone who was not a family member. It also would have presumably created a certain closeness between mistress and maidservant. Yet only one year after her first testimony González did not seem to remember her slave's name, calling her merely "a Black slave."[64] González was at this time aged 31, so senility should not have been a problem.[65] González evidently remembered the name of her other servant, the daughter of a couple who lived with her and her spouse. Was González attempting to protect Catalina from the Inquisition? This would seem doubtful given that González "informed on a long list of Conversos."[66] The voluminous documentation of her supposed judaizing practices never mentions any ritual immersion of Catalina. González also supposedly refused to let the servants and slaves wash the family's dishes with the same cloths with which they washed their own dishes, on which they ate non-kosher food, as mentioned in the previous chapter. This suggests that there were limits to the inclusion of these non-Jewish women. It is possible that González did not realize that Catalina should not be performing rituals for her. On the other hand, numerous cases indicate that marranos were willing to be flexible with ritual requirements in order to observe their religion as best as possible. González may well have thought that having Catalina light the sabbath candles would diminish or eliminate the perception that the act had any ritual purpose.

One informer testifies before an Inquisition official in Potosí in the early part of the seventeenth century to having seen a Mulato servant prepare meat for his master according to Jewish methods. According to halakhic principle, any Jew who is not deaf, insane or a minor may be permitted to slaughter an animal for eating, so long as the procedure is done correctly.[67] All other aspects of the preparation of meat may be done by anyone, Jewish or not, so long as halakha is followed. As always, when discussing potential marranos, normative Jewish law may not have been known at all. The Jewish methods of slaughter appeared in the standard Edicts of the Faith heard in churches throughout both the Spanish and Portuguese empires, so it is hard to know whether the testimony in this case conveys authenticity:

> travelling through the territory of Buenos Aires and taking in his company a mulato, his servant, he [the denouncer, Francisco González Pacheco] had seen that in order to roast a leg of sheep he [the mulato] removed the sciatic nerve, and laughing at the mulato and calling him a Jew, the mulato responded to him: "I am not a Jew, but I served the Portuguese Diego López de Lisboa on this said route and he always ordered me, when there was need to roast some leg of sheep or lamb, not to roast it without first removing the sciatic nerve, because he said it roasted better."[68]

The sixteenth-century Portuguese High Court judge Gil Vaz Bugalho, of Évora, seemingly a devoted marrano, on one occasion needed to have a chicken slaughtered. His wife, also apparently a dedicated marrano, was sick, however. An Old Christian woman took the chicken in hand, prepared to perform the deed. Bugalho, worried that the act be done according to the proper ritual, "insisted that she not kill it, that his woman slave would kill it. The slave was late, the woman insisted." Finally, Gil Vaz gave in, as the slave never appeared. Still, he commanded the Old Christian woman to go get a well-sharpened knife, as required by halakha.[69] If the evidence is to be believed, clearly his slave knew the proper procedure and the judge preferred her doing it correctly.

Not infrequently, evidence arises concerning allegedly marrano households where fresh meat was drained of blood, the eating of which is forbidden by Jewish law (Gen. 9:4; Lev. 7:26-27, 17:10-14). Since slaves performed most, if not all of the kitchen chores, they were often alleged to carry out this process of ensuring that meat was kosher. To add to the examples mentioned in the previous chapter, one witness testifies that she saw that in the household of Elena de Silva, an alleged judaizer from Mexico City, "her slave, a black woman named Luyssa put the meat that they had to eat in clean water the night before."[70] Without further evidence, whether the slaves knew the significance of what they were doing remains an open question.

The washing of the corpse before burial constituted a requirement of Jewish law as well as a widespread practice of New Christians attempting to maintain their Jewishness.[71] It was also a widespread custom among Catholics, though without official ritual status and lacking the required details on which Judaism insisted. Haim Beinart writes that "there is not a trial [of a Judeoconverso from Ciudad Real in Castile] in which death is mentioned that does not contain a description of the washing of the corpse by the bereaved family."[72] In some instances the family delegated the task to slaves. The famous marrano martyr Luis de Carvajal the younger testifies before his inquisitors in Mexico City on 11 August 1589 that among those present at his father's death was "the Black Luis, who has declared that he washed his father when they buried him in the convent of Santo Domingo."⁷³ Though they buried him in a convent to keep up Christian appearances, the Carvajal family nonetheless had their patriarch's corpse properly prepared for interment according to crypto-Jewish custom. The family memoir of the Dutch Sefardi Ishac de Pinto (1671) testifies that such enforced duplicity occurred in other cases. Pinto records how his grandfather, Manuel Alvares Pinto,

> died in April 1635 and left instructions for his body to be temporarily interred in the Discalced [Carmelite] Monastery in Antwerp, and from there to be sent by his sons to his ancestral vault in the Augustinian Monastery of Lisbon. In secret, he ordered his sons to have him buried in a Jewish burial-ground. They considered the second order to be the one which he wanted carried out. The reason why he publicly ordered his body to be deposited in the Monastery was to save appearances. After we were settled in Rotterdam, at my urging, they sent for his body.⁷⁴

In the case of the Carvajals, the family entrusted the practice of ritual preparation to a slave, who probably had no knowledge of the nature of his task. Indeed, as in many of these cases, perhaps the act was merely the custom among Catholics that was being carried out. A Conversa in 1640s Mexico City, Beatriz Enriquez, tells her inquisitors that when her niece, Leonora Vaez, passed away, two Black slave women washed her body.⁷⁵ The following is the only case I have seen whose details hint at a 'Jewish' form of washing done by slaves. Testifying nearly a decade earlier against Beatriz's daughter Raphaela, one witness declares that when a child of Raphaela's had died at around the age of two and a half, she saw how they "threw him on a little buffet [sideboard] and undressed him and then a mulata named Maria de la Concepçion, who lives in the same house, brought hot water and a cloth and began to wash the said boy and she washed all of him, wrapping [?] him from top to bottom [or from front to back], with the said cloth."⁷⁶

Several elements of this ceremony derive from standard Jewish practice: the use of lukewarm water to wash the body and the washing of each limb downward. The details of preparing the corpse for burial do not seem to have been outlined in Jewish law — even the Shulkhan Arukh fails to discuss them — but stem from medieval folk practice and mystical texts.

The fact that marranos bathed the corpses of their deceased in fresh water distinguished this ritual from the similar washing of corpses among Angolans, who used herbal baths in order to ensure that the soul of the dead would not return to this world.⁷⁷ Some Jewish sources in fact mention the use of perfumes to beautify the corpse and make it more presentable. It is possible, however, that the slaves who were asked to carry out the ritual by their marrano masters thought at the time that they were performing an act equivalent to the Angolan herbal corpse bath, or even that the marrano masters knew of this Angolan custom and thought that therefore the slaves would not suspect that this was a Jewish custom. One wonders why this ritual bathing was assigned so often to slaves (another case is discussed below). It could be that these actions were seen as domestic chores or repulsive ones, suitable mostly for the help. In everyday life, it was frequently a slave who bathed the master or mistress. Among open Jews, the ritual preparation of the corpse, in contrast, was perceived as a great honor performed for the deceased and might even be done by family members. At any rate, only pious individuals are to participate in this ritual practice, assuredly not unconverted slaves.

Not all Judaizing masters withheld knowledge of their Judaism from their slaves, rather they entrusted it with them and sought their inclusion in its practices. Unlike with some of the resistant slaves cited in the previous chapter, participation in the crypto-Jewish master's culture sometimes also came from the volition of the slave, whatever the mixture of motives. From seventeenth-century Mexico, Solange Alberro cites "the mulato slave Juan, who serves the wandering hawker Francisco Blandón [the same previously mentioned Blandón accused of circumcising his Mulato lover's son; who] knew how to prepare the foods of his master according to the precepts of the Jewish religion, behavior which reveals an atmosphere of trust and complicity between the two."[78] Ignes de Faria, who frequented the house of the Portuguese High Court judge Gil Vaz Bugalho (mentioned above), testifies to the Inquisition in 1538 about the far-reaching Jewish commitments of the family, which included observance of the dietary precepts of the "Old Law" and Jewish, or, rather, crypto-Jewish holidays and fasts. Bugalho even initiated a project of translating the Bible into Portuguese, for which he sought and received the help of New Christians who knew Hebrew and Aramaic. Ignes de Faria relates to the inquisitors how she once heard Bugalho's daughter, decked out in her Sabbath finery — gold chains and a fur throw — explain to the Black slave Maria "that Saturday was her Sunday."[79] Sometimes it was not even the masters who transmitted Judaism, but others. Maria de la Cruz of Mexico, a 16-year-old slave of Old Christian masters, apparently acquired her knowledge of Jewish practices from other slaves who themselves belonged to crypto-Jews.[80]

All things considered, it is extremely difficult to prove that crypto-Jewish masters "judaized" to their Afroiberian slaves. It seems much more likely that slaves who indeed participated in crypto-Jewish customs did so unaware of their significance. Exceptions existed, as can be seen from some of the cases mentioned above (and see chapter 7). I now turn to an exploration of the case of one Judeoconverso household on which a relatively large amount of data remains, enough to further delineate some of the relationships between owners and slaves that have been raised.

Slaves in/and the Judeoconverso Family: Exploring the Construction of Social Boundaries through Ritual in Bahia

For a variety of reasons, the Portuguese Inquisition never opened a branch in Brazil. Still, the New Christian population of the colony generated its share of complaints and worries, legitimate or otherwise. A growing litany of religious complaints of various kinds led the Lisbon Inquisition to send, between 1591 and

1595, official inquisitional investigators to the captaincies of Bahia, Pernambuco, Itamaracá and Paraíba in order to better ascertain the actual conditions in the territory. In this section I offer a brief microhistorical study of the Antunes family and their slaves. The extended Antunes clan owned a number of engenhos, that is, sugar mills and lands. The patriarch and his wife, both New Christians, owned an estate they called Matoim, which was also the name of the closest Bahian town. Their homestead, as well as those belonging to their children, sat on the banks of the Matoim River or on some of the islands that dotted its opening into the Bay of All Saints, the bay after which the captaincy was named.[81] The banks of the bay all around comprised the area known as the Recôncavo. The unfortunately meager source material derives mostly from the testimony given independently to the visiting inquisitor Heitor Furtado de Mendonça by a number of the members of this family, as well as by unrelated neighbors.

The testimony refers to various slaves, as will be seen. Though they are not always specified as being of African origin, this should be presumed, as the region around the city of Salvador, on the northeastern corner of the bay, was emptied of its Amerindian inhabitants fairly quickly after the city's founding in the middle of the sixteenth century.[82] It is precisely around this time, with the increasing success of Brazilian sugar after 1580, that the importation of African slaves jumped precipitously. In 1572, the slaves on two Jesuit plantations (engenhos), one in Bahia, the other in neighboring Sergipe, comprised 5.3 and 6.3 percent Africans, respectively. By 1591, Africans — Angolans, Congos, Mocanguas and Anziquos (all from Central Africa) — made up 26 percent of the slave population of the plantation in Sergipe. Meanwhile, one private farm (fazenda) in Bahia claimed a 70 percent African slave population by 1585.[83] Yet according to Sweet, contemporary observers estimated that during the 1580s Bahia possessed some 3,000 slaves from Africa, compared with over 8,000 Christianized Amerindian slaves.[84] From the extant testimony we learn that the extended family's slaves were a mixture of individuals born in Africa and born in Brazil.

One oft-mentioned crypto-Jewish custom was to pour out water from vases and pitchers at the death of a family member. The Shulkhan Arukh, Yoreh De'ah 339:5, mentions pouring out "all the water contained in vessels in the vicinity of the deceased," and various sources provide superstitious explanations, such as "the fear that the angel of death would stir up the water and either clean his knife in it or drip a drop of blood in it."[85] The latter explanation appears already in the Spanish Yeḥiel b. Asher's Turei Zahav, Yoreh De'ah (339:4) and in the later fourteenth-century anonymous compilation Sefer Kol Bo, along with the notion that the water is spilled out in order to make the death known to the community.

A New Christian from Matoim, Lianor, voluntarily confesses to the visiting inquisitor in the Recôncavo, the lands surrounding the Bay of All Saints, on 1 February 1592. She says that in the eighteen years of her marriage many occasions led her "to throw out of the house and to order thrown out all the water of the pots and vases which were in the house [...] when someone died on her such as a son or daughter or slaves."[86] Other members of the family seem to have performed this rite as well. The same day on which Lianor talks to the visiting inquisitor, her sister

Isabel Antunes, also a resident of Matoim, makes a similar confession: "it was four years ago that a young slave boy died on her ranch [fazenda] and she ordered the mother of the said slave to throw out all the water of the house."[87] Forty three-year-old Beatris Antunes, Lianor's sister, confesses the previous day, 31 January, to having performed or ordered done the same act only for relatives, such as "a son or daughter, brother or sister or father."[88] Also on 31 January, Lianor's niece, Custódia, daughter of her sister Beatriz Antunes and Sebastião de Faria, confesses. Stating that she is twenty three, she relates that two years earlier, at the death of a male slave, she emptied out the water from the vessels in the house, as her mother had taught her. According to Custódia, her mother had said that doing so "was good for the relatives of the deceased who remain alive." Custódia's grandmother, Ana Rodrigues, also taught her this practice. Custódia claims not to have known that this was a Jewish practice. In response to the visiting inquisitor's questions, she insists that her mother never taught her the Law of Moses or its ceremonies and was a good Christian; she instructed Custódia in the above custom "innocently." Neither does Custódia recall her grandmother Ana Rodrigues ever mentioning that this was a Jewish ceremony.[89] On 6 February, yet another person from Matoim appears for confession in the Recôncavo, the half-Christian Lucas dEscovar, similarly stating that "it was more or less three years that, some slaves having died on him in his house, he spilled out and ordered spilled out all the water of the pots which were in the house and that this he did three or four times at the deaths of three or four slaves without knowing that it was a Jewish ceremony but only had seen his said mother [Violante Antunes, daughter of Heitor Antunes and Anna Rõiz or Rodrigues] doing the same."[90] Finally, appearing on 11 February, the last day of the 30-day grace period for voluntary confessions, Ana Alcoforada, another niece of Lianor's, confesses to doing the same thing on diverse occasions for "seven or eight slaves."[91]

According to halakha, one did not mourn at the death of one's slave. Nonetheless, the often close connections between master and slave might override such technicalities. The Mishna (Berakhot 2:7), redacted in the 2nd century CE, relates the tale of how Rabbi Gamliel mourned on the death of his beloved slave Tabi. Though chastised for this, he responds that "my slave Tabi is not like other slaves; he is kosher," meaning, presumably, that he had become Jewish Of course, most of the New Christians cannot be assumed to have been familiar with halakhic norms. In previous chapters I have brought examples of masters who expressed sadness or loss at the death of a slave, but this is not necessarily the same as mourning, and certainly does not imply the performance of ritualized acts of mourning. In the case of various members of the Antunes family, a ritual act was performed not only at the death of an immediate relative but also for slaves (though ritual acts do not necessarily indicate feelings of sadness or loss). For "a son or daughter or slaves," as Lianor herself put it, without distinguishing between the categories of relationship.

In fact, five of the six confessants that 1 February 1592, share ties of either blood or matrimony, as do others who appear shortly before and after. Nuno Fernandes, Lianor's brother or half-brother, even returns for a second, more detailed confession on 9 February.[92] Perhaps the various family members come together from Matoim for the express purpose of confessing. Coincidence or another motive having no relation to the inquisitor's presence might have drawn them all to him at this moment. They might have come to clear their conscience of these authentic shards of Judaism of which they understood little or nothing. Or they could have appeared to attempt some pre-emptive damage-control (and draw lighter sentences) by making limited confessions pre-arranged between them. This one obscure custom is not the only thing they all discuss with the visiting inquisitor. Lianor's niece Ana Alcoforado (granddaughter of Ana Rodrigues and Heitor Antunes) may not have been aware of it, but her own husband Nicolao Faleiro de Vasconcelos (or Vascongocellos) had in fact come before the visiting Inquisitor already in July of 1591, on the first day of the 30-day grace period in which the people of Salvador and one league around might confess to the visiting inquisitor Mendonça. In his audience, Vasconcelos reports that on two occasions his wife Ana told him to empty the water from the containers in the house outdoors at the death of one of their slaves, though he only complied the second time. Vasconcelos also testifies that not only has Ana never done anything that made him suspect any negative intentions against Catholicism, but that her aunt Lianor, as well as the rest of Lianor's siblings, are all good Christians. Vasconcelos, an Old Christian (though married to a descendant of New Christians), declares that he discovered that emptying out the water as a ritual act comprises a Jewish practice from the Edicts of Faith posted on the church doors only the day before. Had he known this, he says, he never would have consented to the practice.[93] On 20 August 1591, Maria Pinheira, another resident of Salvador, denounces this same practice of Dona Lianor's in terms nearly identical to Lianor's own confessions.[94]

Clearly, something deeper was going on. The day after Vasconcelos' appearance before the visiting inquisitor, several other Old Christians denounce Lionor and Beatriz Antunes and their mother Ana Rodrigues for calling themselves "Maccabees," for preparing food in "the Jewish manner," for eating at a low table as a sign of mourning, for blessing the children "in the Jewish manner," among other supposed signs of judaizing. The family's matriarch, Ana Rodrigues or Roiz, in particular, is mentioned by numerous confessants as a vocal judaizer, openly rejecting and badmouthing Catholic icons and rituals.[95] Several witnesses declare that when her husband Heitor Antunes died, Ana Roiz buried him in virgin soil, according to the Jewish custom.[96] Antunes also came in for passionate denunciation as a judaizer by various witnesses.[97]

Ana Rodrigues had been married to the merchant Heitor Antunes, who had arrived in Brazil in 1557. According to a document presented by the colony's governor, Mem de Sá, with whom Antunes seems to have been close — the two arrived in Brazil on the same ship — Antunes was a knight of the king's house.[98] In 1559 and 1560 Antunes seems to have acted as one of the collectors of the tithe on sugar in Bahia.[99] The couple, Antunes and Rodrigues, bought their plantation and mill, Matoim — Heitor Antunes' ownership is mentioned in a document from 1571 — and gave birth to seven children, all of whom married Old Christians except the youngest, Nuno Fernandes.[100] Elias Lipiner cites a contemporary historian, Gabriel Soares de Sousa, describing the importance of the estates of both father and sons along the Matoim River.[101]

Antunes is said (by Vasconcelos and others) to have been reputed to have possessed another, more dangerous pedigree than his connection with Mem de Sá and the Portuguese knighthood, descent from the Maccabees, the illustrious second-century BCE family that fought successfully against Judaea's hellenistic governors.[102] Many Judeoconversos sought to counter denigration by Iberian Catholics by pointing to descent from the ancient Israelites, the Davidic royal house, a particular tribe or the Maccabees, by identifying with the oppressed Israelites in Egypt or Queen Esther.[103] Gaspar Fernandes, who worked with the husband of Lianor's sister, was another of the Old Christian confessants who mentions the Maccabean descent of the Antunes family. He claims recalling that he heard that once when the elderly Ana Rodrigues was ill, some of her daughters brought a crucifix to her bed as part of their efforts to heal her and she shouted at them to get rid of it. We have here yet another attestation either of religious syncretism or of divergent attitudes within a single family toward the family's religiosity, as Lipiner also concludes. Indeed, one of the daughters retorted to their mother by reminding her of their Old Christian spouses: "Listen mother to what you say [...] we are married to men who are gentlemen [fidalgos] and leaders of the land!"[104] This statement bore especial truth in regard to Sebastião or Bastião de Faria, who had married Beatriz Antunes. He had become a wealthy and powerful landowner in the captaincy, to whom the Jesuit fathers sold slaves, and who earned a street in his name in the nearby city of Salvador.[105] On the other hand, Nuno Fernandes, the one child of Antunes and Rodrigues who married a New Christian, was allegedly seen by some of his Black women slaves striking a crucifix that he kept under his bed.[106] Even Faria's wealth and heroic military exploits could not overcome the murmuring of Old Christians against his marriage to the daughter of 'the Jew' Heitor Antunes and the frequent visits of New Christian merchants and sugar purchasers to his homestead.[107]

On the same day in 1592 that so many younger members of her family confess to the visiting inquisitor, Ana Rodrigues, aged eighty or so, does likewise. She relates that she frequently blessed her grandchildren with the blessing that "the blessing of God and me should cover you" while placing her hands on their heads. Laying hands on the child's head entails part of the parental blessing customarily given by Jews on sabbaths and festivals. When a son had passed away, some thirty five years earlier, she threw all of the water out of the house, as she had learned, "because they cleaned the sword of the blood that was on it." That is, Rodrigues references the precise reason given in the Shulkhan Arukh, though she cannot or will not explain the meaning of this statement to the inquisitor.[108] It should be noted that even the explanation regarding the angel and the sword appeared in at least some of the Edicts of the Faith and therefore does not prove that Rodrigues knew the significance of what she was doing or had learned the significance from older relatives.[109] She claims that "she did not know that [these things] were Jewish, because they were taught her by an Old Christian godmother of hers, Inês Rodrigues, midwife, widow, whose husband was a carpenter, who is now already dead, and at the time she was very old and lived in front of the confessant in the said Interior, in Portugal, who taught this to her, saying it is good, and because of this she [Ana] did it."[110] It seems likely that Ana Rodrigues's pinning the blame on a deceased Old Christian was a wily and common tactic, giving the inquisitor some formalistic answer whose senselessness essentially mocked the goal of his investigation. It appears that many of the confessants to the visiting inquisitor attribute their lapsed religiosity to time in the Brazilian backlands, something Carole Myscofski reads as "admittance of the act but rejection of guilt."[111] Rodrigues and these other confessants drew on the very real dissipation of Catholic influence away from the urban centers in both the Old and New Worlds. Whether or not Rodrigues really understood the significance of her actions remains impossible to prove, though it is plausible that she did. Whether she had passed on to her children anything more than not-understood or unconscious behaviors is also uncertain.

Gracia de Siqueira, who declares herself to be a friend of Beatriz Antunes, Ana's daughter, denounced her friend because some seventeen years earlier, when Gracia had been living on Beatriz's sugar mill, the latter came to her house one day and "told this denouncer that she didn't eat rabbit and gave her a rabbit that had been killed when the Blacks had caught a few in the forest and she said that she would bring it to the house of this denouncer so that she could eat it and this the denouncer did."[112] Rabbit is not kosher. Further, this incident shows the kind of interchanges of goods and services between slaves and masters that characterized the unequal but communal life of such a plantation. Many of those who denounce Ana Rois state that "public reputation" or "public rumor" circulated that she practiced Jewish rites. Six denouncers, mostly residents of Salvador, testify that a synagogue existed on Matoim, and four of them, Manoel Bras, Diogo Dias, Anna Vaz and Ines de Barros even locate it in the house of Heitor Antunes.[113] In the words of Dias:

> from the time of his youth he heard always said in this city [Salvador] in public voice and rumor commonly said by the mouths of all as a thing certain and true that in Matoim in this captaincy the former Heitor Antunes New Christian merchant, who was master of a mill/plantation on the said Matoim [River], had in his house a synagogue and Tora and that in his house New Christians gathered and judaized and kept the Jewish law.[114]

Ines de Barros says that the synagogue stood in "a separate cottage in which on certain days [Heitor Antunes] and other New Christians gathered."[115] Did Lianor or others of her family know about these denunciations? (Were the rumors so much in the atmosphere that the family members had no need to know of specific denunciations?) Did denunciations such as these prompt the 'spontaneous' confessions of the Antunes family members in an attempt, as Lipiner suspects, to preserve their ownership of their estate?[116]

Their 'voluntary' confessions failed. Lianor and Beatriz were both shipped to Lisbon and condemned to burning. Because of the nobility their father had been granted, the sentences of the two sisters were commuted to the confiscation of their goods. Penitenced, they returned to Brazil, where Beatriz died in 1597 and Lianor in 1644, aged eighty.[117] The elderly Ana Roiz was imprisoned in 1593 and, despite the many efforts of Sebastião de Faria and Anrique Minz Teles, died in the Brazilian jail used by the Inquisition. She left the world "outside of the guild and Union of the Holy Mother Church," according to the 1604 sentence, which ordered an effigy of her to be made, shipped to Lisbon and burned there in an auto da fe.[118]

An additional mortuary custom surfaced in the course of the inquisitorial visit. Only a year and a half before the rash of confessions (mid-1590), the young daughter of one of Lianor's female slaves died and Lianor provided a cloth to use as a shroud, "commanding that they enshroud her in it like this whole, not tearing it or throwing any of it away." Though she does not say so, Lianor must have learned this from her mother as well, who taught her also that "it was not good to sew on the shroud of the dead with a needle and thread with which sewing is done in the house and also [..] that it was not good to throw [away] a branch or a piece of shroud in which one will enshroud a dead person."[119]

The significance of these practices appears unclear. Renée Levine Melammed, who cites examples of Castilian Judeoconversas donating material for shrouds or even sewing them on their own, makes no reference to the notions mentioned by dona Lianor.[120] But the shroud for the dead had apparently become the focus of special importance in Judaism. According to the thirteenth-century Nachmanides, in an advance of manners, the famous Rabban Gamliel (1st century C.E.) introduced "the custom of covering the whole dead person with a piece of linen," previous to which cadavers had been buried uncovered.[121] Drawing on the kabbalistic masterpiece, the Zohar, an Ashkenazic collection printed specifically for members of burial societies, Rabbi Aharon Bereḥya's canonical Ma'avar Yabbok (Mantua, 1626), states that a dead man "will first be completely covered by a shroud of white swaddling and then wrapped in his prayer shawl," indicating "the extreme importance given to clothing the dead."[122] Similar emphasis on the integrity of the wrapping appears among accused judaizers in Iberian territories. Manuel Galindo, for example, a resident in Évora, Portugal, was accused in the sixteenth century of preparing deceased New Christians for burial in "the Jewish manner," which included "wrapping them in a cloth of new linen."[123] Seymour Liebman generalizes this practice, writing that among crypto-Jews "the cadaver was [...] dressed in a shroud of new, pure linen" and that "people sought assurance that the linen was made by Jews [sic]."[124] Perhaps the notions of Lianor and her mother Ana Roiz were merely superstitious extensions of the desire to give honor to the dead.

The practices involving not throwing away pieces of the shroud and not sewing the shroud with needles used in the house, I suspect, relate to another dimension of Jewish conceptions of death and the dead: ritual impurity. According to halakha, utensils that have been in contact with a dead body become impure, taking on the impurity of the dead.[125] Bringing a needle and thread back into the everyday realm of the household — into life — would risk symbolically bringing back the impurity of the dead; carelessly throwing away a piece of shroud could make impure an entire room or house. Here the emphasis on maintaining the integrity of the shroud may have had less to do with keeping it whole than with ensuring that impurity does not spread. Of course, these New Christians may not have even known the significance of their acts, which nonetheless admit no alternative explanation known to me.

Clearly these women in Brazil included their slaves in the circle of those intimate enough to warrant the performance of these rites of mourning, which their mothers had taught them.[126] (Lianor's mother's other daughter, Beatriz, on the other hand, seemed less inclined to include her slaves in her circle of family.) These slaves even received a 'proper' and 'respectful' burial, not necessarily a given for slaves of this period (as mentioned in the previous chapter), though one could say that Lianor's inclusiveness stems as much from impersonal "superstitious" motivations (fear of the consequences of improper burial) as affection.

At the same time, Nicolao Faleiro as well as Maria Pinheira base their denunciations of Lianor on what they had heard from Balthesar Diaz de Zambujo, a slave who had previously worked for Lianor and her husband. Nicolao admits "that he does not know whether he was in his right mind (se estava elle em seu sizo), however he knows that he took him [the slave] for a liar and that he appeared in order to raise false testimonies."[127] Finally, on 26 August 1592, the inquisitor Mendonça calls the already-imprisoned Francisca da Costa to testify. Her deposition includes the following statements:

> There was a year in which she was at the house of Anrique Monis married with Dona Lianor New Christian and in this time that she was at his house Isabel, a Brazilian Black, and Maria, a Black from Guinea, slaves of the said Anrique Monis, told her that his said wife Dona Lianor and her sisters and mother were Jewesses and that Friday afternoons they all gathered and entered a house that was a pantry and did not come out of it until the following Saturday and that they were in it celebrating [...] and that they did not know what they did and that they always did this before the Holy Inquisition came to Brazil and that after the Inquisition entered they did not see them do this anymore [...] and that when this denouncer was at [Dona Lianor's] house the Holy Inquisition was already here and she did not see them do such, but, and she took care in this, it seeming to her bad that the whole year that she was in her house the said Dona Lianor never on any Sunday or holiday ordered her slaves to church, and likewise the said slave women told her that the said Dona Lianor and her sisters and mother commanded the water to be spilled from the pots and rooms of the house when someone died in the house, the Black women were ladinas.[128]

This denouncer's narrative rambles, as do many of the confessional narratives produced for the Inquisitions, but its end, emphasizing, seemingly out of the blue, that these Black slaves spoke Portuguese (were ladinas), makes sense: they were already to some degree Christianized and therefore Lianor's neglect of their religion (at best) and judaizing (at worst) became that much more criminal in her eyes. The two slave women never went themselves to denounce their owners, however, for reasons we cannot ascertain without further information, likely irretrievable.

A slave's ability to perform tasks in proper Jewish fashion according to instructions should not be confused with consciously adopting such practices herself. One needs to know whether a slave understood that a practice was (crypto-)Jewish and participated nonetheless. Such cases existed, but proving them requires solid evidence, which is too often lacking. In chapter 7, I turn to a handful of such cases of conscious 'Jewishness' on the part of Afroiberians, whether merely rhetorical or in practice.

CHAPTER 6

Judaizers and Blacks: Alliances, Real and Imagined

Jailed Judaizers and their Jailers' Servants

One of the phenomena frequently reported by — and extremely worrisome to — inquisitional authorities was the way Afroiberian slaves helped judaizers in the Inquisition's prisons. The jails of two local Inquisitions, Mexico City and Lima, generated many accounts of such perceived collaborative subversion of Inquisition operations. Given that the Inquisition's operations, including its trial proceedings and prisons, were supposed to be secret, the conveyance by servile messengers of information and goods back and forth between prisoners and the outside world posed an enormous threat. The records provide us detailed and colorful views of the delicate, tenuous, clandestine yet known cooperation between hounded Judeoconversos and slaves, whether belonging to them or even to their inquisitional persecutors. The interactions between Judeoconverso prisoners, their friends and relatives outside, and Afroiberian slaves were fraught with dangers of all sorts, and not only from the inquisitional authorities. Neither party seemed certain that it could trust the other. The incidents and activities discussed here reveal the ambivalence and ambiguity of motivation, desire and manipulation on both sides.

Slaves who worked for the Inquisition or for municipal officials had the ability to come and go as they pleased within the jails and among those imprisoned within them. In one trial from 1630s Cartagena de las Indias, we hear of the slave of the alcaide (jailor) who "had offered to Juana de Hortensia to bring her to sleep with" a prisoner in his cell.[1] Some jailers helped certain prisoners in various ways, for a bribe or as a kindness. Some slaves did likewise for the same reasons. In addition, slaves might not necessarily have felt the same loyalty to the Inquisition held by jailers, who were direct employees of the institution, and may have been prone to greater sympathy with its victims. A jailhouse conversation between two prisoners reported by another prisoner in 1642 Mexico City alludes to the perceptions held regarding those who staffed the prisons. From their cells, two women of the Rivera family of alleged judaizers discuss asking the jailer for a favor, even if they have to promise him "a shirt, and underwear, or a jewel." Ysabel de Rivera says that this will be "impossible," that, among other things, the jailer "is always angry." Another of the Rivera women replies that "it was much better to negotiate with the black man or the black woman," i.e., slaves employed in the prison. But their mother Blanca replies, "they are negros, and do not have to do favors / no han de hacer cosa buena."[2] On the one hand there is the feeling that the Black slaves are better to deal with, because they are more pliable or willing to respond to requests. The older mother, a marginally poor woman whose father had been involved with the slave trade (see below), is not so sure, whether due to racism or to a more realistic vision of the minimal leeway slaves have within the slave system or to an understanding that slaves might have no reason to do Whites kindnesses.

The quotidian interactions between imprisoned Judeoconversos and slaves were many-sided. On the one hand, it is clear that prisoners were permitted to continue their lifestyle if they were financially able, so that their slaves continued to serve them while in jail or they might have money with which to pay slaves for favors. At the same time, this situation made the ordinary dependence of the masters on their slaves somewhat more desperate. Both aspects can be seen in the following anecdote related by Beatriz Enriquez to her inquisitors in 1646 Mexico City, after already having sat imprisoned since 1642:

> at night while they gave the signal in this house this confessant [Beatriz] spoke through the window of her cell with a black named Antonia who was her slave who put herself in the corridor in front in order to speak to her giving her salt and no more and requesting her to bring some fruit and shoelaces [?] which the black woman sent her among the clean clothes that she washed for her and that the speaking to her took place between three or four times and on one of these [occasions] this confessant asked her regarding her brother Diego rrodriguez and Juan Duarte, and she said to the said black woman that she should tell them on behalf of this confessant that they should confess the truth and she did not bring her a Response other than by means of signals at midday from the corridor [when] she said that the parent of her master who was Ju[li]o [?] duarte had thrown her out and had not wanted to Respond.[3]

In this case, Enriquez's slave Antonia did what her mistress asked of her, though even so she could not overcome an obstacle like the fear or self-interest of relatives on the outside. The willingness or cooperation of slaves could not be guaranteed, however, especially if their owners sat in limbo. Beatriz's sisters, Rafaela and Micaela, also imprisoned, are among a group of women conversing together at one point. One asks after a relative on the outside, to which another replies that she doesn't know because "the mulata had given birth and her black woman had not overcome it because she had fled."[4]

The help of slaves touched on more than just delivering news or messages. After Luis Gomez Barreto had been subject to torture in the course of his first trial by the Cartagena tribunal (1636), the inquisitors "sent one of his slaves to serve and assist him." The jailer "had a little black [boy] brought of up to fourteen or fifteen years old by his looks called manuel of the angola nation slave of the said Luis Gomez Barreto [...] in order to serve his said master."[5] One wonders at the feelings produced in the broken master and the involuntarily helpful slave by such a situation, which for the latter may have differed from their previous relationship only in that now the master also lived without control over his own life. While the local inquisitors in Cartagena may have here revealed a human sympathy for the victim of their administration, Inquisition officials in Madrid responded with anger. When the members of the Suprema reviewed the trial, they pounced on this action, communicating to the local inquisitors their explicit fears:

> A person of his household is not given to the accused to assist him because of the disadvantage that he might bring him some paper, or message to the defendant, but rather [he should be given] another person concerning whom this suspicion won't be had; and that which could have been done in [light of] the impediment of the accused was to give him for a companion one of the prisoners in the secret jails at that time who is not in [Gomez Barreto's alleged] conspiracy nor [is] Portuguese at any rate whoever is put in his company should have taken an oath of secrecy, and if he came from outside to ask him whether he carried from there, whether he brought some message or notice for some prisoner of said jail, and such was not done with the slave of this accused [...] and if in effect the slave entered, neither the time he was [in with Gomez Barreto] nor when he left is said.[6]

It turns out that in this case, as is revealed in his second trial (1652), Gomez Barreto's social status had enabled him to forge a certain degree of friendship with the inquisitors who ended up trying him in his first trial as well as with the jailer of the Inquisition's secret jails in Cartagena.[7]

The efforts of Gomez Barreto's wife, Barbara Pereira, to find someone who would bring food and other items to him in jail during his first trial reveal much. Pereira turned to her (their?) Black slave, Sebastian Bran, possibly because at the time of her husband's imprisonment he was married to a Black woman slave, Isabel, who happened to belong to and work for the jailer. Pereira requested the couple's aid, but, she told the inquisitors, to no avail. Bran, her slave, refused, saying "that the jailer alone entered where her said husband was imprisoned."[8] Nonetheless, Bran remained in their service through at least 1643, according to the testimony of the new jailer, Diego Fernandez de Amaia.[9] Furthermore, Amaia told the inquisitors, Bran had indeed brought food for Gomez Barreto many times, a fact that was widely known. Frequently

> said black of the house of the said Luis Gomez arrived at the house of the said jailer and brought under his cape, hides a large totuma [a hard-shelled squash] which is a kind of pot and within it they brought stew and other things to eat to the said Luis Gomez Barreto this witness knows this because this witness saw

him many times bringing the said totuma and being with it in the house of the said jailer and seeing him/it enter the kitchen and because one day he went up to said black and lifted his cape and saw that inside the said totuma he brought a stew of cooked chicken covered with a plate and over it some kind of chopped [meat?] or jigote [fig?] covered with another plate and that this was a known thing among all the [Inquisition] ministers [...] and the slave women of the said jailer [...] the one called Isavel and the other Lucreçia [...] and another called Mariquilla.[10]

Francisco de la Cruz, slave of the imprisoned Mexican Judeoconverso Simon Vaez Sevilla, was given two reales by his master's cellmate Gaspar Alfar in order to buy him "a booklet (cartilla, for letter-writing?) at the counters (mesillas)," that is, from one of the vendors at the open market, which Cruz did. Despite the fact that Cruz himself was incarcerated at the time, for crimes of his own, as a slave whose labor could be claimed by the Inquisition, he was given the kind of mobility prisoners who had been free citizens lacked. Another prisoner gave him a peso to buy him two tins of jam (or fruit preserves, caxetas de conserba).[11]

Slaves did more than take care of the physical necessities of the imprisoned, whether they were their masters or not. The above Francisco de la Cruz, hearing many of the prisoners in the Mexico City tribunal's jail talking with one another, warns them "to be quiet because people were around."[12] Francisco, also known as Queretano, does not know his own age but surmises that he is older than twenty five and considers himself "more ladino than bozal."[13]

It is clear, then, that prisoners frequently communicated with one another and with the outside world, often by means of slaves. The communications touched on a great variety of topics, not least of all inquisitorial matters pertinent to the prisoners' trials and efforts to get word to or have word from loved ones on the outside. Francisco de Leon Xaramillo, a 28-year-old Portuguese "circumcised judaizer," was accused of passing messages out of the Mexico City Inquisition jail. He supposedly communicated with his mother, Isabel Nuñez, notifying her regarding his case and that of his father, Duarte Leon Xaramillo, his brothers and sisters — all also incarcerated. Xaramillo communicated by means of one of the Black slaves who worked in the jail, sending out through him tins of food with messages secreted inside to his mother, whom the slave knew. The slave evidently did not dare deliver the message but sold the goods for 6 reales. The inquisitors take this opportunity in the summary of the case to warn the jailers about the need for "caution and vigilance" concerning what can happen with those of the "perverse nation" of Judeoconversos.[14] Duarte Leon wrote to his wife Ysabel Nuñez by means of a Black slave, or so Rafaela Enriquez claims Nuñez told her. Rafaela also says that Blanca and Margarita de Rivera told her that they had messages from Ysabel Nuñez, brought to them by the same slave. These messages were brought to Tomás Tremiño de Sobremonte, all at the cost of much money.[15] In Lima, one of Manuel Bautista Peres's domestic slaves, Antonio, carried at least one message to him in his jail cell in 1635 or 1636. Peres also managed to send messages out, with the "connivance of tribunal employees and the help of slaves" or his own servants.¹⁶

Simon Vaez Sevilla, sitting in the Inquisition jail in Mexico City and knowing that the Inquisition had confiscated his property, had to ask his slave Francisco for information concerning the most basic matters of his own life: "how was his house and hacienda, and who lived in it?"¹⁷ In addition, Vaez asks about news that might affect his trial and those of others, "if the fleet had come and if a new Viceregent had come and if it was said that a pardon had arrived [so] that they would be released from the jail" and whether the Inquisition had arrested many people.¹⁸ Switching his visits to nighttime for more privacy, Francisco tells the inquisitors that Vaez "always asked him about his wife and son and about the fleet and pardon."¹⁹ Vaez also asks after "Gasparillo the black, and after the other black called Juan Francisco and he told him that Gasparillo had died in the hospital and Juan Francisco was in the house of Don Garcia."²⁰ It would appear that Vaez inquired out of affection, but whether Francisco placed these queries before those regarding Vaez's wife and son, which follow immediately, because he remembered them in this order or because this was the order in which Vaez raised them cannot be determined. Ysavel Criolla claims that this same Francisco told her that Juana Enriquez wanted her to tell another prisoner, Simon Lopez, "that if he had a hacienda in Cacatecas that he should watch out for it."²¹ Beatriz Enriquez relates another such episode:

> one morning putting into a basket the bread that this confessant [Beatriz] and the other people had for eating, francisco queretano the black emptied the bread into the said cell in the presence of Juan gomez assistant of the Jailer and between the bread there came [out] a written note which the said thomas nuñez de Peralta [Beatriz's husband] took and he read that it came written in portuguese with couplets and verses asking them how they were and how it goes for them without knowing whose the paper could be, and then the black passed the corridor that was in front of the cell in which this confessant was and he asked this confessant whether she had taken the paper and this one answered that yes, and she asked the black who [illegible] said paper and without responding to her he went.²²

Some of these communications imply assigning to slaves an enormous amount of knowledge and trust. Simón Váez asks Cruz "if the Señores [of the Inquisition] had found the money that he had hidden."²³ In some cases the masters act as if the slaves represent blank machines of transmission. The imprisoned friend of Simón Váez, for instance, supposedly tells the Black Ysavel Criolla, slave of Vaez, "that she should tell Juanica that he [Simon Vaez] was suffering for her."²⁴ This message to Juana Enriquez, Vaez's wife, also a prisoner in the same jail, resonates with unarticulated emotion. The friend even uses an intimate diminutive — Juanica — for the name of the wife of the love-starved husband in whose name he sends the message. There is no room here for squeamishness in the face of the slave woman who hears and is to transmit the message, who already knows so much about her master.

To get a sense of the exigencies of cases like these, I will now focus on one situation, about which a rather copious amount of testimony came forth. The septuagenarian Black slave Sebastián Domingo, alias Munguía, of the Congo nation, worked in the Mexico City Inquisition's secret jails during the 1640s.[25] Born in Congo territory, he was at first a slave to one Luis de Mesquita, a factory manager (obrajero) in the province of Tlaxcala.[26] In the summer of 1642 he acted as a messenger between Thomas Nuñez de Peralta, accused of judaizing, and his wife Beatriz Enriquez, the latter one of the five daughters of Blanca Enriquez, an elder who was said to be a leader of the Mexican crypto-Jewish community; Peralta was also the brother-in-law of Simón Váez Sevilla. Most of the Enriquez family was arrested and tried by the Mexico City tribunal. Here we see how the suspicion bred by the inquisitional process bled into relations between Whites and members of the servile class, on whom the former became even more dependent when incapacitated by incarceration. The tale of the transmission of messages is recounted by several of the individuals involved, giving us a sense of their differing perspectives. Peralta's version comes in his audiencia of 20 August 1642:

> it was two months more or less that this confessant being very afflicted in his cell there came to him a black called Sebastian who helps the jailer, and through the grille of the cell he told him that his wife [...] tells him that he should help him [...], and this confessant answered him that he should tell her that he was very sad, and melancholic, and that she should write a note as he said in order to certify whether the message that the said black brought was authentic, asking him [Sebastian] if he had seen his said wife he said that yes and that she gave him the said message, and one, or two days later the said black returned and brought to this confessant a small paper two fingers wide, and a hand's-breadth long saying to him that his said wife had given his message, and she had given him [Sebastian] the said paper which this confessant remembers that [someone] wrote to him [Peralta] that a Thomas Rodriguez de Peralta understood that [someone] had done the damage to him [i.e., denounced him] because he had to name him when they had sequestered his goods, and that if this confessant was Free God would liberate him, that the Virgin our lady made this confessant see that the letter[ing] of this [...] note was not his wife's, and he was frightened, [...] he was suspicious [regarding] from whom the note could be and in particular [because?] the said black filled an inkwell (of which he made a presentation) with a quill, and a half sheet of white paper telling him [Peralta] that his said wife sent it to him so that he respond on it, to that which she had sent

to him, and he recalled that the day the said black gave him the first message that he requested a point [?] telling him that his wife asked for it, and this confessant gave it to him, and sent it and in conformity with that which he [Peralta] said wrote [illegible; this?] confessant in a notebook [quartilla] of a half sheet to his said wife notifying her that he was very plagued, and that he neither recognized nor knew who the said Thomas Rodriguez de Peralta was, and that she should declare more, and notify him [illegible] everything she knew, and that he was dazed by the Justice discovering whom could be the said Man, and that she should write it in her own Hand because he did not recognize that of the said paper, and the said black brought it, and this confessant remained with the mentioned inkwell, and Quill, and he tore up the paper that he had received = And that in three, or four days the said black returned, and brought him another paper in a notebook saying to him that his said wife sent it to him in which she notified him to be certain that they imprisoned him due to the said Thomas Rodriguez de Peralta, and that he should calm himself and secure his health, and [put his] hope in God that he will leave with Honor as he had been born with it, and the said black also brought him another half sheet of paper, and this confessant warned him that this second paper was of the same lettering as the First, and not by the hand of his wife with which his suspicion grew without knowing who could have written it which [note] he ripped up like the First, and he responded to it with the said black, and that he had had three audiences, and had declared in them his Homeland [Patria], Parents, and grandmother, and had complained about Dona Maria de Rivera, and about francisco nieto discrediting them as enemies, and that she should endeavor to find out whether Pedro duarte had done him some damage [i.e., had denounced him] he being a blonde youth of thirty five years old more or less, a merchant who goes and comes to/from Spain because he was his enemy, and a man of evil tongue and he [Peralta] remembers that he wrote in the said paper to his said wife that she should be [illegible; certain?] that this confessant will bring up testimony neither against her nor against her sisters nor against anybody and that she should go speak to the Sir Inquisitor Don francisco de Ara and commend his [Peralta's] trial to him because he seemed to him benevolent and inclined to do well by him and also it was good to gain as a friend the secretary Eugenio de Saravia and had not given other reasons that she should write having so many days = And within a few days said black returned, and brought to this confessant, another, third paper of the same lettering as the two mentioned in which they wrote him consoling him and giving him [to understand] that from the charge that they made against him in the audiences he would deduce who had done him evil, and this confessant seeing that it was not the lettering of his wife remained more confused, and with greater suspicions and fears than before, and on a piece of paper that remained with him from the half sheet this confessant wrote saying that he had received the letter that had come with the purple silk, and that it had not reached their hands, another that said having written to him before that one which one this confessant wrote thusly due to the suspicion that he had that the said papers were not from his wife, and that for this [letter] the bearer would go relating it through the said black, who would convey what was going on around here, neither did he ever have a response, nor did this confessant go back and write more, nor did he receive more messages, and those mentioned and the said papers the said black gave them to him when the assistant [spouse?] of the jailer entered to remove the crockery, or to clean the said cells and when he gave the said inkwell and quill the said black said to him that the jailer should not see it and thus he had hidden it under a beam that it was about twelve days more or less that the said black bringing him a light at night this confessant asked him whether he knew anything regarding his said wife, and how she was, he responded that she was well, and in her house, which he had not believed because a few days before in this part [of the jail] he heard some sighs and complaints in front of his cell and has presumed that she was a prisoner, and in particular because this confessant having given his clothes for washing to the black woman who enters with the jailer when it was returned clean, he recognized that it had been exchanged with that of his wife, because she brought him a high [collared?] shirt that he had left among others in his house, and some knittings [made] with needles that his said wife used with which it was certified that she was a prisoner in this holy office, and that he requested and beseeched by the love of God she be treated with mercy and piety for [her] being a very shy woman, and sick and he believes that she will have natural shame with the result of confessing her sins and those of this confessant, but as he desires that our Lord has opened the eyes of her understanding to tell the truth, and save her soul he intends to jointly save that of his wife and thus declares and confesses that even with her he has never done any fast of the said Law of Moses [....] and that when he received the messages, and papers, inkwell and quill from the said black, and responded to them orally, and in writing he didn't understand what he did [...] for if he had understood he would not have done it [...] if he erred in this he begs pardon for not knowing that he committed a sin in doing it. and that having written in the last paper that was in the purple silk he said it because the last paper they wrote him came wrapped and tied with a strand of purple silk, and that the last time that the said black spoke to this confessant saying how his wife was fine and in her house he promised that he would bring him another paper if this confessant gave him a shirt, and this confessant gave it to him [...] even though it [the paper] was not given nor did he return to speak more.[27]

Peralta's confusion regarding the messages stemmed from the fact that when Beatriz begged Gaspar Vaez to write Peralta, the latter had the slave do so, "in the letter of the black man [fue de letra de negro], this confessant and the black woman Antonia dictating." In other words, Sebastian/Munguia was supposedly literate enough to pen a letter.[28] If this is the case, why did he not inform Peralta of this fact, in order to assuage the prisoner? Was it because Peralta did not wish to confide his unease to this unknown slave? Or perhaps Peralta was trying to defend his wife from the inquisitors, pretending that she had not written letters to him?

Sebastian/Munguia's account of the whole relationship differs considerably. As I will explain, at the time he was already in trouble with the Inquisition, hence his current 'job.' He was then also caught transmitting the messages described in all this testimony. His deposition comes from his own trial. He claims that Peralta called to him through the open door of his cell when he had been sweeping the jail patio on one occasion, asking for some fire or heat. Peralta supposedly then begged him, "for the love of God," to do something for him, which Sebastian/Munguia "promised to do." Peralta then allegedly told him "that if a black of his comes and brings a paper for him from his wife he should bring it to his cell." Within two days, a black boy of ten to twelve years, dressed in a green choker, torn outfit and barefoot, came to call on Sebastian/Munguia, sent as an intermediary by a black woman slave of Peralta's. Whether this boy belonged to Beatriz or was Antonia's son (or both), we get a vivid sense of the kind of clothing provided to slaves of even fairly well-off households. The boy informs Sebastian/Munguia that she wants to see him, and the latter went to meet her at the given address where she awaited him. The slave tells Sebastian/Munguia that her mistress would give him 50 pesos "if he managed to bring a note to the master of the said black woman," Thomas Nuñez de Peralta." Sebastian/Munguia replies to the slave "who is called Antonia and is chubby and young, that he cannot leave the holy office [complex] because he was serving the jailer," but she pleads, "for the love of God do it and began pulling this confessant by the cape in order to bring him to her house and notwithstanding the pleas that the said black Antonia made to this confessant he did not want to go and he remained at this holy office and house of the jailer and that this happened about seven at night he does not remember what day of the week." Antonia comes back another day, also in the evening, enters into the Inquisition complex, finds Sebastian/Munguia, makes him sit down, sits next to him, and gives him a note for Peralta. According to Sebastian/Munguia, perhaps trying merely to protect himself, he and Peralta never exchanged a word when he delivered or picked up the messages.[29] From the testimony it is clear how each party presents the story in a light that defends his own actions.

While Peralta claims that he was being duped by an unknown message writer, Gaspar Vaez Sevilla testifies that indeed Beatriz Enriquez, his aunt, "had communication with" her husband "by means of a black man" while Peralta was imprisoned, "that he received papers and wrote papers, according to what he told" Vaez. But, says, Vaez, Peralta "neither wrote them to nor read them from the said doña Beatriz, and neither to [Vaez's] mother doña Juana [Beatriz's sister], nor did he know who should write them nor did the confessant give her the message to write, the witness [Vaez] awaiting that the said doña Beatriz should send him to the said Peralta."[30] Vaez claims that Antonia was romantically interested in Sebastian/Munguia.[31] This is a possibility, but it could be that her interest was feigned in order to execute the commands of her owners.

Indeed, using as a go-between the Black slave Antonia de la Cruz, who belonged to her and her husband, Thomas Nuñez de Peralta, Beatriz got in touch with the Black slave she leaves unnamed, "who served in the jails of the Holy Office," according to the testimony of Beatriz's sister Juana from the same trial.[32] Beatriz claims, in her own testimony from her own trial, that the whole idea of these communications came from her slave Antonia: "[Beatriz] being greatly afflicted and disconsolate by the imprisonment of her husband Thomas nunez de Peralta by this holy office, one black woman of hers, a slave named Antonia, a creole of Çacatecas, having much knowledge regarding him, began to console [Beatriz], saying that she would bring a black man she knows in the Inquisition and that [Beatriz] should give a note [papel] for her said husband."[33] If there is any truth to Beatriz's statement, which could well be an attempt to deflect culpability, Antonia, who in 1642 declares herself to be around twenty five years old, played the role of empathetic partner, whether out of duty or sincere involvement in the emotional life of her mistress.[34] In addition, it is Antonia's connections and social knowledge that saves the day here. From her testimony it appears that Antonia engaged in healing, even later, while in the Inquisition jails, where the jailer brought patients to her and sent her to treat others, including imprisoned members of the extended Enriquez circle of accused judaizers.[35] Once again we see how a slave with skills is pressed into service by the Inquisition, gaining thereby certain privileges and a modicum of status. If Antonia's depositions from this date onward are at all accurate, it appears that many of the prisoners, understanding her mobility, entrusted her to convey oral and even written messages to one another, information that Antonia reveals fully to her inquisitors. Various prisoners reward her for her messenger services with little gifts and even money.

This is true of other slaves as well, who use their social network in order to carry out their masters' orders. One of Simon Vaez's slaves, the Black Ysavel Criolla, has her mother, Leonor, then a slave to yet another supposed judaizer, Juan Mendez de Villaniciosa, contact someone on the outside to come speak with Simon Vaez.[36] It is noteworthy that Beatriz, in referring to Antonia, almost always calls her "la negra" or "la negra Antonia" throughout her testimony, and not merely

"Antonia." It seems from testimony in other cases that Beatriz made similar attempts to communicate through slaves with other prisoners. Beatriz Enríquez testifies (19 September 1642) during the trial of Juan de León about some of her efforts to communicate by means of a Black slave with the accused while he sat in prison. Beatriz made this whole attempt "even though it was difficult, and that it had cost her much money." With the help of relatives and friends, such as Jorge Jacinto, husband of Blanca Juarez, Beatriz prepared a package for Juan de León: "some pieces of cotton soaked in ink and a small pen, all wrapped in a sheet of white paper and twenty pesos in reales."[37] It could well be, then, that she is merely attempting to shift culpability for concocting this scheme onto her slave Antonia.

Antonia, for her part, claims that it was Beatriz who approached her with the idea: "one day the said Doña Beatriz Enriquez said to this deponent, does she know some person who lives in the Inquisition and this one saying to her, no she does not know anyone, being recently arrived from the mines of san luis Potosi." Suggesting that Antonia get to know some youth in the employ of the tribunal, Antonia responded by saying that "she didn't want to involve herself in this." Nonetheless, Beatriz allegedly implored her to forge a relationship with someone working on the inside. Antonia eventually meets a "half mulato" whom she asks whether he works for the Inquisition. He tells her that his sister, a Black slave, came from Puebla to make a life in Mexico City with her spouse, who works for the Inquisition. This Mulato introduces Antonia to the Black who works for the inquisition — right at the front door of the institution's building, a sign of how little attention slaves and non-Whites might attract — and she shows him to her mistress's house (actually that of Beatriz's sister Juana and brother-in-law Simon Vaez) in order to get the process rolling.[38] Antonia declares (with pride?) that she alone of all the household's slaves knows about these messages "because of how much she is trusted by" her masters.[39]

According to Juana Enríquez, who claims she has never seen him, Beatriz described this Inquisition slave to her as "an old, bald Black man who did not speak much Spanish."[40] Antonia describes him as "between ladino and Boçal."[41] The slave

> arrived at the same time as always,[42] and this confessant [Beatriz] asking him if he knew the said Juan de León, he responded that he did, giving his proper signs [i.e., describing him correctly] and saying that he had all the prisoners at hand, because he gave them [food] to eat, and this confessant beseeching him to take to him [Juan de León] the said paper and message to write, he took it and the said twenty [pesos] which the said Jorge Jacinto had given for him, and the said Black did not return for two days, this confessant went back to call him with the said Black woman [Antonia], and having come he said that he had not dared to give the said paper or the message to write to the said Juan de León because he was a dead man [the many and damning charges against De León were published on

August 29, not even a month before Beatriz's testimony], and for so little [money] he did not look at his face, and likewise he had not wanted to go in with him, and that he had thrown away the paper and the message to write, and as this confessant begged him greatly how important it was to her that he give the paper to the said Juan de León, the said Black said to her that for a very good profit he would do it, that she should give him twenty pesos and he would return for the paper, and this confessant gave him the said twenty pesos, and afterwards she sent to Jorge Jacinto, that he should give these [pesos] to her and write the paper, mentioning to him what happened with the said Black, and the said Jorge Jacinto wrote another paper for the said Juan de León and paid this confessant the twenty pesos which he had supplied for him [the slave], and the said Black having come at the same time as always, he took the said paper of Jorge Jacinto for the said Juan de León, and as he did not return that day nor the next, this confessant sent to see him the said Black woman, who returned saying that the Black man responded that he could not go to see this confessant, that he had given the said paper to the said Juan de León from whom he already had an answer, that she should send him [the slave] monies and go to him, and this confessant gave notice of this to the said Jorge Jacinto, who gave her another ten pesos which this confessant sent to the said Black man with the said Black woman and she went and gave them to him, and he responded that he would then take the answer, and this happened the Saturday before they would arrest her [Beatriz], with which she has no more seen the said Black nor has anything else happened between them other than what she has mentioned.[43]

Among other functions, Sebastian/Munguia offers Beatriz emotional support, telling her on one occasion when there is hope that someone close to Beatriz might be freed from the Inquisition "that she should be of good spirit."[44]

Antonia would supposedly meet Sebastian/Munguia in an alley around seven in the evening in order to communicate and/or give or receive the messages "because she knew that at those hours, he helped empty out the chamber pots."[45] Antonia doesn't seem to have been the most effective secret agent, however. One day Antonia arrives at the Inquisition complex herself. One of the inquisitors asks her what she is seeking. She answers that she seeks a morena named Luçia. The inquisitor disappears into the building, from which Sebastian/Munguia soon emerges. Antonia gives him one of the written messages and he "said to her that she should go so that they should not see her speaking with him," accompanying her out by way of the yard, inserting her into a little door when he sees that people are about and telling her to hide herself before making himself scarce. No doubt Antonia's indiscrete appearance led Sebastian/Munguia to tell Beatriz and the others at their next meeting that he would no longer deliver messages for them, something he announced "very disturbed." At this point, Simon Vaez allowed the slave to remove as much as he wanted from a small sack of money.[46]

Given the degree to which the inquisitors frowned on such illicit communications, it makes sense that, as Juana Enríquez testifies, the slave "charged her [Beatriz] that no one should know about this, that he ran a great risk."[47] Sebastian/Munguia also tells Antonia "for the love of God not to say anything regarding that he was taking and bringing papers," for should she talk, "they would put him and her in a dungeon in this inquisition where they are very dark and that it wasn't good to be in them."[48] In the face of the great risk involved for all the parties, compensation became a major issue. Beatriz's estimate, related by her sister Juana, "that she had given to the said Black a hundred or a hundred and fifty pesos," sounds realistic.[49] Antonia claims her mistress "twice gave to the said black man fifty pesos," while on four other occasions she gave him an unspecified amount of money. Sebastian/Munguia himself testifies that the very first time Antonia communicated with him she announced that her mistress was summoning him and would give him fifty pesos if he would carry a message.[50] One time, according to Antonia, Beatriz gave Sebastian/Munguia "many coins, which the said black man put in his pouches. But they were so many that they did not allow him to walk quickly. In order to go he had to hold the pouches in his hands." No doubt afraid of its evidential power, Sebastian/Munguia is said to have given over his earnings to a Black woman for hiding; he himself confesses eventually that he buried some of it in the alcove where he lived in the jailer's house and what he received from Antonia he gave to a compatriot, a Chinese man.[51] Beatriz, on the other hand, testifies that though he demanded a hundred pesos "in Reales" after his first delivery, she paid him only thirty, promising more if he continued delivering messages.[52] Notwithstanding the importance to her of these deliveries, she negotiated the price down significantly. In a deposition given during his own trial, Sebastian/Munguia discusses an occasion on which "because they would not pay him his money this confessant became very angry and enraged."[53] He probably wanted to continue to earn such good money, despite the obvious risks, yet he also would have appeared to have the upper hand in such a negotiation. Beatriz, in contrast, had little or no money, her husband's goods having been confiscated by the tribunal. One witness, most likely Sebastian/Munguia himself, repeatedly uses the verb rogar [to pray, beg] to describe Beatriz's requests to the slave, on whose willingness to help she is completely dependent. One witness (Sebastian/Munguia?) says that on one occasion Beatriz told the slave "that she would give him as much money as he should like if he would bring a response from a certain prisoner and also gave him two pesos in order to buy chocolate."[54] She ends up paying the slave twenty pesos after each delivery, "with which he left very content," according to her.[55] With the final delivery, Beatriz gives the slave in addition "an embroidered shirt from Rouén which this confessant bought for ten pesos."[56] Sebastian/Munguia, for his part, claims, on the one hand, that Beatriz gave him a shirt the time when she wouldn't or couldn't pay him his money, and, on the other hand, that it was Peralta who promised him a shirt for conveying the messages but never actually gave it to him.[57] In her own testimony Antonia adds that one day Sebastian came to her house "to order a loaned skirt for his wife."[58] According to Sebastian/Munguia's response to the charges against him, he received money only on two occasions and only enough to buy for himself first "some shoes" and then "long johns of blue cloth and other shoes and some sweets."[59] Such items would likely cost less than fifty pesos. In comparison, the Black slave Juan, testifying in 1601 in the trial of Diego Díaz Nieto, says that the prisoners for whom he carried messages "did not give him anything other than that when they should get out, they would pay him and reward him because at present, as prisoners, they did not have what to give him." Others (those on the outside?) gave him "bread and fruit and coins" and the like.[60]

Sometimes even greater compensation was offered to the slaves, perhaps the ultimate reward, liberty. At one point, according to the deposition of an unnamed witness (most likely Antonia herself), Beatriz seems quite excited because she heard that a certain prisoner very close to her might be released, the inquisitors having come up with no charges. She gives the Sebastian/Munguia the usual twenty pesos, to which her brother-in-law adds more coins, yet "not content with this the said Beatriz promised liberty to her said black woman," i.e., Antonia.[61] Referring to an occasion on which Beatriz sent her to discover how Peralta was doing in prison, Antonia says that Beatriz gave her a necklace of a row of pearls from China, "giving her word that she would give her liberty."[62] The Black slave Francisco de la Cruz asserts that his imprisoned master, Simon Vaez Sevilla, told him "that he should come see him every day and that he would give him a letter of liberty [i.e., of manumission]."[63] Ysavel Criolla claims that one day Simon Vaez promised her and Francisco Queretano (de la Cruz) "freedom when he leaves" jail.[64] In her response to the charges of the various witnesses Beatriz seems to confirm having made this promise to Antonia.[65] On the other hand, Antonia testifies that a close friend of her masters warned her that if she revealed anything of these jailhouse communications the inquisitional tribunal would give her two hundred lashes.[66]

The differences between the parties in their depictions of their interactions are revealing. Despite the good service this slave performed for Beatriz, she claims to her inquisitors that she does not even know his name, though she provides them what would seem to be an accurate and operable description: "tall, old, bald and with a bad face [de mala cara]."[67] According to one unnamed witness (Sebastian/Munguia?), however, Beatriz clearly expressed her gratitude to the slave with emotion, for on at least one occasion she "embraced the said black man and told him to return for the response."[68] Does she really not know his name, and is this ignorance a sign of class or racialist blindness, or is she trying to protect him, however ineffectively, by making the inquisitors work to find him? In any case, a month later, having conveyed already a great deal of information about herself and many others, she remembers his name or decides to give it.[69] It should be noted that Beatriz repeatedly disputes Sebastian/Munguia's testimony, declaring many of his statements to be false. She calls him both a spinner of tall tales (embustero) as well as fearful. She also disputes the veracity of assertions that seem to have been made by other slaves/servants, possibly Maria Bautista and/or Antonia.[70] For his part, Sebastian/Munguia, who was incarcerated based on the testimonies that arise from these trials of various Judeoconversos, at first denies several of the statements concerning him raised by others, but changes his testimony over the course of a few days of interrogations; it is clear that indeed he performed many of the missions requested of him.[71] It seems the question of compensation might have become a source of tension between Beatriz and Sebastian/Munguia. Perhaps Beatriz resented the fact that she had sunk to the point where an unknown slave could dictate financial terms to her. Is it also possible that beyond trying to make herself look as innocent as possible, she is trying to salvage before the White inquisitors some class or racial status that would be marred by her abject dependence on a group of slaves? Perhaps Sebastian/Munguia had simply taken advantage of her: he claims, for instance, that she gave him a fighting knife to give to her husband but that instead he sold it.[72]

Antonia de la Cruz was incarcerated as well. The inquisitors have some harsh words to say about her and suspect her assertions. "[B]eing a slave, vile person, and by nature intrepid, and being of bad habits, she was sent from this city, to be sold, to that of Çacatecas, as is done with the slaves of bad nature, and of whom it is truly possible to believe that she lies against her said masters and other persons against whom she deposes."[73]

The inquisitors order her to be threatened with torture, stripped and, if necessary, submitted to the mancuerda (where the wrists are tied with cords and the torturer would throw his weight to produce a rack-like effect). She is then to be brought back for further testimony. This is done. Insisting that everything she has said is true, Antonia does not change a word of her testimony. It is not clear that the inquisitors did anything more than take Antonia to the torture chamber and strap her to the rack.[74] After this judicial procedure that supposedly produced proof that Antonia had been telling the truth, the tribunal seemed content to make ample use of her statements in trials against various alleged judaizers.

Despite the difficulty of cutting through the varying testimonies, the loyal relations between slave and mistress seemingly continued during their mutual imprisonment. Antonia takes the shirt that Ysavel Texosso gave to her as a reward for one of her jailhouse services, as well as the necklace given her by Beatriz, and sells them, through her godmother, the Mulata Ynes, in order to buy shoes for her incarcerated mistress.[75] In an audience shortly thereafter Antonia relates that she "has told her mistress doña Beatriz Enriquez that they had brought her [Antonia] to this Holy Office a prisoner in a dungeon so that she should tell about the messages, and that she had not wanted to tell, that she began to cry."[76] The pent up feelings of fear of the Inquisition, fear of her mistress, continued affection, stress, guilt and betrayal explode, however comingled. Other slaves also remained loyal to their masters. Juliana, the Angolan slave of María de Rivera, never denounced her owners, their families and acquaintances, "[e]ven though they had whipped her, and even though she knew all about their religious practices, even as the Inquisition tortured her."[77]

Sebastián/Munguía probably requested as much money as possible for these risky tasks because the reason he served in the Inquisition jails in the first place was as punishment for his 'crime' of being married twice — doubling the risk he took in passing messages to and from the jails. Having been married in 1624 in New Veracruz with the Black slave Felipa de la Cruz, his master later put him up for sale "because of his bad habits." But "there was nobody who wanted to buy, saying he was married." His master brought Sebastián/Munguía to Puebla de los Ángeles, where he sold him to an obrajero (factory manager). Supposedly, some friends told the slave that his wife Felipa had been sold from New Veracruz and had died, so that Sebastián/Munguía eventually yielded to the importunities of his new master to marry one of his slaves, Ysabel, in order "to assure his money, fearing lest he run away."[78] The above explanation may well be true, but one should keep in mind here, as many scholars have pointed out, that African marital and sexual customs differed from those practiced in Christendom, while, on the other hand, the difficult exigencies of enslavement led to behaviors, modes of coping, that might not have 'normally' arisen. Coming from the Congo nation, Sebastián/Munguía likely saw multiple partnerships as something perfectly reasonable, a sign of largeness of spirit and communality rather than treacherous adultery. If such partnerships could be sanctioned and sanctified by the Catholic Church, so much the better.[79] Yet, perhaps significantly, not a single one of the other witnesses, even Antonia, also a slave, knows him by his African name, Munguia.

In any event, the Mexico City Inquisition arrested Sebastián/Munguía a second time for "violating the secret of the secret jails," i.e., transmitting information and/or messages, something he was said to have done "with ample malice and damaging intention." Not only had he brought messages back and forth, but he also conveyed, "in a very important manner, knowledge of those who were imprisoned [...] and the state of their proceedings." "Being ladino," Sebastian/Mungia understood exactly what he had done.[80] Antonia relates already in 1642 that his wife had informed her of Sebastian's arrest.[81] The inquisitors gathered enough evidence for them to convict him on seven charges.[82] Sebastian/Munguia found himself a penitent at the 30 March 1648 auto de fé in Mexico City. Sebastián/Munguía's new punishment: appearing at the auto carrying a green candle, with a rope around the neck and a penitent's hat on his head, he made a light abjuration; he received 200 lashes and six years at the oars in the galleys in Spain. Probably due to his age, the authorities freed him from the galley sentence, selling him instead for 100 pieces of common gold, which went to pay the Inquisition's expenses for his trial. After six years, he was to be returned to his master.[83]

Speaking 'African'

The worries these jailhouse communications provoked for the inquisitors has been mentioned. I will now contextualize them further. One of the 'judaizers' accused and tried in Puebla, Mexico, in 1648, doña Blanca Juarez, participated in jailhouse conversations with other prisoners under aliases and used "the language of Angola in Guinea to communicate with the maidservants and slaves who serve in the secret jails."[84] In her testimony to the Mexico City tribunal, Ysavel de Silva says that Beatriz Enriquez speaks the language of Angola very well and implies that her husband Thomas Nuñez de Peralta, as well as Rafaela Enriquez and her daughters Ana [Suarez?] and Blanca understand it too.[85]

First comes the question of which language is meant here. It could be Kimbundu, a Central African tongue very similar to the neighboring language of Kikongo, which by the seventeenth century became known as Angolan and "operated as the lingua franca of the entire region, even among interior peoples," no doubt among slave traders as well.[86] Where did these individuals learn this language? Are their skills in it exaggerated by the witnesses to the Inquisition? Given that Blanca Enriquez was born in Puebla and most probably never travelled to Portuguese West Africa, she must have learned it from her family's slaves in Mexico. Alberro writes in reference to Blanca Juárez that "some families devoted themselves to the slave trade and sometimes the children of Portuguese born on African land were raised by black women slaves who taught them their language. Subsequently, the richest of these went along surrounded by slaves, and domestic requirements such as those which imposed prudence in some periods kept alive the use of this language."[87] Blanca's husband was Jorge Jacinto Bassan, a slave trader. Blanca and her sister Ana had a half-sister who had been born in Lima, Peru, Violante Xuarez, an illegitimate daughter of their father, Gaspar Xuarez, who perhaps traded in slaves.[88] Rafaela Enriquez testifies that her maternal grandfather — Diego is the only part of his name that she can recall — died in Angola.[89] This is Diego Lopez, who had died in Angola or Guinea, presumably involved in the slave business. Others in the circle of Mexico City Judeoconversos had connections to the slave trade as well. Blanca de Rivera's father, Enrique Rodriguez Obregon, worked as a "sailor/longshoreman [Cargador] of blacks from Angola to this New Spain."[90]

We do not know much about how or why these Judeoconversos picked up African languages. Did they learn it to better command their slaves? Did they wish to understand them and their culture? If nothing else, their knowledge of the slave language bespeaks the proximity, if not intimacy, in which the master's children (themselves masters) lived with their servants.[91] Such intimacy troubled colonial authorities for a variety of reasons, in this case, due to the possibilities of conveying knowledge. But such facility in the language of the previously idolatrous servile class additionally posed an obstacle to the smooth acculturation of these servants, as well as to the smooth decimation of their idolatrous culture, and an unwanted, unnecessary flirtation on the part of the master class with the servants' culture. According to Maria Odila Leite Silva Dias, in 1698 the governor D. Artur de Sá e Menezes "was dismayed by the habit that São Paulo women had acquired of speaking Tupi with their native Indian servants: 'the majority of those people cannot express themselves in any other language, especially the female sex, and all the servants, and serious harm is resulting from this shortcoming.'"[92]

Not only did many Judeoconversos involved in the slave trade not know an African language, not all those chased or caught by the Inquisitions desired these dangerous liaisons with slaves. After María de Rivera's sisters had been imprisoned by the Inquisition in Mexico City, in May 1642, "she attempted to find the Blacks who in 1635 had brought numerous messages to the prisoners of the Inquisition, but when she presented the penitents from that time [i.e., those former prisoners] with the proposal of requesting their help in order to find the slaves, it was poorly received by them [the former prisoners] and she was unsuccessful in establishing contact with [her sister] Clara."[93] Despite the possibility of helping new victims of the Holy Office, these former prisoners justly continued to be wary of drawing onto themselves the Inquisition's wrath by abetting communications the Inquisition considered illicit. In addition, the sources imply that the former prisoners protected these slaves. As seen above, slaves also at times resisted the requests made of them, or at least so they told the inquisitors. Ysavel Criolla, slave of Simon Vaez, relates that one day her master, imprisoned in the Inquisition jails, called to her. "This confessant not wanting to speak with him and for this [reason] asking him not to call to her because she had a companion [with her] and she did not want her to see her [engaged] in some job" that might not be above-board.[94]

Communicating with slaves aroused the inquisitors' wrath, whether it was done in Angolan, Portuguese or Spanish. A revealing passage in a report about the Lima auto de fe of 23 January 1639 — in which Francisco Maldonado de Silva was burned at the stake — corroborates the connections described in the cases from Mexico:

> Before publicizing the auto, all the Blacks who served in the jails were enclosed in a part where they would not be able to hear, know or understand about the publication, so that they should not give notice to the accused parties, for even though the Inquisition used for this [service in the jails] unassimilated, non-Spanish-speaking Blacks [bozales], just taken from the boats (less is not possible in this kingdom), the Portuguese use assimilated [Blacks, i.e., ladinos], who, as they bring them from Guinea, knew their languages, and by this means they are much helped in their communications, with other skills, like that of [using] the lemon and the alphabet of knocks, a remarkable thing.[95]

This passage describing the preventative segregation of the jail's Black slaves indicates that some Inquisition jails in the Americas followed a policy of using slaves who did not speak or understand Spanish, to prevent unwanted communication of just the sort mentioned here, but also, no doubt, because they were cheaper than acculturated slaves.

Here again we see that, from the Inquisitions' perspective, knowledge of African slave languages was a dangerous vehicle, despite the ironic contradiction in the description that the problem inhered in the slaves and prisoners sharing both Iberian and African tongues — but this doubling only multiplied the situation's dangers. Jewish polyglotism — itself a kind of cosmopolitanism and foreignness

— often served as a pre-modern form of the charge of double loyalty. In the jails of the Inquisitions this linguistic excess and alterity overlapped with that of the empire's largest and most downtrodden caste. In addition, the tribunals had to deal with the somewhat amusing fact that often the prisoners could and did communicate with one another between their cells. In the context of the Lima tribunal Irene Silverblatt quotes accusations from the trial of Manuel Bautista Peréz that New Christians of Jewish background "could speak their languages in front of Old Christians, and Old Christians would not understand a word." Bautista Peréz and a friend of his who was also imprisoned would "speak to each other in a language only understood among themselves, talking about the Law of Moses." This was "a secret language," and "Old Christians just heard normal words, not that out-of-the-ordinary language," in which the Judeoconversos spoke with "duplicity and scheming, so that the prisoner and the rest of his ancestry and kin could converse about conspiracies and heresies."[96] Though possible, it is doubtful that any of these Judeoconversos knew enough Hebrew to converse in it. Are these references to Judeo-Spanish, which, with its smattering of Hebrew, would have sounded both similar and unintelligible to Spanish-speakers? Does this charge raise Old Christian hallucinations of Hebrew? Is it possible that Bautista Peréz and other Portuguese Judeoconversos involved with the slave trade knew enough of an African language to speak it with one another? In any case, the language described bears all the hallmarks of a magical, unfamiliar and, hence, suspect tongue.

That the Inquisitors at Lima went to such precautionary lengths to prevent unwanted communications shows the degree of their fears. An earlier letter from the inquisitors at Lima, 18 May 1637, notes how some prisoners "tear their shirts and sheets and on the shreds write that which they desire with the smoke of the candles, and to the Black bozales who enter the ministries, they [the prisoners] give them over so that they [the slaves] will take them, and in this manner some have come into our hands."[97]

The problem was not new to those who ran the jails. Already in the 1570s action was taken against two Black women who worked in the prison kitchen,

> the one called Antonia, and the other Marica, regarding certain messages and documents which they carried from certain prisoners out of the jails, and verifying what happened surrounding this and the damage that might have been involved, Antonia was given 200 lashes by the secret jails, and Marica the same amount, and they were returned to their owners, ordering them not to enter this Holy Office.[98]

Nonetheless, the problem continued. The 1641 letter from the inquisitor at Lima, Antonio de Castro y del Castillo (cited in part above in note 95), reiterates many of the same complaints, as they arose in the trial of Manuel Bautista Pérez:

> The servants for these people were Black bozales, which is the service around here, and the accused were even traders in this

merchandise, bringing large parties of them from Cartagena, they spoke to them in their language, and they gave messages to be taken from the ones to the others, and many times they gave them papers written with the juice of lemons [....] Other times accounts in figure, in old papers, which were known ciphers among them were sent with the Blacks who took out the plates.[99]

The inquisitors did what they could to stop the flow of such communications. In Cartagena in 1654, Juan, a Black slave of the jailer, received two hundred lashes and a metal ring affixed to one leg as a sign of his imprisonment, and also had to serve at a hospital for his whole life for "having carried messages from the outside to the prisoners," many of whom at that time were Portuguese and accused judaizers.[100] To prevent such occurrences, the practice was instituted, at least by the Cartagena tribunal, of giving prisoners paper — to take notes regarding their case, to detail challenges to the accusations against them, to list names of those they wished to denounce — that was numbered, to enable tracking, in the hope of preventing its use for messages outside the jail.[101] It is unclear when this practice began. In the jails of the Mexico City tribunal as well, some efforts were made to stop jailhouse communications by means of slaves. Maria de Rivera, conversing from her cell with her mother Blanca and sisters in 1642, is said to have mentioned that "a black who was here [working in the jails] in the past did all that [imprisoned judaizers Thomas Tremiño (sic) de Sobremonte and his wife] ordered, [and] that so said Tremiño and his wife also. And that because of this the jailer now did not permit either the [current] black man or black woman to enter within."[102] Sobremonte, whose name is usually given as Treviño de Sobremonte, was, next to Váez Sevilla, probably the wealthiest New Christian merchant in the viceroyalty and also one of the most prominent members of the Mexico City marrano group. Castigating the slave Sebastian/Mungia for his crimes, the Mexico City inquisitors reveal an informed and global perspective:

> [T]he said black Sebastian, having communication with other blacks within and outside the patios and corrals of this Inquisition, which blacks infallibly belong to people who, being observers of the Law of Moses, desire to know about the prisoners in said jails, and they value the said blacks, people whom ordinarily are held to be of little or no account, with whom they relate concerning their own color and nation. And by this route the observers of the said Law procure the achieving of their designs, as with notable damages has been experienced in the Inquisitions of Lima, Cartagena and here.[103]

Hence among the punishments meted out to Sebastian/Mungia was "that he be publicly castigated [with lashes] to give others a lesson." Other lessons also can be learned from the Mexico City inquisitors' summary here. First, the situational configuration — Inquisition, imprisonment and slave mobility — led Judeoconversos to value overmuch people whom the official ideology assigned little value. Second, as if this were not dangerous enough, Judeoconversos, themselves a liminal and dangerous population, were thus led to empathy and camaraderie with these other Others, bonding over shared ethnic and phenotypical marginalization ("with whom they relate concerning their own color and nation").

Judeoconversos, Portuguese and Blacks: Rebellious Others

Recurring violations of the Inquisition jails' secrecy terrified authorities in the context of Spanish worries regarding national security leading up to and following the Portuguese rebellion of 1640 against Castile, which generated a war lasting some twenty eight years. These worries frequently manifested a particular wariness of enemy alliances forming along ethnic and racial lines. Already in 1634, Captain Esteban de Fonseca, a Jew who left Amsterdam to return to Spain, testified, when caught by the Inquisition that "18 ships are going [from Holland to Havana] & with them another ship called the Three Towers (las tres Torres), well known on account of its greatness. Its captain is a Jew named Diego Peixotto alias Mosen Coen, who induced the company [the WIC?] to make the crew (who are negroes) come to them to learn the language. It is also said that a landing is to be made under a flag of truce, pretending that they had escaped from the Hollanders, & in this way they can learn all that is going on."[104] On 10 March 1641, a royal decree from King Felipe IV to Mexico asks officials to keep a close eye on Portuguese residents but not to provoke them because of their "mixture" with "the natives of [the Indies] and Spaniards, slaves and persons who serve them."[105] The next year again the king issued a royal decree concerning Portuguese foreigners in Mexico (10 February 1642), based, possibly, on information supplied by the Bishop of Puebla, Juan de Pálafox y Mendoza: "they are very intermingled with the Blacks, with whom they have a great union, and they [the Blacks] respect them."[106] The same year, the viceregent the Marques de Mancera advised the Counsel of the Indies of fears that the Portuguese in Charcas, Paraguay, Tucumán and Buenos Aires, together with those of Callao and Lima, were intending to rebel via Cartagena by using the city's high number of Blacks, "with the fondness that the blacks have for them, being the first that they came to know."[107] Exaggerations of this kind built upon Spanish fears, but contained elements of truth. The suggestion of a particular respect or fondness in which Afroiberians held Portuguese seems paradoxical, to say the least, given that most slave traders were Portuguese. Is it possible that Afroiberians admired New Christians as subalterns suffering from the same imperial system that oppressed them? (I revisit this theme in the next chapter.) The accused judaizer Ysavel de Silva probably alludes to (and feeds) worries about the connections of judaizers with Africans when she testifies in the mid-1640s "that there was no Portuguese Captain of blacks [...] who did not enter the houses of doña Ana xuarez, Doña Micaela, Doña Rafaela and Doña Cathalina enriquez because they had tables for playing naypes. [...] And that of all the captains of blacks who have come to this city one could give a very large Relation [regarding] their being observers of the law of Moses or not."[108]

Another seventeenth-century communication fretted about the same combination of anti-Spanish hostilities: the Portuguese in the Indies "are more [numerous] than the castillians, and most are conversos, and people who by religion and origin have such hatred toward Castille, and being full of the greatest number of slaves, the best that there are, [...] even without external aid they are so many that, helped by their slaves, they will be more powerful that the castillians."[109] It should be noted that the idea that Portuguese outnumbered Spaniards is preposterous factually but telling psychologically. Fears of alliances of opposition connected to worries about other forms of ideological infection. Spanish fears constituted more than mere paranoia and anti-Jewish sentiment, however. In the 1570s Sir Francis Drake had allied with some Black cimarrones to ambush several mule trains laden with silver and gold. The Spanish responded worriedly about "This league between the English and the Negroes," because, "being so thoroughly acquainted with the region and so expert in the bush, the Negroes will show them methods and means to accomplish any evil design they may wish to carry out."[110] Due to similar worries, in the 1590s, Peruvian Viceroy Garcia de Mendoça prohibited Blacks from carrying arms.[111] A 1615 report from Lima warns about the potential dangers of Perú's various non-White groups, who evinced no great love for their overlords, "should they attempt a general insurrection, because their number greatly exceeds that of the Spaniards."[112] From the authorities' vantage point, slave resistance and uprisings were all too real a threat in New Spain.[113]

The insurrectionary intent of Judeoconverso-Afroiberian relations may on some level have been real. It could well be that this is the reason why the anonymous description of the Spanish Viceroyalty of Peru from around 1615, quite possibly written by a Portuguese Judeoconverso merchant named Pedro de León Portocarrero,[114] elaborates on the physical and martial potential of the colony's Blacks: "They are always in fear that the blacks should not rise up; for this reason, consent is not given to them to carry arms. Some blacks of officials [oidores] and captains and other ministers of justice are permitted to bear a sword and the blacks who go for firewood to the mountains and for herbs to the field and the mule drivers are allowed a knife."[115]

Still, the detailed accusations of treasonous relations between members of these minorities lack corroborating evidence. The description of Peru's policy regarding Blacks/slaves and weapons may simply have been a matter of curiosity for this text's author, a worthy fact to be mentioned in a traveler's description. We do not know whether some of the accused judaizers in Mexico indeed possessed, as the inquisitional authorities claimed in early 1643, "a list of the slaves which were and are on all the sugar plantations," and even if they, whether this was anything more than a commercial tool.[116] Similarly, no external evidence has been found to corroborate the allegation made in the late 1630s by the Lima tribunal that Manuel Bautista Peréz and others were "stockpiling gunpowder earmarked for a second Dutch invasion of Peru's major port city, Callao."[117] The implication, coming as it did amid talk of the judaizers' connections with still-subjugated but rebellious

Portugal and Dutch efforts to take Brazil, needed little elaboration. In a letter that Maria Ventura thinks might have been written in 1641, just after the secession of Portugal, an official in Potosí wrote to the Spanish king, warning that Brazilian Portuguese were "entering [Spanish territory] every day to capture and take indians from among those recently converted to our holy catholic faith, burning churches and committing infinite sacrileges." In this era of persistent contestation over colonies and control of their trade, Spanish fears may have been well-grounded.[118]

Spanish concerns regarding 'Portuguese' connected directly not only to anxieties regarding their rebellious activities and intentions, but also to more diffuse perceived patterns of sedition, including their contraband trade, which was seen as undermining Spanish imperial designs. These anxieties to no small degree generated the New World autos de fé of the late 1630s and 1640s. It is no coincidence that many of the New Christians arrested by the tribunals in Lima and Cartagena were engaged in trade and particularly in the trade in slaves.

When Spain swallowed Portugal in 1580, the extreme cruelty of the Portuguese Inquisition generated an exodus of New Christians back to Spain, irony of ironies. From this time on, Spanish officials harped on the treacherous potential of the 'Portuguese' diaspora population. Often, this alleged treachery entailed the commercial prominence of the New Christian community. Jonathan Israel reminds us that the Portuguese New Christian Duarte de Paz, living in Italy in the 1530s before emigrating to Istanbul in the early 1540s, whose history of loyalties reveals much ambivalence, wrote a letter to the Portuguese ambassador in Rome in 1545 detailing some of the European opinions regarding Portuguese New Christians. Paz gave

> an account of a dinner at which he had been present, attended by the French ambassador and other French notables in which the Emperor Charles V and Portuguese crown had been severely taken to task for driving the Portuguese New Christians to emigrate to Turkey. The reason given was the Turks had previously been thoroughly backward compared to the Europeans but now, thanks to the Portuguese Jews, were provided with all the industries, "officios mecanicos [mechanical professions]," and up to date weapons they needed.[119]

Spanish doubts about this population's threat no doubt increased with the significant entry of Portuguese New Christian bankers and merchants into the Spanish "system of royal asientos and contracts for tax farming, supplying stores and munitions to fleets and fortresses, and for the supply of slaves to Spanish America," beginning in the reign of Felipe III (1598-1621).[120] As early as 1606, Francisco Valverde Mercado, governor of Panama, reported to the Council of the Indies in Madrid that

> today the traders of the Indies are Portuguese because they have the asientos [monopoly contracts] for supplying slaves, and the

dispatch of the fleets and flotillas with proper provision, on which all commerce depends, and of this nation there have been many Jews merchants around here who live according to their Law [of Moses] and they, upon becoming wealthy, go to other realms before they fall into the hands of the Inquisition.[121]

A 1615 Spanish treatise laid the blame for the country's weakening economy directly on the "commerce of the 'Portuguese,' [who controlled the Spanish slaving asiento from 1580 to 1640,] and especially their shipping unregistered cloth and spices, along with slaves, via Angola and Guinea."[122] "From the most vile negro of Guinea to the most precious pearl," all trade passes through the hands of the "Portuguese" merchants, reads an oft-quoted line from a 1636 letter that the inquisitors in Lima nervously wrote to Madrid.[123] By 1641, in the wake of the Portuguese secession, the Spanish had banned the importation of all products by Portuguese or from Portuguese colonies.[124] The fact that in the face of the dire financial crisis beginning to cripple the empire in the 1620s Spanish authorities became desperate to obtain the wealth and commercial power of Portuguese Judeoconversos, appointing some to significant positions within and around the government, failed to assuage the enmity against them. It likely exacerbated it. Furthermore, the converso wealth that could not be securely assimilated for the empire by open invitation perhaps heightened the temptation to grab it through the arm of the Inquisition, the flip side of the pressures leading to the vast sweeps of the 1630s and 1640s.

Political and economic anxieties bled easily into theocratic worries, and the other way around. In 1632, in Madrid, allegations erupted that a group of Portuguese conversos were ritually flogging a figure of Christ. The resulting trials culminated in an auto de fé in which two of the accused were executed. Shortly thereafter, the even more tragic accusation arose (again) of the ritual murder of a Christ-like Catholic child. Purported Jewish deicide had resurfaced once more; these people simply could not be trusted. In his immense compilation of the laws of the Spanish Indies and meditation on the theological meaning of these territories, Política indiana, Juan de Solózano Pereira fretted over the possibility that the empire's African and Amerindian New Christians — he calls them "Peru's simple people" — would be led astray by the judaizing heresies of the Portuguese. Judeoconversos, he argues, actively sought to undermine the faith of these two populations of neophytes.[125]

In the 1590s, Portuguese merchants, many of them Judeoconversos, began flocking to the provinces of Chile and Peru, drawn by commercial opportunities and the fountain of silver pouring wealth out of Potosí. Some of these individuals may well have been fleeing intensifying religious persecution in Brazil, where the Inquisition sent several official investigators (visitadores) in 1591 and 1593. In late 1602, King Felipe III issued a decree warning against the infiltration into Chile and Peru of so many Portuguese New Christians (often by means of the slave ships and without permission), whose questionable religious orientation might infect the spiritual education of the Amerindians, and ordering their expulsion. Worries that these merchants engaged in contraband trade and neglected to pay the required royal fees likely constituted an equal motivation, as was true throughout this era.[126] In and around Buenos Aires, a sweep and expulsion performed in 1603 needed to be carried out again in 1605. Lists of foreigners were compiled by Spanish colonial officials in Potosí in 1581 and again in 1610 and in Cartagena in 1630.[127] In 1631, royal officials in Madrid ordered the audiencia of Charcas, responsible for the mining center of Potosí, to "move against the Portuguese who have entered the Indies through Buenos Aires, of whom many are to be found in Potosí."[128] In Lima, a census of the slave and free non-White population was conducted in 1636, possibly motivated by related security concerns.[129]

The sweep of alleged marranos in Mexico City beginning in the late spring of 1642 followed royal decrees from January 1641 that ordered the expulsion of all Portuguese who sympathized with the secession organized by the Duke of Bragança and the confiscation of all their goods; the immigration of all Portuguese to New Spain was ordered terminated immediately.[130] Robert Ferry calculates that of the 121 individuals arrested for suspicions of judaizing between 1642 and 1649, 48 were Portuguese, or nearly 40 percent of the total.[131] The inquisitors' anxieties produced enough convictions between these dates that no fewer than four autos de fe were held. On 10 February 1642 a royal decree (from which I cited another section above) had ordered further preemptive measures, warning of the many "landed and commercial class" Portuguese who resided in New Spain without license, perceived as brazen in their expressions of disloyalty and charged with having "a strong relationship with the blacks, as much for having many slaves as for having raised them and brought them from Angola and [the blacks] see them as parents."[132] Again, fears of collaboration between the different aggrieved minorities not only agitate the Crown, but appear already materialized. Most fascinating is the language used in this royal document regarding relations between the slaves and those who transported them across the notoriously treacherous middle passage, which can be read as familial and emotional. From the perspective of the threatened Spanish monarch, the Portuguese slavers stand in the eyes of their African merchandise as caretakers, as parental figures — not the belligerent relationship ordinarily posited between slaves and their enslavers. Here, not only do the slaves not resent or hate their enslavers, but they look up to them, respect and admire them. Whether there is more to this intriguing ethnographic projection than situational anxiety is difficult to say.

While inquisitors might claim that Judeoconversos maintained suspicious closeness with African slaves, those working for the Inquisitions were not averse to maintaining their own beneficial relationships with Judeoconversos, even profiting from their slaving connections. In testimony given in Cartagena in 1649 regarding events of the previous decade, one witness recalls how the local tribunal's notary and Inquisitor, Juan de Uriarte, was suspected of overly friendly connections with some of the prominent Portuguese New Christian merchants, in particular Luis Gomes Barreto, who were then arrested and tried by Uriarte's tribunal. Slaves seemed to be one of the items of merchandise in which both these Judeoconverso slave traders and this inquisitor shared an interest and which seemed to pass between them in ownership and service. In addition, and troublingly, the witness, Juan Ramos Perez, nuncio of the local tribunal, "knows that it was much rumored that Juan de Uriarte was served by servants of the Prisoners and that papers of the faith [i.e., dealing with Inquisition matters] would be given to the cashier of Manuel de Fonseca Henriquez to copy, [he] being a servant of the Prisoner and dutch by nation."[133] The Inquisition, in Cartagena, for instance, periodically investigated incoming slave ships in a search for contraband. One such investigation, in 1635, brought forth a confession from one witness to a bribing scheme that allegedly went back 13 years, arranged supposedly by Blas de Paz Pinto and another New Christian slave trader, in which slaves were given to Spanish officials, including the Governor, Lieutenant-General, the factor in Cartagena and others, so that they would look the other way regarding contraband goods.[134]

What remains unclear is the feelings of the Africans and Afroiberians who aided Judeoconversos imprisoned by the Inquisition. Whether they empathized with the suffering of their mistresses and their peers, were merely carrying out the commands of their social superiors or simply sought to earn some much-needed cash — or some unquantifiable combination of all three motivations — cannot be said definitively. From the other direction, it seems impossible to disentangle the sentiments of the imprisoned members of the master class in their awkward dependence on the help and good wishes of their social inferiors from the micro-politics of property and race that structured their mutual relations in ordinary situations. Crisis breeds strange bedfellows, of course, and it may well be that the kind of variegated inter-group relations discussed in this and the previous chapters reiterate the degree to which little can be said to have been ordinary about the surreal mixture of freedom and unfreedom that characterized life for so many Afroiberians and Judeoconversos in the colonial Iberian Atlantic world.

CHAPTER 7

Esperanza Rodríguez, a Mulata Marrana in Mexico City, and Other Afroiberian 'Jews'

The mixing of Judeoconversos and Afroiberians was not just cultural. On a more embodied level, in the Inquisition trials, as well as in other sources, one sees various mentions of New Christian men having relationships, sex and children with Black and Mulata women. Leonor de Carvajal, sister of the well-known Mexican judaizer Luís de Carvajal, confessed that they had a Mulata half-sister, Agustina de Quiñones.[1] The Portuguese dealer in slaves Luis Franco Rodríguez, an alleged judaizer tried in Cartagena in 1624, had two daughters, Felipa and María, despite his never having been married. They were born of "a single mulata who is called Ysabel Górez who lives in the said city of Çaragoza."[2] Relationships between Judeoconverso women and Black or Mulato men have not left any documentary record, as far as I have found. Intriguingly, none of these children seem to have been crypto-Jews. This fact of course raises questions about proselytization of slaves; if Judeoconversos did not induct their own offspring into Marranism in these cases, it is doubtful that they would have sought out the participation of slaves.

Cases of relationships or marriages with non-Whites are known from Europe as well. In their important 2011 book on the small Sephardic communities that existed in the early 17th century on the West African coast (today's Senegal), Peter Mark and José de la Horta discuss a Portuguese merchant whose success there enabled him to move to Amsterdam. Moisés de Mesquita (also known as António Lopes de Mesquita) indeed makes a fascinating figure. Seemingly born in Oporto, Portugal, he spent some years on the African coast as a young trader before arriving in Amsterdam by 1622. There he became wealthy enough to donate a Torah scroll to the Bet Israel synagogue in the 1630s and was elected a parnas in 1647. Making De Mesquita's rise even more remarkable is the fact that he was a Mulato.[3] De Mesquita stands as probably the most prominent Mulato in Jewish history, even though we know precious little about him. Despite drawing information from my 2004 book, Jews and Blacks in the Early Modern World, Mark and De la Horta pass over a fact I discussed there, though at the time I myself had been unaware of the background of De Mesquita that they uncovered. In light of Mark and De la Horta's research, what is for me one of the most noteworthy aspects of his time as parnas is that in that first year, 1647, he signed off on an ascama (communal ordinance) creating a new, separate row in the Ouderkerk cemetery for the burial of non-Jewish Blacks and Mulatos. Only Blacks and Mulatos who were born to parents married according to Jewish law or who married a White Jew according to Jewish law would be permitted burial in the "regular" section of Ouderkerk.[4] All this takes us to topics beyond the scope of this study, however.

In the family genealogy prepared by Isaac de Matatia Aboab (ca. 1676), with later notes and additions by his son, Matatia Aboab, we find that among the ancestors of the author's wife, Sara Curiel (daughter of David Curiel/Lopo Ramirez), her paternal great-grandparents, Duarte Nunes and Gracia Nunes, bore ten children, among them Phelipa Duarte, who married Domingos Lopes. Their daughter Branca Duarte bore five children. The fifth was Duarte Ramirez de Leão, alias Binyamin Benveniste, "who married a bastard [black woman] named Beatris da Costa."[5] The woman's race seems to have been added in to the genealogy later (by Matatia Aboab?). Together this couple had ten children, all technically Mulatos.

None of this is surprising. Relationships between Portuguese New Christians and African women happened both in West Africa and in Portugal, in the former region between outsider merchants and local women, often daughters of chieftains, and in Portugal between men and women slaves or former slaves. Yet, as in many of the instances of comingling, the question of voluntary participation is critical, and messy. As Mary Louis Pratt warns, "It is easy to see transracial love plots as imaginings in which European supremacy is guaranteed by affective and social bonding; in which sex replaces slavery as the way others are seen to belong to the white man; in which romantic love rather than filial servitude or force guarantee the willful submission of the colonized. [....] The allegory of romantic love mystifies exploitation out of the picture."[6] Still, the use made of these same avenues (relationships, marriages) by those 'below' should not go unappreciated. Under this sign they might romanticize or take advantage of trans-racial relationships as a means of escape upward, into Whiteness. Discussing later Sephardic concubinage on Curaçao, Eva Abraham-van der Mark notes how

> For a black woman, having a relationship with a white man was one of the very few ways to acquire upward social mobility in Curaçao's caste-like society. But only a minority of those who had such a relationship ever reached the status of kerida ["beloved," that is, a concubine installed in her own house] and for most of these, life was not easy. Nevertheless, they were envied by their sisters because of their light-colored children. The fact that these sometimes were given a better education and achieved higher positions in society must have been their reward.[7]

Suzana Maria de Souza Santos argues that the willingness of the Bahian New Christian Miguel Nunes de Almeida to acknowledge paternity of the children born to his slave woman, and guarantee their status as his heirs, went against the norm of the surrounding slave society.[8] Not all trans-racial relationships united a 'master' and 'slave'; statuses and motivations were messier than a constant dyadic schema imagines. In any event, the offspring of these unions embody the creolization so famously assigned to Latin America, though the same crossing of borders occurred in Europe and the Mediterranean as well.

Afroiberian Judaizers?

Other ties of pragmatism or affection came to bind non-Whites to Judaism or the marrano Law of Moses, particularly when they were in the employ of judaizing conversos. As mentioned before, documents speak of Mulatos — a handful? dozens? — who affiliated in one way or another with the small Sephardic communities along the West African coast, while evidence regarding Mulatos and Blacks who were born or (were) converted into Sephardic communities in Amsterdam or Suriname has long been known.[9] While it might be more surprising that Afroiberians would open themselves to the dangers of judaizing in Spanish or Portuguese territories, some few indeed did so. Thus, Beatriz Enriquez tells her inquisitors that a Mulata slave of Maria de Campos, named Catalina, "also was found guilty of Judaism," like her mistress.[10] The means by which Afroiberians came to know of crypto-Judaism varied, as did their motivations, which on the whole paralleled those of interested Afroiberians in non-Catholic territories. As always, each case needs to be investigated thoroughly, to attempt a determination of whether such affiliation was real, genuine, substantive or not. After a brief review of several such instances, I devote the remainder of the chapter to an in-depth analysis of the case of Esperanza Rodrigues of Mexico City, one such Afroiberian crypto-Jew.

In the Sevillan auto de fe of 28 February 1623, a Berber Mulato named Domingo Vicente appeared among the penitents. Condemned for professing the law of Moses, he received 200 lashes on the afternoon of 1 March.[11] Yet two years later the same Mulato involved himself in a public act of defiance. On 27 November 1625, a poster appeared on the door of the parochial church of San Isidoro, which read: "Long live Moses and his Law, for all the rest are madness." The following night, some local residents watched from a window opposite the church and saw a man arrive at the postered door. Rushing out, they caught him in the act of pasting up another similar proclamation. Taken by them to the Inquisition, the perpetrator turned out to be the previously castigated Mulato Domingo Vicente. His punishment this time consisted of a public humiliation: led on a donkey to the scene of the crime, he was propped up with his right arm shackled aloft against the wall, remaining thus for an hour, after which he served four years in the galleys and then faced life imprisonment.[12] If the account of his crimes is accurate, Vicente must have either believed fervently in Judaism or possessed an enormous and careless rebellious streak. Left unclear is the origin of his Jewishness or affinity for Judaism, its extent and content. At the time of his exploits he was not a slave, though he might have been in the past. Perhaps he had been born of a black mistress of a Jewish New Christian. Perhaps he was a North African Jew dark enough to earn the racial category of Mulato. Perhaps he had been the servant of secret Jews whose religious passion he adopted. Once again, answers do not present themselves from the documentation I was able to check.

Luis de Páez, a Black, was denounced in 1651 by a priest who claimed that while living on the island of Santo Domingo Páez observed the Law of Moses, did not confess with regularity and, when he did confess, related false information. It is not clear when he arrived in Cartagena nor when he was arrested by the Cartagena tribunal. In 1654 the inquisitors ordered him inspected to see if he were circumcised. The two doctors and surgeon who carried out the examination could not determine whether the condition of Páez's penis derived from a natural condition or an intentional operation. He died before his trial concluded, hospitalized for deteriorating health.[13] In 1655, the case was suspended by the Cartagena Tribunal.[14]

In 1572, five New Christians and a Mulato priest said to be "part New Christian," all from the town of Beja, Portugal, were arrested by the Évora tribunal. They were accused of organizing denunciations of 26 Beja Old Christians for judaizing. The imprisoned Old Christians, in turn, denounced many others, both Old and New Christians, leading to numerous executions, deportations and other punishments. According to a manuscript description of this so-called "Conspiracy of Beja" that circulated among New Christians, the Old Christian confessions of judaizing demonstrated the essential unfairness of inquisitorial procedure.[15] Here it can be seen that not all Judeoconversos were necessarily White. If there is truth to the events as narrated, this partly New Christian Mulato may have been part of an attempt to undermine and act against the Inquisition.

Here and there we find evidence of Afroiberians whose Jewish leanings come from birth into the converso community. One case stems from Bahia in the early 1590s. "In one of his confessions in the jail of the Lisbon Tribunal, Bento [Teixeira] refers to the mulatto women Maria and Brasília born from a New Christian man and an African slave from Guinea. Apparently these two mulatto women, who also embraced Judaism, would gather with other crypto-Jews in the house of the 'rabino' Francisco Pardo to practice some Judaic rites."[16]

In some of the cases in which Afroiberians found themselves tried by the Inquisitions as judaizers enough documentation exists to enable a fuller elaboration of the extent and nature of the attachment to Judaism or Judaic practices, in some instances even the motivations. Social and/or commercial contacts with judaizing New Christians may have been a motivation in some cases. In others, projected visions of the benefits of this subaltern religion/culture may have played a role. Joanna Barreta, one-quarter New Christian, Mulata (parda), found herself imprisoned in 1713 by the Inquisition in Brazil, after having been denounced by many people for living under the law of Moses, "with the intention of being saved in it and for observance [...] of the fast of the great day (the day of expiation [i.e., Yom Kippur]), praying the oration of the Our Father without saying Jesus at the end, keeping the Sabbaths as holy days and not eating the meat of pig, rabbit or fish with skin [i.e., without scales]."[17] In short, the behaviors alleged in her case were no different than those of many crypto-Jews of non-Black background, a sign of her 'real' Jewish belief and practices? Only in 1718, after five years of imprisonment, did she confess to maintaining the practices for which she had been denounced. Condemned to abjuring her heresies at the Lisbon auto da fé of 26 June 1720, to imprisonment and the wearing of the penitential habit, she was granted license to return to Rio de Janeiro that September.

Manoel Rodrigues Monsancto of Pernambuco and his wife, as well as his woman slave Beatriz, an African, her Mulata daughter Rachel and her other daughter, married to a Mulato, the son of a Judeoconverso named Solis, were all denounced to the Inquisition in Lisbon in 1646 by the Catholic priest, Manoel de Moraes, himself suspected of being a Calvinist.[18] According to the arrested priest, Manoel Rodrigues, "on arriving in Amsterdam, was circumcised and declared that he had always been a Jew in Brazil, he and his entire house."[19] Another case:

> Among the 78 victims of the auto-da-fé of July 9, 1713, there were 37 men and 41 women. One of the women was the freed Negro slave Marianna, forty years of age, a native of Angola and a resident of Rio de Janeiro; there was also the mulatto Marianna de Andrade, daughter of Catherina, a native and resident of Rio de Janeiro. Both were accused of Judaizing activities and sentenced to carcere e habito perpetuo, perpetual imprisonment and wearing of the penitencial habit. The younger woman was probably the daughter of a Marrano and his Negro slave, who had been converted to Judaism.[20]

Other cases show that charges of judaizing could work even against Afroiberians. Manuel Gonçalves Doria, a Mulato who was awarded knighthood in the Portuguese Order of Santiago around 1627, had his appointment delayed because of accusations that his maternal grandmother, Isabel Fernandes, had either been sentenced as a judaizer herself or descended from New Christians. It turned out from a second investigation into his genealogy, however, that the charge had derived from an enemy of his who seems to have arranged the choice of witnesses in the first investigation. Nonetheless, the pertinent advisory body, as well as the king, denied Doria authorization for the awarding of his honor.[21]

Solange Alberro adduces many cases which, she argues, prove that "the Jewish-Christians," i.e., Judeoconversos, came "to constitute the valued and admired reference" for "these pariahs who are the slaves and the freemen of African origin," linked by them "to the Portuguese rebels [against Spain], victims of oppression like the blacks and mulatos, but who participate without room for doubts in the splendor which confers prestige and social power."[22] These cases hint at the range of possible attributes Jewishness or Judaism might have held for these exiled, destitute Africans: wealth, power, the capacity of defiance.

A few months after a wave of autos de fe in 1651 Mexico City, one slave, Diego de la Cruz denounced himself to the Holy Office, declaring "that he had desired to adopt the Old Law in order to be rich since 'this was the cause by which the Portuguese [i.e., perceived Jews or judaizers] had so much money.'"[23] Such views of material reward had many adherents among non-Blacks as well, of course, and constituted a popular vestige of ancient anti-Jewish rhetoric among non-Jews and of a redemptive logic of resentment among Jews.[24] Such class consciousness among Judeoconversos themselves arises occasionally in Inquisition sources. Testifying against the Mexican Conversa Rafaela Enriquez, an unnamed witness relates the following conversation: Rafaela was chatting at her house with a female friend one day. In walked another acquaintance, someone who "had not wanted to help [fund] by means of a charitable donation the wedding of someone very close to the woman who spoke" with Rafaela. So Rafaela's friend commented pointedly "that God did not have to give goods to the Portuguese because they did not know how to act well toward" one another. The newcomer responded, in resoundingly theological language, that "he did not want to give his hazienda and remain poor, for no one poor is able to be saved."[25] On the other hand, another Mexico City New Christian, Maria de Rivera, supposedly taught another alleged judaizer a prayer that included the following lines:

> Give me honesty
> Against the dishonesties of this world
> Don't give me riches
> That I should grow haughty [me ensoberbesca]
> Nor poverty that brings me down
> Only an alm with which to serve you [God].[26]

Toward the end of the fifteenth century, Pedro de Villanueva of Quintanar, Castile, denied to the inquisitors that his grandfather, Fernán Sánchez de Villanueva, who had converted to Catholicism, had said that "like a good Jew his only wealth was the Law of Moses."[27]

As Alberro suggests, wealth was not the only attraction the Law of the Jews held for downtrodden Afroiberians. The hopes of poor slaves for material ease need no explanation, but the rhetorical use of 'Judaism' by slaves operated on more ideational levels as well. In the 1650s, a slave in Mexico, the Mulato slave Sebastián de los Reyes, wielded the already martyred judaizer Thomas Treviño de Sobremonte as an exemplar.[28] Sobremonte, a wealthy merchant, had become renown for his defiance and even mockery of the Inquisition, up to and including at his dramatic public execution. When drunk, the Mulato slave Sebastián would rave: "I'm not a Christian, I am Treviño."[29] Even years later, another slave in Mexico, a Black woman named Maria de la Cruz or Maria de Armijo, spat out, among other statements deemed to be heretical blasphemies, "that if she had not confessed her crime, it would have been worse than [it was with] Tremiño." The legend of Treviño's life (and/or death) obviously made quite an impression. Maria was said to be over twenty five years old and might actually have seen Treviño's martyrdom first hand.[30] Such sympathetic glances at the fate of crypto-Jews came from non-Afroiberians as well. The Carmelite Ana de Guillamas, tried in Mexico in 1598 as a 'false' visionary (an alumbrada), stated that while she prayed one time "the devil had spoken to her [...] and said, 'Poor Carvajal who was killed without guilt.'"[31] Guillamas was probably referring to Luis de Carvajal, executed the year before, and it is not surprising that she dissociates herself from having originated this thought. New Christians, obviously, were those who most fervently upheld the notion that the victims of the Inquisitions were martyrs.

Some Afroiberians, like others, could not help but be influenced by the riveting fates of Judeoconversos: insiders often persecuted as outsiders, insiders who yet might challenge and even defy the powers-that-be. Hence the disgust with which one mid-seventeenth-century inquisitor described one such scene of cultural contamination:

> Certain Portuguese judaizers presented a Comedy in this city [Mexico City], the author of which was this evil man [whom Blanca Enriquez praised as a "great Jew"], and he gave the foremost seats to two jews who had been reconciled by this H[oly] Office, standing were many other Catholics, and honored, having waiting for those two reconciled to begin the Comedy. After it finished he took them to his house and entertained them, an action so evil that it caused admiration in one Black boçal, slave of one of the Presenters [Actors?], who said (though a barbarian) that they had been at the Comedy in such beautiful seats, just as those seated men had been taken out [as penitents in the auto de fé] in S. Domingo [cathedral] with green candles and yellow caps [capisayos]. Such is the rupture [rotura] and shamelessness with which this infamous jewish people proceeds."[32]

Jews or Judaism, then, sometimes appeared "good for thinking with" (Lévi-Strauss) for Afroiberians as a means of needling their Christian overlords.[33] One wonders, for instance, exactly what was meant by the Mulata servant of a New Christian in Pernambuco, who in 1599 "extolled the New Christians."[34] A startlingly explicit formulation of the logic at work here can be found in the twentieth-century family memoirs of an Afroamerican woman from Philadelphia. Her mother, she writes, would fight prejudice by claiming to belong to whatever group was being denigrated.

> [H]er strategy is usually confined to strangers or people who do not know her very well. Her strategy is to counteract prejudice against any group by immediately informing the speaker that she is a part of whatever group is under attack. If it is the Jews, she is a Jew; if it is the Italians, she is an Italian; if it is the Catholics, she is a Catholic. And there are no exceptions. One day I asked her about Native Americans, and she said, "Well, I just say that my grandfather was one, or my daughter is married to one, or something like that."[35]

A similar tendency manifested itself among Moriscos, Muslims forcibly converted to Christianity during and after the Spanish Reconquista. The slaves Brianda and Andrés Cano, both punished by the tribunal of Córdoba, Andalucía, between 1575 and 1576 for performing Muslim ceremonies, both proffered the transparent provocation "that the Christians are Jews / que los cristianos son judíos."[36] Blanca Becerra, "black in color," slave of Jorge Becerro from Ubeda near Córdoba, probably had something similar in mind when she repeated even after being castigated that "the better law was that of the Jews and not that of the Christians." Being a minor helped this slave escape with no penalty other than a light abjuration of her delinquencies sometime between 1571 and 1572. In addition, variance between the testimony of the witnesses injured the prosecution's case, with "most of them saying that she said that the Jews were better people and more charitable than the Christians," a perhaps more pointed statement, whether she believed it or not.[37]

Utterances like these must be seen in a comparative light. Insulting the dominant religion entailed a tack taken a variety of individuals. In the mid-sixteenth century at least eight Muslim Africans who had been imported to Lisbon found themselves arrested and tried by the Inquisition. Most had asserted "the superiority of Islam over the religion of their Catholic masters, pointing out, among other things, that Christians did not bathe before prayers. Several others expressed the belief that God had no son and that Jesus was the servant of Mohammed."[38] Though here the religion wielded rhetorically was their own, mistreated slaves often put comparative polemics to good use in self-defense. In 1661, one Black slave in Mexico, Nicolás Bazán, begged the inquisitor to ignore the blasphemy he had uttered while enduring a horrific, if altogether common torture administered by his master, assuring him that his suffering as a Christian "'redeemed by Christ's blood at the hands of fellow Christians' was so painful that 'not even among Turks and Moors was a comparable martyrdom endured.'"[39] This appeal was meant to include the slave within the Catholic body politic, as he should have been according to theology, and to remind the inquisitor that Christians were supposed to behave better than 'barbarian' non-believers. White Christians also wielded such polemics when critiquing what they saw as problems within the Christian body politic. A Mexican alumbrado of the sixteenth century, Juan Núñez de León, was accused of having publicly announced that "the Jews kept their God better than the Christians."[40]

Certain cases show how the various facts or fantasies about 'Judaism' were picked up from the environment and came to be put to use. The fifty-year-old Francisca de Carvajal, slave of doña María de Carvajal, "dark black," was apprehended by the Inquisition of Córdoba, Andalucía, sometime in 1598 or 1599 for blasphemy.[41] Because of variations in her testimony, the inquisitors held several audiences with her. In the third one she confessed that on an occasion other than the one pertaining to her crime, when quarreling with some women, they asked her why she did not attend mass, to which she replied "that she did not want to go, that the law of Moses was better than that of God, which she said with the rage that she had because she had heard the law of Moses named in the autos without knowing what it was and without having the intention of following it."[42] Her reference indicated the recent autos de fe in Córdoba aimed at extirpating the alleged conspiracy of judaizing in the area, in which numerous 'judaizers,' real or otherwise, had appeared (25 March 1597: 71 'judaizers' reconciled, 1 burned at the stake; 8 March 1598: 32 'judaizers' reconciled, 1 burned in absentia). Such a confession notwithstanding, in the heat of an argument the law of Moses served this slave well and spontaneously as a tool with which to belittle the Christianity that, for whatever reasons, so frustrated her. Regarding Francisca de Carvajal, as with many of the Afroiberians mentioned above, there is no question of knowledge of Judaism; it simply stands for the anti-norm, which the powerless wield against the norm disempowering them.

Sincere non-White judaizers must have perplexed and enraged Christian ecclesiastical authorities. Such a reaction erupted in 1579, when a Spaniard from Córdoba visiting in Venice sighted in the Ghetto a young Black boy wearing the yellow Jew's cap. Rebuking him, the good Christian visitor, Don Ferdinando de las Infantes, became further exercised on hearing from a local Jew how slaves bought in Constantinople were circumcised, "made of their own law," and brought West (the quote and paragraph are brought in the previous chapter). Don Fernando informed the local Inquisition, which arrested several people, though they could not find the Black youth in question. One of those whom they did interrogate was the

> dark-skinned Samuel Maestro, [who] appeared to be the child of a well-to-do Jew by a middle-aged servant of Ferrara who was "neither white nor black" and was said to be Jewish herself. [....] "Are you not ashamed," the pious Spaniard remonstrated, "you were born black, you have this grace given you by God to be able to turn Christian, and you have become a Jew?"[43]

Christianity, seen as a remedy for Blackness, became conveniently confused with Whiteness. Not surprisingly, such a confusion proliferated in this era. The Jesuit Alonso de Sandoval, in his 1627 tract on Africans and Christianity, argues that given their treatment at the hands of Europeans, most Africans would never voluntarily consent "to receive that water [of baptism] and be like whites."[44] An incident from early New France, i.e., Canada, then very much Jesuit territory, reflects similar notions. One minister to the natives, Father LeJeune, wrote the following back home in 1632:

> I have become a teacher in Canada: the other day I had a little Savage on one side of me, and a little Negro or Moor on the other, to whom I taught their letters... The little Negro was left by the English with this French family which is here. We have taken him to teach and baptize, but he does not yet understand the language well; therefore, we shall wait some time yet... His mistress asking him if he wanted to be a Christian, if he wanted

to be baptized and be like us, he said "yes," but he asked if he would not be skinned in being baptized. I think he was very much frightened, for he had seen these poor Savages skinned. As he saw that they laughed at his questions, he replied in his patois, as best he could: "you say that by baptism I shall be like you: I am black and you are white, I must have my skin taken off then in order to be like you" (this comment followed by general laughter).[45]

The boy's imputation that the priests encouraged the belief in the whitening power of baptism was not false. The famous António Vieira stated in his Epiphany Sermon of 1662: "An Ethiope if he be cleansed in the waters of the Zaire is clean, but he is not white; but if in the water of baptism, he is both."[46]

From the Catholic perspective, Judaism, a deviation from Christianity, turned logically into a deviation from Whiteness. The ostensibly separate discourses of 'religion,' 'race' and 'politics' become entangled, revealed in their entanglement. Conversion 'upward' meant, comprised entrance into the circle of those 'chosen' for acceptance, recognition and citizenship, or so went the rhetoric.[47] In both senses, from the Christian point of view, not only did Judaism not offer non-Whites salvation — terrestrial or celestial — but it stood as a diversion, distraction and mirage for them on their path to the Christian city of heaven.

Esperanza Rodríguez

I turn now to the case of Esperanza Rodríguez, "a mulata, dark, born in the city of Puebla and resident of Mexico City, widow of Juan del Bosque, of the German nation, deceased, is 50 years old, more or less, tall, aged, greying," who was tried as a judaizer by the Mexican Inquisition in the mid-1640s.[48] Also accused were her Mulata daughters, María Rodríguez del Bosque, age 20, Isabel Rodríguez del Bosque, age 25, and Juana Rodríguez del Bosque, age 29.[49] All were arrested in the summer of 1642, along with numerous other alleged marranos, many of whom knew and associated with one another. Esperanza also had two sons, Juan and Diego, the latter a carpenter, neither seemingly connected to marranism. The denouncers of the Rodríguez/Del Bosques include many individuals from the extended circle of judaizers, real or alleged, around the Enriquez clan of Mexico City, many of whom had been born in Seville, like Esperanza Rodríguez, and to many of whom she was related. Solange Alberro writes that Rodríguez's case reflects "a direct participation in Judaism," unlike some of the cases where Judaism was feigned or instrumentalized for various reasons, as I have tried to show in previous chapters.[50]

Esperanza Rodríguez, the daughter of the New Christian Francisco Rodríguez and Isabel, a woman from Guinea, had been a slave of Doña Catalina Enríquez, who had emigrated from Seville to Veracruz. Originally Esperanza had belonged to a Sevillan woman named Ynes Lopez, who may have been the mother of

Francisco Rodríguez, but who definitely was the mother of Catalina Enríquez. As will be seen, the genealogy of Esperanza and her extended family is rather complicated, with the different sources sometimes contradicting each other regarding various family relationships. Ynes gave Esperanza to Catalina and she came along with Catalina to the Americas, residing in Cartagena, Havana, Veracruz, Guadalajara and then, after Esperanza's husband died, Mexico City. Having won her freedom, Esperanza worked as a dressmaker, as did all her daughters.[51] Blanca Enriquez, one of the spiritual leaders of the Mexico City marranos, told Beatriz, her daughter, that Catalina observed the law of Moses.[52]

Esperanza Rodríguez's mother, Isabel, a Black / negra from the West African region called by the Spanish Guinea, had died in Seville when Esperanza had been six or seven. Esperanza asserts that her mother died a free woman.[53] Though Rodríguez at first tells the inquisitors that she does not know anything about her father, she eventually reveals that he had been Francisco Rodríguez, a New Christian of Seville, accused of judaizing.[54] At one point, Esperanza tells the inquisitors that her mother had been the slave of this Francisco Rodrigues, though other testimony states that she was originally the slave of a woman named Ynes Lopez, who might have been Francisco Rodriguez's mother.[55] According to the son-in-law of Blanca Enriquez, Thomas Nuñez de Peralta (married to her daughter Beatriz), Esperanza "was brought up with" Blanca, who, the matriarch of the extended Enríquez clan.[56] A close family friend of Blanca Enriquez, Blanca Mendez de Rivera, from the same generation as Esperanza and Blanca, says that she "knew [Esperanza] from the city of Seville" and that Esperanza had been the daughter of a female slave (Isabel) belonging to a Portuguese widow named Ynes Lopez.[57] Ynes Lopez had been married to a Portuguese merchant of Seville named Rodrigo Fernandez Salçedas and had immigrated to Veracruz, where she passed away. Catalina Enriquez was their daughter, Francisco Rodríguez's sister and thus Esperanza's aunt.[58] Lopez had given the young Esperanza to Catalina as part of the latter's dowry.[59]

Whoever owned Isabel, Esperanza's mother, she seems to have been unmarried, along with some 80 percent of the slave women in Seville.[60] In the late 16th century the city hosted the second highest population of Africans in Europe, after Lisbon. Yet despite an extremely high rate of endogamous marriages among the slave and free Afroiberians, a growing population of Mulatos developed, making Esperanza a typical child of a common, unofficial and clearly tolerated White-Black, free-slave kind of concubinage.

[Fig. __: Genealogy of Esperanza Rodríguez and the Extended Enriquez Family, from Seville to Mexico City]

Though the full genealogy remains unclear, Ynes Lopez and the Mexico City Enríquez clan were related to one another, while Esperanza Rodríguez also shared blood ties, not to mention long-standing familiarity, with various members of the extended set of families. Ynes Lopez's first cousins included the daughters of clan matriarch Blanca Enriquez. Pedro de Espinosa, husband of Ysabel de Silva (Blanca's sister), was the son of Simon Rodríguez, who was the brother of Esperanza's father, Francisco Rodríguez.[61] The husband of Esperanza's owner,

Catalina Enríquez, was Pedro Arias Maldonado, first cousin of Antonio Rodríguez Arias, Blanca's husband. A merchant, Arias Maldonado conducted trade with partners in Mexico City and Havana. Antonio was called "the famous Jew" by the inquisitors. He and Blanca were married at Arias Maldonado's house in Seville. Maria de Rivera, daughter of Blanca de Rivera, both supposedly involved in the Enriquez clan's judaizing activities, had married Manuel de Granada. Manuel's father had been Antonio de Granada (or at least so Esperanza Rodríguez thinks she recalls his name), who passed away in Seville. Esperanza's mother had cooked for him. Esperanza states that these Granadas are relatives of hers through her father, Francisco Rodríguez.[62] Esperanza's son, Diego, was married to Geronima de Miranda, whose cousin was Gaspar de Robles, another accused judaizer in the Enriquez family circle.[63] Other ties also existed.

Esperanza Rodríguez's story is both remarkable and typical for an age of incipient globalization and ethnic-racial intermingling. She had remained in Seville, in the house of Pedro Arias Maldonado and Catalina Enriquez until the age of seventeen or eighteen. At the end of this period she spent a year in a convent of the nuns of Nuestra Señora de Socorro (Our Lady of Help), along with her mistress Catalina, as Arias Maldonado had gone to Havana. The convent, dedicated to Santa María del Socorro, was one of four such institutions in Seville founded by the Franciscan Order of the Immaculate Conception. According to its 1522 founding deed, the convent was to follow the constitution of the Hieronymite order and be subject to the Monastery of Saint Jerónimo de Buenavista. Many scholars have noted the attraction of conversos to and their prevalence in the Hieronymite order, with its more internal, Pauline approach to religiosity.[64] This affiliation led the order to ban New Christians in 1489.

Arias Maldonado was killed in Havana and soon after Catalina left with Esperanza for the Caribbean in order to recover his estate. They arrived in Cartagena de las Indias around 1602 and shortly thereafter left for Havana.[65] Rodríguez married Juan Baptista del Bosque in Havana around 1606.[66] The couple remained together in Havana for about a year, at which point she accompanied Baptista del Bosque back to Cartagena, where he worked as a sculptor for around five years. Her owner, Catalina, seems to have remained in Havana during this time. Rodríguez and her husband then left Cartagena and met up with Catalina in Veracruz, but after fifteen days left for Mexico City, where the couple resided for four or five years. In Mexico City Rodríguez ran a shop. At some point Bautista del Bosque got work in the port city of Acapulco and Rodríguez went to be with him. After two and a half years they returned to Mexico City. After another four or five years they transferred to Guadalajara, where they lived for ten or twelve years and where Rodríguez again operated a store.[67] Baptista del Bosque died around 1629 in Guadalajara, about five years after their arrival there.[68] Their long marriage, terminated only because of Del Bosque's death, seems to reflect an impressively stable relationship. Rodríguez moved back to Mexico City with all her children sometime between 1634 and 1636.[69] Joan Bristol rightfully suggests that Esperanza made this move in order to reunite with her extended clan from Seville.[70]

An Extended Family of Fervent Marranos?

According to the inquisitional testimony of many witnesses, the Enriquez family matriarch Blanca comes across as a fervent marrano, knowledgeable about crypto-Jewish practices, possibly even capable in Hebrew. Ysavel de Silva testifies that Blanca's mother, Juana Rodríguez, had been imprisoned by the Inquisition already back in Seville.[71] Also supposedly tried by the Seville tribunal were Francisco Rodriguez, Esperanza's father, Ynes Lopez and her sister Ana Enríquez, and Blanca Enríquez.[72] Many other members of the interlocking network of families appear to have been active judaizers back in Spain and Portugal as well, while some lived as open Jews in Italy. A comprehensive portrait is beyond the scope of this chapter, but the following examples from Mexico City hopefully will more than suffice. Various people are said to have gathered on Saturdays at the house of Juana Enriquez, Blanca's daughter, in order to celebrate the sabbath.[73] Blanca and her daughters are said to have fasted on Fridays.[74] Before fasts, Blanca would bathe and put on clean clothes.[75] Maria Baptista, a Mestiza who worked in the house of Blanca Enriquez as a servant or slave, and served as well her daughter Beatriz Enriquez, relates that she saw that in the houses of Micaela and Rafaela Enriquez (Beatriz's sisters) meat was soaked in water to remove the blood, while the throats of chickens were cut in her own house, and that Ysavel de Silva (Espinosa), Blanca's sister, "ordered her black Margarita" to do these tasks, basic requirements of keeping kosher.[76] Pedro Tinoco describes to his inquisitors how his grandmother Blanca Enriquez once called him alone to her and had him prepare bread, following her instructions, such as using a new knife. But this was bread unlike "the ordinary bread that the catholics eat," and she explained to him that this was "the bread of bitterness that the Israelites ate in the desert" and that now must be eaten by those who observe the Law of Moses, clear allusions to matzah and Passover.[77] In addition to making matzah with her daughter Beatriz several times, Blanca gave her as well an extended explanation of the history and meaning of this bread "without yeast nor salt," which the ancient Israelites "ate together with much parsley and many herbs and which in memory of this the observers of the Law of Moses have to eat three days before the Passover of the Resurrection that the Christians celebrate." Blanca used only new utensils when preparing her matzah — a traditional precaution of Jews to ensure complete kashrut for Passover. Blanca (and Beatriz) even knew some of the terminology involved, as well as the halakhic requirement of removing and burning a bit of the dough: "having burned [?; açetado] the sacrifice of the Jala [challah bread], which was that little piece of massa [matzah] that she removed from the middle of what she had in the new saucepan." Blanca made from her dough only the three tortitas ritually required for the central Passover seder plate.[78]

Among others, Gaspar Váez Sevilla (son of Juana Enríquez and the wealthy merchant Simon Váez Sevilla) tells the inquisitors that he and other family members observed "the great fast," i.e., Yom Kippur.[79] At least when Blanca Enríquez fell sick, relates Catalina Enríquez, she and her sisters gathered to celebrate "the fast of the great day" at their mother's house, each bringing a candle to light "as a ceremony of the said law," and covering each candle with a box. Blanca recited some prayers which the others did not understand. Catalina's sister Beatriz prayed barefoot (on Yom Kippur leather was not worn and, hence, most shoes). Robert Ferry nicely connects going barefoot with Catholic practice, as taken up by Teresa de Jesús, among many others.[80] This all took place the evening of the holiday. The next day, all simply fasted until nightfall, each then going home to break the fast with a supper of fish.[81] In his own testimony, Pedro Tinoco recounts one such occasion when all those present "got on their knees, the said Blanca Enriquez, standing and putting her hands over their heads, recited the blessing of Abraham, Isaac & Jacob," also saying "other words that this confessant did not understand well."[82] Beatriz Enriquez relates that after the blessing "each asked forgiveness of the other, the younger ones then embracing the elders."[83]

According to the testimony of one witness, one year thirteen members of the clan plus six other intimate associates observed the fast of the Queen of Esther, a popular marrano 'festival' in honor of this ancient proto-Conversa heroine.[84] Juana Tinoco (daughter of Catalina Enríquez) says that the fast of Queen Esther was at least sometimes conducted in her house.[85] One witness, Ysavel de Silva, tells the inquisitors that she heard that when Beatriz Enríquez was ill at one point, her sisters, including Catalina, said prayers for her that included the word "Adonay."[86] Mixing Catholic practice with Jewish intentions, Beatriz relates how Blanca and her daughters would light candles, usually three, at the supper of certain fasts. In Beatriz's case, "the one in honor of the God of Israel, the second for the health of her spouse and good tidings [buenos suçessos] and the third for herself."[87] When Violante Suarez says she asked her aunt Micaela Enríquez to make her a scapular of Our Lady of Mercy — a cloth shawl covering both the front and back; part of the habit of many religious orders — the latter responded that she couldn't, for she and all of her sisters followed the law (of Moses). Around the same time, Violante's aunt Beatriz Enriquez supposedly mentioned to her that a man who lived in Mexico City had asked to marry Beatriz but that her mother Blanca would not allow it "because he was not an observer of the said law of Moses."[88]

When Blanca Enríquez passed away, according to the Mestiza Maria Baptisa, Juana Enríquez "sent to her house" for a piece of new linen cloth (tocro de lino) and "cut a tora [sic] for the said deceased."[89] Esperanza Rodríguez, among others (see below), washed Blanca's head after she died, in order to clean off the blood that had come from "a little dove that they had placed" there.[90] Washing the head was a component of the traditional Jewish ritual for preparing the corpse for burial. After the funeral, "peeled, hard-boiled eggs" were distributed among her children and grandchildren.[91] Eggs comprise a food rich in symbolism, used on many ritual occasions; a sign of fertility, future possibility and eternity, their roundness alludes to the natural cycles of life, the fact that they can be easily broken but never reconstructed a kind of reminder of the fragility of life. During mourning, they are eaten by traditional Jews before getting to the more common main dishes.[92] Other witnesses corroborate the distribution and eating of eggs, including Pedro Tinoco, who says that during the first days of mourning they would eat hard-boiled egg from which the shell had been removed, without salt, "according to their custom,

[...] as a sign of sadness for the relatives of the deceased."[93] Various family members supposedly gathered at Blanca's house on the third day after her death, to share a supper of fish and eggs together.[94] Like other marranos, Beatriz says this is called "the Bird of Light / Ave Luz," which, whether referring to the eggs themselves or the whole mourning ritual, is either a sign that Beatriz knew the Hebrew term for mourning, avelut, whether she understood it or not — a hyperliteralistic Inquisition scribe then made it Spanish, ave luz — or constitutes a misunderstanding or creative translation of this term Hebrew term.[95]

Blanca Enriquez is alleged to have instructed various family members in religious matters. Pedro Tinoco testifies that his grandmother advised him to observe the Law of Moses, "in which it is necessary to be saved" and which "was better than that of my lord Jesus Christ which this confessant observed."[96] Isabel Tinoco, Pedro's sister, tells the inquisitors that she observed the law of Moses because her grandmother Blanca taught it to her when she was a girl. A few days after her instruction, Isabel says, she asked Blanca if she had taught others, to which her grandmother replied that she had taught the Law of Moses to Catalina, Isabel's mother, as well as Isabel's brothers Pedro and Miguel; that her sister Juana "knows the law;" to Isabel's aunt Juana and her son Gaspar Baez; to Isabel's aunt Rafaela and her two daughters Ana and Blanca; to Isabel's aunts Michaela and Beatriz.[97] Beatriz Enriquez states that when she was around the age of twelve her mother Blanca told her that "she should believe in the one sole true God and should observe the law of Moses" and that she has also taught the law to all her other daughters.[98] Beatriz recites for the inquisitors two prayers that her mother taught her, which she said daily, the first in the morning when arising and the second at night before retiring.[99]

Ysavel de Silva claims that Raphaela Enríquez called her sister Juana Enriquez "Queen of the Jewesses and that all the women kissed her feet." It seems Silva, who is here reporting jailhouse conversations, means this in a concrete, ritual sense; she also speaks of "the vice-queen (virreyna) who had arrived."[100] Some in the community considered Gaspar, the infant son of Juana Enríquez and Simón Váez Sevilla, to be the messiah they awaited as conversos. When this turned out not to be the case, other women were considered as potential mothers of the messiah, including, ultimately, Juana Enríquez.[101] While the deceased Blanca Enriquez was burned only in effigy at the 11 April 1649 auto de fé, her daughter Catalina was executed alive, along with Catalina and Maria de Rivera, Ysabel de Silva and all too many others. Various other members of the clan came out of the Inquisition trials with their lives intact, more or less, and relatively lighter punishments.

Becoming Marrano

As for Esperanza Rodríguez, she appears to have been a familiar and active participant in the Enriquez family's circle of judaizers. Thomas Nuñez de Peralta, husband of Beatriz Enriquez, tells the inquisitors that his mother-in-law Blanca Enríquez told him on one occasion that Esperanza was God-fearing and "a good woman," a code word for her being an observer of the Law of Moses.[102] Various permutations of the same basic story about Rodríguez's coming to Judaism circulated. Ysavel Antunes, a close associate of the Enríquez family, imprisoned as a judaizer by the Mexico City tribunal, confesses that she and Rodríguez declared themselves to one another as observers of the Law of Moses "on many occasions," and that Rodríguez told her "how she had been taught it by them in Seville," that is, how she had been taught the Law of Moses by members of her family.[103] Clara de Rivera also relates that when Rodríguez and her daughters visited the house of Clara's mother, Blanca Mendez de Rivera, Rodríguez told them "that she had been taught [the Law] in Seville."[104] Blanca Mendez de Rivera claims that she and her daughters declared themselves to Rodríguez as observers of the Law of Moses, and vice versa, "on different occasions" and that Rodríguez had told her that she had been taught the Law of Moses in Seville by a Portuguese widow named Ynes Lopez. Later, Blanca deposes that Ynes Lopez had told her herself about teaching Rodríguez.[105] According to Raphaela Enríquez, Rodríguez was taught the Law of Moses by "a mistress of hers, the mother of a Doña Catalina who is in vera cruz."[106] Ysavel de Silva thinks she heard from Blanca Enriquez that Rodríguez's mother Isabel "also knew of the said law. And had been a prisoner in the Inquisition of Seville three days."[107] In their summary of the case and sentencing the inquisitors make no mention of Isabel's judaizing, however.[108]

Rodríguez's first encounter with a 'judaizer,' as far as she tells it to her inquisitors, was striking. It took place more than thirty years earlier, in Seville, yet her memory of it seems fraught with emotion still. The incident only emerges in her response to the charges read to her by her inquisitors, that is, relatively late in her trial. She says that an old Portuguese woman, Maria Hernandez, lived right next door and the young Esperanza could see into her house through the kitchen window. Esperanza watched her conduct fasts at nighttime, or so she claims. One day Hernandez asked her to give an afternoon snack to her son, about seven years old. The young Esperanza gave him a piece of bread with a slice of ham. Discovering this, Hernandez smacked it away, knocking it to the ground, shouting at her son not to eat pig. Offended, Rodríguez said that she must be a Jewess if she is not allowed to eat pig meat. Hernandez "made her cry," Rodríguez tersely reports. All of this seems to have caused Rodríguez's masters amusement ("they laughed to/among themselves").[109] On the one hand, given other testimony, including her own, that she was taught the Law of Moses by either Ynes Lopez or Catalina Enríquez, this anecdote about a neighbor may just be an attempt to dissemble. On the other hand, regardless of the names involved, the manner in which Rodríguez reports the episode reveals the deep and confusing emotions caused to this young slave girl by the contradictory religious dictates motivating the different individuals, herself included, and by her relatively powerless position resulting from her less than full knowledge in a situation in which she is still expected to know how to act.

After her arrest, when pressed for her genealogy by the inquisitors, Rodríguez, who so far has said nothing about her New Christian father, insists she has no memory of them: "as she does not know who her father was, neither does she know who her grandparents were."¹¹⁰ But her silence does not last lost. Rodríguez, finally giving information (accurate or not) to the inquisitors after a few months in prison, relating that Ynes Lopez began teaching her the Law of Moses when she was about twelve or thirteen. Rodríguez, possibly trying to stall the inquisitors' search for information, first divulges matter from years earlier, information that incriminates others rather than herself, and that incriminates people already deceased. One afternoon, says Rodríguez, Lopez, along with her cousins Margarita and Beatriz Enríquez (Lopez's daughter Catalina Enríquez was also present), called the young Esperanza over and tried to persuade her not to believe in Christ nor in his mother Maria, nor to make anything of the sacred images of the religion built around them. The latter attack aimed at various images of Mary that Esperanza possessed (currosas estampadas [...] de bulto). Esperanza was told that one should believe only "in a single God who was called aDonay." If she were to accede to these requests, her mistress "would give her freedom, she would be very happy, and greatly fortunate." The young Esperanza supposedly "replied to them with the art of confusion that she would look into this," but their importunities and promises of benefits, combined with Esperanza's young age, ignorance and vulnerability led her to yield, which caused them "particular joy."¹¹¹ Catalina Enríquez, who "also showed pleasure," said that "with her husband Pedro arrias she would do it [so that Rodríguez] would be given liberty."¹¹² In testimony given after having heard the charges against her and responding to them, Rodríguez says that it was Margarita Enríquez who had promised her liberty, "a thing greatly desired by slaves," and at the time she had been "between nine and ten years old."¹¹³

Because of the testimony of Rodríguez and others, Ynes Lopez was relaxed in absencia at the 11 April 1649 auto de fé in Mexico City.¹¹⁴ Lopez's daughter Catalina Enríquez also appeared at the same auto, aged 80 years old, where she was reconciled with a formal abjuration. Her goods were confiscated at her arrest She is accused of having judaized continuously since the age of twelve. In her confessions, she claims that after her incarceration she saw in her dreams a crucified Christ surrounded by innumerable lights and resplendent glories. This, she asserts, indicates her good intentions. Her many confessions and desperate pleas for mercy did not prevent her from dying while still in prison. Though the inquisitors granted that she died "with signs of penitence," her goods were nonetheless confiscated.¹¹⁵

Rodríguez seems to have been active as a judaizer and known as such by many. She is said to have made and attended various fasts, including those devoted to Queen Esther, which lasted three days, the number of days the biblical Esther fasted before calling on King Ahasuerus to beg the king to save the Jews from the wicked Haman.¹¹⁶ Many witnesses testify to gathering for fasts at Rodríguez's house or going there simply to pass the fast day. Pedro de Espinosa thinks that his wife, Ysavel de Silva, confided in Rodríguez that he was an observer of the Law of Moses, a sure sign of trust, and, in any case, he himself declared being an observer of the Law of Moses with Rodríguez, her daughter Juana and her son Diego, and vice versa, at Rodríguez's house.¹¹⁷ Antonio Lopez de Orduña relates that he and Rodríguez declared themselves to one another.¹¹⁸ Catalina Enríquez (the daughter of Blanca, not the former mistress of Rodríguez) claims that one day, "a long time ago," Rodríguez paid her a visit. Offering her guest a drink of chocolate, Rodríguez declined, saying that she couldn't because "she was doing a fast of the law of Moses."[119] Catalina's sister Beatriz Enríquez claims that Rodríguez declared herself in her presence and names Esperanza as someone who was present at one fish supper, at least, held on a "meat day / dia de carne," one of many conducted by the extended family.[120] It seems Rodríguez hosted one such supper of fish after the death of Leonor de Roxas, attended by some fifteen individuals from the Enríquez clan's circle.[121] During cuaresma of 1642, according to Juana Enríquez, when her sister Beatriz was badly ill, Rodríguez was one of the women who fasted for the return of her health.[122] When Catalina Enríquez (Blanca's daughter) was informed of the death of her father, Antonio Rodríguez Arias, she happened to be in the company of most of the women of the clan, including Rodríguez, who was among those who fasted on the third day after the death.[123] Rodríguez was present at Blanca Enríquez's final hours.[124] Catalina Enríquez, Ysavel de Silva and Beatriz Enríquez relate separately to the inquisitors that after Blanca's death Rodríguez was among the women who washed the body, dressed it in a new shirt set aside for this purpose and arranged the deceased on the bed.[125] Juana Enríquez claims to have been told by her mother Blanca before her death "to buy four or five yards of Ruan [fabric]," which she sent "to the house of Esperanza Rodríguez so that she would make a shroud for her said mother."[126] Rodríguez was present at the gathering of the Enríquez clan that took place the day Blanca Enríquez was buried (in the Carmen convent).[127] Rodríguez was one of the attendees at the fast of mourning held the day after the burial of Diego Antunes.[128]

In her own depositions, Rodríguez confirms many of the above allegations and adds details of her own.[129] Rodríguez testifies that she and Blanca Enríquez declared themselves to one another many times back in Seville, as was also the case with Justa Mendez, Blanca de Rivera's sister, and Mendez's spouse. In both Seville and in Mexico City, Rodríguez "saw" Blanca Enríquez conduct so many fasts of the Great Day, of Queen Esther and ordinary fasts that she can't count them all.[130] Rodríguez and Blanca Enríquez were clearly close to one another. Rodríguez testifies that Blanca would visit her house in Mexico City.[131] According to Rodríguez, Blanca Enríquez's mother, a Portuguese "Jewess" named Juana Rodríguez "was very happy to see this confessant become Jewish."[132] This statement reflects either this woman's great desire to see this Mulata slave girl join the family religion, perhaps because of special qualities she recognized in her, perhaps because of Rodríguez's New Christian paternal blood (or both), or it might reflect Rodríguez's great desire to be wanted. Rodríguez was present at the "Jewish" wedding of Maria de Rivera and Manuel de Granada (in Seville?) and she confesses that she and the Riveras declared themselves to one another "various times and that they did fasts together many times, that she couldn't come up with a definite number of these fasts because they were so many."[133] The Rivera women apparently spent various fasts at Rodríguez's house, as did Ysabel Duarte, widow of Diego Antunes, with her son Manuel.[134] Not only did Rodríguez and Juana

Enríquez (daughter of Blanca) declare themselves to one another "very many times," but Juana, from whom Rodríguez frequently received dress work, was her godmother (comadre) in the realm of their Catholic existence.¹³⁵ Rodríguez claims that when she married Juan Bautista del Bosque, her coreligionists Blanca Enríquez and her former mistress Catalina Enríquez held it to be a bad thing, as "he was not Jewish but German."¹³⁶

If accurate, the testimony of Juan de León/Salomón , provides a glimpse into the social network of Esperanza Rodríguez. One day he went to visit the elderly Blanca Enríquez, with whom he maintained close relations, and who lived at the time with her daughter Beatriz. He found there with them "an old mulata named doña Esperanza Rodríguez." That is, Rodríguez happened to be in the company of some of her relatives, however distant. In the presence of this Mulata, Blanca Enríquez narrated to De León/Machorro some things about his grandfather, Rodrigo Rodríguez, who had died in Antequera, Spain or Nueva Granada. Thus, Blanca Enríquez

> came to tell the said Esperanza Rodríguez who this confessant [León/Machorro] was and that he kept the said Law of Moses, to which the said Esperanza Rodríguez responded that she had heard about or [had] known the said Rodrigo Rodríguez, grandfather of this confessant, and then the said doña Blanca told him how the said Esperanza Rodríguez was an observer of the said Law of Moses, and the said Esperanza Rodríguez said that it was indeed true that she kept the said Law.¹³⁷

Esperanza Rodríguez is obviously the "unnamed mulata judaizer," about whom Solange Alberro speculates; "having gained the respect of honored judaizers among the 17th-century Mexican community, [she] even organized in her house fasts that were well-attended."¹³⁸

It must be noted that Rodríguez, like so many New Christians and acculturated Africans, knew how to cross herself and say the Pater Noster, Ave Maria, Credo and Salve Regina well in Spanish. She also insists that she heard mass and confessed regularly.¹³⁹ Before her two youngest daughters began observing the Law of Moses, Rodríguez would spend entire days on which she was fasting at the church of Santa Clara with them, "in order to dissemble and distract herself" from her hunger.¹⁴⁰

From her teachers Rodríguez seems to have learned much and well. She is accused of explaining to her daughter Ysavel that when one fasts "one should not be menstruating but be very clean" and that one should observe the sabbath — on Saturday, of course — by not working. Rodríguez allegedly knew enough to inform Ysavel de Silva regarding the burning of candles on the fast of the Great Day — the marrano Yom Kippur — "that she never had burned them because it was an invention." In other words, that burning candles in this manner was borrowed from Catholic practice.¹⁴¹ In fact, Jews light candles at the evening entrance of the holy day. Rodríguez is said to have told her daughters that on fast days "one must not enter the churches of the christians" (though she allegedly frequently did exactly this, as was just mentioned).[142] Supposedly, Rodríguez taught her daughters, Ysavel and Maria, the following prayer, to be said daily:

> With the weapons of Adonai
> I go armed.
> With the cape of Abraham
> I go covered.
> With the faith of Ishmael
> in my prayer,
> wherever [God?] wants that I go and come
> Good and bad people I will meet.
> The good should come to me
> The bad should be intimidated by me
> that I not fear the rod of justice
> neither the jailer nor the [Inquisition] agent
> that he will not be able to harm me
> nor initiate evil
> nor [do] more evil than that which
> Haman did to Mordechai.
> Con las armas de Adonai
> ando armadas.
> Con la capa de Abraham
> ando couijada.
> Con la fee de Ysmael
> en mi oracion.
> por donde quiera que fuere y Viniere
> Buenos y malos encontrare.
> Los Buenos se me llegaran
> Los malos se me arredraran
> que no temere bara de justiçia
> ni alcalde ni familiar
> que no me podra maleçer
> ni mal empeçer
> ni mas mal de lo que passo
> Aman sobre Mordocheo.[143]

This prayer contains some intriguing features. Marrano prayers took three forms: (1) traditional prayers handed down from one generation to the next, regardless of how distorted; (2) original prayers formulated by individuals based on specific needs, desires, situations; (3) combinations of the two forms. As far as I can recall, Rodríguez's prayer does not have traditional antecedents, though some of its lines hearken to known Jewish prayers. For instance, the line referring to meeting good and bad people and being kept safe from the latter vaguely echoes a prayer from the morning service, the Yehi Ratzon, that derives from the ancient sage, Rabbi Yehuda HaNasi, while the general tenor of the prayer vaguely resembles other morning prayers said by other ancient sages, all listed in the same talmudic passage (BT Berakhot 16b-17a).[144] Rodríguez's prayer obviously refers explicitly to functionaries of the Inquisitions, whose malevolent powers God is asked to avert. As was not uncommon in marrano discourse, the marrano sees herself here as Mordechai, persecuted by the powerful servant to the Crown, Haman, who represents the Inquisition. Through the surprising appearance of the figure of Ishmael, the prayer reminds us of the importance of Moorish or Islamic tropes in anti-establishment Iberian discourse. This marrano seems to envision herself and her group as downtrodden in the same way as is Ishmael, the son from the 'wrong' side of the family. Many scholars have pointed to the symbolic importance of the Moriscos in the Iberian imaginary. Irene Silverblatt mentions that Moriscas were "commonly held to be experts in occult matters."[145] A Mexican Mulato, Francisco Ruíz de Castrejon, who was accused in 1597 of witchcraft and making a pact with the devil, was allegedly called by his Amerindian acquaintances Mahoma, that is Mohammed.[146] The imprisoned priest Francisco de la Cruz characterizes part of his own anti-establishment mysticism, including a one-time dialogue with God against Rome, as one in which both De la Cruz and God speak "in the way that moriscos who are not very ladinos pronounce the Castillian language."[147] As far afield as the Philippines, a festival of "Moors and Christians," re-enacting and celebrating the triumph of reconquista was regularly held into the seventeenth century.[148] Both of these features — anti-Inquisition rhetoric/magic and Morisco/Muslim symbology — percolate through the religious-magical practices of Afroiberians, as discussed in an earlier chapter. That they surface in a prayer of a Mulata judaizer in New Spain, whose African mother might have worshipped according to the Law of Moses in the formerly Muslim city of Seville, not only makes perfect sense, but adds poignant nuance to the heritage of her religious discourse.

Testifying to Esperanza's parental pedagogy, her daughters also seem to have been involved to some degree in the Enríquez clan's judaizing activities, especially the oldest, Juana. Juana's husband, Blas Lopez, allegedly told Blanca Enríquez that he married her because "she was of a good heart," in other words, that she was an observer of the Law of Moses.[149] Esperanza supposedly told Blanca Mendez de Rivera that she had taught Juana the Law while the latter was still a child and tells her inquisitors the same thing, though she later changes her testimony and claims that Blas Lopez had taught Juana.[150] Juana herself testifies that she learned the Law of Moses from her spouse and his family around 1632, over the course of a period of about fifteen days.[151] Isabel Antunes offers a similar story, saying that Juana "was taught [the Law] by Blass Lopez her husband, being in Guadalaxara, where she married him."[152] Esperanza "showed great joy that this confessant [Juana] observed" the Law and that "her husband had taught it to her."[153] Shortly after this Juana and Blas Lopez celebrated their first "fast of the great day" together.[154] In this same deposition Juana makes it sound as if until this point she was unaware that her mother also observed the Law of Moses, but it seems likely that Rodríguez had ensured that Juana married a marrano. (Is it possible that Lopez was related to the same Ynes Lopez to whom Esperanza's mother had belonged and who had brought the young Esperanza into judaizing?). The next September Juana and Esperanza celebrated the Great Day fast together, washing their heads, putting on clean clothes and supping that evening on eggs and vegetables. The next day they fasted at home through the afternoon.[155] Pedro Tinoco thinks he recalls Juana attending one or more of the quasi-ritual suppers held as Blanca Enriquez grew increasingly ill and close to death, while Juana says that she participated in the fast of mourning held the day after the burial of Diego Antunes.[156] Juana confesses to attending suppers with her mother after her first Great Day fast, at which she, her husband and her mother all declared themselves to one another.[157] According to Blanca Mendez de Rivera, Juana confessed herself to her and her daughters as a marrano, and they to her.[158] Ysavel de Rivera says that one day when she and her sister Margarita were fasting they went to the house of Rodríguez at mid-day, where they continued the fast with Esperanza and Juana.[159]

When Rodríguez finally taught Ysavel and Maria the Law of Moses she conveyed to them exactly what she had learned from Ynes Lopez and her cousins: "that they should not believe in the most holy Virgin nor in Christ nor should they adore the Images."[160] After having fasted on behalf of Blanca Enríquez and after having been taught the Law of Moses by Rodríguez, her daughters Ysavel and Maria were said to have declared themselves to Ysavel and Margarita de Rivera. Both Ysavel and Maria Rodríguez del Bosque would sleep over at the house of Ysavel de Rivera, who was about their age.[161] Simon Suarez de Espinosa claims that his wife, Juana Tinoco, the younger Catalina Enríquez's daughter, told him that Rodríguez had taught the Law to her daughters Ysavel and Maria.[162] When Maria de Rivera and all of her daughters were arrested by the Inquisition, her son Rafael de Granada went to Juana Rodríguez's house, a sign of their closeness.[163]

The nature and extent of the Rodríguez del Bosque sisters' crypto-Jewish knowledge does not seem particularly vast. Juana knows that certain things are ceremonies of the Law of Moses: fasting on the Great Day until nightfall; eating hard-boiled eggs after a death; fasting after a death; the closest friend(s) or relative(s) of the new widow/er send food; to pour out the water at the house of the deceased. The sisters evince certain theopolitical interests, at least as their situation deteriorates. After their imprisonment, some of the Rodríguez del Bosque sisters and Enríquez sisters carry on extended conversations from their cells. Among the many topics they discuss is a mysterious man, a gentleman (muy hidalgo) of illustrious lineage, from Bragança, who is present in the kingdom to liberate them. He is in contact with the king of France and of Portugal, even has orders from the Spanish king to remedy the ongoing abuses. The women talk about God giving long life to the king of Portugal, that the kingdom should thrive; that of all places they could only live safely in Portugal.[164] I was not able to determine the identity of this mysterious savior, but he would seem to be connected, whether in the sisters' minds or in reality, with the Duke of Bragança and his recent secession from Spain.

Within the Bosom of the Clan: From Slave to Elder

According to Blanca Mendez de Rivera, just after Blanca Enríquez passed away (in late 1641), Esperanza Rodríguez told her that Blanca Enríquez's daughter Beatriz gave her seventy pesos for her and her daughters to observe fasts in honor of the soul of Blanca Enríquez. Ysabel and Maria supposedly told Blanca de Rivera about these fasts as well. Rodríguez also allegedly told Blanca Mendez de Rivera some days later, at the latter's house, how after having received the seventy pesos she had instructed her two younger daughters, Ysabel and Maria, in the Law of Moses, in order that they be able to carry out the necessary fasts along with their older sister Juana, who evidently was already inside the judaizing circle. Blanca de Rivera goes on to claim that Esperanza, Ysabel and Maria then declared to one another their mutual allegiance to the Law of Moses.[165] According to Beatriz herself, she gave Rodríguez seventy pesos.[166] Esperanza's daughter Juana testifies that Beatriz gave Esperanza "eighty or ninety pesos," which she saw the former bring.[167] Catalina Enríquez was given by their mother Blanca the key to a trunk containing money, from which Catalina distributed 400 pesos as alms with her own hands to various individuals, including Esperanza Rodríguez. Beatriz herself says that the alms were to go to observers of the Law of Moses.[168] According to her daughter Juana, Rodríguez "fasted three or four Mondays" for the sake of the soul of Blanca Enríquez.[169]

The fact that Beatriz Enríquez offered Rodríguez money to perform a spiritual favor sheds some light on the latter's relationship to the crypto-Jewish community. On the one hand, leaving money for the reciting of certain prayers or psalms on behalf of the dead comprised standard practice within both Judaism and Catholicism. Blanca Enríquez left money so that masses should be said on her behalf in at least two local churches.[170] Beatriz asserts that paying people to perform fasts is a "custom" among observers of the Law of Moses.[171] Blanca de Rivera states that Beatriz Enríquez asked other daughters and grandchildren of Blanca Enríquez to observe similar fasts, offering them a mere peso or a few, openly given and accepted as alms, while Beatriz testifies that Maria de Rivera was sent two pesos so that her two daughters should fast.[172] On the other hand, Rodríguez, as both a beloved former slave and a Mulata, may have stood unclearly defined in relation to this clan of marranos. Despite the many attestations of familiarity cited above, the intimacy of relations do not seem to have been consistent among all members of these marrano circles. The husband of Beatriz Enríquez, Thomas Nuñez de Peralta, for instance, claims never to have communicated with Rodríguez, while Raphaela Enríquez fails to include her in the list of those present after the burial of Blanca Enriquez.[173] Beatriz Enríquez herself testifies that though she knew from others that Rodríguez was an observer of the law of Moses and that Beatriz had had various interactions with her, the two women had never declared themselves to one another until the death of Beatriz's mother, Blanca.[174] Raphaela Enríquez says that though she knew Rodríguez, the two never spoke about judaizing matters.[175] Blanca Mendes de Rivera, who knew Rodríguez already in Seville, claims that neither "she nor her daughters ever did a fast in [Rodríguez's] company, but when they declared themselves to one another they said that they had done the fasts."[176] Ysavel de Rivera allegedly asked Ysavel Rodríguez del Bosque whether her two brothers were Jews. When Rodríguez del Bosque replied in the negative, Rivera exclaimed that "Esperanza Rodríguez was worthless and that they would have to bring the demons because she had not taught [her sons] / era para poco, y se la auian de llevar los diablos porque no los auia enseñado."[177]

Even within these ostensibly tightly knit crypto-Jewish circles race or social status appears to have surfaced as a factor. Though her father was a Judeoconverso, almost every witness for the Inquisition who refers to her mentions her status as a Mulata. In other words, they choose to highlight her mother's Afroiberian lineage (just as I do, I must confess). Beatriz Enríquez says, seemingly distantly, that she also distributed monies to "a mulata called esperanza Rodríguez." Others, such as Blanca and Clara de Rivera, identify her as "a mulata called Esperanza Rodríguez," putting her racial status before her personal name, while Catalina Enríquez (Blanca's daughter) says merely "an old mulata." Though this marker most likely was inserted in order to aid the inquisitors in identifying the person being discussed, perhaps even to provide psychological distance between the witness and the person being denounced, one cannot help but wonder if and how the consciousness of this racial difference affected the everyday relations between the involved parties.[178] On two occasions it appears that race became an issue within this crypto-Jewish community itself. According to one unnamed witness, Rodríguez and her daughter Juana once visited Blanca Enríquez, who was speaking openly of 'Jewish' matters with her daughter Beatriz and them. When Antonio Caravallo (Ysavel de Silva's husband) entered and understood the topic of conversation, he asked Beatriz "in secret [...] how they dared to speak such things in front of the said Esperanza Rodríguez." Beatriz assured the new guest that Rodríguez and her daughter were trustworthy, were 'our people' ("que segura era la gente"), but it is quite possible that his initial reaction was based on the assumption that a Mulata only could have been an outsider, not to be included in discussion of such dangerous subjects.[179] In the final publication of the charges Caravallo's complaint bears even more distance: "how did they speak in such a manner in the presence of these three people?" Similarly, one day, testifies Manuel Nuñez Caravallo, he went to visit his relatives, the sisters Elena and Ysavel de Silva. Esperanza Rodríguez was there with one of her daughters. The two "acted familiarly / trataban familiarmente" with the Silva sisters. After Rodríguez and her daughter left, he asked, "who were those people with whom they acted with such familiarity. They responded that they were from mine [i.e., of my people / de los mios], which is the same as saying that they were observers of the Law of moses."[180] In their summary of the case and issuing of the sentence, the inquisitors fill in what they think went unsaid, stating that Caravallo's perplexity arose from the Rodríguez' "being a few mulata dogs / siendo unas perras mulatas."[181]

Paying Rodríguez so much money for the service of conducting fasts on behalf of the late Blanca Enriquez might signify that Rodríguez held a marginal status within the community; in other words, family members did not require such an amount, as they acted on an unquestionably personal level. Rodríguez's poverty may well have moved Beatriz Enríquez to offer her such a sum of money as an act of charity, unless Blanca had specified the amount. Indeed, according to Maria de Rivera, also accused of judaizing, and other witnesses, Blanca had ordered before her death the distribution of some 400 pesos to the poor among the marrano community (as already mentioned) and these witnesses list Esperanza Rodríguez explicitly as one of the recipients.[182] The Blancas de Rivera together received 60 pesos. Yet, according to Beatriz Enríquez, and Rodríguez confirms this independently, it is Rodríguez who showed up at Beatriz's house to ask for 70 pesos, indicating that Beatriz was unaware of the arrangement. Beatriz even queried Rodríguez, who had to explain why she wanted such an amount.[183] When Blanca Enríquez died, various clothes of hers were distributed to poor observers of the Law of Moses, including a mattress that was given to Rodríguez.[184] One unnamed witness told someone else that one could send alms to Rodríguez, as he/she had "sent alms several times to the said Esperanza Rodríguez as a poor observer [of the Law]."[185] According to Juana Rodríguez del Bosque, the payment from Beatriz was only "one of the times that the said Esperanza Rodríguez her mother took money" from the Enríquez women. Raphaela Enríquez claims that "she has given various alms" to Rodríguez, meaning or including, the "three or pesos" she sent Esperanza from the money Rafaela received from Manuel Albarez five or six times to distribute to poor observers of the Law of Moses, so that they would fast on his behalf. Juana Enríquez testifies that she gave alms to Esperanza three times, later adding that after the death of Blanca Enríquez she gave Esperanza at different times eight or nine pesos.[186] One unnamed witness sums up the relationship bluntly: "because the said Esperanza Rodríguez, and her daughters, profess [the Law of Moses], all the rich observers of [the Law] give them alms, and do them much kindness ("las hazen mucho bien")."[187] At any rate, the fact that Rodríguez told Blanca Mendez de Rivera that she had been given seventy pesos on the occasion of Blanca's death to conduct these fasts with her daughters shows that it meant a great deal to her.[188]

Rodríguez's poverty is easy enough to deduce. When she and her daughters were arrested by the Mexico City tribunal, their goods are inventoried together. Among these goods is "an ordinary guitar."[189] Perhaps one of the women or Rodríguez's deceased husband knew how to play. Like a fair number of her goods, it is listed as broken. The inquisitional inventory deems many of the items belonging to her to be old.[190] Even as free urban Mulatas the Rodríguez women lived in the multicultural American world; hence their possession of "nine small, old pictures of different saints, painted by indians," an "old turkish woman of black damask," "three small measures of silk from China," various skirts, muffs and cloths from Rouen, "a little desk from Japan."[191] The only enumeration of the value of the Rodríguez estate, or at least of some of its items, yields a total of 17 pesos.[192] When deposing in connection with the trial of Beatriz Enríquez, Juana Rodríguez del Bosque describes with seeming excitement how her mother Esperanza spent the money she received for the above-mentioned fasts, retrieving, for instance, a little rug that she had had to pawn.[193] Their stark financial situation lends motivation to Juana's exaggeration of the amount her mother received to fast for Blanca Enríquez. It also makes understandable how on two occasions Rodríguez sent one of her grandsons "to request from [Juana Enríquez] three pesos for her household, and the other time two pesos which she sent her said grandson to request, saying that [Juana Enríquez] would pay it in sewing. But [Juana Enríquez] sent to her saying that she did not want it paid in sewing but rather that [Rodríguez] should commend her said mother [Blanca] to God."[194]

In fact, there was more to the relationship between Rodríguez and the other judaizers than mere charity. One unnamed witness deposes that Rodríguez, among other poor marranos, was given money on different occasions by a judaizer who was having an extramarital affair, so that Rodríguez would fast for the sake of his/her gaining forgiveness for this sin ("por la intençion de la dha persona").[195] According to Rodríguez herself, Ana Xuarez one time sent her two pesos by means of Pedro Tinoco (her aunt Catalina's son) so that Rodríguez (and her daughter/s? — the language is plural) would fast on her behalf, "that God should enlighten her [la alumbrasse] because she was about to give birth." On another occasion, Rodríguez claims, Blanca Enriquez herself sent her a peso (again, through Pedro Tinoco) to fast "for the peace of her house."[196] The use of the term alumbrar here is intriguing. Rodríguez uses it elsewhere in her depositions, but as far as I could see it is rarely mentioned by any of the judaizers associated with the Enríquez clan. Is Xuarez requesting divine illumination in order to teach her future child properly? Enríquez's request might well contain an allusion to the messianic beliefs that some family members attached to certain newborn children, who were hoped/expected to become the new savior, such as the son of Juana Enríquez and Simón Váez Sevilla. Perhaps she is referring to the mystical understandings of the Virgin Mary's annunciation from Gabriel and the light it produces.[197] It is likely, therefore, that Rodríguez was considered a particularly powerful spiritual presence because of her age, knowledge and close connections to Blanca Enríquez and the fonts of their collective heritage in Seville. The inquisitors themselves are convinced of the high esteem in which she was held. In their summary of the case and sentencing they state that Rodríguez was "held to be a holy Jewess" or "Jewish saint" ("tenida por s^{ta} judia"), "was esteemed as a perfect Dogmatizer / perfecta Dogmatiçadora" and they speak of "the respect with which she was treated among the Jews," indeed pointing to the alms given to Rodríguez as evidence.[198]

In a circle of White merchants, some of a prominent and even internationally recognized stature, Esperanza Rodríguez stands out as an anomaly in terms of both economic status and race. It is understandable if Rodríguez had aspirations for a better life and more secure social status. Unusual for a woman and half-White, she knew how to read and write, having been taught during her year at the convent in Seville.[199] When discussing her grandchildren — having been prompted by the inquisitors to do so — some of her strong character and worldliness shines through the usually dry language. She offers seeming apologetics when mentioning that her eldest daughter Juana had children by different men, yet notes proudly that the father of Juana's son was "Don Nicolas de Alarcon, son of the former governor of Soconusco," a region in southern Mexico near Guatemala, and that the father of her daughter was "Hernando Cassado, servant of Don fran^co de Arevalo Suazo," clearly emphasizing the high social connections.[200] When relating the story of her youth and arrival in Mexico to the inquisitors, she points out, as if the social connections rebound to her credit, that she arrived in the Americas (at Cartagena) on a fleet led by "general Juan de Sulas de Valdes nephew of the Señor Inquisitor Don Juan de Llaro y Valdes who was the godfather or companion [compadre] of the said Doña Catalina her mistress. And by her order the said general brought her until Cartagena."[201] When relating her husband's work experience, she states that one of his employers in Acapulco had been "the third Marquesa of Guadalcaçar."[202]

Unlike most of the Mexico City judaizers, especially the younger generation, Rodríguez tends to use in her testimony the term "Jewish" rather than "observer of the Law of Moses," whether applying it to herself or to others; people teach others "to be Jewish," before some men are permitted to marry into the family they were "made to be Jewish," which most likely refers to being taught some of the tradition rather than to being circumcised. Rodríguez seems to regard herself self-consciously as 'a Jew,' an upholder of a significant and legitimate tradition rather than a follower of a cowering, subterranean cult. An indication of what all this meant to her can be gleaned from a moralistic tale told one night at her house by Diego Tinoco, who grew up as an open Jew somewhere outside of Spanish territories, when Esperanza, her daughters and he had been discussing the Law of Moses:

> In an ossuary in a certain place where Jews live in freedom, a spanish catholic stayed in order to sleep. he saw rising up two deceased jewesses, discussing how the following day another jewess had to die from a fall. The said catholic, making an inquiry in the city after the said woman and seeing that she had not died that day, returned to sleep in the same place, and turned to see the same jewesses who spoke, saying that the [other] jewess did not have to die from the fall for having given alms to another jew, from which it resulted that the catholic became a jew.[203]

In this story, related by a group of marranos to bolster their own faith and practice, Judaism is figured as the embodiment of ancient statements repeated around and on Rosh HaShana, the Jewish New Year, and Yom Kippur, the Day of Atonement, that charity saves one from death (Proverbs 11:4; BT Bava Batra 10a). The death which charity can stave off is, as the Talmud exhorts, the spiritual punishment meted out in the afterlife. In Tinoco's tale Judaism comprises the possibility of escape from a punishing fate, a path for transcending strict judgement through goodness and good deeds.[204]

Such sentiments likely had an even more particular resonance for a woman such as Esperanza Rodríguez who was part Afroiberian and a former slave. When asked regarding her maternal grandparents by the inquisitors, she retorts that "her said mother being a black woman born in Guinea, she therefore has no notice of who her parents were."²⁰⁵ Her emotions here might be both sarcastic defiance and genuine sadness. Accepting the Judaism urged on her by her owners-relatives closed a gap in social status that separated her from them. She recounts how after she had acceded to believing in Adonay "she sat down with Ynés and her cousins to have a light meal with special foods that these Jews ate before fasts – fish, salad, and beans. [...] they gave her 'a lot because she had condescended to [take] their advice.'"²⁰⁶ Another insight into the motivating factors of her devotion to her new religion might be obtained from the statement made to her by her mistress Ynes Lopez and Lopez's cousins when they tried to convince her around age thirteen that "whoever believes in that which they say [i.e., the Law of Moses] cannot be a slave / no podia ser esclaba."²⁰⁷ The reasoning Rodríguez relates is not merely an effort at manipulation of a young slave girl. It constitutes a form of cognitive self-liberation, a stance of symbolic marronage wielded by those who so often historically were constrained by external circumstances. The same logic was proffered already by Philo and Paul. It also finds expression within 'normative' Jewish circles before and during Esperanza's own lifetime. Commenting on the commandment to bore a hole into the ear of a Hebrew slave who chooses not to go free after the sixth year (Exod. 21:6; Deut. 15:17), the ancient Mekhilta (parshat Bo) explains that this is a fitting punishment for the ear that heard at Mt. Sinai God announcing, "for the children of Israel are slaves to me and not slaves to slaves [i.e., other people]," and the ear's owner, who refuses to act on this epiphany. The fifteenth-century Isaac Abravanel cites this midrash in his commentary to Deut. 15:17. Rabbi Ishac Athias of Amsterdam, a contemporary of Esperanza Rodríguez, concludes his discussion of why Jews use non-Jewish servants with a nod to the same biblical statement: "He commanded you that pagan servants serve you in perpetuity, in order that your own brothers don't serve you, who are the children of Israel, all elected for My service, and as such it is necessary to be unoccupied [that is, unemployed, available, free to serve divine needs and seek holiness]. And whoever serves such a Master needs not serve humans."²⁰⁸ How attractive such a rhetoric of overturning must have appeared to someone who managed to escape a fate of servitude.

The Tragic Sense of Humor of the Cosmos

Perhaps it was the women of the Rodríguez del Bosque family who resorted to the dealer in cocoa Luis Núñez Pérez, a fellow prisoner listed in the same Relación sumeria, who "not only was a Jew, but rather a superstitious prophet," who, among other suspect practices, "promised safety from imprisonment to certain Jewesses. He also later assured them "that he hadn't denounced them another time when he was a prisoner, but rather a man or a Black woman [had]; what was certain was that hardly had he separated from them when they were immediately arrested by this Holy Office."²⁰⁹ In jail, Rodríguez claims to have suffered from delirium, giving this as the reason in late September 1644 that she did not confess immediately upon her imprisonment. It is not clear whether this illness, as she calls it, is identical with the rational fear she then describes having experienced that if she confessed she would be burned or gravely punished, a fear she says was put in her by the devil.[210] In light of what struck the inquisitors as Rodríguez's willful observance of Jewish practices, they decided to apply "the most serious penalties established by the law, relaxing her person to justice and to the secular arm," Inquisition-speak for execution.[211] In her later meetings with the inquisitors, however, Rodríguez repeatedly expresses repentance for her judaizing and remorse for having shunned "the Law of Our Lord Jesus Christ," begging the Inquisition for mercy. Evidently, the inquisitors were convinced of the sincerity of her remorse. According to the 1646 summary of that year's autos-de-fe, Rodríguez

> Was imprisoned as a Jewess, observer of the law of Moses, with confiscation of goods. Was negative a long time and, becoming tightfisted [i.e., not giving what was wanted], pretended to be crazy, allowing herself to eat lice; saying and doing actions and words with which she pretended to be taken for such [crazy], like the gathering of her shirts and tearing them up, making a large doll, with her mantilla [a lace scarf], girdle, stuffed arms and capillos [cloths used in Mexico as a hat or mantilla] on the head; and kissing it, making as if she gave it the breast, saying it was her baby, and that they would look after him and they would not kill him; and other times, hiding it herself deliberately, she implored and cried that he should return; thinking, by this route so beyond reason, to escape from confessing her grave sins and speaking against the many accomplices who she knew kept the said law of Moses.[212] Ultimately, becoming more agreeable, she admitted being a Jewess judaizer and begged mercy.
>
> Was admitted to reconciliation and sentenced to the auto in the form of a penitent; green candle in the hands; confiscation of goods, which she did not have; formal abjuration; sambenito, and perpetual imprisonment,[213] and in public humiliation and in perpetual banishment from all the West Indies and from the city of Seville and town of Madrid, Court of His Majesty.[214]

Like all those reconciled, Rodríguez was to leave Mexico on the first available fleet to Spain and present herself to the Inquisition in Seville within a month to be assigned the place where her sentence was to be served. A former slave who had sought to improve her lot, she was forbidden now to wear or possess "gold, silver, pearls, nor precious stones, nor silk, camlet [chamelote, a strong, impermeable woven fabric that originally might have been made of camel or goat hair], nor fine cloth, nor to ride on horseback."[215]

Rodríguez's eldest daughter, Juana Rodríguez del Bosque,

> Was imprisoned as a Jewess, observer of the law of Moses, with confiscation of goods. She confessed to being a Jewess judaizer

and begged mercy. Before her imprisonment she agreed with certain Jews and her mother and sisters not to speak against accomplices in the Inquisition, and after imprisonment she communicated in the jails with many of the prisoners, in order to know what they had deposed against her and whether it was contrary to what she had confessed.[216]

Juana was also reconciled, with a sentence slightly different than her mother's, a rope around the throat at the auto, only six months imprisonment, and 100 lashes. She too had no goods to be confiscated.

Juana's sister Isabel found herself accused of the same crime of judaizing and likewise begged mercy.[217]

> She herself, of her own will and cause, made application to Esperanza Rodríguez, her mother, that she teach her the law of Moses, having heard said that a certain famous Jewess [Blanca Enriquez], deceased, had left money so that another Jewess, her daughter [Beatriz Enriquez], would dispense it in order to make abstinence for her soul, taken away from the avarice that is innate in the Hebrews and their descendants. And being a prisoner, she feigned revelation from the Heavens and that she had heard a voice which exhorted her to confess and discharge her conscience, and the revelation was the communications of the jails which she had with other prisoners, under false names, discussing and confirming among themselves about their lawsuits, laying out the way in which they had behaved in them; threatening with notable temerity a certain minister [of the Inquisition?], that she, through the hand of a Jew, would have his face cut.[218]

Isabel also had no goods to confiscate. She received the same sentence as her sister Juana.

María Rodríguez del Bosque, the youngest sister, likewise confessed to the same crime of judaizing, received the same sentence as her older sisters, and likewise had no goods to be taken from her.[219] Of María we read that

> She had notable rebelliousness in confessing her sins, and with threats of denouncing her said mother to this Holy Office for what she had seen her do in the observance of Judaism, she obliged her to teach her the law of Moses [!]. Making up, when she judaized, with some famous Jewesses, she and they made mockery and ridicule of the processions of the Catholics, speaking ill of them. And all that she got out of her apostasy and of the monies she received for making fasts of the said law of Moses was but a damask doubloon of China, blue and red, which

she brought to the jails, so that, as a witness, it would convince her of her evildoing. And in them [the jails], stubborn and rebellious, she communicated with her sisters and other Jews and Jewesses, using false names and serving as intermediary, giving assurances from some prisoners to others, that they shouldn't confess, and if they should, it should be about what they had arranged.[220]

Esperanza Rodríguez delivers the renunciation required of her by the Inquisition, stating formally that she understands the proceedings and promises to live as a good Christian. All in all, she denounces more than 70 individuals in order to appease her inquisitors.[221] On 29 October 1646, still imprisoned after some 4 years, she pens a note to the inquisitors begging to be allowed to serve out her life imprisonment together with her daughters. The same day, she is granted this permission, as well as to leave the place of her incarceration on holidays to hear mass with the other penitents.[222] It is not clear what happened to the inquisitors' original banishment of her from the Americas. In the cases of the Rodríguez del Bosque women one sees at work some of the various forms of resistance and mutual cooperation taken up by those caught in the Inquisitions' net.

With perhaps little choice, Esperanza opted to identify herself as a daughter of her Judeoconverso father, though little surfaces regarding their relationship. It is possible that her mother, Isabel, had already chosen to throw her lot in with crypto-Judaism. These choices may have reflected positive affection for this religious complex or mere efforts to escape a slave status or both. All in all, the story of Esperanza Rodríguez, at least insofar as it can be gleaned from Inquisition documents, offers a glimpse of a rich if idiosyncratic example of how a part-Afroiberian went about forging the kind of "new kin-like ties" that helped remake the "natal network of kin" lost in enslavement.[223]

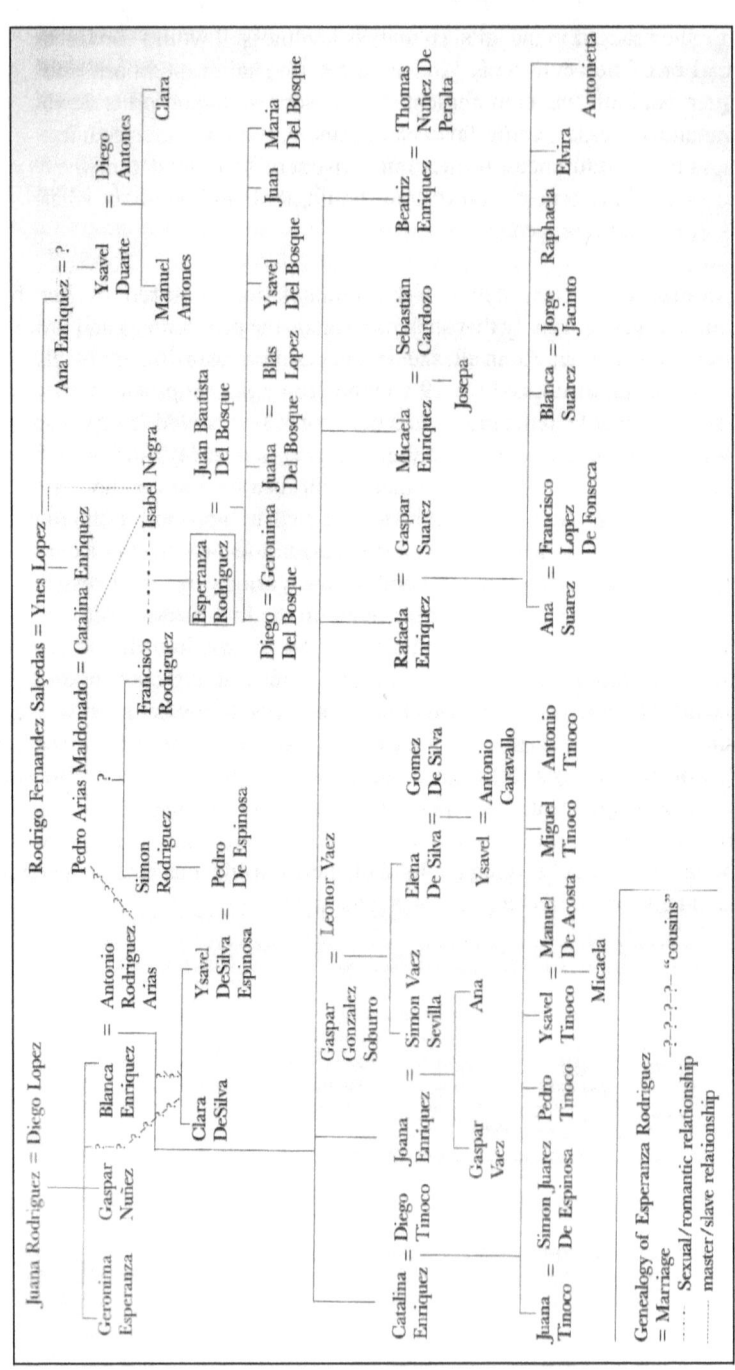

Genealogy of Esperanza Rodriguez and the Extended Enriquez Family, from Seville to Mexico City

Postscript I

The woman who knows giving birth will not feel the [Inquisition's] torture / La mujer que savia parir no sentía el tormento.[1]

So proclaimed the Mexican Marrana Blanca Enriquez to her young relative Ysavel de Silva when recounting her months-long imprisonment by the tribunal of the Seville Inquisition and displaying the marks of the torture she had received at its hands. To give birth in this imperfect world is to become familiar with pain. To make life is to come to know the handiwork of decay, of degeneration, of death. To generate the future, to have felt its powerful potential, to have seen that creation is not only possible but survivable, is to become — to varying degrees — inured to the forces trying to prevent that future. To a large extent, trust in the future may well be nurtured best through a connection to a past that will be met on the road through that future. Like so many Judeoconversos and Afroiberians, Amerindians "venerate their memories constantly with great love [in] the hidden depths of their hearts," in the words of seventeenth-century Quito Bishop Peña Montenegro.[2]

Still, the past wields only so much power on its own in the face of so overwhelming a present. Introducing, in the portentous quincentennial year of 1992, his monumental three-volume study and transcription of the excruciatingly drawn-out Inquisition trial of the messianistic friar Francisco de la Cruz, Vidal Abril Castelló lauds in excited capital letters the "NEW GOD WHICH AMERICA AND SPAIN DISCOVERED IN THEIR RECIPROCAL RELATIONS DURING THE 16TH CENTURY. IT IS THE AUTHENTICALLY EVANGELICAL GOD OF BROTHERHOOD AND OF SOLIDARITY, OF EQUALITY AND RECIPROCITY OF RIGHTS AND DUTIES, OF LIBERTY AND TOLERANCE."[3]

While I, too, am fascinated by this new Mestizo god and long followed his/her revolutionary efforts, I wish these utopian hopes had come to fuller fruition. It seems more accurate to say that we have seen more promise than fulfillment, or fulfillment only for a select few. It also seems important to note that part of this god's 'mestizo' quality inheres precisely in the collusion his/her followers aroused between her/his 'secular' and 'religious' arms, even as these arms struggled against one another.

Early modern 'race' stands as a significant bridge for scholarship between the 'raceless' culturally oriented medieval world and the 'scientific' racism of the modern world. Like its later progeny, early modern race was both biological and cultural, essentialist and situational, rigidly defined and permeable, political and theological. The Inquisitions maintained and stoked anti-Jewish stereotypes, just as various European/White institutions and individuals maintained and stoked anti-Black prejudices, in order "to relegate" each group "to being 'objects of phobia,'" as Marie Theresa Hernández explains the theory of journalist Abraham Nuncio regarding the use of regional legends and folklore about Amerindians by those in power in Nuevo León.[4] I have tried in the preceding chapters to show how constructs — ethnic, religious, racial — were used also by groups other than the dominators. Belonging to a collective, real or imagined, held out powerful identity-forming possibilities, both for negative, external, ascriptive purposes regarding others as well as for positive, internal purposes for oneself.

New Christians of Jewish and African origin suffered for centuries from their being positioned by the dominant majority and other minorities as 'in-between' (Certeau, The Mystic Fable) yet also cultivated on their own such in-betweenness as a defensive barrier, a privileged space, an unsharable uniqueness. To borrow terminology from Hernández, they were 'maybe' Christians, 'maybe' Spaniards, 'maybe' Whites.[5] Though many, perhaps even most individuals from these groups no longer practiced many or any particulars of their traditions, the entire group remained, seemingly permanently, 'designated' as Jews or Africans. As has been argued, correctly, some New Christians expressed skepticism toward religious and political orthodoxies.[6] Many individuals also expressed egalitarian views in opposition to dominant ethnic and/or racial hierarchies. I have not found, however, that Judeoconversos voiced distinct urgency for tolerance other than for themselves under the tyranny of the Catholic Inquisitions (or later against a perceived authoritarian Jewish establishment), nor that Afroiberians argued for an end to anti-converso/Jewish state-church activities. While marranos might have depended for their survival on verbal and behavioral circumlocutions for expressing their identity, these expressions merely articulate that which almost everyone else would have said in any case. Several New Christian women accused in Mexico City of judaizing in the early 1640s, relate that it was enough to say "so-and-so is like us, or, they are good, or, they do as we do, and they are known, and they declare sufficiently, and it is made understood how they keep and observe the said law of Moses."[7]

'We' are the norm, though devalued and denied, and therefore need to stick together.

Many parallels attend these efforts at separate survival. Just as the enslaved and 'colored' might have sought in their get-togethers (juntas) a means of escaping misery, as María Méndez, also known as María Quelembe, of Cartagena, put it in her 1634 Inquisition trial,[8] so too might marranos have seen in judaizing practices and beliefs a mode of being true to themselves and their past. While those of African origin might have sought an escape, literally or figuratively, back to their homeland from which they had been wrenched, for Judeoconversos, on the other hand, flight from Iberian territories, which was often achievable, likely entailed an undesired self-exile from the homeland in which they continued to live but that had in a deep sense been wrenched away from them by the rise of militant Catholic xenophobia. Many Judeoconversos and Afroiberians therefore sought, "through the use of specific knowledges, liberty, goods and to oppose slavery,"[9] though the kind of slavery members of each group faced differed. The insulting term used for Judeoconversos, marranos is said to derive from a word for pig, but the more likely etymology is that given in anti-Jewish literature; that marranos feign (marran) Christianity. One way or another, the plights and categories of marranos and Maroons echo with seeming significance. It is not coincidental that one finds among dedicated members of both subaltern groups efforts to recreate real or symbolic structures of self-governance and even royal households, messianic or realist.[10] Though in my book I do not dwell on the martial efforts of slaves to undo their captivity, often and surprisingly successful despite the disparity of military might, Judeoconversos also at times attempted to make use of more normative forces, diplomacy, wealth and even physical/military resistance, with perhaps less success. Yet each group had at its disposal mostly the weapons of the weak (a term from James C. Scott). For most Afroiberians or Judeoconversos, the most one could hope to do might involve casting a spell over one's master or doing violence to a crucifix. Symbolic marronage may well have permitted psychic survival, even if it did not undo the objective conditions of oppression.

From the perspective of the dominant elite, the advances of globalization birthed their own shadow realm. It makes great sense that not only in the hegemonic imaginary but also in the antipodal discourse of magic and resistance the various Others took on exaggerated dimensions. Hence in Peru, as Irene Silverblatt shows, "Jewish symbols and the insights of moriscas [...] were common ingredients in devilish brews," and the same women who wielded them "were also experimenting with indigenous lore." Magical practitioners made purposeful use of the bones of Amerindians, who "never [had been] baptized," who "had never been touched by the Christian world," or chanted incantations to and used the bones of "men who had been either hanged or decapitated."[11]

Hybridity, cultural and discursive mestizaje were never neutral comminglings nor mere imitations by those below. The borrowings, forced and voluntary, the mimesis by the subaltern constantly sought a renegotiation of the terms.[12] This is how Margaret Olsen reads Alonso de Sandoval's 1647 De instauranda Aethiopum salute (originally published in 1627 under a different title). Beyond the creation of lengthy texts, this is the inner movement beneath Afroiberian citations in everyday conversation of Jews and Jewishness and Judeoconverso wielding of Blacks and Blackness. As simultaneous insiders and outsiders, these groups shared certain perspectives of the dominant majority, but inevitably from a dissonant position. Fuchs calls it the "deliberate enactment of imitation as a strategy for inclusion."[13] This is not to say that they automatically questioned or opposed the prejudices of the mainstream, which would be little more than a retrojected romantic hope, but that their echoes of such views meant something else as well. Such mimesis, especially when utilizing another Other, might take both positive or negative forms. When, in 1566, Felipe I prohibited Moriscos from owning Black slaves, various fifteenth-century morisco noblemen, such as Don Francisco Núñez Muley, protested their right to do so and the importance of doing so in order to protect Morisco society from the erosion that would come from rampant servitude.

Muley's insistence on the entitlement of Moriscos to own Black slaves accompanied his ardent defense of Morisco cultural difference, which he and the others correctly saw Spain as trying to eradicate.[14] One scholar finds that in sixteenth-century Santiago de Guatemala, "Marginal individuals, in particular, foreigners such as Portuguese, were likelier to recognize mulatto children than were those in a better social position."[15] On the Caribbean island of Montserrat, the Irish immigrants who made up two thirds of the population by the late seventeenth century were relegated to second-class status by the English elite. By the early eighteenth century, the Irish constituted the island's primary sugar producers and slaveholders.[16]

Examples such as these are a variant of what Michel de Certeau has in mind when analyzing how "users make (bricolent) innumerable and infinitesimal transformations of and within the dominant cultural economy in order to adapt it to their own interests and their own rules:"

> Submissive, and even consenting to their subjection, the [American] Indians nevertheless often made of the rituals, representations, and laws imposed on them [by the Spanish colonizers] something quite different from what their conquerors had in mind; they subverted them not by rejecting or altering them, but by using them with respect to ends and references foreign to the system they had no choice but to accept. They were other within the very colonization that outwardly assimilated them; their use of the dominant social order deflected its power, which they lacked the means to challenge; they escaped it without leaving it. The strength of their difference lay in procedures of "consumption."[17]

Likewise, James Scott famously illuminated the modes of resistance taken by those in a position of weakness in relation to the larger structures of domination: within certain limits, peasants and all subaltern "human actors fashion their own response, their own experience of class, their own history."[18] Here is the prolonged, persistent struggle or dance between the dominant cultural system and the groups and individuals under and within it, each with its own forms of weaponry, each ceaselessly attempting to make use of, to seduce, to trick, to exert control over the other. It is important to recall, as Scott and Gil Anidjar remind us, that the agency of (dominated) individuals functions in a context of (dominating) institutional agencies, whose power and effects often mock a pretense to symmetry between the parties.[19] Even so, the dominant sociocultural system is never totally homogeneous, it is also made use of by those who participate in producing it, though this may not prevent its being received as a monolith.

It must also be remembered that Europeans in the Americas were "strangers in a strange, often dangerous, and hostile world" where "European power and control was often weak, especially during the early, most crucial stages of culture formation."[20] From a different context and perspective, Mieke Bal underscores that

"Insecurity is not a prerogative of the dominated. The burden of domination is hard to bear. Dominators have, first, to establish their position, then to safeguard it. Subsequently, they must make both the dominated and themselves believe in it."[21] In addition, both Certeau and Scott, focusing on the 'everyday' and on resistance, in opposition to empire and imperialist elites, fail to note that subaltern self-fashioning can be decidedly reactionary, mirroring, consuming and wielding empire's most exclusionary and divisive aspects. Who 'wins' is perhaps not clear until long after the struggles subside; perhaps not even then, as contestation continues over the re-presentation of the struggles.

All this points to ways of reading the recurring violence against Christian discourse and images (the crucifix, images of Christ, the Virgin, etc.) often attributed to Judeoconversos but also to Afroiberians and other Others. The same goes for the range of magical acts wielded by slaves and downtrodden minorities against their masters. These acts seem difficult to believe for moderns, who are inclined to take all this supernatural stuff less than seriously. In a recent study of Purim and Jewish violence, Elliott Horowitz offers the first extended scholarly treatment of alleged marrano violence against Christian icons.[22] Such alleged violence, at one and the same time physical and semiotic, may be part of a larger issue. For one thing, given the intertwining of body and spirit in the pre-modern world, physical violence constituted a legitimate avenue for problem-solving, in the judiciary system or in religious disputation. Discussing the matter of the treatment of Amerindians, Anthony Pagden points out that most of the encomenderos in the New World "had come from a stratum of society where violence was endemic, and where religious beliefs frequently assumed highly unorthodox forms in which outbursts of frustration might easily express themselves by physical attacks on holy images."[23]

In a world thoroughly or highly determined by religious matters, which to varying degrees encompass what today would fall under politics, seemingly minor differences take on disproportional symbolic importance; the world does depend on theological or metaphysical construction. Readers need only recall the intense physical violence wreaked in Europe by Protestants against Catholic churches, their statuary and imagery, or 'idols,' in particular.[24] Calvinists effected similar destruction in Pernambuco after they conquered it from the Portuguese/Brazilians in the early seventeenth century. In the Iberian orbit, William Monter notes that "[o]utrages to the crucifix were often alleged against Jews, but more often practiced by Moriscos," and he provides some pertinent examples.[25] Playing out their own issues regarding gender and femininity through a ritual semiotics, a number of the ilusas or alumbradas in colonial Mexico were accused of desecrating "religious sites and symbols — altars, hosts, and crucifixes — with sexual acts."[26] The blasphemies and sacrileges alleged to have been uttered or performed by crypto-Jews can fruitfully be compared to those of Afroiberian slaves. Here, the semiotics of ritual went from the suffering caused by slavery, a beating by a master, for instance, to a pointed renunciation of the master's religion; in other words, became a denunciation, a challenge, an undoing of the discourse making such injustice possible, of the discourse insisting on such injustice as part of the logic of its own maintenance. In many cases similar, sometimes even the exact same kind of charges are made against Afroiberians: denying Christ or the power of the priests, desecrating the host, mocking, abusing and even destroying sacred images.[27] Hence, around 1608, two Mexican Mulatos who "kept company with Indians" and had spent time in an isolated region that served as a destination for runaway slaves were "accused of removing from a church sacred images that they then spit on and stepped on."[28]

For individuals accused from all of these groups it is fair to ask whether their actions were misunderstood. For instance, Afroiberians may not have intended mockery or attack on Catholic icons but merely to Africanize them for the sake of their own spiritual lives, while New Christians may have been attempting to sincerely worship as Catholics but in a manner that reflected their particular subject position and the insights gained therefrom. At the same time, it is clear that minorities and dominated groups, while politically dependent, were not necessarily timid about self-expression. With some colorful examples, Horowitz shows the frequency and unselfconsciousness of early modern Jewish responses to (perceived) Christian domination, responses that were often physical and violent, to which many others could be added.[29]

Horowitz is misleading, however, in characterizing violence against Christian icons as "part and parcel of what [Cecil] Roth memorably described as 'the religion of the Marranos.'"[30] For one thing, Roth takes a particularly romantic and maximalist stance regarding marrano religiosity, one that lends it far more coherence and systematicity than might be warranted. For Horowitz to quote him here betrays a desire to establish a persistent and homogeneous tradition of violence.[31] There is no such thing as 'the religion of the marranos,' but rather numerous variants produced by individual families, groups of individuals and even isolated individuals, some of which bear as tenuous a resemblance to one another as they each might bear toward normative Judaism. Some marranos may have seen fit to act out their well-earned hostility toward the Catholicism imposed on them by twisting the mandated adoration of crucifixes and other icons into its opposite, a psycho-theologically mandated denigration. Many other marranos, most of them, in fact, were never accused of such behavior. To generalize or to err with sloppy phrasing as Horowitz does here is reckless. He cites Gitlitz, who reasons that since allegations of violence against Christian icons were so widespread and often based on first-hand reports, they must have had some truth to them.[32] This logic does not hold up and returns us to the crux of the hermeneutic conundrum of the Inquisitions. A priori acceptance of accusations because of their ubiquity cannot be sustained as a rule. Blood libels against Jews were also a widespread allegation, but this does not mean that they were true. Gil Anidjar argues convincingly that late medieval accusations of desecration of the host by Jews had more to do with Christian fixations on the blood of Christ and projection onto the Jewish Other.[33] As Catherine Gallagher and Stephen Greenblatt note, "For a Jew to attack the Host seems strange, since there would appear to be no reason to attack something you believe to be a mere piece of bread."[34] Indeed, the medieval examples brought by Horowitz could just as easily reflect Christian anxieties and unconscious projections of what they thought Jews would want to do, perhaps what Christians themselves wanted to do or feared was something they wanted to do. It is possible that even the anti-Christian violence reported to the Inquisitions and 'documented' by them continues to reflect a kind of collective wish-fulfilment. Again, Gallagher and Greenblatt, "The Jews are inevitably guilty in such stories because they do not believe and because at the same time they are made to act out, to embody, the doubt aroused among the Christian faithful by eucharistic doctrine."[35]

This is not to suggest that the extremity and perversity of oppression from above could not have generated such subaltern anti-establishment hostility. In many cases no doubt it did. Re-enacting the crucifixion of Christ might have suited Judeoconversos or Afroiberians who had internalized their own subversive role in Catholic discourse, particularly in a Catholic discourse that seemed to wield the cross as the ultimate weapon. As Pierre Bourdieu suggests, the symbolic violence of domination "is the coercion which is set up only through the consent that the dominated cannot fail to give to the dominator (and therefore to the domination) when their understanding of the situation and relation can only use instruments of knowledge that they have in common with the dominator."[36] This shared conceptual-emotional vocabulary helps explain the kind of symbolic violence from below with which we are concerned. Here, too, subversive intent and refashioning is not hard to see, whether we judge it effective or not, for in whipping crucifixes or similar acts, the individual may have been refashioning the intense, inner, emotional life that monastic as well as mystical Catholicism insisted in different ways on "organizing" by/into "apt performance of conventional behavior" into anti-normative ritualized emotional behavior. Thus weeping, guilt or penance, for example, as expressed in self-mortification, flogging or inquisitorial torture was inverted to become a near-ecstatic flagellation of the demonic embodiment of oppression, Christ or the host.[37] Another plausible Christian source for the practices in question can be found in the medieval monastic practice of ritual humiliation of saints' relics as part of prayers to God for help against an enemy (known as a "clamour"). This inversion ritual included placing relics and a crucifix on the floor on a hair shirt, thus in some sense punishing the relics/saints for not having done their duty as intercessors. In the hands of laypeople imitating the monkish rite this clamor included actual striking of the altar supporting the relics.[38] These scenarios offer a mental set and setting of circumstances remarkably similar to the incidents involving Judeoconversos and other aggrieved subalterns.

My insistence on maintaining the possibility that such subaltern violence happened but also was imagined/projected stems from a desire to uphold the cogency of both logics. The violence of the dominators produced violent reactions as well as the imagination/projection of violent reactions. Both occurred; that is, subaltern violence was real at times and also absent at times yet projected. I will return to this matter below, but I suggest that it stems from the effects of the domination itself. Recent scholarship of Amerindian and Afroamerican responses to colonization recognize the post-traumatic symptoms manifested in these societies and cultures over the course of the following centuries. The emotional and psychic consequences of slavery for Afroamericans has long been a staple of scholarship. There is a tendency in scholarship regarding Judeoconversos to treat only the religious ramifications of the group's similar but peculiar post-traumatic situation. Hardly alone in this, Norman Simms is right to highlight the individual and familial pathologies to emerge as a consequence of the continued non-integration of personality and culture forced onto devoted crypto-Jews and even frequently onto religiously disinterested New Christians.[39] Given the insanity of their situation, it is noteworthy that compensatory anti-Black racism, an easy place to channel displaced anger, was not more evident (as is true of the relative lack of anti-Jewish or anti-Judeoconverso prejudice among Afroiberians), just as the frequency of melting into a quiet Catholic life is noteworthy. David Graizbord's research in the archives of various inquisitional tribunals leads him to think that "Portuguese tribunals classified [Judeoconverso] defendants' racial identities much more specifically than did their Spanish counterparts."[40] I do not believe this distinction to be true for attitudes toward Africans or Amerindians, certainly not after the sixteenth century, though some scholars have suggested that Spaniards thought of themselves as being less racist than the Portuguese. I also do not believe that the evidence brought in this book reveals Portuguese Judeoconversos to have been more race-conscious than Spanish Judeoconversos or than Iberian Catholics.

Recalling some of the examples from the preceding chapters pressures for definition of the discursive modality of the various statements or conceptions regarding Others. Some quite clearly convey a theopolitics. When Afroiberians denounced their masters or others as alleged judaizers they played on the empire's theopolitics, whether they shared it or were just manipulating it to their advantage; likewise for the contrary vector, when Afroiberians adopted aspects of crypto-Judaism. While many such theopolitical acts might not constitute direct instantiations of religious discourse or practice, nearly all reflect "a community whose members construct their identity with reference to a religious discourse and its attendant practices."[41] Other utterances seem to reflect a world view less specifically religious if at all. Though I have purposely chosen not to take up the exploration of New Christian slave traders — a study very much in need of execution, but that would have necessitated writing a different book — not one of the investigations of New Christian slave traders with which I am familiar has managed to excavate any sentiments vis-à-vis Africans directly related to individual New Christians' self-conception, much less delineate even the most basic outlines of their religious lives independently of very problematic Inquisition sources.[42] When Juan de León/Salomón Machorro laments that colonial Blacks receive better treatment than 'honorable' men, we must ask whether he is referring to New Christians or Whites in general.[43] Even if the former, whether this is a statement of ethnocentrism that is 'secular' or 'religious' may depend on a variety of factors. The distinction, in any case, may not be particularly important, given the ways religious and secular discourse overlapped in forging notions of race and Otherness, overlapped in what Kathryn Burns rightly calls a "spiritual economy."[44]

Let us recall some basic definitions of what we mean when we speak of religiosity or belief in connection with individuals and groups from the early modern Atlantic world. On the most general level, the interactions and statements depicted within this study reflect an ongoing cultural drama — albeit one that its participants perceive only fragmentarily — that illustrates how members of a group draw on the symbols of their group (a symbolic economy always imbricated with those of other groups) to face crises and make meaning of life and the world. Countervailing rhetoric notwithstanding, all of the three monotheisms were essentially communal, to some degree even ethnic demarcations. Among other things, marrano and Afroiberian religiosity served as repositories of social memory. Elizabeth Castelli, working on early Christian martyrdom, suggests that religion offers a critical theory of suffering.[45] Collective memories of suffering, as well as religious discourses themselves, frequently serve as levers for liberation; psychic liberation of the self and socio-theopolitical liberation of the group.[46] Both Catholicism and Judaism sought a "maximalist" unity, where "there could be no radical disjunction between outer behavior and inner motive, between social rituals and individual sentiments, between activities that are expressive and those that are technical."[47] In distinct opposition, those Judeoconversos and Afroiberians who resisted their own Christianization all to some degree made a virtue of necessity, that is, made the modalities that were necessary for their survival — splitting their subjectivity into inner and outer; refashioning the symbols of the dominators into usable symbols for themselves, the dominated; foregrounding elements of their religious culture that aided, encouraged and glorified the avoidance, subversion or even destruction of 'false' Catholicism — into new virtues. One prominent converso tack — whether among those of Jewish or African background — comprised a subjectivization or relativization of truth claims. Spinoza expresses this possibility of overturning the purportedly natural modalities of domination when he declares goodness to flow from subject position rather than the other way around: "We neither strive for, nor will, nor want, nor desire anything because we judge it to be good; on the contrary, we judge something to be good because we strive for it, will it, want it, and desire it" (Ethics [1677], pt. 3, prop. 9, note). Spinoza's proposition relativizes belief on both subjective and institutional levels, as was done by numerous marranos, Afroiberians and others. As long as one lives well according to one's religion, it is not so important which religion one follows. In other words, no one religious system, no matter how dominant or imposed on people, can claim absolute truth. Part of the evidence for this sort of 'modern' proposition was experiential and emotional; the unjust suffering forced on 'us' as different and subaltern justifies the very difference that served as an excuse for the dominant power to oppress us.

Spinoza's allegedly marrano relativism pointedly reminds us, however, not to mistakenly think that all pre-modern individuals lived exclusively by or in religious discourse and practice; or, alternatively, religious discourse and practice by no means prevented cognition and experience of the world that today we would distinguish as secular. What is, I think, remarkable about many of the individuals who appear in the preceding pages is the lucidity of their understanding of their situation from the perspective of what today we would call sociology or politics. Perhaps this lucidity, a kind of practical knowledge — which is not the same thing as the ability to effect desired changes — stems from the improvisational skills developed by so many Judeoconversos and Afroiberians in order to survive the very mobility foisted upon them by the incipient modernity of the European empires: "the ability both to capitalize on the unforeseen and to transform given materials into one's own scenario."[48] Perhaps most importantly, their capacity for mutation, for self-metamorphosis — into pretend faithful Catholics, into pretend well-behaved slaves, into pretend Whites — carried with it the threat of the kind of difference and distance that could transform into satanic opposition yet was also a sign that such rebellion had already transpired.[49]

Postscript II

Throughout the relations established among facts, or the elevation of certain of them to the value of symptoms of a whole period, or the "lesson" (moral or political) which organizes the discourse as a whole, in every history a process of meaning can be found which "always aims at 'fulfilling' the meaning of History:" "Historians are those who assemble not so much facts as signifiers."
—Certeau, The Writing of History, 39-40, quoting Roland Barthes

In his book, The Culture of Literacy (1994), Wlad Godzich [...] writes that he was conceived and born in a Nazi concentration camp. [...] Godzich tells his reader that although four members of his family died because of Nazi persecution, there were others who collaborated with the enemy.
—Hernández, Delirio, 207

I suspect all of us have survivor's guilt, aware of those who did not make it, of aspects of ourselves that died as well.
—Michael Eigen, Toxic Nourishment, 160

[H]esitation signifies that one is contemplating [doing an] injustice.
—Cicero, On Duties, I,31 (p. 13)

Come with a good will
Or not at all.
—Mother Goose

Love's the only engine of survival.
—Leonard Cohen, "The Future"

Tying up Toxic Loose Ends

What at first glance appears to be a distant and obscure history of the seventeenth century turns out to persist into the present.

Standing as a near constant is the tension and wavering between at least two competing visions: the homogeneity of collectives as opposed to their internal non-coherence. Blacks suffered from slavery. Portuguese New Christians enslaved and sold Blacks. Jews suffered from Christian persecution. Whites and Blacks oppressed Amerindians. New Christians of Jewish and Black background suffered exclusion, denigration and worse at the hands of Old Christians. Identity versus multiplicity, identity as multiplicity. Can an identity — singular, the same as itself — be multiple, that is, many, different from each other? The question comes with perhaps even greater force when polyglot colonial situations are discussed. For the many scholars of Jewish matters since the nineteenth century who have mentioned Afroiberian judaizers, the phenomenon seems to signify little more than something exotic, that is, aberrant and, therefore, insignificant, on the one hand, or to signify the obvious attractions of Judaism even in the bowels of Christendom and particularly to those who have 'nothing.' These scholars do not seem to have noticed how race may have refracted the stance of Judeoconversos toward Afroiberians in the fractious context of colonialism. Scholars of things Iberian have on the whole not noticed how race refracted the Catholic behavior vis-à-vis Judeoconversos of those subalterns the scholars wanted to be nothing more than Catholics, while many scholars of the African diaspora have been too busy focusing on the supposedly exclusive victimization of Afroiberians to recognize their religious collusion as Catholics against those seen as Jews.[1]

The behavior and attitudes of marranos/Jews continue to shock some Iberian Catholic and Spanish or Portuguese nationalist scholars. The peak of the Nazi period produced many feverish speculations. A relatively sympathetic 1939 book on the Portuguese New Christian Diego López cites as a factor in his rise to commercial, military and political prominence his "qualities of shrewdness and the power of insinuation, very typical of his Jewish blood." The author resuscitates a charge from a medieval forged letter (that he treats in one of the chapters within) to the effect that López was a "hidden Jew, who spared nothing in knocking down the sacred orders in order to be better defended and to profane the sacraments, a thing neither new nor incredible among those of his class."[2] The Spanish scholar Guillermo Díaz-Plaja writes in a 1940 book that what is most characteristic "of the Jewish soul is the desire, conscious or unconscious, but which leads dissolved in the persecuted blood, of liquidating or of attacking the classical forms, that is to say, those decisive for the stable equilibrium of the society in which it lives." This is nothing less than a Jewish "eagerness for sabotage." Such race-thinking enables the author to produce an essay titled "A Possible Racial Factor in the Baroque."[3] Covering the Jews who flocked to Dutch Brazil and the difficulties facing White colonization in the tropics, another patently partisan book from the same year rehashes medieval folklore to the effect that "The immunity of the Jews to the plague is a verified historical fact," citing one historian who "observed categorically: 'This illness never attacks the Jews,'" as well as supposed medical sources going back to 1505.[4] Later periods also yielded similarly bitter fruit. One Peruvian scholar writing in the 1960s about a seventeenth-century converso who penned an anonymous description of Peru called this involvement in contraband and espionage a "primary form of semitic reaction," "a negative gesture of undermining the society which has welcomed them." Though self-contradictory, our scholar alleges that "The accommodating character and atavistic caution of the Jews permitted them to lead a double religious life."[5] Similarly Lucía García Proodian, who treats Judeoconversos in the American colonies and enjoys highlighting their role in the trading of slaves. Her analysis conveys her anti-Jewish feelings without veil. Her second section, for instance, purports to trace the "Continuity of the Hebrew Tradition." Its first chapter, "Temperament and Character," a dubious scholarly category to begin with, turns immediately to the Jews' predominant (primerísimo) trait: "Love of Money." Her treatment of converso women — marranos all, of course — she titles "Woman and the Life of Ostentation." Such scholarship repeatedly calls all New Christians Jews, in a willfully biologistic obfuscation.[6]

At the same time, from the other direction, a woman from a synagogue my wife and I attend was at our house one day. In the course of conversation about Jews and Blacks and my research she asked to see a copy of my first book, Jews and Blacks in the Early Modern World. Showing it to her — I was opening to the first page of the Introduction to show her how I state there that extreme Black charges against Jews regarding slavery are often suspect — she said, in an offhanded way, "oh, I was told by someone at shul [synagogue] that your work is anti-Semitic." (I am not sure whether I had already told her that one of my essays was put online by a rabidly anti-Jewish Black nationalist website.[7]) All this confirmed my wife's worries that the book would make me public enemy number one in the Jewish world. But the deeper meaning is more frightening. After all, what is 'anti-Semitic' about a book treating, in a scholarly methodology of relatively moderate tone and fact-based argumentation, Sephardic relations with Blacks? Likely for some Jews any conclusion that deems Jews to have been less than angelic in some way, that dares raise a critical voice suggesting that Jews behaved like others, that airs dirty laundry in public — verges on anti-Semitism.

Despite such conclusions, there is no 'disposition' for members of a group to respond to their group's persecution or oppression in a given manner.[8] Yirmiyahu Yovel's attempt to harness studies of marranos in order to explain the philosophy of Baruch/Benedict Spinoza rests on a problematic, if not dangerous thesis regarding marranos of the opposite order from Iberian anti-Jewish thinkers but that nonetheless shares a tendency toward generalization. This thesis imagines that marranos display "a this-worldly disposition; a split religious identity; a metaphysical skepticism; a quest for alternative salvation through methods that oppose the official doctrine; an opposition between the inner and outer life, and a tendency toward dual language and equivocation."[9] Historically, given the hermeneutical and epistemological difficulties of dealing with Inquisition records and the extreme situations that produced the converso problem and that it in turn produced, I believe Yovel's thesis is simply inaccurate, as new historical studies make increasingly clear. On another level the danger of such theses lies in the ease with which they become generalized into essentialist understandings about the group under discussion. Many Judeoconversos evince none or few of the above characteristics, while many non-marranos of the era, New Christian or otherwise, do manifest them. Similarly, Afroiberians showed a wide range of reactions to their captivity, mistreatment and exclusion. Gayatri Chakravorty Spivak argues that individuals living in postcolonial situations are "interested either in proving that they are ethnic subjects and therefore the true marginals or that they are as good as the colonials."[10] The peculiar 'in-betweenness' of Christian Afroiberians and Judeoconversos is their simultaneous existence under both colonial and incipient post-colonial conditions, being subject and marginal according to one term of domination ('race') yet included according to another term ('religion').

Irene Silverblatt sees the rise of "race thinking, nationalist sentiments, bureaucratic rule, colonialism — and the nascent capitalist order girding them" in the sixteenth- and seventeenth-century Spanish empire.[11] I fully agree, though I would include Portugal. Yet the truth of this does not mean that subaltern populations and their individual members did not also collude, wittingly or not, in the perpetuation and manipulation of prejudices, as I hope to have shown. Indeed, some dominated groups willingly allied with dominating groups against other dominated groups, some members of every dominated group willingly aided, served or joined the forces of domination, either on specific occasions or for life.[12] Bourdieu comments on this perhaps disappointing propensity:

> the deadly passions of all racisms (of ethnicity, sex or class) perpetuate themselves because they are bound to the body in the form of dispositions and also because the relation of domination of which they are the product perpetuates itself in objectivity, continuously reinforcing the propensity to accept it, which, except in the case of a critical break (that performed by the 'reactive' nationalism of dominated peoples, for example), is no less strong among the dominated than the dominant.[13]

Characterizing "Black-Jewish" relations in the seventeenth century, therefore, almost inevitably retrojects today's socio-economic and political tensions. The very question itself divulges this fact. Yet, despite some significant and vast differences between the two eras and situations, it is hard not to recognize some similarities. As two groups of intermediaries or go-betweens that served vastly different purposes for the empires, Judeoconversos and Afroiberians stood very much in conflict, often quite direct, with one another. Added to this was a very real religious and theopolitical divergence. Nonetheless, it is difficult to detect much, if any, particular animus between members of the two groups.

'Progressive' alliances, proclivities or moments might indeed have existed in the seventeenth century. Tobias Green, in his study of New Christians in the Cabo Verde islands, speculates that the local New Christians may have been more inclined than others to interact with and even adapt to surrounding African cultures.[14] Historian of colonial Brazil, Stuart Schwartz, uses the theopolitical miscegenation of early eighteenth-century Bahia as a narrative of proto-Enlightenment self-emancipation in which the colonial world's "peculiar social contexts (in this Brazilian case, the presence of many New Christians [and widespread African practices]), the opportunities for 'liberty' of conscience and action, and the difficulty of imposing conformity tended to diminish the authority of Church and State, or force those institutions toward accommodation with local realities."[15]

The scenarios highlighted by Green and Schwartz may well have been real, but they cannot be projected onto the totality of 'Judeoconverso life' or 'Afroiberian experience' any more than their negative counterparts.

Analysis must be able to free itself from structuralist binarisms, attentive to the different modes in which power circulates from above to below, from bottom against top, attentive to the multiplicity, partial awareness and even uncertainty that might characterize personal motivation, self-consciousness and self-justification.[16] Discussing "the range of experiences of indigenous women in [colonial] Potosí," Jane Mangan highlights how one finds women "who suffer, manage, and thrive," and she insists that the object of her inquiry can be understood "only by treating this complexity."[17] Walter Mignolo has proposed approaching colonial situations with diatopical or pluritopical perspectives.[18] Pointing with condemnation at 'empire,' harping on 'asymmetries of power' erects the dominators and their instruments as metaphysical principles, totalizing and incontestable, erases through negativity the agency and efficacy (those these are not the same) of those who resist or oppose from below or from within, and seemingly seeks to absolve resisters and opponents from moral standing. On the one hand, even if, as Michel Foucault and others have argued, power circulates diffusely, this does not mean that its local forcefulness and effectiveness cannot be measured, described. Agency and responsibility continue to exist even where power is less generously to be found. The agency of those 'under' power's sway and the circulation of power do not make up a zero sum game. This is the tension laid out by Talal Asad between history from the perspective of the dominant power (global capitalism) and the 'active' subaltern history favored by anthropologists.[19] It would seem self-evident that neither pole can exist in isolation. Asad himself concludes with a query: "People are never only active agents and subjects in their own history. The interesting question in each case is: In what degree, and in what way, are they agents or patients?"[20]

The rub lies elsewhere as well. The question is not just what range of reactions did individuals or groups have to oppression, colonialism or the like. On the level of hermeneutics many scholars continue to operate as if there must be a single explanation for historical events, as if one must choose between ideological or materialist readings. Here, too, I would suggest, mutual exclusivity should not hover like a specter. Some acts of violence might be acts of resistance, some might be efforts to improve nothing more than the life of the actor. Some might be neither. Some might be both. A New Christian or zambo might well have been torn between both of these motivations as well as others, such as romance, hatred, jealousy or unpremeditated impulse. The same multiplicity holds even more for explanations of group behavior or complex phenomena such as colonization, racism or resistance to domination. Generalizations should make us wary, however well-intentioned or rationalized as necessary for the production of 'digestible' historiography.

One modern scholar, introducing a new translation of a seventeenth-century Spanish chronicle about the discovery and conquest of Nueva Granada, concludes that "all history, at bottom, is a study in human nature."[21] If by 'human nature' we mean something like what the portmanteau term implies, something both cultural and natural, both constructed and real, something meaningless enough to extend to any number of conditions/situations yet meaningful enough that most of us use the term on occasion, then I might well agree. This human nature-culture/subject-object operates within a real world whose parameters are quite concretely given. The confluence of multiplicity within the individual and heterogeneity between groups does not result in a simple symmetry of equal and equally free players. Rather, the variety of forces and claims need to be deconstructed with their origins, vectors and effects in mind. This is our job as scholars and citizen-activists; insofar as we are allowed by external circumstance, we must choose our allies, our candidates, our barricades. (And how many choose even when not permitted, even when the penalty is tremendous?[22]) When confronting empire and its injustices, its naive defenders opposing alterity in the name of some right to determine the lives of others, I see it as imperative to foreground the right to be left alone and the relative unfreedom of the subaltern. When confronting subaltern romantic locals and nativists and anti-imperial fascists, I see it as imperative to identify and fight the dangers of undoing helpful universalisms in the name of small-minded particularism. We are more in-between than we imagine. "If I press my nose to someone's window, it isn't to see everything in his house. There is much that would not satisfy my curiosity enough to repay the effort. The privacy I want to invade is that which allows me to learn the denouement of some story about which I have my own psychological urgency, and for which I lack an ending." (Janna Malamud Smith, Private Matters)

I confess to having been significantly influenced by scholars, particularly feminists, who meditate on the meanings of anger in scholarship and wonder what the scholar who feels it is to do with it.[23] Examining the early modern Atlantic inevitably leads to anger over the ubiquitous instances and systemic use of denigration, mistreatment, cruelty and homicidal violence again Others. Even the downtrodden were not (are rarely, if ever) free from the above sins. (It can be asked to what degree a lack of responsive anger or its dismissal signifies a desire for histories "purified" of "our" own transgressions.) Yet looking mostly for historical examples of resistance to domination, to oppression — their own or that of others — who will mirror the scholar's own tendencies, often leads to romanticization and a blindness to the ways in which subalterns willingly acquiesce and submit to the systems in which they find themselves. I have tried to overcome this blindness, to intentionally face it, while not forgetting the very real power of the dominators, of the empire-builders, and the abuses to which their power leads.

Early modern Iberian political and religious triumph and expansion brought about its own tarnishing: immense wealth that barely improved the lives of most citizens if at all; a "pathological fear of uncleanness — of pollution by secret Judaizers, but also of Protestant 'heretics,' 'demoniac witches,' and sexual 'perverts' — underlay almost everything in Spanish life;" a rampant and justified paranoia regarding denunciation by others for the slightest deviation, real or imagined, and a concomitant internal paranoia concerning whether one was deviating from the norms oneself; a fetishistic obsession with reputation, honor, glory, that is, with how one was seen by others.[24] The seemingly society-wide depths of projection of problems onto Others, of endless, obsessive-compulsive self-scrutiny, of willful obfuscation and denial stand in ironic proportional contrast to the very heights of victory, conquest, domination achieved by Spain and Portugal, achievements which should have brought about mostly security, confidence and satiety. It is difficult to refrain from drawing parallels to the empire built with sometimes similar methods by the United States toward sometimes similar ends, currently collapsing from internal misrule, fear of numerous Others and ignorance about the sources of true wealth.

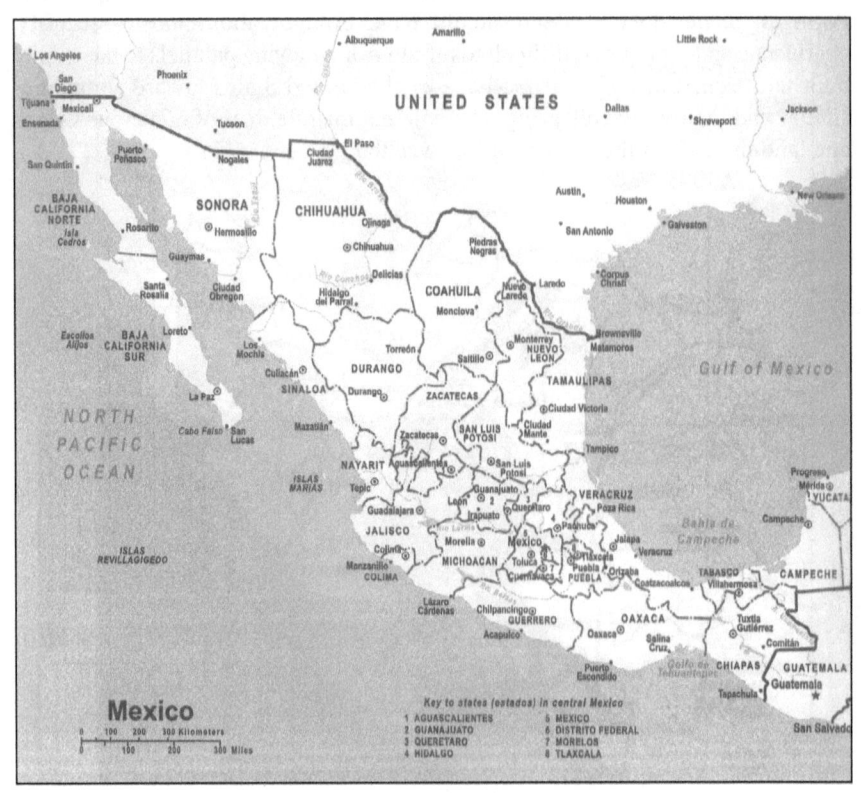

Map of Mexico

Afterword

In the ten years since Swimming the Christian Atlantic came out, numerous new studies have been produced which touch on the same material. While it would be impossible to mention everything important published on New Christians, the Inquisitions, the slave trade, Africans in the Americas, and other intersecting topics, I would like to point to some of the most relevant investigations, particularly those that expand on and offer new perspectives on themes treated in my study.

New Christian/Jewish trans-Atlantic trading networks have received renewed attention by many scholars. Two exemplary dissertations are Reginaldo Jonas Heller, "Diáspora atlântica: A nação judaica no Caribe, séculos XVII e XVIII" (PhD Dissertation, Universidade Federal Fulminense, 2008); and Daniel Strum, "The Portuguese Jews and New Christians in the Sugar Trade: Managing Business Overseas: Kinship and Ethnicity Revisited (Amsterdam, Porto and Brazil, 1595-1618)" (PhD Dissertation: Hebrew University of Jerusalem, 2009). A March 2005 colloquium at Johns Hopkins University, Atlantic Jewry in the Age of Mercantilism, resulted in a volume of essays that has already become canonical: Richard L. Kagan and Philip D. Morgan (Eds.), Atlantic Diasporas: Jews, Conversos, and Crypto-Jews in the Age of Mercantilism, 1500-1800 (Baltimore: Johns Hopkins University Press, 2009).

Recuperating the centrality of Africa to studies of the early New Christian diaspora and trading system has been one of the main innovations of recent scholarship, following on the heels of a similar reorientation in Atlantic-world studies in general. Peter Mark and José da Silva Horta's important book on the small and short-lived Sephardic and New Christian communities along the West African coast in the late 16th and early 17th centuries, The Forgotten Diaspora: Jewish Communities in West Africa and the Making of the Atlantic World (New York: Cambridge University Press, 2011), has added significantly to our knowledge. Similarly, vital as a portrait of New Christian slave traders is Tobias Green, The Rise of the Trans-Atlantic Slave Trade in Western Africa, 1300-1589 (Cambridge University Press, 2011). Green considers many of the same questions that I raise here regarding New Christian identity or subject position as it was shaped by colonialism, imperialism, and mercantilism in his publication, "Pluralism, Violence and Empire: The Portuguese New Christians in the Atlantic World," Francisco Bethencourt (ed.), Cosmopolitanism in the Portuguese-Speaking World, European Expansion and Indigenous Response, Vol. 27 (Leiden: Brill, 2017), 40-58. Claude B. Stuczynski, "Portuguese Conversos and the Manueline Imperial Idea: A Preliminary Study," Anais de história de além-mar 14 (2013): 45-61, provides a complementary abstract and political view.

A significant number of analyses of the Spanish and Portuguese Inquisitions have come out. Particularly relevant to the cast of characters appearing in chapter 3 — treating Cartagena, Blas de Pas Pinto, and the commercial network of Manuel Bautista Perez — is Ana E. Schaposchnik, The Lima Inquisition: The Plight of Crypto-Jews in Seventeenth-Century Peru (Madison: The University of Wisconsin Press, 2015). Stuart B. Schwartz, All Can Be Saved: Religious Tolerance and Salvation in the Iberian Atlantic World (New Haven: Yale University Press, 2008), excavates from the documentary record the widespread skepticism toward religious and political orthodoxies that percolated throughout the Atlantic world, voiced not just by New Christians, but by "ordinary" people of all backgrounds and classes.

Understanding the complexities of New Christian identity or self-perception has remained a difficult but critical task. Recent studies have wielded a variety of approaches but agree that religiosity alone does not provide the solution and that historical variation, the complex self, malleable social frames, and opportunism must be taken into account. Among the freshest and most informed meditations stand Miriam Bodian, "Hebrews of the Portuguese Nation: The Ambiguous Boundaries of Self-Definition," Jewish Social Studies 15,1 (Fall 2008): 66-80. There is also David Graizbord, "Religion and Ethnicity Among 'Men of the Nation:' Toward a Realistic Interpretation," Jewish Social Studies 15,1 (Fall 2008): 32-65; and his publication, "Who and What was a Jew? Some Considerations for the Historical Study of New Christians," Anais de História de Além-Mar 14 (2013): 15-44, as well as Juan Ignacio Pulido Serrano, "Plural identities: the Portuguese New Christians," Jewish History 25,2 (2011): 129-51, and Claude Stuczynski, "Harmonizing Identities: The Problem of the Integration of the Portuguese Conversos in Early Modern Iberian Corporate Polities," Jewish History 25,2 (2011): 229-257. Seth D. Kunin, Juggling Identities: Identity and Authenticity Among the Crypto-Jews (New York: Columbia University Press, 2009), takes these questions into late modernity by means of the crypto-Jewish community of New Mexico.

I suggest that New Christians and former conversos produced a body of textual work that often lauded and shared the assumptions of Portuguese and Spanish imperialism (as does Stuczynski). A different view is offered now by Gabriel Mordoch, "New Christian Discourse and Early Modern Portuguese Oceanic Expansion: The Cases of Garcia da Orta, Fernao Mendes Pinto, Ambrosio Fernandes Brandao, and Pedro de Leon Portocarrero" (PhD Dissertation, Ohio State University, 2017), who reads a number of chronicles and geographic descriptions authored by New Christians as expressing skepticism and implicit criticism toward Iberian imperial triumphalism. I discuss in the same chapter the incredible series of atlases produced by Johannes or Jan Jansonius, to which a number of Sephardic authors contributed. Additional research on the contributions of David Nassy to these atlases has now been advanced by Natalie Zemon Davis, "Regaining Jerusalem: Eschatology and Slavery in Jewish Colonization in Seventeenth-Century Suriname," The Cambridge Journal of Postcolonial Literary Inquiry 3,1 (January 2016): 19-22.

Turning to matters of group perceptions and prejudice, race, and religious Othering, María Elena Martínez, Genealogical Fictions: Limpieza de Sangre, Religion and Gender in Colonial Mexico (Stanford: Stanford University Press, 2008), still stands as one of the most important interventions. She shows how anti-Jewish attitudes and strategies of control and exclusion morphed into the racial caste system of the Iberian colonial worlds. At the time Swimming the Christian Atlantic went to press, only her dissertation was available. Martínez's untimely death stole from the scholarly world a promising investigator and interpreter. Continuing her work, in some sense, is Max S. Hering Torres, who has tackled with welcome sophistication topics related to limpieza de sangre / purity of blood and early modern questions regarding race. See, for instance, Max S. Hering Torres, María Elena Martínez, and David Nirenberg (eds.), Race and Blood in the Iberian World (Zürich: Lit Verlag, 2012), and Nikolaus Böttcher, Bernd Hausberger, and Max S. Hering Torres (eds.), El peso de la sangre: Limpios, mestizos y nobles en el mundo hispánico (Mexico City: El Colegio de México, 2011). These scholars argue against an ahistorical notion of "race" that is then retrojected into early modern situations, preferring the idea that complex, varying, and often flexible understandings of human groups — not based solely on deterministic biological criteria — served as the bases for differing forms of control and exclusion. Based on this body of work, for example, Mark and Horta challenge the application of race as a construct to West Africa from the moment of Portuguese arrival in the late 15th century into the 17th century. Important distinctions also need to be noted between the anti-Jewish and anti-Black attitudes and social strategies of the early Iberian empires.

My own thinking on many of the aforementioned issues has evolved, due in no small part to the contributions of my colleagues. An example of a recent related work of mine is Jonathan Schorsch, "New Christian Slave Traders: A Literature Review and Research Agenda," in Sina Rauschenbach and Jonathan Schorsch (eds.) The Sephardic Atlantic: Colonial Histories and Postcolonial Perspectives (New York: Palgrave Macmillan, 2019): ch. 2. Ranging more widely and dealing mostly with the openly Jewish Atlantic is my "Revisiting Blackness, Slavery and Jewishness in the Early Modern Sephardic Atlantic," in Yosef Kaplan (ed.) Religious Changes and Cultural Transformations in the Early Modern Western Sephardi Communities, (Leiden: Brill, 2019): 512-40. In addition to the Introduction to The Sephardic Atlantic, "Postcolonial Approaches to the Early Modern Sephardic Atlantic," which Rauschenbach and I co-authored, many of the other essays in this volume discuss pertinent topoi. Along with the rest of the publications listed here, they will reward readers who care about this cluster of issues with which we as scholars and as a species continue to wrestle.

New York City
2018

Notes

Introduction

1. Nicholas B. Dirks, *Castes of Mind: Colonialism and the Making of Modern India* (Princeton: Princeton University Press, 2001), 43-60, 125-227.
2. Alida C. Metcalf, *Go-betweens and the Colonization of Brazil, 1500-1600* (Austin: University of Texas Press, 2005), 2.
3. Webb Keane, *Christian Moderns: Freedom and Fetish in the Mission Encounter* (Berkeley: University of California Press, 2007), 29.
4. Peter Van der Veer (ed.), *Conversion to Modernities: The Globalization of Christianity* (New York: Routledge, 1995).
5. Jorge Cañizares-Esguerra, *Puritan Conquistadors: Iberianizing the Atlantic, 1550-1700* (Stanford: Stanford University Press, 2006).
6. Barbara Fuchs, *Mimesis and Empire: The New World, Islam, and European Identities* (Cambridge: Cambridge University Press, 2001). Similar linkages of Old and New World conceptualizations and methods of conquest are offered by Jonathan Boyarin, *The Unconverted Self: Jews, Indians, and the Identity of Christian Europe* (Chicago: University of Chicago Press, 2009).
7. David Eltis, "Identity and Migration: The Atlantic in Comparative Perspective," in *The Atlantic World: Essays on Slavery, Migration, and Imagination*, eds. Wim Klooster and Alfred Padula (Upper Saddle River, NJ: Pearson/Prentice Hall, 2005), 111.
8. Gil Anidjar, "Blood Works: The Fluidity of the Bio-Political c. 1449," paper, conference on Cultural Mobility, Wissenschaftskolleg, Berlin, May 2004, 11; idem, "Lines of Blood: *Limpieza de Sangre* as Political Theology," in *Blood in History and Blood Histories*, ed. Mariacarla Gadebusch Bondio (Firenze: Sismel Edizioni il Galluzzo, 2005).
9. Bruno Latour, *We Have Never Been Modern*, trans. Catherine Porter (Cambridge: Harvard University Press, 1993), 49, with a quote inserted from Irene Silverblatt, *Modern Inquisitions: Peru and the Colonial Origins of the Civilized World* (Durham: Duke University Press, 2004), 119.
10. Latour, *We Have Never Been Modern*, 40. And not, therefore, a "phantasm," as Silverblatt has it (*Modern Inquisitions*, 18). Without wanting to enter into an enormous and dangerous topic, my perspective is that race/ethnicity is real, i.e., "natural," insofar as different population groups often manifest different biological conditions: immunities to particular diseases or lack thereof, manifest specific patterns of disease (lactose intolerance, Sickle Cell Anemia, Tay-Sachs disease, etc.). Different population groups might also manifest statistically notable somatic uniquenesses: eye shape, particularly light skin, height, etc. The problem — racism — arises from, itself entails a socio-cultural response to such axiologically meaningless natural differences.
11. R. Douglas Cope, *The Limits of Racial Domination: Plebeian Society in Colonial Mexico City, 1660-1720* (Madison: University of Wisconsin Press, 1994).
12. Irene Silverblatt, Modern Inquisitions: Peru and the Colonial origins of the Civilized World (Durham: Duke University Press, 2004), 101-15.
13. Silverblatt, *Modern Inquisitions*, 111.
14. Catalina de Erauso, *Lieutenant Nun: Memoirs of a Basque Transvestite in the New World*, trans. Michele Stepto and Gabriel Stepto (Boston: Beacon Press, 1996).
15. Judaizing as a charge had a long history before the Spanish Inquisition. There is debate about whether its usage remained consistent with earlier understandings. To 'judaize' meant for non-Jews "to adopt the customs and manners of the Jews," especially religious practices (Shaye J. D. Cohen, "'Those Who Say They Are Jews and Are Not': How Do You Know a Jew in Antiquity When You See One?" in Shaye J.D. Cohen and Ernest S. Frerichs [eds.], *Diasporas in Antiquity*

[Atlanta: Scholars Press, 1990], 32). Though not considered a crime in the ancient world, 'judaizing' seems to have functioned, already soon after its neutral coinage by ancient Greeks, as a term of demarcation, identification, categorization. It served to place one in an agonistic contest between ethnicities and beliefs. Rabbi Yitsḥak Arama (1420-1494), familiar with the inquisitional mentality and its consequences, used the term to refer to "performing acts which were customary among Jews with the intention of being a Jew and returning to Judaism" (Arama, *Akeidat Yitsḥak* [Salonika, 1522], Deut., 262a; translation from Haim Beinart, *Conversos on Trial: the Inquisition in Ciudad Real*, Hispania Judaica, no. 3 [Jerusalem: The Magnes Press/The Hebrew University, 1981], 24, n.15). Historically it had not always been so easy to distinguish Jews and Christians and *that* was precisely the problem requiring from the medieval period on social constructions distinguishing the two (dress codes, spatial segregation, extreme ideational opposition, etc.). Scholar Karen King defines Christian orthodoxy as the delicate balance between being too Jewish and not Jewish enough. On the medieval history of the term 'judaizing,' see Róbert Dán, "'Judaizare' — The Career of a Term," in R. Dán and A. Pirnát (eds.), *Antitrinitarianism in the Second Half of the Sixteenth Century* (Budapest: Hungarian Academy of Sciences, 1982), 25-34.
16. Samuel Eliot Morison, *The European Discovery of America*, vol. 1: *The Northern Voyages, A. D. 500-1600* (New York: Oxford University Press, 1971), vol. 2: *The Southern Voyages, 1492-1616* (New York: Oxford University Press, 1974); Josiah Blackmore, *Manifest Perdition: Shipwreck narrative and the Disruption of Empire* (Minneapolis: University of Minnesota Press, 2002).
17. Quoted in Michel de Certeau, *The Practice of Everyday Life*, trans. by Steven F. Rendall (Berkeley: University of California Press, 1984), 117.
18. Robert Harbison, *Reflections on Baroque* (Chicago: University of Chicago Press, 2000), 1, 187; Serge Gruzinski, *The Mestizo Mind: The Intellectual Dynamics of Colonization and Globalization* (New York: Routledge, 2002), 114, 128.
19. Carlos Ginzburg, *Wooden Eyes: Nine Reflections on Distance* (New York: Columbia University Press, 2001), 15. He cites Adriano Prosperi, "'Otras Indias': Missionari della controriforma tra contadini e selvaggi," in *Scienze, credenze occulte, livelli di cultura: Convegno internazionale di studi (Firenze, 26-30 giugno 1980)* (Firenze: L.S. Olschki, 1982), 205-34.
20. See, for instance, the cases brought in James H. Sweet, *Recreating Africa: Culture, Kinship, and Religion in the African-Portuguese World, 1441-1770* (Chapel Hill: University of North Carolina Press, 2003), 96-101.
21. Catherine Gallagher and Stephen Greenblatt, *Practicing New Historicism* (Chicago: University of Chicago Press, 2000), 14-16; see also ch. 2 ("Counterhistory and the Anecdote").
22. Henry Kamen, *The Spanish Inquisition: A Historical Revision* (New Haven: Yale University Press, 1998); Irene Silverblatt, "Colonial Conspiracies," *Ethnohistory* 53,2 (Spring 2006): 260-1.
23. Silverblatt, "Colonial Conspiracies," 261.
24. Solange Behocaray de Alberro, "Negros y mulatos en los documentos inquisitoriales: rechazo e integración," in Elsa Cecilia Frost et al (eds.), *El Trabajo y los Trabajadores en la Historia de México: Ponencias y comentarios presentados en la Reunión de Historiadores Mexicanos y Norteamericanos, Pátzcuaro, 12 al 15 de octubre de 1977* (Mexico City/Tucson: El Colegio de México/University of Arizona Press, 1979), 144-49; idem, *Inquisición y sociedad en México, 1571-1700* (Mexico City: Fondo de Cultura Económica, 1988), 467-72.
25. Yosef Hayim Yerushalmi, From Spanish Court to Italian Ghetto: Isaac Cardoso, A Study in Seventeenth-Century Marranism and Jewish Apologetics, 2nd ed. (Seattle: University of Washington Press, 1981 [orig. 1971]), 11-12.
26. Yerushalmi, Spanish Court to Italian Ghetto, 1-42.

Chapter 1

1. Judaizing refers to the teaching or promulgating of Jewish beliefs and/or practices, and thus carried a heavier penalty than merely maintaining such practices oneself.
2. Gwendolyn Midlo Hall, *Slavery and African Ethnicities in the Americas: Restoring the Links* (Chapel Hill: University of North Carolina Press, 2005), 20.
3. David G. Sweet, "Black Robes and 'Black Destiny': Jesuit Views of African Slavery in 17th-Century Latin America," *Revista de Historia de America* 86 (July-December 1978): 105-6.
4. Cope, Limits of Racial Domination, 4; Jack D. Forbes, *Africans and Native Americans: The Language of Race and the Evolution of Red-Black Peoples* (Urbana: University of Illinois Press, 1993), chs. 4 and 8.

5. On the "invention" of the mulato, see Luiz Felipe de Alencastro, *O trato dos viventes: formacao do Brasil no Atlantico Sul* (São Paulo: Cia das Letras, 2000), 345-53; Martínez López, María Elena, "The Spanish Concept of *Limpieza de Sangre* and the Emergence of the 'Race/Caste' System in the Viceroyalty of New Spain," (PhD Dissertation, University of Chicago, 2002), 211-17 (now Marí Elena Martínez, *Genealogical Fictions: Limpeza de Sangre, Religion and Gender in Colonial Mexico* [Stanford: Stanford University Press, 2008]); Forbes, *Africans and Native Americans*, chs. 5 and 6.
6. Stuart Hall, "Pluralism, Race and Class in Caribbean Society," in *Race and Class in Post-Colonial Society* (Paris: UNESCO, 1977), 158, 162.
7. Personal communication; Feb. 2008.
8. Erauso, *Lieutenant Nun*, 28.
9. Letter of 1646 cited by José Toribio Medina, *Historia del Tribunal del Santo Oficio de la Inquisición de Cartagena de las Indias* (Santiago de Chile: Imprenta Elzeviriana, 1899), 242, n. 1.
10. Kenneth Brown, "Lope de Vera (1619-1644) y Lope de Vega (1562-1635)," *Fronteras e interculturalidad entre los sefardíes occidentales*, eds. Paloma Díaz-Mas and Harm den Boer, (Amsterdam: Rodopi, 2006), orig. *Foro Hispánico* 28 (2005), 70. Brown cites Lope de Vega Carpio, *Cartas completas*, ed. Ángel Rosenblat (Buenos Aires: Emecé, 1948), 1:91, 139-31.
11. Vidal Abril Castelló, *Francisco de la Cruz, Inquisición, actas*, 3 vols., Corpus Hispanorum de pace, v. 29, 32-34, 35-37 (Madrid: Consejo Superior de Investigaciones Científicas, 1992-97), 1:565.
12. Cope, *Limits of Racial Domination*; Schwartz, "Spaniards, *Pardos*, and the Missing Mestizos: Identities and Racial Categories in the Early Hispanic Caribbean," *New West Indian Guide* 71,1&2 (1997): 5-19.
13. Herman Bennett, Africans in Colonial Mexico: Absolutism, Christianity, and Afro-Creole Consciousness, 1570-1640 (Bloomington: Indiana University Press, 2003), 27.
14. Certeau, The Practice of Everyday Life, xix.
15. Jeremy Lawrance, "Black Africans in Renaissance Spanish Literature," in Earle and Lowe, *Black Africans in Renaissance Europe*, 76, cites the following sources: Sebastián de Cobarruvias Orozco's famous dictionary, *Tesoro de la lengua castellana o española* (Madrid, 1611), 562: "Aunque negros, gente somos"; *Vocabulario de refranes y frases proverbiales* (1627), ed. Louis Combet (Bordeaux, 1967), 33, which offers the phrase in the period's literary imitation of African dialect *habla de negros*, making even stronger the argument that this utterance reflects the protesting voice of actual Africans: "Aunke somo negro, onbre somo, alma tenemo."
16. See, for instance, Cope, *Limits of Racial Domination*, chs. 1-2 and 4; Christopher H. Lutz, *Santiago de Guatemala, 1541-1773: City, Caste, and the Colonial Experience* (Norman, Okla.: University of Oklahoma Press, 1994), ch. 3. According to Lutz, who seems to have made no effort to track African ethnicities, Black slaves in Santiago de Guatemala married most frequently with free Blacks (115).
17. Bennett, Africans in Colonial Mexico, 82.
18. Leo J. Garofalo, "The Ethno-Economy of Food, Drink, and Stimulants: The Making of Race in Colonial Lima and Cuzco (PhD Dissertation, University of Wisconsin-Madison, 2001), 453.
19. Maria da Graça A. Mateus Ventura, *Negreiros portugueses na rota das Índias de Castela (1541-1556)* (Lisbon: Edições Colibri/Instituto de Cultura Ibero-Atlântica, 1999), 26.
20. A recent and important statement of the growing trend in scholarship that argues the importance of acknowledging and studying the ethnicity of the slaves brought to the Americas can be found in Hall, *Slavery and African Ethnicities in the Americas*. Hall deals mostly with eighteenth-century Louisiana but provides excellent coverage of other Atlantic locales and earlier periods, as well of the translatability of her methodology and conclusions to these spheres, while yet remaining wary of feeling pressure to concoct unitary global results. See also Paul E. Lovejoy, "Trans-Atlantic Transformations: The Origins and Identity of Africans in the Americas," in *The Atlantic World: Essays on Slavery, Migration and Imagination*, ed. Wim Klooster and Alfred Padula (Upper Saddle River, NJ: Pearson/Prentice Hall, 2005), 126-46; idem, "The Muslim Factor in the Trans-Atlantic Slave Trade," in *Slavery on the Frontiers of Islam*, ed. Paul E. Lovejoy (Princeton: Markus Wiener, 2002); Michael A. Gomez, *Black Crescent: The Experience and Legacy of African Muslims in the Americas* (Cambridge University Press, 2005); idem, *Exchanging Our Country Marks: the Transformation of African Identities in the Colonial and Antebellum South* (Chapel Hill: University of North Carolina Press, 1998); Douglas B. Chambers, "Tracing Igbo Identity into the African Diaspora," in *Identity in the Shadow of Slavery*, ed. Paul E. Lovejoy (London: Continuum, 2000), 55-71; idem, "'My Own Nation': Igbo Exiles in the Diaspora," *Slavery and Abolition* 18,1 (April

1997): 72-97; Walter Rucker, "Conjure, Magic, and Power: The Influence of Afro-Atlantic Religious Practices on Resistance and Rebellion," *Journal of Black Studies* 32,1 (Sept. 2001): 84-103; David Northrup, "Igbo and Myth Igbo: Culture and Ethnicity in the Atlantic World, 1600-1850," *Slavery & Abolition* 21 (2000): 1-20; Kenneth Bilby, "Swearing by the Past, Swearing to the Future: Sacred Oaths, Alliances, and Treaties among the Huianese and Jamaican Maroons," *Ethnohistory* 44, 4 (1997): 655-689; idem, "The Kromanti Dance of the Windward Maroons of Jamaica," *Nieuwe West-Indische Gids* 55, nos. 1/2 (1981): 52-101; Maureen Warner-Lewis, *Trinidad Yoruba: From Mother Tongue to Memory* (Tuscaloosa: University of Alabama Press, 1996); Colin Palmer, "From Africa to the Americas: Ethnicity in the Early Black Communities of the Americas," *Journal of World History* 6 (1995): 223-36; Karen Fog Olwig, "African Cultural Principles in Caribbean Slave Societies," in *Slave Cultures and the Cultures of Slavery*, ed. Stephan Palmié (Knoxville: University of Tennessee Press, 1995), 23-39; John Thornton, "'I Am the Subject of the King of Congo': African Political Ideology and the Haitian Revolution," *Journal of World History* 4 (1993): 181-214; idem, "African Dimensions of the Stono Rebellion," *American Historical Review* 96 (1991): 1101-1113; Richard Cullen Rath, "African Music in Seventeenth-Century Jamaica: Cultural Transit and Transmission" *William & Mary Quarterly* 50 (Oct. 1993): 700-27; Andrew Apter, "Herskovits's Heritage: Rethinking Syncretism in the African Diaspora," *Diaspora* 1:3 (1991): 235-60; Joseph E. Holloway (ed.), *Africanisms in American Culture* (Bloomington: Indiana University Press, 1990); B. Kopytof, "Religious Change among the Jamaican Maroons: The Ascendance of the Christian God within a Traditional Cosmology," *Journal of Social History* 20 (1987): 463-84; Daniel C. Littlefield, *Rice and Slaves: Ethnicity and the Slave Trade in Colonial South Carolina* (Baton Rouge: Louisiana State University Press, 1981).
21. Some of the works listed in the previous note also treat Iberian territories. See Luz Adriana Maya Restrepo, *Brujería y reconstrucción de identidades entre los africanos y sus descendientes en la Nueva Granada, siglo XVII* (Bogota: Ministerio de Cultura, 2005); Patrick James Carroll, *Blacks in Colonial Veracruz: Race, Ethnicity, and Regional Development*, 2nd ed. (Austin: University of Texas Press, 2001); Armin J. Schwegler, *"Chi ma nkongo:" Lengua y ritos ancestrales en El Palenque de San Basilio (Colombia)* (Frankfurt: Vervuert, 1996); Palmer, "From Africa to the Americas"; George Brandon, *Santería from Africa to the New World: The Dead Sell Memories* (Bloomington: Indiana University Press, 1993); Adriana Perez and Norma Garcia Cabrera (eds.), *Abakuá: Una secta secreta: Selección de textos* (Havana, 1993); Edna M. Ramos Castro, *Negros do trombetas: Etnicidade e história* (Belém: NAIA/Universidade Federal do Pará, 1991); María Elena Cortés Jácome, "La memoria familiar de los negros y mulatos: Siglo XVI-XVIII," in *La memoria y el olvido, segundo Simposio de Historia de las mentalidades, segunda jornada: Infames, elegidos y memoria* (México, D.F.: INAH, 1985), 125-33.
22. Nicole von Germeten, *Black Blood Brothers: Confraternities And Social Mobility for Afro-Mexicans* (University Press of Florida, 2006); Elizabeth W. Kiddy, "Ethnic and Racial Identity in the Brotherhoods of the Rosary of Minas Gerais, 1700-1830," *The Americas* 56:2 (October 1999): 221-52; Ignacio Camacho Martínez, *La hermandad de los mulatos de Sevilla* (Seville, 1998); Mieko Nishida, "From Ethnicity to Race and Gender: Transformations of Black Lay Sodalities in Salvador, Brazil," *Journal of Social History* 32,2 (Winter 1998): 329-48; Isidoro Moreno Navarro, *La antigua hermandad de los negros de Sevilla: Etnicidad, poder y sociedad en 600 años de historia* (Seville, 1997); Joaquín Rodriguez Mateos, "De los esclavos y marginados: Dios de blancos y piedad de negros, La cofradía de los morenos de Sevilla," in *Actas II Congreso de Historia de Anadalucía, Historia Moderna* (Córdoba, 1995), 569-82; Luis Gómez Acuña, "Los cofradías de negros en Lima (siglo XVII): Estado de la cuestión y análisis de caso," *Páginas* 129 (October 1994): 28-39; Isabel Castro Henriques, "Formas de intervenção e de organização dos africanos em S. Tomé nos séculos XV e XVI," in *Actas do II Colóquio Internacional de História da Madeira, Funchal, Setembro 1989* (n.p.: Centro de Estudos de História do Atlântico, 1990), 797-813; Patricia A. Mulvey, "Black Brothers and Sisters: Membership in the Black Lay Brotherhoods of Colonial Brazil," *Luso-Brazilian Review* 17 (1982): 253-79; idem, "Slave Confraternities in Brazil: Their Role in Colonial Society," *The Americas* 39 (1982), 39-68; A. J. R. Russell-Wood, "Black Mulatto Brotherhood in Colonial Brazil: A Study in Collective Behavior," *Hispanic American Historical Review*, 54,4 (1974): 567-602; H. Sancho de Sopranis, *Las cofradías de morenos en Cádiz* (Madrid, 1958); Miguel Gual Camarena, "Una cofradía de negros libertos en el siglo XV, *Estudios de Edad Media de la Corona de Aragón* 5 (Zaragoza, 1952): 457-466.
23. Ben Vinson III, *Bearing Arms for His Majesty: The Free-Colored Militia in Colonial Mexico* (Stanford: Stanford University Press, 2001), esp. ch. 1; idem, "Race and Badge: Free-Colored Soldiers in the Colonial Mexican Militia," *The Americas* 56,4 (April 2000): 471-96; Herbert S. Klein, "The Colored Militia of Cuba, 1568-1868," *Caribbean Studies* 6,2 (1966): 17-27.

24. Examples include: Francis A. Dutra, "A Hard-Fought Struggle for Recognition: Manuel Gonçalves Doria, First Afro-Brazilian to Become a Knight of Santiago," *The Americas* 56,1 (July 1999): 91-113; idem, "Blacks and the Search for Rewards and Status in Seventeenth-Century Brazil," *Proceedings of the Pacific Coast Council on Latin American Studies* 6 (1977-79): 25-35; A. C. de C. M. Saunders, "The Life and Humour of João de Sá Panasco, o Negro, Former Slave, Court Jester and Gentleman of the Portuguese Royal Household (fl. 1524-1567) in F.W. Hodcroft et al. (eds.), *Mediaeval and Renaissance Studies on Spain and Portugal in Honor of P.E. Russell* (Oxford: Society for the Study of Mediaeval Languages and Literature, 1981), 180-91.
25. Baltasar Fra Molinero, "Juan Latino and His Racial Difference," in Earle and Lowe, *Black Africans in Renaissance Europe*, 337-9; see also V. B. Spratlin, *Juan Latino, Slave and Humanist* (New York: Spinner Press, 1938); José Vicente Pascual, *Juan Latino* (Peligros, Granada: Comares, 1998); Calixto C. Masó, "Juan Latino: Gloria de España y de su raza" (PhD Dissertation: Northeastern Illinois University, 1973).
26. Laura A. Lewis, *Hall of Mirrors: Power, Witchcraft, and Caste in Colonial Mexico* (Durham, NC: Duke University Press, 2003), 2.
27. Cited by Diana Luz Ceballos Gómez, *Hechicería, brujería, e inquisición en el Nuevo Reino de Granada: Un duelo de imaginarios*, 2nd ed. (Medellín: Editorial Universidad Nacional de Colombia, 1995), 141. Seville is a city in Colombia as well as in Spain. The term creole here would make more sense for the former, a colonial site, but either city could be meant.
28. Lewis, *Hall of Mirrors*, 32.
29. Maya Restrepo, *Brujería*, 421. To try to improve the conditions of slaves and enable communication with their masters, Sandoval compiled a list of individuals brought from Africa who spoke the different languages and could serve as interpreters.
30. Frederick P. Bowser, *The African Slave in Colonial Peru, 1524-1650* (Stanford: Stanford University Press, 1974), 249.
31. María del Carmen Borrego Plá, *Palenques de negros en Cartagena a fines del siglo XVII* (Seville: Escuela de Estudios Hispano-Americanos de Sevilla/Consejo Superior de Investigaciones Científicas, 1973), 24; Maya Restrepo, *Brujería*, 49.
32. Cited in the next chapter. Slaves designated as *arara* or *arda*, from the area of present-day Dahomey, from the Gulf of Benin, had been transshipped through São Tomé and were probably Ewe or Fon in origin (Maya Restrepo, *Brujería*, 147; Borrego Plá, *Palenques en Cartagena*, 21). Araras bore marks of scarification, making them less attractive to Spanish purchasers and therefore cheaper. Because of their low price, but also their intelligence and clean habits such slaves were considered preferable for domestic work (Maya Restrepo, *Brujería*, 289-90, citing Alonso de Sandoval; Borrego Pla, *Palenques de negros*, 23-24).
33. Boleslao Lewin (ed.), *Descripcion del Virreinato del Peru: Cronica inedita de Comienzos del Siglo XVII*. Instituto de Investigaciones Historicas: Coleccion de Textos y Documentos, Serie B, No. 1 (Rosario, Argentina: Universidad Nacional del Litoral, 1958), 40.
34. Cited and translated in Robert J. Ferry, "Don't Drink the Chocolate: Domestic Slavery and the Exigencies of Fasting for Crypto-Jews in Seventeenth-Century Mexico," *Nuevo Mundo Mundos Nuevos* 5 (2005); http://nuevomundo.revues.org/document934.html. This document is unpaginated. Regarding what may well be the same case, Laura Lewis reports that a Black slave did not immediately believe certain accusations against his allegedly judaizing master, but said that "he would have to confirm the story by asking yet another black, who was from 'the same land and would tell him the truth'" (Lewis, *Hall of Mirrors*, 197, n. 93).
35. Some exceptions to the general avoidance of dealing with these in-between categories: Claudio Esteva-Fabregat, "African Women, Zambos, and Mulattoes," ch. 7 of *Mestizaje in Ibero-America* (Tucson: University of Arizona Press, 1995 [1987]). For the modern, non-Hispanic world, Naomi Zack, *Mixed-Race* (Philadelphia: Temple University Press, 1993); a response to Zack, Lewis R. Gordon, *Existentia Africana: Understanding Africana Existential Thought* (New York: Routledge, 2000), ch. 5.
36. Lutz, *Santiago de Guatemala*, 117, 122.
37. Stuart B. Schwartz, "The Formation of a Colonial Identity in Brazil," in Nicholas Canny and Anthony Pagden (eds.), *Colonial Identity in the Atlantic World, 1500-1800* (Princeton; Princeton University Press, 1987), 16.
38. Lewis, *Hall of Mirrors*, 76-7; Lutz, *Santiago de Guatemala*, ch. 3. Hence one Mexican viceroy told his successor in 1673, according to Anthony Pagden, "Identity Formation in Spanish America," Nicholas Canny and Anthony Pagden (eds.), *Colonial Identity in the Atlantic World, 1500-1800* (Princeton; Princeton University Press, 1987), 70, "behavior counted for as much as color provided that the shades were not too marked."

39. Lutz, Santiago de Guatemala, 59, 80.
40. Sweet, Recreating Africa, 110, 249, n. 22.
41. Nora E. Jaffary, False Mystics: Deviant Orthodoxy in Colonial Mexico (Lincoln, Neb.: University of Nebraska Press, 2004), 4.
42. Jaffary, False Mystics, 5, 100-6; Martha Few, Women Who Live Evil Lives: Gender, Religion, and the Politics of Power in Colonial Guatemala (Austin: University of Texas Press, 2002).
43. See, for example, John Thornton, Africa and Africans in the making of the Atlantic world, 1400-1800. Second ed. (Cambridge, UK: Cambridge University Press, 1998), 256-7; Michael N. Pearson, Port Cities and Intruders: The Swahili Coast, India, and Portugal in the Early Modern Era (Baltimore: Johns Hopkins University Press, 1998), 150; Asunción Lavrin, "Indian Brides of Christ: Creating New Spaces for Indigenous Women in New Spain," Mexican Studies 15,2 (Summer 1999): 225-60.
44. Iosef Fernandez, Apostólica y penitente vida de el V.P. Pedro Claver, de la compañía de Jesús. Sacada principalmente de informaciones juridicas hechas ante el Ordinario de la Ciudad de Cartagena de Indias. A su religiosísima provincia de el Nuevo Reyno de Granada. Por el padre Iosef Fernandez de la Compañía de Jesús natural de Taraçona (Zaragoça: Diego Dormer, 1666), 222.
45. Bowser, African Slave in Colonial Peru, 28; Jonathan I. Israel, Race, Class and Politics in Colonial Mexico, 1610-1670 (Oxford: Oxford University Press, 1975), 66. Bennett, Africans in Colonial Mexico, 49, agrees with Bowser, while Alberro, Inquisición y sociedad en México, 26, calls Africans neophytes.
46. Agostinho Marques Perdigão Malheiros, A Escravidão no Brasil, Ensaio Histórico-Jurídico-Social. 2 vols. (Petrópolis: Editora Vozes, 1976), 2:24. In contrast, sticking to the technical church definition, A. J. R. Russell-Wood suggested to me that Africans were not considered neophytes, as the papal bulls used the language of reconquest and the Africans, even sub-Saharans, had had the opportunity to hear the Law of Christ, unlike the American natives (personal communication, August 1998).
47. Silverblatt, Modern Inquisitions, 121-2.
48. "So those who are born of clean whites cannot be called Neophytes, which means cristãos novos, nor descendants of such, but only those who in some sense descend from black people should be given this name" (translated in Tobias, "Masters of Difference: Creolization and the Jewish Presence in Cabo Verde, 1497-1672" [PhD Dissertation: University of Birmingham, UK, 2006], 261).
49. Regarding guilds: in Santiago de Guatemala, "In the case of the cobbler's guild, at least, nothing precluded the admittance of mulattos. Apparently, other guilds also lacked prohibitions against mulatto members" in the sixteenth century (Robinson A. Herrera, Natives, Europeans, and Africans in Sixteenth-Century Santiago de Guatemala [Austin: University of Texas Press, 2003], 129); in Portugal, the Goldsmiths' guild excluded Blacks, mulatos and Amerindians (?) at least as of 1622 (Didier Lahon, "Black African Slaves and Freedmen in Portugal During the Renaissance: Creating a New Pattern of Reality," in Earle and Lowe, Black Africans in Renaissance Europe, 278-9); in Cartagena, at the beginning of the seventeenth century, a law was passed: "We prohibit under the most severe penalties that no black or pardo may exercise any mechanical art or profession, which should remain reserved for white people" (Maya Restrepo, Brujería, 449; Nina S. de Friedemann, La saga del negro: Presencia africana en Colombia [Santa Fe de Bogotá: Pontificia Universidad Javeriana, 1993], 56). On military honors: Dutra, "Hard-Fought Struggle for Recognition: Manuel Goncalves Doria"; idem, "Blacks and the Search for Rewards and Status."
50. Martínez López, "Limpieza de Sangre and the Emergence of the 'Race/Caste' System," 339-48; quote from 347.
51. A good summary of the early history of the Church's attitude toward and legal consideration of Africans can be found in G. Jean-Pierre Tardieu, Los negros y la iglesia en el Perú: Siglos XVI-XVII, 2 vols. (Quito: Ediciones Afroamérica/Centro Cultural Afroecuatoriano, 1997); C. R. Boxer, The Church Militant and Iberian Expansion 1440-1770, The Johns Hopkins Symposia in Comparative History, no. 10 (Baltimore: The Johns Hopkins University Press, 1978); Bennett, Africans in Colonial Mexico, ch. 2. On Africans and Amerindians: Silverblatt, Modern Inquisitions, 119-27.
52. James Sweet cites Sandoval on the "incorrect" magical understandings of their baptism held by many slaves (Recreating Africa, 197).
53. A. C. de C. M. Saunders, A Social History of Black Slaves and Freedmen in Portugal, 1441-1555 (Cambridge: Cambridge University Press, 1982), 40, 110; Gonzalo Aguirre Beltrán, La Población Negra de México, 1519-1810 (México: Ediciones Fuente Cultural, 1946), 5.

Notes to Chapter 1   229

54. Katia M. de Queirós Mattoso, *To Be a Slave in Brazil, 1550-1888* (New Brunswick/London: Rutgers University Press, 1994 [1979]), 32. According to one source, slaves coming from Guinea, from the Xolofe or Mandinga nations usually had not been baptized, while those arriving from the Congo or Angola had "some manner of instruction" (Nancy E. van Deusen, "The 'Alienated' Body: Slaves and Castas in the Hospital de San Bartolomé in Lima, 1680 to 1700," *The Americas* 56,1 [July 1999]: 6, n. 21, citing *Instrucción para remediar, y assegurar, quanto con la divina gracia fuere posible, que ninguno de los negros... carezca del sagrado Baptismo* [Lima, 1628]).
55. Luís Alberto Anaya Hernández, *Judeoconversos e Inquisicion en las Islas Canarias* (Las Palmas: Universidad de Las Palmas de Gran Canaria/Ediciones del Cabildo Insular de Gran Canaria, 1996), 127. The author unfortunately lumps together 190 Blacks, 2 Mulatos, 123 Moriscos and 24 people of unknown origin to produce a single sample of 339. Obviously, the rates for Blacks and Moriscos could differ significantly.
56. Colin A. Palmer, "Religion and Magic in Mexican Slave Society, 1570-1650," in Engerman, Stanley L. and Eugene D. Genovese (eds.), *Race and Slavery in the Western Hemisphere: Quantitative Studies* (Princeton: Princeton University Press, 1975), 313.
57. Ceballos Gómez, Hechicería, brujería, e inquisición, 147, n. 10.
58. Quoted in Castelló, *Francisco de la Cruz*, 1:362. Yet he also told his inquisitors that he doubted "whether it was licit to possess blacks as slaves" (ibid., 1:617). On the less than effective though persistent efforts to Christianize slaves in Brazil, see Sweet, *Recreating Africa*,197-202.
59. Ceballos Gómez, Hechicería, brujería, e inquisición, 147, n. 10.
60. On some of the complexities and history of the term, *ladino*, see Ceballos Gómez, *Hechicería, brujería, e inquisición*, 24, n. 10; Maya Restrepo, *Brujería*, 220, 379-80, 390-2.
61. Walter D. Mignolo, The Darker Side of the Renaissance: Literacy, Territoriality, and Colonization (Ann Arbor: University of Michigan Press, 1995), 54.
62. Luis Fernando Calero, *Pastos, quillacingas y abades, 1535-1700*, Biblioteca Banco Popular (Bogotá: Banco Popular, 1991), 168.
63. Alencastro, *Trato dos viventes*, 186.
64. Sweet, *Recreating Africa*, 7. As will be seen in later chapters, some Whites even found African religious or magical approaches helpful for their own needs.
65. Javier Villa-Flores, "'To Lose One's Soul': Blasphemy and Slavery in New Spain, 1596-1669," *Hispanic American Historical Review* 82,3 (2002): 435-68; Palmer, "Religion and Magic." Palmer, citing Philip Curtin and K. A. Busia, compares the blasphemous oaths uttered by slaves during beatings or mistreatment, with an Ashanti oath meant to prevent bodily harm from others and/or to secure the intervention of the central authority (ibid., 318).
66. Palmer, "Religion and Magic."
67. Bennett, *Africans in Colonial Mexico*, 9, 53; Solange Alberro, *Inquisición y sociedad en México*, 8-9, 455. Jean-Pierre Tardieu, who wrote extensively on Peru's African population as well as on its Inquisition, tallied only 119 cases involving individuals of African descent tried by the Lima tribunal between 1571 and 1702 (Tardieu, *Negros y la iglesia en el Perú*, 1:566). Lima and environs hosted a relatively enormous Afroiberian component, yet this number hardly approaches 50 percent of those accused by the tribunal. For Cartagena, Blacks and Mulatos comprise 9.3 percent of those imprisoned in the seventeenth century (T. Escribano Vidal, "Los cambios estructurales en el tribunal novogranadino: Segunda mitad del siglo XVII," in Joaquín Pérez Villanueva and Bartolomé Escandell Bonet [eds.], *Historia de la inquisición en España y América*, 3 vols. [Madrid: Biblioteca de Autores Cristianos/ Centro de Estudios Inquisitoriales, 1984-2000], 1:1202). The same can be said for Brazil. Of the 1,076 people imprisoned by the Portuguese Inquisition in Brazil over the course of its existence (1536-1821), only 27 men and 10 women identified as either Black or Mulato are to be found (Anita Novinsky, *Inquisição: Prisioneiros de Brasil - séculos XVI-XIX* [Rio de Janeiro: Editora Expressão e Cultura, 2002], 33-5). Clearly Alberro is tallying a much wider range of "involvement" of Afroiberians. Is she including all those who were denounced or who served as witnesses?
68. Lewis, *Hall of Mirrors*, 30.
69. Debate exists over whether medieval attitudes toward Jews and the possibility of their converting "out of" Jewishness can be understood through the modern lens of race. Most scholars would agree, I think, that the lines between Christian and Jew hardened after the twelfth century and again after the Reconquista. See Jonathan M. Elukin, "From Jew to Christian? Conversion and Immutability in Medieval Europe," in *Varieties of Religious Conversion in the Middle Ages*, ed. James Muldoon (Gainesville: University Press of Florida, 1997), 171-89; Jerome Friedman, "Jewish Conversion, the Spanish Pure Blood Laws, and Reformation: A Revisionist View of Racial and Religious Antisemitism," *Sixteenth Century Journal* 18 (1987): 3-31; Yosef H. Yerushalmi,

Assimilation and Racial Anti-Semitism: The Iberian and the German Models (New York: Leo Baeck Institute, 1982); Leon Poliakov, *The History of Anti-Semitism* (New York: Vanguard Press, 1965), 2:87-232.
70. This perspective may have been expressed first in writing by Benedict (alias Baruch) Spinoza, in his *Theologico-Political Treatise*, trans. Martin D. Yaffe (Newburyport, MA: Focus, 2004), 64.
71. Studies of the Jews of medieval Sepharad — a biblical toponym retroactively applied to Spain — are too numerous to mention. Also too many to list are treatments of the experience of the New Christians or Judeoconversos, of whom marranos or crypto-Jews comprise a subset, which inevitably intertwines with the story of the Sephardic communities beyond Iberian lands with which conversos had family and commercial relations and into which many later reintegrated; some recent and classic surveys include: Renée Levine Melammed, *A Question of Identity: Iberian Conversos in Historical Perspective* (New York: Oxford University Press, 2004); Pier Cesare Ioly Zorattini, *L'identità dissimulata: giudaizzanti iberici nell'Europa cristiana dell'eta moderna* (Firenze: L.S. Olschki, 2000); David M. Gitlitz, *Secrecy and Deceit: The Religion of the Crypto-Jews* (Philadelphia: Jewish Publication Society, 1996); Norman Roth, *Conversos, Inquisition, and the Expulsion of the Jews from Spain* (Madison: University of Wisconsin Press, 1995); José Faur, *In the Shadow of History: Jews and Conversos at the Dawn of Modernity* (Albany: State University of New York Press, 1992); Haim Beinart (ed.), *Moreshet Sepharad: the Sephardi Legacy*, 2 vols. (Jerusalem: Magnes Press/Hebrew University, 1992); Julio Caro Baroja, *Los judíos en la España moderna y contemporánea*, 3 vols. (Madrid: Istmo, 1986); Antonio Dominguez Ortiz, *Los judeoconversos en España y América* (Madrid: Istmo, 1971); B. Netanyahu, *The Marranos of Spain: From the Late 14th to the Early 16th Century According to Contemporary Hebrew Sources* (New York: American Academy for Jewish Research, 1966); João Lúcio de Azevedo, *História dos cristãos novos portugueses* (Lisbon: Clássica Editora, 1921).
72. Among many other sources: the economic essays in Richard L. Kagan and Philip D. Morgan (eds.), *Atlantic Diasporas: Jews, Conversos, and Crypto-Jews in the Age of Mercantilism, 1500-1800* (Baltimore: Johns Hopkins University Press, 2009); Daviken Studnicki-Gizbert, *A Nation upon the Ocean Sea: Portugal's Atlantic Diaspora and the Crisis of the Spanish Empire, 1492-1640* (New York: Oxford University Press, 2007); *Familia, religión y negocio: El sefardismo en las relaciones entre el mundo ibérico y los Países Bajos en la edad moderna*, ed. Jaime Contreras, Bernardo J. García García, and Ignacio Pulido (Madrid: Fundación Carlos de Amberes/Ministerio de Asuntos Exteriores, 2002); several essays in *The Jews and the Expansion of Europe to the West, 1450-1800*, ed. Paolo Bernardini and Norman Fiering, European Expansion & Global Interaction, Vol. 2 (New York: Berghahn Books, 2001); Daniel M. Swetschinski, *Reluctant Cosmopolitans: The Portuguese Jews of Seventeenth-Century Amsterdam* (London: Littman Library of Jewish Civilization, 2000), 102-64; Jonathan I. Israel, *Diasporas Within a Diaspora: Jews, Crypto-Jews and the World Maritime Empires (1540-1740)*, Brill's Series in Jewish Studies, 30 (Leiden: Brill, 2002); idem, *European Jewry in the Age of Mercantilism, 1550-1750*, 3rd ed. (London: Littman Library of Jewish Civilization, 1998); José Alberto Rodrigues da Silva Tavim, *Os judeus na expansão portuguesa em Marrocos durante o século XVI: Origens e actividades duma comunidade* (Braga: Edições APPACDM Distrital de Braga, 1997), 253-374; Stephen Alexander Fortune, *Merchants and Jews: the Struggle for British West Indian Commerce, 1650-1750* (Gainsville: Center for Latin American Studies/University of Florida Press, 1984); Gedalia Yogev, *Diamonds and Coral: Anglo-Dutch Jews and Eighteenth-Century Trade* (New York: Holmes and Meier Publishers, 1978).
73. Miriam Bodian, "'Men of the Nation': The Shaping of *Converso* Identity in Early Modern Europe." *Past and Present*, no. 143 (May 1994): 48-76.
74. Julia Adams, *The Familial State: Ruling Families and Merchant Capitalism in Early Modern Europe* (Ithaca: Cornell University Press, 2005). She discusses only Holland, England and, minimally, France, while Jews appear a single time in the index, but her arguments could easily be extended to the Iberian powers.
75. Silverblatt, *Modern Inquisitions*, 115.
76. José Antônio Gonsalves de Mello, *Gente da nação: Cristãos-novos e judeus em pernambuco, 1542-1654* (Recife: Fundação Joaqium Nabuco/Editora Massangana, 1989), 7.
77. Seymour B. Liebman, *New World Jewry, 1493-1825: Requiem for the Forgotten* (New York: Ktav Publishing House, 1982), 87.
78. Lina Gorenstein, "Na cidade e nos estaus: Cristãos-novos do Rio de Janeiro (séculos XVII-XVIII), in Gorenstein and Carneiro, *Ensaios sobre a intolerância*, 100-1.
79. Cited in Stanley M. Hordes, *To the End of the Earth: A History of the Crypto-Jews of New Mexico* (New York: Columbia University Press, 2005), 76.

80. Rafael Carrasco, "Solidaridades judeoconversas y sociedad local," in *Inquisición y conversos*. Conferencias pronunciadas en el III Curso de Cultura Hispano-Judía y Sefardí de la Universidad de Castilla-La Mancha, Celebrado en Toledo del 6 al 9 de septiembre de 1993 (Madrid: Asociación de Amigos del Museo Sefardí/Caja de Castilla La-Mancha, 1993), 66.
81. Daniel M. Swetschinski, "Conflict and Opportunity in 'Europe's Other Sea': The Adventure of Caribbean Jewish Settlement," *American Jewish History*, Vol. LXXII, no. 2 (December 1982), 217.
82. Emphasis added; Green, "Masters of Difference," 28.
83. See Maria da Graça A. Mateus Ventura, *Portugueses no Peru ao tempo da união ibérica: Mobilidade, cumplicidades e vivências*, 2 vols. in 3 pts. (Lisbon: Imprensa Nacional-Casa da Moeda, 2005); Israel, *Diasporas Within a Diaspora*; several essays in *Jews and the Expansion of Europe to the West*; Bernardo López Belinchón, *Honra, libertad y hacienda: Hombres de negocio y judíos sefardíes* ([Alcalá de Henares:] Universidad de Alcalá, 2001); Maria da Graça Mateus Ventura, *Negreiros Portugueses na Rota das Índias de Castela, 1541-1556* (Lisbon: 1999); Carmen Sanz Ayán, *Los banqueros de Carlos II* (Valladolid: Universidad de Valladolid, 1988); James C. Boyajian, *Portuguese bankers at the court of Spain, 1626-1650* (New Brunswick, NJ: Rutgers University Press, 1983). Though sometimes ideologically problematic — failing to distinguish between New Christians, Marranos and Jews, for instance — other Iberian studies remain extremely valuable: José Gonçalves Salvador, *Os cristãos-novos em Minas Gerais durante o ciclo do ouro, 1695-1755: relações com a Inglaterra*, Biblioteca Pioneira de estudos brasileiros (São Paulo: Pioneira/São Bernardo do Campo, SP/Instituto Metodista de Ensino Superior, 1992); idem, *Os cristãos-novos e o comércio no Atlântico Meridional (com enfoque nas capitanias do sul 1530-1680)*, Biblioteca Pioneira de estudos brasileiros (São Paulo: Livraria Pioneira Editora, 1978) — dedicated to "the indefatigable descendants of Israel"; Enriqueta Vila Vilar, *Hispanoamerica y el comercio de esclavos: los asientos portugueses* (Seville: EEHA, 1977).
84. See, among other studies, Alencastro, *Trato dos viventes*, 77-116; Mateus Ventura, *Negreiros portugueses*; Vila Vilar, *Hispanoamerica y el comercio de esclavos*.
85. The best treatment remains Seymour Drescher, "Jews and New Christians in the Atlantic Slave Trade," in Bernardini and Fiering, *Jews and the Expansion of Europe to the West*, 439-70.
86. Stuart Schwartz, *Sugar Plantations in the Formation of Brazilian Society: Bahia, 1550-1835* (Cambridge: Cambridge University Press, 1985), 265. Anita Novinsky claims that "Jews" owned and operated about 60 percent of the sugar mills in Bahia ("Jewish Roots of Brazil," in Judith Laikin Elkin and Gilbert W. Merkx [eds.], *The Jewish Presence in Latin America* [Boston: Allen & Unwin, 1987], 36), but her data derives in part from Inquisition records, which, as Schwartz points out, "are surely not an unbiased source in this regard."
87. Gorenstein, "Na cidade e nos estaus," 104.
88. Ventura, *Negreiros portugueses*, 31. One could argue that when it came to "Jews" the Spanish crown wanted to have it both ways, a kingdom free of Jews or Judaism but advantaged by "Jewish" experience and connections in commerce, a kingdom of non-Jewish Jews.
89. Israel, *European Jewry*, 50; on the colonies, see idem, *Diasporas Within a Diaspora*, 130, 38.
90. Israel, European Jewry, 21; Israel, Diasporas Within a Diaspora, 49-52.
91. The trial was eventually suspended without his being charged. Medina, *Historia de la Inquisición de Cartagena*, 123. Some of the ways Portuguese tried to oppose, subvert or critique Spanish racializing of their New Christian ancestry are laid out in Silverblatt, *Modern Inquisitions*, 132-6.
92. Pearson, *Port Cities and Intruders*, 137-8, 142-3; quote from 142.
93. Marc Saperstein, "The Rhetoric and Substance of Rebuke; Social and Religious Criticism in the Sermons of Ḥakham Saul Levi Morteira," *Studia Rosenthaliana* 34,2 (2000): 144-45; the original Hebrew appears on 145, n. 28.
94. Argumentos contra los נוצרים en forma de verso, printed in Kenneth Brown and Harm den Boer, *El barroco sefardí Abraham Gómez Silveira: Arévalo, prov. de Ávila, Castilla 1656 - Amsterdam 1741: Estudio preliminar, obras líricas, vejámenes en prosa y verso y documentación personal* (Kassel: Edition Reichenberger, 2000), 182, n. 158.
95. Epistola Al Excelentissimo Señor Don Fernando de Mascareñas, Conde de la Torre, in Sol de la vida, 84.
96. The symbol appears explicitly within the work as well (for instance, Vega, *Confusión de confusiones*, 205, 257).
97. Spinoza, Theologico-Political Treatise, xviii-xix.
98. See, inter alia: Bella Herson, Cristãos-novos e seus descendentes na medicina brasileira (1500-1850) (São Paulo: Editora da Universidade de São Paulo, 1996); Pilar Huerga Criado, En la raya de Portugal: Solidaridad y tensiones en la comunidad judeoconversa (Salamanca: Ediciones

Universidad de Salamanca, 1994), 95-128; Bruce A. Lorence, "Professions Held by New Christians in Northern and Southern Portugal during the First Half of the SeventeenthCentury," in Tamar Alexander et al. (eds.), History and Creativity in the Sephardi and Oriental Jewish Communities (Jerusalem: Misgav Yerushalayim, 1994), 315-26; Maria José Pimenta Ferro Tavares, Os Judeus em Portugal no Século XV, vol. I (Lisboa: Universidade Nova de Lisboa/Faculdade de Ciências Sociais e Humanas, 1982); vol. II (Lisboa: INIC, 1984), 1:261-88; Antonio Dominguez Ortiz, La clase social de los conversos en Castilla en la Edad Moderna, ed. facsímil. (Granada: Universidad de Granada, 1991 [orig. 1955]).
99. Eltis, "Identity and Migration," 122; he cites Michael Angels and Denis de Carli, "A Curious and Exact Account of a Voyage to Congo in the Years 1666 and 1667," in Awnsham Churchill and John Churchill, *A Collection of Voyages and Travels*, 6 vols. (London, 1744-46), 1:491-2.
100. Bodian, "Men of the Nation:" 49-50.
101. Thomas F. Glick, "On Converso and Marrano Ethnicity," in Benjamin R. Gampel (ed.), *Crisis and Creativity in the Sephardic World, 1391-1648* (New York: Columbia University Press, 1997), 74.
102. José Faur, *In the Shadow of History: Jews and Conversos at the Dawn of Modernity* (Albany: State University of New York Press, 1992), 41; see also idem, "Four Classes of Conversos: A Typological Study," *Revue des Etudes Juives* 149 (1990): 113-24.
103. Robert Garfield, "A Forgotten Fragment of the Diaspora: the Jews of São Tomé Island, 1492-1654," in *The Expulsion of the Jews: 1492 and After*, ed. Raymond B. Waddington and Arthur H. Williamson (New York: Garland Publishing, 1994), 76.
104. Alberro, *Inquisición y sociedad*, 434; she cites Stanley Hordes, "The Crypto Jewish Community of New Spain, 1620-1649" (PhD Dissertation: Tulane University, 1980), 210. Patterns related in Inquisition records from the era of peak anti-Portuguese and anti-judaizing may not reflect general marital behavior in the colony accurately.
105. Stuart B. Schwartz, All Can Be Saved: Religious Tolerance and Salvation in the Iberian Atlantic World (New Haven: Yale University Press, 2008), 190.
106. Gorenstein, "Na cidade e nos estaus," 106.
107. Quoted in David Leon Graizbord, "Conformity and Dissidence among Judeoconversos, 1580-1700" (PhD Dissertation, University of Michigan, 2000), 144.
108. Gretchen D. Starr-LeBeau, *In the Shadow of the Virgin: Inquisitors, Friars, and Conversos in Guadalupe, Spain* (Princeton: Princeton University Press, 2003), 62.
109. Yirmiyahu Yovel, *The Marrano of Reason* (Princeton: Princeton University Press, 1989). A view of Marranism as justified, even sanctified dissimulation can be found in Perez Zagorin, *Ways of Lying: Dissimulation, Persecution, and Conformity in Early Modern Europe* (Cambridge: Harvard University Press, 1990), ch. 3.
110. Albert Memmi, *The Colonizer and the Colonized* (Boston: Beacon Press, 1967 [1957]); Jonathan Boyarin, *Storm from Paradise: the Politics of Jewish Memory* (Minneapolis: University of Minnesota Press, 1992). The same is true for the first African slaves used by the Spanish in the Americas. Writing in the historical mode of recuperation of the 1960s, James Lockhart cites their contributions: "[t]hey were an organic part of the enterprise of occupying Peru from its inception," Blacks "were for the main part the Spaniards' willing allies... And this willingness is understandable. Though Negroes were subordinated to Spaniards, they were not exploited in the plantation manner; except for mining gangs, Negroes in Peru counted as individuals." Lockhart's assessment is quoted, in turn, by Herman Bennett, un-self-consciously, as a still under-appreciated facet of the African origins of the western hemisphere (James Lockhart, *Spanish Peru 1532-1560: A Colonial Society* [Madison: University of Wisconsin Press, 1968]; Bennett, *Africans in Colonial Mexico*, 2, 199-200, n. 9). Using the tactic of ethnic diversity among subaltern populations that goes back at least to Plato, in both New Spain and Perú, Ladino Afroiberians served *encomenderos* as "intermediaries and supervisors over indigenous laborers' (Bennett, *Africans in Colonial Mexico*, 21).
111. See, for instance, Elena Lourie, Crusade and Colonisation: Muslims, Christians and Jews in Medieval Aragon (Hampshire: Variorum, 1990).
112. Diana Luz Ceballos Gómez, "Grupos sociales y prácticas mágicas en el Nuevo Reino de Granada durante el siglo XVII," *Historia Crítica* 22 (Jul.-Dec. 2001): 54-5; Anidjar, "Blood Works."
113. Jonathan Israel, "Menasseh ben Israel and the Dutch Sephardic Colonization Movement of the Mid-Seventeenth Century (1645-1657)," in *Menasseh ben Israel and his World*, ed. Yosef Kaplan, Henry Méchoulan and Richard H. Popkin (Leiden: E.J. Brill, 1989), 146.
114. New Christians were allowed to emigrate to the colonies of Spain and Portugal only in 1601, after "the payment of the enormous bribe of 200,000 ducats to Phillip III, [...] the king promising

that [the prohibition on emigration] would never again be enforced. [...] This 'irrevocable' permission was canceled in 1610 [...and again] restored in 1629" (Cecil Roth, *A History of the Marranos*, 4th ed. [New York: Hermon Press, 1974], 197) Oddly enough, before all this, beginning in 1548, "one of the penalties imposed by the tribunals of the mother-country upon convicted but 'penitent' heretics was that of deportation — generally across the Atlantic" (ibid., 283).
115. Gomes Solís, *Memoires*, 12, 16; cited in Israel, *European Jewry*, 57.
116. Novinsky, Cristãos novos na Bahia, 59.
117. The delicacy of the situation of some Jews can be glimpsed by juxtaposing two of the multiplicitous images of Jews. On the one hand, the "foreignness" of the Jews opened them up to charges from nationalists that their profits were not necessarily benefiting their host country, as the French mercantilist Montchrétien maintained in his *Traicté de l'oeconomie politique* (1615). The "Marranos" in France, he wrote, were "sucking wealth out of the country rather than bringing it in" (Israel, *European Jewry*, 56). On the other hand, the Spanish mercantilist Francisco Rétama acknowledged that Jewish economic profits benefit their protectors as well when he advised Felipe III that he could "sap the economic strength of Spain's enemy, the Dutch Republic, by employing agents in Holland to incite feeling against the Jews and provoke their expulsion to Germany or Poland" (ibid., 57).
118. Cited in Yitzhak Baer, *A History of the Jews in Christian Spain*, trans. from the Hebrew by Louis Schoffman, 2 vols. (Philadelphia: Jewish Publication Society of America, 1961), 1:68.
119. Yom Tov Assis, "The Jews in the Crown of Aragon and its Dominions," in Haim Beinart (ed.), *Moreshet Sepharad: the Sephardi Legacy*, 2 vols. (Jerusalem: Magnes Press/Hebrew University, 1992), 1:50.
120. Green, "Masters of Difference."
121. Gitlitz, Secrecy and Deceit.
122. See, for instance, Irma Salinas Rocha, *Nostro grupo* (Mexico City: Editorial Jus, 1970), cited by Hernández, *Delirio*, 71.
123. José Toribio Medina, El tribunal del santo oficio de la inquisición en las provincias del Plata (Buenos Aires: Editorial Huarpes, 1945), 118.
124. Rafael Gracia Boix, *Autos de fe y causas de la Inquisición de Córdoba* (Córdoba: Publicaciones de la Excma Diputación Provincial, 1983), 138. For now, I am simply taking such statements at face value, though of course there is much that is suspect about them, as I discuss below.
125. N. Taylor Phillips, "Family History of the Reverend David Mendez Machado," *PAJHS* 2 (1894): 47. The American family's Ashkenazic patriarch, Jonas Phillips, had married a Sephardic woman, Rebecca Mendez Machado.
126. Juan Blázquez Miguel, *Inquisición y criptojudaismo* (Madrid: Kaydeda, 1988), 149.
127. José Antonio Gonsalves de Mello, Confissões de Pernambuco (1594-1595): Primeira visitação do Santo Ofício às partes do Brasil (Recife: UFPE, 1970), 10-11.
128. Cited in Boleslao Lewin, Singular proceso de Salomón Machorro (Juan de León): Israelita liornés condenado por la inquisición (México, 1650) (Buenos Aires: Published by the author, 1977), 267.
129. Lewis, *Hall of Mirrors*, 30, shares my reading of this definition; see also Forbes, *Africans and Native Americans*, 132-33.
130. Fuchs, Mimesis and Empire, 91-3; Silverblatt, Modern Inquisitions, 205-6; George E. Brooks, Eurafricans in Western Africa: Commerce, Social Status, Gender, and Religious Observance From the Sixteenth to the Eighteenth Century (Athens: Ohio University Press, 2003), xxi, 51-2.
131. Kathryn Burns, *Colonial Habits: Convents and the Spiritual Economy of Cuzco, Peru* (Durham: Duke University Press, 1999), ch. 1 ("Gender and the Politics of Mestizaje").
132. George E. Brooks, Landlords and Strangers: Ecology, Society, and Trade in Western Africa, 1000-1630 (Boulder: Westview Press, 1993), 186.
133. Letter from the tribunal of Llerena to the *Suprema*, 25 July 1581; cited in Jaime Contreras and Gustav Henningsen, "Forty-Four Thousand Cases of the Spanish Inquisition (1540-1700): Analysis of a Historical Data Bank" in Gustav Henningsen and John Tedeschi (eds.) in association with Charles Amiel, *The Inquisition in Early Modern Europe: Studies on Sources and Methods* (Dekalb, Il: Northern Illinois University Press, 1986), 124. Similarly, in Holland, arriving New Christians were deemed "Roman Catholics without faith and Jews without knowledge, but wishing to be Jews" (quoted in Brooks, *Eurafricans*, 90). The *Libro del Alborayque* (ca. 1460) also harps on Judeoconverso in-betweenness (Bodian cites a passage in "Men of the Nation," 53).
134. Giorgio Rota, "False Moriscos and True Renegades: Spaniards and Other Subjects of the King of Spain in the Records of the *Santo Uffizio* of Venice (How to Become a Renegade)," in *España*

y el Oriente islámico entre los siglos XV y XVI (Imperio Otomano, Persia y Asia central), ed. Encarnación Sanchez García, Pablo Martín Asuero and Michele Bernardini (Istanbul: Editorial Isis, 2007), 182.
135. Günter Böhm, *Los sefardies en los dominios holandeses de America del Caribe, 1630-1750* (Frankfurt: Vervuert, 1992), 22-3; Mello, *Gente da nação*, 50-1; Isaac S. Emmanuel, "Seventeenth-Century Brazilian Jewry: a Critical Review," *American Jewish Archives* 14,1 (April 1962): 39.
136. Mello, *Gente da nação*, 478-9.
137. Yosef Kaplan, "The Travels of Portuguese Jews from Amsterdam to the 'Lands of Idolatry' (1644-1724)," in Yosef Kaplan (ed.), *Jews and Conversos: Studies in Society and the Inquisition* (Jerusalem: World Union of Jewish Studies/The Magnes Press/The Hebrew University, 1985), 197-224.
138. Graizbord, "Conformity and Dissidence among Judeoconversos, 1580-1700," 128, for instance; see now idem, *Souls in Dispute: Converso Identities in Iberia and the Jewish Diaspora, 1580-1700*, Jewish Culture and Contexts (Philadelphia: University of Pennsylvania Press, 2003).
139. Cited by Hordes, *End of the Earth*, 109.
140. Anita Novinsky, *Cristãos-novos na Bahia, 1642-1654* (São Paulo: Pioneira/EDUSP, 1972), 65; Angela Maria Vieira Maia, *À sombra do medo: Cristãos velhos e cristãos novos nas capitanias do açúcar* (Rio de Janeiro: Oficina Cadernos de Poesia, 1995), 111-21.
141. Vieira Maia, *Sombra do medo*, 115.
142. Novinsky, *Cristãos-novos na Bahia*; see also idem, "Marranos and the Inquisition: On the Gold Route in Minas Gerais, Brazil," in *Jews and the Expansion of Europe to the West*, 215-41.
143. Gorenstein, "Na cidade e nos estaus," 108-9.
144. Testimony of Beatriz Enriquez, 22 January 1644; AGN Mexico, Inq. 393/12/3, fol. 264r.
145. Quoted in Herman Prins Salomon, "Spanish Marranism Re-examined," *Sefarad* 67,1 (Jan.-June 2007): 127.
146. Novinsky, *Inquisição*, 49.
147. Quoted in Graizbord, "Conformity and Dissidence among Judeoconversos," 245.
148. Hordes, To the End of the Earth, xvii.
149. Novinsky, "Marranos and the Inquisition," 222.
150. Jailhouse conversation reported by Ysavel de Silva, herself already arrested for judaizing, testimony of 9 July 1643; AGN Mexico, Inq. 402, exp. 1, leg. 2, fol. 109r.
151. The accused was Blas de Paz Pinto, treated in chapter 3; AHN Inq., leg. 1601, no. 18, fol. 40; reprinted in I ic Croitoru Rotbaum, *Documentos coloniales: Originados en el santo oficio del tribunal de la inquisición de Cartagena de Indias (Contribución a la historia de Colombia)*, v. 2 of *De Sefarad al neosefardismo* (Bogota: Tipografia Hispana, 1971), 231.
152. Cited, for instance, by Díaz-Plaja, *Espíritu del Barroco*, 72. It is hard not to see that era's accusations of Jewish love of money, gold and silver, à la Nietzsche's *Genealogy of Morals*, as bad-faith projections.
153. Graizbord, "Conformity and Dissidence among Judeoconversos," 208, 297.
154. Jean Pierre Dedieu, "The Archives of the Holy Office of Toledo as a Source for Historical Anthropology," in Henningsen, Gustav and John Tedeschi (eds.) in association with C. Amiel, *The Inquisition in Early Modern Europe: Studies on Sources and Methods* (Dekalb, Ill.: Northern Illinois University Press, 1986), 159.
155. Gustav Henningsen, "The Archives and the Historiography of the Spanish Inquisition," in Henningsen and Tedeschi, *Inquisition in Early Modern Europe*, 54.
156. Ellis Rivkin, "How Jewish Were the New Christians?" *Hispania Judaica* 1 (1980): 104-15.
157. António José Saraiva, *The Marrano Factory: The Portuguese Inquisition and Its New Christians, 1536-1765*, trans., revised and augmented by H. P. Salomon and I. S. D. Sassoon (Leiden: Brill, 2001), which is a translation and expansion of the 1985 edition of Saraiva's *Inquisição e cristãos-novos* (1969); Alencastro, *Trato dos viventes*, 25.
158. A not uncommon example: In 1495, a Judeoconverso couple paid the tribunal of Toledo 2,000 *maravedís* to reclaim for themselves and their descendants the right to use and wear silk, gold, silver and precious stones, to possess arms and to mount horses, privileges otherwise forbidden to individuals penitenced or condemned by the Inquisition, their children and grandchildren (Salomon, "Spanish Marranism Re-examined," 121).
159. Salomon, "Spanish Marranism Re-examined," 123.
160. Colin A. Palmer, *Slaves of the White God: Blacks in Mexico, 1570-1650* (Cambridge: Harvard University Press, 1976). See also Palmer, "Religion and Magic."
161. Bennett, Africans in Colonial Mexico; Sweet, Recreating Africa; Maya Restrepo, Brujería.

Notes to Chapter 2   235

162. Ruth Behar, "Sex and Sin, Witchcraft and the Devil in Late-Colonial Mexico," *American Ethnologist* 14 (Feb. 1987): 34-54; Diana Luz Ceballos Gómez, *"Quyen tal haze que tal pague:" Sociedad y prácticas mágicas en el Nuevo Reino de Granada* (Bogotá: Ministerio de Cultura, 2002); idem, "Grupos sociales y prácticas mágicas en el Nuevo Reino de Granada durante el siglo XVII,"*Historia Critica* 22 (Jul.-Dec. 2001): 51-75; Few, *Women Who Live Evil Lives*; idem, "Women, Religion, and Power: Gender and Resistance in Daily Life in Late-Seventeenth-Century Santiago de Guatemala," *Ethnohistory* 42 (Fall 1995): 627-37; Lewis, *Hall of Mirrors*; Silverblatt, *Moon, Sun, and Witches: Gender Ideologies and Class in Inca and Colonial Peru* (Princeton: Princeton University Press, 1987), ch. 9; idem, *Modern Inquisitions*.
163. Sweet, Recreating Africa, 9.
164. Dedieu, "Archives of the Holy Office of Toledo," 164.
165. Dedieu, "Archives of the Holy Office of Toledo," 168.
166. Maria Cristina Corrêa de Melo, "A Organização do Processo Inquisitorial: alguns Paralelismos com o Processo comum," *Inquisição*, Vol. 1: *Comunicações apresentadas ao 1.º congresso luso-brasileiro sobre inquisição realizado em Lisboa, de 17 a 20 de Fevereiro de 1987* (Lisboa: Sociedade Portuguesa de Estudos do Século XVIII/Universitária Editora, 1989), 397.
167. H. P. Salomon and I. S. D. Sassoon, Introduction, Saraiva, *Marrano Factory*, xi-xii.
168. Novinsky, "Marranos and the Inquisition," 225.
169. Villa-Flores, "Blasphemy and Slavery in New Spain," 450.
170. Graizbord, "Conformity and Dissidence among Judeoconversos,"298.
171. Henry Kamen, *The Spanish Inquisition: A Historical Revision* (New Haven: Yale University Press, 1997), 189. Silverblatt thinks the statistics in Peru were comparable (*Modern Inquisitions*, 71).
172. Saraiva, J.-P. Dedieu and Salomon suspect that both Inquisitions tacitly accepted that "accusations of Judaizing brought against persons of demonstrably clean Old Christian stock were not to be entertained" (Salomon, "Spanish Marranism Re-examined," 138).
173. Jaime Contreras and Gustav Henningsen, "Forty-Four Thousand Cases of the Spanish Inquisition (1540-1700): Analysis of a Historical Data Bank" in Gustav Henningsen and John Tedeschi (eds.) in association with Charles Amiel, *The Inquisition in Early Modern Europe: Studies on Sources and Methods* (Dekalb, Il: Northern Illinois University Press, 1986), 114.
174. According to Henry Kamen, the Toledo tribunals "may have dealt with over eight thousand cases in the period 1481-1530," the "overwhelming majority" of which were not brought to trial. Of those tried by the Barcelona tribunal between 1488 and 1505, 99.3 percent were Judeoconversos, while those tried by the Valencia tribunal between 1484 and 1530 included a percentage of Judeoconversos totalling 91.6 (Kamen, *The Spanish Inquisition*, 57, 59). Where Kamen strays, in my opinion, is in his polemical interpretation of the "low" numbers of those martyred — "unlikely that more than two thousand people were executed" up to 1530 (ibid., 60) — as a sign of the normalcy and beneficence of the Spanish Inquisition.
175. Quoted in Henningsen and Tedeschi, "Introduction," Henningsen and Tedeschi (eds.), *Inquisition in Early Modern Europe*, 3.
176. Carlo Ginzburg, "The Inquisitor as Anthropologist," in *Clues, Myths, and the Historical Method* (Baltimore: Johns Hopkins University Press, 1989), 156-67.
177. Howard Adelman, "Inquisitors and Historians and their Methods," unpublished paper, June 1990, 30.

Chapter 2

1. Certeau, The Practice of Everyday Life, xix.
2. In this I agree with Bennett, *Africans in Colonial Mexico*, 68.
3. Cited by Kevin Ingram, "Secret Lives, Public Lies: The Conversos and Socio-religious Non-conformism in the Spanish Golden Age" (PhD Diss.: University of California San Diego, 2006), 99-100.
4. Elvira Pérez Ferreiro, *El Tratado de* [Gaspar de] *Uceda contra los estatutos de limpieza de sangre: Una reacción ante el establecimiento del estatuto de limpieza en la orden franciscana* (Madrid: Aben Ezra Ediciones, 2000), 75. Thus Fray Diego of Burgos (15th cen.) was said to have stated: "It pleases me more to stem from the lineage of Jews whence stemmed our lord Jesus Christ than from the lineage of the devil whence the gentiles stem" (cited in Faur, *In the Shadow of History*, 35). Similarly, one Luis García "continued to say that a New Christian was far better than an Old

one, since the new one sprang from the lineage of Christ and the old ones from the Gentiles" (cited in Stephen Gilman, *The Spain of Fernando de Rojas* [Princeton: Princeton University Press, 1972], 136).
5. Saunders, "The Life and Humour of João de Sá Panasco," 190.
6. Moses Maimonides, *The Guide of the Perplexed*, trans. and ed. Shlomo Pines (Chicago: University of Chicago Press, 1963), 2:618-619.
7. Martínez López, "*Limpieza de Sangre* and the Emergence of the 'Race/Caste' System," 339-48, offers an important discussion of the late seventeenth-century evaluation by the Supreme Council of the Inquisition of the question of whether descendants of Amerindians and/or Africans needed to be subjected to the regime of the purity of blood laws, as well as whether they could be considered Old Christians. Basing itself on numerous sources, the *Suprema* accepted Amerindians as both pure of blood and Old Christians, while Afroiberians "gradually drop out of the discussion and toward the end are hardly mentioned at all" (347).
8. "Contas, contas, bulraria, bulraria" (quoted in Gitlitz, *Secrecy and Deceit*, 156; Gitlitz takes this from Antonio Baião, *A Inquisição em Portugal e no Brasil. Subsidios para a sua historia. A inquisição no seculo XVI* [Lisbon: Edição do Arquivo Historico Portugues, 1921], 143).
9. Baião, *Inquisição em Portugal e no Brasil*, 114, 117.
10. Elena de' Freschi Olivi is the woman (cited in Brian Pullan, *The Jews of Europe and the Inquisition of Venice, 1550-1670* [Oxford: Basil Blackwell, 1983], 286).
11. Gustav Henningsen, "The Eloquence of Figures: Statistics of the Spanish and Portuguese Inquisitions and Prospects for Social History," in *The Spanish Inquisition and the Inquisitorial Mind*, ed. Angel Alcalá (Boulder: Social Science Monographs/Columbia University Press, 1987), 227. Henningsen is referring to findings in Jaime Contreras, *El santo oficio de la inquisición de Galicia: Poder, sociedad, y cultura* (Madrid, 1982).
12. Quoted in Vieira Maia, *Sombra do medo*, 122; see Laura de Mello e Souza, *The Devil and the Land of the Holy Cross: Witchcraft, Slavery, and Popular Religion in Colonial Brazil* (Austin: University of Texas Press, 2004), 61, for other examples.
13. The accused is María de Zárate, Francisco Botello's wife, charged in 1656 for judaizing (quoted in Boleslao Lewin, ed., *Proceso de María de Zárate: Racismo inquisitorial* [Puebla, 1971], 99). Clearly she is ignoring or unaware of the existence of black madonnas. The son of African slaves, Benito (1526-1589) went on to become a Franciscan whose charitable deeds became legendary.
14. Schwartz, *All Can Be Saved*, 106.
15. Juan de León (aka Salomón Machorro); 1646 (quoted in Boleslao Lewin, ed., *Confidencias de dos criptojudíos en la cárcel de la Inquisición* [Buenos Aires, 1975], 78).
16. Quoted in Renée Levine Melammed, "María López: A Convicted Judaizer from Castile," in Mary E. Giles, ed., *Women in the Inquisition: Spain and the New World* (Baltimore: Johns Hopkins University Press, 1999), 70 and 314, n. 73.
17. Mathias de Bocanegra, *Auto general de la fee, celebrado [...] Dominica in Albis 11. de Abril de 1649*. El P. Mathias de Bocanegra de la Compañia de IESUS (Mexico: Antonio Calderon, Impressor del Secreto del S. Officio, n.d.), s.v. Leonor Vaez Sevilla.
18. Bocanegra, *Auto General*, s.v. Doña Ana de Leon Carauajal.
19. Ruth Behar, "Sex and Sin, Witchcraft and the Devil in Late-Colonial Mexico," *American Ethnologist* 14 (Feb. 1987): 43-4.
20. Elias Lipiner, *Izaque de Castro: o mancebo que veio preso do Brasil* (Recife: Fundação Joaquim Nabuco/Editora Massangana, 1992), 51.
21. Cited in Lipiner, *Izaque de Castro*, 50. The continuation of the testimony buttresses the accuracy of the allegations: "The governor attending to this, he [the bachelor] was taken to one of these [ships] and this witness, going after a few hours to say goodbye to the ships because he was in the infantry, and understanding that this nephew of the said Matheus Lopes went to Pernambuco to judaize, made efforts to throw him off of the ship, saying that he had no written license; and he defended himself [by saying] that he went as a prisoner by order of the governor, he [Pero Ferraz] could not get him to disembark, before there were with him two others of his nation, all protesting that this man went with the order of the governor; by which grew on the witness the understanding that the imprisonment was feigned in order that this New Christian could go to Pernambuco. And, the witness relating all this to the said governor and the suspicions that he had, the said governor responded: They fooled me like a child."
22. Audience, Tuesday, 19 October 1649; cited in Lewin, *Singular proceso de Salomón Machorro*, 413.
23. Laura Lewis writes that the Spanish "religious discourse that made 'innocents' out of Indians, thus simultaneously made blacks 'guilty'" (Lewis, *Hall of Mirrors*, 29).

24. That they were all fellow Sephardim comes across easily enough from their names: Afonso Rodrigues Cardoso, Diogo de Pina, Bento Osorio, James Lopes da Costa, Duarte Esteves de Pina and Diogo Gonçalves de Lima (E. M. Koen, W. Hamelink-Verweel, S. Hart, and W. C. Pieterse, "Notarial Records in Amsterdam Relating to the Portuguese Jews in That Town up to 1639," *Studia Rosenthaliana*, running series beginning with 1,1 [1967-present]; 5,1 [January 1971]: 124 [doc. 419]). While other notarial deeds explicitly mention that the declarer appears at someone else's behest, the same seems likely here.
25. GemeenteArchief Amsterdam, Notarial Archive 62, fol. 194v. I cite and discuss this deed in Schorsch, *Jews and Blacks*, 189-90.
26. Martínez López, "*Limpieza de Sangre* and the Emergence of the 'Race/Caste' System," 377-8, 381.
27. T. F. Earle, "Black Africans versus Jews: Religious and Racial Tension in a Portuguese Saint's Play," in Earle and Lowe, *Black Africans in Renaissance Europe*, 345-60. Though Earle may well be correct in pointing out the drama's tactful omission of calls for anti-Jewish/converso violence or extermination, a jarring sign of the continuing binarism informing many studies of race and of the aporias that too often inhibit their authors is the final sentence that Earle affixes to this description of one Afroiberian's participation in the dominant majority's anti-Jewishness: "In the injustice and horror of a slave society, [Álvares] stands out as a beacon of hope."
28. James Lockhart and Enrique Otte, *Letters and People of the Spanish Indies*, rev. ed. (Cambridge: Cambridge University Press, 1988), 143-44; Herrera, *Natives, Europeans, and Africans in Sixteenth-Century Santiago de Guatemala*, 34.
29. José Ramos Tinhorão, *Os Negros em Portugal: Uma presença silenciosa* (Lisbon, 1988), 172-173.
30. Quoted in Isidoro Moreno Navarro, *La antigua hermandad de los negros de Sevilla: Etnicidad, poder y sociedad en 600 años de historia* (Seville: Universidad de Sevilla/Consejería de Cultura de la Junta de Andalucía, 1997), 85.
31. Baltasar Fra Molinero, *La imagen de los negros en el teatro del Siglo de Oro* (Madrid: Siglo Veintiuno Editores, 1995), 44. Simón Aguado is the author of *Entremés de los negros*, seemingly written in 1602.
32. Quoted in Souza, *The Devil and the Land of the Holy Cross*, 206.
33. Solange Behocaray de Alberro, "Negros y mulatos en los documentos inquisitoriales: rechazo e integración," in Elsa Cecilia Frost et al (eds.), *El Trabajo y los Trabajadores en la Historia de México: Ponencias y comentarios presentados en la Reunión de Historiadores Mexicanos y Norteamericanos, Pátzcuaro, 12 al 15 de octubre de 1977* (Mexico City/Tucson: El Colegio de México/University of Arizona Press, 1979), 153-4.
34. Baião, *Inquisição em Portugal e no Brasil*, 113.
35. Mello, *Gente da Nação*, 185.
36. Few, "Women, Religion, and Power," 633.
37. Lucien Wolf, *Jews in the Canary Islands, being a Calendar of Jewish Cases Extracted from the Records of the Canariote Inquisition in the Collection of the Marquess of Bute, translated from the Spanish and edited with an Introduction and Notes* (London: The Jewish Historical Society of England/Spottiswoode, Ballantyne & Co., 1926), 40.
38. Testimony of Mariana de Guzman, 15 December 1637; AGN Mexico, Inq. 402, exp. 1, leg. 2, fol. 17r. She is testifying against members of the extended Enriquez family.
39. Testimony of Maria de la Conçepçion, also against members of the Enriquez family, for whom she washed laundry, 17 March 1643; AGN Mexico, Inq. 402, exp. 1, leg. 2, fol. 206r. When Rafaela Enriquez asked her "whether she knew of some person or Indian to whom she could give some Pesos in order to give them to her husband Gaspar Suares," Conçepçion responded that "she was raised since infancy in a convent and did not know these *bellaquerias*" (ibid., fol. 207r.). The Mulata Conçepçion hints here at the opposing religious trajectories that separate alleged judaizers from "good" Christians, even if Mulatos, as well as the racial differences that distinguish her from Amerindians.
40. Testimony of 17 March 1643; AGN Mexico, Inq. 402, exp. 1, leg. 2, fol. 209r. De Ortega says that she came to the Inquisition to depose "having heard in the edicts of faith that those were things that should not have been done."
41. Testimony of Mariana de Guzman, 15 December 1637; AGN Mexico, Inq. 402, exp. 1, leg. 2, fol. 17r.-v.
42. Testimony of 17 March 1643; AGN Mexico, Inq. 402, exp. 1, leg. 2, fol. 206v. Conçepçion also states that the Black slave Ynes told her that "Blanca Enriquez ordered her to put the cut meat in water the afternoon before in order to remove the blood." Additionally, armed with the knowledge gained from recently having heard the Edicts of Faith read in church, Conçepçion relates, regarding

many of the women in the Enriquez family, that "she noticed that they ate meat and fish cooked with oil," instead of lard. This case can be added to many others that seem to indicate that marranos preferred unacculturated *bozal* slaves precisely because they would not yet have learned to distinguish "Jewish" practices from the Christian perspective. In some ways *bozales* were preferred by Spaniards in general, deemed as they were to be more submissive than *ladino* slaves who had learned some of the ways of their masters.

43. A great deal has been written about Maldonado de Silva, whose trial and death at the stake became a cause célèbre among contemporary Jews, such as Menasseh ben Israel, who cited his martyrdom in *Mikveh Yisrael / Esperança de Ysrael* (1650). Günter Böhm devotes the entire first volume of his history of the Jews of Chile to an analysis and transcription of the trial (*Historia de los judíos en Chile*, vol. 1, *Período colonial* [Santiago: Andrés Bello, 1984]). Medina gives Silva's case a whole chapter in his *Inquisición en Chile*. Surprisingly, Böhm himself refers to the Mulata Maria Martinez as "a mulata slave / una mulata esclava," though the documents clearly indicate that she has been freed: "*orra*," i.e., "*horra*," meaning "manumitted" (*Judíos en Chile*, 86). More background on Martínez is given by Silverblatt, *Modern Inquisitions*, 172-74.

44. The *sambenito* was the cloak worn by the penitent at the *auto de fé*. It often had depictions specific to the type of crime the wearer allegedly committed. Punishments sometimes had the criminal wear the *sambenito* for years after as well. When a penitent had finished the term of such a punishment, the *sambenito* was to be hung at the local church, so that all could know that the person had been found guilty of the crime.

45. Böhm, *Judíos en Chile*, 86-7.

46. We know from elsewhere in his trial documents that Silva owned four slaves as of the end of 1625: "a Black called Simón from the caste of Angola, more or less twenty years old, [...] a young Black called Francisco from the caste of Angola, more or less twelve years old, [...] a mulata slave called Catalina of the age of more or less fifty, [...] and a Black called Isabel from the caste of Angola of the age of twenty four [...] with a daughter at the breast of the age of a year" (cited in Böhm, *Judíos en Chile*, 57-8). The trial documents shed no light, however, on the nature of the relations between the servants and Silva and his wife. It is known that Silva's father, Diego Nuñez de Silva, made his Black slave his apprentice.

47. The latter is more likely; see Miriam Bodian, *Dying in the Law of Moses: Crypto-Jewish Martyrdom in the Iberian World* (Bloomington: Indiana University Press, 2007), 117-52.

48. This tactic had been recommended already by the fourteenth-century trainer of inquisitors, Nicolau Eimeric (Saraiva, *Marrano Factory*, 45).

49. *Tefilin* or phyllacteries, are two ritual boxes containing scrolls with portions of the Bible, which Jewish men traditionally place on their forehead and left arm during morning prayers except on sabbath and holidays.

50. See Elias Lipiner, *Gonçalo Anes Bandarra e os cristãos-novos* (Trancoso/Lisbon: Câmara Municipal de Trancoso/Associação Portuguesa de Estudos Judaicos, 1996), 34-40; quotes from 35 and 36.

51. Lewis, *Hall of Mirrors*, 40: "[F]ree blacks threatened each other with the Inquisition."

52. David Fergusson, "Trial of Gabriel de Granada by the Inquisition in Mexico 1642-1645: translated from the original by David Fergusson; edited with notes by Cyrus Adler," *Publications of the American Jewish Historical Society* 7 (1899); reprinted in Martin A. Cohen, ed., *The Jewish Experience in Latin America: Selected Studies from the Publications of the American Jewish Historical Society*, 2. vols. (Waltham, MA/New York: American Jewish Historical Society/KTAV Publishing House, 1971), 1:375.

53. The woman was Briolanja Fernandes, illegitimate daughter of Diogo Fernandes and his servant Madalena Gonçalves (cited from her trial transcript by Mello, *Gente Da Nação*, 159).

54. *La vida de Lazarillo de Tormes y de sus fortunas y adversidades*, ed. Alberto Blecua (Madrid: Clásicos Castalia, 1972 [1554]), 93-4.

55. Quoted in José Toribio Medina, *Historia del Tribunal del Santo Oficio de la inquisición en Chile* (Santiago de Chile, Fondo Histórico y Bibliográfico J. T. Medina, 1952 [orig. 1890]), 202. Though Medina often quotes directly from the trial transcripts, one gets the feeling that even much of the unmarked text comes either verbatim or in close paraphrase from the manuscript sources he found in the archives, as in this passage.

56. Testimony of Thomassina de Mendoca, 21 August 1635; AGN Mexico, Inq. 402, exp. 1, leg. 2, fol. 16r. She is referring to the sisters Juana and Rafaela Enriquez, whose extended family will be treated at length in chapter 4. Rafaela herself made a similar charge against Juana and her husband Simón Váez Sevilla, claiming that they frequently ordered their slaves whipped for various "childish reasons," but only on Fridays (cited and translated in Ferry, "Don't Drink the Chocolate").

It could be that these acts of mistreatment were a cover for Friday-night rituals, though this is doubtful, or that the allegations are exaggerations meant to insinuate wrongdoing for the Inquisitors. The cruelty of New Christian masters, real or alleged, as raised in the various incidents and citations given in this chapter does not stand out at all from the behavior of Old Christian masters, as recounted and analyzed in any number of works on Afroiberian slavery.

57. Arnold Wiznitzer, *Jews in Colonial Brazil* (New York: Columbia University Press, 1960), 21; Gitlitz, *Secrecy and Deceit*, 163.
58. Antonio came to Lisbon at age 8 (*ca.* 1713) because his mother had been summoned there from Rio de Janeiro by the Inquisition.
59. "Traslado do processo feito pela inquizição de Lisboa contra Antonio Jozé da Silva poeta brazileiro," *Revista Trimensal do Instituto Historico Geographico Brazileiro* (Rio de Janeiro) 59,1 (1896): 9.
60. "Processo contra Antonio da Silva," 10.
61. Originally, the Spanish king explicitly permitted intermarriage with Amerindians in a 1501 decree, instructing the governor of Santo Domingo two years later to encourage the marriage of Spanish Christians and Indians "so that both parties can communicate and teach each other, and the Indians become men and women of reason" (Magnus Mörner, *Race Mixture in the History of Latin America* [Boston: Little, Brown, 1967], 26). Again in 1514 the Crown permitted Spaniards to marry Amerindians (37). For political reasons, both the Spanish and Portuguese policies encouraged intermarriage with women of the indigenous nobility (37, 50). As early as 1538, however, the Spanish Crown issued commands to an expedition in Cartagena de las Indias ensuring that "no soldier slept with any Indian who was not a Christian." The Portuguese in Brazil operated under similar orders, whether or not they followed them (25). According to Mörner, the Spanish Crown "on the whole opposed intermarriage with the African element," mostly to prevent slaves "from obtaining freedom for their children or even for themselves, in this way" (38). The Church as well as the Crown also opposed interracial concubinage, as they did any form of concubinage (40). In any event, it seems most White settlers preferred White women, when they were available, even those of "ill repute" or lower-class status, to indigenous women (26-7, 37, 49; C. R. Boxer, *Race Relations in the Portuguese Colonial Empire: 1415-1825* [Oxford: Clarendon Press, 1963], 40, 99): "there is no doubt but that from the days of the Conquest, most successful Spaniards in the New World aspired to have a white wife as the legitimate female head of their household" (Boxer, *Race Relations*, 38). Exceptions proliferated, of course, among them the "heretical" views cited here (Alfredo Margarido," As mulheres outras nas ilhas atlânticas e na costa occidental africana nos séculos XV a XVII," and Maria Helena Vilas-Boas e Alvim, "A mulher e a expansão na perspective de alguns cronistas e historiadores seus coevos," in *O rosto feminino da expans*o portuguesa: Congresso internacional realizado em Lisboa, Portugal, 21-25 de Novembro de 1994: Actas* [Lisbon: Comissão para a Igualdade e para os Direitos das Mulheres, 1995], 1:357-74, 261-8).
62. Brooks, *Eurafricans*, 79.
63. Letter of 20 April 1599; quoted in José Toribio Medina, *Historia del Tribunal de la Inquisición de Lima, 1569-1820*, Prólogo de Marcel Bataillon, 2nd. ed., 2 vols. (Santiago de Chile: Fondo Histórico y Bibliográfico J. T. Medina, 1956 [orig. 1887]), 1:288.
64. Cited in Alfonso Toro, *Los judíos en la Nueva España: Documentos del siglo xvi correspondientes al ramo de inquisición* (México City: Archivo General de la Nación/Fondo de Cultura Económica, 1982 [1932]), 104, 117.
65. Quoted in Medina, *Inquisición de Lima*, 1:151. Hernandez appeared as a penitent at a public *auto de fé*, heard his sentence read to him, performed a light abjuration and began his two-year banishment from Lima and four-year banishment from Panamá. Were he to break the terms of his sentence, he would face double the time in the galleys at the oar and without salary.
66. Cited in Rafael Gracia Boix, *Autos de fe y causas de la Inquisición de Córdoba* (Córdoba: Publicaciones de la Excma Disputación Provincial, 1983), 38.
67. Quoted in Medina, *Inquisición de Lima*, 1:233.
68. Cited in Gracia Boix, *Inquisición de Córdoba*, 44. She had to attend mass as a penitent. I have cited examples only from the Spanish world; for examples from the Portuguese orbit, and a brief and similar analysis, see Ronaldo Vainfas, *Trópico dos pecados: Moral, sexualidade e Inquisição no Brasil* (Rio de Janeiro: Editora Campus, 1989), especially 368-372, "Fornicação, Misoginia e Preconceito Racial."
69. Rachel Mizrahi Bromberg, *A inquisição no Brasil: Um capitão-mor judaizante* (São Paulo: Centro de Estudos Judaicos da F.F.L.C.H./USP, 1984), 97.
70. Yom-Tov Assis, "Sexual Behaviour in Mediaeval Hispano-Jewish Society," in *Jewish History:*

Essays in Honour of Chimen Abramsky, ed. Ada Rapoport-Albert and Steven J. Zipperstein (London: P. Halban, 1988), 39-40.
71. Assis, "Sexual Behaviour," 41.
72. Saunders, "The Life and Humour of João de Sá Panasco, o Negro," 185; Alberto Ferreiro, "Simon Magus, Dogs, and Simon Peter," in *The Devil, Heresy and Witchcraft in the Middle Ages: Essays in Honor of Jeffrey B. Russell*, ed. Alberto Ferreiro (Leiden, Netherlands: Brill, 1998), 45–90.
73. Cited in Lipiner, *Izaque de Castro*, 103. Already in the first decade of the century Fray Prudencio de Sandoval voices the same sentiment; see Yosef Hayim Yerushalmi, *Assimilation and Racial Anti-Semitism: The Iberian and German Models*, Leo Baeck Memorial Lecture, 26 (New York: Leo Baeck Institute, 1982), 16. José de Acosta wields the trope of Jer. 13:23 in reference to barbaric peoples in general (*De procuranda indorum salute (Predicación del evangelio en las Indias)*, ed. Francisco Mateos [Madrid: I. G. Magerit, 1952], 1.2.57-8). The increasingly "biological" tendencies of Iberian *limpieza de sangre* lead some (former) converso physicians to similarly essentializing theories. The physician Juan de Huarte, of converso origin, supports his Lamarckian understanding of how Jews pass on their medical prowess by pointing to the intrinsic nature of Blackness in "Ethiopians," both qualities impervious to changes in climate (*Examen de ingenios para las sciencias* [Amsterdam: Juan de Ravestein, 1662 (orig. pub. 1575)], 230-251 [ch. 12]); see also Diego Gracia Guillén, "Judaism, Medicine, and the Inquisitorial Mind in Sixteenth-Century Spain," in *The Spanish Inquisition and the Inquisitorial Mind*, ed. Angel Alcalá (Boulder: Social Science Monographs, 1987), 375-400; David B. Ruderman, *Jewish Thought and Scientific Discovery in Early Modern Europe* (New Haven: Yale University Press, 1985), ch. 5 ("Converso Doctors and Race").
74. Cited in J. Caro Baroja, *Los judíos en la España moderna y contemporánea*, 4th ed. (Madrid: Ediciones Istmo, 2000), 1:215.
75. Elizabeth Feist Hirsch, *Damião de Gois: The Life and Thought of a Portuguese Humanist* (The Hague: Nijhoff, 1967), 154.
76. My translation. *The Mirror of the New Christians (*Espelho de Christãos Novos*) of Francisco Machado*, ed. and trans. Mildred Evelyn Vieira and Frank Ephraim Talmage (Toronto: Pontifical Institute of Mediaeval Studies, 1977), 75.
77. My translation. Ibid., 323.
78. Quoted in Luis G. Martínez Villada, *Diego López de Lisboa* (Córdoba: Imprenta de la Universidad, 1939), 16. Medina has it differently: "son of a converso and mulato physician" (*Inquisición en Chile*, 367). As in other examples, it is unclear whether *mulato* refers to Blackness or to Jewish-Christian or New Christian-Old Christian miscegenation.
79. Silverblatt, *Modern Inquisitions*, 48.
80. Stuart B. Schwartz, "Questioning Slavery and Accepting Africa: Dissidence, Tolerance, and Syncretism in the Iberian Atlantic World," Unpublished conference paper, delivered at the conference on Slavery, Enlightenment, and Revolution in Colonial Brazil and Spanish America, Fordham University, 5 May 2006.
81. Sweet, *Recreating Africa*, 208.
82. Poncet defended Ethiopian Christianity against such charges. Cited in Ronald S. Love, "Adventures in Abyssinia: The Relation of Charles Poncet, 1698 to 1700," *Itinerario* 28,3 (2004): 54. For the Jesuit view, see Donald M. Lockhart and M.G. Da Costa (eds. and trans.), *The Itinerário of Jerónimo Lobo* (London: Hakluyt, 1984), 176-77, 180.
83. Sweet, *Recreating Africa*, 35. As will be seen in the next chapter, Angola was cited by a number of conversos charged by the Inquisitions as a site of judaizing.
84. Israel, *Diasporas Within a Diaspora*, 129.
85. Cited in Green, "Masters of Difference," 190; see also 260.
86. By 1506, only around 600 were said to have survived the rampant tropical diseases. The possible survival of Judaism among this intermarried group and its descendants has received much tendentious coverage. *Jewish Child Slaves in São Tomé: Papers, Essays, Articles and Original Documents Related to the July 1995 Conference*, ed. Moshé Liba (Wellington, NZ: New Zealand Jewish Chronicle Publications, 2003); Robert Garfield, "A Forgotten Fragment of the Diaspora: the Jews of São Tomé Island, 1492-1654," in *The Expulsion of the Jews: 1492 and After*, ed. Raymond B. Waddington and Arthur H. Williamson (New York: Garland Publishing, 1994), 73-87; idem, "Public Christians, Secret Jews: Religion and Political Conflict on São Tomé Island in the Sixteenth and Seventeenth Centuries," *Sixteenth-Century Journal* 21,4 (1990): 645-54.
87. The trader André Donelha, cited in George E. Brooks, *Landlords and Strangers: Ecology, Society, and Trade in Western Africa, 1000-1630* (Boulder: Westview Press, 1993), 210; see also Peter Mark and Jose Da Silve Horta, "Two Early Seventeenth-Century Sephardic Communities on

Senegal's Petite Cote," *History in Africa* 31 (2004): 233-4.
88. Brooks, *Eurafricans*, 61; idem, *Landlords and Strangers*, 159, 178-9, 185-7, 221-2. On Cabo Verde, see Green, "Masters of Difference."
89. Malyn Newitt, "Mixed Race Groups in the Early History of Portuguese Expansion," in *Studies in the Portuguese Discoveries I: Proceedings of the First Colloquium of the Centre for the Study of the Portuguese Discoveries*, ed. T. F. Earle and Stephen Parkinson (Warminster: Aris & Phillips/Comissão nacional para as Comemoracões dos Descobrimentos Portugueses, 1992), 42.
90. Brooks, *Eurafricans*, 50; idem, *Landlords and Strangers*, 191.
91. Translated in Green, "Masters of Difference," 260, n. 412; regarding the women of the island adapting (to) local fashion, see Arlindo Manuel Caldeira, "As mulheres no quotidiano da ilha de São Tomé nos séculos XV e XVI," in *Rosto Feminino da expansão portuguesa*, 1:502. Meanwhile, one Black cleric of Cabo Verde, Thome Vaz Mascarenhas, was accused in 1652 of living in a "dissolute and scandalous manner" and "having partiality and dealings with" the local New Christians (Green, "Masters of Difference," 312, n. 182).
92. Brooks, *Landlords and Strangers*, 159; Green, "Masters of Difference," 81, 86, 101, 203. According to Green, no contemporary document actually identifies "Jews" among the lançados, though with later persecution many New Christians did become lançados ("Masters of Difference," 63, 82, 202-3). Alfredo Margarido understands the accusations of judaizing as stemming from the cultural parallels such as circumcision ("Mulheres outras," 368).
93. Alencastre, *Trato dos viventes*, 25-6; Garfield, "Forgotten Fragment," 78, 83; Green, "Masters of Difference," 85.
94. Brooks, *Eurafricans*, 85, 89-90; idem, *Landlords and Strangers*, 221-2; Mark and Horta, "Two Early Seventeenth-Century Sephardic Communities," 233-4, 245-6. An anonymous memorandum of 1612 identified 15 supposed Jews or judaizers (85). In 1629, a Portuguese expedition dispatched by the king (Spain and Portugal were united at the time) destroyed an alleged synagogue at Rufisque, some 100 miles north of the Gambia River, and arrested several "Jews" there (89-90).
95. Green, "Masters of Difference"; Mark and Horta, "Two Early Seventeenth-Century Sephardic Communities"; Filipa Ribeiro da Silva, "A inquisição na Guiné, nas Ilhas de Cabo Verde e São Tomé e Príncipe," *Revista Lusófona de Ciência das Religiões* 3,5-6 (2004), 167-8; Brooks, *Eurafricans*, 90, drawing on a number of earlier studies; see also 91-3; Caldeira, "Mulheres no quotidiano da ilha de São Tomé," 491-506. As always, the hundreds of denunciations and confessions must be treated with caution. It must be kept in mind that between 1536 and 1821, only three trials for judaizing resulted in sentences (Silva, "Inquisição," 172). The article of Mark and Horta lacks any skepticism regarding the claims of open Judaism or of judaizing found in the sources. For a similar response and modification, see Tobias Green, "Further Considerations on the Sephardim of the Petite Côte," *History in Africa* 32 (2005): 165-83. Regarding the Dutch view, Wim Klooster kindly alerted me to a description of Angola and Congo (in question and answer form) that was sent from Luanda to the West India Company's Zeeland Chamber in late 1641 or early 1642: Q: "Les Portugais lé-bas sont-ils catholiques romains ou juifs [nouveaux chrétiens]?" A: "La plupart et les principaux des habitants portugais sont de nouveaux chrétiens. Cependant, on ne sait pas s'ils sont juifs, parce qu'ils professent ouvertement la religion et la foi catholique romaine / Most of the Portuguese inhabitants and the most prominent ones are new Christians. However, we do not know if they are Jews, because they openly profess the Roman Catholic religion and faith" (Louis Jadin, *L'ancien Congo et l'Angola 1639-1655 d'aprés les archives romaines, portugaises, néerlandaises et espagnoles* [Bruxelles, Rome: Institut Historique belge de Rome, 1975], 162). All of the region's Judaism was allegedly extirpated by the middle of the seventeenth century with the Jews' conversion by Spanish Capuchin missionaries.
96. The quote is from Carole A. Myscofski, "Heterodoxy, Gender, and the Brazilian Inquisition: Patterns in Religion in the 1590s," *Journal of Latin American Lore* 18 (1992), 87. The flip side is the manner in which any non-conformist behavior or belief by New Christians was ascribed to "judaizing;" on this see John Edwards, "Religious Faith and Doubt in Late Medieval Spain: Soria circa 1450-1500," *Past and Present* 120 (August 1988): 3-25.
97. Baião, *Inquisição em Portugal e no Brasil*, 118-9; Elias Lipiner, *O Sapateiro de Trancoso e o alfaiate de Setúbal* (Rio de Janeiro: Imago Editora, 1993), 263-4.
98. Mercedes García-Arenal reports a similar exchange from 1534 between a Morisco blacksmith and his neighbor, who accused him of not being a good Christian. Says the blacksmith, "If they made you a Moor by force, would you be a good Moor?" When the neighbor answers in the negative, Mendoza continues, "Well, then why do you want me to be a good Christian?" (*Inquisición y moriscos: Los procesos del tribunal de Cuenca* [Madrid: Siglo Veintiuno Editores, 1978], 100; she cites Luis Mármol Carvajal, *Historia del rebelión y castigo de los moriscosdel reino de*

Granada [orig. 1600], reprinted in Biblioteca de Autores Españoles, vol. 21 [Madrid: Atlas, 1946], 157). Rodrigues' analogy might be a spontaneous application of clever logic drawing on shared topical examples but might on the other hand be derived from tropes that circulated precisely because they grew out of well-known and -debated questions of central concern.
99. Baião, *Inquisição em Portugal e no Brasil*, 121-2.
100. J. Capistrano de Abreu, *Primeira Visitação do Santo Oficio as Partes do Brasil: Denunciações da Bahia, 1591-1593* (São Paulo: Homenagem de Paulo Prado, 1925), 568.
101. Schwartz, *All Can Be Saved*, 95.

Chapter 3

1. *Descripción del Peru*, 121; for an English translation of the text, see "Anonymous Description of Peru (1600-1615)," in Irving A. Leonard (ed.), *Colonial Travelers in Latin America* (New York: Alfred A. Knopf, 1972), 97-117.
2. Antonio Vázquez de Espinosa, *Compendio y descripción de las islas occidentales* [1629], the original manuscript transcribed by Charles Upson Clark, Smithsonian miscellaneous collections, 108 (Washington, D.C.: Smithsonian Institution, 1948), 220.
3. *Descripcion del Peru*, 121-2.
4. C. R. Boxer, *The Portuguese Seaborne Empire, 1415-1825* (London: Hutchinson, 1969), 337; Gonzalo Aguirre Beltrán, *La población negra de México: Estudio etnohistórico* (Mexico City: Fondo de Cultura Económica, 1989), 45-6.
5. On the slave trade and economy in Spanish South America, see Herbert S. Klein and Ben Vinson, *African Slavery in Latin America and the Caribbean*, 2nd ed. (New York: Oxford University Press, 2007); Bowser, *The African Slave in Colonial Peru*; Leslie Rout, *The African Experience in Spanish America, 1502-present* (New York: Columbia University Press, 1976); Rolando Mellafe, *La introducción de la esclavitud negra en Chile: Trafico y rutas* (Santiago de Chile: Universidad de Chile, 1959); Maya Restrepo, *Brujeria*, 64-213.
6. *Descripcion del Peru*, 122.
7. Pedro Simón, *Noticias historiales de las conquistas de Tierra Firme en Las Indias Occidentales*, 6 vols., Biblioteca Banco Popular, vol. 105 (Bogotá: Banco Popular, 1981), 5:307.
8. Walter Rodney, "Portuguese Attempts at Monopoly on the Upper Guinea Coast, 1580-1650," *Journal of African History* 6 (1965): 309; cited in Philip D. Curtin, *The Atlantic Slave Trade: A Census* (Madison: University of Wisconsin Press, 1969), 108.
9. Cited in Ventura, *Portuguese no Peru*, 1:57.
10. Iosef Fernandez, *Apostolica y penitente vida de el V.P. Pedro Claver, de la compañia de Iesus. Sacada principalmente de informaciones juridicas hechas ante el Ordinario de la Ciudad de Cartagena de Indias. A su religiosisima provincia de el Nuevo Reyno de Granada. Por el padre Iosef Fernandez de la Compañia de Iesus natural de Taraçona* (Zaragoça: Diego Dormer, 1666), 105.
11. Quoted in Medina, *Inquisición de Cartagena*, 139.
12. Translated by H. P. Salomon, "The Portuguese Background of Menasseh Ben Israel's Parents as Revealed through the Inquisitorial Archives at Lisbon," *Studia Rosenthaliana* 17,2 (July 1983), 113.
13. Enriqueta Vila Vilar, "Extranjeros en Cartagena (1593-1630)," *Jahrbuch für Geschichte von Staat, Wirtschaft und Gesellschaft Lateinamerikas* (Koln Wein, 1979): 155, 175-76. The most comprehensive analysis of the Portuguese presence in the adjacent and perhaps most prosperous Spanish colony is Ventura, *Portugueses no Peru*.
14. The quote is from Ceballos Gómez, *Hechicería, brujería, e inquisición*, 141.
15. A list of foreigners in Cartagena, compiled in 1630, calls him forty years old (reprinted in Ventura, *Portugueses no Peru*, 3:40). The list, *Relación y abecedário de los estrangeros que se hallan en la ciudad de Cartagena...*, is reprinted in ibid., 3:31-77.
16. Letter to Manuel Bautista Perez from Simon Dias Pinto, 17 April 1634, AGN Peru, Inq., Leg. 34, fol. 173r.
17. Studnicki-Gizbert, *Nation Upon the Sea*, 57.
18. Ventura, *Portugueses no Peru*, 1:171, 208, 400-1. Bautista Peres and Duarte established their firm in Lima in 1627 (ibid., 1:287). Further details on Bautista Peres and his trade network, including Pinto, can be found in Linda A. Newson and Susie Minchin, *From Capture to Sale: The Portuguese Slave Trade to Spanish South America in the Early Seventeenth Century* (Leiden: Brill, 2007).

19. Ventura, *Portugueses no Peru*, 1:296.
20. I ic Croitoru Rotbaum, *Documentos coloniales originados en el santo oficio del tribunal de la inquisición de Cartagena de Indias (Contribución a la historia de Colombia* [vol. 2]) (Bogota: Tipografia Hispana, 1971), after p. 136.
21. Ventura, *Portugueses no Peru*, 3:41.
22. Ventura, *Portugueses no Peru*, 1:337, 401-2.
23. According to Spanish legislation of the colonies, Portuguese were considered foreigners (Lewis Hanke, "The Portuguese in Spanish America with Special Reference to the Villa Imperial de Potosí," *Revista de Historia de América* 51 (June 1961), 10 n. 34).
24. Álvarez Alonso, *Inquisición de Cartagena*, 118-9.
25. AHN Inq. 1021, fols. 1-4v., *Relación del auto de fé que los señores inquisidores licenciado Don Martín de Cortázar y Azcárate y Doctor Damián Velázquez de Contreras, celebraron a 25 del mes de Marzo de 38 años, a honra y gloria de Dios y exaltación de la fe católica y extirpación de las herejías, en la ciudad de Cartagena de las Indias*; reprinted in Anna-María Splendiani, *Cincuenta Años de Inquisición en el Tribunal de Cartagena de las Indias, 1610-60*, 4 vols. (Bogotá, 1997), 3:39.
26. The Cartagena tribunal's summary of the charges against Pinto appear in the *Relación de la causas de fé* from 1636; AHN Inq. 1020, fols. 503r.-507v.; reprinted in Splendiani, *Tribunal de Cartagena*, 2:438-43.
27. AHN Inq. 1020, fol. 504r.; Splendiani, *Tribunal de Cartagena*, 2:439.
28. AHN Inq. 1020, fol. 504r.; Splendiani, *Tribunal de Cartagena*, 2:439.
29. AHN Inq. 1021, fol. 28r.-v., *Relación de las causas de fe del santo oficio de la inquisición de Cartagena, que este año de mil y seiscientos y treinta y ocho remite a su alteza el licenciado Juan Ortiz, fiscal de dicha inquisición*, reprinted in Splendiani, *Tribunal de Cartagena*, 3:63-4.
30. AHN Inq. 1021, fol. 32v., *Relación de las causas de la fe*; Splendiani, *Tribunal de Cartagena*, 3:68.
31. The text pertaining to Judaism is reprinted in Medina, *Inquisición de Cartagena*, 52-5.
32. AHN Inq. 1020, fol. 504r.; Splendiani, *Tribunal de Cartagena*, 2:439.
33. AHN Inq. 1620/18, fol. 265-67; reprinted in Croitoru Rotbaum, *De Sefarad*, 283.
34. Croitoru Rotbaum, *De Sefarad*, 283.
35. AHN Inq. 1620/15; reprinted in Croitoru Rotbaum, *De Sefarad*, 308-12.
36. AHN Inq. 1020, fol. 503v.; Splendiani, *Tribunal de Cartagena*, 2:439.
37. Green, "Masters of Difference," 219, citing AHN, Inquisición, Legajo 1608, Expediente 24, folio 25v: "*...alavo a Dios para server a VM...*", and see Green's notes for the other examples of the expression.
38. AHN Inq. 1620, fol. 504r.-v.; Splendiani, *Tribunal de Cartagena*, 2:439-40.
39. AHN Inq. 1620, fol. 505r.; Splendiani, *Tribunal de Cartagena*, 2:440.
40. AHN Inq. 1620, fol. 505v.; Splendiani, *Tribunal de Cartagena*, 2:441. The time of the torture session appears on fol. 506r.
41. AHN Inq. 1620, fol. 505v.; Splendiani, *Tribunal de Cartagena*, 2:441. The weekday fasts of marranos comprised a rather flexible system, some fasting on Tuesdays and Thursdays, some one day a week, others any day(s) they chose (see Gitlitz, *Secrecy and Deceit*, 396-7).
42. AHN Inq. 1620, fols. 505v.-506r.; Splendiani, *Tribunal de Cartagena*, 2:441.
43. The *Suprema* or Supreme Council of the Inquisition noted this and numerous other flaws in its review of the 1636 trial of Luis Gomes Barreto, conducted by the Cartagena tribunal (AHN Inq. 1620/9; reprinted in Croitoru Rotbaum, *De Sefarad*, 275-6).
44. See, for instance, AHN Inq. 1021, fols. 1-48r., reprinted in Splendiani, *Tribunal de Cartagena*, 3:39-85.
45. AHN Inq. Leg. 1620, quad. 7, no. 1, *Testimonio de Los confessionas que ha hecho diego lopez cirujano presso en las carzeles secretas destes s^{to} offi^o de la ynq^{on} de cartag^{na} de las yndias por brujo Hereje Apostata de mas s^{ta} ffe catolica* (1634), fol. 2r. López is treated in Manuel Tejado Fernandez, *Aspectos de la vida social en Cartagena de Indias durante el seiscientos* (Seville: Escuela de Estudios Hispano-Americanos, 1954), esp. ch. 5.
46. Jairo Solano Alonso, *Salud, cultura y sociedad: Cartagena de Indias, siglos XVI y XVII* (Bogota: Fondo de Publicaciones de la Universidad del Atlántico/Colección de Ciencias Sociales Rodrigo Noguera Barreneche, 1998), 71, 75-6.
47. Concerning Santiago de Guatemala, see Herrera, *Natives, Europeans, and Africans*, 90.
48. Ceballos Gómez, *Hechicería, brujería, e inquisición*, 70. The author does not describe the nature of her sources.
49. Solano Alonso, *Salud, cultura y sociedad en Cartagena*, 103-15, 119-231; Ceballos Gómez, *Hechicería, brujería, e inquisición*, 71.

50. *Testimonio de Diego López*, AHN Inq. 1620/7/1, fols. 1-3r. All reproduced in Tejado Fernandez, *Vida social en Cartagena*, 307-23 (Appendix 3, "Testimonio de las confesiones del mulato Diego Lopez").
51. A full treatment of Eguiluz, born on the island of Santo Domingo to a Biafran mother, and her circle is offered by Maya Restrepo, *Brujería*, 599-615, 623-5, 629, 647-9, 704.
52. Maya Restrepo, *Brujería*, 590-4.
53. *Testimonio de Diego Lopez*, AHN Inq. 1620/7/1, fols. 3v.
54. *Testimonio de Diego Lopez*, AHN Inq. 1620/7/1, fols. 32v-33r.
55. *Testimonio de Diego López*, AHN Inq. leg. 1620/7/1, fol. 51.
56. *Testimonio de Diego Lopez*, AHN Inq. 1620/7/1, fols. 13v.-14r.; quoted in Tejado Fernandez, *Vida Social en Cartagena*, 316.
57. On "knowing other people's lives" in the inquisitional context, see Joseph H. Silverman, "On Knowing Other People's Lives, Inquisitorially and Artistically," in Mary Elizabeth Perry and Anne J. Cruz (eds.), *Cultural Encounters: the Impact of the Inquisition in Spain and the New World* (Berkeley: University of California Press, 1991), 157-75.
58. *Testimonio de Diego Lopez*, AHN Inq. 1620/7/1, fols. 14r., 17v.; quoted in Tejado Fernandez, *Vida social en Cartagena*, 316, 319-20.
59. Ceballos Gómez, "Grupos sociales y prácticas mágicas," 54.
60. Sánchez, seeing what López is doing, and knowing "that the accused [Diego] was a friend of the said Blas de Paz, asked him if he came to speak with his friend."
61. *Testimonio de Diego Lopez*, AHN Inq. 1620/7/1, fols. 17v.-18r.; quoted in Tejado Fernandez, *Vida social en Cartagena*, 320.
62. *Testimonio de Diego Lopez*, AHN Inq. 1620/7/1, fols. 16v.-17r.; cited in Tejado Fernandez, *Vida social en Cartagena*, 318-9.
63. AHN Inq. 1021, fol. 3r.-v., *Relación del auto*; Splendiani, *Tribunal de Cartagena*, 3:39.
64. Daviken Studnicki-Gizbert, "*La Nación* among the Nations: Portuguese and Other Maritime Trading Diasporas in the Atlantic, Sixteenth to Eighteenth Centuries," in Richard L. Kagan and Philip D. Morgan (eds.), *Atlantic Diasporas: Jews, Conversos, and Crypto-Jews in the Age of Mercantilism, 1500-1800* (Baltimore: Johns Hopkins University Press, 2009), 88-90.
65. Willis Johnson, "The Myth of Jewish Male Menses," *Journal of Medieval History* 24 (1998): 273-95; John L. Beusterien, "Jewish Male Menstruation in Seventeenth-Century Spain," *Bulletin of the History of Medicine* 73,3 (1999) 447-56; Sander L. Gilman, *Jewish Self-Hatred: Anti-Semitism and the Hidden Language of the Jews* (Baltimore: Johns Hopkins University Press, 1986), 64-5. Elliott Horowitz cites Irvin Resnick to argue that the myth first appeared in the thirteenth-century work of Jacques de Vitry, *Historia orientalis* (Elliott Horowitz, *Reckless Rites: Purim and the Legacy of Jewish Violence* (Princeton: Princeton University Press, 2006), 194). Johnson emphasizes that "medical theorists, from Galen (130-199) to Arnold of Villanova (1240-1311), described menstrual and haemorrhoidal bleeding as interchangeable. This bleeding was part of a natural process in which the body rid itself" of unhealthy humors ("Myth of Male Menses," 288; see also Thomas Laqueur, *Making Sex: Body and Gender from the Greeks to Freud* [Cambridge: Harvard University Press, 1990], 107).
66. Johnson, "Myth of Jewish Male Menses," 275. On the symbolic potency of Judas, see, for example, Othlon de Saint-Emeran (11th cen.): "these things that have been said concerning Judas the traitor extend to the entire Jewish people" (David Nirenberg, *Communities of Violence: Persecution of Minorities in the Middle Ages* [Princeton: Princeton University Press, 1996], 62, n. 79).
67. Johnson, "Myth of Jewish Male Menses," 275.
68. Juan de Quiñones, *Memorial de Juan de Quiñones dirigido a Fray Antonio de Sotomayor, inquisidor general, sobre el caso de Francisco de Andrada, sospechoso de pertenecer a la raza judía, discutiendo sobre los medios de conocer y perseguir a ella* (Madrid: Biblioteca Nacional, VE, box no. 16, 1632); translated in Georgina Dopico Black, *Perfect Wives, Other Women: Adultery and Inquisition in Early Modern Spain* (Durham: Duke University Press, 2001), 3; on Quiñones and his tract, see also Yerushalmi, *From Spanish Court to Italian Ghetto*, 122-33.
69. Toward the end of the fifteenth century, Torquemada had convinced Ferdinand and Isabella to reinstate a 1412 statute forbidding the employment of Jewish physicians. In Mallorca, conversos had been prohibited from practicing medicine, pharmaceutics or phlebotomy in 1488 (Antonio Contreras Mas, *Los médicos judíos en la Mallorca bajomedieval: Siglos XIV-XV* [Palma de Mallorca: Miquel Font Editor, 1997], 105).
70. *Discurso contra los judíos traducido de lengua portuguesa en castellano por el Padre Fray Diego Gavilán Vela* (Salamanca, 1631); cited in Dopico Black, *Perfect Wives*, 218, n.2. This text is discussed and excerpted at length in Josette Riandère La Roche, "Du discours d'exclusion des

Notes to Chapter 3   245

juifs: Antijudaïsme ou antisémitisme?" in *Les problèmes de l'exclusion en Espagne, XVI-XVII siècles*, ed. Agustín Redondo (Paris: Sorbonne, 1983), 51-75. The original Portuguese version is Vicente da Costa Mattos, *Breve discurso contra a heretica perfidia do iudaismo, continuada nos presentes apostatas de nossa sante Fe, com o que conuem a expulsao dos delinquentes nella dos Reynos de sua Magestade, co suas molheres & filhos: conforme a Escriptura sagrada, Santos Padres, Direito Ciuil, & Canonico, & muitos dos politicos* (Lisbon: P. Craesbeeck, 1622); for Jewish menstruation, see 131r-v. The translator to Spanish, Gavilán Vela, was the Bishop of Lugo. According to Yerushalmi, the same accusation later appeared in Francisco de Torrejoncillo, *Centinela contra judíos* (Pamplona, 1691), 174 (*From Spanish Court to Italian Ghetto*, 128). Franco da Piacenza, a Jewish convert to Christianity, included in his 1630 catalogue of "Jewish maladies" the charge that Jewish men and women of the lost tribe of Simeon menstruated four days a year. "In placing the menstruating male Jew in the exotic world of the lost tribes (the New World), he substantiated the charge of Jewish difference while freeing himself from the stigma of difference" (Gilman, *Jewish Self-Hatred*, 75). See also Pedro Aznar Cardona, *Expulsión justificada de los moriscos españoles* (1612), cited in Beusterien, *Jewish Male menstruation*, 451-2. Even the English member of Parliament Edward Spencer used such notions. Arguing that the Jews should only be readmitted to England if they repent for their crucifixion of Christ, he asked rhetorically: "have not all of you a bloody issue about your bodies, [...] and doe not the Italians say, *they smell a Jew before they discerne him with their eyes?*" (Edward Spencer, *A Briefe Epistle to the Learned Manasseh Ben Israel. In Answer to his, Dedicated to the Parliament. September. 6* [London: John Downame, 1650], 10).
71. T. Malvenda, *De Antechristo* (Rome, 1604), 513; quoted in Henry Méchoulan, *El honor de dios: Indios, judíos y moriscos en el siglo de oro* (Barcelona: Editorial Argos Vergara, 1981), 158.
72. David B. Ruderman, "The Community of Converso Physicians: Race, Medicine, and the Shaping of a Cultural Identity," in David B. Ruderman, *Jewish Thought and Scientific Discovery in Early Modern Europe* (New Haven: Yale University Press, 1995), 290; Méchoulan, *Honor de dios*, 138-41. Neither Méchoulan nor Yerushalmi gives the date of Huarta's proposal, though it might stem from his *Problemas filosóficos* (Madrid: Iuan Goncalez, 1628), 12 and following. Physicians from other suspect minorities suffered from growing Iberian intolerance as well. By the late sixteenth century, Morisco physicians were being accused of poisoning and maiming their Old Christian patients, as often had been alleged regarding converso doctors, and there was a growing demand that Moriscos be excluded from medical schools (Stephen Haliczer, *Inquisition and Society in the Kingdom of Valencia, 1478-1834* [Berkeley: University of California Press, 1990], 258).
73. Shlomo ibn Verga, *Shevet Yehuda*, ed. A. Shochat (Jerusalem: Mosad Bialik, 1947 [orig. 1554]), 129; cited in Yosef Hayim Yerushalmi, *Freud's Moses: Judaism Terminable and Interminable* (New Haven: Yale University Press, 1991), 32.
74. AHN Inq. 1020, fol. 503r.; Splendiani, *Tribunal de Cartagena*, 2:438; AHN Inq. 1601/18, fols. 40-43v.; Croitoru Rotbaum, *Documentos*, 231-4.
75. I surmise Rufina's illiteracy from the fact that, according to Diego López, she several times asked him to spy on Paz Pinto for her by trying to determine the book from which the people in the latter's house seemed to be praying, "since you know how to read," i.e., *she did not* (*Testimonio de Diego Lopez*, AHN Inq. 1620/7/1, fol. 19v., see also fol. 20r.).
76. In 1777, the Inquisitors of Cartagena complained that the Edicts of the Faith needed to be copied by hand because the city's only press had been sold by its desperately poor owner (Letter of the Inquisitors José Umeres and Juan Félix de Villegas, 11 October 1777; Medina, *Inquisición de Cartagena*, 378, n.1). Medina's history of printing in Cartagena thus begins only in 1809, without mention of any early modern publishing in the city (J. T. Medina, *La imprenta en cartagena de las indias 1809-1820* [Santiago de Chile: Imprenta Elzeviriana, 1904].
77. Maya Restrepo, *Brujería*, 602, 612. According to a 1622 letter, consignment to the "general hospital" to serve the patients alongside the Capuchin brothers seems to have been the punishment meted out to four other Afroiberian practitioners of magic, because "nowhere [else] did they want to receive them" (Medina, *Inquisición de Cartagena*, 122).
78. Solano Alonso, *Salud, cultura y sociedad en Cartagena*, 65-6; Pedro López de León, *Pratica y teorica de las apostemas en general y particular. Questiones, y praticas de cirugia, de heridas, llagas, y otras cosas nuevas, y particulares* (Sevilla: Luys Estupiñan, 1628). The idea of Jewish male menstruation does not appear in the most oft-used text of surgery, Juan Fragoso, *Cirugia universal* (Madrid, 1581), reprinted and expanded in several editions.
79. Ceballos Gómez, "Grupos sociales y prácticas mágicas," 55.
80. Ceballos Gómez, *Sociedad y prácticas mágicas*, 465. Maya Restrepo, on the other hand, convincingly argues that Eguiluz was familiar, as were other Black or Mulata Caribbean *brujas*,

with the magical recipes and incantations proffered in the Mediterranean/European magical discourse attributed through the centuries in a variety of ever-morphing texts to King Solomon (*Brujería*, 615-38).
81. *Testimonio de Diego Lopez*, AHN Inq. 1620/7/1, fol. 16v.
82. Croitoru Rotbaum, *Documentos*, 232, who reproduces all of the charges against Pinto, 231-234.
83. Ina Johanna Fandrich, *The Mysterious Voodoo Queen, Marie Laveaux: A Study of Powerful Female Leadership in Nineteenth-Century New Orleans* (New York: Routledge, 2005).
84. Ceballos Gómez, *Sociedad y prácticas mágicas*, 299.
85. *Testimonio de Diego Lopez*, AHN Inq. 1620/1/7, fol. 15r.
86. *Testimonio de Diego Lopez*, AHN Inq. 1620/1/7, fol. 15r.
87. "[S]iempre dixo la dcha Rufina con admiraçion que si tocaba en esta materia que de Ruina ha de aver" (*Testimonio de Diego Lopez*, AHN Inq. 1620/1/7, fol. 10r.).
88. *Testimonio de Diego López*, AHN Inq. 1620/1/7, fol. 25r.
89. *Testimonio de Diego Lopez*, AHN Inq. 1620/1/7, fol. 22r.-v.
90. *Testimonio de Diego Lopez*, AHN Inq. 1620/1/7, fol. 22r.-v.
91. "y aviendole dho que no le dixo que se baxasse abaxo que no querian estos hombres que nadie viesse sus q^{tas} en dhos libros dando Con esto a entender a este que era Libro donde estaban Armadas quentas Con lo qual aquel dia no se effetuo La Compra de las liquidas que yba a Comporar por el alboroto que se avia Caussado Con el Libro, si bien tubo effecto de alli a un mes sin volver a su cassa" (*Testimonio de Diego Lopez*, AHN Inq. 1620/1/7, fol. 22v.-23r.).
92. *Testimonio de Diego Lopez*, AHN Inq. 1620/1/7, fol. 24v.
93. Ceballos Gómez, *Hechicería, brujería, e inquisición*, 141-42.
94. Ceballos Gómez, *Hechicería, brujería, e inquisición*, 131-32, but see the whole section on this episode, 125-54. All of the above motivations came into play with many forms of African magic used by slaves; on the Portuguese world, see Sweet, *Recreating Africa*, 164-88.
95. Ceballos Gómez, *Hechicería, brujería, e inquisición*, 135.
96. Ceballos Gómez, *Hechicería, brujería, e inquisició*, 132.
97. Sweet, *Recreating Africa*, 14, 171.
98. *Testimonio de Diego Lopez*, AHN Inq. 1620/1/7, fol. 32v.
99. Maya Restrepo, *Brujería*.
100. Silverblatt, "Colonial Conspiracies," 263.
101. Michael Taussig, *Shamanism, Colonialism, and the Wild Man: A Study in Terror and Healing* (Chicago: University of Chicago Press, 1987), 218.
102. Maya Restrepo, *Brujería*, 503-4; on the Portuguese world, see Sweet, *Recreating Africa*, 134-7, 145-59. Maya Restrepo shows, for instance, how Eguiluz utilized ritual gestures, verbal and otherwise, drawn from the Yoruba-influenced traditions surrounding the spirit/diety Exu (*Brujería*, 647-9). White admiration of African spiritual/magical powers was widespread. At the beginning of the eighteenth century, one poor Mexican *castiza* (half White, half Mestizo), Marta de la Encarnación, told an acquaintence that "she had traveled 'in spirit' to a sinful man she knew, 'transformed as if she were a black woman [*negrita*] and told the man the story of his whole life and sins, warning him that he must amend his ways'" (cited in Jaffary, *False Mystics*, 48). This woman's subliminal desire to be Black (she herself may have had some African ancestry) likely is connected to a positive perception of the relevant African prowess. Two other accused Mexican mystics shared similar visions/fantasies (ibid., 103-4).
103. *Testimonio de Diego Lopez*, AHN Inq. 1620/1/7, fol. 2r.
104. *Testimonio de Diego Lopez*, AHN Inq. 1620/1/7, fol. 32v.
105. Sweet, *Recreating Africa*, 175. Much of the magic practiced by Whites also pertained to romance and sexuality; see Behar, "Sex and Sin."
106. *Testimonio de Diego Lopez*, AHN Inq. 1620/1/7, fol. 37v.
107. Maya Restrepo, *Brujería*, 605; for examples of "politically"-motivated attacks by members of other groups (*juntas*) of magical practitioners, on domestic slaves, for example, see 556-62. Similarly, Lutz, *Santiago de Guatemala*, 43, reads the frequent larcenies committed by non-Whites of Santiago de Guatemala as acts targeting the city's Spanish elites.
108. "Los mios no lo son sino los de Paula que nos anima a Todas y de semejantes cassos" (*Testimonio de Diego Lopez*, AHN Inq. 1620/1/7, fol. 35v.). Maya Restrepo reads the frequent acts of infanticide as resistance to enslavement and the slave system, and the use of various body parts of the dead as a component of African medico-magical practice (*Brujería*, 697-705; see also Sweet, *Recreating Africa*, 67).
109. "no fiarsse la dha Paula de ning^{na} negra sino de su^a zamba" (*Testimonio de Diego Lopez*, AHN Inq. 1620/1/7, fol. 36r.). The term zamba here probably refers to Eguiluz's assistant of mixed

African and Amerindian background, Juana Zamba. Ultimately, Eguiluz was sentenced twice by the Cartagena tribunal, the second time in 1642, in trials that produced some 405 folios of documentation (Maya Restrepo, *Brujería*, 506).
110. *Testimonio de Diego Lopez*, AHN Inq. 1620/1/7, fol. 6r.-v., 26r. A free Black woman, Potenciana de Abreu, also of Cartagena, describes a nearly identical mark — ritual scarification? a marriage pledge? a pact of resistance? — in her own 1635 inquisition trial (AHN Inq. 1020, fol. 467v.; Splendiani, *Tribunal de Cartagena*, 2:420).
111. The Dominican friar Francisco de la Cruz also claimed to receive visits from a demon who appeared in the guise of an Amerindian (Castelló, *Francisco de la Cruz*, 1:517). In the 1620s, Juan de Mañozca y Zamora, one of the founders of the Cartagena tribunal in 1610 and inquisitor at Lima from 1624-1639, complained that the viceroyalty's many magical practitioners who were not themselves Amerindian "were immersed in the customs and knowledge of the colony's natives" (quoted in Silverblatt, "Colonial Conspiracies," 261). This cultural interchange is traced in Silverblatt, "Colonial Conspiracies," esp. 261-8; Garofalo, "The Ethno-Economy of Food, Drink, and Stimulants, 400-67. Maya Restrepo, *Brujería*, 659, reads the exchange of botanical and psychopharmacological expertise between Afroamericans and Amerindians as being more reciprocal, as does Gonzalo Aguirre Beltrán for Mexico (*Medicina y magia: El proceso de aculturación en la estructura colonial* [Mexico City: Instituto Nacional Indigenista, 1963]). Of course, the symbolic importance of things Amerindian for non-Amerindians entailed a continuation of the more basic cultural adoption of Amerindian comestibles, including coca or the native Andean alchoholic beverages, known to the Spanish as chicha, which was drunk and even sold by Africans and Spaniards alike (Jane E. Mangan, *Trading Roles: Gender, Ethnicity, and the Urban Economy in Colonial Potosí* (Durham: Duke University Press, 2005), 83-6). The inquisitor Mañozca y Zamora seems to have been of New World origin himself, having graduated from the University of Mexico in 1596 before studying canon law at Salamanca (Medina, *Inquisición de Cartagena*, 114). Due to irregularities, he was eventually removed from his position as inquisitor in Lima.
112. *Testimonio de Diego Lopez*, AHN Inq. 1620/1/7, fol. 6v. This particular spirit, Taravira, was in all other cases assigned to *women* (Maya Restrepo, *Brujería*, 569). Rufina's accord with her demon, Huebo, includes her having to permit it/him to penetrate her anally (*Testimonio de Diego Lopez*, AHN Inq. 1620/1/7, fol. 34r.). For an interpretation of these companion spirits as a reconfiguration of personal sexuality, among other aspects of personhood, independent from the slave/racial economy, see Maya Restrepo, *Brujería*, 564-71. The repeated appearance of anal penetration suggests a counter-rhetoric of overturning, opposition and reversal. On the other hand, Sweet argues that same-sex relations were both common in Central African cultures and a response to the lack of available women in many slave settings, the latter clearly not the case here (Sweet, *Recreating Africa*, 50-8).
113. *Testimonio de Diego Lopez*, AHN Inq. 1620/1/7, 33r. Is this merely another name for the spirit Huebo or another spirit?
114. Maya Restrepo, *Brujería*, 502.
115. Ventura, *Portugueses no Peru*, 1:138.
116. Nathan Wachtel, *La Foi du souvenir: Labyrinthes marranes* (France: Editions du Seuil, 2001), 83; Boyajian, *Portuguese Bankers*, 122. Bautista Peres stood among the wealthiest New Christian merchants of the Americas, estimated, along with Simon Váez Sevilla of Mexico City, to possess a fortune of over 200,000 pesos (AGN Inq. 409, fol. 381; Israel, *Diasporas Within a Diaspora*, 98; according to Boyajian, *Portuguese Bankers*, 124, Bautista Peres' estate was "valued at about 650,000 ducats"). Pinto traded with Bautista Peres and Duarte through two brothers of the latter, Pedro Duarte and Paolo Rodrigues (Maria da Graça A. Mateus Ventura, "Los Judeoconversos portugueses en el Perú del siglo XVII: Redes de complicidad," *Familia, religión y negocio: El sefardismo en las relaciones entre el mundo ibérico y los Países Bajos en la edad moderna*, ed. Jaime Contreras, Bernardo J. García García and Ignacio Pulido [Fundación Carlos de Amberes/ Fernando Villaverde Ediciones, 2002], 400), as well as directly. On the African connections of Bautista Peres and Duarte, see Green, "Masters of Difference," 223-7, 230-1. One of the New Christians who traded slaves and other commodities with Pinto and Sebastián Duarte was Tomás Rodrigues Barassa, associate and relative of Diogo Barassa, "one of the most powerful Portuguese residents in Cacheu," on the West African coast (ibid., 217). According to Green, Pinto was so well known in Guinée that in 1637 "4 people testified in Cacheu that they recognized his handwriting" (ibid., 226).
117. Green, "Masters of Difference," 226.
118. Green, "Masters of Difference," 231, n. 305.

119. Salo W. Baron, *A Social and Religious History of the Jews*, 18 vols. (New York/Philadelphia: Columbia University Press/Jewish Publication Society of America, 1952-83), 15:301; Dominguez Ortiz, *Judeoconversos*, 136; Israel, *Diasporas Within a Diaspora*, 135; Green, "Masters of Difference." The prominence of "Jewish" slavers seems to lead Maria Ventura to claim that in old Veracruz, Mexico, "one of the principle destinations of the slaving routes, there existed a river named *Espanta Judios* [Scare off the Jews]" (Ventura, *Negreiros portugueses*, 37). One wonders whether similar considerations led to the naming of the "Jewess' shoal / Baixo da Judia" off of the Cape of Good Hope mentioned in at least one Portuguese shipwreck narrative (Blackmore, *Manifest Perdition*, 45-6). On the other hand, these toponyms could be wielding Jews as either (1) a demonic force whose animating hostility is attached to dangerous nautical passages or (2) as a metaphor for those too cowardly to face a difficult nautical situation.
120. Israel, *Diasporas Within a Diaspora*, 102. Elsewhere he cites a 1608 tract by the Spaniard Pedro de Avendaño Villela which claims that it was the Portuguese New Christians "who navigate the coast and rivers of Guinea to ply the trade in negros" (135-36). The fact is that many slavers, even among the Portuguese, were not conversos.
121. Israel, *Diasporas Within a Diaspora*, 104; see the following pages, including the many individuals who had been in/through Angola, 106-7. Here Israel's terminology is unfortunately vague; it remains the case that credible scholarship has yet to delineate the ethnic or religious loyalties of most of these slave traders.
122. *Relación y abecedário de los estrangeros que se hallan en la ciudad de Cartagena*, reprinted in Ventura, *Portugueses no Peru*, 3:31-77.
123. Jonathan Israel cites Eva Uchmany to the effect that Angola and Guinea were places where "many Portuguese New Christians were inducted, 'converted' or confirmed in crypto-Judaism" (Israel, *Diasporas Within a Diaspora*, 106; Eva A. Uchmany, "The Participation of New Christians and Crypto-Jews in the Conquest, Colonization and Trade of Spanish America, 1521-1660," in Bernardini and Fiering, *Jews and the Expansion of Europe to the West*, 198; Toby Green, "The Role of the Portuguese Trading Posts in Guinea and Angola in the 'Apostasy' of Crypto-Jews in the 17th Century," in *Creole Societies in the Portuguese Colonial Empire*, eds. Philip J. Havik and Malyn Newitt (Bristol: Bristol University Press, June 2007), 25-40.
124. Lewin, *Singular Proceso de Salomón Machorro*, xii-xviii.
125. Printed in Tejado Fernández, *Vida social en Cartagena*, 186.
126. Israel, *Diasporas Within a Diaspora*, 105, citing Lucía García de Proodian, *Los judios en America: Sus actividades en los Virreinatos de Nueva Castilla y Nueva Granada s. XVII* (Madrid: Instituto Arias Montano, 1966), "Appendice documental," 287. Irene Silverblatt brings more such examples in "New Christians and New World Fears in Seventeenth-Century Peru," *Comparative studies in society and history; an international quarterly* 42, no. 3 (July 2000): 545, n. 71.
127. Green, "Masters of Difference," 146.
128. Testimony of an unnamed witness; AGN Mexico, Inq. 402, exp. 1, leg. 2, fol. 364r. It is unclear whether the term *Capitanes de negros* refers to mere masters of slaves or actual ship captains.
129. *Testimonio de Diego Lopez*, AHN Inq. 1620/1/7, fol. 33v.
130. "Vino a ver a este en Compañia de Ger^{ma} sobrina de Ju^o Tellez que tambien era bruja y este la dixo que aguardas mulata como no buelles a mi cassa pues tienes alla los quatroçientos pessos que te he dado p^a tu libertad a que La susodcha Respondio no tengas pena que yo tengo trazado Con que amansar a mis amos Y porque lo heches dever tu lo Veras Y este La dixo pues conque y ella le Respondio Yo Te embiare una [...] seña [?] porque Paula de Eguiluz me ha enseñado un conjuro de doña Maria de Padilla quieres oyr le Y este dixo que no Y el dia sig^{te} suçedio que la dcha Rufina le embio un Razimo de ubas a este y fue Assi que sus amos Se aquietaron" (*Testimonio de Diego Lopez*, AHN Inq. 1620/1/7, fols. 33v.-34r.). This may or may not refer to the time Eguiluz offered to give Rufina a bit of eucharist to mix in a chocolate drink in order to tame her mistress (ibid., 47v.-48r.).
131. The inconsistency of López's claims is difficult to resolve. Did she prefer her relatively secure slave condition under "tamed" masters? Did López really give her the funds as he claims? Did she prefer to spend the money on other things? For example, she is said to have paid Eguiluz six pesos to teach her the above-mentioned spell, while later she supposedly paid one Black slave of Catalina de Castro, in silver, to put certain herbs at the threshold of the house of the Black Juana de Hortensia in order to kill her (ibid., 34r., 45v.).
132. "Rufina le dixo avia hecho un conçierto Con otro diablo que le avia traydo Paula de Eguiluz llamado Huebo y era El dho Conçierto que el dho diablo avia de Tomar La figura de la dha Rufina Y en ella avia de asistir en su cassa a todos los actos p^a en que fuesse llamada assi para El serviçio de La cassa Como para asistir con diego lopez Arias su amo quando La fuesse a buscar para sus

torpezas Y que enpago desto avia de Comer cal La dha Rufina y dexarse conoçer carnalm^{te} por el vaso trasero Con el dho demonio huebo y que avia venido en el dho Contrato por poder mas Librem^{te} salir de su Cassa quando quisiesse" (*Testimonio de Diego Lopez*, AHN Inq. 1620/1/7, fol. 34r.). Such magical means of coping with one's servitude as cited here are attested throughout the Americas; see Palmer, "Religion and Magic, 322-3; Sweet, *Recreating Africa*, 164-71.
133. *Testimonio de Diego Lopez*, AHN Inq. 1620/1/7, fol. 46r.
134. The information is supplied by Rufina, the free Mulata of Doña Mariana de Armas; AHN Inq. 1020, fols. 389v.-390r.; Splendiani, *Tribunal de Cartagena*, 2:351.
135. Maya Restrepo, *Brujería*, 35; see also 542-75.
136. Maya Restrepo, *Brujería*, 580.
137. *Testimonio de Diego Lopez*, AHN Inq. 1620/1/7, fol. 20v.
138. Ventura, "Judeoconversos portugueses en el Perú," 405, n. 21; idem, *Portuguese no Peru*, 1:171, 3:40.
139. *Testimonio de Diego Lopez*, AHN Inq. 1620/1/7, fol. 20v.
140. He sold pearls to Simon Rivero and through him (AHN Inq. 1601/8, fols. 20-21; cited in Croitoru Rotbaum, *Documentos*, 148).
141. Ventura, *Portugueses no Peru*, 1:398-99. On Duarte, see Mellafe, *Introducción de la esclavitud*, 169-81.
142. Ventura, *Portugueses no Peru*, 1:396. On Bautista Peres's life, career and commercial activities, see ibid., 1:347-457, 2:16-93; Wachtel, *Foi du souvenir*, 79-101; Studnicki-Gizbert, *Nation upon the Ocean Sea*, throughout; Boyajian, *Portuguese Bankers*, 122-4; Silverblatt, *Modern Inquisitions*, 47-53, 132-5, 145-8, 152, 157 and elsewhere. Inquisition sources allow Studnicki-Gizbert to surmise that Bautista Peres's residence in Lima was "a good-size manse" housing, among others, "close to two dozen adult African slaves and their children: servants, maids, cooks, liverymen, porters, and stable hands." Besides trading in slaves, he ran a general store in town and a hacienda outside of Lima at which worked 50 slaves that he had imported (*Nation upon the Ocean Sea*, 77, 109, 200, n. 45). Mentions of Pinto in the business letters between Peres, Duarte and others reprinted by Maria Mateus Ventura can be found in *Portugueses no Peru*, 3:138, 142, 145-6, 148, 151, 163, 166-7, 185, 294, 296, 302-3; letters to/from Pinto: 3:170-2, 179-82.
143. Ventura, *Portuguese no Peru*, 1:171, 3:41. Among the items Pinto fed his sick slaves were wine, oranges, grains and sugar. These were not cheap commodities but also did not guarantee the recovery of the slaves' health (letter of Brás de Paz Pinto to Sebastião Duarte, 13 January 1634, AGN Inq., S.O., Co. caja 30, exp. 299, fols. 251-2; Ventura, *Portugueses no Peru*, 1:431 and 3:172). Rolando Mellafe draws on a *Memoria de las medicinas que han llevado para los negros del capitán don Sebastián Duarte*, in the Archivo Nacional de Santiago, that offers a detailed glimpse of the kinds of treatments Pinto might have used (Mellafe, *Introducción de la esclavitud*, 177).
144. AHN Inq. 1601/8, fol. 21; cited in Croitoru Rotbaum, *Documentos*, 148.
145. *Testimonio de Diego Lopez*, AHN Inq. 1620/1/7, fol. 20v.; Boyajian, *Portuguese Bankers*, 123.
146. Ventura, *Portugueses no Peru*, 1:381; see also Mellafe, *Introducción de la esclavitud*, 174. The biographer of Pedro Claver, on the other hand, provides a harsh depiction of the general mistreatment of the slaves in the interest of increasing profits (Fernandez, *Apostolica y penitente vida de el V.P. Pedro Claver*, 105-7).
147. Ventura, *Portugueses no Peru*, 1:399.
148. On the Branes, several groups living around the Cassamance River in West Africa (today's Senegal and Gambia), see Alonso de Sandoval, *Un tratado sobre la esclavitud*, Intro., transcription and translation [of *De instauranda aethiopum salute* (1647)] by Enriqueta Vila Vilar (Madrid: Alianza Editorial, 1987), 107-8, 119.
149. Letter of 13 January 1634, AGN (Peru) Inq., S.O., Con., box 30, exp. 299, fol. 251r.; reprinted in Ventura, *Portugueses no Peru*, 3:170.
150. Ventura, *Portuguese no Peru*, 1:171, quoting the *Relação e abecedário dos estrangeiros que se acharam na cidade de Cartagena*.
151. AHN Inq. 1601/8, fol. 21-26v.; cited in Croitoru Rotbaum, *Documentos*, 149-55.
152. Ventura, *Portugueses no Peru*, 2:541.
153. AHN Inq. 4822/8, fol. 217; cited in Álvarez Alonso, *Inquisición en Cartagena*, 321; Medina, *Inquisición de Cartagena*, 230.
154. *Testimonio de Diego Lopez*, AHN Inq. 1620/1/7, fol. 41v.
155. See, for instance, AHN Inq. 1620/1/7, fol. 29r.-v., 32r.-v.
156. AHN Inq. 1020, fol. 420v., Splendiani, *Tribunal de Cartagena*, 2:377.
157. AHN Inq. 1601/18, fols. 31-7, 40-4; Croitoru Rotbaum, *Documentos*, 223-9, 231-6. The date is

given on AHN Inq. 1601/18, fol. 46r. The unnamed witness states that "he has been brought to this *audiencia* various times" (AHN Inq. 1601/18, fol. 43v.; Croitoru Rotbaum, *Documentos*, 234).

158. AHN Inq. 1601/18, fols. 30, 37, 46r.; Croitoru Rotbaum, *Documentos*, 223,229, 236. The official presiding over these sessions, the prosecutor (*fiscal*) of the local tribunal, the *licenciado* Juan Ortiz, summarizes that the accused have been "reconciled in their trials of faith which remain in the secret chamber of the Inquisition of the city of Cartagena de Indias to which I refer, Done in said secret chamber on five august one thousand six hundred and fifty and one years." This is why these sessions are inserted with material from 1636 and thereabouts, the period of the earlier trials.
159. *Testimonio de Diego Lopez*, AHN Inq. 1620/1/7, fol. 24r.
160. *Testimonio de Diego Lopez*, AHN Inq. 1620/1/7, fol. 23v. This is the same Sánchez who complains that the Inquisition does not arrest judaizers such as Pinto.
161. *Testimonio de Diego Lopez*, AHN Inq. 1620/1/7, fol. 30v.
162. According to Esquivel's testimony, 1649 (AHN Inq. 1601/3/8, fol. 46v.; Croitoru Rotbaum, *Documentos*, 327). He owed her the money for "*escritura*," which could mean letter-writing, though he was himself literate, or for some kind of notarial service.
163. Ceballos Gómez, "Grupos sociales y prácticas mágicas," 57.
164. *Testimonio de Diego Lopez*, AHN Inq. 1620/1/7, fol. 23r.
165. Solano Alonso, *Salud, cultura y sociedad en Cartagena*, 251-3; Ventura, *Portuguese no Peru*, 1:208-9. Neto's work was recently published, for the first time: Juan Méndez Nieto, *Discursos Medicinales* (Salamanca: Universidad de Salamanca/Junta de Castilla y León, 1989).
166. For instance, the royal physician Luis Mercado (1525–1611) published *De la facultad de los alimentos y medicamentos yndianos*, no longer extant, while Pedro López de León cites Amerindian cures, the practices of Blacks and American medicinal plants (Alonso, *Salud, cultura y sociedad en Cartagena*, 130, 179, 200-9). Natalie Zemon Davis, *Women on the Margins: Three Seventeenth-Century Lives* (Cambridge: Harvard University Press, 1995), 184-89; Sweet, *Recreating Africa*, 145; Jonathan Schorsch, "American Jewish Historians, Colonial Jews and Blacks, and the Limits of *Wissenschaft*: A Critical Review," *Jewish Social Studies* 6,2 (Winter 2000): 111; James Delbourgo, "Slavery in the Cabinet of Curiosities: Hans Sloane's Atlantic World," www.thebritishmuseum.ac.uk/the_museum/news_and_ debate/news/hans_sloanes_ atlantic_world.aspx, 16; Lawrence Levine, "The Sacred World of Black Slaves: The Quest for Control, Slave Folk Belief," in *Black Consciousness* (Oxford: Oxford University Press, 1977), 65; Michel Laguerre, *Afro-Caribbean Folk Medicine* (South Hadley, Mass.: Bergin and Garvey Publishers, 1987); Karol K. Weaver, *Medical Revolutionaries: The Enslaved Healers of Eighteenth-Century Saint Domingue* (Campaign, IL: University of Illinois Press, 2006).
167. López testifies that one night Rufina created a late-night ruckus outside his house, causing him and another man to go out to investigate. Coming across her, López asks what she is doing there. "That's a good question," she responds, "as you have not seen me in some time." He explains that his wife just gave birth and, being the first time, he is helping. "Your Honor will be very content because he has a daughter, but before much time you will not have her," states Rufina in a mixture of sarcasm and threat. "By your life, leave her be," replies López. "There is no remedy, because my devil *Rompe sanctos* has thrown the three stones [a method for trying to determine a desired outcome?]," Rufina concludes the conversation and leaves. Minutes later he catches her in his arms, though this time she is flying through the air with her devil. López summarizes for the inquisitors: "Within two days, as the above-mentioned transpired, the infant died" (*Testimonio de Diego Lopez*, AHN Inq. 1620/1/7, 33r.).
168. *Testimonio de Diego Lopez*, AHN Inq. 1620/1/7, fol. 33v.
169. *Testimonio de Diego Lopez*, AHN Inq. 1620/1/7, 36r.-v.
170. *Testimonio de Diego Lopez*, AHN Inq. 1620/1/7, fol. 52v.
171. AHN Inq. 1020, fol. 420r., Splendiani, *Tribunal de Cartagena*, 2:377.
172. *Testimonio de Diego Lopez*, AHN Inq. 1620/1/7, fol. 24v.
173. *Testimonio de Diego Lopez*, AHN Inq. 1620/1/7, fol. 24r.
174. *Testimonio de Diego Lopez*, AHN Inq. 1620/1/7, fol. 44v.; AHN Inq. 1020, fol. 379v.-380r., reprinted in Splendiani, *Tribunal de Cartagena*, 2:341.
175. AHN Inq. 1020, fol. 419v., Splendiani, *Tribunal de Cartagena*, 2:377.
176. Ceballos Gómez, "Grupos sociales y prácticas mágicas," 57-8.
177. AHN Inq. 1020, fols. 418r.-422r., Splendiani, *Tribunal de Cartagena*, 2: 375-9.
178. AHN Inq. 1020, fols. 420v.-421r.; Splendiani, *Tribunal de Cartagena*, 2:378. Ceballos Gómez explicates the societal distinctions between the types of magic (Ceballos Gómez, "Grupos sociales y prácticas mágicas," 61-2).

179. See the *Relación de las causas de fe* from 1634, AHN Inq. 1020, fols. 418r.-422r., reprinted in Splendiani, *Tribunal de Cartagena*, 2:375-9.
180. AHN Inq. 1020, fol. 422r.; Medina, *Inquisición de Cartagena*, 216.
181. AHN Inq. 1021, fol. 8r. *Relación del auto*, reprinted in Splendiani, *Tribunal de Cartagena*, 3:43; AHN Inq. 1021, fol. 14r., 15r.-16r., 28v., *Relación de las causas de fe*, Splendiani, *Tribunal de Cartagena*, 3:48, 50, 64. As mentioned in the previous chapter, similar charges of New Christian alliance with the Dutch arose in "Portuguese" West Africa.
182. AHN Inq. 1021, fol. 28v.-29r., *Relación de las causas de fe*, Splendiani, *Tribunal de Cartagena*, 3:64. Fonseca Enríquez claims that Rodríguez Mesa possessed the logbook and served as the treasurer of the group.
183. AHN Inq. 1620/11, fol. 59; cited in Tejado Fernández, *Vida social en Cartagena*, 181.
184. Vila Vilar, "Extranjeros en Cartagena," 164, n. 54.
185. Ventura, *Portuguese no Peru*, 1:298; excerpt from the confession of Captain Estevan de Ares de Fonseca in Caro Baroja, *Judíos en la España*, 3:362-64.
186. AHN Inq. 1020, fols. 481v.; Splendiani, *Tribunal de Cartagena*, 433-4.
187. AHN Inq. 1601/18, fol. 41r.; Croitoru Rotbaum, *Documentos*, 232.
188. *Testimonio de Diego Lopez*, AHN Inq. 1620/7/1, fols. 19v.-20r.
189. Caro Baroja, *Judíos en la España*, 2:431-2; in Appendix 13, 3:331, Caro Baroja brings the letters' mention by the lawyer from Alcarez, Ignacio del Villar Maldonado, *Sylva responsorum iuris* (Madrid, 1614). The letters were proven to be a forgery by I. Loeb, "La correspondance des juifs d'Espagne avec ceux de Constantinople," *Revue des Études Juives* 15 (1887): 262-76. They are reprinted as well in Azevedo, *História dos cristãos-novos*, 464 (Appendix 10). The version printed in Loeb and Azevedo does not call for the physical destruction of churches or their idols.
190. Translated in Studnicki-Gizbert, *A Nation Upon the Ocean Sea*, 166.
191. Recorded in AHN Inq. 1600/16; Croitoru Rotbaum, *Documentos*, 486-525.
192. See AHN Inq. 1601/3/1-2; Croitoru Rotbaum, *Documentos*, 281-6. See also the testimony of the many witnesses interviewed during yet another *visita* of Inquisitor Don Pedro de Medina Rico in 1649 (AHN Inq. 1601/3/8; Croitoru Rotbaum, *Documentos*, 288-475). Complicity of varying sorts in slave trading also seems to have occurred. Uriarte and Ortiz were accused by Don Joseph de Bolibar, knight of the Order of Santiago and bailiff of the Cartagena tribunal, of using moneys sequestered by the Inquisition from the Portuguese conversos to buy over 200,000 ducats of clothes and slaves from Angola and Guinea on one occasion, while on another purchasing from Angola and Guinea more than 450 slaves whom they sold in Cartagena for a profit of 60,000 pesos (AHN Inq. 1601/3/8, fols. 90r.-91v.; Croitoru Rotbaum, *Documentos*, 367-9; see also AHN Inq. 1601/3/8, fol. 128r.v., 165r.-166r., 187r.-191r.; Croitoru Rotbaum, *Documentos*, 402, 435-6, 456-9). Ortiz, it seems, had been a merchant before working for the Inquisition (Medina, *Inquisición de Cartagena*, 167). Another time, Uriarte, as the one in charge of the sequestered goods of João Rodrigues Mesa and Blas de Paz Pinto, ordered a girl slave of Juan Cotel to be sold at auction, though refusing to provide the required written order, as requested by both Bolibar and Andred Fernandez de Castro, the tribunal's receiver. Cotel had owed the slave as part of his debts to either Rodrigues Mesa or Pinto, but Uriarte wanted the sale kept unofficial since Cotel also bore a debt to Uriarte's wife (AHN Inq. 1601/3/8, fol. 101r.-v.; Croitoru Rotbaum, *Documentos*, 379).
193. AHN Inq. 1601/3/8, fols. 82v.-83r.; Croitoru Rotbaum, *Documentos*, 359-60. For example, it seems Pinto was to have given some strings of pearls from the merchant Miguel Fernandez Pereira to Don Francisco Rexi, a consultant to the Cartagena tribunal, "who was his lawyer and with whom he communicated this" payment, still never paid as of 1649. See also AHN Inq. 1601/3/8, fol. 113v., 154r.; Croitoru Rotbaum, *Documentos*, 390, 424 and AHN Inq. 1600/16, fols. 12r.-v.; Croitoru Rotbaum, *Documentos*, 503.
194. AHN Inq. 1021, fol. 9r., *Relación de las causas de fe*, reprinted in Splendiani, *Tribunal de Cartagena*, 3:43.
195. As had happened with the Lima tribunal as well (Silverblatt, "Colonial Conspiracies," 268).
196. AHN Inq. 1620/7/1, fol. 17v.-18r.; AHN Inq. 1601/18, fol. 41v.; Croitoru Rotbaum, *Documentos*, 233.
197. AHN Inq. 1620/7/1, fol. 18v.-19r.; AHN Inq. 1601/18, fol. 42r.-v.; Croitoru Rotbaum, *Documentos*, 233.
198. AHN Inq. 1601/18, fol. 43r.-v.; Croitoru Rotbaum, *Documentos*, 234. João Rodrigues Mesa is also accused of being the "doctrinizer [*dotrinatisador*] of the Law of Moses and its rabbi" (AHN Inq. 1601/18, fol. 31; reprinted in Croitoru Rotbaum, *Documentos*, 223). Already the *Relación de las causas de fe* prepared for the 1638 *auto* "improved" the accusations against Pinto

somewhat. Going to investigate the gatherings at Pinto's house, López claims not to have been allowed in and to have waited in the next-door house of Don Martin Felix or Feliz, who says to him, referring to the closed curtains of Pinto's house and the men assembled therein: "i do not know how the señores of the holy office sleep nor what they do, as they do not castigate these, and the said Feliz was pondering this, saying that in that House a synagogue was conducted and the whole afternoon the said don martin feliz was muttering about this with this Prisoner" (*Testimonio de Diego Lopez*, AHN Inq. 1620/7/1, 19r.). This Martin Felix/z appears never to have been interrogated. In the *Relación de las causas de fe*, the inquisitors' summation of the charges, this individual muttering supposedly produced by the daytime gatherings becomes a seemingly general "scandal and murmuring in which it was said that they had a synagogue" (AHN Inq. 1021, fol. 20v., Splendiani, *Tribunal de Cartagena*, 3:55).
199. AHN Inq. 1620, fols. 506r.-507r.; Splendiani, *Tribunal de Cartagena*, 2:441-3.
200. AHN Inq. 1601/3/8, fol. 207r., 208r.; Croitoru Rotbaum, *Documentos*, 473, 474.
201. AHN Inq. 1021, fols. 1-48r., reprinted in Splendiani, *Tribunal de Cartagena*, 3: 35-85. The *Relación del auto*, the first part of this report, read aloud at the *auto*, completely passes over the torture applied to Paz Pinto and the cause of his final and fatal illness, euphemizing the torture in the standard manner as "the charitable admonition" (AHN Inq. 1021, fol. 3v., Splendiani, *Tribunal de Cartagena*, 3:39).
202. AHN Inq. 1620, fol. 507v.; Splendiani, *Tribunal de Cartagena*, 2:443.
203. AHN Inq. 1021, fol. 5r.-v., *Relación del auto*, reprinted in Splendiani, *Tribunal de Cartagena*, 3:41.
204. From a letter by visiting inspector inquisitor Pedro Medina Rico, 31 May 1649; quoted by Medina, *Inquisición de Cartagena*, 225, n. 1. Ironically, at one point in 1636 Paula de Eguiluz was called in by the Cartagena inquisitors to minister to Manuel Alvarez Prieto, whose arms had been broken by torture (Croitoru Rotbaum, *De Sefarad*, 312-3). Taussig, basing himself on Henry Charles Lea, states that Eguiluz was initially sentenced to burning at the stake as one of the leaders of the large group of Black magical practitioners in the port of Tolú (about 65 miles south of Cartagena). After six years of imprisonment, her sentence was commuted to the punishment just described (Taussig, *Shamanism*, 219).
205. Caesar E. Farah (trans. and ed.), *An Arab's Journey to Colonial Spanish America: The Travels of Elias al-Mûsili in the Seventeenth Century* (Syracuse: Syracuse University Press, 2003), 19.

Chapter 4

1. AHN Inq. 1601/18, fol. 61v.; Croitoru Rotbaum, *Documentos*, 248-9.
2. Trial and Criminal Cause against Sebastian Domingo alias Mungia black man [from the] Congo, 22 August 1642; AGN Mexico, Inq. 399, exp. 2, fol. 312r. Sebastian will be treated at length in chapter 6.
3. AHN Inq. 1737, exp. 1, leg. 3, fols. 79r-82v; cited in Ferry, "Don't Drink the Chocolate," n. 11.
4. Mangan, *Trading Roles*, 98. Beyond the direct orbit of the Inquisition, in 1673 the municipal council of Bahia, Brazil, ordered the guilds participating in that year's Corpus Christi procession to "provide Negroes who would carry [the dragon] in the processions" (cited in Appendix item 18, C. R. Boxer, *Portuguese Society in the Tropics: The Municipal Councils of Goa, Macao, Bahia, and Luanda, 1510-1800* [Madison/Milwaukee: University of Wisconsin Press, 1965], 181).
5. Quoted in Clara E. Cohan, *Los marranos en el Paraguay colonial* (Asunción: Intercontinental, 1992), 182.
6. Tejado Fernandez, *Vida social en Cartagena*, 276.
7. Trial and Criminal Cause against Sebastian Domingo alias Mungia black man [from the] Congo, 22 August 1642; AGN Mexico, Inq. 399, exp. 2, fol. 312r.
8. Cited in Lewin, *Singular Proceso*, 297.
9. Lewin, *Proceso de María de Zárate*, 73.
10. Medina, *Inquisición en Chile*, 528, n.13. Only three months later did the tribunal conclude its case against the corpse's former inhabitant, finding him guilty of following the erroneous and heretical teachings of the Santiago Jesuit Juan Francisco de Ulloa (528-530).
11. Medina, *Inquisición en Chile*, 309.
12. Testimony of Beatriz Enriquez, 13 September 1644; AGN Mexico, Inq. 393/12/3, fol. 267v.
13. Fergusson, "Trial of Gabriel de Granada," 372, 375. As far as I could see, Elvira does not make another appearance in the trial record as translated by Fergusson; I did not check the original.

14. María Isabel Pérez de Colosía Rodríguez, *Auto inquisitorial de 1672: El criptojudaísmo en Málaga* (Málaga: Diputación Provincial de Málaga, 1984), 39.
15. Medina, *Inquisición de Lima*, 1:232.
16. Cited in Medina, *Inquisición de Cartagena*, 92, n.1
17. Montesinos, Fernando, *Auto de la fe celebrado en Lima a 23. de enero de 1639. Al tribunal del Santo oficio de la inquisición de los reynos del Perú, Chile, Paraguay, y Tucuman* (Lima: Pedro de Cabrera, 1639), 3 [unpaginated].
18. Medina, *Inquisición de Cartagena*, 91-2.
19. Mathias de Bocanegra, *Auto general de la fee, celebrado [...] Dominica in Albis 11. de Abril de 1649*. El P. Mathias de Bocanegra de la Compañia de IESUS (Mexico: Antonio Calderon, Impressor del Secreto del S. Officio, n.d.), unpag.
20. See also Maureen Flynn, "Mimesis of the Last Judgment: The Spanish *Auto de Fé*," *Sixteenth Century Journal* 22,2 (Summer 1991): 281-97.
21. Montesinos, *Auto de la fe celebrado en Lima* (1639), 55 [unpag.].
22. Saraiva, *Marrano Factory*, 20, paraphrasing the letter. The Portuguese style of writing the name these events differs slightly from the Spanish.
23. Quoted in Medina, *Inquisición de Lima*, 1:216.
24. Cited in Medina, *Inquisición de Lima*, 2:21.
25. Quoted in Pérez de Colosía Rodríguez, *Auto inquisitorial de 1672*, 156. María Isabel Pérez de Colosía Rodríguez writes that in addition "the Inquisition showed particular interest in implicating in its repressive activity the privileged classes, reflecting perfectly this collaborationism in the ceremony of the *auto de fé*" (*Auto inquisitorial de 1672*, 72). Similar ethnological statist interests appear in the celebration of festivals; see Curcio-Nagy, *The Great Festivals of Colonial Mexico City*, 42-3.
26. The language is that of Green, "Masters of Difference," 88.
27. Baião, *A Inquisição em Portugal e no Brasil*, 114; Lipiner, *O Sapateiro de Trancoso*, 182: "[Q]uando foi o auto que se fez na Ribeira, em que queimaram o [Diogo de] Montenegro, ela [Catarina] com isso se mostrava agastada." The Inquisition forced its prisoners to watch these public acts as well, for their spiritual edification and in order to inspire fuller and more sincere confessions.
28. Baião, *Inquisição*, 117.
29. This narrative might be compared to an incident related in passing during a winding tale about an official of Nueva Granada about to be executed for murder in 1580s Bogotá told by a local chronicler in the 1630s, Juan Rodríguez Freile. Having mounted the scaffold, the accused, a Doctor Cortés de Mesa, recognized the executioner as "a former slave of his own whom he had himself saved from the gallows and had appointed city executioner. At the sight he turned pale and speechless, and would have collapsed but for the archbishop and a surgeon who had likewise mounted the platform." Cortés begged the archbishop for a last favor. "'Don't let that negro behead me.' 'Remove the negro,' commanded the archbishop, and he was pushed off the platform" (Juan Rodríguez Freile, *The Conquest of New Granada*, trans. William C. Atkinson (London: Folio Society, 1961), 114). Clearly the setting is fraught with emotions for this man, about to killed. The shock of the starkly opposing trajectory of a former slave and the humiliation of having him in particular end Cortés' life would have been intense enough, but it is possible that the executioner's Blackness added to the perceived insult. The upstaged executioner's feelings about all this are not recorded by the chronicler.
30. Baião, *Inquisição em Portugal e no Brasil*, 121-122.
31. David Nirenberg, *Communities of Violence: Persecution of Minorities in the Middle Ages* (Princeton: Princeton University Press, 1996), 177.
32. Huerga Criado, *En la raya de Portugal*, 92.
33. Renée Levine Melammed, "Judaizing Women in Castille: A Look at Their Lives Before and After 1492," in Le Beau, Bryan F. and Menachem Mor (eds.), *Religion in the Age of Exploration: the Case of Spain and New Spain* (Creighton University Press, 1996), 17; Huerga Criado, *En la raya de Portugal*, 91.
34. Renée Levine Melammed, "Some Death and Mourning Customs of Castilian *Conversas*," in *Exile and Diaspora: Studies in the History of the Jewish People Presented to Professor Haim Beinart* (Jerusalem: Ben-Zvi Institute of Yad Izhak Ben-Zvi/the Hebrew University of Jerusalem/Consejo de Investigaciones Científicas, Madrid, 1991), 120-1. One study of Cordoba at the end of the fifteenth century shows that 54 percent of the city's working Christian women were employed in domestic service. Of this group, 75 percent were servants, with slaves following in numerical importance. Men made up 46 percent of the servant class, traditionally considered a feminine

occupation (Escobar Camacho, José Manuel, Manuel Nieto Cumplido and Jesús Padilla Gonzalez, "La mujer cordobesa en el trabajo a fines del siglo XV," in Cristina Segura Graiño (ed.), *Las mujeres en las ciudades medievales*: Actas de las III jornadas de investigacion interdisciplina (Madrid: Seminario de Estudios de la Mujer/Universidad Autonoma de Madrid, 1984), 157). The employment of Christian servants and the owning of Christian slaves by Jews faced increasingly restrictive legislation in medieval Castile. After the promulgation of the *Siete Partidas* of Alphonso X in 1261, Jews (along with Muslims and heretics) in Spain were forbidden outright to possess Christian slaves (Code IV, Title 21), though they could employ Christians as laborers, agricultural help and as guards or escorts during travel (Code VII, Title 24). In the first quarter of the fourteenth century, Castile effectively banned Jews from using Christian wet-nurses, prohibiting Christian women from nursing or rearing Jewish children (E. H. Lindo, *The History of the Jews of Spain and Portugal* (New York, 1848; repr. New York: Burt Franklin, 1970), 126), legislation reiterated in 1335 by the Council of Salamanca, which buttressed the prohibition with the penalty of excommunication (ibid., 139), and in 1380 by King Juan I, who decreed that Christians may not nurse the children of Jews (or Muslims), under penalty of a 600 maravedi fine (163). Among the laws passed at Briviesca in 1387, was one that forbade Jews (and Muslims) to have live-in Christian servants, under penalty of the confiscation of their goods — a third of which would go to the informer who turned them in (168). Towards the end of 1411, some members of Juan II's council proclaimed the same ban again (193). The next year, legislation issued in the name of the king himself (but signed only by the queen, the king being still under eight years old) decreed that "No Jews or Moors are to have Christian lacqueys or domestics, or any other persons to serve them, execute their orders, perform their household work, cook their victuals, or do any thing for them on Sabbaths, as lighting fires, carrying wine or similar articles; nor have Christians to nurse their children, nor to be their herdsmen, gardeners, or shepherds" (197). Six months later, however, the King signed similar laws that made the ban on servants total, extending it to include Muslims and other non-Christians (203). Later examples are by no means lacking. The repeated issuing of such laws indicates that the problematic behavior continued. To my knowledge no law was ever passed forbidding Judeoconversos from owning slaves, a significant fact.

35. Renée Levine-Melammed, "The Conversos of Cogolludo," *Proceedings of the Ninth World Congress of Jewish Studies*, Division B, Vol. I (Jerusalem: World Union of Jewish Studies, 1986), 138.
36. Quoted in Medina, *Inquisición en Chile*, 203, n.6. For more on servants in converso households, beatings, and denunciations, see Stephen Haliczer, *Inquisition and Society in the Kingdom of Valencia, 1478-1834* (Berkeley, Calif.: University of California Press, 1990), 219-20, 232.
37. Alastair Hamilton, *Heresy and Mysticism in Sixteenth-century Spain: The Alumbrados* (Toronto; Buffalo: University of Toronto Press, 1992), 68.
38. Mary Elizabeth Perry, *The Handless Maiden: Moriscas and the Politics of Religion in Early Modern Spain* (Princeton: Princeton University Press, 2005), 93.
39. Andrée Aelion Brooks, *The Woman Who Defied Kings: The Life and Times of Doña Gracia Nasi - a Jewish Leader during the Renaissance* (St. Paul: Paragon House, 2002), 31. The testimony of the wetnurse, Blanca Fernandez, can be found transcribed at Watson Manuscript Library, University College, London, box CC, folders 2 and 8 of Wolf's papers. I was unable to get to this document myself. Brooks's other reference, Renata Segre, "Sephardic Refugees in Ferrara: Two Notable Families," *Crisis and Creativity in the Sephardic World, 1391-1648* (New York: Columbia University Press, 1997), 182, does not say what Brooks wants it to.
40. Testimony of the cleric Diego de Sandoval, 5 May 1642; cited and translated in Robert Ferry, "Don't Drink the Chocolate," unpaginated.
41. Salomon, "Spanish Marranism Re-examined," 134-5; the second quote is Salomon's conclusion. A nun accused the Moras' nieces of having said that the Moras "did not employ maidservants because maidservants tattle on their masters" (136).
42. Quoted in Maria José Pimenta Ferro Tavares, "Para o estudo dos judeus de Trás-os-Montes, no século XVI: A 1ª geração dos cristãos-novos," *Cultura—História e Filosofia* 4 (1985): 378.
43. See the excerpted transcription of Sebastian Rodriguez's processo in Croitoru Rotbaum, *De sefarad*, 294-6. The free Blacks and Mulatos in Mexico City as well specialized in domestic service.
44. Saraiva, *Marrano Factory*, 140; H. P. Salomon, *Portrait of a New Christian: Fernão Álvares Melo [1569-1632]* (Paris: Fundação Calouste Gulbenkian/Centro Cultural Português, 1982), 48.
45. See Jennifer A. Glancy, *Slavery in Early Christianity* (Minneapolis: Fortress Press, 2006), 136-8; M. I. Finley, *Ancient Slavery and Modern Ideology* (New York: Penguin Books, 1980), 108-9. So, for instance, Jerome holds that the Christian martyr Apollonius was denounced by a slave. In a

fifth-century hagiography, *The Life of Eupraxia*, a nun who had been a slave informs on her fellow nun, the young girl Eupraxia, because of the latter's particularly stringent and effective asceticism.
46. Ceballos Gómez, "Grupos sociales y prácticas mágicas," 59.
47. AHN, Inq. 1020, fol. 337v.; reprinted in Splendiani, *Tribunal de Cartagena*, 2:310; quoted in Ceballos Gómez, "Grupos sociales y prácticas mágicas," 59, n. 17. Juana de Ortensio, the woman in question, was punished in the Cartagena *auto de fé* of 1633.
48. Manuel Barrios (ed.), *El Tribunal de la Inquisición en Andalucía: Selección de textos y documentos* (Sevilla: Editorial Castillejo, 1991), 80. Barrios takes this text from *La Inquisición en memorias de cosas sucedidas en Sevilla*, which he unfortunately fails to identify.
49. The portions of these standard proclamations having to do with Jewish practices are reproduced in many places, among them, in English, Wolf, *Jews in the Canary Islands*, 25-8.
50. Quoted in Haim Beinart, *Conversos on Trial: the Inquisition in Ciudad Real*. Hispania Judaica, No. 3 (Jerusalem: The Magnes Press/The Hebrew University, 1981), 132, n.103; see also Renée Levine Melammed, *Heretics or Daughters of Israel? The Crypto-Jewish Women of Castile* (New York: Oxford University Press, 1999), 78. This case, too complex to treat here, will reappear in chapter 5. Melammed brings examples from many other cases where servants were involved. It needs to be remembered that not every listener reacted the same way to official Inquisition indoctrination. Some, for instance, would have agreed with Bartolomé Fernández, who heard the Edicts of the Faith read in a church in Santa Fe, Nueva Granada, and who supposedly "said that many mestizos and Indians would not even understand them and that such edicts served only to pen people in like pigs in pigpens." He escaped the Cartagena Tribunal around 1614 with a penalty of a light abjuration of his sins/crimes (Medina, *Inquisición de Cartagena*, 99).
51. Quoted in Bernardo López Belinchón, *Honra, libertad y hacienda: Hombres de negocios y judíos sefardíes* ([Alcalá de Henares, Madrid]: Universidad de Alcalá, 2001), 220, n. 14.
52. Silverblatt, *Modern Inquisitions*, 132.
53. In ancient Athens, acts of impiety, such as causing damage to sacred olives or robbing a temple could be tried based on information from slaves. "It was perhaps only in relation to religious offences that such power over their masters was granted to slaves," (Robert Parker, "Law and Religion," *The Cambridge Companion to Ancient Greek Law*, ed. Michael Gagarin and David J. Cohen [New York: Cambridge University Press, 2005], 64-5; Virginia Hunter, "Introduction: Status Distinctions in Athenian Law," *Law and Social Status in Classical Athens*, ed. Virginia Hunter and Edmondson [Oxford: Oxford University Press, 2000], 7-8). According to Plato's recasting of Athenian law, slaves had the right to denounce offenses against the public, though denunciation of her own master is not specified (Glenn Raymond Morrow, *Plato's Law of Slavery in its Relation to Greek Law* [Urbana: University of Illinois Press, 1939], 123). On the Roman Republican and empire, see Leonhard Schumacher, *Servus Index: Sklavenverhör und Sklavenanzeige im republikanischen und kaiserzeitlichen Rom*, Forschungen zur antiken Sklaverei, 15 (Wisbaden: Franz Steiner, 1982).
54. Nicolau Eimeric and Francisco Peña, *El manual de los inquisidores*, Introduction, translation from Latin into French and notes by Luis Sala-Molins, translated from French by Francisco Martín (Barcelona: Muchnik Editores, 1983), 250-1.
55. John Leddy Phelan, *The Kingdom of Quito in the Seventeenth Century: Bureaucratic Politics in the Spanish Empire* (Madison: University of Wisconsin Press, 1967), 256.
56. Myscofski, "Heterodoxy," 80.
57. Beinart, *Conversos on Trial*, 131, n.101. The torture would ostensibly produce trustworthy evidence.
58. Erika Rummel, *Jiménez de Cisneros: On the Threshold of Spain's Golden Age* (Tempe, Ariz.: Arizona Center for Medieval and Renaissance Studies, 1999), 30.
59. Saraiva, *Marrano Factory*, 35.
60. Quoted in Croitoru Rotbaum, *De Sefarad*, 278-9.
61. On the fates of providers of false testimony, see Geraldo Pieroni, *Os excluídos do reino: A inquisição portuguesa e o degredo para o Brasil colônia* (Brasília/São Paulo: Editora Universidade de Brasília/Imprensa Oficial do Estado, 2000), ch. 13.
62. Barrios, *Inquisición en Andalucía*, 81. This text comes from the same unidentified source mentioned above.
63. Medina, *Inquisición en Chile*, 625.
64. AHN Inq. 1021, fols. 91v.-92r., 122r.-v.; Splendiani, *Tribunal de Cartagena*, 3:130-1, 156-7. Because Cassanga was no longer in Panama City and could not be found, Rodríguez, who continued to deny everything despite being tortured, was let off with a relatively light sentence, which included a fine of 200 pesos, receiving 200 lashes and two years banishment from Cartagena as well as Madrid.

65. AGN Mexico, Inq. 396/3/6, fol. 510v. The slave, Antonia de la Cruz, belonging to Thomas Nuñez de Peralta and Beatriz Enriquez, and her activities, will be treated further. It seems the inquisitors did not do more than take her to the torture chamber and show her the instruments of torture, a step recommended in the various inquisitors' manuals.
66. Audience of Francisco de la Cruz, 19 October 1643; AGN Mexico, Inq. 396/3/6, fol. 528v. Though insisting that his previous declarations were accurate, Francisco, unlike Antonia, was subjected to a few turns of the rack. This got Francisco to reveal the place where his master, Simon Vaez Sevilla, had hidden money and jewels (fol. 532v.). It seems that in this case the inquisitors thought Francisco was withholding further information, not telling falsehoods.
67. Ysavel Criolla, slave of Simon Vaez, also given torture, "being a slave and vile person" (AGN Mexico, Inq. 396/3/6, fol.539v.).
68. Wolf, *Jews in the Canary Islands*, 39.
69. Quoted in B. N. Teensma, "Fragmenten Uit Het Amsterdamse Convoluut Van Abraham Idaña, Alias Gaspar Méndez del Arroyo (1623-1690)," *Studia Rosenthaliana* 11,2 (July 1977): 146.
70. Jonathan I. Israel, "The Jews of Spanish North Africa, 1600-1669," *Transactions of the Jewish Historical Society of England*, Vol. 26 (1974/1978), 81. Israel is citing the *Breve Relacion y compendioso epitome de la general Expvlsion de los Hebreos de la Iuderia de la Ciudad de Oran* (n.p., n.d.), fol. 4.
71. Cited in Thornton, *Africa and Africans in the Making of the Atlantic World*, 177.
72. Edgar Roy Samuel, "The Curiel Family in 16th-century Portugal," *Transactions of the Jewish Historical Society of England* 31 (1988/1990): 125, 127.
73. Encarnación Marín Padilla, *Relación judeoconversa durante la segunda mitad del siglo XV en Aragón: La ley* (Madrid: n.p., 1988), 166.
74. Ceballos Gómez, *Sociedad y prácticas mágicas*, 298-99.
75. Abreu, *Denunciaçoes da Bahia*, 313.
76. Testimony of Thomassina de Mendoca, 21 August 1635; AGN Mexico, Inq. 402, exp. 1, leg. 2, fol. 16v. She is referring to the extended Enriquez family, on whom see chapter 7.
77. Silverblatt, *Modern Inquisitions*, 49.
78. Ceballos Gómez, *Sociedad y prácticas mágicas*, 389-90.
79. Testimony from Cartagena de Indias, 1643; I ic Croitoru Rotbaum, *Documentos coloniales originados en el santo oficio del tribunal de la inquisición de Cartagena de Indias (contribución a la historia de Colombia)* (Bogota: Tipografia Hispana, 1971), 339.
80. Quoted in Bruno Feitler, "Jews and New Christians in Dutch Brazil, 1630-1654," in Kagan and Morgan, *Atlantic Diasporas*, 141.
81. Testimony again Hector Nunez and his family, London, 1591; Charles Meyers, "Lawsuits in Elizabethan Courts of Law: the Adventures of Dr. Hector Nunez, 1566-1591: a Precis," *The Journal of European Economic History* 25, no. 1 (Spring 1996): 11, 157.
82. Garachico, the Canary Islands, 1665; Wolf, *Jews in the Canary Islands*, 204.
83. Baião, *Inquisição*, 118.
84. Abreu, *Denunciações da Bahia*, 544.
85. Guaman Poma complains precisely about the erasure of difference in the colonies by means of conviviality, though from the opposite class direction: "For the magistrates and priests or Spaniards and knights and the principal Indian lords, legitimate lords since the time of their ancestors, sit down to eat and entertain and talk and drink and game with riffraff, ruffians, highwaymen, robbers, liars, laborers and drunkards, Jews and Moors and lowly persons, Indian menials. And they tell these people their secrets and converse with these mestizos and mulattos and blacks. And so there are in this life many lords and ladies not worth a fig" (translated in Fuchs, *Mimesis and Empire*, 93).
86. Quoted in Castelló, *Francisco de la Cruz*, 1:426.
87. Filipe de Moura was the witness; cited in Mello, *Gente da Nação*, 147.
88. AGN Inq., vol. 398, exp. 1, Proceso contra Simón Váez Sevilla (1642), fol. 266v.; Alberro, *Inquisición y sociedad*, 559. Simón Váez Sevilla, the wealthiest and most well-connected New Christian in New Spain, is said to have headed the largest group of crypto-Jews in New Spain, which met annually for the great fast of Yom Kippur at their hacienda (Seymour B. Liebman, "The Religion and Mores of the Colonial New World Marranos," in Anita Novinsky and Maria Luiza Tucci Carneiro (eds.), *Inquisição: Ensaios sobre mentalidade, heresias e arte: Trabalhos apresentados no I Congresso Internacional — Inquisição. Universidade de São Paulo. Maio 1987* [São Paulo: Editora da Universidade de São Paulo, 1992], 55, 59); on Váez Sevilla and his commercial and familial network, see Hordes, *End of the Earth*, 35-43, 52-60. This extended clan will be treated most directly in chapter 7.

89. Or, as a twentieth-century Jewish author put it, "The kitchen was the temple in which Mother was priest and Maggie Doyle [the Irish maid], Levite" (Harriet Lane Levy, *920 O'Farrell Street: A Jewish Girlhood in Old San Francisco* [Berkeley: Heyday Books, 1996 (orig. 1937)], 136). Eva Abraham-van der Mark notes how in nineteenth-century Curaçao the kitchen where their mother may have worked stood as the borderland beyond which the illegitimate "colored" children could not enter the world of their White father and into which the mistresses of the house, "socialized into pretending complete ignorance," dared not venture. One Sephardic woman was repeatedly told by her grandfather: "A lady should never enter the kitchen" ("Marriage and Concubinage among the Sephardic Merchant Elite of Curaçao," in Janet Momsen [ed.], *Women and change in the Caribbean* [London: Indiana University Press/James Currey, 1993], 43). Even "powerless" servants and slaves could thus sometimes negotiate a modicum of power or a proprietary turf for themselves.
90. In 1528, in the Canariote town of Santo Cristobal la Laguna, "Sebastian, black slave of Alonso Rodriguez, deposes that his master cuts off all the fat from the meat before cooking it, and that on two Saturdays he put on a clean shirt; and that he does not eat pork, nor allow the inmates of his house to do so. Deponent does not know whether his master is a convert" to Christianity (quoted in Wolf, *Jews in the Canary Islands*, 87). Of the 21 witnesses who testify against doña Ysabel Alvarez de Alarcon before the Inquisition in Granada sometime prior to the 15 October 1595 *auto de fé* in which she was reconciled for following certain Mosaic practices, all were women, "except one Black male slave of the accused." He, along with the rest of the denouncers, testified to having seen his mistress "having made fasts without eating or drinking the whole day until night, and not eating bacon and fish without scales" (Jose Maria Garcia Fuentes [ed.], *La inquisición en Granada en el siglo XVI: Fuentes para su studio* [Granada: Departamento de Historia Moderna de la Universidad de Granada, 1981], 480).
91. For instance Matias Rodrigues de Olivera, a fifty-one-year-old bachelor from Portugal living in Mexico, *ca.* late 1640s (Arnold Wiznitzer, "Crypto-Jews in Mexico during in the Seventeenth Century," *American Jewish Historical Quarterly* 51 [1961/2]; reprinted in Cohen, *Jewish Experience in Latin America*, 1:157) or Alvaro Gonçales of La Palma, the Canaries, sentenced in 1526 (Haim Beinart, "Jews in the Canary Islands: a Re-evaluation," *Transactions of the Jewish Historical Society of England* 25 [1973/1975], 54).
92. Canary Islands, 1520; translated in Wolf, *Jews in the Canary Islands*, 22.
93. Beinart, "Jews in the Canary Islands," 54, n. 51.
94. Quoted in Beinart, "The Jews in the Canary Islands," 54, n.47.
95. Translated in Wolf, *Jews in the Canary Islands*, 5-6.
96. Yosef Karo, *Shulkhan Arukh*, Yoreh De'ah, section 267:11.
97. Translated in Wolf, *Jews in the Canary Islands*, 23.
98. Baião, *Inquisição em Portugal e no Brasil*, 121.
99. "Traslado do Processo feito pela Inquizição de Lisboa contra Antonio Jozé da Silva," 246.
100. Ciudad Real, 1511; printed in Haim Beinart, *Records of the Trials of the Spanish Inquisition in Ciudad Real*, 4 vols. (Jerusalem: Israel Academy of Sciences and Humanities, 1974-1985), 2:165.
101. It should be noted that in some respects Catholic masters also bore a religious subject position antagonistic to that of their slaves. It is intriguing the degree to which some Catholic masters wielded their own sincere faith and the "interests" of Jesus, Mary and/or the saints in making sure that their slaves know their proper, submissive place in the Christian social hierarchy. See, for instance, Villa-Flores, "Blasphemy and Slavery in New Spain," 459-60.
102. Translated in Wolf, *Jews in the Canary Islands*, 24.
103. In 1515, Portuguese King Dom Manuel sought to address the poor burial conditions of slaves in the Lisbon area: "We are informed that the slaves who die in this city, those brought from Guinea, as well as others, are not well buried, as they should be, in the places where they are thrown, and that they are thrown on the ground in such a manner that they remain uncovered, or completely above ground without any thing of theirs to cover them, and that the dogs eat them; and that most of these slaves are thrown in the dunghill [...] and likewise also in other places by the country estates of the suburbs"(Victor Ribeiro, *A Santa casa da misericordia de lisboa [subsidios para a sua historia], 1498-1898* [Lisbon: Typographia da Academia Real das Sciencias, 1902], 183); Ed. Freire de Oliveira, *Elementos para a história do município de lisboa* [Lisbon, 1885], 1:509). In 1547, the cabildo of Vera Cruz, in New Spain, issued an ordinance prohibiting "masters from throwing the cadavers of slaves in the river, since the practice was a health hazard" (Palmer, *Slaves of the White God*, 42). In Brazil slaves' corpses were often left to rot in shallow graves, where they might be rooted out by dogs or wild animals, or they were dumped on beaches and left to the tides (A. J. R. Russell-Wood, *The Black Man in Slavery and Freedom in Brazil* [London: Macmillan, 1982], 132).

104. Bennett, *Africans in Colonial Mexico*, is largely about this process.
105. Translated in Wolf, *Jews in the Canary Islands*, 23.
106. Translated in Wolf, *Jews in the Canary Islands*, 23.
107. Medina, *Inquisición en las provincias del Plata*, 247-8.
108. Mello, *Gente da Nação*, 25.
109. Mello, *Gente da Nação*, 193.
110. "Processo contra Antonio Jozé da Silva," 246.
111. Huerga Criado, *En la raya de Portugala*, 92-3. The same seems to have been true of the servile denunciations made against an extended family of Judeoconversos in Quintanar, Castile, in the 1570s (Salomon, "Spanish Marranism Re-examined," 133).
112. Testimony of Ysabel de Silva, 27 July 1643; AGN Mexico, Inq. 402, exp. 1, leg. 2, fol. 113r.
113. Cyrus Adler, "Trial of Jorge de Almeida by the Inquisition in Mexico," *Publications of the American Jewish Historical Society*, 4 (1896); reprinted in Cohen, *The Jewish Experience in Latin America*, 334.
114. Lúcia Helena Costigan, *Through Cracks in the Wall: Modern Inquisitions and New Christian Letrados in the Iberian Atlantic World* (Leiden: Brill, 2010), 104.
115. Charges against Maria de Rivera, 1642; AGN Mexico, Inq. 403, exp. 3, fol. 379r.
116. Cited in Lewin, *Singular Proceso de Salomón Machorro*, 253. León/Machorro's Jewish background was strong: he lived in Pisa from the age of two, moved soon after to Livorno, where he learned Judaism and regularly attended synagogue, "wearing a talit;" around 1621 he was sent to Smyrna, Turkey, to study with his uncle, Abraham Israel; altogether he spent some four years in the synagogues of Chios, Smyrna and Algiers (AGN Inquisición 416, fols. 519-20; Lewin, *Singular Proceso de Salomón Machorro*, 129, 132).
117. Cited in Lewin, *Singular Proceso de Salomón Machorro*, xxxiii.
118. Testimony of Beatriz Enriquez, 24 July 1642; AGN Mexico, Inq. 393, exp. 12, leg. 3, fol. 211r. Robert Ferry notes how in this case merely modifying the ritual sufficed when getting rid of the slaves or hiding the ritual from them proved impossible ("Don't Drink the Chocolate").
119. Quoted in Toro, *judíos en la Nueva España*, 256.
120. Cited in Lipiner, *Sapateiro de Trancoso*, 106. Francisco's mother supposedly taught Mendes and his wife a little song, then current among Portuguese New Christians, that lauded Israel and denigrated Edom (Christendom) and Ishmael (Islam), which they sang at secret gatherings of New Christians. It was said that Francisco had written letters to and received a response from Luís Dias, the self-proclaimed yet much-followed Messiah from Setúbal, Portugal. They had allegedly obtained the names of God written in Hebrew, which they claimed possessed great virtue, from the servant of an openly Jewish rabbi traveling through Évora. Lipiner suggests that these names of God derived from the banner of David HaReuveni, the self-proclaimed representative of the Lost Tribes who had recently visited Portugal and stirred up messianic hopes among the converso population. The servant belonged to Rabbi Abraão ben Zamiro or ibn Zimor, of Safim, Morocco, a prestigious rabbi and supporter of the Portuguese against the Muslims in North Africa, who provided clandestine aid to the crypto-Jews in Portugal (242-3).
121. Testimony of Beatriz Enriquez, 14 November 1642; AGN Mexico, Inq. 393/12/3, fol. 243r.-v.
122. Testimony of 29 December 1644; AGN Mexico, Inq. 393, exp. 12, leg. 3, fols. 96r.-v.
123. Testimony of 1 July 1642; cited in Lewin, *Singular proceso de Salomón Machorro*, 45.
124. Testimony of Beatriz Enriquez, her daughter, 24 July 1642; AGN Mexico, Inq. 393, exp. 12, leg. 3, fol. 211v.
125. Testimony of Antonio Lopez de Orduna, 1 September 1642; AGN Mexico, Inq. 393, exp. 12, leg. 3, fol. 177v. Nothing regarding the avoidance of meat appears in the *Shulkhan Arukh*. In fact, the eating of meat is specifically permitted once the deceased is buried (*Shulkhan Arukh*, Yoreh De'ah, sec. 378:8-9. Perhaps because a mourner is required to refrain from celebration and even joy during the seven days of mourning (*Shulkhan Arukh*, Yoreh De'ah, #391), the custom developed of not eating of meat, considered a pleasure. Abstaining from meat may have been a custom observed among marranos, though Gitlitz, *Secrecy and Deceit*, does not mention it. Various witnesses state that fish suppers are "a ceremony of the said law when an observer of [the law] dies" (testimony of Catalina Enriquez, Mexico City, 20 July 1643; AGN Mexico, Inq. 393, exp. 12, leg. 3, fol. 153r.). Orduna states explicitly that he heard said "that it is a ceremony of the said law that when a person dies who observes [the law] the relatives of the deceased do not eat any meat item for the first few days" (ibid., fol. 177r.).
126. Testimony of Beatriz Enriquez, 24 October 1642; AGN Mexico, Inq. 393/12/3, fol. 228v.
127. AHN Inq. 1601/18, fol. 31; reprinted in Croitoru Rotbaum, *Documentos*, 223.
128. Summary of charges against Maria de Rivera, 1643; AGN Mexico, Inq. 403, exp. 3, fol. 439v.

129. Testimony of Beatriz Enriquez (Leonor's aunt), 19 January 1645; AGN Mexico, Inq. 393/12/3, fol. 275r. Rafaela Enriquez corroborates this: "they had placed, in order to comply with the Catholics who would be able to see it, especially the slave women, the image of a crucified saint" (testimony of 5 January 1645; ibid., 402, exp. 1, leg. 2, fol. 286v.).
130. Fergusson, "Trial of Gabriel de Granada," 471. Granada also related how one of their Black women slaves supposedly saw his aunt, Margarita, and others flogging a crucifix, to the point where it broke, something that caused them to burn it in order to destroy the evidence (432).
131. Melammed, *Heretics or Daughters of Israel*, 88.
132. Cited in Gitlitz, *Secrecy and Deceit*, 319. Robert Ferry speculates that "for *observant women*, the risk of appearing conspicuously idle in observance of the Sabbath and other holy days was diminished since their slaves regularly did most if not all domestic labor" ("Don't Drink the Chocolate"), but he is wrong to think that rituals such as bathing, lighting candles or eating chicken/meat in honor of the sabbath might not threaten to raise suspicions even among slaves. As I am trying to make clear here, it is not the case that "descriptions of other ritual activities mention slaves and secrecy only occasionally."
133. Response to the charges of various witnesses, AGN Mexico, Inq. 393/12/3, fol. 423v.
134. As the judaizer Alvar Gonçales did to his "Moorish" slave Inés once he began worrying that the Inquisition might arrest him; Las Palmas, the Canary Islands, *ca.* early 1520s (Beinart, "Jews in the Canary Islands," 54).
135. Cited and translated in Ferry, "Don't Drink the Chocolate."
136. Cited in Hordes, *End of the Earth*, 56. Antonia will appear again at length in chapter 6.
137. Adler, "Trial of Jorge de Almeida," 319. Almeida, or Almeyda, had lived as a Jew in Ferrara in the 1570s before returning to Spain and then leaving, with his mother and two brothers, for New Spain (Seymour B. Liebman, *The Jews of New Spain* [Coral Gables, Florida: University of Miami Press, 1970], 172-3).
138. Cited in Lewin, *Singular proceso de Salomón Machorro*, 333. Another case of a slave being sold by a New Christian family in Portugal appears in the Lisbon denunciations of 1541. At least two slaves belonging to the family, including one Mulato, had told others about the family's Jewishness. The sale of the slave came under the condition that he never return to Portugal (Baião, *Inquisição*, 112). Non-converso households also faced problems generated by the behavior or gossip of slaves. The mystically inclined Francisco de la Cruz relates to his inquisitors (Peru, 1571) that his angel told him, because of various Blacks and Mulatos stirring up trouble with gossip about the romantic affairs of their masters and masters' acquaintances, "that I should tell doña Elvira to throw out of her house all of the free blacks that she had in it" (Castelló, *Francisco de la Cruz*, 1:428).
139. Cited in Lewin, *Singular proceso de Salomón Machorro*, 333. This conversation was reported to the inquisitors, along with many, many others between these two prisoners as well as other prisoners, by yet another prisoner, Gaspar Alfar. The sheer volume and detail (which often can be corroborated through other testimonies) force the conclusion that Alfar lacked morals far more than surveillance skills. On Alfar, who, among other things, feigned being a priest in Rome and Seville and went to the Indies without a license to serve as a priest but administered all the sacraments nevertheless, see Boleslao Lewin, *Confidencias de dos criptojudíos en las cárceles del Santo Oficio, México, 1645-1646* (Buenos Aires: n. p., 1975), 12-15. Elsewhere, Alfar reports that León/Machorro named the slave's mistress, María de Rivera, as well as the slave, Juliana (cited in Ferry, "Don't Drink the Chocolate").
140. Testimony of Beatriz Enriquez, 19 September 1642; AGN Mexico, Inq. 393/12/3, fol. 220v.
141. Their conversations also were reported by Gaspar Alfar (testimony of 13 June 1642; AGN Mexico, Inq. 396, exp. 3, fol. 570v.); see also testimony of Miguel de Almonaçir, 24 May 1642, AGN Inq. 413, no exp., fol. 25v.; cited in Ferry, "Don't Drink the Chocolate."
142. Botello was again arrested, due to the denunciation of his adopted son, José Sánchez, in 1656. In the 8 October 1659 *auto de fe* the Inquisition burned him to death at the stake (Lewin, *Proceso de María de Zárate*, 31).
143. Cited in Lewin, *Singular processo de Solomón Machorro*, 400. Lewin transcribed a slightly different version of Botello's dream from another manuscript source in *Confidencias de dos criptojudíos*, 133-4.
144. Ferry, "Don't Drink the Chocolate." Laura Lewis provides a list of Afromexican slaves who denounced their masters of judaizing: AGN Inq. 296, exp. 3, 1612; 316, exp. 26, 1617; 510, exp. 128, 1625; 435 (1), fs. 78, 254, 1650; 435 (2), f. 410, 1650; 458, exp. 34, 1658, 520, exp. 101, 1685 (Lewis, *Hall of Mirrors*, 204, n. 176, 231, n. 95). These cases are all supplemental to those I have discussed here.

145. Tardieu, *Negros y la iglesia en el Perú*, 1:567, n. 3.
146. Huerga Criado offers this argument regarding Portugal (*En la raya de Portugal*, 92).

Chapter 5

1. Wolf, *Jews in the Canary Islands*, 43.
2. For an insightful analysis of African divination under the slave system, see Sweet, *Recreating Africa*, 120-37.
3. Mark and Silva Horta, *Forgotten Diaspora*; Green, "Masters of Difference"; idem, "The Role of the Portuguese Trading Posts in Guinea and Angola in the 'Apostasy' of Crypto-Jews"; Mark and Silva Horta, "Two Early Seventeenth-Century Sephardic Communities."
4. Testimony of 24 January 1645; AGN Mexico, Inq. 402, exp. 1, leg. 2, fol. 291r. Her acquaintance merely adjusted his blessing, "no, rather, [her days should be] like the following day, because it was that of the great fast."
5. Alberro, *Inquisición y sociedad en México*, 561.
6. Ferry, "Don't Drink the Chocolate," n. 27.
7. Haim Beinart, "Legajo 2135 N° 1. The Inquisition in Valladolid in the Times of the Inquisitor-General Fray Antonio de Sotomayor (1621-1643)," *Mémorial I.-S. Révah: Études sur le marranisme, l'hétérodoxie juive et Spinoza*, ed. Henry Méchoulan and Gérard Nahon (Paris-Lousain: E. Peeters, 2001), 85. On the use of slaves for physical attack and murder of enemies, see Debra G. Blumenthal, "Implements of Labor, Instruments of Honor: Muslim, Eastern and Black African Slaves in Fifteenth-Century Valencia" (Ph. D. Diss, University of Toronto, 2000), 203-217. Lewis, *Hall of Mirrors*, 56, 67-72, offers numerous examples of slaves in Mexico carrying out the colonialist orders of their Spanish masters against Amerindians.
8. Baião, *Inquisição em Portugal e no Brasil*, 115. "No dia 3 [de Feb.] compareceu Jorge Gonçalves, bombardeiro, morador, na Pampulha que vindo de passeiar, e passando perto do pomar de Alonso Barreira, christão novo, vio nelle andar um negro e disseram todos que aquillo parecia mal. Porém Alonso Barreira veio a casa d'elle, acompanhado por um escravo e um Ratinho e, como elle não estives-se, perguntara á sua mulher pelo ladrão do marido, ao que esta respondeu que o seu marido era tão ladrão como quem lh'o chamava e o negro puchara então da espada para ella. Alonso Barreira tinha zanga á testemunha por ter ido dizer ao cura de Santos o Velho que ella mandava os negros cavar ao Domingo."
9. This was often one of the results of shipwrecks (Blackmore, *Manifest Perdition*, 74, 92), though Blackmore does not dwell on this.
10. Gretchen D. Starr-LeBeau, *In the Shadow of the Virgin: Inquisitors, Friars, and Conversos in Guadalupe, Spain* (Princeton: Princeton University Press, 2003), 65.
11. Wolf, *Jews in the Canary Islands*, 22.
12. "tambien embio parte del al ospital de nuestra Señora a los pobres con una esclaba suya, Ysavel o antonia, Y tambien a los Pobres de la carceles con las mismas esclabas" (as testified in August 1642 to his inquisitors by Thomas Nuñez de Peralta, who heard it from his wife Beatriz Enriquez, daughter of Blanca Enriquez; AGN Mexico, Inq. 393, exp. 12, leg. 3, fol. 59v.).
13. Response to the charges against her, 20 September 1647 (?); AGN Mexico, Inq. 393/12/3, fol. 324r.
14. Huerga Criado, *En la raya de Portugal*, 91-2.
15. Ferry, "Don't Drink the Chocolate."
16. Huerga Criado, *En la raya de Portugal*, 92-3.
17. Translated in Ambrósio Fernandes Brandão, *Dialogues of the Great Things of Brazil (Diálogos das grandezas do Brasil)*, Attributed to Ambrósio Fernandes Brandão, trans. and annotated by Frederick Holden Hall, William F. Harrison and Dorothy Winters Welker (Albuquerque: University of New Mexico Press, 1987), 157-8; for the original Portuguese, see Ambrósio Fernandes Brandão, *Diálogos das grandezas do Brasil*, ed. José Antônio Gonsalves de Mello, 3rd ed. (Recife: Fundação Joaquim Nabuco/Editora Massangana, 1997), 119-20.
18. Translated in Fernandes Brandão, *Dialogues of the Great Things of Brazil*, 158-59; the original Portuguese: *Diálogos das grandezas do Brasil*, 121.
19. Testimony of Ysavel de Silva, 30 June 1643; AGN Mexico, Inq. 402, exp. 1, leg. 2, fol. 96r.
20. Toro, *Judios en la Nueva España*, 170-1.
21. She had been arrested in 1591. The two former maids, Maria Antunes and Antónia, among other Old Christian character witnesses, were never questioned by the inquisitors (Salomon, "Portuguese Background," 117; ANTT, Inq. de Lisboa, no. 2203).

22. Querétaro was the name of a commercial center north of Mexico City.
23. Testimony of Francisco de la Cruz, 3 September 1643; AGN Mexico, Inq. 396/3/6, fol. 524r.-v.
24. See Croitoru Rotbaum, *Documentos* 506, for instructions from 1645 Cartagena on dealing with the sequestered slaves of accused persons.
25. Böhm, *Historia de los judíos en Chile*, 71, 58.
26. Böhm, *Historia de los judíos en Chile*, 135. "[S]e le secuestraron todos sus bienes, y porque entre ellos se secuestraron los bienes que yo llevé de dote, [...] que los bienes que están embargados del dicho mi marido que son, en la plaza de la dicha ciudad, tres cuartos de solar y dos negros llamados Simón y Francisco, y otros bienes que constará por el embargo, para que los venda en pública almoneda rematándolos en le mayor ponedor, y de su procedido me pague y haga pagar toda la cantidad que recibió conmigo en dote [...]."
27. Böhm, *Historia de los judíos en Chile*, 271. Silva's widow received but a fraction of the purchase price, the rest being treated as confiscated goods and used to pay for the Inquisition's expenses in maintaining Silva in jail (138).
28. Juan de Uriarte was the official, denounced in the late 1640s by the Governor Alonso Ordoñez de Arçe Cavallero, among others. "Y despues voluio el dicho don Juan de Araoz y le dijo a este declarante que le auia dicho el dicho Francisco Piñero que quando le sequestraron los bienes tomó y ocultó el dicho Juan de Uriarte quatro o cinco barretones de oro y que tambien tenia un taleguillo de perlas pinjantes y algunas cadenas de oro y negros que no se pusieron en el ynuentario y se ocultaron" (Croitoru Rotbaum, *Documentos*, 304). See also the 1643 testimony of the jailer Diego Fernandez de Amaia: "y tanbien sucedio en este tiempo sauer el dicho Francisco Rodriguez de Solis que el dicho Juan de Uriarte hauia sacado por interpuesta persona una esclaba negra de mucho valor de la almoneda de sus bienes de que fue depossitario Diego de Orozco por un precio muy corto y el dicho Francisco Rodriguez de Solis quiso pedir dicho esclabo por el [....]" (ibid., 341).
29. Pullan, *Jews of Europe and the Inquisition of Venice*, 75, n. 12.
30. Maria José Pimenta Ferro Tavares, "The Portuguese Jews after Baptism," in *Studies on the History of Portuguese Jews from Their Expulsion in 1497 through Their Dispersion*, ed. Israel J. Katz and M. Mitchell Serels (New York: Sepher-Hermon Press/The American Society of Sephardic Studies, 2000), 20; she cites Pier Cesare Ioly Zorattini (ed.), *Processi del S. Uffizio di Venezia contro Ebrei e Giudaizzanti (1579-1586)*, vol. 7 (Firenzi: Olschki, 1987), 34-41, 61 and 151.
31. Pier Cesare Ioly Zorattini, "The Ribeiros: a Sixteenth Century Family of Conversos between two Inquisitions: Lisbon and Venice," in Novinsky and Tucci Carneiro, eds., *Inquisição*, 310; Pullan, *Jews of Europe and the Inquisition of Venice*, 104.
32. Trial of Habraham Bendana Sarfatim, ANTT, *Inquisição de Évora*, livro 563 [Reduzidos], fol. 294. I am most grateful to José Alberto Tavim for this reference.
33. Perry, *Handless Maiden*, 94.
34. Jonathan I. Israel, "The Jews of Spanish North Africa, 1600-1669," *Transactions of the Jewish Historical Society of England* 26 (1974/1978): 80.
35. Translated in Israel, "Jews of Spanish North Africa," 80; the Spanish original appears on 85.
36. Green, "Masters of Difference," 252.
37. Schorsch, *Jews and Blacks*, chs. 7-9.
38. Tardieu, *Negros y la iglesia en el Perú*, 1:567, n. 3.
39. Cited in Lipiner, *Izaque de Castro*, 32.
40. Mattoso, *To Be a Slave in Brazil*, 107-8. This may be the force of the accusation that one New Christian merchant in Cabo Verde, Pedro de Bairros, "has a stronghold in his house with 100 blacks" (trans. in Green, "Masters of Difference," 290, n. 92).
41. Cited and translated in Ferry, "Don't Drink the Chocolate."
42. On Portuguese judaizers maintaining newly imported, non-Spanish-speaking African slaves, *bozales*, see below.
43. Anita Novinsky, "A Critical Approach to the Historiography of *Marranos* in the Light of New Documents," *Studies on the History of Portuguese Jews from their Expulsion in 1497 through their Dispersion*, ed. Israel J. Katz and M. Mitchell Serels (New York: Sepher-Hermon Press, 2000), 113. She cites ANTT No. 7487.
44. Quoted in Mello, *Gente da nação*, 119.
45. Quoted in Mello, *Gente da nação*, 63.
46. Testimony of Ysavel de Silva, 19 October 1643; AGN Mexico, Inq. 393, exp. 12, leg. 3, fols. 93v.-94r.; also brought in ibid 402, exp. 1, leg. 2, fol. 117v.
47. On Olivera's slave-trading, see: summary of the case against him, AGN Mexico, Inq. 409, exp. 1, fol. 206v.; Israel, *Diaspora Within a Diaspora*, 99.

48. Testimony of 12 February 1644; AGN Mexico, Inq. 409, exp. 1, fol. 100r.-v.; cited in Wiznitzer, "Crypto-Jews in Mexico During the Seventeenth Century," 157. Maria de los Reyes alleges that when a 14-year-old Mulato belonging to Olivera died, as well as a Black woman two days later, their master did not have either given the last rites (testimony of 22 January 1643; AGN Mexico, Inq. 409, exp. 1, fol. 98v.). In his response to the charges, Olivera denies neglecting the slaves' final sacraments (ibid., fol. 140v.). An inspection ordered by the inquisitors found Olivera to be circumcised (AGN Mexico, Inq. 409, exp. 1, fols. 126r.-127r.).
49. Pullan, *Jews of Europe and the Inquisition of Venice*, 75, n.13 and 216. This, according to Pullan, stands as the "only well-authenticated case of a servant being converted to Judaism" in the records of the Venician Inquisition (75, n.13).
50. Célia Maria Ferreira Reis, "A visitação de Marcos Teixeira aos Açores em 1575," *Inquisição*, Vol. 1: *Comunicações apresentadas ao 1.⁰ congresso luso-brasileiro sobre inquisição realizado em Lisboa, de 17 a 20 de Fevereiro de 1987* (Lisboa: Sociedade Portuguesa de Estudos do Século XVIII/Universitária Editora, 1989), 284.
51. Cited in Lipiner, *Izaque de Castro*, 180.
52. Seymour B. Liebman, "The Religion and Mores of the Colonial New World Marranos," in Anita Novinsky and Maria Luiza Tucci Carneiro (eds.), *Inquisição: Ensaios sobre mentalidade, heresias e arte: Trabalhos apresentados no I Congresso Internacional — Inquisição. Universidade de São Paulo. Maio 1987* (São Paulo: Editora da Universidade de São Paulo, 1992), 56. As Liebman provides no more details than this, the geographic and temporal provenance of the subjects remain unclear. Even in territories where marranos could freely practice Judaism, tension surrounded the decision to circumcise sons, especially if agreement between spouses did not exist. See, for instance, the notarial deed from Amsterdam in which testimony is given concerning Margrita Faras, who threatened to send her small son, fathered by Manuel Thomas, to Portugal "in order to have the friends of Manuel Thomas arrested by the Inquisition, because Thomas had had the child circumcised" ("Notarial Records Relating to the Portuguese Jews in Amsterdam up to 1639," *Studia Rosenthaliana*, 17,2 [July 1983]: Nr. 2235, November 11, 1620).
53. Elias Lipiner mentioned to me one such case from Portugal, but I have never been able to identify it or verify his claim.
54. Alberro, *Inquisición y sociedad*, 436; Wiznitzer, "Crypto-Jews in Mexico," 137; Bocanegra, *Auto General*, s.v. Francisco Lopez Blandon: "Mostrò el falso zelo que tenia de su muerta ley, circuncidando a␣vn hijuelo suyo avido en vna Mulata, por tenerle señalado con señal de judio, esperando que siendo de edad capaz le podria reduzir al judaismo."
55. *Relacion sumaria del auto particular de fee, que el tribunal del santo oficio de la inquisition de los Reynos, y Provincias de la Nueuva España, celebró en la muy noble, y muy leal Ciudad de Mexico, a los diez y seis dias del mes de Abril, del año de mil y seiscientos y quarenta y seis.* [...] escribela el doctor Don Pedro de Estrada y Escovedo Racionero de la Santa Iglesia Cathedral de Mexico, y de los Presos y del Real Fisco del mismo Tribunal (Mexico: Francisco Robledo, Impressor del Secreto del Santo Oficio, n.d.), 18v.
56. Beinart, *Records*, 2:163.
57. Testimony of 12 February 1644; AGN Mexico, In. 409, exp. 1, fol. 100v.
58. AGN Mexico, Inq. 409, exp. 1, fol. 168r.
59. The principle that a male slave is subject to the same ritual obligations as a woman derives from BT Ḥagigah 4a.
60. Beinart, *Records*, 2:250; see also Melammed, *Heretics or Daughters of Israel*, 78-79.
61. Trans. in Melammed, *Heretics or Daughters of Israel*, 78.
62. Melammed, *Heretics or Daughters of Israel*, 80.
63. Beinart, *Conversos on Trial*, 278-9.
64. Beinart, *Conversos on Trial*, 279.
65. At the beginning of her trial, González testifies that she is thirty years old (Beinart, *Conversos on Trial*, 243). The Black maidservant whose name she couldn't recall had come up a year later when González is asked who accompanied her to alleged judaizing meetings at the house of a neighbor ("Dixo que vna negra, esclaua desta confesante, y Catalina [Gonsales, donzella (see 242)], su criada, hija de Marcos Amarillo, la qual la lleuaua la rueca o vna canastilla de maçorcas para devanar e lana de orillas para desmotar, e que todo lo tornava en la noche a su casa por haser, porque como holgauan los dichos sabados, no hazia cosa ninguna" [279]).
66. Beinart, *Conversos on Trial*, 240.
67. BT Ḥulin 2a.
68. *Autos y diligencias obrados en el Tribunal de Lima relativos al licenciado Diego López de Lisboa* [1637]; cited in Medina, *Inquisición en las provincias del Plata*, 368. Covarrubias Orozco's

Notes to Chapter 5   263

dictionary (Madrid, 1611) defines the term *landrecilla* (sciatic nerve), interestingly enough, almost exclusively by means of Jewish practice ("la cual landrecila los judíos la sacan de la pierna del carnero, y no lo comen en memoria de habérsele secado a Jacob aquel niervo, cuando luchando con el ángel le tocó en él y quedó algo cojo y tardo en el *incessu*, como se cuenta, *Génesis*, c. 32").

69. António Borges Coelho, "Repressão Ideológica e Sexual na Inquisição de Évora entre 1533 e 1668: as Primeiras Gerações de Vítimas Cristãs-Novas," in Novinsky and Tucci Carneiro, eds., *Inquisição*, 1:443.
70. Testimony of Thomassina de Mendoca, 21 August 1635; AGN Mexico, Inq. 402, exp. 1, leg. 2, fol. 15v. Further examples appear below.
71. See Melammed, "Some Death and Mourning Customs," 158.
72. Beinart, *Conversos on Trial*, 281.
73. Quoted in Toro, *Judíos en la Nueva España*, 251.
74. H. P. Salomon, "The 'De Pinto' Manuscript: a 17th century Marrano Family History," *Studia Rosenthaliana* 9,1 (January 1975): 23; the Portuguese original appears on 51.
75. Testimony of 19 January 1645; AGN Mexico, Inq. 393/12/3, fol. 275r.
76. Testimony of Maria de Cuniga, 25 February 1633; AGN Mexico, Inq. 402, exp. 1, leg. 2, fol. 7r. A different witness testifies that it was the child of Elena and Gomes de Silva who died and that Juana Enriquez, Rafaela's sister, mandated for the process some "clean water" (ibid., fol. 15r). Another Mulata who was present, Geronima Ramirez, commented on the meticulous process, "What for were they washing him if the earth was to eat him?" (ibid., fol. 10v.). Responding to the same question from another woman at the scene, Raphaela's sister, Juana Enriquez, said that this was the custom for all those who die, "in order that their flesh be tightened / *se les aPretasen las carnes*" (ibid., 12v.). I confess I do not understand this explanation.
77. Sweet, *Recreating Africa*, 193.
78. Alberro, "Negros y mulatos en los documentos inquisitoriales," 146. This assumes that said trust and complicity was not merely a product of the Inquisition trial itself.
79. Lipiner, *Sapateiro de Trancoso*, 193; Baião, *Inquisição em Portugal e no Brasil*, 106. Perhaps the daughter had a special relationship with this particular slave, as another denouncer, this one anonymous, testifies to having seen "that the judge's wife ordered cut the throat of a duck because they don't eat meat from a butcher [which would not have been slaughtered in a kosher manner], even though they would put it [meat from the butcher] on the table in order to let the servants understand that they, the masters, also ate it [butcher's meat]" (Lipiner, *Sapateiro de Trancoso*, 199).
80. Liebman, *Jews of New Spain*, 250.
81. On New Christians among Bahia's planter class, see Schwartz, *Sugar Plantations*, 265-6, 274-5.
82. Schwartz, *Sugar Plantations*, 82.
83. Sweet, *Recreating Africa*, 22-3. On the lives and conditions of slaves on the Recôncavo sugar plantations, see Schwartz, *Sugar Plantations*, 132-59, 346-412.
84. Sweet, *Recreating Africa*, 23. Another modern scholar estimates that Salvador and environs had some 4,000 Blacks at the beginning of the seventeenth century (cited in Pieroni, *Excluídos do reino*, 268).
85. Levine Melammed, "Some Death and Mourning Customs," 157.
86. J. Capistrano de Abreu (ed.), *Primeira Visitação do Santo Oficio as Partes do Brasil: Confissões da Bahia, 1591-92* (Rio de Janeiro, 1935), 138.
87. Abreu, *Confissões da Bahia*, 141.
88. Abreu, *Confissões da Bahia*, 132. Beatris and her husband, Bastiam de Faria (an Old Christian), employed a Mulato, Fernão Luis, as a teacher of their children (Abreu (ed.), *Denunciações da Bahia, 1591-1593*, 465).
89. Ronaldo Vainfas (ed.), *Confissões da Bahia: Santo oficio da inquisição de Lisboa* (São Paulo: Companhia das Letras, 1997), 271-3. This is a more recent edition of Abreu's compilation.
90. Abreu, *Confissões da Bahia*, 156. Violante's daughter Isabel had confessed on 1 February 1592, stating that she had followed her aunts and grandmother in emptying out the water once when her a daughter of hers died. She also taught a slave woman to do the same. All this she did "without having a bad intention in her heart" (Vainfas, *Confissões da Bahia*, 294-6).
91. Abreu, *Confissões da Bahia*, 173.
92. Abreu, *Confissões da Bahia*, 166.
93. Vainfas, *Confissões da Bahia*, 51-4. The visiting inquisitor does not believe Vasconcelos' claim of ignorance.
94. Abreu, *Denunciações da Bahia*, 379.
95. See Elias Lipiner, *Os judaizantes nas capitanias de cima: Estudos sobre os cristãos-novos do*

Brasil nos séculos XVI e XVII (São Paulo: Editôra Brasiliense, 1969), 125-6. A few additional details of the Antunes family saga are brought in Ronaldo Vainfas and Angelo A. F. Assis, "A esnoga da Bahia: Cristãos-novos e criptojudaísmo no Brasil quinhentista," in *Os judeus no Brasil: Inquisição, imigração e identidade*, ed. Keila Grinberg (Rio de Janeiro: Civilização Brasileira, 2005), 45-64.
96. Lipiner, *Judaizantes*, 126-7.
97. Lipiner, *Judaizantes*, 128-9.
98. Lipiner, *Judaizantes*, 122.
99. Lipiner, *Judaizantes*, 123.
100. Lipiner, *Judaizantes*, 141, n. 40, 122-3.
101. Lipiner, *Judaizantes*, 133.
102. Vainfas, *Confissões da Bahia*, 53.
103. Bodian, "Men of the Nation," 62-3. Though knowledge and celebration of Hanuka was extremely rare among Marranos (Gitlitz, *Secrecy and Deceit*, 376-7), another Portuguese New Christian and possible marrano, Miguel da Silveira (1576-1636?), composed a long panegyric devoted to the family's exemplary ancient exploits, *El Macabeo: Poema heroico* (Naples: Egidio Longo, 1638).
104. Lipiner, *Judaizantes*, 125, where he brings the quote as well.
105. Lipiner, *Judaizantes*, 133.
106. Abreu, *Denunciações da Bahia*, 257, 313.
107. Lipiner, *Judaizantes*, 134.
108. Vainfas, *Confissões da Bahia*, 282, 284.
109. See the text cited in Pieroni, *Excluídos do reino*, 100. As the text of the Edicts of the Faith changed with changing inquisitorial knowledge, a historical study of them remains an important desideratum.
110. Vainfas, *Confessōes da Bahia*, 283.
111. Myscofski, "Heterodoxy," 87.
112. Confession of 7 September 1591, Abreu, *Denunçiações da Bahia*, 493.
113. Abreu, *Denunciações da Bahia*, 315, 392, 420-1, 475, 492-3, 537.
114. Abreu, *Denunciações da Bahia*, 475, see also 395.
115. Abreu, *Denunciações da Bahia*, 537.
116. Lipiner, *Judaizantes*, 123. So-called spontaneous or voluntary confessions were those given by people without their having been summoned from the inquisitors. Given the intense pressures to avoid incrimination, such confessions really were neither entirely spontaneous nor voluntary.
117. Lipiner, *Judaizantes*, 142, n. 53.
118. Lipiner, *Judaizantes*, 137.
119. Abreu, *Confissões da Bahia*, 141.
120. Levine Melammed, "Some Death and Mourning Customs," 159.
121. Sylvie Anne Goldberg, *Crossing the Jabbok: Illness and Death in Ashkenazi Judaism in Sixteenth-through Nineteenth-Century Prague* (Berkeley: University of California Press, 1996), 82; Nachmanides, *Torat ha-Adam* (Warsaw, 1876), 46; BT Mo'ed Katan 27, 10b.
122. Goldberg, *Crossing the Jabbok*, 112.
123. Borges Coelho, "Repressão ideológica e sexual na inquisição de Évora," 444.
124. Liebman, "Religion and Mores of the Colonial New World Marranos," 62; on the importance of linen, see Gitlitz, *Secrecy and Deceit*, 282-283.
125. Lev. 10:1-24; Num. 10:2; Rashi on BT Pesaḥim 14b, 17a; Maimonides, *Avot*, Hilkhot Tumat ha-Met.
126. Abreu, *Confissões da Bahia*, 139. As do Isabel Antunes and Lianor's niece Ana Alcoforada, Lianor asserts that she did not know that this, among other acts to which she confessed, was a Jewish ritual, a fact she claims to have learned only with the recent publication of the Edict of Faith by the same visiting inquisitor (Sunday, 12 January). Her mother, Ana Rōiz, she insists, had in turn learned the custom from Inês Rodrigues, Ana's neighbor (and godmother / *comadre*?), an Old Christian in the interior of Portugal, who failed to mention that this was a Jewish ceremony. As mentioned, Beatriz gives the same story (Vainfas, *Confissões da Bahia*, 276). Lianor also confesses to other 'Jewish' practices: not eating meat for eight days after the death of a daughter (abstaining from meat is not a traditional practice; the official initial mourning period is seven days), ordering the throwing out of the hind quarters of calves (which contain the forbidden sciatic nerve), not eating lamprey (though she would eat other fish that lacked scales), covering the blood poured out from a chicken killed by her slave with sawdust. Beatriz likewise confesses to not eating meat for eight days after a relative's death, to throwing out the hind quarters of calves, to

not eating lamprey, among other Jewish acts. She repeatedly uses the term *"nojo,"* when describing the reason that certain things were avoided, that is nausea, disgust, loathing (Vainfas, *Confissões da Bahia*, 275-76). With seemingly touching sincerity Lianor tells the inquisitor that when she discovered from the Edict of Faith the Jewish nature of these acts, she, "seeing that she was of the Nation [of Portuguese Jews, i.e., a descendant of Judeoconversos] and that she had done these things innocently, became very sad, seeing that it might be considered that she was a Jewess" (Vainfas, *Confissões da Bahia*, 139). The inquisitor finds all this rather hard to believe, ordering Lianor not to leave the city without his permission.

127. Abreu, Denunciações da Bahia, 244.
128. Abreu, Denunciações da Bahia, 561.

Chapter 6

1. Testimonio de Diego López, AHN Inq. 1620/7/1, fol. 16r. Another jailer's slave who was tried by the Inquisition was Juan, a slave from Mozambique, who served Gaspar de los Reyes Plata, the alcaide for the Mexico City tribunal. In 1601 he testifies in the second Inquisition trial of Diego Díaz Nieto against the accused, for whom he had carried messages and other items. See Uchmany, Vida entre el judaísmo y el cristianismo, 207-10; José Toribio Medina, Historia del tribunal del santo oficio de la inquisición en México (Santiago de Chile: Imprenta Elzeviriana, 1905), 124.
2. Testimony of Gaspar Alfar, 21 May 1642; AGN Mexico, Inq. 396/3/6, fols. 563r.-v.
3. Testimony of 9 August 1646; AGN Mexico, Inq. 393/12/3, fol. 288r.
4. Testimony of Ysavel de Silva, 6 July 1643; AGN Mexico, Inq. 402, exp. 1, leg. 2, fol. 102v.
5. Quoted in Croitoru Rotbaum, De Sefarad, 271. Among the foods sent to the imprisoned Barreto by his relatives were Kola nuts (Maria Cristina Navarrete, "Cotidianidad y cultura material de los negros de Cartagena en el siglo XVII," America Negra 7 (1994), 78). Had Barreto, a slave trader, developed a fondness for this tropical West African food while doing business in Africa or does this merely indicate the extent of trans-Atlantic commerce in African edibles.
6. Quoted in Croitoru Rotbaum, De Sefarad, 280.
7. For example, the food for the wedding of the daughter of the Inquisition notary don Juan de Uriarte was prepared in the house of Gomez Barreto and his wife, Barbara Pereira, a fact not unconnected with the friendship Barbara Pereira maintained with Uriarte's wife Antonia (see Croitoru Rotbaum, Documentos, 330). "El señor Inq-or argos era muy amigo y que tambien tenia alguna amistad llana conel señor Inq-or D. Damian de velazques == y en la misma manera tubo amistad con el señor Inq-or Don Ma-n de cortazar y conel señor Inq-or Agustin de Ugarte sarabia" (quoted in Croitoru Rotbaum, De Sefarad, 283). Elsewhere Gomez Barreto states that on occasions when he spent time at the ranch of Blas de Paz Pinto, the inquisitor Argos was present, among many other guests, and that when visiting the ranch of a woman named Maria de Soto, Argos also came, along with the inquisitor Domingo Velez de Asas and Diego Fernandez de Amaya, warden of the secret jails (ibid., 283-284). The Governor, Alonso de Arçe Cavallero, was married to Barbara Pereira's niece (Croitoru Rotbaum, Documentos, 339).
8. Quoted in Croitoru Rotbaum, Documentos, 330.
9. Croitoru Rotbaum, Documentos, 339.
10. Croitoru Rotbaum, Documentos, 339.
11. Testimony of Francisco de la Cruz, 3 September 1643; AGN Mexico, Inq. 396/3/6, fols. 526r., 528r. As mentioned previously, Vaez Sevilla was one of the most powerful merchants and wealthiest New Christians in the Americas; see, among other sources, Eva Alexandra Uchmany, "Simón Váez Sevilla," Estudios de Historia Novohispana 9 (1987): 67-93; a longer version appears in Michael (Tel Aviv) 8 (1983): 114-61.
12. Testimony of 3 September 1643; AGN Mexico, Inq. 396/3/6, fol. 527r.
13. Ibid., fol. 527v.
14. Relacion del tercero auto particular de fee [...] à los treinta del mes de Março de 1648. años (Mexico: Iuan Ruyz, 1648), 22.
15. Testimony of Raphaela Enriquez, 3 January 1645; AGN Mexico, Inq. 402, exp. 1, leg. 2, fol. 281v.
16. Silverblatt, Modern Inquisitions, 244, n. 121.
17. Testimony of Francisco de la Cruz, 3 September 1643; AGN Mexico, Inq. 396/3/6, fol. 524v.
18. Ibid., fols. 525r.-v. Francisco makes it clear that he would visit Vaez's cell while the jailer was eating his meals.
19. Ibid., fol. 526r.

20. Ibid., fol. 525r.
21. Testimony of 22 October 1643; AGN Mexico, Inq. 396/3/6, fol. 548r.
22. Testimony of 9 August 1646; AGN Mexico, Inq. 393/12/3, fol. 288r.-v.
23. Testimony of Francisco de la Cruz, 19 October 1643; AGN Mexico, Inq. 396/3/6, fol. 532v. Francisco tells him that they hadn't but under torture he later reveals the location.
24. Testimony of Antonia de la Cruz, 21 October 1643; AGN Mexico, Inq. 396/3/6, fol. 520v.
25. "[D]e edad al parecer de sesenta años, negro, esclavo, de nación congo guineo" (cited in García, Documentos ineditos, 216). This might be the same slave referred to by Gabriel de Granada in his audience of 5 November 1643, when he related that "he also heard his said mother say that by means of this same negro slave [of the alcaide] Luis Perez Roldan used to communicate with his wife Isabel Nuñez" (Fergusson, "Trial of Gabriel de Granada," 61). Some of the documents have his name as Mungia.
26. Summary of the trial against him (AGN Mexico, Inq. 399, exp. 2, fol. 343v.).
27. AGN Mexico, Inq. 393, exp. 12, leg. 3, fols. 55r.-57v.; see also AGN Mexico, Inq. 399, exp. 2, fol. 312r.-313r.
28. Testimony of Beatriz Enriquez, 19 September 1642; AGN Mexico, Inq. 393/12/3, fol. 219v.
29. Testimony of 1 September 1642; AGN Mexico, Inq. 399, exp. 2, fols. 317r.-319v.
30. Testimony of Gaspar Vaez Sevilla, 15 February 1644; AGN Mexico, Inq. 393, exp. 12, leg. 3, fol. 113r.
31. Testimony of Gaspar Vaez Sevilla, 15 February 1644; AGN Mexico, Inq. 393, exp. 12, leg. 3, fol. 115v.
32. Testimony of 17 March 1643; cited in Lewin, Singular proceso de Salomón Machorro, 114.
33. Testimony of 19 September 1642; AGN Mexico, Inq. 393/12/3, fol. 219r. Antonia tells the inquisitors that she is from San Luis Potosi, a province of Mexico (AGN Mexico, Inq. 396/3/6, fol. 492r.), but Beatriz bought her in Çacatecas, where Antonia had been taken to be sold (below we will see why).
34. AGN Mexico, Inq. 396/3/6, fol. 492r. Francisco de la Cruz, slave of Simon Vaez Sevilla, tells the inquisitors that he is revealing how he helped the Judeoconverso prisoners "because he is a baptized christian, and that he begs pardon and mercy for this his sin, and that he did it as a poor slave, desirous of liberty" (ibid., fol. 527v.). Attesting to choice use of language, Francisco relates how one imprisoned Judeoconversa implored him "not to say anything even if they should crucify him" (ibid., fol. 533v.).
35. 10 October 1643; AGN Mexico, Inq. 396/3/6, fols. 501v.-502r., 503r., 504v., 507r., etc.
36. Testimony of Francisco de la Cruz, 22 October 1643; AGN Mexico, Inq. 396/3/6, fol. 536r. Ysavel also healed people and was used for this purpose by the jailor (testimony of Ysavel Criolla, 20 October 1643; ibid., fols. 540v.-541r.).
37. Cited in Lewin, Singular proceso de Salomón Machorro, 88.
38. Testimony of 1 September 1642; AGN Mexico, Inq. 396/3/6, fol. 493r.-v.
39. AGN Mexico, Inq. 396/3/6, fol. 497r. Perhaps knowing of this trust, after the slaves Antonia and Luçia are summoned to testify before the Inquisition in late August 1642 Beatriz's sister Micaela calls them to her house. The two slaves are afraid to enter, however, because Micaela has told her Black slaves Çiçilia and Maria that "they had to kill [Antonia] with a dagger," a threat that they convey to Antonia (ibid).
40. Cited in Lewin, Singular proceso de Salomón Machorro, 115.
41. AGN Mexico, Inq. 396/3/6, fol. 493v.
42. According to Juana Enriquez, the slave always arrived at midday (Inq. 393, exp. 1, leg. 3, fol. 184r.-v.).
43. Testimony of Beatriz Enriquez, 19 September 1642; AGN Mexico, Inq. 393/12/3, fols. 220v.-221r.; cited in Lewin, Singular proceso de Salomón Machorro, 88-9. Francisco de la Cruz, known as Queretano, the Black slave of Simon Vaez, performed nearly identical functions for his jailed master (see, among other sources, the testimony of Francisco de la Cruz, 3 September 1643; AGN Mexico, Inq. 396/3/6, fols. 524v. and passim; testimony of Antonia de la Cruz, 21 October 1643; ibid., fols. 519r.-520v.).
44. Testimony of an unnamed witness (Beatriz's slave Maria Bautista or Antonia herself?); AGN Mexico, Inq. 393/12/3, fol. 392r.
45. Testimony of Sebastian Domingo, 1 September 1642; AGN Mexico, Inq. 399, exp. 2, fol. 319r.
46. Testimony of Antonia de la Cruz, 1 September 1642; AGN Mexico, Inq. 396/3/6, fol. 495r.-v. Simon Vaez's generous payment is also mentioned in the testimony of an unnamed witness, possibly Sebastian/Munguia himself (AGN Mexico, Inq. 393/12/3, fol. 391r.).
47. Testimony of 17 March 1643; AGN Mexico, Inq. 393, exp. 12, leg. 3, fol. 184v.; cited in Lewin, Singular proceso de Salomón Machorro, 115.

48. Testimony of Antonia de la Cruz, 2 September 1642; AGN Mexico, Inq. 396/3/6, fol. 499v.
49. Testimony of 17 March 1643; AGN Mexico, Inq. 393, exp. 12, leg. 3, fol. 184v.; cited in Lewin, Singular proceso de Salomón Machorro, 115.
50. Testimony of 1 September 1642; AGN Mexico, Inq. 399, exp. 2, fol. 318r.
51. Testimony of 1 September 1642; AGN Mexico, Inq. 396/3/6, fol.494r.; testimony of 2 September 1642; ibid., fol. 498v.; testimony of Sebastian, where he denies giving money to a Black woman (testimony of 3 September 1642; ibid., Inq. 399, exp. 2, fol. 325v.), testimony of 4 September 1642; ibid., fol. 328r. According to the testimony of Jorge Jacinto Bassan from the trial of Beatriz Enriquez, he provided her money to pay the slave carrying the messages (AGN Mexico, Inq. 393, exp. 12, leg. 3, fol.162v.).
52. Testimony of 19 September 1642; AGN Mexico, Inq. 393/12/3, fol. 220r.
53. Testimony of 1 September 1642; AGN Mexico, Inq. 399, exp. 2, fol. 320r. After walking out on them Sebastian/Munguia flung away the paper that they had given him. This might be the message he claims to have lost.
54. AGN Mexico, Inq. 393/12/3, fol. 388r.
55. Testimony of Beatriz Enriquez, 19 September 1642; AGN Mexico, Inq. 393/12/3, fol. 221r.
56. Testimony of Beatriz Enriquez, 19 September 1642; AGN Mexico Inq. 393/12/3, fol. 221r.
57. Testimony of 1 September 1642; AGN Mexico, Inq. 399, exp. 2, fols. 326v., 323r.
58. Testimony of 2 September 1642; AGN Mexico, Inq. 396/3/6, fol. 499v. Sebastian/Munguia denies this (testimony of 3 September 1642; ibid., Inq. 399, exp. 2, fol. 326v.).
59. Testimony of 3 September 1642; AGN Mexico, Inq. 399, exp. 2, fol. 325v.
60. Quoted in Uchmany, Vida entre el judaísmo y el cristianismo, 209-10.
61. AGN Mexico, Inq. 393/12/3, fol.391r. On the next folio (and day?) Beatriz's promise is repeated: Sebastian/Munguia "said to the said black woman [Antonia?] that her master said to her that if he should leave [the jail] well he had to give [her] liberty" (AGN Mexico, Inq. 393/12/3, fol. 392r.) All this is repeated with only slight variation in the testimony of Antonia de la Cruz (AGN Mexico, Inq. 396/3/6, fols. 496r., 498r.). In her testimony, Antonia seems pretty insistent that she is telling the truth and that her mistress knows all this to be true (ibid., fol. 496r.). Sebastian/Munguia denies that Peralta promised Antonia her freedom, saying only that Sebastian/Munguia heard this from her, but he does state that Beatriz indeed promised to free Antonia if her husband was released from prison (testimony of 3 September 1642; ibid., Inq. 399, exp. 2, fol. 326r.).
62. Testimony of 10 October 1643; AGN Mexico, Inq. 396/3/6, fol. 507r. It is unclear whether this refers to an episode mentioned above or to something that transpired after they were all arrested. Ysavel Criolla says that it was a necklace of pearls (testimony of 20 October 1643; ibid., fol. 546r.).
63. Testimony of 3 September 1643; AGN Mexico, Inq. 396/3/6, fol. 524v.
64. Testimony of Ysavel Criolla, 20 October 1643; AGN Mexico, Inq. 396/3/6, fol. 543r.
65. AGN Mexico, Inq. 393, exp. 1, leg. 3, fol. 421v.
66. Testimony of 1 September 1642; AGN Mexico, Inq. 396/3/6, fol. 492v.
67. Testimony of 19 September 1642; AGN Mexico, Inq. 393/1/3, fol. 219v.
68. AGN Mexico, Inq. 393/12/3, fol. 386v. In his own testimony during his own trial Sebastian/Munguia says that the first time he and Beatriz meet, after he has already conveyed a message for her, "seeing this confessant she thanked him greatly for his having brought the said paper" (testimony of 1 September 1642; AGN Mexico, Inq. 399, exp. 2, fol. 319r.). He also declares that Antonia embraced him on one occasion (testimony of 5 September 1642; ibid., fol. 329v.).
69. Testimony of 18 November 1642; AGN Mexico, Inq. 393/12/3, fol. 245v.
70. AGN Mexico, Inq. 393/1/3, fols. 421r.-v.
71. Testimony of 3-11 September 1642; AGN Mexico, Inq. 399, exp. 2, fol. 324v.-333r. The inquisitors eventually order Sebastian/Munguia tortured, in order to draw out definitive testimony. He "persevered," though through how much is not stated, and repeated his previous testimony enough to satisfy the inquisitors (ibid., fol. 336v.).
72. Testimony of 4 September 1642; AGN Mexico, Inq. 399, exp. 2, fol. 328r.
73. 16 October 1643; AGN Mexico, Inq. 396/3/6, fol. 510v.
74. 17 October 1643; AGN Mexico, Inq. 396/3/6, fols. 513r.-518v. Ferry notes that Antonia's testimony came only after she had been caught colluding in the exchange of messages, in other words, long after her owners had been arrested by the Inquisition.
75. Testimony of 21 October 1643; AGN Mexico, Inq. 396/3/6, fol. 521r. Likewise, her master, Thomas Nuñez de Peralta, "sent her among the dirty laundry some new shoes that didn't fit him" (ibid., fol. 521v.). Francisco de la Cruz testifies that in prison Beatriz Enriquez gave him for various services an old shirt, which he sold, and two reales (Testimony of 19 October 1643; ibid., fol. 533r.). He calls her fat — "dª Beatriz la gorda."

76. Testimony of 21 October 1643; AGN Mexico, Inq. 396/3/6, fol. 521r.
77. Robert Ferry, "Don't Drink the Chocolate." Still, Ferry, who does not appear skeptical of Inquisition records, does not consider that perhaps some, much or perhaps even all of the testimony regarding the Blancas de Rivera is not credible. I.e., Juliana may not have denounced them because there was nothing to denounce.
78. Trial and Criminal Cause against Sebastian Domingo, alias Mungia, AGN Mexico, Inq. 399, exp.2, fols. 345r.-346r.; García, Documentos ineditos, 216-7.
79. See, for instance, Bennett, Africans in Colonial Mexico, esp. 61-78, 156-80; Sweet, Recreating Africa, 35-50.
80. Trial and Criminal Cause against Sebastian Domingo, 22 August 1642; AGN Mexico, Inq. 399, exp. 2, fol. 312r.-v.; García, Documentos ineditos, 216-7.
81. Testimony of 2 September 1642; AGN Mexico, Inq. 396/3/6, fol. 500r.
82. AGN Mexico, Inq. 399, exp. 2, fols. 335v.-336r.
83. AGN Mexico, Inq. 399, exp. 2, fol. 350r.; García, Documentos ineditos, 216-7.
84. Cited in García, Documentos ineditos, 235. Perhaps Blanca Juarez was also the object of the reference to an imprisoned judaizer with whom Isabel Nuñez used to communicate in the Inquisition jails, other than her son, mentioned earlier: "se comunicó con otros presos, con los nombres supuestos de Clavellina, Zapatilla, y la Angola, por saber hablar la lengua Guineota." See Bocanegra, Auto general de la Fee, s.v. Ysabel Nuñez. Whoever this Judeoconversa was who adopted the code name "the Angolan Woman," she adopted the identity of an Angolan.
85. AGN Mexico, Inq. 393, exp. 12, leg. 3, fol. 93v.
86. Sweet, Recreating Africa, 19, 250, n. 2, basing himself on the work of Joseph Miller.
87. Alberro, "Negros y mulatos en los documentos inquisitoriales," 146.
88. Relacion del Tercero Auto Particular de Fee, 40v.
89. Testimony of 2 January 1643; AGN Mexico, Inq. 402, exp. 1, leg. 2, fol. 246v.
90. Estrada y Escovedo, Relacion sumaria del auto particular de fee, 10v.
91. On the other hand, Juana Enriquez and Simón Váez Sevilla owned may slaves — Robert Ferry says at one point "as many as two dozen, both adults and children," and elsewhere "at least 18" ("Don't Drink the Chocolate") — yet they are not alleged to speak Angolan. This couple was accused of whipping their slaves frequently and hence the question of intimacy or lack thereof may have varied radically depending on, among other factors, the personalities of the owners.
92. Maria Odila Leite da Silva Dias, Power and Everyday Life: The Lives of Working Women in Nineteenth-Century Brazil (New Brunswick, NJ: Rutgers University Press, 1995 [1984]), 62.
93. AGN Mexico, Inq. 387, exp. 11, Memoria del día en que entraron los presos de esta Complicidad, desde el año de 1639 hasta el de 1647; 403, exp. 3, Proceso contra María de Rivera (1642), fols. 339-341v; Alberro, Inquisición y sociedad en México, 558.
94. Testimony of Ysavel Criolla, 20 October 1643; AGN Mexico, Inq. 396/3/6, fol. 543r.
95. Montesinos, Auto de fé celebrado en Lima, 5 [1639 ed., unpag.]; the text is reproduced in full in Böhm, Historia de los judíos en Chile, 375-429. A letter from the Inquisitor Antonio de Castro y del Castillo, Lima, 8 June 1641, explained how the lemons were used: "many times they give them [their Black slaves] papers written with the juice of lemons, which they request for ailments that they feign or for the enhancement [sainete] of their food, and even though it seems that the papers go out blank, put to the fire the letters emerge, a secret discovered by the señor Licenciado Juan de Mañosca" (quoted in Böhm, Historia de los judíos en Chile, 372).
96. Quoted in Silverblatt, "Colonial Conspiracies," 271-2; she cites AHN Inq. 1647/13, fols. 53r.-v. and 266.
97. Quoted in Böhm, Historia de los judíos en Chile, 132.
98. Quoted in Medina, Inquisición de Lima, 1:138-9.
99. Carta del inquisidor don Antonio de Castro y del Castillo, Lima, 8 June 1641; quoted in Böhm, Historia de los judíos en Chile, 372.
100. Medina, Inquisición de Cartagena, 274.
101. Splendiani, Tribunal de Cartagena, 2:350, n. 916.
102. Testimony of Gaspar Alfar, who reported these conversations, 16 June 1642; AGN Mexico, Inq. 396, exp. 3, fol. 576v. Adding to the discussion of New Christians' allegedly dangerous linguistic abilities, Sobremonte, who traded in the northern mining regions of New Spain as well as in Oaxaca, knew Nahuatl, as Stanley Hordes cites a letter sent him by one of his agents in this language, warning him about the Inquisition (End of the Earth, 43). Seymour B. Liebman mentions, without giving details, that Sobremonte's trial revealed that he had had "a sexual relationship" with an Amerindian woman (Seymour B. Liebman, "The Mestizo Jews of Mexico," American Jewish Archives 19,2 [November 1967]: 155).

103. Trial and Criminal Cause of Sebastian Domingo, 22 August 1642; AGN Mexico, Inq. 399, exp. 2, fol. 313r.
104. Cyrus Adler, "A Contemporary Memorial Relating to Damages to Spanish Interests in America Done by the Jews of Holland (1634)," PAJHS 17 (1909): 49. Moses Coen Henriques, alias Antonio Vaez Henriquez, as well as Diego Peixotto, is said to have been the leader of the Dutch conquest of Pernambuco earlier in the year. It is unclear which language was taught the crew by the Jews. Portuguese? Hebrew? Fonseca's testimony is filled with partial truths, exaggerations and errors. This passage is cited by Edward Kritzler, Jewish Pirates of the Caribbean (London: JR Books, 2009), 139, who turns it into the following: Moses Cohen Henriques schemed "to capture Havana with African warriors disguised as slaves: 'The landing is to be made under a flag of truce, pretending they escaped from the Hollanders, and [once inside the city] under cover of night, they would arm themselves and slaughter the soldiers.'"
105. Sobre el levantamiento de los portugueses en Buenos Aires, December 1649, Cartas de la Audiencia, 18 May 1650, AGI Santo Domingo, 57, r. 2, n. 31, fol. 5v. My thanks to Daviken Studnicki-Gizbert for sharing this document with me.
106. AGN, Reales Cédulas Originales, vol. 1, núm. 288, f. 528; also in AGI Mex. 1067, lib. 12, fols. 35-137v; cited in Alberro, Inquisición y sociedad en México, 551. Such ethno-racial anxieties were nothing new. Already in the 1530s Spanish authorities worried that mestizos on Santo Domingo — who are said to be bellicose, mendacious and friends of every evil — would cause rebellion among Blacks and full-blooded natives and therefore should be removed from the island when still young (Schwartz, "Spaniards, Pardos, and the Missing Mestizos," 10-1).
107. Enriqueta Vila Vilar, "La Sublevación de Portugal y la trata de negros," Ibero-amerikanisches Archiv 2,3 (1976): 186, quoting Lima, 23 de julio de 1642 (AGI, Indiferente, 763).
108. Testimony of 21 August 1645; AGN Mexico, Inq. 402, exp. 1, leg. 2, fols. 123r.-v.
109. Álvarez Alonso, Inquisición en Cartagena, 117, citing a letter from AGI Con. 5171, without identifying the date or author. On the other hand, generalization based on nationality or ethnicity is always dangerous. It appears that two Portuguese slave traders in Mexico City who spoke Angolan revealed the plot of the planned 1612 slave uprising; see Luis Querol y Roso, "Negros y mulatos de Nueva España, historia de su alzamiento de 1612," Anales de la Universidad de Valencia 12,90 (1935): 121-162. On the context of Spanish political-economic-theological anxieties, see Silverblatt, "Colonial Conspiracies"; idem, "New Christians and New World Fears in Seventeenth-Century Peru," Comparative Studies in Society and History; An International Quarterly 42,3 (July, 2000): 545, n. 71.; Stuart B. Schwartz, "Panic in the Indies: The Portuguese Threat to the Spanish Empire, 1640-1650," in Werner Thomas and Bart De Groof (eds.), Rebelión y resistencia en el mundo hispánico del siglo XVII: Actas del Coloquio Internacional Lovaina, 20-23 de Noviembre de 1991 (Leuven: Leuven University Press, 1992), 205-26.
110. Cited in Robin Blackburn, The Making of New World Slavery: From the Baroque to the Modern, 1492-1800 (London: Verso, 1997), 140.
111. Medina, Inquisition in Lima, 1:203.
112. Relación del estado en que se hallaba el Reino del Perú, hecha por el Excmo. Señor Don Juan de Mendoza y Luna, Marqués de Montesclaros, al Excmo. Señor Principe de Esquilache, su sucesor, reprinted in Colección de las memorias o relaciones que escribieron los virreyes del Perú acerca del estado en que dejaban las cosas generales del reino, ed. Ricardo Beltrán Rózpide (Madrid, 1921), 1:169.
113. Colin Palmer, Slaves of the White God, 119-44; David M. Davison, "Negro Slave Control and Resistance in Colonial Mexico, 1519–1650," HAHR 46 (1966): 235-53. Spanish anxieties regarding internal tranquility in the colonies led to many attempts to segregate Afroiberian and Amerindian populations over the course of the sixteenth century.
114. The author's identification was made by Guillermo Lohmann Villena, "Una incógnita despejada: La identidad del Judió portugués," Revista Histórica (Lima, Peru) 30 (1967): 26-93; reprinted as "Una incógnita despejada: La identidad del Judió portugués autor de la 'Discriçión General del Piru,'" Revista de Indias (Madrid) 30 (1970): 315-87. The article, though evincing thorough archival research, drips with retrogressive anti-Jewish overtones, making suspect some of its sweeping assertions about persistent Jewish identity.
115. Descripcion del Peru, 40. According to Hanke, the Descripcion was submitted to the Dutch Estates General ("Portuguese in Spanish America," 29).
116. AHN Inq., libro 1054, Cartas del Tribunal del Santo Oficio de México al Consejo, fol. 31; cited in Alberro, Inquisición y sociedad en México, 573.
117. Silverblatt, "Colonial Conspiracies," 271.
118. Quoted by Ventura, Portugueses no Peru, 3:19. According to Stanley Hordes, communiqués to

New Spain related the slaughter of three thousand Spanish residents of Brazil. In November of 1641, Pálafox warned the viceroy of New Spain that the wealthy Portuguese merchants there planned to buy up "all the flints and arquebuses, thus secretly controlling all the arms [...] Veracruz is the principal key to these kingdoms and there are currently in that port more Portuguese than Spanish" (End of the Earth, 50-1). In 1642, the Mexican Inquisition tried the exiled Irishman and possibly an agent of the Count Duke of Olivares, Guillén Lombardo de Guzmán or William Lampart, who was accused of plotting insurrection, including the abolition of slavery and opening the holding of political offices to former slaves and mestizos (Schwartz, "Questioning Slavery and Accepting Africa").
119. Jonathan Israel, Diasporas Within a Diaspora, 54; he cites Lúcio de Azevedo, História dos cristãos novos, 446-47.
120. Israel, Diasporas Within a Diaspora, 101; James C. Boyajian, Portuguese Bankers at the Court of Spain, 1626-1650 (New Brunswick, 1983).
121. Quoted in Uchmany, "Participation of New Christians and Crypto-Jews," 197, 202. Despite fears of New Christian 'judaizing,' neither Spain nor Portugal made any effort to control or curtail New Christian commercial activity, other than through the indirect, inefficient, ineffective and always reactive means of the Inquisition, a sure sign of the economic self-interest motivating state policy.
122. Alonso de Cianca, Discurso breve [...] en que se muestra y da a entender la causa que a enflaquecido el comercio de las flotas de Nueva España y Tierra Firme (N.p.: n.d. [c. 1615]), 1-6; quoted in Israel, Diasporas Within a Diaspora, 102; see also Israel's essay in the same volume, "Buenos Aires, Tucumán and the River Plate Route: Portuguese Conversos and the 'Commercial Subversion' of the Spanish Indies (1580-1640)," 125-50.
123. Letter of 16 May 1636, printed in Medina, Historia del Tribunal de Lima, 2:46.
124. Israel, Diasporas Within a Diaspora, 225, 272.
125. Juan de Solózano Pereira, Política indiana (1647), in Biblioteca de autores españoles, vols. 252-56 (Madrid, 1972), bk. 1, vol. 2:262.
126. See, for example, a letter to this effect from the governor of Chile to the king (cited in Raúl A. Molina, "El Primer banquero de Buenos Aires: Jerarquia alcanzada por su descendencia: Diego de Vega," Revista de Historia Americana y Argentina 2 (1961): 61).
127. The last reprinted in Ventura, Portugueses no Peru, 3:25-77. Medina prints a 1611 letter from the Lima tribunal urging quick and severe action against Portuguese of the Hebrew nation (Inquisición de Cartagena, 341-2).
128. Hanke, "Portuguese in Spanish America," 22; his translation.
129. Bowser, African Slave in Peru, 341, offers a different explanation.
130. Hordes, End of the Earth, 51; Israel, Race, Class and Politics in Colonial Mexico, 210-16. It should be recalled that the Spanish Crown was fighting other rebellions that burst out in 1640, when Catalonians rose up and allied themselves with France and various nobles attempted a secessionist plot in Andalucía. Furthermore, Portuguese had been very active in the major Mexico City uprising of 1624, in part out of frustration with the antagonistic stance of the viceroy Diego Carrillo Mendoza y Pimentel (Israel, Race, Class and Politics in Colonial Mexico, 123, 135-60).
131. Ferry, "Don't Drink the Chocolate." Jonathan Israel provides similarly high percentages in his tally of those tried between 1620 and 1650 but suggests that 150 individuals were arrested between 1642 and 1646 on charges of judaizing (Israel, Race, Class and Politics in Colonial Mexico, 125-6, 130).
132. AGI Mex. 1067, lib. 12, fol. 135-137v, in my translation; cited in Hordes, End of the Earth, 51. Hence an Inquisition document of December 1643 tallies the number of slaves who had belonged to the arrested crypto-Jews, a total of 53 (AHN Inq. 1737, exp. 1, leg. 3, fols. 79r-82v; cited in Ferry, "Don't Drink the Chocolate," n. 11), hardly an immense number.
133. AHN Inq. 1601/3/8, fol. 72v.; Rotbaum, Documentos, 351.
134. Green, "Masters of Difference," 231, n. 305.

Chapter 7

1. Seymour B. Liebman, The Enlightened: The Writings of Luis de Carvajal, el Mozo (Coral Gables, FL: University of Miami Press, [1967]), 144; Liebman cites AGN, Inquisición, tomo 560 (1652), Expediente 21.
2. Cited in Tejado Fernandez, Vida social en Cartagena, 151.

3. At least he was called a Mulato in an Inquisition document, which I have not yet examined directly. Peter Mark and José da Silva Horta, The Forgotten Diaspora: Jewish Communities in West Africa and the Making of the Atlantic World (New York: Cambridge University Press, 2011), 187, 211.
4. Jonathan Schorsch, Jews and Blacks in the Early Modern World (New York: Cambridge University Press, 2004), 196, 201.
5. I. S. Revah, "Pour l'Histoire des Nouveaux-Chretiens Portugais: La Relation Généalogique d'I. de M. Aboab," Boletim Internacional de Bibliografia Luso-Brasileira 2,2 (April-June 1961): 299.
6. Mary Louise Pratt, Imperial Eyes: Travel Writing and Transculturation (London/New York: Routledge, 1992), 97.
7. Abraham-van der Mark, "Marriage and Concubinage among the Sephardic Merchant Elite of Curaçao," 43.
8. Suzana Maria de Souza Santos, "Uma família cristã-nova portuguesa na Bahia Setecentista," Lina Gorenstein and Maria Luiza Tucci Carneiro (eds.), Ensaios sobre a Intolerância: Inquisição, Marranismo e Anti-semitismo (São Paulo: Humanitas/FFLCH/USP, 2002), 155.
9. See Mark and Silva Horta, Forgotten Diaspora; Schorsch, Jews and Blacks.
10. Testimony of 9 August 1646; AGN Mexico, Inq. 393/12/3, fols. 289r.-v.
11. José María Montero de Espinosa, Relación histórica de la judería de Sevilla, establecimiento de la inquisición en ella, su estinción, y colección de los autos que llamaban de fé celebrados desde su erección (Sevilla: D. Juan J. Franco, 1849), 71. Montero de Espinosa does not identify his sources, but it would appear that he quotes from the published and unpublished Relaciones concerning the various autos de fe held in Seville.
12. Montero de Espinosa, Relación histórica de la judería de Sevilla, 91-2. This is probably the same unnamed Berber Mulato cited by Manuel Barrios, El tribunal de la inquisición en Andalucía: Selección de textos y documentos (Sevilla: Editorial Castillejo, 1991), 79, from the unidentified La Inquisición en memorias de cosas sucedidas en Sevilla. Notice about Domingo Vicente is surprisingly absent from Antonio Domínguez Ortiz's supposedly thorough account of the Sevillan Inquisition's autos of the seventeenth century (Autos de la inquisición de Sevilla [Siglo XVII] [Seville: Servicio de Publicaciones del Ayuntamiento de Sevilla, 1981]), despite the fact that he admits relying for certain points on Montero de Espinosa, whom he nonetheless criticizes for being disorderly and unscientific (14).
13. "Copia de la relación de causas del año de 1654 desde 27 de Abril, que fue con los galeones del cargo del Marqués de Monte Alegre, hasta Junio de 1655," AHN Inq. 1021, fols. 404r.-405r.; Splendiani, Tribunal de Cartagena, 3:405-6. Splendiani calls this "the first case of a black accused of judaizing" by the tribunal. I was not able to determine if any records from Páez's trial remain extant.
14. Medina, Inquisición de Cartagena, 292.
15. Saraiva, Marrano Factory, 76-7; Salomon, Portrait of a New Christian, 24-5; Azevedo, Cristãos-novos, 137. Various versions of the episode were published. I am following the reconstruction by Saraiva and Salomon. Saraiva describes other cases of "perjurers" who denounced Old Christians, seemingly with the intention of undermining Inquisition "justice," but at the least in order to wreak vengeance on members of the class persecuting New Christians. Irene Silverblatt discusses a similar episode from 1630s Lima, supposedly orchestrated by a New Christian named Antonio de Acuna, who allegedly advised others to give false testimony against Old Christians in order to show that the inquisitors operated according to ethnic stereotypes rather than real evidence (Modern Inquisitions, 42-3).
16. Costigan, Through Cracks in the Wall, 101.
17. Quoted in Egon and Frieda Wolff, Judeus, judaizantes e seus escravos (Rio de Janeiro: Egon and Frieda Wolff, 1987), 36.
18. Wiznitzer, who cites this material, has in one place "a mulatto Jew, the son of Salim" (Jews in Colonial Brazil, 60) and in another "son of the Jew Solis" (ibid., 150). Only the latter accords with the transcribed trial record ("Processo de Manoel de Moraes, sacerdote e theologo, natural da villa de S. Paulo, estado do Brazil, residente que foi nas partes do norte, preso nos carceres da inquisição de Lisbôa [1647]," Revista do Instituto Historico e Geographico Braziliero [Rio de Janeiro], 70,1 [1908]: 25).
19. "Processo de Manoel de Moraes," 25. I was not able to track down information on the others denounced.
20. Wiznitzer, Jews in Colonial Brazil, 150.
21. Dutra, "Manuel Gonçalves Doria," 98, 105-6. Doria was being rewarded with knighthood for his exploits in helping fight off the Dutch attacks on Bahia in 1624-5.
22. Alberro, "Negros y mulatos en los documentos inquisitoriales," 144.

23. Cited in Alberro, "Negros y mulatos en los documentos inquisitoriales," 144.
24. See, for some examples from sixteenth-century Aragón, Padilla, *Relación judeoconversa*, 15; from Spain, Graizbord, "Conformity and Dissidence among Judeoconversos," 311; from sixteenth-century Portugal, Lipiner, *Sapateiro de Trancoso*, 267.
25. Early 1640s; AGN Mexico, Inq. 403, exp. 1, leg. 2, fol. 364r. Indeed, the scribe or one of the inquisitors underlined the last statement as if to call attention to its heretical character.
26. Charges against Maria de Rivera, 1642; AGN Mexico, Inq. 403, exp. 3, fol. 379r.
27. Salomon, "Spanish Marranism Re-examined," 117.
28. Beatriz Enriquez related that Margarita de Rivera told her that Sobremonte "knew many prayers of the Law of Moses and that hearing, she was left with her mouth open, because he was very learned in the matters of the Law" (testimony of Beatriz Enriquez, 7 January 1645; AGN Mexico, Inq. 393/12/3, fol. 270v.).
29. Cited in Alberro, "Negros y mulatos en los documentos inquisitoriales," 146.
30. See *Auto General de la Fee* [...]*Celebrado En la Plaça mayor de la muy noble, y muy leal ciudad de Mexico, à los 19. de Noviembre de 1659. años* (Mexico: La Imprenta del Secreto del Santo Officio, n.d.), s.v. Maria de la Cruz.
31. Cited in Jaffary, *False Mystics*, 33.
32. From the summary regarding Pedro de Mercado, in Bocanegra, *Auto general de la fee celebrada*, unpag.
33. Basing himself largely on Alberro, José Piedra has likewise found that most of "the self-accusations [of prominent black citizens of New Spain] are of being Jewish, and it remains difficult to separate fact from fiction, particularly because many blacks enjoyed a symbiotic cultural relationship with Jews" (José Piedra, "Literary Whiteness and the Afro-Hispanic Difference," in Dominick LaCapra [ed.], *The Bounds of Race: Perspectives on Hegemony and Resistance* [Ithaca Cornell University Press, 1991], 286, n. 14). Ironically, Piedra erases the negative side of this "symbiosis," ignoring the cases Alberro brings which show Afroiberians adopting the anti-Jewish prejudices of their new religion and society (a few cited in previous chapters).
34. Mello, *Gente da nação*, 25.
35. Kathryn L. Morgan, *Children of Strangers: The Stories of a Black Family* (Philadelphia: Temple University Press, 1980), 102-103.
36. Cited in Gracia Boix, *Autos de fe y causas de la inquisición de Córdoba*, 160.
37. Quoted in Gracia Boix, *Autos de fe y causas de la inquisición de Córdoba*, 83.
38. Sweet, *Recreating Africa*, 89.
39. Quoted in Villa-Flores, "Blasphemy and Slavery in New Spain," 436.
40. Quoted in Jaffary, *False Mystics*, 33. Needless to say, the inquisitors suspected Núñez of crypto-Judaism.
41. She is called *atesada*, meaning "double black" or "jet black."
42. Quoted in Gracia Boix, *Autos de fe y causas de la Inquisición de Córdoba*, 359.
43. Cited in Pullan, *Jews of Europe and the Inquisition of Venice*, 74-75, from Archivio di Stato, Venice, Santo Uffizio, b. 44, proc. Samuel Maestro, 30 April to 6 Aug. 1579. Testimony given to the Lisbon Inquisition by a visitor to Amsterdam records a 1611 encounter with Diogo Dias Querido, a prominent trader whose career had moved between Brazil, Amsterdam and the West African coast. The visitor met Querido at the synagogue: "there were three blacks at the door of the synagogue, making a great fuss because the Jews had perverted (sic) one of their black friends and turned him into a Jew" (Green, "Masters of Difference," 190). On Querido, see Schorsch, *Jews and Blacks*, 93; Green, "Masters of Difference," 189-91). What remains unclear from this testimony is whether the fuss is positive or negative, though it is probable that the understanding that the Black's conversion was a perversion belonged to the denouncer.
44. Sandoval, *Tratado sobre esclavitud*, 397; cited in Margaret M. Olsen, *Slavery and Salvation in Colonial Cartagena de Indias* (Gainesville: University Press of Florida, 2004), 111. See also Olsen's sensitive parsing of a passage in Sandoval's *De instauranda Aethiopum*, in which an African priest who converted to Christianity explains to a Muslim that Whites are free and Blacks enslaved because God created Whites first and sent those created last to serve their elders/betters (Olsen, *Slavery and Salvation*, 129-30).
45. Masarah van Eyck kindly informed me of this quotation; *The Jesuit Relations and Allied Documents: Travels and Explorations of the Jesuit Missionaries in New France, 1610-1791*, the original French, Latin, and Italian texts, with English translations and notes, ed. Reuben Gold Thwaites, 73 vols. in 36 (New York: Pageant Book Co., 1959), 5:63.
46. Cited in Boxer, *The Church Militant*, 36. These sentiments were not limited to the Iberian Catholic sphere. Perhaps the best indication that the valences involved in such distinctions contained

*meta*physical import is the revealing title of a mid-seventeenth-century English translation of a conversionary tract aimed at Jews by the formerly Jewish "Samuel of Morocco:" Thomas Calvert, *The Blessed Jew of Marocco: or, A Blackmoor Made White Being a Demonstration of the True Messias out of the Law and Prophets by Rabbi Samuel* (York: Thomas Broad, 1649). In this case, Jews are themselves seen as non-White; see Schorsch, *Jews and Blacks*, chs. 7 and 8.

47. For a view from other places and era, see Gauri Viswanathan, *Outside the Fold: Conversion, Modernity, and Belief* (Princeton: Princeton University Press, 1998); Van der Veer, *Conversion to Modernities*.

48. The accused and members of her family appear under the year 1647 in the *Relación de los Reos que este Tribunal del Santo Oficio de la Iquisición de México ha Penitenciado y castigado, con otros, por la observancia de la ley de Moisén, en dos autos de fe que han celebrado; y bien desterrados perpetuamente de estos reinos y provincias [...] con testimonio de sus sentencias, edades y señas exteriores para presentarse con dichos testimonios en el Tribunal del Santo Oficio de la dicha ciudad de Sevilla* [...], (1647; reproduced in Genaro García, *Documentos ineditos o muy raros para la historia de Mexico*, 3rd ed. (Mexico City: Editorial Porrúa, 1982), 70-74), as well as in the *Relacion sumeria del auto particular de fee, que el trbunal del santo officio de la Inquisicion de los Reyes, y Provincias de la Nueva España, celebro en la muy noble, y muy leal Ciudad de Mexico a los diez y seis dias del mes de Abril, del año de mil y seiscientos y quarenta y seis* (1646; García, *Documentos*, 137-177). In the latter, we are informed that Juan Bautista had been a sculptor and assembly worker (escultor y ensamblador; García, *Documentos*, 155). Esperanza's age is given there as seventy four.

49. García, *Documentos*, 70-74. The youngest daughter's description: "María Rodríguez del Bosque, mulata, white, single, [...] born in Guadalajara [...] age 20, tall, fat, black eyes, of good appearance." Isabel: "mulata, white, single, born and resident in Mexico City, [...] age 25, thin, good body, and black eyes." Juana: "mulata, white, married to Blas López, Portuguese, observer of the law of Moses, fugitive many years, born in the city of Cartagena of the Indies, and resident of Mexico City, [...] age 29, of good body and appearance, round-faced, somewhat fat." Blas López is listed as a tailor and assembly worker (ibid., 160).

50. Alberro, "Negros y mulatos en los documentos inquisitoriales," 156. More information and general background regarding this extended clan of supposed marranos can be found in Wiznitzer, "Crypto-Jews in Mexico During the Seventeenth Century"; Nathan Wachtel, "Marrano Religiosity in Hispanic America in the Seventeenth Century," Paolo Bernardini and Norman Fiering (eds.), *The Jews and the Expansion of Europe to the West, 1450 to 1800* (New York: Berghahn Books, 2001), 149-71; Solange Alberro, "La familia conversa novohispana: Familia hispana," Pilar Gonzalbo Aizpuru (ed.), *Familias novohispanas, siglos XVI al XIX*, Seminario de historia de la familia, Centro de Estudios Históricos (Mexico City: Colegio de Mexico, 1991), 227-42; and idem, "Crypto-Jews and the Mexican Holy Office in the Seventeenth Century," Bernardini and Fiering (eds.), *Jews and the Expansion of Europe*, 172-85. Excerpts from the trial of Blanca Mendez de Rivera, a member of the extended clan, is reprinted in Richard L. Kagan and Abigail Dyer (ed. and trans.), *Inquisitorial Inquiries: Brief Lives of Secret Jews and Other Heretics* (Baltimore: Johns Hopkins University Press, 2004), ch. 7.

51. Testimony of Esperanza Rodríguez, 7 August 1642; AGN Mexico, Inq. 408, exp. 2, leg. 1, fol. 458r.

52. Testimony of Beatriz Enriquez, a cousin of the Catalina Enriquez who was Rodríguez's mistress, 19 September 1642; AGN Mexico, Inq. 393/12/3, fol. 222v.

53. Testimony of 7 August 1642; AGN Mexico, Inq. 408, exp. 2, leg. 1, fol. 458r.

54. Testimony of 7 August 1642; AGN Mexico, Inq. 408, exp. 2, leg. 1, fols. 458r., 469r. and elsewhere. "[L]ibre y antes esclava de doña catalina Enríquez, reclusa en este Santo Oficio por judaizante; e hija de Isabel, negra de Guinea, que murió en Sevilla, y de Francisco Rodríguez, hebreo, cristiano nuevo; de oficio y ocupación costurera" (García, *Documentos*, 155).

55. Response to the charges against her, AGN Mexico, Inq. 419, exp. 6, fol. 107v.

56. AGN Mexico, Inq. 393, exp. 12, leg. 3, fol. 68r.

57. Testimony of 18 July 1642; AGN Mexico, Inq. 408, exp. 2, leg. 1, fol. 410r.; testimony of 18 November 1642; ibid., fol. 411r.-v. Ysavel de Silva also deposes that Rodríguez had grown up with Blanca Enriquez (testimony of 25 June 1643, ibid., 415, exp. 6, fol. 519r). In a depositions of her own, Rodríguez confirms having grown up in Seville with both Blanca de Rivera and Blanca Enriquez (testimony of 21 April 1643; ibid., fols. 357v.-468r.) and that she knew Blanca de Rivera "very well" in Seville, along with her oldest daughter Maria, who was then very little (response to the charges against her, ibid., 419, exp. 6, fol. 72r.). Indeed, Rodríguez, in her response to the charges against her, seems to say that Blanca and Margarita de Rivera are relatives of her former

mistress, Catalina Enriquez in Veracruz, but that that Catalina and Margarita, at least, had a falling out (ibid. 419, exp. 6, fol. 106v.-107r.).
58. Testimony of Esperanza Rodríguez, 7 August 1642; AGN Mexico, Inq. 408, exp. 2, leg. 1, fol. 458r.; Bocanegra, *Auto general*.
59. Testimony of Esperanza Rodríguez, 30 January 1643; AGN Mexico, Inq. 408, exp. 2, leg. 1, fol. 465v.
60. Ignacio Camacho Martínez, *La Hermandad de los mulatos de Sevilla: Antecedentes históricos de la Hermandad del Calvario* (Seville: Área de Cultura del Ayuntamiento de Sevilla, 1998), 53.
61. Testimony of Esperanza Rodríguez, 21 April 1643; AGN Mexico, Inq. 408, exp. 2, leg. 1, fol. 469r.
62. Testimony of 21 April 1643; AGN Mexico, Inq. 408, exp. 2, leg. 1, fol. 467r.
63. Testimony of Esperanza Rodríguez, 21 April 1643; AGN Mexico, Inq. 408, exp. 2, leg. 1, fol. 470v. Geronima's mother had been a Mexican mestiza who married Henrique de Miranda, whom Esperanza knew from Seville as well as from Cartagena.
64. Albert A. Sicroff, "Clandestine Judaism in the Hieronymite Monastery of Nuestra Señora de Guadalupe," *Studies in Honor of M. J. Benardete* (New York: Las Américas Publishing Co., 1965), 89-125; Ingram, "Secret Lives, Public Lies," 68-69; Marie-Theresa Hernández, *The Virgin of Guadalupe and the Conversos: Uncovering Hidden Influences from Spain to Mexico* (New Brunswick, NJ: Rutgers University Press, 2014), ch. 2.
65. Testimony of Esperanza Rodríguez, 7 August 1642; AGN Mexico, Inq. 408, exp. 2, leg. 1, fol. 459v.
66. Testimony of Esperanza Rodríguez, 7 August 1642; AGN Mexico, Inq. 408, exp. 2, leg. 1, fol. 458v. It could be that Rodríguez is getting the dating muddled. She says she and her mistress arrived in Cartagena in 1602, where they stayed only about "fifteen or twenty days," before sailing for Havana. Arriving there, she married Del Bosque "within eight days" (ibid., fols. 459v.-460r.).
67. Testimony of Esperanza Rodríguez, 7 August 1642; AGN Mexico, Inq. 408, exp. 2, leg. 1, fol. 460v.-r. Ysavel de Silva testifies to having been aware that Blanca Enriquez maintained contact with Rodríguez during the latter's time in Guadalajara (testimony of 25 June 1643, ibid., 415, exp. 6, fol. 519r.).
68. Testimony of Esperanza Rodríguez, 7 August 1642; AGN Mexico, Inq. 408, exp. 2, leg. 1, fols. 458v., 460v.
69. Testimony of Esperanza Rodríguez, 7 August 1642; AGN Mexico, Inq. 408, exp. 2, leg. 1, fol. 460v.
70. Joan Bristol, Unpublished paper, "Moving through Community: Examining the Travels of Esperanza Rodriguez in Seventeenth-Century Mexico," presented at the Society for the Study of American Women Writers, Denver, November 2018, 3. I thank the author for sharing her work with me.
71. Testimony of 25 June 1643; AGN Mexico, Inq. 415, exp. 6, fol. 519v. As had Blanca (see below).
72. I have not yet been able to verify any trials in the extant documentation of the Seville Inquisition.
73. Testimony of Antonio Lopez de Orduña, 1 September 1642; AGN Mexico, Inq. 393, exp. 12, leg. 3, fol. 176v.
74. Testimony of Gaspar Vaez Sevilla, 13 February 1644; AGN Mexico, Inq. 393, exp. 12, leg. 3, fol. 111v.
75. Testimony of Beatriz Enriquez, 24 July 1642; AGN Mexico, Inq. 393, exp. 12, leg. 3, fol. 211r.
76. AGN Mexico, Inq. 393, exp. 12, leg. 3, fol. 192r.
77. Testimony of 27 May 1643; AGN Mexico, Inq. 393, exp. 12, leg. 3, fols. 132r.-v. Pedro was the son of Catalina Enriquez and Diego Tinoco. The latter had lived openly as a Jew in some non-Spanish territory (AGN Mexico, Inq. 410, exp. 4, leg. 5, fols. 524v.) or was born in such a place (according to Margarita de Rivera; testimony of 8 July 1642; ibid., fol. 527v.). Catalina testifies that Diego was circumcised (testimony of 9 November 1643; ibid., fol. 527r.). Somehow, Catalina and Margarita de Rivera knew of his being circumcised, though Catalina is not sure whether this was told to her directly (by Catalina Enriquez?) or to her mother Blanca (testimony of Catalina de Rivera, 30 June 1642, ibid., fol. 528r.; testimony of Margarita de Rivera, 8 July 1642, ibid., fol. 527v.).
78. Testimony of Beatriz Enriquez, 14 November 1642; AGN Mexico, Inq. 393/12/3, fol. 243r.-244r.
79. Testimony of 17 February 1644; AGN Mexico, Inq. 393, exp. 12, leg. 3, fol. 117v. Ysavel de Silva says that one year the Fast of the Great Day was held in Blanca's home as "she was alone and had no black woman in the house because they had left" (testimony of 30 June; ibid 402, exp. 1, leg. 2, fol. 89r.).
80. Ferry, "Don't Drink the Chocolate," n. 16.

81. Testimony of 28 May 1643; AGN Mexico, Inq. 393, exp. 12, leg. 3, fol. 148v.-149v. Describing her first "fast of the great day" under the tutelage of her mother Blanca, Juana Enriquez says that they "ate the supper of vespers of the said fast / çenaron la bispera del dho ayuno" (testimony of 13 October 1642, ibid., fol. 183v.), using the Christian term for marking sacred hours and prayer services. She is describing the meal before the fast, rather than following it. Beatriz, her sister, uses the same language (testimony of 24 July 1642; ibid., fol. 210v.).
82. Testimony of 6 June 1643; AGN Mexico, Inq. 393, exp. 12, leg. 3, fols. 139r.-v. This was the parental blessing of the child, which traditionally invokes Joseph's sons, Ephraim and Menasseh, for boys and Sarah, Rebecca, Rachel and Leah for girls. Catalina Enriquez, Pedro's mother, describes the scene identically, with one difference (Testimony of 28 May 1643; ibid., fol. 149r.): each went one by one before Blanca to receive her blessing. Again, this occurred on the festival eve. Beatriz Enriquez says that they went in order of age and that it was the blessing "that Jacob gave to his grandchildren and sons" (testimony of 14 November 1642; ibid., fol. 238v.).
83. Testimony of 14 November 1642; AGN Mexico, Inq. 393/12/3, fol. 238v.
84. Charge by an anonymous witness read to Gaspar Vaez Sevilla, 16 February 1644, and confirmed by him the following day; AGN Mexico, Inq. 393, exp. 12, leg. 3, fols. 113r.-v., 117r.-v. On Esther, Purim and the fast dedicated to her, see Gitlitz, *Secrecy and Deceit*, 116-17, 377-79, 470.
85. Testimony of 23 July 1642; AGN Mexico, Inq. 393, exp. 12, leg. 3, fol. 142r.
86. AGN Mexico, Inq. 393, exp. 12, leg. 3, fols. 78v.-79r.
87. Testimony of 14 November 1642; AGN Mexico, Inq. 393/12/3, fols. 237r.-v. At one supper that took place on *quaresma*, according to Rodríguez, the food that remained "was given out to the black serving women and girls" (response to the witnesses, 15 September 1644, ibid., 419, exp. 6, fol. 112v.).
88. Testimony of Violante Xuarez, 27 November 1642; AGN Mexico, Inq. 393, exp. 12, leg. 3, fol.172r.-v.; and see the testimony of Beatriz Enriquez, 3 September 1643; ibid., fol. 253r.-v.
89. AGN Mexico, Inq. 393, exp. 12, leg. 3, fol. 193r.
90. Charges against Esperanza Rodríguez, AGN Mexico, Inq. 419, exp. 6, fol. 59v. The inquisitors characterize this as a "ceremony used by the Jews with their deceased." There is a kabbalistic healing ceremony in which one or two birds are placed on the body of the sufferer in order to draw out the illness. Despite inquiries, I was not able to obtain concrete sources on this quasi-magical operation.
91. Charge by an anonymous witness read to Gaspar Vaez Sevilla and confirmed by him, 16 February 1644; AGN Mexico, Inq. 393, exp. 12, leg. 3, fol. 113r.
92. *Shulkhan Arukh*, Yoreh De'ah, sec. 378:9.
93. Testimony of 28 May 1643; AGN Mexico, Inq. 393, exp. 12, leg. 3, fol. 135r.; testimony of Catalina Enriquez, 28 May 1643; ibid., fol. 150r.
94. Testimony of Antonio Lopez de Orduña, 1 September 1642; AGN Mexico, Inq. 393, exp. 12, leg. 3, fol.177r. Below we hear of a gathering on the third day after a death in order to fast. It could be that the supper occurred at the end of the fast. The prominence of marking the third day of a death derives from Christianity, which marked the day with a special mass for the deceased. This day commemorated the three days which Jesus passed in the sepulcher and as a prefiguration of the resurrection there is a special prescription in the Apostolic Constitutions (VIII, xlii): "With respect to the dead, let the third day be celebrated in psalms, lessons, and prayers, because of him who on the third day rose again" (*The Catholic Encyclopedia* [New York: Robert Appleton Company, 1911], s.v. Masses of Requiem). Eating fish on the third day might hearken to the broiled fish that the astonished disciples gave to the resurrected Jesus, who had asked for meat (Luke 24:41-43). Ysabel de Rivera speaks of a fast carried out on the seventh day after the death of her sister Blanca's husband, various Enriquez sisters being present (AGN Mexico, Inq. 402, exp. 1, leg. 2, fol. 28v.). Blanca de Rivera testifies that it is a custom of observers of the Law of Moses to eat a fish supper on the ninth day after the death of a relative, as was done after the death of her spouse, with Blanca Enriquez and her daughters in attendance (ibid., fol. 35r.). In medieval Catholicism, the novena or ninth day of mourning was marked with special significance.
95. Testimony of 14 November 1642; AGN Mexico, Inq. 393/12/3, fol. 241v.; see also Gitlitz, *Secrecy and Deceit*, 293. Esperanza Rodríguez also knows this name (testimony of 21 April 1643; ibid., 408, exp. 2, leg. 1, fol. 472r.). I thank Maynard P. Maidman for suggesting the *avelut* connection and thereby extricating me from my perplexity about *ave luz*. Wiznitzer, "Crypto-Jews in Mexico During the Seventeenth Century," 1:153, comes to the same conclusion.
96. Testimony of 23 May 1643; AGN Mexico, Inq. 393, exp. 12, leg. 3, fol. 131r. For a time, Pedro lived with his grandmother (testimony of Catalina Enriquez, 3 August 1643, ibid., fol. 153v.).

97. Testimony of 9 September 1642, AGN Mexico, Inq. 393, exp. 12, leg. 3, fol. 167v.-168r. Ysavel de Silva asserts that Catalina Enríquez, her sisters and their daughters are not only Jewesses but witches (*hechizeras*), using drinks and other means to bewitch men (*atontarles*, that is, to turn them into fools), cause them to hallucinate or make them attracted to the spell-casting woman. Catalina supposedly carried a bag (*bolsa*) containing the tooth and navel of an infant, some powders, and two *raysitas* (I cannot figure out what this last item might be) called feminine and masculine, the latter bearing some colored hairs. A slave of Rafaela Enríquez allegedly told Ysavel de Silva that when her mistress was going to sleep with a man (not her husband) she placed two vanilla beans under the pillows. These comprise typical elements of romantic magic (testimony from 1646; AGN Mexico, Inq. 393, exp. 12, leg. 3, 99r.-100r.). Carrying a *bolsa* with magical powers, containing "any number of substances, including folded pieces of paper with Christian orations written on them, rocks, sticks, roots, bones, hairs, animal skins, feathers, powders, consecrated particles, and so on," comprised both an African and an old European practice. A *bolsa* might protect its wearer from harm, assure luck, help slaves escape or relieve suffering (Sweet, *Recreating Africa*, 179-81).
98. Testimony of Beatriz Enríquez, 24 July 1642; AGN Mexico, Inq. 393, exp. 12, leg. 3, fol. 209v.; 24 October 1642, ibid., fol. 225v.
99. Ibid., fol. 210r.
100. Testimony of 6 July 1643; AGN Mexico, Inq. 402, exp. 1, leg. 2, fol. 102r.
101. On the messianic expectations of this extended clan see Wachtel, "Marrano Religiosity in Hispanic America in the Seventeenth Century," 161-64.
102. AGN Mexico, Inq. 393, exp. 12, leg. 3, fol. 68r.
103. Testimony of 30 July 1642, AGN Mexico, Inq. 393, exp. 12, leg. 3, fol. 156r.; ibid., 408, exp. 2, leg. 1, fols. 432v.-433r.
104. Testimony of 28 May 1642; AGN Mexico, Inq. 408, exp. 2, leg. 1, fol. 406v.
105. Blanca de Rivera knew Lopez, who was deceased by the time of her deposition. Testimony of 18 July 1642; AGN Mexico, Inq. 408, exp. 2, leg. 1, fol. 410r.-v.; testimony of 18 November 1642; ibid., fol. 411r.-v.
106. Testimony of 18 July 1642; AGN Mexico, Inq. 408, exp. 2, leg. 1, fols. 425v.-426r.
107. Testimony of 25 June 1643, AGN Mexico, Inq. 415, exp. 6, fol. 519r. Elsewhere Silva testifies that Blanca Enriquez had been imprisoned, along with the slave Isabel, by the Seville tribunal "for six or eight months. And that all that the inquisitors said was that they should tell the truth and that [Blanca] had said to [Ysavel de Silva] as well that from the beginning to the end she had defied [the truth, i.e., denied all allegations]. And that they had put her to the torture, and she signified the arms on which they had given it to her, with signs that this confessant saw. And how much better was it to suffer that than to lose honor and estate." Others also had seen Blanca's scars, such as Blanca Méndez de Rivera and Isabel Duarte (*Inquisitorial Inquiries: Brief Lives of Secret Jews and Other Heretics*, ed. and trans. Richard L. Kagan and Abigail Dyer [Baltimore: Johns Hopkins University Press, 2004], 162, n. 27, 163). According to the summary of the 11 April 1649 *auto* by Bocanegra, Ynes Lopez was sentenced as a judaizer by the Seville tribunal, but earned reconciliation (Bocanegra, *Auto general de la fee celebrada*, unpag.).
108. AGN Mexico, Inq. 419, exp. 6, fol. 118r.
109. AGN Mexico, Inq. 419, exp. 6, fol. 108r.
110. Testimony of 7 August 1642; AGN Mexico, Inq. 408, exp. 2, leg. 1, fol. 458r.
111. Testimony of 30 January 1643; AGN Mexico, Inq. 408, exp. 1, leg. 1, fol. 464v.-465r. The underline was made by the inquisitorial scribe. In her response to the charges against her, Rodríguez says all this happened when she was "eight or ten" (ibid., 419, exp. 6, fol. 72r.).
112. Testimony of 30 January 1643; AGN Mexico, Inq. 408, exp. 2, leg. 1, fol. 465v.
113. Testimony of 24 September 1644, AGN Mexico, Inq. 419, exp. 6, fol. 113v.-114r. Note that if Rodríguez's mother Isabel indeed knew something of crypto-Judaism, it is not she who is credited — or blamed — for transmitting it to her daughter.
114. "Enseñó à muchas personas de su pare*tela, y estrañas la ley de Moysen, y à Esperança Rodríguez mulata su esclava ofreciandola la libertad, y ayunado con todos ellos, y otras personas, lo qual calló en su causa, y se le probó, conque murió en los mesmos delictos, è impenitente. Salió su Estatua al Auto, con vn Sãbenito, y Coroza de cõdenada con vn letrero de su nombre [....]" (Bocanegra, *Auto general de la fee celebrada*, unpag.).
115. Bocanegra, *Auto general de la fee celebrada*, unpag. Catalina's husband, Pedro Arias Maldonado was also sentenced in absentia at this *auto*.
116. Charges against Esperanza Rodríguez, AGN Mexico, Inq. 419, exp. 6, fol. 62r.
117. Testimony of 18 November 1642; AGN Mexico, Inq. 408, exp. 2, leg. 1, fol. 413r.-v.

Notes to Chapter 7   277

118. Testimony of 1 September 1642; AGN Mexico, Inq. 408, exp. 2, leg. 1, fol. 451v.
119. Testimony of 24 October 1642; AGN Mexico, Inq. 408, exp. 2, leg. 1, fol. 421r.
120. Testimony of 19 January 1645; AGN Mexico, Inq. 393/12/3, fol. 278r.; 7 November 1642; ibid., fol. 235v.
121. Testimony of Pedro de Espinosa, 18 November 1642; AGN Mexico, Inq. 408, exp. 2, leg. 1, fol. 414v.
122. Testimony of 23 February 1643; AGN Mexico, Inq. 393, exp. 12, leg. 3, fol. 185r.
123. Testimony of Catalina Enriquez, 22 June 1643; AGN Mexico, Inq. 393, exp. 12, leg. 3, fol. 152v.; ibid., 408, exp. 2, leg. 1, fol. 423r.
124. Testimony of Catalina Enriquez, 28 May 1643; AGN Mexico, Inq. 393/12/3, fol. 149v.; elsewhere given as testimony of 18 May 1643; ibid., 408, exp. 2, leg. 1, fol. 421v.
125. AGN Mexico, Inq. 393/12/3, fols. 80v., 149v., 294v. Intriguing differences accompany the question of who washed the body of Blanca Enriquez. Her daughter Beatriz says that it was Blanca de Rivera and Rodríguez who were supposed to do so (testimony of 19 September 1647; ibid., fol. 294v.). Raphaela Enriquez says that it was Blanca de Rivera, some of Blanca's daughters and Rodríguez (response to charges, 28 September 1647; ibid., 402, exp. 1, leg. 2, fol. 343r.). Also involved in preparing Blanca's corpse was Maria Baptista, the "mestiça of the said house," as well as a Black slave woman of Rafaela Enriquez named Sicilia (only mentioned in the testimony of Antonio Lopez de Orduña, ibid., 393/12/3, fol. 177v.; and in the testimony of Maria Baptista, ibid., fol. 192v.). It seems from Maria Baptista's deposition that it was she, Rodríguez and the slave Sicilia who actually washed the body (ibid., 193r.). As in other similar cases, it is unclear whether such arrangements reflect sentiments of intimacy, convenience or necessity. Like Blanca (and Rodríguez, for that matter), Maria Baptista was an older woman, aged fifty in 1643 (testimony of Maria Bautista, March 1643; ibid., fol. 191r.). Beatriz Enriquez testifies that before she died Blanca took from her desk an agnus dei to give to Maria, something that seems to greatly upset one of Blanca's daughters, who ran out of the room. It is not clear if Beatriz is describing her own reaction or that of one of her sisters nor whether the reaction stems from a feeling that this gift is too good for Maria Bautista (and should have gone to one of the daughters) or from sadness over Blanca's impending death (testimony of 29 October 1642; ibid., fol. 234r.-v.). It should be noted that Ysavel de Silva claims that when Blanca Enriquez was at the moment of death, she, all her daughters and Ysavel Tinoco threw out the two women who were present who were not observers of the Law of Moses, one of whom was Maria Baptista (testimony of 30 June 1643; ibid., 402, exp. 1, fol. 90r.). Finally, Rodríguez testifies that she noticed that after Blanca's death, Maria Baptista was "very angry that they made her eat things fried in oil" rather than in lard (testimony of 21 April 1643; ibid., 408, exp. 2, leg. 1, fol. 473r.). Baptista later testifies before the Inquisition.
126. Testimony of 17 March 1643; AGN Mexico, Inq. 408, exp. 2, leg. 1, fol. 441v.; also mentioned in the testimony Ysavel de Rivera, 22 September 1642; ibid., fol. 429v. Rodríguez confirms that Juana sent to have this garment made five days before Blanca's death (testimony of 21 April 1643; ibid., fol. 472v.).
127. Testimony of Gaspar Vaez Sevilla, 13 February 1644; AGN Mexico, Inq. 393, exp. 12, leg. 3, fols. 110v.-111r.; testimony of Catalina Enriquez, 28 May 1643; ibid., fol. 150r. Though Blanca Enriquez is not named in Vaez Sevilla's testimony, it is clearly her funeral being described. Among other clues is the discussion of the burial of her body along with some of her teeth that had fallen out while she was alive, which someone reported the tribunal was going to investigate, to the point of disinterring the body, considering it a Jewish practice to make sure all body parts were properly buried (in order to be whole for the future resurrection of the dead). Her fallen teeth are mentioned by other witnesses who describe her death and the burial. Ysavel de Silva claims that Blanca "expressly ordered" that these teeth be buried with her (testimony of 30 June 1643; AGN Mexico, Inq. 415, exp. 6, fol. 521r.).
128. Testimony of Juana del Bosque, 15 September 1642; ibid., 408, exp. 2, leg. 1, fol. 403v.
129. Beginning with her testimony of 21 April 1643; AGN Mexico, Inq. 408, exp. 2, leg. 1, fol. 466v. and passim.
130. Testimony of 21 April 1643; AGN Mexico, Inq. 408, exp. 2, leg. 1, fols. 467v.-468r. All this was true as well with Blanca Enriquez's sister, Clara de Silva (ibid., fols. 468r.-v.).
131. Testimony of 21 April 1643; AGN Mexico, Inq. 408, exp. 2, leg. 1, fol. 469r.
132. Testimony of 21 April 1643; AGN Mexico, Inq. 408, exp. 2, leg. 1, fol. 468r. Is it possible that Juana Rodríguez was related to, was even the mother of Esperanza's father, Francisco Rodríguez?
133. Testimony of 21 April 1643; AGN Mexico, Inq. 408, exp. 2, leg. 1, fols. 467r., 466v. Rodríguez claims that when Margarita de Rivera married her cousin Miguel Nuñez de Huerta they didn't

even bother with the Christian wedding procedures, usually performed at some point just for appearances (ibid., fol. 467r.-v.).
134. Testimony of Esperanza Rodríguez, 21 April 1643; AGN Mexico, Inq. 408, exp. 2, leg. 1, fols. 471r.-472r.
135. Testimony of Esperanza Rodríguez, 21 April 1643; AGN Mexico, Inq. 408, exp. 2, leg. 1, fol. 470r. The constant maximalization of the character of the connections between Rodríguez and the others may point to a need on her part to assert her centrality, her firm standing within this White judaizing circle to her White inquisitors or to herself.
136. Testimony of 21 April 1643; AGN Mexico, Inq. 408, exp. 2, leg. 1, fol. 468r.
137. Cited in Lewin, *Singular proceso de Salomón Machorro*, 201-2. León/Machorro continues by saying that on another occasion Blanca Enríquez informed him that Rodríguez's daughter, Juana, whom he had never met, was also a secret Jew.
138. Alberro, *Inquisición y sociedad*, 436.
139. According to the Inquisition's scribe; deposition of Esperanza Rodríguez, 7 August 1642; AGN Mexico, Inq. 408, exp. 2, leg. 1, fol. 459v. After months in jail, when first moved to confess her sins/crimes, Rodríguez says that "satan [*el Demonio*] had blinded her," a phraseology perhaps more common to Afroiberians before the Inquisition than Judeoconversos (testimony of 30 January 1643; ibid., fol. 464r.).
140. AGN Mexico, Inq. 419, exp. 6, fol. 70r.
141. Publication of charges against Esperanza Rodríguez, AGN Mexico, Inq. 419, exp. 6, fols. 80v., 81v.; charges against Esperanza Rodríguez, ibid., fol. 60r.-v. In the latter document, the person/people on whose testimony these charges are based is/are not named. The trial record against Rodríguez is not complete, though some of the missing material appears in the documentation of other trials. In her response to the accusations against her, Rodríguez denies having said these things (ibid., fol. 70r.).
142. Response to the charges against her, AGN Mexico, Inq. 419, exp. 6, fol. 70r.
143. Charges against Esperanza Rodríguez, AGN Mexico, Inq. 419, exp. 6, fol. 60r.-v. In her response to the charges against her, Rodríguez confirms that she taught this prayer to her daughters, but that they recited it only when they fasted (ibid., fol. 70r.). A slightly differing version appears in the publication of charges against Rodríguez, ibid., fol. 81r.: "Con las armas de Adonai/andare armada/con la capa de Abrahan/andare cobijada/con la fe de Ysmael/en mi coraçon/por donde quiera q fuere/y viniese, buenos y malos encontrare/los buenos se me allegaiar/y los malos se me arredraran/que no temere vara de justicia/ni alcalde, ni familiar/que no me podra maleser/ni mal empecer/ni mas mal de lo que paso/Aman sobre Mardoqueo."
144. As rendered quite traditionally in a fifteenth-century Ladino siddur for women, God is asked "non me traygas [...] ni a lugar de menos precio," and "que me escapes [...] de desverʷuensamentos de façes y de desvergüensán façes, de ombre malo [...] de vesino malo, de encuentro malo [...] de ui io grave y de dueño de uicio duro, quier que es de mi ley quier que non se a de mi ley" (*Siddur Tefillot: A Woman's Ladino Prayer Book [Paris B.N., Esp. 668; 15th c.]*, A Critical Edition by Moshe Lazar [Lancaster, CA: Labyrinthos, 1995], 4).
145. Silverblatt, "Colonial Conspiracies," 262, 275, n. 12.
146. Lewis, *Hall of Mirrors*, 143.
147. Quoted in Castelló, *Francisco de la Cruz*, 1:46.
148. See Robert Ricard, "Otra contribución al estudio de las fiestas de 'moros y cristianos,'" *Miscelanea P. Rivet, Octogenario Dicata* (Mexico: Universidad Nacional, 1960), 2:871-79; Nicolás Cushner, "Las fiestas de 'moros y cristianos' en las Islas Filipinas," *Revista de Historia de América* 52 (Dec. 1961): 518-20.
149. Testimony of Beatriz Enriquez, 19 January 1645; AGN Mexico, Inq. 393/12/3, fol. 278r. Blanca de Rivera states that Lopez was Portuguese (testimony of 18 July 1642; ibid., 408, exp. 2, leg. 1, fol. 410v.).
150. Testimony of Blanca de Rivera, 18 July 1642; AGN Mexico, Inq. 408, exp. 2, leg. 1, fol. 410v.; testimony of Esperanza Rodríguez, 21 April 1643; ibid. 408, exp. 2, leg. 1, fol. 471v.
151. Testimony of 13 July 1642; AGN Mexico, Inq. 408, exp. 2, leg. 1, fol. 400v.; testimony of 15 September 1642; ibid., fol. 401r.
152. Testimony of 30 July 1642; AGN Mexico, Inq. 408, exp. 2, leg. 1, fol. 433r.
153. Testimony of 15 September 1642; AGN Mexico, Inq. 408, exp. 2, leg. 1, fol. 401v.
154. Testimony of 15 September 1642; AGN Mexico, Inq. 408, exp. 2, leg. 1, fol. 401v.
155. Testimony of 15 September 1642; AGN Mexico, Inq. 408, exp. 2, leg. 1, fol. 401v. All this took place in Guadalajara. Going out to the river to distract themselves, they eventually got trapped in an unwanted social call by a couple they knew, who would not let them return home despite their

excuses. They decided that it was better to break the fast than to attract suspicion and remained and ate (ibid., fols. 401v-402r.; testimony of Esperanza Rodríguez, 21 April 1643; ibid., fol. 471v.).
156. Testimony of 28 May 1643; AGN Mexico, Inq. 393, exp. 12, leg. 3, fol. 136r.; testimony of Juana del Bosque, 15 September 1642; ibid., 408, exp. 2, leg. 1, fol. 403v.
157. Testimony of 15 September 1642; AGN Mexico, Inq. 408, exp. 2, leg. 1, fol. 401v.
158. Testimony of 18 July 1642; AGN Mexico, Inq. 408, exp. 2, leg. 1, fol. 410v.
159. Testimony of Ysavel de Rivera, 12 October 1642; AGN Mexico, Inq. 408, exp. 2, leg. 1, fol. 429v.
160. Testimony of Esperanza Rodríguez, 21 April 1643; AGN Mexico, Inq. 408, exp. 2, leg. 1, fol. 470v.
161. Testimony of Ysavel de Rivera, 22 September 1642; AGN Mexico, Inq. 408, exp. 2, leg. 1, fol.428v.-429r. Maria was also known as Cota. Ysavel de Rivera claims to have been 19 or 20 in 1642, Maria Rodríguez/Del Bosque 20 and her sister Ysavel 25.
162. Testimony of 9 June 1644; AGN Mexico, Inq. 408, exp. 2, leg. 1, fol. 449v.
163. Testimony of Juana del Bosque, 15 September 1642; AGN Mexico, Inq. 408, exp. 2, leg. 1, fol. 402v.
164. As reported by Ysabel de Silva, also imprisoned for judaizing; testimony of 9 July 1643; AGN Mexico, Inq. 402, exp. 1, leg. 2, fols. 107v.-108r., 109r.
165. Testimony of 18 July 1642; AGN Mexico, Inq. 393, exp. 12, leg. 3, fols. 10r.-v.; 408, exp. 2, leg. 1, fol. 411r. Thomas Nuñez de Peralta, Beatriz Enriquez's husband, confirms in his own testimony merely that Beatriz "gave her some money that should go to doing well for the soul of her mother / le dio algunos dineros q serian para hazer vien por el alma de su madre" (AGN Mexico, Inq. 393, exp. 12, leg. 3, fol. 68r.), as does Ysavel Antunes (ibid., fol. 156r.). Ysavel de Silva also corroborates that Esperanza and her daughters were given money along with many others, while Pedro Tinoco says he knows that Esperanza was given four pesos to carry out some fasts (ibid., fol. 81r., 137r.).
166. Testimony of 24 July 1642; AGN Mexico, Inq. 408, exp. 2, leg. 1, fol. 446r.
167. Testimony of 15 September 1642; AGN Mexico, Inq. 408, exp. 2, leg. 1, fol. 402r.
168. Testimony of Catalina Enriquez, 28 May 1643; AGN Mexico, Inq. 393, exp. 12, leg. 3, fol. 151r.; testimony of Beatriz Enriquez, 7 January 1645; ibid., 271r. The latter states that up to 20 pesos went to "Justa Mendez, who was secluded in the hospital of the Indians, who was dying," transmitted by a Black slave named Ysavel. What was this crypto-Jew doing in the hospital for Amerindians, which had been founded for that purpose in the mid-sixteenth century, endowed and sponsored by the Crown itself? Or was this hospital no longer solely serving its originally intended population? Rafaela Enriquez says that her husband, Gaspar Suarez, withdrew to this hospital because of various lawsuits and demands to pay debts brought against him (testimony of 2 January 1643; ibid., 402, exp. 1, leg. 2, fol. 249v.).
169. Testimony of 15 September 1642; AGN Mexico, Inq. 408, exp. 2, leg. 1, fol. 402r.
170. Testimoney of Maria de Rivera; AGN Mexico, Inq. 393, exp. 12, leg. 3, fol.30r.
171. Testimony of 24 July 1642; AGN Mexico, Inq. 405, exp. 8, fol. 430r. Ferry thinks that the above-mentioned masses were actually a code word for the judaizing fasts and notes the close parallel between the Catholic practice of paying priests to say masses for the souls of those who had died ("Don't Drink the Chocolate").
172. AGN Mexico, Inq. 393/12/3, fols. 13v.-14r., 325r. Pedro Tinoco, for instance requests "three or four pesos" (testimony of Beatriz Enriquez; ibid., fol. 257r.).
173. AGN Mexico, Inq. 393, exp. 12, leg. 3, fols. 68r., 127v. Núñez de Peralta's statement might be assessed in light of the assertion of Raphaela that "it is very normal that men do not declare themselves [observers of the Law of Moses] to women / es muy de ordinario no declararse los hombres con los mugeres" (ibid., 129r.).
174. Testimony of 24 July 1642; AGN Mexico, Inq. 393, exp. 12, leg. 3, fol.213r.
175. Testimony of 13 January 1643; AGN Mexico, Inq. 408, exp. 2, leg. 1, fol. 426r. Rodríguez offers a different story, saying that she and Raphaela, as well as her sister Catalina, confessed their Jewishness to one another around 1630. One source of the distance alleged by Raphaela could be Rodríguez's knowledge that both Raphaela and Catalina were carrying on extramarital affairs, or so Rodríguez told the inquisitors (testimony of 21 April 1643; ibid., fol. 469v.).
176. Testimony of 18 July 1642; AGN Mexico, Inq. 408, exp. 2, leg. 1, fol. 410v.
177. Publication of the charges against Esperanza Rodríguez, AGN Mexico, Inq. 419, exp. 6, fol. 82r.
178. Testimony of 24 July 1642; AGN Mexico, Inq. 393, exp. 12, leg. 3, fol. 213r.
179. Charges against Esperanza Rodríguez, AGN Mexico, Inq. 419, exp. 6, fols. 67v.-68r.
180. Testimony of 13 January 1643; AGN Mexico, Inq. 408, exp. 2, leg. 1, fol. 435r. According to

Ysavel de Silva, the response was that Rodríguez and her daughter "were from our people / eran de los nuestros" (testimony of 10 July 1643, ibid., 415, exp. 6, fol. 524r.).
181. AGN Mexico, Inq. 419, exp. 6, fol. 121r.
182. "[E]sta confesante creyo, y entendio que la dha d^a Blanca enriquez se los avia dado, a la dha doña Beatriz su hija, para repartir entre pobres, observantes de la dha ley de Moisen" (AGN Mexico, Inq. 393, exp. 12, leg. 3, fols. 28v., 30r.; see also the testimony of Antonio Lopez de Orduña, 1 September 1642, ibid., fol. 175v.).
183. "Y tambien Repartio de este dinero hasta en cantidad de setenta ps. a una mulata llamada esperanza Rodríguez q aun q esta confessante sabia por Relacion q era obserbante de la ley de moissen, y la havia tratado en diferentes cossas nunca se havia declarado con ella hasta q murio la dha d. Blanca enriquez su madre q fue la dha esperanza Rodríguez a cassa de esta confessante, Y pidiendole del dho dinero la cantidad q arriba Refiere Para aiunarles por el alma de la difunta esta confessante la Pregunto q Para q queria tanto dinero junto a q la dha esperanza Rodríguez Respondio que Para ella, Y Para sus hijas Por q, Ya las havia enseñado al ley de moissen Conte q^i esta Confessante le dio les dhos setenta ps. declarandose con ella, Y ella Con la dha esperanza Rodríguez por obserbantes de la dha ley" (testimony of Beatriz Enriquez, 24 July 1642; AGN Mexico, Inq. 393, exp. 12, leg. 3, fol. 213r.). In her response to the witnesses, Rodríguez mentions that "she requested the money" from Beatriz (15 September 1644; ibid., 419, exp. 6, fol. 113r.).
184. Testimony of Ysabel Antunes, 14 December 1644; AGN Mexico, Inq. 402, exp. 1, leg. 2, fol. 152r. Rodríguez also received the two shirts which she had wet in order to wash the blood off of Blanca Enriquez's head, which Rodríguez seems to have asked to have (responses to the charges against her, ibid., 419, exp. 6, fol. 69v.) or, elsewhere in the same responses, two shirts and two sheets (ibid., fol. 110r.).
185. Charges against Esperanza Rodríguez, AGN Mexico, Inq. 419, exp. 6, fol. 63v.
186. Testimony of Juana del Bosque, 15 September 1642; AGN Mexico, Inq. 408, exp. 2, leg. 1, fol. 404r.; testimony of Raphaela Enriquez, 18 July 1642; ibid., fol. 426r.-v.; testimony of Juana Enriquez, 17 March 1643; ibid., fol. 441r.; 22 June 1643, ibid., fol. 441v. Rodríguez claims that she doesn't recall receiving alms on one occasion from Juana, but from Juana's sister Beatriz (response to the witnesses, 15 September 1644, AGN Mexico, Inq. 419, exp. 6, fol. 111v.).
187. Publication of the charges against Esperanza Rodríguez, AGN Mexico, Inq. 419, exp. 6, fol. 88v.
188. Testimony of Blanca de Rivera, 18 July 1642; AGN Mexico, Inq. 408, exp. 2, leg. 1, fol. 410r.
189. AGN Mexico Inq. 392, exp. 2, fol. 2r.
190. Descriptions such as *maltratado, quebrado, mui roto, muy viejo* abound.
191. AGN Mexico Inq. 392, exp. 2, fol. 3v.-4v.
192. AGN Mexico, Inq. 392, exp. 3, fol. 6r.
193. AGN Mexico, Inq. 393, exp. 12, leg. 3, fol. 145r.; repeated in Inq. 408, exp. 2, leg. 1, fol. 402v. It should be noted that Juana claims that Rodríguez also bought with this money an engraving or plate (*lamina*) of "our lady of the conception" and a purple christening robe.
194. Testimony of Juana Enriquez, 17 March 1643; AGN Mexico, Inq. 408, exp. 2, leg. 1, fol. 441r.
195. Charges against Esperanza Rodríguez, AGN Mexico, Inq. 419, exp. 6, fol. 65r.-v.
196. Testimony of 21 April 1643; AGN Mexico, Inq. 408, exp. 2, leg. 1, fols. 469v.-470r.
197. See, for instance, Jaffary, *False Mystics*, 118.
198. AGN Mexico, Inq. 419, exp. 6, fol. 120v.
199. Testimony of Esperanza Rodríguez, 7 August 1642; AGN Mexico, Inq. 408, exp. 2, leg. 1, fol. 459v. A note to the inquisitors in her handwriting, rather strong and legible, appears among the trial records (ibid., 419, exp. 6, fol. 130r.).
200. Testimony of 7 August 1642; AGN Mexico, Inq. 408, exp. 2, leg. 1, fol. 458v.-459r. "y aunque la dicha su hija tiene oltro niño y niña son de diferentes padres el hijo es de Don Nicolas de Alarcon hijo del governador que fue de soconuz[...]." Juana's husband was much older; Esperanza says he is 70. At some point he had gone to Caracas to work with cocoa, but never returned; they think he is dead (testimony of 21 April 1643; ibid., fol. 471v.).
201. Testimony of 7 August 1642; AGN Mexico, Inq. 408, exp. 2, leg. 1, fol. 460r. I could not confirm the identification of these two figures.
202. Testimony of Esperanza Rodríguez, 7 August 1642; AGN Mexico, Inq. 408, exp. 2, leg. 1, fol. 460r.
203. Publication of the charges against Esperanza Rodríguez, AGN Mexico, Inq. 419, exp. 6, fol. 96v.
204. A remarkably similar tale is recounted to the same effect by an unnamed modern informant of Middle-Eastern background (Susan Starr Sered, "Food and Holiness: Cooking as a Sacred Act Among Middle-Eastern Jewish Women," *Anthropological Quarterly* 61,3 [1988]: 129). I have not investigated the origins of the story, which may have been well-known among Sephardim.
205. Testimony of Esperanza Rodríguez, 7 August 1642; AGN Mexico, Inq. 408, exp. 2, leg. 1, fol.

458v. Her lack of any siblings, aunts or uncles from her mother's side might also explain her search for a community among her owners' family.
206. Joan Bristol, Unpublished paper, "Focusing Different Lenses on Esperanza Rodriguez, a mulata Jew in Seventeenth Century Mexico," presented at the Future(s) of Microhistory Symposium, University of Rochester, November 2017, 6, citing from her Inquisition trial, AGN Mexico, Inq. 408, exp. 2, leg. 1, fol. , 460.
207. Testimony of 30 January 1643; AGN Mexico, Inq. 408, exp. 2, leg. 1, fol. 465r.; repeated in the summary and sentence of the inquisitors, ibid., 419, exp. 6, fol. 117v. Ironically, or suitably, depending on one's perspective, the young Esperanza responds as one commanded, whether as a young slave girl to her masters or as a servant only of God: "she responded that she would do that which they commanded and would believe in that God of aDonay."
208. Ishac Athias, *Thesoro de preceptos adonde se encierran las joyas de los seys cientos y treze preceptos, que encomendó el señor a su pueblo israel. Con sv declaracion, razon, y dinim, conforme a la verdadera tradicion, recibida de Mosè y enseñada por nuestros sabios de gloriosa memoria* (Amsterdam: Semuel ben Israel Soeyro, 5409 [1649]; orig. Venice: Gioanne Caleoni, 1627), 67a.
209. *Relacion sumeria del auto particular de fee*, in García, *Documentos*, 163. The 30 year-old Portuguese-born Pérez was said to be circumcised.
210. Testimony of 24 September 1644, AGN Mexico, Inq. 419, exp. 6, fol. 114r.
211. Charges against Esperanza Rodríguez, 2 September 1644, AGN Mexico, Inq. 419, exp. 6, fol. 68v.
212. This behavior supposedly went on for six months (summary of the case and sentencing, AGN Mexico, Inq. 419, exp. 6, fol. 121v.
213. According to E. William Monter and John Tedeschi, the "compilers of inquisitorial handbooks were unanimous in their opinion that this sentence [of life imprisonment] should be commuted when, after three years, the convicted heretic had shown signs of real contrition" (E. William Monter and John Tedeschi, "Toward a Statistical Profile of the Italian Inquisitions, Sixteenth to Eighteenth Centuries," in Henningsen and Tedeschi, *The Inquisition in Early Modern Europe: Studies on Sources and Methods*, 157, n. 73). Various cases show that such penal theory did not always triumph in practice.
214. *Relacion sumeria del auto particular de fee*, in García, *Documentos*, 155-156. Rodríguez might well be the "mulata loca" whom Francisco de la Cruz describes calling for him and asking "when the news of leaving [the jails] and the pardon arrives," a question she asked the other slaves as well (Testimony of 19 October 1643; AGN Mexico, Inq. 396/3/6, fol.535r.).
215. Summary and sentence, AGN Mexico, Inq. 419, exp. 6, fol. 126v.
216. *Relacion sumeria del auto particular de fee*, in García, *Documentos*, 160-1.
217. In the *Relación sumeria*, Isabel is said to be 24, not 25, and Juana's aunt, not sister (hermana de padre y madre de la dicha Juana del Bosque; ibid., 160).
218. *Relacion sumeria del auto particular de fee*, in García, *Documentos*, 160.
219. María is said to be 19, not 20, in the *Relación sumeria* (ibid., 169).
220. *Relacion sumeria del auto particular de fee*, in García, *Documentos*, 169.
221. Joan Bristol and Tamara Harvey, "Creole Civic Pride and Positioning 'Exceptional' Black Women," Mary McAleer Balkun and Susan C. Imbarrato (eds.) *Women's Narratives of the Early Americas and the Formation of Empire* (New York: Palgrave Macmillan, 2016), 57.
222. AGN Mexico, Inq. 419, exp. 6, fol. 130r.-v.
223. The quotes are from Sweet, *Recreating Africa*, 33.

Postscript I

1. Testimony of Ysavel de Silva, 25 June 1643, AGN Mexico, Inq. 415, exp. 6, fol. 519r. My translation is intentionally loose.
2. Quoted in Taussig, *Shamanism*, 377.
3. Castelló, *Francisco de la Cruz*, 1:24.
4. Hernández, *Delirio*, 48.
5. Hernández, *Delirio*, 204.
6. For instance, Yirmiyahu Yovel, *The Marrano of Reason* (Princeton: Princeton University Press, 1989), 34-6.
7. Testimony of Maria de Rivera, AGN Mexico, Inq. 393, exp. 12, leg. 3, fols. 25v.-26r.; see also the testimony of Catalina Enriquez, ibid., fol. 150v.
8. Maya Restrepo, *Brujería*, 577.

9. Maya Restrepo, *Brujería*, 593.
10. See, for example, Elizabeth W. Kiddy, "Who is the King of Congo? A New Look at African and Afro-Brazilian Kings in Brazil," in Linda M. Heywood (ed.), *Central Africans and Cultural Transformations in the American Diaspora* (Cambridge: Cambridge University Press, 2002), 153-82; Marina de Mello e Souza, *Reis negros no Brasil escravista: História da festa de coroação de rei Congo* (Belo Horizonte: Editora UFMG, 2002).
11. Silverblatt, "Colonial Conspiracies," 262, 263, 275, n. 13.
12. I find the conclusions of Fuchs, *Mimesis and Empire*, 164-6, insightful and convincing.
13. Fuchs, *Mimesis and Empire*, 165.
14. Baltasar Fra-Molinero, "Juan Latino and His Racial Difference," in Earle and Lowe, *Black Africans in Renaissance Europe*, 334-5; on Muley, see Fuchs, *Mimesis and Empire*, 101-7. Morisco protest proved ineffectual. By the mid-1570s, fourteen percent of the morisco population of the city of Granada, mostly women, had been enslaved.
15. Herrera, *Natives, Europeans, and Africans*, 115.
16. Donald H. Akenson, *If the Irish Ran the World: Montserrat, 1630-1730* (Montreal: McGill-Queen's University Press, 1997), 117-53; Richard S. Dunn, *Sugar and Slaves: The Rise of the Planter Class in the English West Indies, 1624-1713* (Chapel Hill: University of North Carolina Press, 1972), 130.
17. Certeau, *Practice of Everyday Life*, xiii-xiv; see also Pierre Bourdieu, *Pascalian Meditations* (Stanford: Stanford University Press, 2000), 185.
18. James C. Scott, *Weapons of the Weak; Everyday Forms of Peasant Resistance* (New Haven: Yale University Press, 1985), 42.
19. Gil Anidjar, "Secularism," *Critical Inquiry* 33 (Autumn 2006): 68-9.
20. Hall, *Slavery and African Ethnicities in the Americas*, 167.
21. Mieke Bal, *Lethal Love: Feminist Literary Readings of Biblical Love Stories* (Bloomington: Indiana University Press, 1987), 110.
22. Horowitz, *Reckless Rites*, 174-81. Gitlitz, *Secrecy and Deceit*, 162-4, also discusses the phenomenon, coming to conclusions very similar to Horowitz.
23. Anthony Pagden, *Fall of Natural Man*, 36. Pagden cites various Inquisition cases.
24. Carlos M. N. Eire, *War Against the Idols: The Reformation of Worship from Erasmus to Calvin* (Cambridge: Cambridge University Press, 1986), 105-65; Natalie Zemon Davis, "The Rites of Violence," *Past and Present* 59 (1973): 51-91.
25. William Monter, *Frontiers of Heresy*, 228.
26. Jaffary, *False Mystics*, 10.
27. For New Spain, see Villa-Flores, "'To Lose One's Soul,'" 435-68; for the Portuguese world, see Sweet, *Recreating Africa*, 210-14.
28. Lewis, *Hall of Mirrors*, 108.
29. Horowitz, *Reckless Rites*, 197-8, 271-2.
30. Horowitz, *Reckless Rites*, 181.
31. Though Horowitz tells us (*Reckless Rites*, 181) that this converso behavior did not descend from rabbinic tradition, the narrative of his entire book seems to establish Jewish violence from ancient times to modern as a coherent cultural feature.
32. Gitlitz, *Secrecy and Deceit*, 162.
33. Anidjar, "Lines of Blood," 4-5; see also William A. Christian, Jr., *Local Religion in Sixteenth-Century Spain* (Princeton: Princeton University Press, 1981), 192-3; Gallagher and Greenblatt, *Practicing New Historicism*, ch. 3 ("The Wound in the Wall").
34. Gallagher and Greenblatt, *Practicing New Historicism*, 99.
35. Gallagher and Greenblatt, *Practicing New Historicism*, 104.
36. Bourdieu, *Pascalian Meditations*, 170. Emphasis added.
37. The quote is from Talal Asad, *Genealogies of Religion: Discipline and Reasons of Power in Christianity and Islam* (Baltimore: Johns Hopkins University Press, 1993), 64; see also ch. 3 ("Pain and Truth in Medieval Christian Ritual"); Kagan and Dyer, *Inquisitorial Inquiries*, 168, n. 46.
38. Patrick Geary, "Humiliation of Saints," in *Saints and their Cults: Studies in Religious Sociology, Folklore, and History*, ed. Stephen Wilson (Cambridge University Press, 1983), 123-40.
39. Norman Simms, *Masks in the Mirror: Marranism in Jewish Experience* (New York: Peter Lang, 2006). Though studded with insights and novel perspectives, Simms' study cannot transcend its own kind of reactive mania, a scattershot lack of methodology, over-the-top generalizations, ahistorical psychologistic speculations, idiosyncratic black-or-white maximalizations and a seeming unconcern for the most basic forms of analyzing historical actors and events (he does not cite a single solid source in Spanish or Portuguese and relies on a disturbingly high number of materials from the internet).

40. Graizbord, "Conformity and Dissidence among Judeoconversos," 321, n. 53.
41. Bruce Lincoln, *Holy Terrors: Thinking about Religion after September 11*, 2nd ed. (Chicago: University Of Chicago Press, 2006), 6. Lincoln defines religious discourse as a "discourse whose concerns transcend the human, temporal, and contingent, and that claims for itself a similarly transcendant status," and religious practices as those "whose goal is to produce a proper world and/or proper human subjects, as defined by a religious discourse to which these practices are connected" (5-6). Depending on the intentions of the actor, the social and institutional discourse that gave rise to it as well as the social/institutional interpretations of his/her act, denouncing a crypto-Jew, for instance, may entail a religious practice.
42. The authors seem to be able to offer only generalizations that merely adduce blood or family connections to judaizers or open Jews. José Gonçalves Salvador, relying on Inquisition records in discussing New Christian slavers living or working in Angola, still only raises the vaguest proofs of judaizing (*Cristãos-novos e o comércio*, ch. 8). Ventura, *Negreiros portugueses*, a fine study, cannot produce a single substantive description of the identity or religiosity of the sixteenth-century slaver Manuel Caldeira, her main subject, whose biography occupies a good chunk of the book (75-117). In a more recent work, *Portuguese no Peru*, Ventura expends much effort trying to lay out the identity and religiosity of the seventeenth-century Lima slaver Manuel Bautista, coming up with convincing evidence (not necessarily original to her) of his judaizing, but nothing explicating his understanding of his own profession. Even Green's outstanding recent contribution, "Masters of Difference," offers only circumstantial evidence of the religiosity or subject position of various New Christian slavers of the West African coast.
43. The formulation, "honorable" men, was of course ubiquitous among European elites and their creole counterparts. In 1598, the officers of the royal *audiencia* in Mexico wrote to the Spanish king, warning of the consequences should the crown fail to uphold the feudal contract with its Mexican subjects. The text is suffused with the moralizing language of race and class: "Honorable men who by chance see themselves, their encomiendas exhausted, [reduced] to great poverty while others who arrived yesterday grow wealthy in the land their forefathers helped to win, taking due account of the value of their services, these men, who are unused to suffering ills, may join up with mulattoes, blacks, and other perfidious peoples and attempt some uprising" (quoted in Pagden, "Identity Formation in Spanish America," 54).
44. Burns, *Colonial Habits*, 3-4.
45. Elizabeth Castelli, *Martyrdom and Memory: Early Christian Culture Making*, Gender, Theory, and Religion (New York: Columbia University Press, 2007).
46. See, for example, Kenneth Surin, "Liberation," in Taylor, *Critical Terms*, 173-85; Carlos Carrete Parrando, "Nostalgia for the Past (and for the Future?) among Castilian *Judeoconversos*," in *Jews, Christians, and Muslims in the Mediterranean World after 1492*, ed. Alisa Meyuhas Ginio (London: Frank Cass, 1992), 25-43. Attempts to sacralize trauma and to preserve its transcendence pose their own dangers; see, for instance, Dominick LaCapra, *History in Transit: Experience, Identity, Critical Theory* [Ithaca: Cornell University Press, 2004], 117-23). This may be seen in the ways that marrano and Afroiberian religiosity — each differing within itself and vastly differing between each other — could become stuck in a kind of repetition compulsion around victimization and projection of totalizing power onto the dominant Other.
47. The term "maximalist" comes from Lincoln, *Holy Terrors*, 5; the quote is from Asad, *Genealogies of Religion*, 63.
48. Stephen Greenblatt, *Renaissance Self-Fashioning: From More to Shakespeare* (Chicago: University of Chicago Press, 1980), 225.
49. The dark early modern obverse of the kind of miraculous medieval transformations treated in Caroline Walker Bynum, *Metamorphosis and Identity* (New York: Zone Books, 2001).

Postscript II

1. For a meditation on simultaneous status as victims and dominators, see Athalya Brenner, "'On the Rivers of Babylon' (Psalm 137), or Between Victim and Perpetrator," in *Sanctified Aggression: Legacies of Biblical and Post Biblical Vocabularies of Violence*, ed. Jonneke Bekkenkamp and Yvonne Sherwood (London: T & T Clark International, 2003), 76-91.
2. Luis G. Martínez Villada, *Diego López de Lisboa* (Córdoba: Imprenta de la Universidad, 1939), 24, 32.
3. Díaz-Plaja, *El espíritu del Barroco*, 65-7, 76. In this fascistic/nostalgic discourse, the Jewish affinity for sabotage and search for the transcendent absolute lives on, an unkillable blood-type as

from the twice-produced horror flick, The Thing (Christian Nyby, 1951; John Carpenter, 1982): "It is not anecdotal to note that Karl Marx is a very characteristic Jew and that in the U.S.S.R. the Jews have a role as a preponderant minority"(Díaz-Plaja, *Espíritu del Barroco*, 66).
4. José Honorio Rodrigues e Joaquim Ribeiro, *Civilização Holandesa no Brasil* (São Paulo: Companhia Editora Nacional, 1940), 153. I hope to return elsewhere to the subject of Jewish immunities in the service of colonialism.
5. Lohmann Villena, "Una incógnita despejada," 55, 85.
6. Lucia Garcia de Proodian, *Los judios en America: Sus actividades en los Virreinatos de Nueva Castilla y Nueva Granada s. XVII* (Madrid: Instituto Arias Montano, 1966). The topic of love of money comes on 112.
7. www.blacksandjews.com. The now dated site is/was possibly affiliated with but certainly adulates Louis Farrakhan and the Nation of Islam. It is anti-Jewish because it goes beyond justifiable critical appraisals of Jewish involvement in slave-trading and Jewish participation in colonial domination over and control of Black populations to indulge in unjustifiable attacks — on Jews as almost innate capitalists and anti-Black racists, on Zionism and Israel — and extreme partisan apologetics, such as denying that Muslims had anything to do with the bombings of 11 September 2001.
8. See, for instance, Bourdieu, *Pascalian Meditations*, 156-63.
9. Yovel, *Marrano of Reason*, x.
10. Gayatri Chakravorty Spivak, "The New Historicism: Political Commitment and the Postmodern Critic," in *The New Historicism*, ed. H. Aram Veeser (New York: Routledge, 1989), 290.
11. Silverblatt, *Modern Inquisitions*, 16.
12. For examples, Stephanie E. Smallwood, "African Guardians, European Slave Ships, and the Changing Dynamics of Power in the Early Modern Atlantic," *The William and Mary Quarterly*, 3rd Series, 64,4 (October 2007): 679-716; John Thornton, "African Political Ethics and the Slave Trade: Central African Dimensions.," http://muweb.millersville.edu /~winthrop/Thornton.html.
13. Bourdieu, *Pascalian Meditations*, 181.
14. Green, "Masters of Difference," 98-9, 112-14.
15. Schwartz, "Questioning Slavery and Accepting Africa."
16. Some revisionist works wind up suffering from a kind of reverse imbalance. Thus, Sweet's fine study does not, ultimately, convince me that "the adoption of African spiritual elements by Catholic priests was no different from the African embrace of [Portuguese] Catholic elements" or that "the impact of Christianity on Africans was no greater than the impact of African beliefs on Christians" (*Recreating Africa*, 225, 230). Or Ramón Grosfoguel: "Slaves' prayers to Catholic saints are strategies of hybridization and *mestizaje* that have nothing to do with 'syncretism.' The hybridization practiced on the subaltern side of colonial difference represents 'subversive complicity,' 'border thinking,' and 'transculturation;' subsistence and resistance in the face of colonial power. The Catholic saints were 'transculturated' and 'transmodernized' so as to subvert and redefine them within a global, non-European cosmology. Each saint was converted into an African God" (Ramón Grosfoguel, "Hybridity and *Mestizaje*: Syncretism or Subversive Complicity? Subalternity from the Perspective of the Coloniality of Power," in *The Masters and the Slaves: Plantation Relations and* Mestizaje *in American Imaginaries*, ed. Alexandra Isfahani-Hammond [New York: Palgrave Macmillan, 2005], 125). Even Certeau's awe-inspiring analysis of mysticism proffers at one point a romanticized homogenization of 'Marrano' mysticism within Catholicism (*The Mystic Fable*, 22-3).
17. Mangan, *Trading Roles*, 11.
18. Walter D. Mignolo, "Colonial Situations, Geographic Discourses, and Territorial Representations: Toward a Diatopical Understanding of Colonial Semiosis," *Dispositio* 14,36-38 (1989): 93-140.
19. Asad, *Genealogies of Religion*, 3-24.
20. Asad, *Genealogies of Religion*, 4. Many of the points I argue above are made in Brian Sandberg, "Beyond Encounters: Religion, Ethnicity, and Violence in the Early Modern World, 1492-1700," *Journal of World History* 17,1 (2006): 1-25, which reached me only as this manuscript was going to press.
21. Freile, *Conquest of New Granada*, 16. The author of the Introduction is not named, but I assume it must be the translator, William Atkinson.
22. Evoking Kierkegaard via Derrida, my colleague Mark C. Taylor calls this "the madness of decision."
23. I have in mind Chava Weissler, *Voices of the Matriarchs: Listening to the Prayers of Early Modern Jewish Women* (Boston: Beacon Press, 1998), 173-6, and some of the literature she cites (255, n. 2).
24. I am paraphrasing somewhat and have taken the quote from Norman Simms, *Masks in the Mirror*, 74-5.

Bibliography

Abbreviations

BT = Babylonian Talmud
exp = expediente / file
JT = Jerusalem Talmud

Archival Sources

AGI = Archivo General de Indias (Seville)
AQ = Archivo de Quito
Con = Contratación / Transactions
Mex = Mexico
AGN Mexico = Archivo General de la Nación, Mexico
AGN Peru = Archivo General de la Nación, Peru
S.O. = Santo Oficio
Con = Contencioso
AHN = Archivo Historico Nacional (Madrid)
Inq. = Inquisition
ANTT = Arquivo Nacional Torre do Tombo
GAA = Gemeente Archief Amsterdam

Relevant Secondary Sources

Adams, Julia, The Familial State: Ruling Families and Merchant Capitalism in Early Modern Europe (Ithaca: Cornell University Press, 2005).
Aguirre Beltrán, Gonzalo, La población negra de México: Estudio etnohistórico (Mexico City: Fondo de Cultura Económica, 1989).
Alberro, Solange Behocaray, de, Inquisición y sociedad en México, 1571-1700 (Mexico City: Fondo de Cultura Económica, 1988).
_____ "Negros y mulatos en los documentos inquisitoriales: rechazo e integración," in Elsa Cecilia Frost et al (eds.), El Trabajo y los Trabajadores en la Historia de México: Ponencias y comentarios presentados en la Reunión de Historiadores Mexicanos y Norteamericanos, Pátzcuaro, 12 al 15 de octubre de 1977 (Mexico City/Tucson: El Colegio de México/University of Arizona Press, 1979).
Alencastre, Luis Felipe de, O trato dos viventes: Formação do Brasil no Atlântico Sul (São Paulo: Companhia das Letras, 2000).
Anaya Hernández, Luís Alberto, Judeoconversos e Inquisicion en las Islas Canarias (Las Palmas: Universidad de Las Palmas de Gran Canaria/Ediciones del Cabildo Insular de Gran Canaria, 1996).
Azevedo, J. Lúcio de, História dos cristãos-novos portugueses, 3rd ed. (Lisbon: Clássica Editora, 1989).

Baião, Antonio, A inquisição em Portugal e no Brasil (Lisboa, 1920 [orig. 1906]).
Behar, Ruth, "Sex and Sin, Witchcraft and the Devil in Late-Colonial Mexico," American Ethnologist 14 (Feb. 1987): 34-54.
Beinart, Haim, "The Conversos in Spain and Portugal," in Moreshet Sepharad / The Sephardi Legacy, ed. Haim Beinart, 2 vols. (Jerusalem: Magnes Press, 1992), 2:43-67.
_____ Conversos on Trial: the Inquisition in Ciudad Real, Hispania Judaica, No. 3 (Jerusalem: The Magnes Press/The Hebrew University, 1981).
_____ "The Jews in the Canary Islands: A Re-evaluation," Transactions of the Jewish Historical Society of England 25 (1973/1975).
_____ (ed.), Moreshet Sepharad: the Sephardi Legacy, 2 vols. (Jerusalem: Magnes Press/Hebrew University, 1992).
Bennett, Herman, Africans in Colonial Mexico: Absolutism, Christianity, and Afro-Creole Consciousness, 1570-1640 (Bloomington: Indiana University Press, 2003).
Bernardini, Paolo, and Norman Fiering (eds.), The Jews and the Expansion of Europe to the West, 1450-1800, European Expansion & Global Interaction, Vol. 2 (New York: Berghahn Books, 2001).
Blackburn, Robin, The Making of New World Slavery: From the Baroque to the Modern, 1492-1800 (London: Verso, 1997).
Blázquez Miguel, Juan, Inquisición y criptojudaismo (Madrid: Kaydeda, 1988).
Bodian, Miriam, "'Men of the Nation': The Shaping of Converso Identity in Early Modern Europe." Past and Present 143 (May 1994): 48-76.
Böhm, Günter, Los Sefardies en los Dominios Holandeses de America del Caribe, 1630-1750 (Frankfurt: Vervuert, 1992).
Borrego Pla, María del Carmen, Palenques de negros en Cartagena a fines del siglo XVII (Seville: Escuela de Estudios Hispano-Americanos de Sevilla/Consejo Superior de Investigaciones Científicas, 1973).
Bowser, Frederick P., The African Slave in Colonial Peru, 1524-1650 (Stanford: Stanford University Press, 1974).
Boxer, C. R., The Church Militant and Iberian Expansion 1440-1770, The Johns Hopkins Symposia in Comparative History, no. 10 (Baltimore: The Johns Hopkins University Press, 1978).
_____ The Portuguese Seaborne Empire, 1415-1825 (London: Hutchinson, 1969).
_____ Portuguese Society in the Tropics: The Municipal Councils of Goa, Macao, Bahia, and Luanda, 1510-1800 (Madison/Milwaukee: University of Wisconsin Press, 1965).
_____ Race Relations in the Portuguese Colonial Empire: 1415-1825 (Oxford: Clarendon Press, 1963).
Boyajian, James C., Portuguese Bankers at the Court of Spain, 1626-1650 (New Brunswick: Rutgers University Press, 1983).
Bromberg, Rachel Mizrahi, A inquisição no Brasil: Um capitão-mor Judaizante (São Paulo: Centro de Estudos Judaicos da F.F.L.C.H./USP, 1984).
Brooks, George E., Eurafricans in Western Africa: Commerce, Social Status, Gender, and Religious Observance From the Sixteenth to the Eighteenth Century (Athens: Ohio University Press, 2003).
Cañizares-Esguerra, Jorge, Puritan Conquistadors: Iberianizing the Atlantic, 1550-1700 (Standford: Stanford University Press, 2006).
Caro Baroja, Julio, Los judíos en la España moderna y contemporánea, 4th ed. (Madrid: Ediciones Istmo, 2000).
Ceballos Gómez, Diana Luz, "Quyen tal haze que tal pague:" Sociedad y prácticas mágicas en el Nuevo Reino de Granada (Bogotá: Ministerio de Cultura, 2002).
Certeau, Michel de, The Mystic Fable, vol. 1: The Sixteenth and Seventeenth Centuries, trans. Michael B. Smith (Chicago: University of Chicago Press, 1992).

_____ The Practice of Everyday Life, trans. by Steven F. Rendall (Berkeley: University of California Press, 1984).
Cohan, Clara E., Los marranos en el Paraguay colonial (Asunción: Intercontinental, 1992).
Contreras, Jaime, Bernardo J. García García, and Ignacio Pulido (eds.), Familia, religión y negocio: El sefardismo en las relaciones entre el mundo ibérico y los Países Bajos en la edad moderna (Madrid: Fundación Carlos de Amberes/Ministerio de Asuntos Exteriores, 2002).
_____ and Gustav Henningsen, "Forty-Four Thousand Cases of the Spanish Inquisition (1540-1700): Analysis of a Historical Data Bank" in Gustav Henningsen and John Tedeschi (eds.) in association with Charles Amiel, The Inquisition in Early Modern Europe: Studies on Sources and Methods (Dekalb, Il: Northern Illinois University Press, 1986).
Cope, R. Douglas, The Limits of Racial Domination: Plebeian Society in Colonial Mexico City, 1660-1720 (Madison: University of Wisconsin Press, 1994).
Costigan, Lúcia Helena, Through Cracks in the Wall: Modern Inquisitions and New Christian Letrados in the Iberian Atlantic World (Leiden: Brill, 2010).
Croitoru Rotbaum, I ic, Documentos coloniales originados en el santo oficio del tribunal de la inquisición de Cartagena de Indias (Contribución a la historia de Colombia [vol. 2]) (Bogota: Tipografia Hispana, 1971).
_____ De sefarad al neosefardismo (Contribución a la historia de Colombia) (Bogota: Editorial Kelly, 1967).
Curtin, Philip D., The Atlantic Slave Trade: A Census (Madison: University of Wisconsin Press, 1969).
Davis, David Brion, Slavery and Human Progress (New York: Oxford University Press, 1984).
Dedieu, Jean Pierre, "The Archives of the Holy Office of Toledo as a Source for Historical Anthropology," in Henningsen, Gustav and John Tedeschi (eds.) in association with C. Amiel, The Inquisition in Early Modern Europe: Studies on Sources and Methods (Dekalb, Ill.: Northern Illinois University Press, 1986).
Díaz-Plaja, Guillermo, El espíritu del Barroco: Tres interpretaciones (Barcelona: Editorial Apolo, 1940).
Díaz-Mas, Paloma, and Harm den Boer (eds.), Fronteras e interculturalidad entre los sefardíes occidentales (Amsterdam: Rodopi, 2006), orig. Foro Hispánico 28 (2005).
Dille, Glen, Antonio Enríquez Gómez (Boston: Twayne Publishers, 1988).
_____ "A Black Man's Dilemma in Las misas de S. Vicente Ferrer," Romance Notes 20 (1979): 87-93.
Dirks, Nicholas B., Castes of Mind: Colonialism and the Making of Modern India (Princeton: Princeton University Press, 2001).
Domínguez Ortiz, Antonio, Autos de la inquisición de Sevilla (Siglo XVII) (Seville: Servicio de Publicaciones del Ayuntamiento de Sevilla, 1981).
_____ "La Esclavitud en Castilla durante la edad moderna," Estudios de Historia Social de España, Carmelo Viñas y Mey (ed.) (Madrid: Consejo Superior de Investigaciones Cientificas, 1952), 2:367-428.
Dutra, Francis A. "A Hard-Fought Struggle for Recognition: Manuel Goncalves Doria, First Afro-Brazilian to Become a Knight of Santiago," The Americas 56:1 (July 1999): 91-113.
_____ "Blacks and the Search for Rewards and Status in Seventeenth-Century Brazil," Proceedings of the Pacific Coast Council on Latin American Studies, vol. 6 (San Diego: San Diego State University, 1977-1979), 25-35.
Earle, T. F., "Black Africans versus Jews: Religious and Racial Tension in a Portuguese Saint's Play," Earle, T.F., and K. J. P. Lowe (eds.), Black Africans in Renaissance Europe

(Cambridge University Press, 2005), 345-60.
———— and K. J. P. Lowe (eds.), Black Africans in Renaissance Europe (Cambridge University Press, 2005).
Eltis, David, "Identity and Migration: The Atlantic in Comparative Perspective," in The Atlantic World: Essays on Slavery, Migration, and Imagination, ed. Wim Klooster and Alfred Padula (Upper Saddle River, NJ: Pearson/Prentice Hall, 2005), 108-25.
———— "Atlantic History in Global Perspective," Itinerario 23,2 (1999): 141-61.
Emmanuel, Isaac S., "Seventeenth-Century Brazilian Jewry: A Critical Review," American Jewish Archives 14,1 (April 1962).
Farah, Caesar E. (trans. and ed.), An Arab's Journey to Colonial Spanish America: The Travels of Elias al-Mûsili in the Seventeenth Century (Syracuse: Syracuse University Press, 2003).
Faur, José, In the Shadow of History: Jews and Conversos at the Dawn of Modernity (Albany: State University of New York Press, 1992).
———— "Four Classes of Conversos: A Typological Study," Revue des Etudes Juives 149 (1990): 113-24.
Feitler, Bruno, "Jews and New Christians in Dutch Brazil, 1630-1654," Richard L. Kagan and Philip D. Morgan (eds.), Atlantic Diasporas: Jews, Conversos, and Crypto-Jews in the Age of Mercantilism, 1500-1800 (Baltimore: Johns Hopkins University Press, 2009), 123-51.
Ferré, Pilar Romeu, "Fuente clara: Un ejemplo de interculturalidad entre los judíos sefardíes en la segunda mitad del siglo XVI," Fronteras e interculturalidad entre los sefardíes occidentales, ed. Paloma Díaz-Mas and Harm den Boer, (Amsterdam: Rodopi, 2006), orig. Foro Hispánico 28 (2005)
Ferreira Reis, Célia Maria, "A visitação de Marcos Teixeira aos Açores em 1575," Inquisição, Vol. 1: Comunicações apresentadas ao 1.º congresso luso-brasileiro sobre inquisição realizado em Lisboa, de 17 a 20 de Fevereiro de 1987 (Lisboa: Sociedade Portuguesa de Estudos do Século XVIII/Universitária Editora, 1989).
Ferry, Robert J., "Don't Drink the Chocolate: Domestic Slavery and the Exigencies of Fasting for Crypto-Jews in Seventeenth-Century Mexico," Nuevo Mundo Mundos Nuevos 5 (2005); http://nuevomundo.revues.org/document934.html, unpaginated.
Few, Martha, "Women, Religion, and Power: Gender and Resistance in Daily Life in Late-Seventeenth-Century Santiago de Guatemala," Ethnohistory 42 (Fall 1995): 627-37.
Flynn, Maureen, "Mimesis of the Last Judgment: The Spanish Auto de Fé," Sixteenth Century Journal 22,2 (Summer 1991): 281-97.
Friedemann, Nina S. de, La saga del negro: Presencia africana en Colombia (Santa Fe de Bogotá: Pontificia Universidad Javeriana, 1993).
Fuchs, Barbara, Mimesis and Empire: The New World, Islam, and European Identities (Cambridge: Cambridge University Press, 2001).
Gadelha, Regina Maria d'Aquino Fonseca, "Judeus e Cristãos-Novos no Rio da Prata: a Ação do Governador Hernandarias de Saavedra," in Novinsky and Tucci Carneiro, eds., Inquisição.
Garcia Fuentes, Jose Maria (ed.), La inquisición en Granada en el siglo XVI: Fuentes para su studio (Granada: Departamento de Historia Moderna de la Universidad de Granada, 1981).
Garfield, Robert, "A Forgotten Fragment of the Diaspora: the Jews of São Tomé Island, 1492-1654," in The Expulsion of the Jews: 1492 and After, ed. Raymond B. Waddington and Arthur H. Williamson (New York: Garland Publishing, 1994), 73-87.
———— "Public Christians, Secret Jews: Religion and Political Conflict on São Tomé Island in the Sixteenth and Seventeenth Centuries," Sixteenth-Century Journal 21,4 (1990): 645-54.

Garofalo, Leo J., "The Ethno-Economy of Food, Drink, and Stimulants: The Making of Race in Colonial Lima and Cuzco (PhD Dissertation, University of Wisconsin-Madison, 2001).
Germeten, Nicole von, Black Blood Brothers: Confraternities And Social Mobility for Afro-Mexicans (University Press of Florida, 2006).
Ginzburg, Carlos, Wooden Eyes: Nine Reflections on Distance (New York: Columbia University Press, 2001).
_____ "The Inquisitor as Anthropologist," in Clues, Myths, and the Historical Method (Baltimore: Johns Hopkins University Press, 1989), 156-67.
Gitlitz, David M., Secrecy and Deceit: the Religion of the Crypto-Jews (Philadelphia: Jewish Publication Society, 1996).
_____ "La angustia vital de ser negro: Tema de un drama de Fernando de Zárate," Segismundo 11 (1975): 65-85.
Glick, Thomas F., "On Converso and Marrano Ethnicity," in Benjamin R. Gampel (ed.), Crisis and Creativity in the Sephardic World, 1391-1648 (New York: Columbia University Press, 1997), 59-76.
Gorenstein Ferreira da Silva, Lina, Heréticos e impuros: A inquisição e os cristãos-novos no Rio de Janeiro — Século XVIII (Rio de Janeiro: Secretaria Municipal de Cultura/Departamento Geral de Documentação e Informação Cultural, 1995).
_____ and Maria Luiza Tucci Carneiro (eds.), Ensaios sobre a intolerância: Inquisição, marranismo e anti-semitismo (Homenagem a Anita Novinsky) (São Paulo:Humanitas/FFLCH/USP, 2002), 65-96.
Graizbord, David Leon, "Conformity and Dissidence among Judeoconversos, 1580-1700" (PhD Dissertation, University of Michigan, 2000).
Green, Tobias, "The Role of the Portuguese Trading Posts in Guinea and Angola in the 'Apostasy' of Crypto-Jews in the 17th Century," in Creole Societies in the Portuguese Colonial Empire, eds. Philip J. Havik and Malyn Newitt (Bristol: Bristol University Press/Seagull/Faiolean, June 2007), 25-40.
_____ "Masters of Difference: Creolization and the Jewish Presence in Cabo Verde, 1497-1672" (PhD Dissertation: University of Birmingham, UK, 2006).
_____ "Further Considerations on the Sephardim of the Petite Côte," History in Africa 32 (2005): 165-83.
Grinberg, Keila (ed.), Os judeus no Brasil: Inquisição, imigração e identidade (Rio de Janeiro: Civilização Brasileira, 2005).
Grosfoguel, Ramón, "Hybridity and Mestizaje: Sincretism or Subversive Complicity? Subalternity from the Perspective of the Coloniality of Power," in The Masters and the Slaves: Plantation Relations and Mestizaje in American Imaginaries, ed. Alexandra Isfahani-Hammond (New York: Palgrave Macmillan, 2005), 115-29.
Gruzinski, Serge, The Mestizo Mind: The Intellectual Dynamics of Colonization and Globalization (New York: Routledge, 2002).
Haliczer, Stephen, Inquisition and Society in the Kingdom of Valencia, 1478-1834 (Berkeley, Calif.: University of California Press, 1990).
Hall, Gwendolyn Midlo, Slavery and African Ethnicities in the Americas: Restoring the Links (Chapel Hill: University of North Carolina Press, 2005).
Hall, Stuart, "Pluralism, Race and Class in Caribbean Society," in Race and Class in Post-Colonial Society: A Study of Ethnic Group Relations in the English-Speaking Caribbean, Bolivia, Chile and Mexico (Paris: UNESCO, 1977).
Harbison, Robert, Reflections on Baroque (Chicago: University of Chicago Press, 2000).
Henningsen, Gustav, "The Eloquence of Figures: Statistics of the Spanish and Portuguese Inquisitions and Prospects for Social History," in The Spanish Inquisition and the Inquisitorial Mind, ed. Angel Alcalá (Boulder: Social Science Monographs/Columbia University Press, 1987).

_____ "The Archives and the Historiography of the Spanish Inquisition," in Henningsen, Gustav, and John Tedeschi (eds.) in association with C. Amiel, The Inquisition in Early Modern Europe: Studies on Sources and Methods (Dekalb, Ill.: Northern Illinois University Press, 1986).

Hernández, Marie Theresa, Delirio — the Fantastic, the Demonic, and the Réel: The Buried History of Nuevo León (Austin: University of Texas Press, 2002).

Hernández Asensio, Raúl, La frontera occidental de la audiencia de Quito: Viajeros y relatos de viajes (1595-1630), Travaux de l'Institut Français d'Etudes Andines, 203 (Lima: Instituto de Estudios Peruanos/Instituto Francés de Estudios Andinos, 2004)

Hernández Cuevas, Marco Polo, Africa en el carnival mexicano (Mexico City: Plaza y Valdés, 2005).

Herrera, Robinson A., Natives, Europeans, and Africans in Sixteenth-Century Santiago de Guatemala (Austin: University of Texas Press, 2003).

Herzog, Tamar, "El baile inquisitorial: unas notas sobre el derecho y el abuso del poder (El proceso de Francisco de la Cruz, Lima 1571-1578)," in Inquisición y conversos: conferencias / pronunciadas en el III Curso de Cultura Hispano-Judía y Sefardí de la Universidad de Castilla-La Mancha, celebrado en Toledo del 6 al 9 de septiembre de 1993 ([Toledo]: Asociación de Amigos del Museo Sefardí: Caja de Castilla-La Mancha, [1994]), 119-29.

Huerga Criado, Pilar, En la raya de Portugal: Solidaridad y tensiones en la comunidad judeoconversa (Salamanca: Ediciones Universidad de Salamanca, 1994).

Ingram, Kevin, "Secret Lives, Public Lies: The Conversos and Socio-religious Non-conformism in the Spanish Golden Age" (PhD Diss.: University of California San Diego, 2006).

Isfahani-Hammond, Alexandra (ed.), The Masters and the Slaves : Plantation Relations and Mestizaje in American Imaginaries (Palgrave Macmillan, 2004).

Israel, Jonathan I., Diasporas Within a Diaspora: Jews, Crypto-Jews and the World Maritime Empires (1540-1740), Brill's Series in Jewish Studies, 30 (Leiden: Brill, 2002).

_____ European Jewry in the Age of Mercantilism, 1550-1750 (Oxford: Clarendon Press, 1989).

_____ "Menasseh Ben Israel and the Dutch Sephardic Colonization Movement of the Mid-Seventeenth Century (1645–1657)," in Kaplan, Menasseh Ben Israel and His World.

_____ Race, Class and Politics in Colonial Mexico, 1610-1670 (Oxford: Oxford University Press, 1975).

Jason, Howard M., "The Negro in Spanish Literature to the End of the Siglo de Oro," Blacks in Hispanic Literature: Critical Essays, ed. Miriam DeCosta (Port Washington, NY: National University Press/Kennikat Press, 1977).

Kagan, Richard L., and Abigail Dyer (eds. and trans.), Inquisitorial Inquiries: Brief Lives of Secret Jews and Other Heretics (Baltimore: Johns Hopkins University Press, 2004).

Kagan, Richard L., and Philip D. Morgan (eds.), Atlantic Diasporas: Jews, Conversos, and Crypto-Jews in the Age of Mercantilism, 1500-1800 (Baltimore: Johns Hopkins University Press, 2009).

Kamen, Henry, The Spanish Inquistion: A Historical Revision (New Haven: Yale University Press, 1997).

Kaplan, Yosef, Judios nuevos en Amsterdam: Estudios sobre la historia social e intelectual del judaísmo sefarí en el siglo XVII (Barcelona: Gedisa Editorial, 1996).

___, Henry Méchoulan and Richard H. Popkin (eds.), Menasseh Ben Israel and His World (Leiden: E. J. Brill, 1989).

_____ "The Travels of Portuguese Jews from Amsterdam to the 'Lands of Idolatry' (1644-1724)," in Yosef Kaplan (ed.), Jews and Conversos: Studies in society and the inquisition (Jerusalem: World Union of Jewish Studies/The Magnes Press/The Hebrew University, 1985), 197-224.

_____ "The Portuguese Jews in Amsterdam: From Forced Conversion to a Return to Judaism," Studia Rosenthaliana 15, 1 (March 1981): 37-51.
Keane, Webb, Christian Moderns: Freedom and Fetish in the Mission Encounter (Berkeley: University of California Press, 2007).
Koen, E. M., W. Hamelink-Verweel, S. Hart, and W. C. Pieterse, "Notarial Records in Amsterdam Relating to the Portuguese Jews in That Town up to 1639," Studia Rosenthaliana, running series beginning with 1,1 (1967-present).
Kurlat, Frida Weber de, "Sobre el negro como tipo cómico en el teatro español del siglo XVI," Romance Philology 17 (1963/1964).
Lahon, Didier, "Black African Slaves and Freedmen in Portugal During the Renaissance: Creating a New Pattern of Reality," in Earle and Lowe, Black Africans in Renaissance Europe, 261-79.
Lewis, Laura A., Hall of Mirrors: Power, Witchcraft, and Caste in Colonial Mexico (Durham, NC: Duke University Press, 2003).
Liebman, Seymour B., "The Religion and Mores of the Colonial New World Marranos," in Anita Novinsky and Maria Luiza Tucci Carneiro (eds.), Inquisição: Ensaios sobre mentalidade, heresias e arte: Trabalhos apresentados no I Congresso Internacional — Inquisição. Universidade de São Paulo. Maio 1987 (São Paulo: Editora da Universidade de São Paulo, 1992).
_____ New World Jewry, 1493-1825: Requiem for the Forgotten (New York: Ktav Publishing House, 1982).
_____ The Jews of New Spain (Coral Gables, Florida: University of Miami Press, 1970).
_____ "The Mestizo Jews of Mexico," American Jewish Archives 19,2 (November 1967): 144-74.
Lipiner, Elias, Gonçalo Anes Bandarra e os cristãos-novos (Trancoso/Lisbon: Câmara Municipal de Trancoso/Associação Portuguesa de Estudos Judaicos, 1996).
_____ Izaque de Castro: o mancebo que veio preso do Brasil (Recife: Fundação Joaquim Nabuco/Editora Massangana, 1992).
_____ Os judaizantes nas capitanias de cima: Estudos sobre os cristãos-novos do Brasil nos séculos XVI e XVII (São Paulo: Editôra Brasiliense, 1969).
López Belinchón, Bernardo, Honra, libertad y hacienda: Hombres de negocios y judíos sefardíes ([Alcalá de Henares, Madrid]: Universidad de Alcalá, 2001).
Lopez Garcia, José Tomás, Dos defensores de los esclavos negros en el siglo XVII (Maracaibo/Caracas: Biblioteca Corpozulia/Universidad Catolica Andres Bello, 1981).
Lutz, Christopher H., Santiago de Guatemala, 1541-1773: City, Caste, and the Colonial Experience (Norman, Okla.: University of Oklahoma Press, 1994).
Maia, Angela Maria Vieira, À sombra do medo: Cristãos velhos e cristãos novos nas capitanias do açúcar (Rio de Janeiro: Oficina Cadernos de Poesia, 1995).
Mangan, Jane E., Trading Roles: Gender, Ethnicity, and the Urban Economy in Colonial Potosí (Durham: Duke University Press, 2005).
Mark, Peter, and José Da Silva Horta, The Forgotten Diaspora: Jewish Com-munities in West Africa and the Making of the Atlantic World (New York: Cambridge University Press, 2011).
_____ "Two Early Seventeenth-Century Sephardic Communities on Senegal's Petite Cote," History in Africa 31 (2004): 231-56.
Martínez López, María Elena, "The Spanish Concept of Limpieza de Sangre and the Emergence of the 'Race/Caste' System in the Viceroyalty of New Spain," (PhD Dissertation, University of Chicago, 2002).
Martínez Villada, Luis G., Diego López de Lisboa (Córdoba: Imprenta de la Universidad, 1939).
Maya Restrepo, Luz Adriana, Brujería y reconstrucción de identidades entre los africanos

y sus descendientes en la Nueva Granada, siglo XVII (Bogota: Ministerio de Cultura, 2005).
Mea, Elvira Cunha de Azevedo, "Orações judaicas na inquisição portuguesa — século XVI," Jews and Conversos: Studies in Society and the Inquisition, ed. Yosef Kaplan (Jerusalem: Magnes Press/Hebrew University, 1985), 149-78.
Medina, José Toribio, Historia del Tribunal de la Inquisición de Lima, 1569-1820, Prólogo de Marcel Bataillon, 2nd. ed., 2 v. (Santiago de Chile: Fondo Histórico y Bibliográfico J. T. Medina, 1956 [orig. 1887]).
_____ Historia del Tribunal del Santo Oficio de la inquisición en Chile (Santiago de Chile, Fondo Histórico y Bibliográfico J. T. Medina, 1952 [orig. 1890]).
_____ El tribunal del santo oficio de la inquisición en las provincias del Plata (Buenos Aires: Editorial Huarpes, 1945).
_____ Historia del Tribunal del Santo Oficio de la Inquisición de Cartagena de las Indias (Santiago de Chile: Imprenta Elzeviriana, 1899).
Melammed, Renée Levine, A Question of Identity: Iberian Conversos in Historical Perspective (New York: Oxford University Press, 2004).
_____ Heretics of Daughters of Israel? The Crypto-Jewish Women of Castile (New York: Oxford University Press, 1999).
_____ "María López: A Convicted Judaizer from Castile," in Mary E. Giles, ed., Women in the Inquisition: Spain and the New World (Baltimore: Johns Hopkins University Press, 1999), 53-72.
_____ "Judaizing Women in Castille: A Look at Their Lives Before and After 1492," in Le Beau, Bryan F. and Menachem Mor (eds.), Religion in the Age of Exploration: the Case of Spain and New Spain (Creighton University Press, 1996), 15-37.
_____ "Some Death and Mourning Customs of Castilian Conversas," in Exile and Diaspora: Studies in the History of the Jewish People Presented to Professor Haim Beinart (Jerusalem: Ben-Zvi Institute of Yad Izhak Ben-Zvi/the Hebrew University of Jerusalem/Consejo de Investigaciones Científicas, Madrid, 1991), 157-67.
_____ "The Conversos of Cogolludo," Proceedings of the Ninth World Congress of Jewish Studies, Division B, Vol. I (Jerusalem: World Union of Jewish Studies, 1986), 135-42.
Mellafe, Rolando, La introducción de la esclavitud negra en Chile: Trafico y rutas (Santiago de Chile: Universidad de Chile, 1959).
Mello, José Antônio Gonsalves de Gente da nação: Cristãos-novos e judeus em pernambuco, 1542-1654 (Recife: Fundação Joaqium Nabuco/Editora Massangana, 1989).
Memmi, Albert, The Colonizer and the Colonized (Boston: Beacon Press, 1967 [1957]).
Metcalf, Alida C., Go-betweens and the Colonization of Brazil, 1500-1600 (Austin: University of Texas Press, 2005).
Mignolo, Walter D., The Darker Side of the Renaissance: Literacy, Territoriality, and Colonization (Ann Arbor: University of Michigan Press, 1995).
Molina, Raúl A., "El Primer banquero de Buenos Aires: Jerarquia alcanzada por su descendencia: Diego de Vega," Revista de Historia Americana y Argentina 2 (1961): 55-123.
Molinero, Baltasar Fra, "Juan Latino and His Racial Difference," in Earle and Lowe, Black Africans in Renaissance Europe, 326-44.
_____ La imagen de los negros en el teatro del Siglo de Oro (Madrid: Siglo Veintiuno Editores, 1995).
Moreno Navarro, Isidoro, La Antigua hermandad de los negros de Sevilla: Etnicidad, poder y sociedad en 600 años de historia (Seville: Universidad de Sevilla/Consejería de Cultura de la Junta de Andalucía, 1997).
Mörner, Magnus, Race Mixture in the History of Latin America (Boston: Little, Brown, 1967).

Mott, Luiz R. B., Rosa Egipcíaca: Uma santa africana no Brasil (Rio de Janeiro: Bertrand Brasit, 1993).
Myscofski, Carole A., "Heterodoxy, Gender, and the Brazilian Inquisition: Patterns in Religion in the 1590s," Journal of Latin American Lore 18 (1992): 79-94.
Newitt, Malyn, "Mixed Race Groups in the Early History of Portuguese Expansion," in Studies in the Portuguese Discoveries I: Proceedings of the First Colloquium of the Centre for the Study of the Portuguese Discoveries, ed. T. F. Earle and Stephen Parkinson (Warminster: Aris & Phillips/Comissão nacional para as Comemoracões dos Descobrimentos Portugueses, 1992), 35-52.
Newson, Linda A., and Susie Minchin, From Capture to Sale: The Portuguese Slave Trade to Spanish South America in the Early Seventeenth Century (Leiden: Brill, 2007).
Nogueira Monteiro, Yara, "Economia e fé: A perseguição inquisitorial aos cristãos-novos portugueses no vice-reino do Peru," in Gorenstein and Carneiro, Ensaios sobre a intolerância, 65-96.
Novinsky, Anita, "The Myth of the Marrano Names," Revue des Études Juives 165,3-4 (2006): 445-56.
_____ Inquisição: Prisioneiros de Brasil - séculos XVI-XIX (Rio de Janeiro: Editora Expressão e Cultura, 2002).
_____ "Marranos and the Inquisition: On the Gold Route in Minas Gerais, Brazil," in Bernardini and Fiering, Jews and the Expansion of Europe to the West, 215-41.
_____ "A Critical Approach to the Historiography of Marranos in the Light of New Documents," Studies on the History of Portuguese Jews from their Expulsion in 1497 through their Dispersion, ed. Israel J. Katz and M. Mitchell Serels (New York: Sepher-Hermon Press, 2000).
_____ "Jewish Roots of Brazil," in Judith Laikin Elkin and Gilbert W. Merkx (eds.), The Jewish Presence in Latin America (Boston: Allen & Unwin, 1987).
_____ Cristãos-novos na Bahia, 1642-1654 (São Paulo: Pioneira/EDUSP, 1972)
Olsen, Margaret M., Slavery and Salvation in Colonial Cartagena de Indias (Gainesville: University Press of Florida, 2004).
Ortíz, Antonio Domínguez, Los judeoconversos en España y América (Madrid: ISTMO, 1971).
_____ La clase social de los conversos en Castilla en la edad moderna (Granada: Universidad de Granada, 1991 [1955]).
Pagden, Anthony, "Identity Formation in Spanish America," in Nicholas Canny and Anthony Pagden (eds.), Colonial Identity in the Atlantic World, 1500-1800 (Princeton; Princeton University Press, 1987), 51-93.
Palmer, Colin A., Slaves of the White God: Blacks in Mexico, 1570-1650 (Cambridge: Harvard University Press, 1976).
_____ "Religion and Magic in Mexican Slave Society, 1570-1650," in Engerman, Stanley L. and Eugene D. Genovese (eds.), Race and Slavery in the Western Hemisphere: Quantitative Studies (Princeton: Princeton University Press, 1975), 311-28.
Panford, Moses Etuah, Jr., La figura del negro en cuatro comedias barrocas (PhD Dissertation, Temple University, 1993).
Pearson, Michael N., Port Cities and Intruders: The Swahili Coast, India, and Portugal in the Early Modern Era (Baltimore: Johns Hopkins University Press, 1998).
Perdigão Malheiros, Agostinho Marques, A escravidão no Brasil, Ensaio histórico-jurídico-social. 2 vols. (Petrópolis: Editora Vozes, 1976).
Perelis, Ronnie, "Marrano Autobiography in its Transatlantic Context: Exile, Exploration and Spiritual Discovery" (PhD Dissertation, NYU, 2006).
Pérez de Colosía Rodríguez, María Isabel, Auto inquisitorial de 1672: El criptojudaísmo en Málaga (Málaga: Diputación Provincial de Málaga, 1984).

Pieroni, Geraldo, Os excluídos do reino: A inquisição portuguesa e o degredo para o Brasil colônia (Brasília/São Paulo: Editora Universidade de Brasília/Imprensa Oficial do Estado, 2000).
Pimentel, Maria do Rosário, "A escrava negra numa sociedade de senhores brancos," in Rosto feminino da expansão portuguesa, 1:557-72.
Popkin, Richard H., and Gordon M. Weiner (eds.), Jewish Christians and Christian Jews: From the Renaissance to the Enlightenment (Dordrecht: Kluwer Academic Publishers, 1994).
Pratt, Mary Louise, Imperial Eyes: Travel Writing and Transculturation (London/New York: Routledge, 1992).
Rabasa, José, Inventing America: Spanish Historiography and the Formation of Eurocentrism (Norman, Ok.: University of Oklahoma Press, 1993).
Rout, Leslie, The African Experience in Spanish America, 1502-present (New York: Columbia University Press, 1976)
Russell-Wood, A. J. R., The Black Man in Slavery and Freedom in Brazil (London: Macmillan, 1982).
Salomon, Herman Prins, "Spanish Marranism Re-examined," Sefarad 67,1 (Jan.-June 2007): 111-54.
Saraiva, António José, The Marrano Factory: The Portuguese Inquisition and Its New Christians, 1536-1765, trans., revised and augmented by H. P. Salomon and I. S. D. Sassoon (Leiden: Brill, 2001).
Saunders, A. C. de C. M., A Social History of Black Slaves and Freedmen in Portugal, 1441-1555 (Cambridge: Cambridge University Press, 1982).
Schorsch, Jonathan, Jews and Blacks in the Early Modern World (New York: Cambridge University Press, 2004).
Schwartz, Stuart B., All Can Be Saved: Religious Tolerance and Salvation in the Iberian Atlantic World (New Haven: Yale University Press, 2008).
_____ "Spaniards, Pardos, and the Missing Mestizos: Identities and Racial Categories in the Early Hispanic Caribbean," Nieuwe West-Indische Gids 71,1&2 (1997): 5-19.
_____ "Panic in the Indies: The Portuguese Threat to the Spanish Empire, 1640-1650," in Werner Thomas and Bart De Groof (eds.), Rebelión y resistencia en el mundo hispánico del siglo XVII: Actas del Coloquio Internacional Lovaina, 20-23 de Noviembre de 1991 (Leuven: Leuven University Press, 1992), 205-26.
_____ "The Formation of a Colonial Identity in Brazil," in Canny and Pagden, Colonial Identity in the Atlantic World, 1500-1800, 15-50.
_____ Sugar Plantations in the Formation of Brazilian Society: Bahia, 1550-1835 (Cambridge: Cambridge University Press, 1985).
Scott, James C., Weapons of the Weak; Everyday Forms of Peasant Resistance (New Haven: Yale University Press, 1985).
Serrano y Sanz, Manuel, Orígenes de la dominación española en América (Madrid: Bailly-Bailliere, 1918).
Silva, Filipa Ribeiro da, "A inquisição na Guiné, nas Ilhas de Cabo Verde e São Tomé e Príncipe," Revista Lusófona de Ciência das Religiões 3,5-6 (2004): 157-73.
Silverblatt, Irene, "Colonial Conspiracies," Ethnohistory 53,2 (Spring 2006): 259-80.
_____ Modern Inquisitions: Peru and the Colonial origins of the Civilized World (Durham: Duke University Press, 2004).
_____ "New Christians and New World Fears in Seventeenth-Century Peru," Comparative Studies in Society and History: An International Quarterly 42,3 (July, 2000): 524-546.
Silverman, Joseph H., "On Knowing Other People's Lives, Inquisitorially and Artistically," in Mary Elizabeth Perry and Anne J. Cruz (eds.), Cultural Encounters: the Impact of the Inquisition in Spain and the New World (Berkeley: University of California Press, 1991), 157-75.

Solano Alonso, Jairo, Salud, cultura y sociedad: Cartagena de Indias, siglos XVI y XVII (Bogota: Fondo de Publicaciones de la Universidad del Atlántico/Colección de Ciencias Sociales Rodrigo Noguera Barreneche, 1998).

Souza, Laura de Mello e, The Devil and the Land of the Holy Cross: Witchcraft, Slavery, and Popular Religion in Colonial Brazil (Austin: University of Texas Press, 2004).

Splendiani, Anna-María, Cincuenta Años de Inquisición en el Tribunal de Cartagena de las Indias, 1610-60, 4 vols. (Bogotá, 1997).

Starr-LeBeau, Gretchen D., In the Shadow of the Virgin: Inquisitors, Friars, and Conversos in Guadalupe, Spain (Princeton: Princeton University Press, 2003).

Studnicki-Gizbert, Daviken, "La Nación among the Nations: Portuguese and Other Maritime Trading Diasporas in the Atlantic, Sixteenth to Eighteenth Centuries," Richard L. Kagan and Philip D. Morgan (eds.), Atlantic Diasporas: Jews, Conversos, and Crypto-Jews in the Age of Mercantilism, 1500-1800 (Baltimore: Johns Hopkins University Press, 2009), 75-98.

_____ A Nation upon the Ocean Sea: Portugal's Atlantic Diaspora and the Crisis of the Spanish Empire, 1492-1640 (New York: Oxford University Press, 2007).

Sweet, James H., Recreating Africa: Culture, Kinship, and Religion in the African-Portuguese World, 1441-1770 (Chapel Hill: University of North Carolina Press, 2003).

Swetschinski, Daniel M., Reluctant Cosmopolitans: The Portuguese Jews of Seventeenth-Century Amsterdam (London: Littman Library of Jewish Civilization, 2000).

Tardieu, G. Jean-Pierre, Los negros y la iglesia en el Perú: Siglos XVI-XVII, 2 vols. (Quito: Ediciones Afroamérica/Centro Cultural Afroecuatoriano, 1997 [orig. 1987]).

Tavares, Maria José Pimenta Ferro, "The Portuguese Jews after Baptism," in Studies on the History of Portuguese Jews from Their Expulsion in 1497 through Their Dispersion, ed. Israel J. Katz and M. Mitchell Serels (New York: Sepher-Hermon Press/The American Society of Sephardic Studies, 2000), 7-28.

_____ "Para o estudo dos judeus de Trás-os-Montes, no século XVI: A 1ª geração dos cristãos-novos," Cultura—História e Filosofia 4 (1985): 371-417.

_____ Os Judeus em Portugal no Século XV, vol. I (Lisboa: Universidade Nova de Lisboa/Faculdade de Ciências Sociais e Humanas, 1982); vol. II (Lisboa: INIC, 1984).

Tejado Fernandez, Manuel, Aspectos de la vida social en Cartagena de Indias durante el seiscientos (Seville: Escuela de Estudios Hispano-Americanos, 1954).

Thornton, John, Africa and Africans in the making of the Atlantic world, 1400-1800. Second ed. (Cambridge, UK: Cambridge University Press, 1998).

Tinhorão, José Ramos, Os Negros em Portugal: Uma presença silenciosa (Lisbon, 1988).

Toro, Alfonso, Los judíos en la Nueva España: Documentos del siglo xvi correspondientes al ramo de inquisición (México City: Archivo General de la Nación/Fondo de Cultura Económica, 1982 [1932]).

_____ La Familia Carvajal (Mexico City: Patria S.A., 1977).

Uchmany, Eva Alexandra, "The Participation of New Christians and Crypto-Jews in the Conquest, Colonization and Trade of Spanish America, 1521-1660," in Bernardini and Fiering, Jews and the Expansion of Europe to the West, 186-202.

_____ La vida entre el judaísmo y el cristianismo en la Nueva España, 1580-1606 (Mexico City: Archivo General de la Nación/Fondo de Cultura Económica, 1992).

Vainfas, Ronaldo, Trópico dos pecados: Moral, sexualidade e Inquisição no Brasil (Rio de Janeiro: Editora Campus, 1989).

_____ and Angelo A. F. Assis, "A esnoga da Bahia: Cristãos-novos e criptojudaísmo no Brasil quinhentista," in Grinberg (ed.), Os judeus no Brasil: Inquisição, imigração e identidade, 45-64.

Van Deusen, Nancy E., "The 'Alienated' Body: Slaves and Castas in the Hospital de San Bartolomé in Lima, 1680 to 1700," The Americas 56,1 [July 1999]: 1-30.

Ventura, Maria da Graça A. Mateus, Portugueses no Peru ao tempo da união ibérica: Mobilidade, cumplicidades e vivências, 2 vols. in 3 pts. (Lisbon: Imprensa Nacional-Casa da Moeda, 2005).

———. "Los Judeoconversos portugueses en el Perú del siglo XVII: Redes de complicidad," Familia, religión y negocio: El sefardismo en las relaciones entre el mundo ibérico y los Países Bajos en la edad moderna, ed. Jaime Contreras, Bernardo J. García García and Ignacio Pulido (Fundación Carlos de Amberes/Fernando Villaverde Ediciones, 2002).

———. Negreiros portugueses na rota das Índias de Castela, 1541-1556 (Lisbon: Edições Colibri/Instituto de Cultura Ibero-Atlântica, 1999).

Vilar, Enriqueta Vila, "Extranjeros en Cartagena (1593-1630)," Jahrbuch für Geschichte von Staat, Wirtschaft und Gesellschaft Lateinamerikas (Koln Wein, 1979): 147-84.

———. Hispanoamerica y el comercio de esclavos: los asientos portugueses (Seville: EEHA, 1977).

Villa-Flores, Javier, "'To Lose One's Soul': Blasphemy and Slavery in New Spain, 1596-1669," Hispanic American Historical Review 82,3 (2002): 435-68.

Villanueva, Joaquín Pérez, and Bartolomé Escandell Bonet (eds.), Historia de la inquisición en España y América, 3 vols. (Madrid: Biblioteca de Autores Cristianos/Centro de Estudios Inquisitoriales, 1984-2000).

Wachtel, Nathan, La foi du souvenir: Labyrinthes marranes (France: Éditions du Seuil, 2001).

———. "Marrano Religiosity in Hispanic America in the Seventeenth Century," Paolo Bernardini and Norman Fiering (eds.), The Jews and the Expansion of Europe to the West, 1450 to 1800 (New York: Berghahn Books, 2001), 149-71.

Wiznitzer, Arnold, "Crypto-Jews in Mexico during the Sixteenth Century," American Jewish Historical Quarterly 51 (1961/2); reprinted in Martin A. Cohen (ed.), The Jewish Experience in Latin America: Selected Studies from the Publications of the American Jewish Historical Society (Waltham, MA/New York: American Jewish Historical Society/KTAV Publishing House, 1971), 88-132.

———. "Crypto-Jews in Mexico during the Seventeenth Century," American Jewish Historical Quarterly 51 [1961/2]; reprinted in Cohen, Jewish Experience in Latin America, 133-77.

———. Jews in Colonial Brazil (New York: Columbia University Press, 1960).

———. The Records of the Earliest Jewish Community in the New World (New York: American Jewish Historical Society, 1954).

Wolf, Lucien, Jews in the Canary Islands, being a Calendar of Jewish Cases Extracted from the Records of the Canariote Inquisition in the Collection of the Marquess of Bute, translated from the Spanish and edited with an Introduction and Notes (London: The Jewish Historical Society of England/Spottiswoode, Ballantyne & Co., 1926).

Wolff, Egon and Frieda, Judeus, judaizantes e seus escravos (Rio de Janeiro: Egon and Frieda Wolff, 1987).

Yerushalmi, Yosef Hayim, Assimilation and Racial Anti-Semitism: The Iberian and German Models, Leo Baeck Memorial Lecture, 26 (New York: Leo Baeck Institute, 1982).

———. From Spanish Court to Italian Ghetto: Isaac Cardoso, A Study in Seventeenth-Century Marranism and Jewish Apologetics, 2nd ed. (Seattle: University of Washington Press, 1981 [orig. 1971]).

Yovel, Yirmiyahu, The Marrano of Reason (Princeton: Princeton University Press, 1989).

Zagorin, Perez, Ways of Lying: Dissimulation, Persecution, and Conformity in Early Modern Europe (Cambridge: Harvard University Press, 1990).

Index

Aboab, Isaac de Matatia 170
Abravanel, Isaac 196
Acevedo, Alvaro Rodríquez de 113
act of faith; *See also* auto de fé 98
Acosta, Antonio de 71
Acosta, Manuel de 71
Adams, Julia 24
Afonso Álvares 53
Afroamerican 10, 88, 175, 207
Afroiberian history 18, 42, 126
Afroiberians; *See also* Blacks, Marranos, Moriscos, Mulato, slaves 1, 2, 7-10, 13, 15, 17-19, 21, 23, 25, 27, 29, 31, 33, 35, 37, 39-43, 45-47, 49, 50, 53, 55, 58-59, 62-66, 95, 100-101, 103, 112, 119, 124, 126, 142, 163, 168-169, 171-175, 177, 179, 189, 201-203, 205-210, 212-214
alcaide (jailor) 143
Alberro, Solange 7, 23, 30, 42, 134, 173, 178, 187
Alencastro, Luis Felipe de 23
alms (almsgiving) 93, 102, 116, 121, 191, 193-195
alumbrado (also alumbrar, alumbrasse, alumbrada) 174, 176, 194
Amerindians 4, 14, 17, 21, 32, 36, 52, 59, 62, 67, 88, 166, 201-203, 205, 208, 212
Amsterdam 5, 26-28, 31, 35, 38, 43, 52, 68, 90, 163, 169, 171, 173, 196, 219
Angola 28, 32, 35, 40, 52, 63, 69, 71, 83-86, 91, 113, 116, 122, 124, 128, 144, 158, 159, 166, 167, 173
Anidjar, Gil 204, 206
Antunes Family (Antunes Beatriz, Diego, Heitor, Isabel, Lianor, Manuel, Violante, Ysavel) 135-139, 184, 186, 189-190
anthropological space 6
anti-Portuguese hysteria 69
arms, the right to bear 20
Arama, Rabbi Yitsḥak 224
Arius (heresiarch) 75
Arroyuelos (Spain) 34
Asad, Talal 215

Assis, Yom-Tov 61
asiento (slave contract) 68, 166
auto de fé 16, 56, 61, 69, 75, 79, 89, 92-93, 98, 100, 105, 117, 158, 160, 166, 171, 175, 183, 185, 239, 245, 256, 258, 260, 263, 273
Auto de São Vicente 53
Auto general de la fee celebrada 277
Azevedo, J. Lúcio de 41

Baer, Yitzhak 41
Badajoz (Spain) 101, 113, 121
Bahia, Brazil 26, 37, 59, 62, 107-108, 114, 126, 134-135, 137, 172, 214
Bal, Mieke 204
Barcelona, Spain 32, 40
Bar Ḥiyya, Abraham 32
Behar, Ruth 42
Beinart, Haim 41, 131-132
Ben Israel, Menasseh 68, 123
Bennett, Herman 16, 23, 42
Bible 55, 64, 79, 134
Blackmore, Josiah 6
blasphemy 23, 35, 43-44, 50, 103, 176
blood purity (pure blood, purity of blood, purity of bloodline) 4, 13, 21, 26, 36, 46, 52, 61, 76, 95, 221
Bocanegra, Mathias de 238, 256
Bodian, Miriam 28, 220
Bourdieu, Pierre 207
Bowser, Frederick 21
Boxer, Charles R. / Boxer, C. R. 67
bozales 82, 95, 160-161
Brandão, Ambrósio Fernandes 220
Bugalho, Gil Vaz 115, 132, 134
Buenos Aires 26, 63, 83, 132, 163, 167
burial (burial practices, burial grounds) 97, 112, 132-133, 140-141, 169-170, 182, 186, 190-191
Burns, Kathryn 208

Cabo Verde (islands) 21, 26, 32, 34, 63-64, 214
Cacheu, West Africa 83, 125
Callao, Peru 17, 163-164

Canary Islands 22, 40, 55, 106, 109, 111, 118-119
Cañizares-Esguerra, Jorge 3
Carlos V of Castile, King 22
Carmen Convent (Mexico City) 186
caste (caste system) 2-7, 11, 13, 15-17, 19-21, 42, 46-47, 54, 71, 93, 95, 99, 104, 161, 221
Castelli, Elizabeth 209
Castelló, Vidal Abril 201
Castile, Spain 22, 37, 40-41, 51, 102, 120, 132, 163, 174
Cartagena (de las Indias, Colombia) 9, 10, 17-19, 21-22, 27, 40-41, 44, 67-73, 75, 77-81, 83, 85-87, 89-93, 95, 98-99, 103, 105, 115, 124, 143-145, 162-163, 165, 167-169, 172, 179-180, 195, 202, 220
Carvajal (Family, Franscisca de, Leonor de, Luis de, y de la Cueva) 33, 36, 114, 132-133, 169, 174
Certeau, Michel de 204
Chaunu, Pierre 45
cimarrón / cimarrones (runaway slaves) 23, 164, 206
circumcision 48, 63-64, 129
Ciudad Real, Spain 103, 116, 129, 131-132
Claver, Pedro 21, 68, 92
colonialism 24, 27-28, 31, 47, 212, 214-215, 219
Colombia 23, 41
concubinage 61, 170, 179
confession 55-56, 58, 71, 83-84, 106, 136-137, 168, 177
conquistador 36
Conspiracy (of judaizers, of Beja) 44, 172
Conversos 8, 10, 15, 25-27, 29-32, 36-38, 41, 44, 48, 53-54, 61-62, 69, 71-72, 90, 95, 97, 101, 104, 131, 164, 166, 171, 180, 183, 219-220
Cope, R. Douglas 4
creole 18, 32, 124, 152
crypto-Jews 9-10, 13, 19, 24, 29, 37-38, 47, 67, 73, 76, 97, 102, 110, 112, 115, 117-118, 126, 129, 134, 140, 169, 172, 174, 208, 219-220
crypto-Judaism 25, 41-42, 45, 126, 129, 171
cultural commuters / cultural intermediaries 2, 29, 107

denunciation / denunciations 9, 17, 42-43, 48, 55-56, 58-59, 62, 64-65, 69, 80, 88, 102, 104, 106, 109, 111-113, 118, 121, 126, 137, 139, 141, 172, 205, 217
desecration 54, 59, 206
diaspora 4, 13, 24-25, 165, 212, 219
domination (Christian, catholic, mercantile, the effects of) 2, 26-27, 204-207, 209, 214-217

Edicts of Faith / Edicts of the Faith / *edictos de fe* 45, 55, 70, 72, 103, 132, 137-138
Eimerich, Nicolas / Nicolau 99, 104
endogamy 17
engenhos; *See also* sugar mills 26, 135
England 31
Esther, Queen (biblical, fast of) 138, 182, 185-186
Ethiopia 63
Ethiopians (ethiopian christians / christianity) 48-49, 52, 62-63
ethnicity (ethno-racial identity) 6, 15, 18, 24, 28-29, 46, 60, 214, 219, 220
ethnocentrism 48, 208
ethnographic / ethnography 2-3, 25, 40, 52, 167
ethnology 8, 74
execution 98, 174, 197, 208

Fanon, Franz 45
fasting 115, 187, 190
Felipe, King (III &IV) 34, 36, 76, 163, 166
Ferry, Robert 118, 121, 167, 182
Few, Martha 42, 55
Foucault, Michel 215
Franciscan (order, convents, theologians) 180

Gallagher, Catherine 7, 206
Glick, Thomas F 28
Gómez, Diana Luz Ceballos 8, 22, 42, 74, 78, 80, 87, 89, 107
Graizbord, David 36, 208, 220
Green, Tobias 32, 71, 83, 214, 219
Greenblatt, Stephen 7, 206
Guiné 26, 63, 83, 125

Halakha 131-132, 136, 140
Harbison, Robert 6
Holy Office (of the Inquisition); *See also* Inquisition 16

Hordes, Stanley 37
Horowitz, Elliott 205

imprisonment 72, 87, 89, 92, 121, 123, 145, 152, 157, 162-163, 171, 173, 190, 196-199, 201
insurrection; *See also* rebellion 18, 164
Islam; *See also* Moriscos 13, 32, 125, 176.
Israel, Jonathan 21, 31, 83, 106, 125, 165
Israel, Menasseh ben 68, 123

Jaffary, Nora 21
Jewish identity 25, 29
Jewish law 33, 52, 57, 61, 63, 125, 130-134, 139, 170
Johnson, Willis 75
judaizers / judaizing; *See also* crypto-Jews, crypto-Judaism 2, 5, 9, 13, 25, 29-30, 33-34, 38-39, 41-45, 47, 50-52, 54-55, 57-59, 61-65, 71, 83-84, 89, 91, 97, 101-104, 106-109, 111-112, 114, 117, 120-121, 125-131, 134, 137, 140, 142-143, 145, 147-149, 151-153, 155, 157-159, 161-167, 171-173, 175, 177-181, 183-184, 187, 189-191, 194-195, 202, 208, 212, 216

languages (foreign, native, secret) 10-11, 19, 22, 159-161
Latour, Bruno 4
Law of Moses 30, 33-34, 57, 60-61, 70-71, 83- 84, 89-90, 92, 114-115, 123, 126, 136, 150, 161-162, 164, 166, 171-172, 174, 176-177, 179, 181-187, 189-193, 195-198, 202
León, Pedro López de 55
Lewis, Laura 42
Liebman, Seymour 25, 129, 140
Lipiner, Elias 137
Lima, Peru 4, 6, 17, 19, 25, 40, 44, 56, 60-62, 67, 69, 71, 83, 96, 98-100, 103, 107, 143, 146, 159-167, 220
Lisbon, Portugal 4, 6, 17, 19, 25, 40, 44, 56, 60-62, 67, 69, 71, 83, 96, 98-100, 103, 107, 143, 146, 159-167, 220
Luso-Africans 34, 63

Machorro, Salomón 34, 52, 114-117, 187, 208
Madrid, Spain 21, 34, 44, 69, 91, 105, 120, 145, 165-167, 197
magic 67, 73, 77, 81-82, 89, 123, 189, 203
magical gatherings 78, 84, 86, 89, 103
magical practices 73, 82, 119
Maimonides 49
Mark, Eva Abraham-van der 170
Maroons 203

Marranos 9-10, 15, 29, 33, 96, 101, 114, 126, 131, 133, 167, 178-179, 181, 183, 191, 194-195, 202-203, 206, 209, 212-213
marronage, symbolic 81-82, 196
master-slave relationship 121, 122
Melammed, Renée Levine 101, 140
merchant capitalism 24
mestizos 5, 15-17, 21, 34, 67, 89, 98, 221
Minas Gerais, Brazil 63, 126
Moriscos 21, 41, 101, 125, 176, 189, 203-205
mourning 84, 115, 136, 141, 182-183, 186, 190
Mulato 10-11, 16-17, 19-20, 34, 50, 53-54, 58, 62, 67, 72, 86, 99, 101, 103, 113-114, 127, 129, 131-132, 134, 153, 169, 171-174, 189
Myscofski, Carole 104, 139
mystics 20, 41

Nação (The Nation) 24
neophyte 21
New Christians 6-7, 9-10, 15, 19, 21, 24-26, 28-31, 33-34, 36-39, 41-43, 47-48, 50-51, 53-54, 57, 60, 62-64, 66, 68-69, 72, 79, 83, 91, 97, 99, 101-102, 104, 109, 112, 114, 118-120, 124-126, 132, 134-137, 139-141, 161, 163, 165-166, 170, 172-173, 175, 180, 187, 202, 206, 208, 212-214, 219-220
New Granada / Nueva Granada 22, 41-42, 68, 82, 187, 216

old Christians 21, 30, 36-37, 49, 53-54, 64, 76, 101-102, 120, 123, 137, 138, 161, 172, 212
othering 2, 47, 221

Padilla, Marín 107
pagan 33
pagan (*gentios*) 33
Pagden, Anthony 205
Palenques 81
Pas Pinto, Blas de 220
Penso de la Vega, Josef 5, 28
Perés, Manuel Bautista 62, 69, 83, 85, 107, 146
Pernambuco 25-26, 33, 37, 51, 54, 90, 108, 113-114, 135, 173, 175, 205
Peru 16, 19, 22, 26, 32-33, 40, 63, 67, 68, 81, 108, 118, 126, 159, 164, 166, 203, 212, 220
Phelan, John Leddy 104

Potosi, Bolivia 26, 67, 96, 131, 153, 165-167, 215
Pratt, Mary Louis 170
prayers 33, 35, 37, 43, 92, 103, 110, 113-114, 129, 176, 182-183, 188-189, 191, 207
Proodian, Lucia Garcia de 213
quarteron 17

Race Restrepo, Luz Adriana Maya 8, 42
rebellion 82, 163, 210
Reconquista 3, 31-32, 41, 176, 189
religion 4-5, 7, 10, 15, 18, 20, 30, 33-35, 38-39, 49, 53, 63, 65, 108, 112, 119, 121, 123, 125, 127, 129, 131, 133-135, 137, 139, 141-142, 164, 172, 176, 178, 185, 186, 196, 205-206, 209, 214, 220-221
religious visions; *See* visions
Rio de Janeiro, Brazil 25-26, 30, 37, 173
Río de la Plata Province, Peru 26, 33, 113
Roth, Cecil 41, 206
Rufina (slave of Raphael Gómez) 9, 73-75, 77-89

sacred objects 20
Sandoval, P. Alonso de 19
Santiago de Chile 59, 62, 97, 101
São Tomé 5, 28-29, 35, 40, 63-64, 128
Saraiva, António José 41, 43, 45
Schwartz, Stuart 16, 20, 26, 30, 214, 220
Sentence (punishment assigned by court) 43, 81, 93, 105, 140, 158, 192, 197-198
Sephardic diaspora 24
Sephardim 11, 24, 26, 31, 52, 90
sex, interracial 59
Shulkhan Arukh 110, 130, 133, 135, 138
social engineering 3, 16
Spinoza, Benedict (Baruch) 213
spiritual economy 208
Spivak, Gayatri Chakravorty 214
Sweet, James H. 23, 42, 81, 135

Torquemada, Tomás de 41
torture 43-44, 51, 70-72, 87, 92, 104, 106, 144, 157, 176, 201, 207
trade 4, 14, 21, 26-27, 31, 63-64, 70, 83, 85, 119, 128, 144, 159, 161, 165-167, 180, 219
Uceda, Gaspar de 48

Valencia, Spain 40
Veer, Peter Van der 3
Vega, Lope de 16

Ventura, Maria 165
visions 51, 172, 249

West India Company 90
witchcraft (accusations of) 18, 23, 37, 41, 44, 56, 57, 67, 77, 80, 89, 189
Wolf, Lucien 110

Yehudah, ha-Levi 32
Yerushalmi, Yosef Hayim 10, 53
Yovel, Yirmiyahu 29, 213

zambos 15, 89
Zaragoza, Spain 27, 40

About the Author

Jonathan Schorsch holds the Chair in Jewish Religious and Intellectual History at the University of Potsdam (Germany), having taught previously at Sarah Lawrence College, Columbia University and Emory University. Among his books are *Swimming the Christian Atlantic: Judeoconversos, Afroiberians and Amerindians in the Seventeenth-Century Iberian World* (2008) and *Jews and Blacks in the Early Modern World* (2004). With Sina Rauschenbach he co-edited *The Sephardic Atlantic: Colonial Histories and Postcolonial Perspectives* (2018).

www.ingramcontent.com/pod-product-compliance
Lightning Source LLC
Chambersburg PA
CBHW020942230426
43666CB00005B/135